Vicksburg

CIVIL WAR AMERICA

Gary W. Gallagher, editor

Vicksburg

The Campaign That Opened the Mississippi

Michael B. Ballard

THE UNIVERSITY OF NORTH CAROLINA PRESS

Chapel Hill & London

© 2004 The University of North Carolina Press
All rights reserved
Set in New Baskerville and Didot types
by Keystone Typesetting, Inc.
Manufactured in the United States of America

The paper in this book meets the guidelines for
permanence and durability of the Committee on
Production Guidelines for Book Longevity of the
Council on Library Resources.

Library of Congress Cataloging-in-Publication Data
Ballard, Michael B.
Vicksburg : the campaign that opened the Mississippi / by
Michael B. Ballard.
    p. cm. — (Civil War America)
Includes bibliographical references and index.
ISBN 978-0-8078-2893-9 (alk. paper)
ISBN978-0-8078-7128-7 (pbk.: alk. paper)
1. Vicksburg (Miss.) — History — Seige, 1863. I. Title. II. Series.
E475.27.B358 2004
973.7'344–dc22   2004001059

Frontispiece:
Vicksburg, circa 1860 (Old Court House Museum, Vicksburg)

cloth   13 12 11 10 09 6 5 4 3 2
paper 13 12 11 10 09 5 4 3 2 1

To

Jan, my bride,

Terry, my best man,

and

Ed, my inspiration

Contents

Sections of illustrations appear after pages 92 and 352.

Maps

Preface

My interest in the Vicksburg campaign dates back to my childhood, when my parents occasionally took my brother and me to the Vicksburg National Military Park, a drive of some three hours from our north-central Mississippi home. I fell in love with the Park, the city, the Mississippi River, and the bluffs. Vastly improved roads make the trip easier now, and I still look forward to each and every journey to the place termed many years ago the "Gibraltar of the Confederacy." The city and the Park on the bluffs have become all the more special since December 2, 2000, when I married Jan on Fort Hill, with my dear friend Terry Winschel, Park historian, as my best man. A cold, brisk west wind made the day that much more memorable, as I realized a long-held dream of getting married at Vicksburg, in the Park.

My serious exploration of the Vicksburg campaign dates back to the 1960s, when I began reading the works of Edwin C. Bearss, who for a time was the Park historian, before moving on to become chief historian of the National Park Service. Ed inspired me to want to know more about the people and events that characterized and shaped this complex campaign. His pioneering work provided a foundation from which I launched my own research.

My attachment to historic Vicksburg and my endless fascination with the epic campaign that defined the course of the Civil War's Western Theater led me in later years to write a biography of John Pemberton, Confederate commander of the district that encompassed Vicksburg from November 1862 to the surrender on July 4, 1863. Pemberton's story stirred my interest all the more. So I decided to broaden my horizon, to produce a one-volume comprehensive overview of the longest campaign of the war, which began on May 18, 1862, and ended on July 17, 1863. In my view, there has been no prior published study that adequately covers that time period in enough detail to give us an appreciation of the magnitude of the Union's determined effort to wrest control of Vicksburg, and with it the Mississippi River, from the Confederacy.

My approach has been to produce what is primarily a tactical and strategic work that also addresses topics in several other areas. This blending of traditional military history methodology with the so-called new military history offers a well-rounded treatment, giving readers a sense of how the Vicksburg campaign fit within the broader sweep of the war and how the conflict affected people behind the lines. The traditional model has been characterized by detailed studies of campaigns and battles, usually from commanders' points of view, while the "new" focuses more on the impact of war on soldiers, civilians, towns, landscapes, politics, and other nonmilitary areas of human existence.

I believe that unifying the paradigms provides a much more accurate view of the realities and ramifications of war. Campaigns and battles do not occur in a vacuum; by their very nature, their effects are widespread and profound. Too close a focus on military operations will restrict our understanding of a conflict and what we can, and should, learn from it.

Within this volume, I have written about battles and commanders, but I have also included information that traditional military histories have generally ignored. Here one will find accounts of precampaign and postcampaign events, civilian-military interactions, guerrilla warfare and its consequences, Union soldier reactions to slavery and slaves, attitudes and concerns of soldiers on both sides, women's experiences and perceptions, the intrusions of war on life in towns and rural areas and on farmland, and the evolution of hard war.

Hard war became sharply defined during the Vicksburg campaign as a result of several factors, though largely through antagonisms fueled by guerrilla activities. I prefer the term "hard war" to "total war." Historians have never been able to agree on what "total war" is; in my view, it is the intent of one side to totally obliterate the other, in both human and physical terms. Hard war is more of an attitude of taking the means of making war from the enemy, and if that involves destroying businesses, taking food from hungry families or burning farm buildings, or retaliating harshly against neighborhoods used as bases by guerrillas, then so be it. Such actions surely get out of hand from time to time, but during the Vicksburg campaign the methods used never developed into total war.

The Vicksburg campaign, then, provides a panoramic portrait of civil war. My mission has not been so much to offer startling new interpretations, though I have challenged some long-accepted analyses, as to expand the historical paradigm of the campaign, which will in turn make our analysis of what happened and why much more meaningful. The campaign consisted of many subcampaigns and many skirmishes and battles, creating a complex tapestry that has caused many historians and buffs over the years to shy away from it. Brief campaigns and single battles, even those that last two or three days, are much easier to understand and analyze. Yet the Vicksburg campaign's significance demands that we pay attention to it and try to grasp its many nuances. The course of the war in the Western Theater, the decisive theater I would argue, cannot be comprehended unless the Vicksburg campaign, in its entirety, is understood.

I offer this study in the hope that it will both increase our historical understanding of this epoch of the Civil War and inspire other historians to investigate in greater depth some of the issues and events that I address but could not delve into further without going beyond my intended one volume. Despite what many may say about the excessive publication of Civil War books, my Vicksburg odyssey has convinced me that we still have much to learn.

I must make two points about the content of this volume. The first deals with material that is not included. I chose not to incorporate a detailed study of the Port Hudson campaign. I believe that to have included Port Hudson would have taken the focus too much off the campaign around Vicksburg proper. I have mentioned Port Hudson and how operations there impacted options and decisions to the north, so that readers can understand the significance of that campaign. There are excellent histories of the Port Hudson campaign available for readers who would like to know more.

Second, I have included numerous quotes in the text without inserting the equally numerous "*sics*" that would be required to indicate misspellings or grammatical errors. I believe in letting those who experienced the campaign speak for themselves, where appropriate, without having their words disrupted with notations of mistakes in their letters and diaries. Where clarification is needed, I have interpolated information in brackets.

I chose not to include a lengthy list of military units that participated in the campaign. This campaign included many different battles and subcampaigns; to identify all of the units, within a breakdown of each action, would require many additional pages. Those readers interested in a general, compiled list should go to the following site on the Internet: http://www.nps.gov/vick/state/unit_reg.htm.

Many people contributed to the completion of this work. Terry Winschel, who was warmly hospitable during my many visits to the Vicksburg National Military Park archives, read the entire manuscript and offered constructive comments. I am also most grateful to a great friend, retired brigadier general Parker Hills, Mississippi National Guard, who resides in Clinton, Mississippi. Over the years, my understanding of the Vicksburg campaign has been richly affected and clarified by frequent conversations with Parker, who is an avid student and tour guide of the many campaign battlefields.

I wish to acknowledge others, many of them valued friends, who contributed in a variety of ways; collectively, they made this study possible. Wiley Sword, Peter Cozzens, Richard McMurry, Mike Parrish, Allan Richard, Alan Whitehead, and Bob Younger all shared important research materials. John Marszalek, my longtime mentor and friend, Larry Daniel, and Gary Gallagher read the manuscript and made valuable suggestions for improvements. A good number of people provided research assistance. Those who made special efforts are Craig Piper and Chris Lynch, who helped with research in Mississippi and Alabama; Yu-Cheng Qin at the University of Iowa; Marilyn McGlothlin at the University of Michigan; Cheryl Schnirring at the Illinois State Historical Library; Richard Sommers and David Richards at the United States Army Military History Institute at Carlisle Barracks, Pennsylvania; Ned Irwin at the East Tennessee State University Library; John White at the Wilson Library of the University of North Carolina–Chapel Hill; Jeff Giambrone and Gordon Cotton at the Old Court House Museum in Vicksburg; Katie Benton at the University of Wisconsin; John Warner in Indiana repositories; Michael Mangus at the Ohio Historical Society; and Elizabeth Joyner, Bob Younger, and Rebecca Drake for providing invaluable assistance with photographs. For outstanding work with maps and photographs, I thank Becky Smith and Russ Houston respectively and with great respect. Becky's talent and patience are quite remarkable and most appreciated. Speaking of patience, I especially applaud the fine assistance and cooperation I have received from the University of North Carolina Press; my gratitude goes to David Perry, Mark Simpson-Vos, and Paul Betz. Without them, this book would never have made it into print.

Finally, I wish to thank my assistants in the Congressional and Political Research Center, Mississippi State University Library, Betty Self and Craig Piper, for their support and most especially for their encouragement. Thanks, too, to Nyssa, one of my student assistants, who photocopied a very long manuscript. My immediate family—Jan and Erin, plus our cats Blackie, Mocha, Josie, and Cappuccino and dog Mollie—and Illinois friends and family, including Ed and Mary Beth, Bailey (the Big Red 1), Charlene and Phil, Chris and John, Kathy, Dianne, Roy and Helen, Vicki and David, Randy and family, Miss Beulah, Eric, Mindy, and especially two beautiful granddaughters, Alex and Addison (Addie), brightened my long campaign journey, seemingly always during times when the long marches became particularly burdensome, and in wonderful ways they never thought about, or were even aware of. For their support, and just being there, words are inadequate to express my love and appreciation.

Vicksburg

1

A Town, a River, & War

While the United States was still a young republic, pioneers moving west noticed attractive land sitting on high bluffs above a sharp hairpin turn in the Mississippi River. An ideal place for a town, some observers said, and a South Carolinian named Elihu Hall Bay thought so too. By 1800, Bay had title to some 3,000 acres of this high ground that had come to be known as the Walnut Hills. The name no doubt evolved from boatmen who came to recognize the "halo of walnut trees high above the river" as a landmark. A future observer of the area would cynically describe it: "After all the big mountains and regular ranges of hills had been made by the Lord of Creation, there was left on hand a large lot of scraps, and these were dumped down at Vicksburg into a sort of waste heap." A kinsman of Bay's named Robert Turnbull later inherited the property and was more interested in planting cotton than a community. These Mississippi Territory hills along the river seemed to take on a life of their own, however, and houses began to appear around the edges of Turnbull's real estate.[1]

Another cotton planter named Newitt Vick, a visionary neighbor of Turnbull's, recognized settlement possibilities and began marking off lots to sell in 1819. A native Virginian, Vick was a circuit-riding Methodist preacher who had brought his family into Warren County, named for Revolutionary War hero Joseph Warren, in 1809, eight years before Mississippi entered the Union as the twentieth state. Vick died of yellow fever before the town that would bear his name, Vicksburg, was officially incorporated in 1825, but his descendants made sure it happened.[2]

Indian land cessions in Mississippi in the early days of statehood increased cotton planting in the state, thereby increasing the need for a river port on the Mississippi where the white gold could be transported to New Orleans and beyond. The village on the bluffs proved an ideal spot for such a port, so Vicksburg grew rapidly, soon ranking second

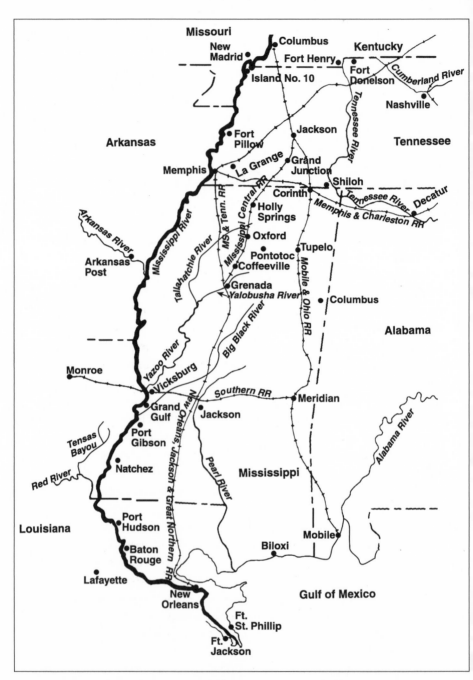

The General Area of the Vicksburg Campaign. Map by Becky Smith.

only to Natchez, its river neighbor to the south, as a center of economic activity. The peculiarities of the river made the city's prominence possible. After the Mississippi passed by the mouth of the Yazoo, it started turning north and "suddenly began to change in temperament; the current began to move rapidly," and just above Vicksburg it looped. Then the "channel made a complete 180-degree turn around the tip of De Soto Point and flowed in a torrent right down the city waterfront." The current was fast and tricky, but due to the "deep water off the bank, regardless of water stage," the long waterfront made a good docking area, and a reliable one, since the water could not eat away at the "solid limestone and shale" at the core of the bluffs. More and more people moved in; goods and services increased; and soon Vicksburg became the county seat of Warren County, taking that honor from the village of Warrenton a few miles downriver.[3]

Because Vicksburg was on a mighty river that led to the outside world, its growth followed different patterns than the county in which it sat. The society that dominated the town was "heterogeneous and fluid," "more dynamic, more complex" than the rural adjacent areas. Like a mini-city, Vicksburg developed into well-defined neighborhoods during its formative years. The business district dominated the landscape on the east bank of the river up to the courthouse bluff. Residential areas then took over and through the years spread among the hills. To the north lay the "Kangaroo," a crude, backstreet area haunted by riffraff, including shady gamblers, prostitutes, and drunken brawlers. When the Kangaroo burned to the ground in the early 1830s, few beyond its occupants mourned its loss.[4]

Despite the welcome growth and accompanying thriving economy, Vicksburg citizens deceived themselves into thinking that they could control the social dynamics various people brought to the city. Worry over undesirables, loosely defined as any outsider, fueled the growth of local militia. Right up to the eve of the Civil War, many residents seemed to fear these outsiders more than the threats of slave revolts that haunted other antebellum white southerners. Underscoring societal tensions was a July 4, 1835, picnic at which a drunken gambler insulted finely dressed militia. The incident triggered violent confrontations between citizens and the clique of gamblers common in river towns. By the time things settled down, the original perpetrator had been tarred and feathered, several on both sides had been shot, and the gamblers who could not escape were hung en masse.[5]

Three years later, civic leaders turned their wrath on river men whose merchandise-laden flatboats competed with the city's more legitimate businesses, owned by local businessmen. Taxes levied on the boatmen had little effect; most carried so much cash that they paid without wincing. So the taxes kept going up until resistance finally brought an armed standoff, which fortunately fizzled before anyone was harmed. A circuit judge later ruled in favor of the river men, but a message had been sent. The city would not stand idly by and be taken advantage of by interlopers.

In spite of the paranoia, Vicksburg continued to grow, surviving the national financial panic of 1837 and a destructive city fire in 1846. The latter year the town watched excitedly as the First Mississippi Regiment was organized locally, with prominent planter Jefferson Davis elected as its colonel. The town that did not want outside intervention had no compunction about sending its sons to intervene in the conflict between Texas and Mexico that resulted in the Mexican War. Their attitudes typified southern support for Texas, where slavery, the major factor that unified white southerners, had been introduced.[6]

The 1850s brought prosperity, and with it came an increasing number of fine homes for which Vicksburg, like Natchez, became famous. The population increased as well; by 1860 Vicksburg would have 4,500 residents, more than the capital city of Jackson, some forty miles to the east. Irish immigrants accounted in large measure for this growth; others came from England and Germany. The city that feared the newcomer had become cosmopolitan in spite of itself. The ethnic influx brought economic diversity to the river city, the federal census reporting some 193 different occupations in 1860.[7]

Despite its progress and its handsome residences, Vicksburg on the eve of civil war was in many respects an eyesore. Several wooden buildings stood unpainted; unfettered hogs roamed unpaved streets and, along with equally free-ranging, mostly homeless, dogs, ripped open anything that promised to be food. Roaches had become a citywide problem. Citizens did occasionally take action; one report in 1860 indicated that 129 homeless dogs had been rounded up and drowned in the river. A few streets were improved, and a magnificent county courthouse dominated the city's skyline.

Yet problems persisted. Four-legged troublemakers and vermin could be more easily dealt with than drunks and prostitutes, undesirables that continued to persist despite the attempted 1830s purge. Like other residents of the slave South, Vicksburgians decided that rather than deal with the unpleasantness all around, they would strengthen community ties by organizing exclusive clubs and doing charity work. Many seemed to resolve their attitudes against "them" by simply pretending that the undesirables did not exist. Women especially busied themselves reaching out to the sick and unfortunate. Unfortunately for those engaged in self-deception, national issues insistently intruded into their private world.

≈ White citizens of Vicksburg reacted schizophrenically to growing crises of the late 1850s. John Brown's 1859 raid at Harpers Ferry, Virginia, produced occasionally violent reactions against slaves suspected of insurrectionary tendencies. On one occasion, fearful townspeople tarred, feathered, and banned to a river skiff a suspected abolitionist. The perpetrating mob felt a sense of slight relief as they saw this perceived threat float away down the Mississippi. An unusually large number of fires along the river and in Vicksburg fueled suspicions of slave mischief. Yet the Unionist majority in the city felt that growing worries over slave revolts might be a plot by the prosecession minority. Certainly they had reason to worry. In Mississippi, secession winds had begun to reach gale force, and while support for separation was hardly unanimous, Unionists were becoming increasingly outnumbered.

In Vicksburg, whatever oratory local secessionists mustered in support of the growing movement in the South, fueled by the presidential election of 1860, was drowned out locally by majority Whig counterarguments. Merchants especially feared the business disruptions that were bound to come if Mississippi left the Union. Yet Vicksburg was not an island that could ultimately go its own way economically or socially. The town's ongoing efforts to shield itself from national dynamics would continue to be illusory and futile.[8]

As November 1860 and the national presidential election approached, tensions increased nationwide and especially in Vicksburg. The national Democratic Party had split, and the Southern wing had chosen John C. Breckinridge of Kentucky as its presidential candidate. Jefferson Davis, a Warren County resident, United States senator, Mexican War hero, and former secretary of war under President Franklin Pierce, came home to campaign for Breckinridge. Ostensibly an opponent of secession, Davis had become more belligerent in tone of late, a reflection of white Southerners' state of mind. Though Davis knew that with the Democrats split Breckinridge could not win, he had decided that Southern honor was more important than victory. He warned that his county and his state would be degraded by submission to Northern demands that slavery not be extended to U.S. territories and new states. These demands threatened the future of the institution of slavery. If Mississippi resisted those threats, Davis said, and the North should respond aggressively, the state would "welcome the invader to the harvest of death."[9]

Davis's position did little to change attitudes of conservative old-line Whigs. While some Vicksburgians listened to secession talk, many more attended a rally in support of the newly formed Constitutional Union Party, an antisecession group that nominated Tennessean John Bell as their candidate. Like Breckinridge, Bell had little chance of winning, especially since Northern Democrats had rallied behind Stephen A. Douglas of Illinois. Many citizens of Vicksburg who abhorred the idea of separation from the Union felt, however, that they had little choice but to go with Bell. They valued compromise and peace more than the vague and risky concept of Southern honor that Davis embraced. They could not see "honor" in the potential loss of their livelihoods and even their lives on the altar of war.

When local ballots were counted, conservative economic interests prevailed, barely. Bell received 309 votes, Douglas 52; and Breckinridge ran a close second with 296. The Republican Party candidate, Abraham Lincoln of Illinois, was not on the ballot.[10] Unionists could rightly claim victory, but hardly a resounding one; the election no doubt startled many Whigs who could see their long-time influence waning. Nation-wide, the feared Republican Party, founded on free-soil, abolitionist principles, won the presidency. Lincoln opposed any further expansion of slavery, and rabid secessionists would seize the moment, making life ever more miserable for secession opponents in the South like those in Vicksburg.

Resistance in the hill city remained strong for a time. Many residents refused to budge on the question of separation until they no longer had a choice. They had a much more realistic view of what war would mean than did the fire-eating secessionists that increasingly dominated Mississippi. The town's "ties with the North—especially the river connection with the Midwest—fear of war stemming from property and personal hazard, genuine love for the Union, and strong partisan, political feelings which made the conservatives distrust the demagogic, secession-inclined Democrats were the forces which worked to hold the city apart from most of the state."[11]

A local paper, predictably named the *Daily Whig*, called for calm in the wake of Lincoln's election. The editor wrote hopefully: "We call upon the people, . . . now that the issue is made, to choose under which banner they will serve—disunion, with all its attendant horrors of rapine, murder and Civil War or Union with the guarantees of the Constitution to protect us, and one-half of the people of the north to sympathise and aid us in maintaining our rights."[12]

The paper almost daily tried to calm fears and promote faith in the righteousness of the Union. When Stephen Douglas stopped by, en route to his plantation in Washington County, Mississippi, north of Vicksburg, the editor reported on Douglas's twenty-minute speech, in which he assured listeners that Lincoln, an old political foe of Douglas's, would be powerless to interfere with Southern slavery. The Congress would control the president, Douglas said, and the Illinois senator went on to praise local support for the Union in this, the "most important point in Mississippi."[13]

A few days later, attendees of a large pro-Union rally in town heard other speakers urge caution. They agreed that if Lincoln insisted on embracing abolitionism, then the South would have a right to leave the Union, but such action should be taken by all states at once. Clearly, they hoped such would not be the case, but if such action became necessary, they wanted it to be orderly and with unanimity, rather than have Mississippi act hastily on its own. Their words indicated, too, a realization that secession might soon be too powerful a movement to be checked.[14]

Resistance to secession continued. When the Mississippi state legislature called for elections to a state secession convention to be held on December 20, pro-Unionists in Vicksburg and Warren County went to work, and their candidates outpolled separatists by 561 to 173. The secessionist editor of a Vicksburg paper called the *Daily Citizen* cried fraud, but to no avail. Two Unionist delegates thus represented Warren County at the convention, which met on January 7, 1861. Despite their local victory, neither Warren delegates nor their supporters had any illusions that Mississippi could be held in the Union. Yet it was a bit of a surprise when one of the two broke ranks and voted with eighty-three other representatives for secession. The other delegate remained loyal to his cause, and was one of fifteen delegates who voted against secession. In addition to the old Whig counties along the river, the hill counties of northeastern Mississippi offered strong opposition; it was an area with a relatively small slave population that, like Vicksburg, would experience firsthand the harshness of war.[15]

Secession had come to Mississippi, and many, especially in the capital, Jackson, rejoiced amid cannon firing and bells ringing. Few such expressions could be found in Vicksburg. No sounds of gunfire or fireworks rang through the hills, but the absence of celebration did not necessarily indicate sulking. However mistaken the pro-Unionists believed their fellow citizens to be, most would not turn their backs on Mississippi. One antisecessionist wrote to the *Whig*: "It is enough for us to know that Mississippi, *our* State, *our* government has taken its position. We, too, take our position by its side. We stand ready to defend her rights and to share her fate."[16]

📰 They would indeed share her fate, more so than they could have imagined at the time. War had not come yet, and many people in Vicksburg had done their best to prevent it from coming at all, but it was coming, and the city on the hills, occupied by so many who opposed it, would be one of its focal points. Ironically, the very thing that gave economic life to the town, the Mississippi, would likewise bring destruction. Mississippi and Vicksburg would learn that people living far upriver in the area known as the Old Northwest, considered the river as much theirs as anybody's, and they would not stand idly by and watch its free access threatened.

Residents in the states of Illinois, Ohio, Wisconsin, Iowa, and other areas of the old Northwest Territory understood clearly the economic ramifications of a closed river. Yet their anger at that possibility reflected much more. Canals and railroads had developed to the point that farmers could get their goods to Eastern markets without the river, though many still used the Mississippi. For these people, the river had always been more than an economic lifeline. Through the years, it had become "a symbol that incorporated their prosperity, their regional pride, and their allegiance to the national union." They wanted to keep the "status quo, express the power of their region, and maintain the economic benefits that had proved beneficial in the past."

The United States, not the Southern states, had controlled the Mississippi for nearly sixty years. Migration and concomitant increases in agricultural production had firmed up dependence on the river and one of its major tributaries, the Ohio. These waterways facilitated shipments to markets in the East, and because the states were united, and the rivers flowed through or by many of them, shippers assumed they would always be there, free and unfettered.[17]

These deeply ingrained attitudes flared into bitter resentment and anger when Mississippi governor John Jones Pettus, a fire-eater who seemed addicted to periodic bungling, committed a major blunder. Pettus and other Southern governors in what was becoming the Western Confederacy, had repeatedly reassured their Northern neighbors that secession would not mean closing the river. Yet the volatile climate of early 1861 fueled rumor and mistrust. One false tale, passed along to Pettus by Thomas Moore, governor of Louisiana, had Northern armed forces hurrying south to occupy military installations along the Mississippi where it passed through Louisiana. Moore had already been sending state troops to take over federal military facilities, even though his state had not yet left the Union.[18]

Never one to react soberly, Pettus rushed state militia to the Vicksburg bluffs to intercept the expected interlopers who never materialized. Included among the troops was a detachment of a Jackson artillery company and a few local Vicksburg troops. On January 11, the trigger-happy ragtag force fired on the *O. A. Tyler*, a harmless steamer. Fortunately, no one was hurt. The next day, alarm bells sounded, and armed men rushed about the bluffs in anticipation of serious action. Supposedly, a boat called the *Silver Wave* was coming downstream, loaded with Yankee troops bent on attacking river towns in the belligerent Southern states. Nothing happened; the *Silver Wave* showed up later with its usual harmless cargo and passengers. After enduring bad weather for a few more days, the would-be Louisiana-Mississippi defenders of river sovereignty went home.[19]

Pettus, ever bearing the torch of secession, continued to prepare for war. Though he knew that pro-Union sentiment was strong in Vicksburg, he had not hesitated to stump the area in the fall of 1860, calling for armed neutrality. He of course fooled no one. Like other fire-eaters he wanted secession, and he did not care if war followed.[20]

Counseled by Jefferson Davis, new provisional president of the Southern Confederacy, to be aggressive, Pettus had been looking at various strategic options regarding perceived threats to his state. He worried about a Federal fort on Ship Island, which lay a few miles south of the Mississippi Gulf Coast shoreline. Enemy boats there could interfere with the state's water commerce. Federal troops soon vacated the place, easing the governor's mind but doing little to temper his drive. Pettus worked hard to secure arms and ammunition for state troops, and generously sent men to other states to aid in the seizure of Federal property, like Fort Pickens in Florida. He prevailed on Governor Moore to send weaponry from Louisiana. Pettus's good intentions sometimes brought his buffoonery to the fore, as when he purchased numerous shotguns for his state troops. When the weapons arrived, they proved to be a collection of pieces of guns, antiques, a veritable useless junk-pile of metal.[21]

Such was the nature of the man who overreacted to groundless rumors. Sensing the ramifications of his big mouth and miscalculations, Pettus called on the state legislature to pass a resolution that Mississippi remained committed to an open river. "This, in my opinion," he wrote lamely, "will materially aid in preserving peace . . . if it can be preserved." The legislature agreed, and the secession convention passed a similar resolution. Politicians urged Pettus to distribute the consoling words to appropriate governors in the North. He did so, no doubt hoping that his bad judgment would be forgiven and his state's olive branch accepted.[22]

In most areas of the Northern river states, it was not. Governor Richard Yates of Illinois said in his inaugural address that his state would never consent to the river flowing even partially through "a foreign jurisdiction." A Cincinnati editor chimed in that the Northwest would come together as one to keep the river open to the Gulf. In Indiana, an editor called the placement of cannon on the Vicksburg bluffs an "act of war." A Wisconsin paper warned the South not to provoke the military spirit of Midwesterners.[23]

In Indiana, the state legislature passed a resolution calling the appearance of the battery "a heinous offence." A Chicago editor asked his readers if they would acquiesce to riding in boats heading downstream that might pass under the shadows of guns at Memphis, Vicksburg, Natchez, and Baton Rouge. John Sherman, an Ohio politician and brother of future general William T. Sherman, reacted to reports that river boats at Vicksburg now had to give an accounting of themselves with a warning that "thousands of men will float down" the Mississippi and "make it free."[24]

Delegates at the Louisiana secession convention joined their Mississippi counterparts in trying to defuse the storm of criticism rolling down the river. The Louisianans unanimously endorsed unfettered access, yet their action did little to soothe hard feelings. Louisiana and Mississippi might talk one way now and act another later, especially if war came, and with each passing day, conflict seemed more inevitable. The gathering storm of conflict created a sense of urgency in mending fences. Pettus's irresponsible act had in fact undercut Confederate government policy aimed at "neutralizing northwest opposition to secession" by promising to keep the river open. A bill enacting such a policy passed the Confederate Congress and was signed by Jefferson Davis on February 25. The congress also passed a trade bill that prohibited most duties on agricultural products, another thinly veiled effort to appease the Old Northwest.[25]

Northerners in northeastern states looked on the Mississippi River question with realistic detachment. Closure of the river might be an irritant, but it would not stop the East-West flow of commerce. The remote possibility of some kind of alliance between the South and Northwest troubled few. Such an alliance would be too costly to the Northwest, and, more to the point, unthinkable. Other Northerners understood the sense of nationhood with which the Midwest viewed the river. William T. Sherman had once called the Mississippi the spinal column of the nation. People along the northern reaches of the river would not stand for anyone damaging that spine; most Easterners understood that and knew that the men of the Old Northwest would fight rather than participate in an unholy alliance.[26]

In Vicksburg, citizens did not seem overly concerned about the Northern rancor that Pettus had ignited. They had been too occupied with fearful expectations ever since the *Silver Wave* incident. The mental stress and excitement of probable invasion by armed men from the North refocused perspectives on secession and war. Union sentiment had not been totally destroyed, but antisecessionists were getting harder to find. Even those who still opposed separation came to accept the reality that the "more abstract concept of political allegiance to a Federal Union could not possibly hope to compete for loyalty against something as close and as compelling as a pattern of life created by fathers and grandfathers and passed down from father to son." Fears of outsiders attacking their town forced many conservatives to place Vicksburg, Warren County, and Mississippi much higher than the United States on their allegiance priority list. The national capital, which lay so far away geographically, seemed even more remote now that it was in the hands of an apparently hostile president and his abolition party.

With war seemingly imminent, and with their obvious vulnerability to attack from the river in mind, city fathers rushed ahead with military preparation. The city council appropriated funds to match a $5,000 gift from a local businessman specified for the construction of an arsenal to be built outside the city limits for safety's sake. Curiously, the state secession convention refused to recommend the hill city's plan to the state military board, which coordinated preparedness statewide. Perhaps delegates felt Vicksburgians were moving too quickly and too much on their own. Whatever the case, the council ignored the snub and moved ahead. A town facing enemy invasion could hardly waste time with bureaucratic wrangling in Jackson.[27]

In addition to munitions, Vicksburg needed more armed defenders, and local companies began springing up. Young men signed up with units that had such picturesque names as Vicksburg Sharpshooters, Hill City Cadets, Jeff Davis Rebels, and Warren Dragoons. Talk of creating a Zouave company quickly faded due to the foreign (French-Algerian) nature of such a thing. Preparations for a war fought to preserve the familiar sharply defined the town's old prejudices. In Vicksburg, words such as honor, glory, and cause could only be applied to the chosen.[28]

Despite the fearful uncertainty of the times, arsenal building, and formation and drilling of combat units, life in Vicksburg settled down as a post–*Silver Wave* lull settled over the hills. Excitement did flurry briefly, when the new, provisional president of the Confederacy, Jefferson Davis, came through on his way to the provisional capital in Montgomery, Alabama.[29]

A rider from Vicksburg had taken the news of his election on February 11 to Davis at his home, Brierfield Plantation. Davis received a warm welcome in a city filled with political enemies a few months earlier, yet another sign of shifting attitudes wrought by a war atmosphere. Davis, the secessionist, had become "that distinguished Soldier[,] Statesman and Patriot" according to a city council resolution. Novice militia companies turned out in uniform and used the occasion to show off their cannon and rifle skills. Davis uttered brief patriotic remarks and, accompanied by the young soldiers, walked to the Southern Railroad of Mississippi where a train scheduled to depart for Jackson had been held up for his convenience. When he reached the capital city, he told the awaiting crowd that his affectionate reception in Vicksburg had "cheered his heart."[30]

Getting ready for war and having a president come to town seemed to produce a surreal atmosphere that smacked of an earlier Vicksburg when residents tried to sanitize the town. This mind-set materialized when girls who worked for a local madam named Mollie Bunch held a ball, not an unusual event, and in other times something that would have been overlooked. The girls forced a reaction when they overstepped their bounds by inviting ministers and other city elites. As a result, the night of the event, fire alarms rang, and indignant citizens took fire-fighting equipment to Mollie's and drenched her home, tore up furniture, and hosed down those attending the shindig. The mob then turned to a tavern and wrecked it, filling city gutters with alcoholic liquids. Authorities looked the other way; after all these perpetrators were only "correcting an evil." The madam and the bar owner tried to get reimbursed, but failed, and the latter lost his liquor license.[31]

The misfortunes of Mollie and the tavern did not occur in a vacuum. Law enforcement officers kept up a hectic pace from February to May 1861. Arrests and incarcerations more than doubled during that time span as if "the city was purging itself in anticipation of war." Rumors continued to abound that enemies up North were up to no good. After all, an Illinois resident had warned President Davis that a secret Mississippi Society planned to infiltrate Southern lands along the river and break levees. To counter such threats, Southerners must not only be right but righteous. Local attitudes seemed to mirror the feeling across the South that secession was God-ordained, and the Confederacy must be pure if it was to be victorious.[32]

So Vicksburgians worked toward that end, all the while preparing for conflict while hoping that somehow it would not come to pass. Rabid secessionists got irritated at the slow pace of preparedness, and their vocal concern perhaps spurred recruiting. Men began leaving town to help out at Fort Pickens, considered an important seaport and not too far away in the Gulf of Mexico off the coast of western Florida. Even as tearful families watched loved ones entrain for places where unpredictable dangers lurked, city leaders assured their people that this revolution would be "bloodless."[33]

Even though the beginning of the war, which at this point seemed likely to start in Charleston Harbor, South Carolina, at Fort Sumter, had been growing closer than most residents of the hill city realized, they had reason for optimism. Trade with the North continued along the riverfront. Locally, most goods were plentiful, and social events continued apace. Businessmen with vision soon stocked Confederate-oriented supplies, like "Jefferson Davis" writing paper and envelopes. The appearance of such things perhaps appeased some local fire-eaters who thought their town did not have an apparent enthusiasm for the Confederacy.[34]

Southern guns firing on Fort Sumter soon gave Vicksburg and the rest of the Confederacy the adrenalin that fire-eaters could not. Just prior to that momentous event of April 12, 1861, a poignant ceremony took place at St. Paul's Catholic Church. Two young girls became novitiates in the Sisters of Mercy, the first time such a ceremony had taken place in the city. Protestants and Catholics turned out for the ceremony, a symbolic, peaceful finale to the history of antebellum Vicksburg.[35]

The ceremony stood in stark contrast to excitement in faraway Charleston. While Southern fanatics had a holiday, life continued peacefully in Vicksburg. The city had wrestled with deception since its inception. It grew up cosmopolitan, yet periodically tried to fend off the world that the river continually brought to its doorstep. The city thrived because of the river, yet the old guard sometimes insisted that a social filter must be placed between the town and the docks. They at times seemed almost hysterical about fending off strangers, especially when slavery seemed threatened. They never succeeded, and the city changed in spite of itself, even though many right up to the eve of war insisted on wearing blinders.

Like the South and the Confederacy in which they resided, Vicksburgians in general still believed that separation would not necessarily mean war. Those opposed to separation initially believed they could turn the tide; when that did not happen, they acquiesced and tried to convince themselves that conflict could be avoided. Separation champions embraced the illusory gods of honor and sovereignty, buzzwords of a deceptive past, no matter the cost, yet seemed convinced that the cost would be small. Perhaps, they thought, the Midwest alliance would work, and everyone would live happily ever after.

In effect, Vicksburg was a microcosm of the secession movement. Secessionists believed that they could somehow have their way by isolating themselves on their own terms. They were about to learn that they could not. Vicksburgians would see soon enough that the river belonged to the nation, and Americans upriver would not consider it otherwise. As John Sherman had warned, they would come and fight, and Vicksburg would be the storm center of their fury. The town and the river had been inexorably linked from the earliest days of the settlement that became Vicksburg. Now they were about to be linked by a war that would leave the town in shambles and the river littered with the traffic and wreckage of conflict. The question was no longer if, but when.

~~~ In faraway Washington, events were unfolding that would focus attention and thousands of troops on Vicksburg. Winfield Scott, an elderly American military icon, hero of the war with Mexico and now commander of all Union armies, had a plan to crush the rebellion. He advocated choking it to death by blockading waterways and ports until the infant Confederacy starved to death. Scott's plan was not long on details, and it seemed to many Northerners anxious to end the war before it could build up steam that such a plan would take much too long to succeed. Scott's idea, dubbed the Anaconda Plan, after the reptile that specializes in squeezing its prey to death, never became official policy, though Abraham Lincoln and his navy secretary, Gideon Welles, a Connecticut native who proved to be most capable, did like certain aspects of it.[36]

After Fort Sumter fell, Lincoln proclaimed a blockade of seaports of all states involved in the insurrection. The president would not sit and wait for results, however. He had in mind an offensive strategy to go along with the blockade. He wanted especially to bottle up all water outlets from the South that might be used to transport Southern cotton and other Confederate products. Likewise, no war matériel or other manufactured goods from foreign ports would be allowed to enter

Southern ports. As for the Mississippi River Valley, Lincoln envisioned military movements from the Gulf and from the North. He would not squeeze the Valley; he would free it from Rebel control.[37]

Gideon Welles moved quickly to implement Lincoln's plan, passing the word to naval officers that "a competent force be posted so as to prevent the entrance and exit of vessels from the ports" that served the Confederacy. Further, vessels from neutral countries must be notified that "only public armed vessels of foreign powers should be permitted to enter" restricted ports. Neutral or foreign vessels already in the ports would be given reasonable time to exit. Welles further dictated that United States commerce must be protected from privateers. The navy must do its part to contribute to the "speedy suppression of the insurrectionary movements and the adjustment of the present unhappy difficulties."[38]

Lincoln meant business, and his firmness set a tone echoed by his home-state governor, Richard Yates of Illinois. On April 24, 1861, Yates, a native Kentuckian with strong pro-Union sentiments, sent Chicago militia to take possession of the strategic port town of Cairo, located at the confluence of the Ohio and Mississippi rivers. Additionally, on May 8, the federal government via the head of customs at Louisville, Kentucky, a city sitting on the southern bank of the Ohio, proceeded to block shipping of weapons and supplies intended for the South. Trains traveling on north-south tracks picked up some of the shipping slack, but both Union and Confederate officials tried to thwart such traffic. All this activity increased tension caused by the war starting at Fort Sumter. While Midwest Northerners blamed Southerners for disrupting river traffic, it had been Union officials who took initial action to block commerce on the Mississippi.[39]

As the Lincoln government moved vigorously, Jefferson Davis and the Confederate Congress did not sit idly by. The congress passed legislation on May 10 to stop all trade with the United States. Cotton, the commodity that the South fooled itself into thinking would rupture Northern resolve and gain European recognition for the Confederate cause, would be the main economic weapon. The self-imposed embargo on cotton by the congress would ultimately fail on both fronts. The 1860 cotton crop had produced an overabundance that flooded markets, and even when that was all gone, the Union and Europeans would find other cotton sources.

Davis perhaps suspected as much, for he sought other ways to thwart Lincoln's blockades. The Confederate president called on privateers to attack Federal shipping, and the response was positive and effective.

Though the Confederacy did not, and never would have, a navy comparable to the Union's, there were many privately owned ships that could, and did, harass Northern shipping lanes with hit and run attacks.

Meanwhile, the expanding Union blockade along the Gulf of Mexico reached the mouth of the Mississippi. South of New Orleans, the Union ship *Brooklyn* arrived on May 26 among the passes that connected the Gulf and the river, becoming the first Federal vessel to block free access from the Gulf into the Mississippi. Of course, a secure blockade would require more than one ship, and soon the *Powahatan*, commanded by Lieutenant David Dixon Porter, a navy veteran from Pennsylvania, foster brother of naval officer David Farragut, and a future key figure of the Vicksburg campaign, steamed up to cover the southwest flank of the pass. Both Porter and Charles Poor, commanding the *Brooklyn*, complained to Navy Secretary Welles that they needed more coal, and also some smaller, faster boats to help cover the numerous other waterways along the coast. Gradually, the situation improved, and with the arrival of the *Massachusetts* in June, the naval commanders began to think of ascending the river.[40]

Before such operations could begin, the Union navy needed a base, and they found one, a piece of land well off the state of Mississippi shoreline. The Rebels held Ship Island, but William Mervine, commander of the Gulf squadron, believed he could take it. Not only did the navy need it; the Confederacy could not afford to lose it. Mervine wrote Welles, "This island is fortified by the rebels, for the purpose of protecting their inter-water commerce with New Orleans, which is very important to them." When the Federal boats approached, the defending Confederates, knowing they were hopelessly outmanned and outgunned, quickly abandoned the island. Governor Pettus begged Jefferson Davis for assistance, but the few troops sent to the coast could do nothing about disputing Federal control of the island, which gave the Union a key operations base for an offensive against the lower Mississippi River Valley.[41]

News of Union naval activity to the south caused much concern in New Orleans. Confederate commanders there worked feverishly to build defenses. Rafts (to be set ablaze to hold off Union boats) and other obstructions were set up along the river and pertinent tributaries. George Hollins, a longtime U.S. Navy veteran from Maryland, who joined the Confederate war effort and took over command of New Orleans defenses on July 31, 1861, ordered wooden vessels converted into ironclad rams and the construction of floating batteries. The Confederates converted three steamboats into battleships, and a tugboat, dubbed the *Manassas*, in honor of a Confederate victory in Virginia, into a ram. Hollins had shown much energy and creativity, but he still faced overwhelming odds. He knew that a major Union attack would probably succeed.[42]

By the fall of 1861, a major Federal effort seemed to be under way. Union boats ascended to a spot called Head of Passes, closer to New Orleans. Hollins decided to take a major gamble. The blockade had begun to have a telling effect on the city's supply situation, so Hollins figured that he had to do something other than sit and wait. He sent his rather motley fleet downriver and surprised the Union ships there, driving them back to the Gulf. While the Confederates could justly celebrate, their victory had been hollow. The Federal retreat had been due to bad leadership more than a lack of firepower. The Union fleet had hardly been damaged and would certainly be back. Hollins received unjust criticism for not following up his victory, and soon found himself traveling to Richmond to serve on a court-martial proceeding. The bottom line was that the Confederates had won a skirmish, and New Orleans was as strapped as ever for supplies. Removing Hollins did not change anything.[43]

While Union pressure on New Orleans remained and would grow, pressure on the upper reaches of the Mississippi made Richmond equally nervous. The militia that Illinois governor Yates sent to Cairo stopped a boatload of lead headed for Tennessee, resulting in scattered outbreaks of violence. By June, Union forces had secured the Missouri River and General George McClellan, overall Federal commander in the West, and an advocate of Scott's Anaconda concept, urged offensive action on the Mississippi.[44]

The pace quickened when orders went out on July 30 to Union vessels on the river where it flowed past lower Missouri, Illinois, and western Kentucky that all southbound traffic must be stopped. Boats headed south would be checked at Cape Girardeau, Missouri, while Federal naval vessels at New Madrid, Missouri, received orders to block all northbound traffic.[45]

The navy's tight grip on the upper reaches of the river convinced Confederate officials that the greatest threat to Southern control of the Mississippi lay in that region rather than at New Orleans. Confederate strategists concentrated on beating back enemy threats on the river in general and on the section between the mouth of the Ohio and Memphis, Tennessee, in particular. William Richard Hunt, Rebel ordnance chief, wrote with much insight to General Leonidas Polk on August 12: "If this war should unfortunately be prolonged, the valley of the Mississippi must ultimately become the great theater, for the enemy now working to subjugate the South knows the value of our great artery of commerce and of the prominent cities upon it too well for us to doubt that he will bend all his energies to control them." Unfortunately for the South, understanding the problem did not necessarily mean a solution would be found.[46]

To address Union pressure on the river, Confederates constructed several fortifications along the Tennessee bank in 1861, the most notable being Fort Pillow north of Memphis. Confederate troops filed off transports at New Madrid, Missouri, on the west bank of the river, just northwest of the Tennessee-Kentucky state line, thus thwarting Union efforts to set up a blockade at that point. From where it passed New Madrid, the Mississippi looped south and then back north, forming a large hairpin turn. At the low end of the turn lay Island No. 10, so named because it was the tenth island south of where the Ohio emptied into the Mississippi. The Confederates, who had ideas of using New Madrid as a base for an invasion of Missouri, turned their attention to Island No. 10 and built fortifications to block southbound Union boats. By late August, a Confederate engineer wrote confidently, "I feel satisfied we can defend the valley of the Mississippi against any number of invaders above us."[47]

Jockeying for position on the upper Mississippi took a dramatic turn when Confederate general Gideon J. Pillow, a political general with limited military ability, was ordered by his superior, General Leonidas Polk, an officer who was an Episcopal bishop and possessed much initiative and very little common sense, to occupy Columbus, Kentucky. Columbus sat on the banks of the Mississippi about halfway between Island No. 10 and Cairo. Union control of the town would give the Yankees a base close to Island No. 10, plus it was the terminus of a railroad that descended into Tennessee. Unfortunately for the Southern cause, Polk's preoccupation with the strategic significance of Columbus, which was debatable, led to the neglect of work going on at Island No. 10. Perhaps Polk had listened too closely to his engineers, for, as events would demonstrate, the island's defenses were not as strong as supposed. Beyond all the military ramifications, Polk's orders to occupy Columbus proved to be a political disaster, for in giving them he had violated, and in effect destroyed, Kentucky's attempts to stay neutral. Polk's action infuriated Jefferson Davis and his government and without doubt boosted pro-Union sentiments in Kentucky and the surrounding region.[48]

Federal strategists likely celebrated Polk's misstep. Now that Kentucky's neutrality was a moot point, Union commanders and troops could enter the state and establish a staging area for invading Tennessee. President Lincoln wanted to send troops to relieve pressure on the many Unionists in East Tennessee and now that could possibly be done. Also, the Tennessee and Cumberland rivers provided natural avenues of invasion into the Volunteer State. Successful ascension of the Cumberland could lead to the capture of Nashville and further penetration into the South, possibly even into Mississippi, and eventually to Vicksburg.[49]

A new Confederate commander now stepped into the picture, and he did not like what he saw. Albert Sidney Johnston, an old and close friend of Jefferson Davis, received orders in early September to take command of Department Number 2, called the Western Department, which consisted of all of Tennessee and Arkansas and that portion of Mississippi west of the New Orleans, Jackson and Great Northern and the Mississippi Central railroads, which included Vicksburg. Additionally, Johnston controlled operations in Kentucky, Missouri, Kansas, and Indian country west of Missouri and Arkansas. Johnston chose to establish his headquarters at Columbus, Kentucky, where he perhaps hoped to get a frontline view of the situation he faced.[50]

One of Johnston's first acts was to wire Governor John Pettus that President Davis had authorized a call for troops from Mississippi to assist in the defense of their state and other areas in Johnston's department. Johnston confided to Pettus, "The defenseless condition of this department was patent from the moment I arrived and had a hasty view of the field. The necessity for a strong and efficient army is present and pressing." Johnston specifically requested 10,000 troops and asked that they be assembled in the Mississippi River towns of Vicksburg and Natchez and the north-central Mississippi town of Grenada, located on the Mississippi Central Railroad, which ran north into Tennessee. Johnston obviously wanted troops that could be moved quickly by water and rail. Pettus complied, and the Army of 10,000, as it came to be known, was born.[51]

The news of military events to the north and to the south in the Mississippi Valley received close attention in Vicksburg. Citizens were not as nervous as residents of New Orleans, nor did they share Sidney Johnston's pessimism. The news of war and military maneuvering seemed to leave unshaken the hopes in Vicksburg that peace might yet come. So the people continued with their odd mixture of optimism and military preparation. Yet beneath any talk of peace lay an ever-hardening resolve to meet the challenge of war.[52]

William Howard Russell, the English traveler who toured the lower South during the early days of the conflict, noticed that conviction lay beneath the myriad discussions of events. The North should not be misled by bombastic Southerners who shrugged off the conflict with stated beliefs that the Yankees would not fight, at least not for long. "The issue to them," Russell observed, "is one of life and death. Whoever raises it hereafter if it be not decided now, must expect it to meet the deadly animosity which is now displayed towards the North." When he stepped off a boat at the Vicksburg docks and walked uphill into the city, he noticed that "the war fever is rife in Vicksburg, and the Irish and German laborers, to the extent of several hundreds have all gone off to the war."[53]

Sumter and Lincoln's call for volunteers to put down the rebellion had caused a wave of Southern patriotism to sweep over Vicksburg, similar to the *Silver Wave* episode. A local paper commented, "The history of nations does not present an example of unanimity among any people comparable to the extraordinary spectacle now presented in the Confederate States. We can speak confidently in Mississippi. In the fervor of patriotic feeling, divisions about mere details have been completely merged. . . . This spirit pervades all sects — all classes — all ages."[54]

Unity and patriotic fervor seemed to overshadow the reality of bloody war. Russell participated in a feast in the city's Washington Hotel, a meal that he thought odd, given the urgencies of civil war. People representing several social levels sat feeding themselves from a seemingly endless supply of foods provided by the owner of the hotel. He thought it strange to hear complaints about the state government coercing owners to give up their slave labor from time to time for the sake of war-related work, perhaps an indication that Southern patriotism had its limits. Then the hotel crowd gathered at the train station to make windy speeches and cheer local young men departing for combat. News of a Confederate victory at Bethel, Virginia, added to the lofty spirits of the occasion. Calls came for cheers for Jeff Davis and states' rights. Russell thought the whole thing had the atmosphere of a sporting event, rather than of serious thought about young men dying in battle.[55]

Vicksburgians seemed to underscore Russell's observations by playing war. A group of elderly city fathers formed the Old Guard, a worthless military unit, but an important symbol intended to show support for the Confederate cause from among those too aged or infirm to fight. A few local immigrants formed a "Foreign Legion", which included those who had trouble speaking English. Two free blacks got attention when they made public their purchase of Confederate war bonds. Such were the unusual scenes wrought by a war that still seemed far away.[56]

Local idiosyncrasies aside, the events in Vicksburg mirrored much of what was going on in the rest of the Confederacy. Distorted ideas of romantic battles and dreams of patriotic, female-pleasing glory overwhelmed the common sense of young white males. Of course, as in the case of Vicksburg's aged Guard, the fever gripped all ages. Some, like the Guard, experienced war thrills vicariously through the young men shooting and being shot at. The latter group would know the truth soon enough: the vague, delusional air of wonderful distant battlefields was a myth. They would kill or be killed, maim or be maimed, all in the name of deceptively defined rights. In 1861, the war was too young for most Southerners, including Vicksburgians, to understand what they were getting into.

Vicksburg women, like their sisters across the South, perhaps had a greater sense of war's reality than men, but they put on proud faces and perpetuated local delusions with projected airs of patriotism and encouragement. The tears they shed when the trains left told a truer story, one that could not be dismissed as just a natural manifestation of their sex. Seeing the number of men-folk dwindling with every train whistle gave the women a glimpse of a future they did not wish to think about. They dried their tears and made blankets and shirts and pants, and a few learned how to handle firearms. They simply coped, as they always had in their male-dominated world.

Despite citizens' best efforts to thwart it, reality insisted on surfacing from time to time. The summer heat of 1861 brought forth old echoes of paranoia. Some complained about Unionists in their midst. A local newspaper editor endorsed having all citizens wear identification badges; vigilance committees spied on fellow citizens; and business owners suspected of being soft patriots received various threats. Perhaps it was merely a case of war nerves; certainly there seemed to be little substance to all the talk. More than anything else, such events seemed to be the spasms of a disappointed city seeing all hopes of peace disappear.

Yet many tenaciously clung to the fable that the war would end before it got to Vicksburg. People did not conserve; they bought and sold as they had before Sumter. A local female academy planned its fall semester as if the threat of war did not exist. Local ministers did not use the time of trouble to call for repentance. Political divisions melted away as secession certainly seemed irreversible. But soon evidences of war began to appear that could not be ignored. The war was close and would get closer.

The muddy waters of the Mississippi that flowed past Vicksburg had been churned less and less by paddle wheelers as summer became fall and symbolic winter winds blew in from the north. River traffic from the Ohio and upper Mississippi gradually slackened to a halt, and boats from New Orleans and other points south brought fewer supplies to Vicksburg docks. Resulting food shortages created hunger problems quickly addressed by the city government and the fledgling Benevolent Society. Gluttonous feasts at the Washington Hotel seemed long past.

The clear signal of troubled times brought by reduced river traffic did not produce immediate panic. Local foundries had plenty of war orders, and their increased business gave work to those whose jobs had been lost due to Union blockades. As Christmas 1861 came and went, an air of nonchalance still hung over the city, despite the threats of a future that could be considerably more detrimental. Ironically, when it came to defending Vicksburg, state and Confederate government authorities seemed to have the same attitude. The first great battle of the war had been won at Manassas, focusing the struggle on Virginia. The victory raised morale and hopes and melted fears and worries all across the Confederacy. By year's end, very little, in fact practically nothing, had been done to prepare defensive works around Vicksburg. The new year brought a resumption of activity that could well cost the city and the Confederacy a high price for such lackadaisical attitudes.

To the south, in New Orleans, the Confederate military situation had undergone a significant change. At the insistence of Louisiana governor Thomas Moore and others, Jefferson Davis had decided in September to replace the latest area commander, the elderly David Twiggs, with Mansfield Lovell, whom Secretary of War Judah Benjamin viewed as "a brilliant, energetic, and accomplished officer." Lovell, who was not a native Southerner and therefore would be regarded with suspicion by locals, would not measure up to the task, and by late 1862 he would disappear from the war stage for good.

President Davis made the change to get Moore and other Louisiana critics off his back. The president did not like criticism, and he reminded Moore regarding the Twiggs situation: "In his selection I yielded as much to the solicitation of the people of New Orleans, I think they should [have] sooner informed me of the mistake they had made." After typically passing the buck, Davis insisted that he had been led to believe that work on New Orleans area defenses had been proceeding adequately. Further, in spite of Moore's complaints of neglect, Davis argued that he had tried to provide needed munitions and armaments.

Davis then concluded his remarks with words that indicated he was less concerned about the fate of New Orleans than about being blamed for the loss of the city. If New Orleans were to fall, he wrote, "which I cannot bring myself to believe when I remember how much has been done for the defense of New Orleans since 1815, both in the construction of works and facilities for transportation — I hope a discriminating public will acquit this Government of having neglected the defenses of your coast and approaches to New Orleans."[57]

The new commander soon understood Governor Moore's agitation. Lovell complained to the War Department that New Orleans was not battle-ready, and the shipments of supplies out of the city to other points should be stopped. Secretary Benjamin responded that Lovell should purchase what he needed rather than suggest blocking commerce. Benjamin's somewhat insulting reply indicated yet again that Richmond had little sense of urgency about the safety of the Crescent City.

Despite Confederate government attitudes, Lovell worked diligently to prepare for expected Union attacks. In early December he wired Benjamin that when all of its heavy guns were put in place, the city should be "a citadel" unless attacked from all sides. Lovell flatly refused to weaken his position by sending 5,000 troops north to the Columbus front. He insisted that he had none to spare, especially since he needed all he had to guard his southern flank against enemy forces in the Gulf as well as his rear to the north. Lovell, from the perspective of his strategic and tactical situation, understood what it took the War Department much too long to learn. Defending fixed positions against potential multiple frontal attacks offered little promise of success, especially if large numbers of troops in those fixed positions were siphoned off to other fronts.[58]

Since the war began, Confederate officers in the Mississippi Valley theater had been analyzing the challenges that lay ahead. Colonel Edward Fontaine, Mississippi's ordnance chief, shared his views in a December 1861 letter to Governor Moore. Fontaine believed that river activity to the north was a clear sign that the Yankees would use the rivers to reach Memphis and, via the Tennessee and Cumberland rivers, Nashville as well. Federal boats to the south would ascend to New Orleans. Fontaine reported that he intended to go to Vicksburg on December 19 to plan fortifications and estimate the number of slaves that would be needed to build them. He thought he could prevent the capture of Vicksburg, but he knew he could not stop Union boats from passing by the city or stopping and shelling it. A fort might protect the railroad terminus across the river from Vicksburg that linked interior North Louisiana to the Mississippi. On the other hand, he could do nothing to prevent the enemy from digging a canal through the neck of land across from Vicksburg, a canal that would allow the Union navy to bypass the city's defenses. Fontaine concluded that rivers north of Vicksburg should be closed and defended by a string of strategically located forts. The colonel's foresight is fascinating, for in his letter he accurately forecast several components of future efforts to capture Vicksburg. His most telling contribution, however, was pushing construction of defensive works, which should have long been completed before December 1861. As was true of its handling of New Orleans, the Confederate War Department's neglect of Vicksburg signaled Richmond's head-in-the-sand attitude regarding the dynamics of the Mississippi Valley campaign.[59]

Abraham Lincoln understood clearly. A few weeks prior to Fontaine's musings, on the night of November 15, 1861, Lincoln met with David Porter, Gideon Welles, George McClellan (now overall army commander), Gustavus Fox (Welles's assistant), and Flag Officer Samuel F. Dupont at McClellan's home in Washington to discuss plans for a naval attack on New Orleans. Porter would later claim that the capture of Vicksburg also came up for discussion. Porter's is the only account of Lincoln's remarks about taking Vicksburg, and Porter had a penchant for playing games with the truth. Yet what Porter claimed Lincoln said has a ring of truth to it and is now too much part of Civil War lore to question.[60]

In fact, Porter's account does not even state the exact date that he heard Lincoln's words, but the November 15 meeting is the most likely. Whatever the case may be, Lincoln presumably pointed at a map and, according to Porter, said: "See what a lot of land these fellows hold, of which Vicksburg is the key. Here is Red River, which will supply the Confederates with cattle and corn to feed their armies. There are the Arkansas and White Rivers, which can supply cattle and hogs by the thousand. From Vicksburg these supplies can be distributed by rail all over the Confederacy. Then there is that great depot of supplies on the Yazoo. Let us get Vicksburg and all that country is ours. The war can never be brought to a close until that key is in our pocket. I am acquainted with that region and know what I am talking about, and, valuable as New Orleans will be to us Vicksburg will be more so. We may take all the northern ports of the Confederacy, and they can still defy us from Vicksburg. It means hog and hominy without limit, fresh troops from all the States of the far South, and a cotton country where they can raise the staple without interference." Porter noted that "Lincoln's capacious mind took in the whole subject, and he made it plain to the dullest comprehension. A military expert could not more clearly have defined the advantages of the proposed campaign." Porter further recalled that Lincoln actively urged the military men in attendance to make the capture of Vicksburg a high priority.[61]

Subsequent events would demonstrate many holes in Lincoln's theory. Supplies from west of the Mississippi never poured into regions east of the river in the amounts that Lincoln, and certainly Jefferson Davis, suspected. Most men, food, and matériel in the Trans-Mississippi area stayed there. The Vicksburg, Shreveport and Texas Railroad, which ran from directly across Vicksburg on the Louisiana side of the Mississippi some eighty miles west to Monroe, did not prove to be the supply artery Confederates envisioned. The Southern Railroad of Mississippi ran east from Vicksburg, intersecting the north-south Mobile and Ohio at Meridian, but from that point roads east were segmented and unfinished, and, all in all, Vicksburg's rail connections with the east never lived up to Confederate expectations. The military significance of Vicksburg lay more in the perceptions of Lincoln and Davis, and in the reality of future military events, than in the city's actual strategic and logistical strengths. Vicksburg became vital, "the key," because both sides ultimately decided it was, and because faulty Union strategy made it seem so. The latter aspect of Vicksburg's stature became obvious during the first stage of the Union navy's lower Mississippi River campaign.[62]

First, New Orleans would have to fall. Several months had passed since the arrival of Union naval forces at the mouths of the Mississippi, and no serious attempt had been made to capture the city. With the dawn of 1862, Union strategists turned their attention to the lower Mississippi. Engineer and brigadier general J. G. Barnard detailed how he felt the campaign should be carried out. He urged an attack by "a combined naval and land [force], operating through the mouths of the river, and making the capture of Forts Jackson and Saint Phillip [located on the river south of New Orleans] an essential feature of the plan." He believed that the forts had to be eliminated, for if they fell, "New Orleans falls, and our gunboats appear at once before Vicksburg, Natchez, and Memphis, and the rebel defense both ways (our armies and flotilla in the Upper Mississippi cooperating) is completely annihilated." Future operations would be carried out along the lines of Barnard's plan, but they would be more protracted and complicated than he envisioned.

George McClellan, the arrogant Pennsylvanian who proved to be incapable of field generalship but who had administrative and planning talents, had similar thoughts. In February 1862, he told Benjamin Butler, a political general who would command Union army forces in the upcoming New Orleans campaign, that the navy's job would be to take care of the forts. Butler was to help in the capture of land works at New Orleans and in other areas the navy could not easily reach, including Baton Rouge, the Louisiana state capital upriver from New Orleans. From Baton Rouge, Butler should attempt to establish contact with Union forces upriver, "always bearing in mind the necessity of occupying Jackson, Miss., as soon as you can safely do so, either after or before you have effected the junction." Butler ignored McClellan's instructions to take Mobile, Pensacola, and Galveston first, all three important Southern ports. Such operations would take too much time, and Butler was ready for action. Butler would make his mark in New Orleans, but he would never reach Jackson or effect a junction.[63]

While Union plans evolved for the capture of New Orleans and the lower Mississippi, Mansfield Lovell worked long hours in his efforts to save New Orleans for the Confederacy. In addition to building an army, he had had to throw together a makeshift navy that would operate under his command. He ordered the building of additional obstructions, but bad winter weather and lack of material hampered his efforts.

The biggest barrier to success continued to be the government in far away Richmond. Constantly harassed by the War Department with numerous requests to send troops and supplies hither and yon, he finally yielded to Secretary Benjamin's demand for 5,000 troops for Columbus. Benjamin explained the War Department's position: "New Orleans is to be defended from above by defeating the enemy at Columbus; the forces now withdrawn from you are for the defence of your own command, and the exigencies of the public defense allow us no alternative." This was quite a gamble, for Davis and Benjamin seemed to be counting on the Union force south of New Orleans to do nothing while the Confederates concentrated their efforts on the Columbus front. Lovell felt a sense of doom, for he realized the danger. After he sent the troops upriver, he knew that "New Orleans is about defenseless. In return we get nothing."[64]

The situation at Columbus was not good either, and with too few men to defend the entire river valley, the War Department felt the gamble with New Orleans's fate was necessary. Sidney Johnston's unrealistic attempt to hold a long line that stretched from the Mississippi eastward to Cumberland Gap in the Appalachians had been foiled by Confederate defeat at Mill Springs, Kentucky, on January 19, 1862. As a result,

Johnston decided he must abandon Columbus; the evacuation was completed by March 2. By then, Johnston seemed to lose all hope of holding Tennessee. He had begged Richmond for boats to assist in the holding of Fort Henry on the Tennessee and Fort Donelson on the Cumberland. Johnston had repeatedly asked for more men and had warned Tennessee governor Isham Harris in November that a determined Yankee invasion could probably not be stopped and would lead to a penetration of the lower Confederacy, especially the Mississippi Valley.[65]

On the Federal side, General Henry Halleck, the brainy, and often controversial, commander of the Department of the Missouri, did his best to keep up pressure on Johnston after General Don Carlos Buell's victory at Mill Springs. Halleck saw Buell's triumph as an opportunity to fulfill one of President Lincoln's desires—relief for Unionists in East Tennessee. In January, Halleck put together operations against Forts Henry and Donelson; the former fell rather easily on February 6. Donelson held out longer, but thanks to inept Confederate generalship and a strong showing by an unassuming Union general named Ulysses S. Grant, native Ohioan and current Illinoisan, the Confederate stronghold on the Cumberland capitulated on February 16. A disgusted Johnston evacuated Nashville without a fight on February 23.[66]

Far away in Vicksburg, the Federal penetration into Tennessee brought much worry. One woman wrote, "The town is fermenting again, about the advance of the Federals down the Tennessee river, and every body is going to war right off." Apart from a patriotic spurt, a pall of uncertainty settled over the city. "Some of the old ladies think they are going to eat us up right away, but I defy the Yankees to scare me," the woman added. "I am not afraid to die and there is nothing worse than death in store for me." She longed for her husband who was with the Confederate army in Virginia and commented on their separation, "If it keeps growing harder every day, before long it will be intolerable." She warned him that his home state "may be polluted by the Vandal's tread."[67]

Having witnessed the folly of scattering his thin forces across a wide area, a strategy that only magnified Yankee superiority in numbers, Johnston pulled his army all the way south to Corinth, Mississippi, an important railroad center in the northeast corner of the state. Meanwhile, victorious Union forces commanded by Grant steamed down the Tennessee and disembarked at Pittsburg Landing and up onto bluffs some twenty miles northeast of Corinth. On April 6, Johnston launched an attack on Grant's position that caught most Union troops by surprise. The Confederates drove the Federals back to the river bluffs; but

Johnston fell, mortally wounded, the attack bogged down, and new commander P. G. T. Beauregard called a halt. Beauregard, hero of Fort Sumter and veteran of early battles in Virginia, had to reform his scattered army. But, the next day, Grant used Don Carlos Buell's newly arrived troops from Columbia, Tennessee, where they had been held up by floodwaters, and one of his own late arriving divisions, to turn the tide and send the Confederates retreating to Corinth.[68]

On the Mississippi, things turned equally sour for the Confederate cause. At shipyards in Carondelet, Missouri, on the Mississippi south of St. Louis, Union naval captain Andrew H. Foote had taken charge of the construction of ironclads that would be known as the city series. Based on the designs of Samuel Pook, these vessels, dubbed Pook's turtles on account of their humpback design and slow speed, were named the *Carondelet, St. Louis, Louisville, Pittsburg, Mound City, Cincinnati,* and *Cairo.* The boats steamed to Cairo to be equipped and assigned crews. Foote also had on hand three boats of traditional construction. The Confederacy could never match this kind of naval power.[69]

The only Confederate works north of Vicksburg that had any chance of stopping Foote's fleet were at Island No. 10. Union forces commanded by General John Pope, another arrogant officer whose self-image exceeded his abilities, captured New Madrid on March 14. William Mackall took command of Confederate forces on March 31, replacing the inept John McCown, a Tennessean and West Pointer who made Pope look good by abandoning New Madrid to the Yankees. Perhaps he would have had to evacuate the place anyway, but McCown had shown no imagination or fighting spirit. Whether Mackall could do any better was problematical. The Confederate naval presence, such as it was, did little to help the situation at Island No. 10. George Hollins, back in the war after being called to Richmond from New Orleans, commanded Confederate boats, and he knew he would be outclassed by Yankee ironclads. He begged to be sent back to New Orleans where his vessels would be more evenly matched with the Federal navy threatening the city. His pleas fell on deaf ears, and his performance in the Island No. 10 campaign demonstrated that his heart was elsewhere. Flanked and entrapped by Pope, with the aid of the Union navy, Mackall surrendered on April 7. Pope had performed well in spite of himself and would soon be sent to Virginia where disaster awaited him in a match with Robert E. Lee. Foote's gunboats performed more admirably than their commander, who would receive a promotion to admiral and then die of Bright's disease in 1863. His ironclads proved that they could pass by Confederate shore batteries relatively unscathed and also play a key role in transporting ground troops to strategic positions. Such tactics would come in handy farther downriver.[70]

The Federal fleet continued on south and encouraged the Confederates to abandon Fort Pillow above Memphis on June 3–4. Union vessels then battered an outclassed hodgepodge of Confederate boats at Memphis on June 6, and the city surrendered, but the clearing of the Mississippi was still over a year away. Union strategists could not seem to decide how best to take advantage of successes that led to control of the river from Cairo to Memphis.

To the south, Union operations finally got under way against New Orleans. David Farragut, a hard-nosed veteran flag officer, received the assignment to lead the fleet upriver. David Porter served under his foster brother and commanded twenty mortar boats, which he believed would be the keys to knocking out Forts St. Phillip and Jackson. Porter's mortars opened fire on April 18. The bombardment, assisted by Farragut's other warships, kept up a continual shelling for several days. Farragut finally grew impatient, and on April 24 he led the fleet past the forts and captured New Orleans the next day. The Confederate vessels, without the leadership of an experience naval commander, performed poorly; but they were so heavily outgunned that better leadership likely would not have mattered.

Mansfield Lovell ordered his troops to evacuate the city to escape capture, and in the process he saved New Orleans from much destruction. Lovell would be criticized for not putting up a fight, but he knew his position was hopeless, and he saw no need of senseless resistance. The Confederates retreated to Camp Moore east of the river via the New Orleans, Jackson and Great Northern Railroad. Meanwhile, due to the quick, unexpected Union takeover, the city they left behind became chaotic. On April 28, the two forts surrendered, and New Orleans was securely in Federal hands. Farragut had demonstrated, as had Foote, that fixed fortifications on the Mississippi could not stop fast moving naval vessels, even wooden ones.[71]

In Vicksburg, all the bad news from upriver and down did not produce panic in a town that still seemingly refused to believe that war would ever come to its neighborhood. The city fathers worried that unsavory refugees from other river cities captured by the Yankees might come pouring into Vicksburg. Accordingly, the mayor asked local militia to be ready to assist police in controlling the expected influx. As events progressed, it was not a flood of refugees that awakened the city from its self-induced slumber. Trainloads of wounded soldiers from Shiloh began arriving, bringing the true horror of war to Vicksburg for the first time. One local lady summed up the obvious: "the war is near us indeed." The wounded, plus the news of the fall of New Orleans, meant that the war was getting closer all the time. David Farragut and his fleet had stopped at New Orleans, but they would soon be steaming upriver. In a few weeks, the Vicksburg waterfront would be playing host to a Union navy squadron that had in mind putting the key in Lincoln's pocket.[72]

2

Summer Stalemate

David Glasgow Farragut brought the war to Vicksburg. Despite disturbing rumors of enemy naval activity on the southern and northern reaches of the Mississippi, Vicksburg citizens clung to the desperate hope that the outside world in general and the war in particular could be kept at bay. By the time he reached Vicksburg, Farragut did not want to be on the Mississippi any more than Vicksburgians and the Confederacy wanted him there. Farragut's long career had been mostly spent on oceans, and he felt confined by riverbanks, even those as far apart as the Mississippi's. At first, Farragut liked Benjamin Butler's idea of focusing on moving up the Mississippi after New Orleans fell. He believed that he could build on the New Orleans victory by easily taking the major towns upriver, Baton Rouge, Natchez, and Vicksburg, and, with another Union naval flotilla coming south, the Mississippi should be free of Rebels within a few weeks at most. Clearing the river would block the west-to-east Confederate supply line, extending from the Mississippi up the Red River, and also cut the railroad across from Vicksburg that ran into interior northern Louisiana. An open river meant a return to the Gulf of Mexico and salt water. The job did not prove to be as easy as expected.

Farragut sent a flotilla ahead, led by Captain Thomas Craven, who personally commanded the sloop of war *Brooklyn*. As Craven's detachment steamed upriver, the crews were well aware of staring eyes, some hostile and some friendly, or pretending to be, from both banks of the river. At one point, a few navy men went ashore to gather information and found some civilians "terribly frightened, but after learning that we were not on a nigger stealing expedition, and their property was safe . . . they gradually calmed down." They found too that partisan bands of guerrillas had frightened many people by threatening retaliation for cooperating with Yankees. The Union navy and army would have many encounters with guerrillas before the river war ended, and many civilians would pay a high price for being in harm's way.[1]

Craven's detachment passed Baton Rouge without incident. He had not been told to shoot at the Louisiana capital, and the Confederacy had not bothered to fortify the place. Upriver from Baton Rouge, the sailors saw smoke boiling from banks on both sides, emanating from burning cotton. Planters loyal to the Confederacy used fire to keep their crops from enemy hands, and the smoke signaled others that the Yankees were coming. Farmers paid dearly for being on the front line of the war with no succor in sight from their government in Virginia.

After Craven's boats and ships passed the mouth of the Red, he decided to go back downriver. Mechanical problems and the failure of Farragut to catch up dictated the decision. On the way back, Craven encountered Samuel Phillips Lee, commander of the *Oneida*, and learned that Farragut wanted the Craven detachment to return to Baton Rouge, while Lee took a few gunboats to Vicksburg. Farragut was heeding warnings that big war ships might be a problem to handle in the high water upstream caused by spring floods, so for a time a massive Union naval effort to clear the lower reaches of the river would have to wait. Waiting could be dangerous, however, for intelligence reports indicated a Confederate buildup at Vicksburg and the construction of a Rebel ironclad somewhere in the Vicksburg area.[2]

Craven found Farragut in Baton Rouge receiving the peaceful surrender of that city. Commander James Palmer of the *Iroquois* proceeded up to Natchez, Mississippi, which also was surrendered without a shot being fired. Farragut intended using Natchez as a base for operations against Vicksburg. Palmer discovered that Lee was still at Natchez; why Lee had not gone on to Vicksburg is not clear. Perhaps the appearance of a Rebel steamer, the *Vicksburg*, above Natchez had sobered his fighting spirit. In any event, Palmer obtained the city's surrender from Mayor John Hunter, who knew the pitiful band of only fourteen Confederates occupying the town could not defend anything. Meanwhile, Union infantry and artillery, sent by Butler to help out as needed, and commanded by General Thomas Williams, disembarked in Vidalia, Louisiana, across the river from Natchez.

Continuing the pattern of crop destruction, planters in the area rushed to destroy cotton, and local citizens, distraught at this disruption of their world and livelihoods, glared at occupying Yankee soldiers with sullen and angry demeanors. A soldier in the 6th Michigan found such reactions amusing, noting, "Between their voluntary destruction of cotton & sugar, the flood & the Yankees our Southern brethren are in a sorry condition." So far, the easy run upstream by Farragut and his lieutenants demonstrated clearly to Louisianans and Mississippians just how far beyond the help of the Confederate government they were. Without a navy comparable to the Union's, the Confederacy could do little to provide security along inland waterways.[3]

Captain Lee, meanwhile, had finally gone upriver, reaching Vicksburg on May 18, whereupon he demanded the surrender of the city. Here the unobstructed expedition up the Mississippi ended. Lieutenant Colonel James Autry, military governor at Vicksburg and acting on behalf of the state government, responded heatedly: "I have to state that Mississippians don't know, and refuse to learn, how to surrender to an enemy. If Commodore [Flag Officer] Farragut or Brigadier-General [Major General] Butler can teach them, then let them try." Autry's reductions in rank for Farragut and Butler were likely intentional insults rather than mistakes. Martin L. Smith, commanding Confederate forces in the city, replied similarly, "Having been ordered to hold these defenses, it is my intention to do so as long as in my power." And Mayor Lazarus Lindsay added, "Neither the municipal authorities nor the citizens will ever consent to a surrender of the city." Thrice rebuffed, Lee retreated south of Vicksburg to wait for Farragut.[4]

In Vicksburg, General Smith, a native New Yorker, whose prewar army service in the South had resulted in marriage to a Southern woman and development of Southern sympathies, increased work on the city's defenses. Smith had been ordered to assume command on May 12 by General Mansfield Lovell, who still commanded the area despite losing New Orleans and being vilified throughout the South. By the time Lee arrived, Smith's force consisted of the 8th Louisiana Battalion, the 27th Louisiana infantry regiment, and six artillery batteries, but he needed more. Smith revitalized the ironclad project, which he found in disarray. He recruited mechanics and accumulated materials for continued construction of the ironclad, dubbed the *Arkansas*. At last a competent naval officer, Isaac N. Brown, "a pushing man," arrived to take over the project, allowing Smith to focus on defending Vicksburg.[5]

Trains chugged into town on the Southern Railroad of Mississippi, bringing troops from the east. Adaptations had to be made to rolling stock and low overhead bridges to give soldiers jammed into cars a safe ride. Surprisingly to the soldiers, many citizens in Vicksburg condemned their presence because they feared more Confederate soldiers would attract more Union attention. Even now, some residents clung to the notion that the war would pass them by, and they did not want to deal with any outsiders, even men defending their city. Soldiers went to work anyway, burning excess cotton, constructing fortifications and campsites, and fighting sickness, especially outbreaks of measles. Many local women swallowed their pride and rushed to help out at hospitals, while dejected young men wondered if they would see the glory of battle before experiencing death in a hospital.[6]

Reinforcements from the East set a pattern for Confederate attempts to save Vicksburg. Earl Van Dorn's army from Arkansas proved to be one of the last major troop transfers from the Trans-Mississippi to the eastern side of the Mississippi River, and it had arrived too late to help at Shiloh. Arkansans had not been happy about losing Van Dorn's men. Jefferson Davis understood that all too well, and though he would encourage and even order the sending of reinforcements to Vicksburg's relief in the future, he never forced the issue. By allowing political considerations to force him into deferring to Trans-Mississippi commanders' wishes not to cross the river, Davis fatally tied the hands of Vicksburg commanders.

At the time, General Smith was so pleased to have additional men that he did not concern himself with where they came from. He worried not only about getting healthy soldiers but also about the fate of many civilians who ignored warnings and refused to leave. He felt relieved when some did flee, taking "to forests, fields, glens, cow-sheds, carriage-houses, shanties, any place, every place for shelter. A sheet, a quilt, a blanket, stretched over their heads for a tent was all hundreds had to cover themselves with." As time passed, Smith accepted the fact that numerous townspeople would never leave, no matter the danger. Their tenacity inspired him: "With great unanimity [they] made up their minds that [their town's] possession ought to be maintained at all hazards, even though total demolition should be the result." Enemy shells tested such resolve.[7]

On May 21, Mayor Lindsay received another message from Lee, who appealed to the mayor's humanitarian spirit: "It becomes my duty to give you notice to remove the women and children beyond the range of our guns within twenty-four hours, as it will be impossible to attack the defenses without injuring or destroying the town, a proceeding which all the authorities of Vicksburg seemed determined to require. I had hoped that the same spirit which [induced] the military authorities to retire from the city of New Orleans, rather than wantonly sacrifice the lives and property of its inhabitants, would have been followed here." The mayor promised to give public notice, and Lee responded rather convolutedly: "[I] have to state that my communication of yesterday in relation to the removal of the women and children was for the purpose of placing it at my option to fire or not, as I might think proper, at the earliest moment, upon the defenses of the town, without producing a loss of innocent life, and to that determination I shall adhere." Whatever he meant, Lee did nothing for the next several days.

Union naval inactivity prompted great concern in distant Washington. Assistant Secretary of the Navy Gustavus Fox notified Farragut that rumors of a retreat back to New Orleans "distressed the President so much that I immediately dispatched the *Dacotah* from Hampton Roads" in Virginia to get word to Farragut that the lower river must be cleared and Memphis taken. War Department strategists counted on Farragut to provide logistical support to the Union army, now threatening Confederates in Corinth. On May 19, Navy Secretary Gideon Welles warned Farragut: "The President of the United States requires you to use your utmost exertions (without a moment's delay, and before any other naval operations shall be permitted to interfere) to open the river Mississippi and effect a junction with Flag-Officer [Charles] Davis, commanding (pro tem.) the Western Flotilla." Farragut did not receive the messages for several days. Meanwhile, he had arrived at Vicksburg, grown angry at city officials' recalcitrance, and noted with disgust that Thomas Williams insisted his infantry and artillery could do nothing along the flooded Louisiana side of the river. Farragut wanted to launch an all-out naval bombardment, but his commanders convinced him to calm down and think about it.[8]

On May 22, Farragut notified Butler of the dangers of bringing war ships any further north than Grand Gulf, a Mississippi town along the river about forty miles or so south of Vicksburg. The river got wider and deeper as it flowed north. Also, Williams refused to send his small force in a suicidal attack against the Vicksburg bluffs. Farragut insisted that the Rebels had many thousands of troops in Vicksburg, which was not true, so shelling the city would accomplish little. Even if city officials surrendered, the navy and Williams's meager force could not hold the place. Given the dilemma, Farragut settled on a blockade to "occasionally harass them with fire until the battle of Corinth shall decide its fate. General Williams is going up the Red River, where he thinks he will be more useful. . . . I shall soon drop down the river again, as I consider my services indispensably necessary on the seaboard. . . . I do not see that I can be of any service here, and I do not see as General Williams will be of any use here with the small force he has." Frustrated, Farragut longed for the sea. The river campaign could wait.[9]

On May 30, Farragut wrote a lengthy report to Secretary Welles from New Orleans, detailing his trip to Vicksburg, "at least 300 miles farther than I was ever from sea water before since the days of my childhood." He reiterated earlier arguments, added additional thousands to his overestimates of Confederate strength, and included false information about large numbers of Confederate rams on the river. Vulnerable supply lines and the likelihood of seasonal low water induced him "to abandon the idea of attacking Vicksburg beyond harassing it, to prevent the erection of more batteries." Finally, in a note to Fox, Farragut cited problems of getting infantry to Memphis, negotiating the hairpin turn at Vicksburg and the desperate need for an ironclad, which would be "worth all the gunboats in the river."[10]

While Farragut attempted to appease Washington, turmoil developed at Vicksburg among naval officers. Lee, left behind, he thought, to oversee blockade operations, learned that James Palmer had assumed command of the Blockading Squadron. Lee lashed out at Farragut, who pointed out Palmer's seniority. So Palmer issued orders, and boring, routine blockade maneuvers began. The command controversy and unproductive blockade strategies, which provided no threat to Vicksburg, had a negative impact on morale. A curious situation had evolved. The Confederate government could in effect do nothing to thwart Union naval operations on the river. The federal government's navy could do no more than accept a stalemate.[11]

≈ While the navy fought boredom, Thomas Williams returned his troops to Baton Rouge. Williams endured problems with the conduct of his soldiers and with Confederate guerrillas. Some of his troops had pillaged earlier in the New Orleans area. An embarrassed Williams admitted that his "officers and men, with rare exceptions, appear to be wholly destitute of the moral sense, and I believe that they believe, in the face of all remonstrances, exhortations, and disgust, expressed in no measured terms, that they regard pillaging not only right in itself but a soldierly accomplishment." These attitudes were not uncommon in the Union army, and combating the issue proved to be a major problem for officers, especially when some among them looked the other way. Union soldiers embraced "hard war," which meant aggressive acts against civilian property, long before it became official policy. The Vicksburg campaign provided many examples of the impact of war on civilians.[12]

On the way to Baton Rouge, Williams and his men had experiences that fueled reckless behavior. Confederates firing at Union troop transports wrought frustration and anger among the intended victims. Such partisan tactics led Federal troops to lump perpetrators into one category: guerrillas. The so-called guerrillas consisted of local militia, private citizens, and occasionally Confederate regulars. Others included outlaw bands or thugs who would attack either side when convenient. To soldiers on the transports, distinctions did not matter, and they could not wait to get ashore and wreak their vengeance. But pillaging and sacking did not always require an excuse. Some of Farragut's sailors earlier raided the Jefferson Davis property on Davis Bend, along the Mississippi south of Vicksburg, for no other reason than the place belonged to Davis.[13]

One particular trouble spot for Williams's troops proved to be Grand Gulf. Williams understood the strategic significance of the town. Maps showed that the Big Black River entered the Mississippi just above Grand Gulf. If smaller Union vessels ascended the Big Black, which ran in a northeasterly direction up through Mississippi, they could destroy the Southern Railroad bridge, which connected Vicksburg with points east. The navy had rejected the idea, primarily because the Big Black was neither wide enough nor deep enough for large ships, and reports indicated that the Confederates had placed cannon to defend southern approaches to the bridge. Nevertheless, Williams decided to unleash his men on Grand Gulf to at least drive out the worrisome Confederate snipers and artillerists there.[14]

When the Union troops landed, Grand Gulf residents protested with arguments that became familiar along the river. Those who fired at the vessels were guerrillas "over whom they had no control." Williams's troops checked on the enemy cannon, and a skirmish broke out. Several men fell, including Williams's aide, George DeKay, riddled by buck shot and partially paralyzed. Though furious, Williams kept his composure and left Grand Gulf standing. In return, grateful citizens consented to Union demands for food. Union forces had not seen the last of trouble at Grand Gulf. Williams would regret not doing more, but he needed to get his small army to Baton Rouge, where rest could remedy their "careworn faces and . . . sagging, emaciated bodies," souvenirs of Vicksburg. Meanwhile, Williams's sortie did nothing to slow guerrilla activities along the Mississippi.[15]

In Vicksburg, Martin Luther Smith remained concerned about holding on to the town despite the reduced enemy pressure. Infantry regiments and cavalry companies and an occasional artillery battery arrived, but the numbers never approached anything close to Farragut's exaggerations. Smith welcomed them all, but he noticed many were "new troops, just mustered into service, and indifferently armed." Smith sent some newcomers to watch the Warrenton area where most of the Union squadron anchored. Work on the city's defenses went slowly and shoddily on account of the inconsistent availability of slave labor. Wrote one disgusted Confederate named Sidney Champion, whose home area east of Vicksburg would become a campaign landmark, "Negroes are running off from home daily and their masters are not returning them." He lamented, "We are willing to sell ourselves to the Lincolnites for the poor Negro. We [a]re in fact 'Negro holists.' Yea— love them better than our sons or husbands. Men are actually coming down after their Negroes fearing they will get sick. Oh; dear—this sort of work will be our ruin before long. The merchants are moving every- thing out in the country—and families are moving out very rapidly— fearing an attack very soon."[16]

Uncertainty prevailed in Vicksburg, especially in Martin Smith's mind, for he received few scouting reports. He basically knew only what he saw, and occasional rumors gave him no solid evidence of enemy intent. He worried more about infantry showing up in force, either in his rear or being transported to Vicksburg's northern and southern flanks by river transports, than about Farragut's navy. He later recalled that, counting from May 26, "The ensuing ten days I consider the most critical period of the defenses of Vicksburg: batteries incomplete; guns not mounted; troops few, and both officers and men entirely new to ser- vice, and not a single regular officer to assist in organizing and com- manding. Had a prompt and vigorous attack been made by the enemy, while I think the dispositions made would have insured their repulse, still the issue would have been less certain than at any time afterwards."[17]

Smith's defensive line as of May 20 included seven batteries, two above the town to protect upriver approaches and five below to meet the more immediate threat posed by Union boats. The five batteries included eighteen guns, a combination of smoothbores, which had limited range and power, and more effective rifled pieces. A rifled 18- pounder would become known in Vicksburg lore as "Whistling Dick" because of the whistling noise shells made after being fired. These weapons were the sum total of all Smith's heavy guns, except for two 42- pounder smoothbores sent up the Yazoo to protect construction of the *Arkansas*. Confederates at Vicksburg likely had heard about the failure of land batteries at Island No. 10 and New Orleans and elsewhere on the river. Smith had reason to feel vulnerable, but the enemy obligingly gave him time, the one thing he needed most.[18]

Smith had no way of knowing that no Union threat was imminent. Federal strategy in the summer of 1862 did not include a combined navy- army attack on Vicksburg. Washington authorities made plans based on their deluded belief that Farragut could, after New Orleans, continue an unfettered cruise up the Mississippi. Vicksburg might prove to be the key, but other keys at Baton Rouge and Natchez had been so easily taken that military minds had not considered the possibility of the river campaign bogging down at Vicksburg. Even if Vicksburg did not fall at once, surely it could be bypassed with relative ease, and, after Corinth had been secured, Farragut and Davis could go back and demolish Smith. In fact, future events would prove that Farragut could have passed by the bluffs relatively unscathed and gone on to Memphis. At the same time, Smith had to deal with the consequences of Richmond's delusions about a secure New Orleans and victory north of Memphis. Vicksburg proper became a low priority, simply because the Confederate front at Columbus was viewed as an impenetrable protective shield. Smith had to pick up the pieces of flawed, failed Confederate strategy.

Smith also found himself caught up in a personnel dispute, but, unlike Farragut, he did not have the power to settle it himself. Smith's difficulties were rooted in the fact that no overall commander had been assigned to the Western Theater since Sidney Johnston's death at Shiloh. With no one on hand to settle differences, territorial disputes often erupted. Mansfield Lovell, headquartered in Louisiana near Baton Rouge, issued grandiose orders as if he still controlled the area that included Vicksburg. P. G. T. Beauregard, now commanding Confederate forces in northeast Mississippi, sent Daniel Ruggles, a crusty Massachusetts native married into a Virginia family, from Corinth to take command at Vicksburg, and Ruggles thought Lovell overstepped his authority. Beauregard pressed Lovell for more troops to be sent to Vicksburg and received no reply, other than Lovell's continual whining that the loss of New Orleans was not his fault. Smith innocently became a figure in this minidrama because he had been appointed by Lovell to take charge at Vicksburg.

Ruggles's arrival meant one commander too many and set the stage for conflict. Lovell, meanwhile, had decided to accompany Louisiana troops en route to reinforce Vicksburg, and he got there before Ruggles. When Ruggles arrived, Lovell complained that he "stepped in here to take command of Smith, myself, and all our troops with a wonderful degree of gravity, and it was only when I asked him what he would do if I withdrew all my troops that he seemed to appreciate the case." Lovell pointedly told Beauregard he had orders directly from Richmond, implying that Beauregard should back off. An infuriated Ruggles traveled east to Jackson and wired Beauregard that Lovell "claims the command and refuses to yield it. Prompt and energetic action is necessary."[19]

Beauregard, like Farragut, realized he had created a serious problem. A history of bad feelings between Ruggles and Lovell compounded the situation, and Lovell pleaded that Ruggles be sent somewhere, "but for heaven's sake don't send him into my department, where he will raise a row in a week." Beauregard finally pointed out to Ruggles that since the Vicksburg troops belonged to Lovell, Lovell should be in command. Ruggles assented and moved his headquarters north to Grenada, which, though connected by rail to Jackson, would be out of Lovell's district. Confusing district boundaries in Mississippi compounded the difficulties, and Beauregard sent new district guidelines from Richmond to Lovell, noting that the strange drawing of lines had Jackson in Lovell's department and Vicksburg in Beauregard's. In an accompanying letter, Beauregard wrote, "I attach only little importance to this matter; all that I desire is success to our arms and to our cause." "The great point," Beauregard said firmly, "is to defend the river at Vicksburg. The question of who does it must be of a secondary consideration."[20]

Beauregard likely felt some trepidation, for Lovell, no doubt anxious to salvage his reputation, seemed to have difficulty grasping reality. He continued to appeal to Richmond for approval of his actions in New Orleans, and begged Beauregard for "arms, arms, arms," so once the water level on the Mississippi fell he could lead a campaign to retake New Orleans. Beauregard gave Lovell nothing, for he worried only about holding Corinth, because, to him, losing that place meant the loss of the entire Mississippi Valley. Beauregard, quite simply, saw Vicksburg as a wasted drain on limited Confederate resources. He bluntly told Lovell, "I can only express my . . . regret at not having here [at Corinth] the available force at present with you, for I care more about my front at this moment than I do for my rear."[21]

Beauregard's comments indicated another serious problem with Confederate strategy in the West. The War Department had a self-destructive concept of attempting to defend too many points with too few troops. Beyond that, the Lovell-Ruggles-Beauregard fiasco underscored problems of ill-constructed departments and command systems. A competent officer like Martin Luther Smith must have wondered how he could hope to be successful against the enemy at his front with so much divisive bickering going on among those from whom he needed support.

While curious developments characterized both Union and Confederate strategy and command problems, the Union navy finally brought the full impact of war to the streets of Vicksburg when Palmer's squadron began a systematic bombardment on May 26. A Confederate soldier commented that falling shells caused "such a miserable squaking & scratching & getting along through the wind [as] I never did hear." Women and children still in town sought refuge in dirt forts. Up until that time, both sides had only fired occasional shots, just enough to create nervous anticipation. A group of civilians watching the show on May 28 stood frozen in terror when a shell seemed to come right at them. As the missile whizzed over their heads, they finally broke and ran, some throwing belongings into a carriage and taking off "to the music of the cannon balls," until out of range. Fire-rafts set adrift from upstream by Confederates at night, giving Rebel gunners a better view in case of enemy activity, added to a surreal atmosphere on the river and bluffs.[22]

During the early days of increased shelling, Rebel artillerymen, who had limited supplies of ammunition, received orders "not to return . . . fire at extreme range, and at ordinary range only at considerable intervals." Smith later wrote, "This policy was adhered to throughout; at first because little ammunition had then arrived; afterward for the reason that our works could not be injured by direct firing, and by saving the men[,] they were fresh night and day to meet close and serious attacks, such as occurred before the termination of the bombardment; besides, the enemy were thus kept ignorant of our real strength as well as the effect of their own shot."[23]

The action became routine, Union vessels taking turns shooting at the city, and Confederate cannon sporadically responding. A curious incident that has never been explained took place on May 27. A Confederate manning one of the southern batteries pulled a lanyard at 8:25 A.M.; around 10:00 a shot rang out from the Confederate batteries north of town; and then at 11:30 another shot echoed from the same direction. At noon, a Rebel boat, the *De Soto*, left the Vicksburg docks and started slowly downriver flying a flag of truce. The *Itasca* approached, and Lieutenant George Bacon allowed two Rebel army officers to deliver dispatches addressed to Palmer, who responded around 2:30 P.M. The nature of this correspondence is not indicated in official Union naval reports or ship logs; General Smith did not mention the incident at all. One may speculate that, in light of what followed later that afternoon, Smith tried to convince Palmer to give up the fight, or at least not to shell residential areas. Whatever the case, Palmer sent two boats to shell Vicksburg from late in the afternoon until after 11:00 P.M. The next day Smith ordered Confederate and other flags removed from sight; he and his officers determined that Yankees were using the flags to gauge firing distances. Then, after a few days, things got very quiet, and

Smith, his men, and Vicksburg's citizens realized to their astonishment that the enemy navy had disappeared.[24]

James Palmer had not heard from Farragut since the latter's departure from Vicksburg, and he worried about Rebel activity in his rear along the Natchez–Grand Gulf stretch of river. On June 10, from near Grand Gulf, Palmer wrote Farragut that he "feared the rebels might be erecting batteries upon the bluffs down the river and thus [would] prevent any transport coming up from New Orleans." Palmer also worried about enemy works spotted along Grand Gulf bluffs. Palmer decided to attack, and on June 7 a battle erupted between two Union gunboats and a Confederate battery, the latter holding its own, scoring forty-two hits. Despite light casualties, the fierceness of the exchange convinced Palmer to pull the rest of the fleet down from Vicksburg. On June 10–11, the blockading squadron bombarded Grand Gulf, and Union patrols went ashore and set several fires in a failed attempt to burn the town. One sailor observed, "The people along here are the most treacherous and rabid secessionists and I think we served them right in destroying the town." The fleet then dropped downriver; the Union river war against Vicksburg seemed in serious regression.[25]

While Palmer waited for news and for coal, he received scouting reports indicating the near completion of an enemy ironclad on the Yazoo. Also, Confederates had supposedly evacuated Fort Pillow above Memphis, and it seemed likely that troops and ordnance there would be sent to Vicksburg. Meanwhile, Palmer sent sick sailors to Baton Rouge and scouts to the Red River. On June 12, the squadron descended to Natchez, and after taking on coal returned to Vicksburg. The perceived threat of enemy batteries in his rear had proved overblown, and the boats chugged north uneventfully, anchoring below Vicksburg on June 14.[26]

From Baton Rouge, Farragut reported to Gideon Welles his usual hyperbolic information: "The rebels are fortifying all the bluffs between here and Vicksburg, at which place (we learn from deserters) the final stand is to be made for the defense of this river. We will leave here, however, for the attack on Vicksburg on the arrival of the army and mortars, which I am now awaiting. I will leave for Grand Gulf to-morrow morning." Thomas Williams agreed to bring his troops back to the Vicksburg front, though he warned that his infantry would be of limited use unless he could get in the rear of the town. No one seemed to know exactly how that could be done.[27]

In Vicksburg, Confederate generals Smith and Lovell decried the lack of coordination in the Western Theater. Lovell and Smith heard rumors of the evacuation of Fort Pillow long after the fact. Memphis fell to Charles Davis's Union fleet on May 6, causing panic in northern Mississippi, and civilians fled east. Smith complained to Lovell that if Beauregard knew all this, he should have shared the information. After all, the Union naval forces to the north might soon show up at Vicksburg. Lovell concurred and sent Smith's complaint to Beauregard, who was already in a bad mood after being forced to evacuate Corinth on May 30. The Louisianan replied heatedly:

> Relative to the intended evacuation of Fort Pillow not having been communicated to you both, I have to state that this movement was the natural consequence of the retreat from Corinth, as will be the loss of all the Mississippi Valley; a fact long since communicated to you. That retreat was made when compelled to do so by the overpowering numbers of the enemy in our front, having but little time to communicate the information even to those around me. I might as well complain of your not having communicated to me your intention to evacuate New Orleans and surrender the forts guarding the river, by which we lost all the cattle in Texas and Western Louisiana intended for this army. Moreover, it was to be supposed that after the retreat from Corinth you would have ample time to make whatever arrangements you thought necessary to suit the new order of things.[28]

Having vented his wrath, Beauregard said he intended to fight if Union commander Henry Halleck advanced on Tupelo, south of Corinth, and if he could muster enough men "to meet him with a chance of success." Otherwise he might fall back further south or move west to Oxford in north-central Mississippi. If he chose the latter, Beauregard's troops could protect Jackson's north flank along the Mississippi Central Railroad. Beauregard preferred that Lovell bring Vicksburg troops to Tupelo where a unified Confederate force might take the offensive. Beauregard favored concentration rather than tying down forces to defend specific places like Vicksburg. He hoped by maneuver to force Halleck to divide his huge army, giving Confederates more offensive options. How all this might be accomplished, Beauregard did not say, but the adoption of his ideas would likely lead to the abandonment of Jackson and Vicksburg, something Jefferson Davis and his advisers would never condone.[29]

Beauregard regarded Vicksburg's "fate as sealed." "You may defend it for a while to hold the enemy at bay," he told Lovell, "but it must follow ere long the fate of Fort Pillow." Meanwhile, all the ordnance and other war matériel taken from Pillow, and "not required at Vicksburg or

Grenada," should be sent to Meridian, or if possible, to Columbus, two eastern Mississippi towns well south of Tupelo and currently out of harm's way. As an aside, Beauregard inquired about the progress of the *Arkansas*. He had little hope the Confederate navy could do anything, concluding: "I fear the Navy Department has many sins of omission and commission to answer for in this war."[30]

Beauregard's gloomy outlook, combined with other deteriorating Confederate fortunes in the West, struck a nerve in Richmond. The thought of losing Vicksburg apparently hit home, and on June 14 Jefferson Davis wrote General Smith a series of anxious questions: "What progress is being made toward the completion of the Arkansas? What is the condition of your defenses at Vicksburg? Can we do anything to aid you? Disaster above and below increase the value of your position. I hope and expect much from you."

Robert E. Lee, at the time an adviser to Davis, told Lovell that he regretted "the smallness of the means you have at your command to defend so extensive and important a district of country," and assured Lovell that his department was "of too much importance to be thought of being abandoned." Lee encouraged him to hold on, find recruits and use his "known activity and energy" to secure Vicksburg. Yet Richmond blundered by shipping weapons intended for Vicksburg elsewhere, and all the talk and slow, limited action reduced the morale of Vicksburg's defenders. The summer weather and camping in the city graveyard had already severely tested their resolve, and now they had to face the return of the Yankee navy and more shelling.[31]

The downturn in Confederate affairs made Governor Pettus nervous, and he complained to Richmond about Lovell's incompetence. President Davis assured the governor that Braxton Bragg had been ordered to Jackson, but a sudden illness had befallen General Beauregard, forcing Davis to appoint Bragg head of the army at Tupelo. Davis then ordered Bragg to send Earl Van Dorn to take command at Vicksburg. "I hope," Davis wrote, "he will answer the popular desire." Davis encouraged the political leader of his home state: "The heroic determination of my neighbors gives assurance that you will use effectively all the means you possess. I would they were larger, and earnestly wish it were consistent for me to be with you in the struggle."[32]

Van Dorn, a Mississippian from Port Gibson and commander of the Army of the West, loser at Pea Ridge in northwestern Arkansas prior to Shiloh, thus took over the Department of Southern Mississippi and East Louisiana. Van Dorn reported to Braxton Bragg, who, as it turned out, permanently replaced Beauregard after the latter developed his mysterious illness. The changes in command did not seem to hurt the Confederate cause in the Vicksburg area. On the contrary, the new team of Van Dorn and Bragg moved with alacrity to meet the challenges of their commands. Van Dorn, especially, perhaps because he hailed from a nearby town and had a dashing reputation, brought new hope to civilians tired of the bombardment of Vicksburg.[33]

On June 22, Bragg authorized the transfer of Daniel Ruggles's 6,000 Grenada troops to Vicksburg. Ruggles must get the troops moving "without delay" and reach Vicksburg "at the earliest possible moment." Kentuckian John C. Breckinridge's 4,000 men boarded a train for the hill city. Ruggles intended to go there himself, but he then received orders to command the Fifth District of Van Dorn's department with headquarters at Tangipahoa, Louisiana. Apparently, Lovell was not the only one who did not want Ruggles around.[34]

Van Dorn arrived in Vicksburg on June 23 and, with his usual flare for the dramatic, wired Davis that the Union navy had returned in force, but he vowed: "Will not give up unless beaten back by superior force. Foot by foot the city will be sacrificed. Of course citizens proud to do so." Van Dorn also asked that the *Arkansas* be placed under his orders, and Davis immediately agreed. This, a seemingly innocent request, proved to be a mistake that eventually severely crippled the defense of Vicksburg and the Mississippi. Van Dorn liked what he saw of Smith's defensive works and noted with relief cannon arriving from various points across the lower South.

Breckinridge's men also arrived and immediately filed into entrenchments. Enemy naval shelling got to some of the new arrivals, and many of the soldiers "could hardly be held in line." Veterans were not immune. A Mississippian wrote, "One feels utterly defenseless unless there is a chance to strike back, which in this case, is out of the question." Smith's brigade manned the batteries, and, with the assistance of detachments from Breckinridge, guarded forward positions facing the river on northern and southern flanks. Light artillery and cavalry guarded flanks north along the Yazoo and south below Warrenton. The regiments alternated duties around town, "which consisted mainly in lying under the shade of the trees in the beautiful grassy lawns, with which the city and its suburbs abounded, and, at night, watching the course of the immense mortar shells fired from the yankee fleets above and below the city."[35]

Aside from dodging shells, the growing numbers of Confederate defenders battled bad water. Water from scum-covered ponds had to be dipped out and filtered with a piece of cloth. The method did not always work, and several men died. Mosquitoes also tormented the soldiers, large ones that could bite through clothing, and chiggers, commonly known as red bugs, provided additional torture. A steady diet of sugar and rice led one man to recall in later years that he could not eat rice for thirty years after the war. Mississippians camped at the city cemetery grew so ill that many came to resemble the "occupants of the tombs which spot the surface of the abode of the dead [rather] than the hearty lads who left the homes of their youth to battle for freedom[']s holy cause."[36]

Troops camped close to the cemetery also found the site cause for introspection about the war. A Louisianan taking "a walk among the Dead" experienced conflicting emotions about the certainty of death. "We shrink from those mournful thoughts," he wrote his wife, "but too true, that is the one [and] only road all nature must travel, yet we hope to have friends, as it were to band [with us] from this desolate shore, into that ever blooming shore of happiness. The hope of Heaven, the promises in the bible, the home of the pure, the good, and the loving is all that can bring true joys to a heart under such circumstances as surrounds us at present."[37]

Troop buildups and the enemy navy's return disrupted but did not eliminate city commerce, and anti-outsider attitudes persisted. Some soldiers complained about "Jew" establishments staying open and increasing prices, including a "war risk" fee added to purchases. Inflated prices, among other things, led to an attitude among soldiers well expressed by a Louisianan: "I expect they [the Yankees] will burn up the place and I don't care if they do." The Washington Hotel closed briefly, while the Prentiss House continued to provide entertainment, though, noted a customer, "it is difficult to speak of the excellence of faire and the comfort of the lodging rooms of a tavern that is not bomb-proof." A shell decapitated Mrs. Patience Gamble. She was known as "a lady whose entire time for months past has been devoted to the relief of the sick and suffering troops. She was killed at her post, while with the fearless soul of a pure woman, ministering to the wants of brave boys, whose mothers and sisters were far away."[38]

Down the Mississippi at Baton Rouge, miles away from the miserable conditions around Vicksburg, David Farragut, sensing he had better do something, suddenly had the confidence to take Vicksburg. No doubt he figured he had ignored the government's expectations long enough. On June 13, he ordered the concentration of his fleet at Vicksburg and welcomed good news that Charles Davis had taken Memphis and might be on his way downstream. Thomas Williams's army, now numbering 5,000, moved upstream, escorted by Farragut's boats, and Farragut, ever concerned about securing his rear, detailed the *Brooklyn* to check reported gun emplacements at the river town of Rodney, Mississippi, south of Grand Gulf.

Rodney had previously been a focal point for a sharp exchange of messages between Mansfield Lovell and Farragut. Federal warnings that the town would be held accountable for Confederate fire from the area on Union ships led Lovell to write Farragut: "The practice of slaying women and children as an act of retaliation has happily fallen into disuse in this country with the disappearance of the Indian tribes, and I trust it will not be revived by the officers of the United States Navy, but that the demolition and pillage of the offending little village of Grand Gulf may be permitted to stand alone and without parallel upon the record." Farragut replied that Confederates should not place guns close to towns. "I do know that the fate of a town is at all times in the hands of the military commandant who may at pleasure draw the enemy's fire upon it, and the community is made to suffer for the act of its military." Farragut affirmed, "We war not against defenseless persons, but against those in open rebellion against our country, and desire to limit our punishment to them, but it may not always be in our power to do so."[39]

The guerrilla issue surfaced with more and more frequency. On one occasion, Farragut authorized action against an enemy telegraph station near the river. A Union detachment went ashore and destroyed the place, and they heard numerous complaints about local guerrillas, "represented . . . as a lawless set, whom the inhabitants of the country and small towns had a greater dread of than they had of the visits of our navy, or even of our army and . . . [they] hoped we would not" hold them responsible for the actions of such "cutthroat bands." The persistence and similarities of such sentiments planted seeds of doubt in Federal minds regarding whether locals did or did not support partisan activity.

Farragut continued preparations for the new campaign and welcomed back his foster brother David Porter, fresh from Gulf duties. Porter had been frustrated, and had in fact become quite angry at Benjamin Butler's bureaucratic morass in New Orleans. Butler had promised help in towing upriver a heavy mortar flotilla put together by Porter, but the promises drowned in a sea of red tape. Porter bitterly told Farragut, "I don't hesitate to say that there has been a deliberate attempt made to deceive and trifle with me, and whosever's fault it is, it should be made known." Porter hated fighting traitors on two fronts, and fumed at the "difficulties of getting up the river with stores, coal, etc."[40]

Farragut forwarded Porter's complaint to Secretary Welles and admitted it had been a mistake ever to involve Butler with naval operations. Porter made it upriver anyway, and since Charles Davis was supposedly coming down from Memphis with his fleet, Farragut hoped the naval concentration could force Vicksburg's surrender. Only the *Arkansas* remained a concern, and a couple of gunboats had been reported at Greenwood, but Farragut did not think them any threat. He assured Welles, "As soon as Vicksburg surrenders the river will be clear from anything but occasional assaults by the guerrillas from the bluffs."

Porter, satisfied that Butler's incompetence had been reported to Washington, looked forward to testing his mortar flotilla at Vicksburg. He hoped the snub-nosed weapons could lob shells over the river heights into the city's defenses and induce surrender. En route his men skirmished with Confederates along the river, and at one stop he had to deal with the unexpected problem of contrabands seeking safety with Union forces. Porter noted, "The only slaves that have come into the flotilla have sought refuge there, and have in no case been taken from the custody of their masters. I must decline returning any slaves to the custody of those claiming to be their masters." Union commanders at this stage of the war ignored slave issues, except when they needed labor, and only then did they welcome freedom-seeking blacks.[41]

While Farragut traveled upstream, his lieutenants tried contacting Davis, both to report *Arkansas* rumors and discuss a Farragut-Williams idea of digging a canal, with slave labor, across the base of the narrow neck of land known as De Soto Point, around which the Mississippi curved in front of Vicksburg. If successful, Union boats could bypass Vicksburg, in effect eliminating, or sharply curbing, the significance of defenses there. The idea sounded promising, but it would prove to be an illusion.[42]

On June 25, Farragut arrived below Vicksburg aboard his flagship *Hartford* and issued a plan of attack for the next morning. He wanted Porter's mortars to bombard Vicksburg's batteries and forts at dawn. The rest of the fleet would then proceed in a double line, with the large warships *Richmond*, *Hartford*, and *Brooklyn* in one column and the smaller gunboats on a parallel course. Shells, rather than solid shot, would be the missiles of the day, since Farragut believed shrapnel would have a greater effect. A detachment would stay above Vicksburg, assuming all got there safely, where they would unite with Davis, while the rest fell back downriver.[43]

Although Farragut's written orders had the sound of immediacy, preparations delayed action until June 28; both Porter and Farragut needed more deployment time than Farragut anticipated. Porter's mortar boats also divided into two lines, nine on the right (east side) and eight on the left (west side) of the river. He later reported, "The position selected here for the mortars was a beautiful one, on the starboard side of the river, at 2,500 yards from the main battery and 2,200 from the water battery. The vessels of the port [left] side, about 700 yards further off, were rather exposed to the enemy's fire, but were so covered up with bushes, that it was not easy to see them at that distance, much less fire accurately at them."

At 3:30 P.M. on the 26th, Porter ordered his gunners to fire. The mortars spoke "deliberately" in order to find their range. When Confederate batteries replied, Porter observed with relief that Rebel shells fell "all around and over" the mortars with none being hit. Confederate gunners, conserving ammunition, soon ceased fire, and the mortars continued periodic target practice free from molestation. Meanwhile, the rest of the Union fleet moved into position.[44]

On June 27, Porter's and Farragut's guns continued sporadic firing, again trying to make adjustments to improve accuracy, and Smith, still conserving ammunition, ordered his guns to reply infrequently. The only notable event of the day occurred around 8:30 P.M. when gunboats tossed incendiary shells into Vicksburg, but the shells did not detonate. Smith's batteries returned a heavy fire that "rained upon . . . [Union] batteries" and "severely tried the patience of both officers and men." Neither side suffered significant damage. Later in the evening Farragut called his officers together to discuss the major assault next morning.[45]

Farragut would have no help from Davis, who had not left Memphis. Davis, recently promoted to flag officer, had led an expedition to clear the White River in Arkansas of Confederate vessels after the fall of Memphis. When he received Farragut's request to come to Vicksburg, he assembled a fleet consisting of his flagship, the *Benton*, plus two gunboats and a half dozen mortar boats. An advance flotilla, commanded by Lieutenant Colonel Alfred Ellet, consisting of five vessels, proceeded downriver. Ellet's fleet had been converted from fast-moving river steamers to rams and had originally been commanded by his recently deceased brother, Charles, who was fatally wounded at Memphis. Ellet, an army officer, anchored above Vicksburg on June 25 near the head of the hairpin loop and made contact across the base of the peninsula with Farragut.[46]

Farragut decided Ellet's boats were not in a position "well calculated for taking the forts," so the June 28 attack proceeded without the rams. Rams would be of limited use anyway, since the primary Union targets were land batteries, not enemy boats. Despite Davis's absence, Farragut felt confident he could force the city to surrender. Ellet notified Davis that Farragut had decided to proceed, adding hopefully that the note "may reach you in time to enable you to participate in the approaching contest." It did not.[47]

Undeterred by Farragut's rejection, Ellet decided to act on his own, and he ascended the Yazoo to check on the alleged Rebel ironclad. At the mouth of the Sunflower River he learned from locals that Rebel boats were farther upstream near Liverpool. Ellet saw oil in the muddy Yazoo waters, which the Confederates intended to set afire if Yankee boats approached. He moved on anyway and spotted several enemy boats on fire and drifting downstream. A Rebel battery could be seen frowning from Liverpool bluffs, and then one of the fired boats exploded. Ellet thought he saw the *Arkansas*, but by then he had decided to retreat.[48]

Farragut, unaware of Ellet's escapade, readied his attack. Nearby, Thomas Williams and his infantry nestled into the unhealthy Louisiana lowlands to observe. Why Williams did not disembark his men below Vicksburg and attack by land from the south, in conjunction with the naval assault, is not known, but he probably still felt undermanned. Both Williams and Farragut seemingly envisioned the army as an occupation force after Vicksburg surrendered.

While waiting, Williams's men, along with some 1,100 to 1,200 blacks "gathered from the neighboring plantations by armed parties," broke ground on the canal project. The general soon concluded that "the labor of making this cut is far greater than estimated by anybody. The soil is hard clay as far as yet excavated (6 ½ to 7 feet) and must be gone through with, say, some 4 feet or more before the water can be let in; for all concur in this, that we must come to sand before the cut can be pronounced a success." Despite Williams's prophetic words, Union strategists clung to the canal idea.[49]

Farragut's fleet got under way in the early morning hours of June 28. David Porter penned a graphic description of battle action. He saw Farragut's *Hartford* at 4:00 A.M. "By that time," he noted, "the mortar steamers had got nearly into position and moved up toward the batteries, throwing in a quick fire. Nearly all the mortars had commenced as the *Richmond* passed, and the shells were falling very well and rapidly, the *Hartford* and gunboats opening their batteries with grape, canister, and shrapnel. The air seemed to be filled with projectiles."[50]

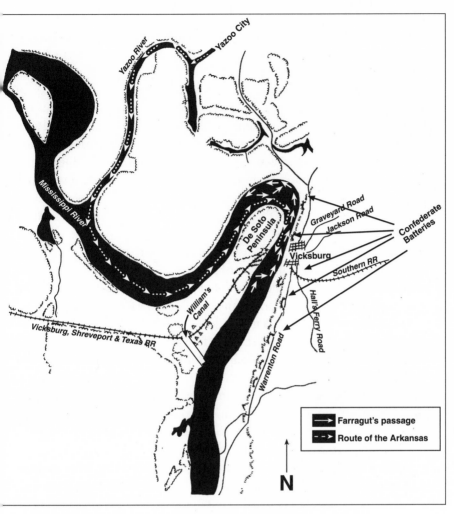

Farragut's Passing of the Batteries, June 28, 1862, and the Arkansas *Attacks, July 15, 1862. Map by Becky Smith.*

In Vicksburg, Martin Smith heard the commotion, watched the action from atop the bluffs, and concluded it was "apparent that the decisive struggle was at hand." Smith counted thirty-five enemy vessels firing rapidly, their shells and the mortar missiles filling the atmosphere around and in Vicksburg. Smith's guns replied "as soon as the vessels were within range and for the first time in full force." He later noted, "The roar of cannon was now continuous and deafening; loud explosions shook the city to its foundations; shot and shell went hissing and tearing through trees and walls, scattering fragments far and wide in their terrific flight; men, women, and children rushed into the streets, and, amid the crash of falling houses, commenced their hasty flight to the country for safety." Dogs, horses, mules, cows, and even birds hastily escaped the impact areas.[51]

One citizen wrote of June 28, "We were aroused by such a roar of artillery as is seldom heard. I jumped from my bed & looked out the window just at the moment when a shell struck in an adjoining yard & by its explosion threw the earth as high as the houses. You may depend upon it; I was dressed & out in a flash, & rushing up to our eminence the nearest by. I feared that the whole of the enemy's fleet had moved up & were out attacking our batteries, while every mortar boat was likewise opening its dogs of war, there was no second of time but in which numbers of cannon were discharged by the enemy, whose roar was mingled with the roar of the answering guns from our batteries." Soon smoke covered the whole riverfront, and "the constant flash of the cannon & roar of the artillery, coupled with running up of the ships of war amidst the whole of it, made the scene wonderfully grand."[52]

Even in the midst of this major assault, which created a dangerous war zone, some Confederate soldiers felt Vicksburg was getting what it deserved. The continuing arrogant attitudes of citizens toward soldiers had had a major impact on Smith's men. Noting the damage, a Louisianan wrote his sister that while some buildings had holes from Yankee shells, many of the men did not care because damaged businesses had been overcharging troops. More to the point, "I wouldn't care if the town was torn down and a few deaths with it."[53]

While Union shells shrieked through the streets, Confederate gunners quickly found the range on Farragut's boats. Aboard the *Richmond*, "shots came crashing through . . . bulwarks, brains and blood flying all over the decks." The mortar steamer *Jackson* received a shell that penetrated its wheelhouse and disabled the steering mechanism. The *Clifton* came to its aid and got hit in the boiler. The resulting explosion scalded six sailors to death and horribly wounded others. Some dove overboard to escape, and at least one drowned. Porter's boat, the *Octorara*, was not hit, but did drift precariously when the steering mechanism jammed. Farragut's *Hartford* had blood-soaked decks; one man fell dead, and thirteen received wounds. Farragut, who suffered a slight contusion, saw his ship's rigging shredded and several guns disabled. Despite casualties and damage, the Union fleet did not lose a ship; on the other hand, the attack achieved nothing, but getting the fleet north of Vicksburg gave Farragut a chance to send one boat to watch for the *Arkansas*.[54]

General Smith proudly reported that none of his guns had been silenced or disabled. If Farragut thought previous shelling had in any way reduced the effectiveness of Vicksburg batteries, return fire proved him wrong. Smith declared that the naval attack "demonstrated to our satisfaction that how large so ever the number of guns and mortar-boats, our batteries could probably be successfully held; consequently that the ultimate success of our resistance hinged upon a movement by land." In addition to the repulse of the enemy navy came the good news that Richmond was sending small arms to Vicksburg, and that welfare donations were accumulating from outside Vicksburg to aid citizens. Beyond the celebratory attitudes in Vicksburg, one fact was obvious. Confederate batteries had done little significant overall damage, even though they were shooting directly into Farragut's flotilla. The perceived effectiveness of the batteries seemed grossly exaggerated.[55]

Yet the Confederates were strong enough to maintain a stalemate with Federal naval power. Farragut and Porter came to the same conclusions as Smith, and Farragut sent word to Davis about the failure to knock out Rebel guns. "I think . . . that as long as they have the military force to hold the back country it will be impossible for me to reduce the place without your assistance and that of the army." Williams obviously did not have the necessary manpower to attack by land, and Farragut assured Henry Halleck that the river could not be cleared "without your assistance." Porter agreed that joint army-navy operations would be essential to taking Vicksburg. "Ships and mortar vessels," he reported, "can keep full possession of the river and places near the water's edge, but they can not crawl up hills 300 feet high, and it is that part of Vicksburg which must be taken by the army."[56]

Union manpower concerns on both sides of the lower Mississippi kept the much-needed infantry from coming to the navy's aid. Soldiers occupying other areas tied down Confederate troops that would have been valuable additions to the Vicksburg garrison, but the failure to make Vicksburg the number one priority meant Federal generals in the West spread resources to the point of accomplishing practically nothing.

Though Farragut understood now that he required Halleck's help, he still felt frustrated and angry about his failure. He had seen things that disturbed him during the assault, and now he sought answers, which convinced him that his officers lacked a clear vision of his plan of operations. Embarrassed by the breakdown in communications, Farragut chewed out officers who had retreated on their own, according to their understanding of things, and set off a fierce debate at a time when he should have been promoting unity and teamwork.[57]

Farragut particularly went after one of the offenders, Craven, for assuming "the right to annul my orders, or act according to your own will." Further, "it was your duty to have followed your flag-officer until his situation justified you in abandoning him as hopeless." Whether Farragut merely disliked Craven or used him to make a point, he lost a commander. Craven asked to be relieved so he could go to Washington and plead his case. He did not return to the Vicksburg campaign.[58]

The Craven situation settled, Farragut turned his attention to cooperating with Davis, who had finally arrived with his fleet from the north. The two talked at length, and Davis wired Ulysses S. Grant, now commanding the Department of West Tennessee, to intervene with Halleck regarding the need for infantry. After taking Corinth, Halleck, responding to cries for help, scattered his army across Tennessee, North Mississippi, and Alabama, and insisted on July 2 that he could not "at the present" send any troops to Vicksburg. He offered some encouragement: "Probably I shall be able to do so as soon as I can get my troops more concentrated. This may delay the clearing of the river, but its accomplishment will be certain in a few weeks." To boost morale, Farragut responded to Halleck's disappointing message by ordering his fleet to celebrate July 4 with "a flag at each masthead at 8 A.M., and a salute of twenty-guns will be fired at noon from each of the vessels of the fleet mounting the number of guns authorizing salutes." Federal sailors would no doubt remember this event exactly one year later.[59]

The July 4 cannonading caught Confederates by surprise. One of Breckinridge's Kentuckians recorded the day's events in his diary: "To our surprise a silence, profound as death, rested upon the combatants until just at noon, when both fleets opened fire with every gun. They rent the heavens with the fury of exploding shells; the shore batteries instantly responded, and for half an hour these tremendous engines of death vomited forth their horrible contents and then ceased as suddenly as they began, not another gun being fired during the day." The brief barrage gave Vicksburg's defenders time to celebrate too — not the Fourth, but news of Robert E. Lee's victory in Virginia over George McClellan on the peninsula east of Richmond.[60]

The celebration did little to brighten Farragut's mood; he felt abandoned by the army and would have agreed with Secretary Welles's description of Halleck as "good for nothing." Farragut complained to Washington: "The forts can be passed and we have done it, and can do it again as often as may be required of us. It will not, however, be an easy matter for us to do more than silence the batteries for a time, as long as the enemy has a large force behind the hills to prevent our landing and holding the place." Davis had seen few troops in Memphis, so help from there seemed unlikely. Williams's canal project progressed; and if it proved successful, Farragut would have to back his fleet downriver while waters rushed through the channel, else they might find themselves stranded in shallow water. Finally, the disgruntled flag officer got around to what was on his mind: "I have almost abandoned the idea of getting the ships down the river unless this place is either taken possession of or cut off." In case of the latter, a few gunboats could keep the river open, but the Rebels would surely fortify positions, like Grand Gulf, downstream. Farragut thus made clear he had tired of this stalemate and wanted to return to his beloved ocean waters.

Charles Davis did not think the canal would work any time soon because the river was falling, and reports of heavy rains upriver would give only temporary relief. On paper, the canal seemed feasible, but Davis did not believe anything but army help would produce victory at Vicksburg. Davis had no desire to get bogged down at Vicksburg, enduring both a frustrating stalemate and the overwhelmingly humid July heat. "I never can describe . . .," he wrote, "the heat, the succession of still and breathless days — long, long, weary, red-hot, gasping days."[61]

Farragut sank more into the doldrums and showed little inclination to do anything during those oppressive days, other than wait for troops. He discounted rumors of Halleck leading a force to Jackson, Mississippi, nor did he believe that Beauregard had arrived in Vicksburg with reinforcements; and he was right on both counts. He turned to routine administrative matters and did not object to Secretary Welles transferring Porter and his mortar fleet to Hampton Roads, Virginia. Perhaps Farragut felt that a reduced force would reduce pressure on him to do anything. He knew the Rebels would be happy, but he understood also that since the navy obviously could not destroy Vicksburg, Porter's departure signified nothing.[62]

Farragut finally decided on a direct approach about his desire to leave by proposing to Welles that Davis assume patrolling responsibilities for the Vicksburg area. Farragut knew that George McClellan had retreated from Richmond, and he hoped his boats would be needed to help defend Washington. Certainly Porter's mortars would be of little use in Virginia. Farragut also argued that Davis's force could easily prolong the stalemate, while his own squadron would be more effective cruising the Gulf. Rebel boats of any consequence, except the rumored ironclad, had been eliminated. His presence on the Gulf would result in "adding to the Union ports after ports," and he would be willing to leave three ships at New Orleans in reserve for emergency service at Vicksburg. He warned Welles that if the Mississippi continued to fall, his big ships might be stuck at Vicksburg until the water rose, which would not be for several months.

While he waited for a reply, Farragut consulted with Williams, Davis, and Ellet about an expedition up the Yazoo to find out once and for all the fact or myth of the *Arkansas*. Ellet still fumed about Confederates earlier firing at his boat; he called them "ruffian bands" that infested the Yazoo riverbanks. Ellet added cannon to his rams and wanted to give his gunners target practice along the Yazoo, especially against snipers.

In Washington, Secretary Welles read Farragut's request and contacted Secretary of War Edwin Stanton to see if any land force could soon be sent to Vicksburg. Stanton in turn asked Halleck, who sounded a familiar refrain: "I cannot at present give Commodore Farragut any aid against Vicksburg. I am sending reinforcements to General [Samuel] Curtis in Arkansas and to General [Don Carlos] Buell in Tennessee and Kentucky." Meanwhile, Welles notified Charles Davis that Farragut would be "instructed to proceed with his fleet to the Gulf for the purpose of conducting operations at some point or points on the coast, and to leave you in control and possession of the Mississippi, or the greater part of it. The point south to which it may be advisable to extend your command will be determined by Flag-Officer Farragut and yourself." Davis, said Welles, should maintain the status quo.[63]

Before Welles's decision reached Farragut or Davis, an unexpected development changed the nature of the campaign. On the morning of July 15, three of Davis's vessels, two gunboats and the ram, *Queen of the West*, steamed toward the Yazoo River's mouth. Williams's sharpshooters lined the decks to discourage Rebel activity along the banks. Specifically, the detachment was "to procure correct information concerning the obstructions and defenses of the river." This was not a good morning for Union vessels to explore the Yazoo; just ahead, the *Arkansas*, having been tested and found worthy, steamed toward the Mississippi.[64]

〰 Lieutenant Isaac Brown, veteran seaman, native Kentuckian who lived in Mississippi, and the hard-nosed, innovative commander of the *Arkansas*, had overcome numerous obstacles to get the ironclad built. He had been supervising the construction of ironclads near New Orleans when the city fell, and he had to abandon his work. When he assumed command of the *Arkansas* project, he found it in a shambles. Inefficiency abounded and bureaucratic ineptness thwarted efforts to get men, machinery, and other necessities to the Yazoo City naval yard, where Brown eventually moved the project from Memphis to complete construction. Local citizens helped, but Brown constantly worried that a Union naval thrust up the Yazoo might force him to abandon this project too. Fortunately, the arrival of Earl Van Dorn and reinforcements at Vicksburg, plus the inability of the Union navy to reduce the city, gave him time.[65]

On June 20, Brown took the ironclad on a successful trial run to Liverpool. The vessel consisted of "200 seamen, landsmen, firemen, soldiers and boys. She mounted 10 guns, viz, two 8-inch columbiads forward, two six-inch astern, and two IX-inch, two 6-inch, and two 32-pounder guns in broadside. She was 165 feet in length, with 35 feet of beam, and drew 11 ½ feet of water. Her plating was of railroad iron, 4½ inches in thickness, and her general appearance was long and rakish." On the evening of July 14, Brown, acting on the orders of his immediate superior, Flag Officer William Lynch, and in accordance with the wishes of General Van Dorn, who had authority over the *Arkansas*, thanks to Jefferson Davis, ordered the boat to proceed down the Yazoo.

Confederate military authorities counted on Brown to break up the enemy naval presence in front of Vicksburg. The *Arkansas* would be one against many, but it lived up to expectations. At 6:00 A.M. on the fifteenth, the ironclad went into battle for the first time when it encountered the three Union boats. A severe fight ensued; the three boats turned and headed for the Mississippi; and Brown chose to pursue the *Carondelet*, which turned back to give battle. The two ironclads slugged it out for nearly an hour before Brown tried to ram the Yankee boat. Suddenly the *Carondelet's* steering malfunctioned, and she drifted helplessly to shore. The *Arkansas* had been penetrated by a couple of shots, and its pilothouse shattered, but Brown refused to back off. The *Carondelet* had extensive damage, having been pierced by some thirteen enemy shells, and had casualties of four killed, sixteen wounded, and ten missing.

Brown followed the two other retreating vessels, and the *Arkansas* steamed into the Mississippi and the teeth of Farragut's and Davis's combined forces, some thirty-three boats and ships. John Wilson, one of Brown's officers, vividly described the *Arkansas*'s descent into the Federal gauntlet: "In passing them we underwent a terrific fire at close range, which we answered actively, bringing every gun into action that would bear upon the enemy. The federal ram *Lancaster*, running out to strike us, received a shot in her drum from one of our bow guns, which caused an escape of steam. Many of her crew leaped overboard and perished in full sight of the fleet. A shell penetrated the broken armor on our port side and exploded, wounding Lieutenant [George] Gift in the right shoulder and killing and wounding most of his gun's crew. I was at the same time cut in the arm and leg by fragments of wood and iron. The heat on the gun deck from rapid firing, and the concussion from shot and shell alike was terrific."

Stifling heat forced men to strip to their underwear, as they continued firing as fast as possible to combat the storm of incoming iron and lead. Union shells took a toll; eight died when a shell that had already killed three bounced across the deck and passed through the lower smokestack. In fact the smokestack took so many hits, the crew had problems keeping up sufficient steam. Yet, despite the heavy rain of shot and shell coming from both sides of the river, Brown's crew managed miraculously to get the *Arkansas* to the cover of Confederate batteries at Vicksburg.[66]

The excursion through the gauntlet of Yankee vessels had been a nonstop battle, and Brown lost sixteen killed and twenty wounded. He was among the twenty, having been hit by flying splinters from the fragmented pilothouse. When the *Arkansas* arrived at the Vicksburg waterfront, "the scene around the gun deck . . . was ghastly in the extreme. Blood and brains bespattered everything, whilst arms, legs, and several headless trunks were strewn about." Citizens and soldiers who had waited so long for the ironclad to appear rushed to the docks, cheering as they went. They beat a hasty retreat soon enough when they saw the horrific aftermath of battle scattered over the boat's deck. Nevertheless, a Confederate soldier summed up the general feeling about the *Arkansas*'s journey: "It was glorious!"[67]

The fight on July 15 had not ended. Union boats had suffered damage and casualties, but by evening, frustrated that this one Rebel ironclad had survived, Union officers deployed to renew the attack. Williams's sharpshooters pinned down Rebels on the Vicksburg waterfront, while Farragut took his squadron back downriver to protect ships there from the enemy ironclad. Infuriated by Brown's escape, Farragut sent word to Davis: "We were all caught unprepared for him, but we must go down and destroy." "It will be warm work," he admitted, "but we must do it; he must be destroyed." While passing downstream late in the evening, Union vessels exchanged fire with the *Arkansas*. Brown lost eight killed and eleven wounded during this phase of the fighting. Total casualties for the Union fleet were eighteen killed, fifty wounded, and ten missing.

That night, from below Vicksburg, Farragut again wrote Davis to urge a joint attack. He frankly told Davis that the latter's ironclads would be expected by "the country" to destroy the Rebel menace. Nevertheless, said Farragut, "I desire to do my part and full share in this matter, and therefore have to propose that we make a combined attack upon him in Vicksburg." Farragut suggested a July 17 morning assault with the two fleets moving upriver and down respectively.

Davis begged to disagree. "I do not think the destruction of the *Arkansas*," he replied, "without any regard to the consequences to ourselves, would be an object sufficient to justify the abandonment of all the other advantages which have accumulated from the long series of triumphs and successes of patient waiting and of successful content on the part of the Army and Navy in the Mississippi River during the last five or six months." After all, he argued, the Union controlled the river except for the small span of space in front of Vicksburg, and the two squadrons had an avenue of communications along Williams's canal site. The government had promised army troops eventually; and when they came, the *Arkansas* would be even less an issue. As long as the Rebel ironclad stayed in front of Vicksburg, it could do little damage. Having said all that, Davis agreed to cooperate in a joint attack, but his boats would not be ready to go until at least the eighteenth.[68]

Farragut and Davis continued debating while Brown supervised repairs on his heavily damaged boat. Farragut reminded Davis that the two of them needed to gain control of the situation, and even though the enemy ironclad might be harmless at the moment, it could move out at any time. Davis's supply line was a bit more secure than Farragut's because guerrilla activity seemed more rampant south of Vicksburg. "Hence the difference in our feelings, and I suppose it accounts in great measure for the difference in our instructions, for while yours advise the prudential course, mine advise exactly the opposite."

July 18 came and went with no action, and finally on the twentieth Davis sought to relieve Farragut's anxiety by ordering his fleet to shell Brown's ironclad from afar and by sending down the ironclad *Essex*, commanded by David Porter's brother, William, the "largest ironclad boat and most powerful ironclad ram" available to Davis. On July 21, Porter personally assured Farragut that he would attack and would be backed up by the *Queen of the West*. The rest of the two fleets would provide cover fire.[69]

On July 22, the *Essex* and the *Queen* got under way, passing the *Benton*, where Davis stood on deck, waving and yelling his wishes for success. Porter pushed on, but could hear no Union fleet response to the roar of Confederate batteries. The *Essex* approached the *Arkansas*, fired a volley, rammed the Rebel ironclad, and ricocheted into the shallows along the riverbank. There it ran aground for several minutes, all the while taking enemy fire from Confederate sharpshooters, field pieces, and heavy batteries. Porter did not try to send men into the cauldron to board the *Arkansas*, but his guns blazed away at practically point-blank range. When he realized Farragut had not come to help, Porter ordered his crew to disengage and move downstream. In spite of the close fighting, Porter had light casualties: one killed and three wounded. The *Queen* also rammed the *Arkansas*, but with no support it too withdrew. Brown's ironclad had suffered additional damage, but it remained in service; his crew suffered twelve additional casualties.[70]

An aggravated Porter lashed out at Farragut and Davis for their lack of support. Farragut denied that he was supposed to help, later claiming that his fleet was to intercept the *Arkansas* should it try to escape downriver. Davis rejected Porter's accusations as false. Davis had never favored the plan; Farragut seemed to have lost interest; and as a result, Porter had been left to his own devices. Reactions to the affair appeared to indicate that communications among Union naval officers continued to be a major problem. On July 22, Farragut wrote Davis that the *Essex* would remain south of the city, and added that General Williams wanted to take his men farther downstream "in consequence of the sickness of his troops."

While disgruntled Union officers struggled with their failure, Gideon Welles's July 18 message reached Farragut on the twenty-third. Farragut probably felt like leaping for joy when he read: "Go down river at discretion." He at once notified Davis and said somewhat smugly that Davis would have to deal with the problem of controlling any *Arkansas* actions below Vicksburg. Rebel fire downstream on Union transports carrying sick to Baton Rouge made Farragut that much more anxious to leave. He intended to take his flotilla all the way to New Orleans, and he warned Davis that if he needed assistance, he should speak up now. Farragut sarcastically extended "best wishes for a speedy release from this embarrassment by an increase of both land and naval forces."[71]

A concerned Davis asked Williams to suspend moving his troops downriver, but Williams responded that disease was wrecking his army; he only had about 800 well enough to report for duty. Williams had decided that major campaigning on the river should be undertaken somewhere other than at Vicksburg. Sick lists had jeopardized both the canal project and the effective guarding of the railroad into Louisiana. Confederates inspecting the canal area later found some 600 fresh grave sites, and about 500 sick and underfed blacks left behind by departing Union forces. The canal had been a miserable failure and a place of human misery.[72]

Finally Davis, unable to find army support, threw up his hands and ordered the *Essex* and the *Sumter*, both anchored south of Vicksburg, to go to Baton Rouge. Without Williams's troops on the peninsula, it would be difficult to maintain communications between boats above and below the city. Davis placed Porter in charge of the stretch of the Mississippi from Vicksburg to Baton Rouge, and ordered him to be vigilant in watching for the *Arkansas*.

On August 1, Charles Davis decided that he had had enough; he ordered his fleet upriver to Helena, Arkansas, south of Memphis, which soon became a major staging area for downriver operations. In a lengthy dispatch to Secretary Welles, Davis detailed a litany of reasons for his decision: (1) the departure of Williams and his men; (2) disruptions in communications in Davis's rear, to the north; (3) reports of a possible junction of Rebel forces under Sterling Price and Thomas Hindman in Arkansas; and (4) steadily increasing sickness among his crews. Therefore, he had left Vicksburg, where he could do nothing. Now he was free to secure supply and communications lines and maintain contact with the army. His action, he argued, did not mean loss of control of the river. "Between this place and Vicksburg," he wrote, "there are no bluffs, no highlands suited to fortifications; guns can only be mounted on the level bank, where, to be sure, the levee often serves as a breastwork. But they will have no advantage of ground, and can be easily dislodged."[73]

Secretary Welles learned of Davis's move several days after the fact. In Washington, he mulled over reports of the *Arkansas* episode, and on August 2 sent similarly worded messages to Farragut and Davis, stating frankly that the news had caused "serious mortification to the [Navy] Department and the country." Any "neglect or apparent neglect of the squadron" must be rectified by the capture or destruction of the *Arkansas*, which he hoped would be a fact by the time his messages arrived. The ironclad would eventually be destroyed, but in a manner not envisioned by Welles, Farragut, or Davis.[74]

In Vicksburg, Farragut's and Davis's departures caused much celebration. Soldiers and citizens had endured continual shelling and sickness, and yet the city stood firm, with relatively few scars to show for the long summer's ordeal. Many residents moved back into abandoned homes; others hesitated, fearing enemy boats might return. The Confederate War Department congratulated Van Dorn and his troops and

Brown and his sailors. The Confederate Congress passed a resolution congratulating Brown and his crew. Van Dorn applauded Brown's odyssey through the Federal fleet that "immortalized his single vessel, himself, and the heroes under his command by an achievement the most brilliant ever recorded in naval annals." The facts cheered the Confederacy: "With one ironclad, a handful of guns, and 7,000 troops, the Confederates had regained control of 250 miles of the Mississippi." By withholding army troops to assist the navy, the Union high command had squandered a wonderful opportunity to take Vicksburg. Yet whatever control the Confederates had of the Mississippi was highly tenuous. Van Dorn and Brown had bought Vicksburg time, not salvation.[75]

Indeed, the first attempt to take Vicksburg had not failed because of Confederate resistance. Circumstances dictated that neither the Union navy nor the Union army acting alone could force the city's surrender. Easy victories along the river south of Vicksburg proved misleading to Federal strategists who thought clearing the Mississippi would come easily. The Farragut-Davis campaign proved to be sobering for Abraham Lincoln and his War Department. Securing the Mississippi required considerably more than naval superiority. Command bickering and lack of focus distorted the vision of both attackers and defenders, guaranteeing the prolonging of what might have been a brief, successful Union operation.

Beyond tactical realities, the war along the river underscored the hardening of attitudes and a harshness that changed the nature of the struggle for the lower river valley. The harder war would become more evident in the second major phase of the Vicksburg campaign in the late fall–early winter months of 1862. Before the second phase began, however, there would be much strategic maneuvering that, while impacting future campaign activities, distracted Union attention from Vicksburg. At the end of this interim period, the city, ever in the back of military minds blue and gray, would reemerge as the magnet of Federal determination to eliminate enemy control of the Mississippi.

3

≋ Counterstrokes & Controversies

The first campaign to take Vicksburg ended with a bold iron-clad and a whimper, and a long interim between the summer and winter campaigns of 1862 began. During this period, the Confederacy lost its only significant weapon on the Mississippi; the ranking Confederate commander in the Vicksburg area fell from favor; the Confederacy lost two key battles in Northeast Mississippi; a new, controversial commander arrived from the Eastern Theater; a Union general found himself restored to command and then learned of subterfuge that threatened his campaign plans; and guerrilla warfare and hard war emerged as key elements in the Union army's invasion of North Mississippi. The autumn of 1862 thus proved to be a time of turmoil for commanders and soldiers in both armies, and for civilians. The stage was set for the second major phase of the Vicksburg campaign.

In Vicksburg, Earl Van Dorn's victory celebration had not lasted long. In the past his major problem had been rushing into things without considering the ramifications. Rather than give the Vicksburg garrison time to rest, regroup, and rebuild, the rash Mississippian decided to go on the offensive before the Yankees renewed efforts to take the city. As long as Baton Rouge remained in enemy hands, the Confederate supply line connecting the Trans-Mississippi with Mississippi and points east was, if not blocked, certainly throttled by Union control of the mouth of the Red River. Taking back the Louisiana capital thus became Van Dorn's top priority.

The general later wrote of his thinking: "It was a matter of great necessity to us that the navigation of Red River should be opened as high as Vicksburg. Supplies much needed existed there, had to be obtained from any other quarter, and strong military reasons demanded that we should hold the Mississippi at two points, to facilitate communications and cooperation between my district and the Trans-Mississippi

Department. The capture of Baton Rouge and the forces of the enemy at that point would open the Mississippi, secure the navigation of the Red River, then in a state of blockade, and also render easier the recapture of New Orleans." Typically, Van Dorn's plans included grandiose, unrealistic schemes beyond the immediate objective. Without a significant naval force, the Confederates could not hope to take back New Orleans, and possibly not even Baton Rouge.

Jefferson Davis, delighted with the results of the summer campaign at Vicksburg, approved Van Dorn's proposal. Davis liked the idea of both redeeming Confederate fortunes in Louisiana and diverting Van Dorn's mind from recent organizational changes in Mississippi. Davis and his advisers had decided to combine two departments that included that portion of Louisiana east of the Mississippi River and most of Mississippi. Van Dorn thought the expansion took the focus off Vicksburg, but Davis patiently explained he only wanted commanders to have more flexibility deploying their forces. Ironically, Davis's words likely influenced Van Dorn to propose the ill-fated Baton Rouge offensive.[1]

Other Confederate strategic plans seemed to support Van Dorn's decision. Braxton Bragg moved the major portion of his army east in late July 1862 to operate with Edmund Kirby Smith in Tennessee. Their combined strength, on paper, of some 54,000 men, could clear central Tennessee of Federals and perhaps open the way for Bragg to carry the war into Kentucky. Bragg left 16,000 men, commanded by Sterling Price, in Mississippi around Tupelo. Bragg hoped that dividing his troops would force Union commanders to disperse their numerical advantage, thus improving Confederate odds. Bragg felt that if he did not move, massed Union forces would crush him and then stroll into Vicksburg as easily as Halleck could and should have done. Van Dorn's effort to take Baton Rouge complemented this scenario by occupying the attention of Federals south of Vicksburg.

On July 26, two days after Bragg began transferring troops by rail to Chattanooga, Van Dorn discussed Baton Rouge plans with John Breckinridge, the former vice president of the United States who would command the expedition. Breckinridge's army, some 4,000 men, traveled to Camp Moore, near Tangipahoa, Louisiana; he could have called off the campaign if he felt his small army were too weak, which it was, but he did not. Scouting reports indicated the Union force in Baton Rouge numbered 5,000 — intelligence surprisingly accurate by Civil War standards. Yet many of Thomas Williams's troops lay ill in Baton Rouge hospitals.[2]

Predictably, Van Dorn, consumed by a sense of urgency, did not consider human factors that could cripple Breckinridge's operation. Breckinridge's men had suffered greatly from the summer campaign and the trip to Louisiana. Breckinridge later wrote how his command had "suffered severely from the effects of exposure . . . from heavy rains without shelter and from the extreme heat." He left Vicksburg with only 3,400 of the 4,000 men he had on paper, and by the time the army reached Baton Rouge, he had 2,600 capable of combat. Breckinridge obviously needed help. A diversion on the river seemed logical; so he immediately thought of the *Arkansas*, and he sent word to Van Dorn.[3]

Responding too quickly, Van Dorn, given command authority over the ironclad by President Davis, ordered the *Arkansas* to Baton Rouge. His timing could not have been worse. The battered boat still had engine problems, and loose iron plating needed to be reattached to the hull. After getting repairs under way, Lieutenant Isaac Brown, still commanding the ironclad, had taken a short leave to his home in Grenada, where he became "violently ill." There he learned that his second in command, First Lieutenant Henry Stevens, had been told by Van Dorn to take the *Arkansas* to Breckinridge's aid. Stevens, aware of the vessel's problems, hesitated, but Van Dorn insisted, "beyond all reason." In Brown's absence, Stevens, perhaps not understanding or caring that Van Dorn had presidential approval to order the *Arkansas* into action, referred the matter to Flag Officer William Lynch in Jackson. Lynch was a senior officer of the Confederate navy whose command included the Mississippi River and its tributaries. He had never been impressed with the *Arkansas*; so he ordered Stevens to get under way, and the crippled boat chugged south out of Vicksburg, four hours before Brown arrived after a desperate trip to Vicksburg to prevent the departure.[4]

Brown later wrote bitterly of how Lynch, "with horses and carriages, furnished by [the] Government in place of a flag-ship, thus commanding in chief for the Confederacy on the Mississippi, sixty miles from the nearest waters," had made such a fateful decision. "This officer," wrote Brown, "whose war record was yet in abeyance, had attained scientific celebrity by dabbling in the waters of the Dead Sea, at a time when I was engaged in the siege of Vera Cruz and in the general operations of the Mexican war. Ignorant or regardless of the condition of the *Arkansas*, fresh from Richmond on his mission of bother, not communicating with or informing me on the subject, he ordered Stevens to obey Van Dorn without any regard to my orders to the contrary."[5]

Having been assured that the *Arkansas* would arrive by August 5, John Breckinridge attacked Baton Rouge early that morning. The battle evolved into a vicious struggle in the streets of the Louisiana capital.

Each side sent about 2,500 men into the fray, and during the fighting Thomas Williams was shot dead. On the Confederate side, General Ben Hardin Helm, husband of Mary Lincoln's half-sister, received serious injuries when his horse fell, and Mrs. Lincoln's brother, A. H. Todd, was killed. Future Mississippi governor Charles Clark also fell with serious wounds that left him crippled.

Breckinridge's troops drove Federal forces deep into Baton Rouge, but superior Yankee artillery and Union gunboat shells forced them to retire, leaving the town in enemy hands. Though he could claim a somewhat empty tactical victory, Breckinridge realized that the Union navy and the absence of the *Arkansas*, which had not been heard from, meant he could do nothing more. His losses numbered over 400 killed, wounded, and missing. Federal casualties totaled more than 380.[6]

Williams's second in command, Colonel Thomas Cahill, called Baton Rouge a "glorious victory" for the Union, but on August 16, Benjamin Butler, fearing a Confederate assault on New Orleans, ordered Baton Rouge evacuated. The Federals left the town in a shambles, and Breckinridge charged the Yankees with committing atrocities. Meanwhile, Butler berated Secretary of War Edwin Stanton for allowing Henry Halleck to break up the army in North Mississippi and for permitting the departure of the navy from Vicksburg. Halleck's decision and the navy's withdrawal had obviously let the Confederates assume the offensive, and Butler feared losing his hold on the lower Mississippi. Yet, even without Baton Rouge, the Union navy still controlled the mouth of the Red River and had the upper hand on the Mississippi.

Meanwhile, John Breckinridge salvaged something for the Confederacy when he ordered a detachment to occupy Port Hudson, a river town sitting above Baton Rouge. The terrain and location of Port Hudson gave Confederates a good river defensive position south of Vicksburg. General John Bowen, the best Confederate field general of the Vicksburg campaign, deployed his Missouri brigade on the banks of the Comite River to watch Baton Rouge. Some historians have argued erroneously that Confederate occupation of Port Hudson gave the Confederates control of the Mississippi from that point north to Vicksburg. While Port Hudson did provide a strategic strong point on Vicksburg's southern flank, the Confederacy had no naval force to dominate the river between the two, and the occupation of Port Hudson further depleted the already scarce Confederate manpower. Van Dorn's best move would have been to abandon the Baton Rouge operation and withdraw all troops back to Vicksburg, especially after the *Arkansas* met its fate.[7]

The *Arkansas*'s crew pushed the dilapidated ironclad downstream at full speed, which forced frequent stops for repairs. The chief engineer could not make the trip; his absence exacerbated attempts to keep the engines running. By the time the struggling boat reached the mouth of the Red, problems had become so serious that Henry Stevens called a council of war. Whatever the arguments pro and con, the mission continued. On August 4, the *Arkansas* steamed into Port Hudson, where the crew gave her a thorough check. Stevens received reports that several Union vessels were anchored at Baton Rouge and that Breckinridge would attack next morning. At dawn the crew heard sounds of battle, and the ironclad steamed back into the Mississippi.

Stevens had planned to ram an old foe, the *Essex*, and then go after other gunboats. As the Confederates neared the last turn before entering a straight path to Baton Rouge, the starboard engine shut down, forcing the boat aground and jamming the hull against cypress stumps. The crew struggled to get the engine going and to pull free, in full view of the enemy navy. Civilian onlookers watched anxiously while the frustrated Confederates worked. Finally, after prying the hull with railroad rails, the crew pulled the boat free and pointed her upstream out of harm's way. That night, work continued on the engines, and sailors replenished the onboard coal supply and prepared for a dawn attack.

The next morning, the *Essex* came after the *Arkansas*. Stevens could see several other boats behind the *Essex*, and he decided to retreat, drawing the *Essex* farther upriver, before turning to fight. Soon the *Arkansas*' port engine failed beyond repair, forcing the boat ashore again, this time with enemy vessels closing fast. Stevens's gunners exchanged a few shots with the *Essex*, but he knew he had to destroy the ironclad before it fell into Yankee hands. The crew set the wardroom and cabin afire and positioned shells to ignite. The wet sailors scrambled for the banks and safety. Behind them fire reached the shells, and the *Arkansas* blew apart.

Henry Stevens had to be helped ashore because of his serious hand burns. He and his men escaped through the Louisiana countryside, "partly on foot, horseback, and in wagons, the planters, their wives and daughters receiving us," wrote one, "all along our route with the utmost kindness." They crossed two rivers and by August 9 reached Jackson. Brown, upset at the loss of his boat, but relieved that his crew had escaped, reported angrily that Confederate guerrillas refused any assistance to the refugee sailors. Brown passed along the news to Breckinridge, adding, "Pray have all such running heroes added to the conscript roll on both sides." So ended the brief, brilliant, and sad career of the *Arkansas*, sent to her doom by an aged flag officer and a reckless army general. Whatever hope Van Dorn had of regaining lost stretches of river sank with the fragmented ironclad.[8]

Though the Baton Rouge campaign fizzled, for a time it relieved pressure on Vicksburg from the southern reaches of the Mississippi, and the river city came to life. The war had come to stay, however, so any hope residents had of normality proved elusive. The unhealthy climate continued to cause problems, more noticeably because of the increase in population due to military occupation. Commanders had trouble finding suitable sites far enough from the river to train troops and yet close enough for quick deployment if the enemy reappeared. Contagious illnesses, such as measles, continued to plague both Vicksburg and neighborhoods across the river. Exchanged Confederate prisoners brought downriver by Union transports filled up the town, and their presence exacerbated illnesses and attracted young women who "swarm the streets every evening about sundown giving quite an animated appearance."

The men regaled locals with stories, but relations between soldier and civilian remained strained. Soldiers who had endured incarceration often found unsympathetic ears in Vicksburg, and such attitudes, along with high prices for food, fed continuing hostile feelings among troops toward city residents.[9]

What soldiers perceived as unsympathetic attitudes often stemmed from fear. Civilians remained in a state of tension from memories of naval shells. Window shutters remained closed; streets contained much less traffic than during prewar days; river commerce had been reduced to a trickle; a few slaves could be seen, probably in search of, or on errands for, masters; stray cats and dogs roamed about. Refugees slowly began returning, thereby relieving food shortages in the countryside between Vicksburg and Jackson. The city council tried to resume meetings but could not get a quorum for several weeks, and they could only "re-affirm their uselessness." Some previously closed stores reopened, and slave trading began anew. Buyers focused on young females less likely to run away or be taken for labor by the army. The military's heavy-handed use of private property for building fortifications angered civilians. Conflicts were "a matter of mind: a tangled web of parochialism, State's Rights, war-weariness, and human perversity." The people of Vicksburg adjusted to shortages, volunteered at hospitals, helped transport munitions, glared at Union prisoners, and realized war would not go away soon.[10]

〰️ While citizens and soldiers coped in Vicksburg, the ramifications of guerrilla, or partisan, warfare in the surrounding region continued. The Confederate government established a policy that exacerbated the fledgling, but increasingly bitter, guerrilla activity on the Mississippi. Confederate adjutant and inspector general Samuel Cooper issued orders to General Richard Taylor on July 30 to report to the Trans-Mississippi.

Taylor, a capable career officer and brother of Jefferson Davis's deceased first wife, received instructions to "prevent the use of rivers and bayous . . . by the enemy" and to cut Union supply lines and communications. In particular, the government instructed Taylor to "embarrass the enemy in the navigation of the Mississippi River" by setting up light artillery at strategic points. Further, and most significantly, Taylor had to inspect partisan military organizations and "direct and control" them so they could effectively assist in protecting private property. While the Confederate government intended to make positive use of guerrilla tactics, Davis and his advisers soon learned that partisan activities could not be easily controlled.[11]

This kind of warfare could not be confined to the river, for its very methods tempted civilians all across the South to strike out at invading Yankees. In North Mississippi, where most of the next major phase of the Vicksburg campaign would be centered, the prospect of the area becoming a battleground resulted in vandalism and guerrilla activities. The earlier siege of Corinth seemed but a foretaste of worse to come. Families terrified by the prospects of being overrun by Yankees loaded wagons and left, "flowing from before the enemy saving what property they can." Union soldiers often arrested civilians on suspicion of espionage or guerrilla activity, further fueling the exodus to other parts of Mississippi and the Southeast.[12]

Federal anger at guerrilla operations produced harsh retribution, sometimes justified, which further ripped the tenuous local social fabric. One family had their carpets stripped from the floor, torn into pieces and scattered about their yard. Dresses were taken and given "to the negro women on the place," a common tactic employed by Union soldiers, who enjoyed infuriating and humiliating slave owners. Federals destroyed furniture, and occasionally had bowel movements in wheat stored on the grounds. Others deposited excrement inside houses, mutilated family photographs, killed poultry, and took slaves. A Confederate soldier captured the essence of hard war in his comment on depredations committed against a Tennessee family: "Truly, this war, by our enemies has been waged against our people, with savage barbarity, and acts of wantonness, characteristic of no people on the face of the earth except the red-necked, clock-peddling, wooden-nutmeg selling Yankees."[13]

Union army interaction with slaves further heightened tensions. Some slaves ran away; owners hid others to keep them from being freed by Yankees. Owners tried to intimidate their slaves by circulating reports that enemy soldiers were shooting slaves. Grant's men laughed at slaves who expressed surprise that these men from the North had no horns, as their masters had told them. William T. Sherman's soldiers in Memphis, however, complained about the "big drove of blackbirds" that flocked to the city, and applauded when contrabands boarded boats for the North. A Confederate wrote of those troubled times, "The Negroes is the absorbing topic. Our Negroes seem to be restless and hard to please. Perhaps they are but seeking a pretext for leaving." Certainly runaways fueled partisan warfare, for white owners adopted guerrilla hit-and-run tactics in retaliation.[14]

General Grant, now finally restored to the command of the Union army in West Tennessee, a command he had lost after Shiloh, had to deal with these problems. Having been surprised by the Confederate attack the first day of that battle, Grant and his army had been whipped; and, though they triumphed the second day, Grant had been berated, especially in the press. Henry Halleck, his immediate superior, had traveled to Tennessee to take personal command of the army. Eventually Halleck would be called to Washington to become general in chief, and Grant, who had been given command of the district of West Tennessee, became departmental commander on October 25. One story circulated that Halleck offered the command to a friend and quartermaster officer, who turned it down. The story is suspicious, but, if true, it demonstrated the underlying hostility between Grant and Halleck. Whatever the truth, the two developed an effective, if strained, working relationship.

As guerrilla activity increased, Grant devoted more time to countermeasures, and Halleck responded to Grant's concerns with a simple solution: "It is very desirable that you should clear out West Tennessee and North Mississippi of all organized enemies. If necessary, take up all active sympathizers, and either hold them as prisoners or put them beyond our lines. Handle that class without gloves, and take their property for public use." "It is time," he wrote, "that they should begin to feel the presence of war on our side." Grant listened, but did not favor such remedies and later claimed he could not recall personally ordering any citizens arrested. When he learned that some officers had arrested white noncombatants to send north, he ordered their release.[15]

Grant's friend and confidant William T. Sherman, the military governor of Memphis, preferred a more direct approach. The fiery Sherman, an Ohioan who would ultimately have more success in the army than in civilian life, had definite ideas about guerrillas. He viewed all locals as guerrillas, skilled at hit-and-run tactics and always acting innocent. Sherman believed in "universal confiscation and colonization." He proposed moving troops from place to place and destroying anything that might be of use to the enemy, though he had not yet embraced the hard-war concepts that marked future operations.[16]

Grant later wired Halleck that guerrilla activity seemed to be on the decline, though many local troublemakers remained. Most of the overt, aggressive guerrillas had apparently been driven south into Mississippi, and Grant hoped to keep them there. Accomplishing that feat proved to be more difficult than he anticipated. Grant continued to handle the issue lightly, for "I deemed it better that a few guilty men should escape than that a great many innocent ones should suffer."[17]

Meanwhile, during the late summer–early autumn lull, sporadic military activity erupted on the Mississippi. On the west side, General Samuel Curtis decided to operate on the Arkansas and White rivers in an attempt to clear both of Confederates. Yet he knew that without naval assistance he could do very little. Curtis wrote on August 6 to Halleck: "The hopes of the West float on the Mississippi, and all my hope of reducing Arkansas and supporting Missouri depend on this river."[18]

A combined navy-army expedition on the Yazoo, August 16–27, met with limited success. Union forces captured the Confederate steamer *Fairplay* and with it some 1,200 Enfield rifles, 4,000 muskets, other small arms, and various kinds of ammunition, plus four pieces of artillery. Embarrassed by the loss of the *Fairplay*, M. L. Smith blamed incompetent sentries, and thereafter he sent cavalry to watch Helena and protect planters on the Mississippi side of the river. Smith did not have the numbers necessary to thwart such Federal operations over the expansive lower Mississippi Valley.

Other developments had an impact on future Vicksburg campaigning. The memory of the *Arkansas* caused concern among Federals; if the Confederates had more ironclads under construction on interior Mississippi waters, control of the Mississippi could be threatened. In September, Halleck warned Grant about reports of additional ironclads being built on the Yazoo. Halleck need not have bothered; there would be no more *Arkansas* to contend with. Even if the Confederacy had had the means, the Union navy's dominance of inland waters would make construction of ironclads precarious.

Union naval developments elsewhere included an effective blockade of Gulf of Mexico ports, which made it "practically impossible to run supplies into the eastern Confederate states from abroad via Texas or Louisiana across the Mississippi." The blockade increased the value of the Vicksburg area in linking the Western Theater to the East. David Dixon Porter was promoted to commander of the Mississippi River Squadron, and Porter named Brigadier General Alfred Ellet to head up a force known as the Mississippi Marine Brigade to help eradicate river guerrilla activity. Both Porter and Ellet would play key roles in future Vicksburg operations.[19]

Meanwhile, Henry Halleck's scattering of Union forces created new challenges for both sides. Samuel Curtis sparred in Arkansas with Thomas Hindman, a volatile Arkansas politician. Hindman's presence led to the establishment of a Union base at Helena. Hindman could roam the hinterland, but he must be kept away from the river. To check Hindman, Curtis demanded more troops.

The Helena base was not popular. One soldier wrote his wife, "I know that a military camp is no place for any decent woman and it would be no pleasure to either you or me but I sincerely hope and trust the day will come when we will have the pleasure of meeting again at home to enjoy life in a way that suits me better than this." Another noted that Helena was very small, very Confederate, and infested with dangerous guerrillas. Unhappy soldiers marched hither and yon, for no reason apparent, and they quickly tired of it and became short tempered with one another. Helena gained a reputation as a volatile locale, symbolic of morale problems caused by troops sitting immobile in the late summer–early fall of 1862.[20]

Halleck soon left for Washington, having been named general of all Union armies on July 11. Curtis, U. S. Grant, and others inherited Halleck's scattered forces, and they faced the challenge of regaining Union momentum to clear the Mississippi. Grant moaned: "I was put entirely on the defensive in a territory whose population was hostile to the Union." This was "the most anxious period of the war" for Grant, because he was trying to hold the Corinth-Memphis corridor without adequate troop strength. He knew future campaigning against Vicksburg depended on stabilizing that area.[21]

Halleck's decision to send Don Carlos Buell to attack Chattanooga had been especially costly to Grant's hopes for assuming the offensive.

Buell intended to get between Braxton Bragg in North Mississippi and Edmund Kirby Smith in Tennessee to disrupt Confederate communications. Richmond authorities deemed Buell's advance a threat and asked Bragg to reinforce Smith. Bragg knew that he must get active in the field or be milked dry of troops. After looking at his bleak supply situation, Bragg decided to move into Tennessee, and ultimately to Kentucky, leaving behind enough soldiers in Mississippi to keep Grant from reinforcing Buell.[22]

Bragg expected Van Dorn, with some 16,000 men, to hold the line on the Mississippi River, while Sterling Price, with "a similar force," stayed in North Mississippi. Bragg told Van Dorn, somewhat cryptically, "It is the wish of the commanding general that you should consult freely and co-operate with Major-General Price. It is expected that you will do all things deemed needful without awaiting instructions from these headquarters. General Price will be instructed to the same effect." In effect, Bragg told his subordinates to do their jobs and leave him alone.

Bragg's departure caused confusion. Van Dorn commanded the District of the Mississippi; Price now commanded all troops in Mississippi not in Van Dorn's district or in the Gulf of Mexico area, commanded by John Forney. In effect, none of the three could take charge and coordinate movements against the enemy. Bragg likely felt these officers would cooperate, but only time would tell.

Perhaps having second thoughts, Bragg tried initially to pull strings from a distance. Anticipating that Union troops in North Mississippi under the command of a Grant lieutenant, General William Rosecrans, might come to Tennessee, Bragg wired Price on August 2, "The road is open for you into Western Tennessee." Price understood the tactical implication, but he had apprehensions; the road might be open eventually, but currently it was not. Price asked Governor Pettus for Mississippi state militia to come to the Tupelo area and perform garrison duty while regular troops took to the field. Whatever his concerns, Price felt obliged to obey Bragg if possible. Price soon learned that his preparations were for naught; Rosecrans was not going anywhere. Union officials had no intention of abandoning North Mississippi and West Tennessee. Grant understood Buell's need for help, but he refused to strip his department to provide it.[23]

Once Bragg learned of Grant's decision, he looked west for strategic assistance to keep Union reinforcements out of Tennessee. On August 11, he wired Van Dorn to press the Federals in West Tennessee: "If you hold them in check we are sure of success here; but should they reenforce here so as to defy us then you may redeem West Tennessee and probably aid us by crossing to the enemy's rear." Van Dorn saw no urgency in doing anything in North Mississippi. At the time that Breckinridge was nearing Baton Rouge, Van Dorn still wanted Price to send reinforcements to the Red River.

Breckinridge's withdrawal from Baton Rouge changed the strategic landscape. Van Dorn now wanted Price to send healthy men to Vicksburg to temporarily fill Breckinridge's depleted ranks; Van Dorn promised to lead them back north to rejoin Price. Price did not know that Van Dorn had any notion of coming north, but he welcomed the news. The changing focus of operations by both sides took the spotlight off Vicksburg, giving the city further respite.[24]

For Confederate strategists, the key question became how long Grant could hold back Rosecrans. Grant yielded to Halleck's pressure in August and sent two divisions to Buell, but he resisted Halleck's request for diversionary action in West Tennessee. Grant knew Price lurked in the Tupelo area, and scouting reports indicated he might be receiving reinforcements intended to keep Grant from sending more men to Buell. On the other hand, Grant knew that if his army got too weak, Price might become emboldened and attack. Price reinforced Grant's thinking by keeping active, to the point that Grant asked Curtis for help in holding North Mississippi Confederates at bay.[25]

Meanwhile, Van Dorn and Price talked further about concentrating and moving into West Tennessee. Before that happened, a leery Price wanted to chase Federals out of Corinth to regain control of the railroads needed for logistical support. He suggested marching to Corinth from Tupelo, since such a move would "hinder and delay" reinforcements to Buell. "We must attack the enemy before they begin to receive their new levies," he argued. "We ought to avail ourselves, too, of the moral force which we would gain by participating in the great forward movement which our armies are now making everywhere." Price was thinking not only of Bragg and Smith's campaign into Kentucky, but also of Robert E. Lee's invasion of Maryland. The feisty Price moaned, "We alone are stationary."

On September 2, Price received an urgent message from Bragg that Buell was marching from Nashville toward Kentucky. Rosecrans must not be allowed to send support. Price decided he must act at once, and so informed Van Dorn, who began shifting troops from Vicksburg to Holly Springs. By moving west and north of Rosecrans's position at Corinth, Van Dorn could both block Sherman in Memphis from sending reinforcements east and force Rosecrans to fight to avoid being flanked. If Rosecrans moved toward Nashville before Van Dorn got to

Corinth, then Price must pursue. Van Dorn told Price, "Separated we can do but little; joined we may do much." Surprisingly, and perhaps for the first time in the war, Van Dorn seemed to be in no hurry. If Price acted quickly, he would have to do so alone.

On September 4, Van Dorn sent Breckinridge's troops to Holly Springs, but Price refused to go there. He knew Bragg expected him to stay where he was to prevent Union troop movements east. Reports indicated that Rosecrans had already shifted most of his troops east of Corinth to Iuka and Eastport, and if true, a move by Price to the west would clear the way for Rosecrans to go east to Tennessee via rail. Also such a movement would expose the flank and rear of Price's army. He thus moved from Tupelo toward Iuka to press Rosecrans.[26]

While Price marched, U. S. Grant had to deal with continuing insistence from Washington that he send more reinforcements to Buell. Grant asked Halleck about freeing up troops by abandoning part of the Memphis-Charleston Railroad east of Corinth. Halleck agreed but Rosecrans objected, arguing that Iuka and Eastport needed to be held. To give up the railroad all the way to Iuka would force evacuation of a hospital and loss of significant supply depots. The discussion ended abruptly when news came that both Van Dorn and Price were on the move.

Van Dorn weighed the evolving strategic situation by pondering a series of "ifs." If Rosecrans had crossed the Tennessee, should not Van Dorn and Price push north into Kentucky? If Rosecrans was marching anywhere, could Price overtake him? If their joint forces moved fast enough, they might block reinforcements for Buell. If Rosecrans had not crossed the Tennessee, Van Dorn and Price could make a combined attack. If Confederates forced Rosecrans to the Tennessee, Sherman might have to evacuate Memphis and move north.[27]

Van Dorn took time from his analysis to appeal to Richmond for permission to command Price's movements, in effect hoping to cancel Bragg's influence on Price. Also, Van Dorn wanted custody of exchanged Confederate prisoners assigned to Price. President Davis agreed that Van Dorn should have some leeway in using these men, but they then must be returned to their old regiments, most of which were Price's. However, any regiment headquartered within Van Dorn's district lines could be assigned to his army. Van Dorn's rank gave "him the command of all the troops with whom he will be operating." But, Davis warned, "nothing in these instructions must be considered as rescinding the orders or interfering with the arrangements of General Bragg." The president concluded his convoluted answer with the added warning that nothing should be done in North Mississippi to endanger Vicksburg or Port Hudson.

Davis soon realized the difficulty of handling situations from a distance. On September 12, Van Dorn, unaware that he had been given command over Price, complained that Price "proposes to follow Rosecrans toward Nashville." Van Dorn wanted to invade West Tennessee, cross the Tennessee and the Cumberland, and go to Kentucky, and that meant "no cooperation" between him and Price. The situation quickly changed when Rosecrans moved west toward Corinth; Price agreed to join Van Dorn in an attack there, and Van Dorn proposed an approach from the west and southwest. Bragg, meanwhile, lashed out at Price and Van Dorn for doing nothing to stop Rosecrans from moving toward Nashville. Though Rosecrans made no such movement, Van Dorn soothed Bragg's anger by sending Breckinridge's division to Tennessee.[28]

Jefferson Davis decided that Bragg's trip to Tennessee had destabilized the command situation in Mississippi, and the president felt "at a loss to know how to remedy evils without damaging" Bragg's plans. Without coordinated operations, "disaster to all must be the probable result," Davis warned. The exchanged prisoners had not arrived, and perhaps Van Dorn should have remained in Jackson. Davis still worried about security at Vicksburg and Port Hudson. For the moment, Van Dorn and Price must cooperate with Bragg's and Smith's operations in Tennessee. Davis's War Department insisted that "nothing should be allowed to obstruct" movements in concert.[29]

≫ While confusion reigned in Confederate circles, Union commanders in North Mississippi reached conclusions that led to battle. Price's advance toward Iuka caused Henry Halleck to wire Grant: "Do everything in your power to prevent Price from crossing the Tennessee River. A junction of Price and Bragg in Tennessee or Kentucky would be most disastrous. They should be fought while separate." Halleck's concerns underscored the reality of the strategic situation; each side had determined to keep the other from sending reinforcements to Tennessee. The common goal brought Price to Iuka in search of Rosecrans and now Rosecrans and Grant to Iuka in search of Price.

Grant decided on a two-pronged operation to trap Price in Iuka. Grant knew Van Dorn lurked to the southwest but not close enough to help Price. Rosecrans took part of the army and swung around Price's left to enter Iuka from the south. Grant traveled with E. O. C. Ord's command, approaching Iuka from the west. The proposed joint attacks against Price did not work because they were not coordinated.[30]

Rosecrans encountered delays, and, though Ord got into position on September 18, Rosecrans did not make contact with Price until the next day. Ord waited, because Grant wanted Rosecrans to strike first to divert Price's attention, a strategy that Rosecrans did not know about. Rosecrans's 9,000 fought viciously with Confederate General Henry Little's two brigades. Little, a special favorite of General Price, fell dead, and the Confederates fought on, holding their own; but reports of Ord's presence forced a reluctant retreat south. Ord's 8,000 remained inert because they could not hear the battle raging south of town just a few miles away. One modern explanation is that geographic features and weather conditions muted the sounds of battle. Whatever the case, Price escaped with about 15,000 men, claiming he suffered only 652 casualties, but the total was probably well over a thousand. Grant's losses totaled 790.[31]

After escaping the enemy trap, Price moved south and then northwest to join forces with Van Dorn. Price's men rested while Van Dorn waited for the promised paroled prisoners. Characteristically, Van Dorn remained confident that he and Price could hold "a large force in check; later we will defeat them, free West Tennessee, and penetrate Kentucky or cross the Ohio." While he waited, Van Dorn adhered to Davis's wishes and sent reinforcements to Port Hudson.[32]

During this pause, Van Dorn received orders to assume command of all troops in the area and take to the field. He must "make proper disposition for the defense of the Mississippi River, and also for an advance into Tennessee." But he received an unwelcome surprise when Gideon J. Pillow, sent by Bragg, showed up to command the returned prisoners, not yet arrived. Van Dorn, no doubt of aware of Pillow's erratic reputation, was not pleased.[33]

The continued uncertainty in his home state caused Jefferson Davis to have second thoughts regarding Van Dorn's ability to operate in North Mississippi and West Tennessee and still secure the lower Mississippi. Several days would pass before Van Dorn learned that Davis had decided to relieve him of command. By the time he did, few would argue with Davis's decision.

Van Dorn finally got under way on October 1 to attack Corinth. The march was not well planned, and Van Dorn had resorted to his old habit of rushing things. The expected former prisoners had still not arrived, though at least Van Dorn did not have to worry about Pillow, who stayed behind. Van Dorn expected to "take Corinth," then go north and cut the railroad to Jackson, Tennessee. Union officers were not surprised. Grant wired Halleck on October 1 that though there had been doubts about Van Dorn's intentions, "it is now clear that Corinth is to be the point, and that from the west or southwest." "My position is precarious," he wrote, "but hope to get out of it all right."[34]

The Federals got out of it all right, but it took two days of hard fighting to beat off the Confederates. Van Dorn launched his first assault on October 3, and his army burst through outer defenses, but then ran into well-entrenched Yankees. The Rebels were tired, hungry, and thirsty, and yet Van Dorn, who predictably ignored logistics and the physical condition of his army, urged his men on. The fighting continued the next day, but the Confederates, also suffering from poor tactical leadership, had to retreat west. Only a savage rearguard action by John Bowen's division saved the army, which escaped to Ripley. Corinth ended Van Dorn's career as an army commander. Confederate losses were serious, totaling over 4,000 (killed, wounded, and missing) out of 22,000 engaged. Rosecrans had some 2,500 total casualties out of 23,000.

Rosecrans wanted to keep up pursuit and deliver a knockout blow, but Grant refused. The usually aggressive general feared that Rosecrans might run into heavily fortified enemy positions at Holly Springs, positions that in fact were held only by the paroled Confederate prisoners, who at last had returned and who could have offered meager resistance. Grant and Rosecrans had had strained relations since the confusion at Iuka, but Grant's refusal to permit pursuit is difficult to defend.[35]

Van Dorn's debacle left Confederate military affairs in a state of confusion. In North Mississippi, Confederates had only a tenuous foothold, whereas Grant had a firm grip. The focus in the Mississippi Valley now began shifting back to Vicksburg. Union river activity in the Yazoo alerted Confederate officials to the need for better defenses along Vicksburg's north flank. Flag Officer Lynch suggested fortifying the Yazoo bluffs to control the mouths of the Yazoo and the Big and Little Sunflower rivers. The Yazoo channel should be obstructed and a barricade at Liverpool below Yazoo City improved. The crew of the defunct *Arkansas* and other sailors without boats were told to arm themselves and protect obstructions. Inland commerce on the Yazoo, which provided logistical support for Confederate troops in Vicksburg, must be protected.[36]

Confederate fortunes seemed on the decline all across the Western

Theater. Compounding the repulse at Corinth, Braxton Bragg lost his nerve after a vicious battle with Buell at Perryville, Kentucky, and retreated back into Tennessee. Further disappointment came from the East when Robert E. Lee and his army barely survived at Antietam and had to retreat into Virginia. Confederate optimism had been replaced by worries over a possibly dangerous winter, especially in the West. Union armies stood poised to take the offensive.

U. S. Grant decided that Van Dorn's rout at Corinth eliminated immediate Union concerns for the Department of West Tennessee. Grant received reinforcements from the Midwest that he had been begging for. He reorganized departmental lines, his new realm becoming the Department of the Tennessee, which included portions of Tennessee and Kentucky west of the Tennessee, plus Cairo, Illinois, and as much of Mississippi as he could conquer and hold.

Grant seemed unclear about what to do next. Van Dorn had been beaten, but the Confederate troops in North Mississippi could not be ignored. Grant worried about another attack on Corinth, and asked for more men, especially those close by in such places as Helena. Grant also bluntly wrote Halleck: "You have never suggested to me any plan of operations in this department, and as I do not know anything of those [plans] of commanders to my right or left I have none therefore that is not independent of all other forces than those under my immediate command." Clearly Grant wanted to expand his command authority and territory.[37]

Grant looked at the region and suggested that railroads leading out of Corinth be destroyed to deter Confederate operations. He wanted to concentrate in the Grand Junction, Tennessee, area, and invade Mississippi along the Mississippi Central Railroad, which descended into the heart of Mississippi. This rail line ran south to Canton, where it continued on through Jackson to New Orleans under the name the New Orleans, Jackson and Great Northern. Success would "cause the evacuation of Vicksburg" and permit Union forces "to capture or destroy all the boats in the Yazoo River." Grant would not move until his numbers increased, but he was planning ahead. Yet he reassured Halleck that he would do whatever he was told, "without criticism."

Halleck, Stanton, and Lincoln no doubt deeply appreciated Grant's attitude, which was more submissive than that of many other generals. They congratulated him on his Iuka and Corinth victories, and he must have at last thought the scars of Shiloh might be fading. Yet he continued to act as if he lacked the full confidence of anyone. Things looked better for him, but he had no intention of doing anything risky.

Meanwhile, Grant seemed to be learning the game of military politics quite well. Halleck stepped up efforts to get more men to Grant; Illinois, Grant's adopted state, sent a flood of volunteers. Illinois would have more troops participating in the Vicksburg campaign than any other state, on either side. Halleck gave Grant first priority for all available troops, and also contacted Samuel Curtis about manpower needs in Arkansas.[38]

Halleck's successes portended well for Grant, but something going on behind the scenes did not. John McClernand, an ambitious politician-citizen-soldier from Illinois, used his Washington connections, including political ties with Abraham Lincoln, to put together a Mississippi River expedition with the purpose of clearing all Rebel resistance below Memphis. Lincoln informed Secretary of War Edwin Stanton and Halleck of the plan in early October. McClernand would raise his own force in the Midwest and personally lead it south.

McClernand had been a prominent U.S. congressman from Illinois when war came, and he entered the army as a brigadier general in 1861. By March 1862, he had been promoted to major general, thanks to his participation in Union victories at Forts Henry and Donelson. McClernand demonstrated that, while not a professional soldier by any means, he learned quickly and had good instincts on the battlefield. His biggest problem, which no doubt benefited his political career, proved to be his own big mouth. He had a talent for irritating those around him, especially superior officers. He also had a tendency to write battle reports that lauded the accomplishments of his men at the expense of other commands. He especially agitated U. S. Grant, a mistake that eventually cost him. By August 1862, McClernand's personal relationship with Grant had deteriorated significantly. McClernand constantly complained about everything, especially Grant's refusal to take the offensive until properly reinforced.[39]

Finally, McClernand got leave to return to Illinois and assist Governor Richard Yates in organizing new troops. McClernand used the time for more than that, traveling to Washington to visit with Federal officials, including Lincoln, about an offensive into the Mississippi Valley. Complaints from his home state and its neighbors over the loss of momentum in the Western Theater made Lincoln receptive to any ideas that included action. Before McClernand arrived in Washington, Lincoln's advisers had suggested a "special force" be raised to take Vicksburg. David Dixon Porter would command the naval part of the operation; Porter did not like West Pointers anyway, though he later developed friendships with Grant and Sherman, so at the time he did not mind McClernand's ploy. Halleck seemed to have little to say about the situation; despite his tense relationship with Grant, subsequent events indicated that he preferred Grant to McClernand.

On his return to Illinois, McClernand began gathering a force that included men intended for Grant. If the expedition should be limited to 20,000, McClernand told Stanton, then a fourth of the number should be experienced troops from Grant's Army of the Tennessee (which McClernand had been part of). McClernand identified thirteen regiments that he wanted assigned to his expedition. He assured Stanton that their places could be taken by new troops "without material detriment to the public service."

On October 21, Stanton sanctioned the campaign by issuing a confidential order for McClernand to proceed to Indiana, Illinois, and Iowa to organize troops and "forward them with all dispatch to Memphis, Cairo, or such other points as may hereafter be designated by the general-in-chief, to the end that, when a sufficient force not required by the operations of General Grant's command shall be raised, an expedition may be organized under General McClernand's command against Vicksburg and to clear the Mississippi River and open navigation to New Orleans." Stanton added a caveat that this force would be subject to Henry Halleck's orders and would be "employed according to such exigencies as the service in his judgment may require." The phrasing left the door open for manipulation of the expedition by Grant and Halleck. Halleck, being regular army, did not like McClernand's pedigree. Also, it is very likely that Halleck resented being left out of the plan, which, though born in secrecy, did not remain so very long.[40]

〰️ While McClernand schemed, an unaware U. S. Grant sorted through rumors of Confederate activity and planned his North Mississippi invasion. On November 1, he notified Sherman that the army would move south to Grenada down the Mississippi Central Railroad, and Grant would accompany the troops and communicate with Memphis by courier. If Grant proceeded south of Holly Springs, Sherman should "put a force on the [Mississippi and Tennessee] railroad [a direct route from Memphis to Grenada] to repair it, start toward Grenada, repairing the road as the troops advance." Grant also encouraged Sherman to demonstrate to the southeast to "give the idea of a formidable movement to the front." By November 3, most of Grant's main invading force was marching from various points to Grand Junction, the assembly and embarkation point. Grant kept Halleck informed of the operation, more as a courtesy than out of a sense of duty, since Halleck had ignored Grant's request for advice.[41]

On November 2, Grant informed Halleck that five divisions were approaching Grand Junction, and the campaign would get under way the next day, the initial target being Holly Springs, and then Grenada. Detachments would be stationed at strategic points en route to guard the rails and telegraph lines. Grant believed that John C. Pemberton, now commanding the Confederate army, had begun withdrawing to the south, and he intended to press the Rebels.

As the Union army concentrated, Grant divided it into two wings, with the popular James McPherson commanding two divisions on the right and Charles Hamilton leading three on the left. Altogether, Grant had some 31,000 men spread along Scott Creek and Wolf River from two and a half miles south of Grand Junction to just west of La Grange.

While Grant readied his advance, he asked Halleck to send Sherman sixteen regiments, plus available cavalry and artillery, to solidify protection of Grant's right flank, and provide an adequate garrison at Memphis. Grant also requested seven more regiments for his invasion force. He seemed a bit skittish about plunging into North Mississippi. Perhaps memories of being surprised at Shiloh haunted him, and perhaps that explains in part why he reined in Rosecrans's pursuit of Van Dorn. Whatever the case, he seemed overly cautious.[42]

Numerous, fully loaded troop transports steamed toward Memphis as the Union buildup to take Vicksburg gained momentum. The hurried transfer of troops caused difficulties. An Iowan explained, "The condition of troops on board a transport is miserable in the extreme. Huddled together like hogs in a pen — jostled and jammed from side to side — compelled to eat and sleep on the filthy decks — without exercise during the day, and trampled upon at night while endeavoring to sleep — with rations of half cooked meat and tasteless pilot-bread, and constantly inhaling the impure atmosphere engendered by the dense crowd on board, and arising from mules and horses on the lower deck."[43]

Halleck continued his good job of rounding up more men, so Grant decided to put off the advance into Mississippi for a week to ten days to assimilate new arrivals. If the Confederates should decide to evacuate Holly Springs before that time, Grant told Sherman, the invasion would begin at once. Grant thought he had enough troops to get the job done, but confided to Sherman, "it is more prudent perhaps to avail myself of our whole strength." Halleck further boosted Grant's confidence by promising assistance from Helena if an expedition to Little Rock did not materialize.

While he waited during the continual influx of reinforcements, Grant turned his attention to improving intelligence gathering. He urged Sherman to send all news regarding Rebel activity in the Holly Springs area. Grant's scouts concluded that the Confederates had some 30,000 men there, but in a disorganized condition. If that were the case, Grant boasted to Sherman, he could "move from here with a force sufficient to handle that number without gloves." Yet Grant still hesitated, a strange departure from his later reputation of forging ahead regardless of enemy activities.

In fact Grant insisted on knowing more about Confederate strength, and he ordered a reconnaissance in force, consisting of two infantry divisions plus cavalry to move toward Holly Springs. Grant assured Halleck, "I have not the slightest apprehension of a reverse from present appearances," a remark similar to sentiments expressed before the Confederate attack at Shiloh. Scouting reports indicated that the Rebels might be pulling out of Holly Springs or that enemy generals were merely meeting to discuss options, not to organize a withdrawal. Grant wanted to know the truth.[44]

Union soldiers marching to Holly Springs enjoyed themselves at first, for at last they had something to do. Weeks of inactivity had left many wondering just how long this war would go on. They enjoyed camping in enemy territory, surrounded by an almost surrealistic world of full moons, campfires, and shadows of men and horses all about. Yet they had tired of grand reviews and drilling; now they enjoyed being on the prowl. They "foraged," a military term for stealing, for food and took other items from families, often ignoring orders to give receipts to Union sympathizers. Most did not believe there were any in Mississippi. Many men carried counterfeit Confederate money they used to swindle white and black noncombatants.

As columns moved south, the country became more desolate owing to the swampy terrain around rivers and the devastation wrought by the appetites of two large armies. Clean water became scarce, and men became frustrated. One night a soldier in the 15th Iowa complained loudly of the unclean habits of the 16th Iowa camped upstream. They are, he wrote, "the nearest to *swine* of anything we have seen to be called men." As soldiers marched, the campaign, at times seeming endless, became more a test of endurance than a source of excitement.[45]

Meanwhile, Grant had his own unhappy situation to bear, for he had finally gotten wind of McClernand's gambit. On November 10, he angrily wired Halleck, "Am I to understand that I [should] lay still here while an Expedition is fitted out from Memphis or do you want me to push as far South as possible? Am I to have Sherman move subject to my order or is he & his forces reserved for some special service? Will not more forces be sent here?" From Halleck came a quick response that no doubt pleased Grant and would have infuriated McClernand: "You have command of all troops sent to your department, and have permission to fight the enemy where you please."

Grant needed the encouraging news. As he grappled with moving his army, he had to deal with several additional issues. Constant foraging by growing numbers of soldiers along the Mississippi-Tennessee border area created hardships among local citizens. Drawing from a precedent set by Halleck a few months earlier in Missouri, Grant told his army: "People not actively engaged in rebellion should not be allowed to suffer from hunger in reach of a country abounding with supplies." On the other hand, the present state of affairs had not been caused by the national government, so it "should not be subjected to the burden of furnishing the necessary relief." Rather, those who "by act, encouragement, or sympathy" had brought on and sustained the rebellion ought to pay the price. Grant therefore decided to force Rebel sympathizers to provide relief, the extent to be determined by guidelines employed by departmental commanders.[46]

Soldiers in the ranks, unimpressed by such guidelines, entertained themselves by ransacking and burning homes and other private property. One Illinoisan stated plainly, "not a foot of rail fence remained unburned[;] the whole line of our march was one flame of fire which consumed fences[,] cotton fields[,] meadows[,] hay stacks and everything combustible." Several Iowans blamed "*Stragglers* from our army, worthless, trifling, *cowardly* wretches," for the destruction. A member of the 15th regiment noted "great mountains of smoke" and blasted "scalawags and stragglers who fire buildings and burn property unauthorized"; they "should be punished with death." One soldier personally counted thirty to forty homes and a church in smoldering ruins. Many others supported any measure that might shorten the war, even the emancipation of slaves. Soldiers feared the antiwar movement organized by "copperheads" back home could prove more destructive than enemy bullets. Copperheads, so named by pro-Unionists after poisonous snakes, were antiwar Northerners who supported peace negotiations with the South.[47]

Grant combated the situation as best he could, putting the onus on his lieutenants for controlling his soldiers. He ordered that "every effort be made to arrest . . . thieves and house-burners," and offenders should be tried and punished quickly. Officers who did not cooperate would be fired and confined in military prison. General Hamilton blamed the problem on stragglers and skulkers, but noted, "All good soldiers share in the odium which such conduct brings upon the army."

From this milieu emerged Grant's subsequent Special Field Orders No. 1 in which he deplored the "gross acts of vandalism" by both wings of the army. "Houses have been plunder'd and burned down, fencing destroyed and citizens frightened without an enquiry as to their status in this Rebellion, cattle and hogs shot and Stock driven off" in disobedience to previous orders. Such, the commanding general warned, were punishable by death. Not only had perpetrators gone outside the bounds of articles of war, but they had also made enemies of locals who, if not friends, were at least noncombatants. Grant blamed officers more than their men and warned they would be held accountable. Order and discipline must be maintained, and any "offenders may be brought to trial or [suffer] immediate dismissal from the service and public disgrace." Stragglers captured by Rebels would be dishonorably discharged, lose benefits, and not be exchanged.[48]

True to his word, Grant often dealt harshly with misbehavior as well as other issues that raised his ire. He fined some Illinois troops for depredations against civilians. Two Minnesotans who committed arson wound up in prison in Illinois for the remainder of the war and forfeited all their pay. Officers who stole cotton and arranged to sell it on the black market occasionally got caught and were punished.[49]

Problems with vandalism and trading irregularities never went away; in fact they grew increasingly complex, but Grant refused to be deterred from his main goal — the capture of Vicksburg. Yet his hesitancy persisted, and he continued asking Halleck for more men, and Halleck reminded Samuel Curtis, now commanding the Department of the Missouri, that if there could be no movement on Little Rock, troops in Helena "must cooperate with General Grant against Grenada." Curtis hesitated and suggested instead sending cavalry from Helena into Mississippi to get in the rear of the Confederate army and destroy railroads around Grenada. Confederates could burn bridges, possibly entrapping Union riders, but the risk seemed worth taking.[50]

The idea caught on. Grant liked it, and Curtis informed General Alvin P. Hovey, commanding temporarily at Helena, to prepare "cavalry and howitzers for a movement which will require great energy, courage, and prudence," the object being to block Confederate retreat routes. Infantry and artillery would provide support in case the cavalry had to withdraw. Halleck firmed up the operation by sending additional troops to reinforce Helena during the raid.

As plans for the Grenada expedition evolved, Grant kept a wary eye on Holly Springs. On November 8, he told James McPherson to probe south from La Grange to Lamar, Mississippi, north of Holly Springs. Grant wrote that he would rather fight the enemy at Holly Springs than follow the Rebels south. If the Confederates retreated across the Talla-hatchie River, Grant did not relish the idea of dealing with enemy troops protected by a river barrier.

McPherson found Confederates "drawn up in line of battle" on the south bank of the Coldwater River, guarding a railroad crossing a few miles north of Holly Springs. Scouting reports indicated more enemy forces scattered from Holly Springs south to Abbeville. Just north of Abbeville, the Tallahatchie flowed under a railroad bridge. On November 9, McPherson informed Grant that the army could easily reach Holly Springs. Grant cautioned that he did not want to risk a fight just yet, for he did not know how strong the Rebels were opposite the Cold-water. McPherson obediently pulled back to La Grange, and Grant continued probing Rebel positions, refusing to be rushed. He might have been more aggressive had he known that McClernand, despite Washington's reassurances to Grant, continued to maneuver for control of an expedition to clear the Mississippi.[51]

John Pemberton, Van Dorn's replacement, also had command problems in North Mississippi. Pemberton, a Pennsylvanian by birth who had come south thanks to his Virginia-born wife's influence, did not arrive in Mississippi a confident man. A graduate of West Point and a veteran of the Second Seminole and Mexican wars, Pemberton had chosen to fight for the Confederacy against the wishes of his Pennsylvania family and had begun the war training new recruits in Virginia. Later he moved to the Suffolk area, the home ground of his wife, and would have been happy serving out the war there. Fate and the War Department sent him to Robert E. Lee's department in South Carolina, and after a short stay he assumed command when Lee was recalled to Richmond. Pemberton did not have Lee's Southern background or his diplomatic skills, and he eventually was relieved after a stormy relationship with South Carolina politicians got out of hand. Jefferson Davis, angered by the treatment Pemberton had received in South Carolina, sent the beleaguered general west to assume the vital role of defending Vicksburg and Port Hudson.[52]

Pemberton received orders on September 30 to proceed to Jackson,

Mississippi, and relieve Van Dorn "for the purpose of permitting him to command the forces ordered to advance into West Tennessee." Richmond authorities had decided that Van Dorn could not both assist Bragg and carry on an effective defense of Mississippi and East Louisiana. The latter role fell to Pemberton, and he had to "consider the successful defense of those States as the first and chief object of your command." Pemberton was also meant to cooperate with Richard Taylor in retaking New Orleans if the opportunity arose. Beyond this basic assignment, Pemberton was expected get his army organized, built up, and prepared for field operations.

By the time Pemberton arrived, he found Van Dorn and the army in North Mississippi licking their Corinth wounds. There would be no advance into West Tennessee, and the circumstances left Pemberton in an uncomfortable situation. He could not technically relieve Van Dorn, for Van Dorn, like Lovell, was senior in rank. Adjutant General Samuel Cooper assured Pemberton that his pending promotion to lieutenant general would eliminate the problem.

Van Dorn of course felt betrayed. He complained to Secretary of War George Wythe Randolph that his department had "not considered the difficulties before me." Further, "I have not received instructions of any kind. I shall act for the best, but I am now an isolated body in the field of Mississippi, relieved of command of my department. I hope this will be corrected."[53]

Richmond's correction created a strange command structure. Pemberton soon received his promotion; Van Dorn retained command of all troops in Mississippi but reported to Pemberton, whose realm now included "forces intended to operate in southwestern Tennessee" (Van Dorn's Corinth army), as well as the District of Mississippi and East Louisiana. Van Dorn shook off his disappointment and organized the North Mississippi army into two corps, commanded by Price and Lovell, and also created a cavalry corps led by William H. Jackson. The situation in reality left Van Dorn without an official position, since Pemberton's assignment made Van Dorn's command of the army superfluous. Van Dorn asked Jefferson Davis for a transfer, and Davis's reply indicated that even the president found the command mess in Mississippi confusing. Davis said he assumed Van Dorn would command one division and Price the other and both would report to Pemberton.

Van Dorn's response to Davis on October 22 must have further confused the president. Van Dorn reviewed his recent performance and justifications for his actions, actions that had led John Bowen to file charges, ultimately dismissed, against Van Dorn, and then added: "General Lovell has now the entire confidence of the troops and gained reputation in the late battle. If I remain, I displace him and he must take a subordinate position in the army lately commanded by him — a mortifying position to which it is not customary to subject a superior officer. I would consider it less injurious to be transferred to another field, wherever you may choose. I have no choice."[54]

Van Dorn told Davis that he abhorred "false reports put in circulation about me" and asked permission to come to Richmond to "justify my actions to you." "If I do not satisfy you that I have done my duty," he concluded, "I shall willingly coincide with you that I am not competent to command." In his determination to restore his reputation, Van Dorn had, intentionally or not, lied about Lovell's role in the Corinth campaign, for Lovell had done nothing of note. Perhaps Van Dorn glossed the truth to draw more sympathy to his situation. Whatever his intent, Van Dorn did not go to Richmond and settled for functioning as overall field commander. Whether Pemberton and Van Dorn worked out such an arrangement or simply made the best of the situation is unclear, but certainly it suited Pemberton, who much preferred an office in Jackson and paperwork to field duties.

Van Dorn found working with an absentee Pemberton to be frustrating. On October 16, he wrote from Holly Springs: "It is advisable that you should come here as soon as possible. Events are gathering near. You cannot be here too soon to prepare for action under whatever policy you may see fit to adopt. If you cannot come at once will you inform me if you desire that I should resist the occupation and fortifying of La Grange or Grand Junction? It is probable this will be done by the enemy in a few days, unless I resist it." Enemy reinforcements were arriving almost daily — so some of Theophilus Holmes's Arkansas troops should be sent to help, "if you would save Mississippi."[55]

On October 18, Van Dorn hopefully informed Davis that Pemberton would "assume command in person of his army in a few days." Since Price and Lovell commanded the two corps, would Davis "do me the kindness to have me ordered to some other field? Anywhere you may be pleased to direct." Davis again responded as if no problem existed, assuring Van Dorn that Pemberton's appointment had no impact on Van Dorn's and Price's status. The president continued, "The wants of Mississippi and your own fame equally render me unwilling to withdraw you from your present sphere of duty at this time."

Content to let Van Dorn take care of things in North Mississippi, Pemberton reviewed his overall command and buried himself in organizational details. Secretary Randolph had specifically mentioned strengthening Port Hudson, and Pemberton shared that concern, despite enemy threats to the north. On October 22, he directed Van Dorn to send troops to Port Hudson, a strange dispersal of manpower given the more immediate threat in North Mississippi. Pemberton's assessment of priorities often seemed illogical.

Confederate strategic thinking in the Vicksburg theater during these fall months of 1862 seemed to be based on the assumption that the top Union priority was William Rosecrans's efforts to drive Bragg out of Tennessee. Pemberton believed it, but Van Dorn did not think so, though his scouts brought in vague, often contradictory, accounts of Grant's actions. Van Dorn thought the enemy ready to advance into Mississippi, and he opposed sending troops elsewhere until the picture cleared. Van Dorn's better understanding of the situation demonstrated how being absent from the field handicapped Pemberton's perceptions. On October 22, Van Dorn bluntly told Pemberton that Bragg's late retreat from Kentucky into Tennessee might free up reinforcements for Grant. Evidence to that effect abounded: "If we are not strengthened here, we shall lose this State." Indeed, Van Dorn thought Pemberton should ask Bragg for help.

Given manpower shortages in the Western Theater, Pemberton did not think he could get additional troops. Some men were volunteering to avoid conscription, and the return of exchanged prisoners offered promise, but not salvation. He told Van Dorn, "If the enemy increases in strength and there is evidence of his intention to advance you will take position behind the Tallahatchie." Pemberton hoped the river barrier would buy time for the government to find reinforcements. As a precaution, Van Dorn sent detachments to check "bridges, fords, and forest, and to see that the forces there guard them properly." He assured Pemberton that if Grant moved further south, the army would retreat beyond the Tallahatchie.[56]

Meanwhile, Confederates along the North Mississippi front rested, foraged, drilled, and waited for campaigning to begin. On November 3, the whole army, some 30,000, passed in review, an event attended by many area civilians anxious not only to see troops but also to ogle generals. Texas cavalry added to the excitement by romping about on horses that had finally arrived from their home state. All in all, thought a Louisiana Confederate, the day produced "a brilliant and imposing spectacle." "The imposing array of men, with their guns glittering in the cold November sunlight, the assembly of fair ladies, the galaxy of dashing and distinguished officers, formed a brilliant and imposing spectacle. It was a combination of the beauty and chivalry of the country."[57]

With the North Mississippi front in a lull for the moment, Pemberton focused his attention on Vicksburg. He ordered inspections of the bluff defenses north of the city on the Yazoo. He brought in male slaves from Jackson to build fortifications and Yazoo River obstructions. He studied staff recommendations regarding batteries and placement of troops. He urged the War Department to send him all conscripts from Louisiana and Mississippi, and asked for help from General Holmes. Pemberton also tried to gain control of partisan units by enrolling them in the regular army.

Richmond allowed Pemberton to detain seven unarmed regiments (which would be supplied with arms) ordered from Holmes to Lee in Virginia. It is worth noting that when Lee needed troops, they were usually sent, whereas when Pemberton needed help from Holmes, the War Department requested reinforcements, but deferred the matter to Holmes. This was one of the few times that Pemberton got any help from Holmes, and it did not come directly or intentionally.[58]

Meanwhile, Pemberton worked to appease disgruntled Missourians, including General Price, and Arkansans, by asking the War Department to send these troops, at their request, to the Trans-Mississippi. Holmes would complete the exchange by providing replacements for Mississippi. But after seeing these impressive soldiers pass in review on November 3, Pemberton, "much pleased with them," changed his mind and kept the troops, though Price would eventually leave. This decision proved to be his most astute during the entire Vicksburg campaign.

Pemberton maintained an optimistic attitude during these early weeks of command and showed a propensity to embrace as gospel any good news, however suspect. He smiled at reports of Federal troops leaving Corinth to reinforce Buell. Van Dorn shot down the rumor; in fact Federals were moving in force into Mississippi. "I move to-morrow across Tallahatchie, or one corps will get across no doubt," Van Dorn advised, and he urged Pemberton to ask Bragg for help. In a separate message, Van Dorn confirmed, "The enemy are advancing. Have driven in my pickets at Grand Junction and La Grange." Van Dorn ordered a retreat and then welcomed reports that the enemy seemed to be holding back.[59]

Van Dorn continued to complain about Pemberton's absence and urged the commanding general to come to the front. Pemberton responded: "Unless it is positively certain that the enemy is advancing on you in full force do not change your position yet. I doubt his intention to do so. I want you to keep all your available cavalry threatening him. I have a train ready if you think it advisable for me to go up."

Pemberton, meanwhile, let Bragg know via Knoxville that an invasion of Mississippi seemed imminent. Bragg replied that his army in Tennessee was marching and might "create a diversion in your favor." Two days later, noting Grant's reluctance, Pemberton told Bragg that "the enemy is in front of Wolf River; not advancing. If I knew your plans I might perhaps assist them." Pemberton had by now decided to relieve the whiny Van Dorn, but, still preferring desk command, changed his mind.[60]

On November 7, Bragg informed Pemberton that cavalry had been sent from North Alabama to Corinth to ease pressure on Van Dorn's front. Meanwhile, Bragg resumed his diversionary offensive in Middle Tennessee and considered striking behind Grant with his whole army, but the Tennessee River stood in the way. Bragg warned Pemberton to pull back behind the Tallahatchie, but not to retreat so far as to expose the arsenal in Columbus, Mississippi, which contained "machinery and stores we cannot replace; so that its loss would be great and irreparable."

Bragg's words led Pemberton to report on November 9 the situation in North Mississippi to Adjutant General Samuel Cooper. The unsettled Confederate general concluded, without giving any credit to Bragg, "I deemed it advisable to withdraw from the indefensible position at Holly Springs and take a strong one behind Tallahatchie, and am fortifying."

The Confederates moved quickly, and on November 10 Van Dorn deployed skirmishers and guards at strategic points south of the Tallahatchie. He cautioned officers to prevent straggling and "destruction of private property in the vicinity of their camps." Obviously civilians had to worry about depredations from both armies. While the army dug in, disturbing news arrived: on November 11, Federal troops from Helena had begun crossing the river into Mississippi. If true, Pemberton's left flank and rear would be threatened.[61]

Confederates now sensed they would be giving up more ground. One soldier detested the retreat, made "to the tune of jostling wagons, braying mules, neighing horses, cursing drivers and the dull heavy tread of marching infantry." Men gathered around campfires and pondered their fate as the cold night air penetrated the blankets wrapped around their shoulders. Others did not mind pulling back in one sense; they could leave to the Yankees certain unpatriotic citizens and storekeepers, who shamelessly overcharged Confederates for everything. Knowing that such people would receive their just due from the enemy eased the misery of bad weather and crawling varmints. The latter could be a challenge, one soldier finding "a huge, many-footed *louse* biting and clawing as though he intended to make a hole through my body; Goodness but he was a whale of a fellow, except the tail and gills and he had claws and bristles to make up for everything of the pisc[a]tory character."

Otherwise, the men spent time reflecting, especially on why Northerners refused to let them alone. Rather than be dictated to, they preferred seeing "every stage of life in these fair lands of our beautiful and glorious Sunny South" perish. They had no desire to go back into a union "from which our people have withdrawn their destinies." Such sentiments were standard fare this early in the war, but no one knew how long such rhetoric could sustain the Southern cause.[62]

~~~ While the Confederates thus watched, waited, and tried to anticipate enemy threats, U. S. Grant perused reports. In a long, rambling letter to Sherman, Grant reviewed what he knew of Rebel strength and reinforcements sent by Halleck. Grant thought of sending Sherman against the enemy's left, or perhaps directing him toward Moscow, Tennessee. Whatever they did, they should "all start together, especially if there should be a movement from Helena as desired."

Grant noted, "We will of course supply ourselves from the country with everything it affords necessary for the army, giving receipts for the same to be settled at the close of hostilities." This was similar to a misleading comment that Grant would make in his memoirs about living off the country later in the campaign. Wagons kept his army supplied now and later, for some 600 wagons, bringing supplies and ordnance, would follow the army into Mississippi. Grant intended to solidify his logistical situation by keeping railroads in his rear open to the north. Living off the land and nothing else never entered his mind.[63]

As December dawned, the North Mississippi front resembled two glaciers, one slowly moving back and the other inching forward. Generals on both sides seemed reluctant to take action that might bring the campaign to a head. The second major phase of the Vicksburg campaign had begun, born of strategic decisions affected by concerns regarding Vicksburg and Port Hudson and Braxton Bragg's campaign in Tennessee and Kentucky. Hard war had become more prevalent, and soldiers too had become more hardened to the war. They needed to be toughened, for the road ahead for both armies would be long. While the Vicksburg campaign was being redefined, the city itself remained safe, but eyes on both sides had now refocused on the river city. Grant intended to accomplish what the navy could not, but he would be frustrated; and the key figure in repelling his initial effort turned out to be an unlikely one — Earl Van Dorn.

U. S. Grant (Author's Collection)

David Farragut (Library of Congress)

David Dixon Porter
(Private Collection of Robert Younger)

Henry Halleck (Library of Congress)

William T. Sherman (National Archives)

James B. McPherson (National Archives)

John A. McClernand (National Archives)

E. O. C. Ord
(Ezra J. Warner, Generals in Blue, *1964)*

William S. Rosecrans (Library of Congress)

Benjamin Grierson (Library of Congress)

Frederick Steele (Library of Congress)

Frank Blair (National Archives)

John C. Pemberton (Library of Congress)

Martin L. Smith (Library of Congress)

*Isaac Brown
(Naval Historical Foundation)*

Joseph E. Johnston
(Vicksburg National Military Park)

Earl Van Dorn (Henry W. Elson, Elson's New History: The Civil War through the Camera, *1912)*

Sterling Price (Library of Congress)

Stephen D. Lee (Mississippi State University Libraries, Special Collections Department, University Archives)

John S. Bowen
(Confederate Veteran, *September 1899*)

William W. Loring
(Vicksburg National Military Park)

Carter Stevenson (Library of Congress)

John Gregg
(Private Collection of Lawrence T. Jones)

4

≋ Race to Vicksburg

As winter winds and rain swept across North Mississippi in November 1862, U. S. Grant knew the deeper he penetrated south, the longer and more vulnerable his supply line became. He had to deal with geographic factors, including rivers, swamps, and hills that, impacted by winter weather, made mobility difficult. Yet with the flank movement from Helena moving forward, he felt confident. Ultimately the pressure of John McClernand's attempt to take over the river campaign led Grant to divide his forces, with William T. Sherman taking a detachment downriver. Grant in effect changed a slow, methodical advance into North Mississippi into a race for Vicksburg, a race between himself and McClernand. He envisioned a two-pronged offensive designed to force outnumbered Confederates to weaken either their front in North Mississippi, or their defenses at Vicksburg. Whichever they chose would bring Union victory he believed. In retrospect the advance into Mississippi was a huge gamble, stretching commonsense logistical considerations to the limit.

The North Mississippi campaign also increased the intensity of the civilian-soldier-guerrilla milieu. The war weighed heavily on civilians who dared remain home rather than taking flight as refugees. Conflicts between Union soldiers and civilians, and the presence of the guerrilla catalyst, produced bitterness and tragedies, the memories of which lingered long after the war ended. Grant and Sherman continually struggled with the problem, but in the end it played out beyond their reach as Federals in the ranks and civilians grappled with the collision of cultures.

On November 14, Grant began implementing his invasion plan and told Sherman to bring two divisions at least and three if possible to Holly Springs, and to go on to Grenada if it were feasible. With the Rebels beyond the south bank of the Tallahatchie, Grant sensed a chance to overwhelm Pemberton's retreating army. As soon as Sherman marched, Grant would move his entire force south from La Grange. The wings would unite at Holly Springs or further south.

Sherman, excited by prospects of battle, heartily endorsed the expedition from Helena, which he believed would weaken Pemberton's left, facilitating Sherman's advance. He could think of "nothing better," he told Frederick Steele, who now commanded at Helena. On November 26, Sherman sent his troops marching southeast from Memphis. Grant got the rest of the army under way, spreading his front across the Mississippi Central to approach the Tallahatchie from Holly Springs. Once the two columns linked, Sherman would command the right wing, McPherson the center, and Hamilton the left. Grant informed Halleck that the march had begun; Halleck responded with caution, "Do not go too far."[1]

Grant, accompanied by his wife Julia, arrived in Holly Springs and established quarters in local mansions. Pleased that no major resistance had been encountered, he checked division alignment, communications links, and the supply situation. In a short time, thousands of rations and other large amounts of stores arrived by rail and were piled up around the Holly Springs depot. Grant depended on his staff, especially his friend from prewar days, John Rawlins, to see to myriad details, but often they did slipshod work. Grant would find as the campaign progressed that Rawlins was about the only one he could depend upon; hence, it was no surprise that Rawlins usually could be found close to Grant.[2]

Union soldiers had troubles of their own. Excited at first about active campaigning, they now complained of the march south as "hard," especially "for new men." Rain-soaked roads often became impassable, forcing troops to take to fields to keep the columns moving. "It seemed to me," wrote one Illinoisan, "that it rained all of the time, the roads were bad, very muddy." "The winter was spent marching and counter marching," he recalled, "guarding the railroads, keeping watch. . . . Several times we were in line of battle but did not fight. We were very short of food, we lived on what we could find in the country." Another Federal recalled the depressing countryside: "It is grievous to see the picture of desolation the country presents. Sometimes we march for miles and not a piece of fence left, houses pulled down or burnt, bridges destroyed; in fact the country is ruined for years to come."[3]

Personal contacts with Confederates produced a variety of reactions. An Illinoisan mocked his conversations with Rebels: "We'ns don't go north to fight you'ns, why do you'ns come down here to fight we'ns, if you'ns would let we'ns alone, we'ns would let you'ns alone." Accents and pronunciations may have been amusing and peculiar, but the words well summed up Rebel feelings. Many Confederates may have been "ignorant and unlearned," but they were gaining a better understanding of where the war was leading. A Mississippian feared for his state: "This war will beggar us all. Our own army carries destruction almost as surely to some kinds of property as that of the enemy."[4]

〰️ As the gap narrowed between the Union front and Confederate works along the south bank of the Tallahatchie, Grant and his generals prepared for action. On November 29, Sherman ordered all noncombatants to leave the army and return to Memphis. Grant cautioned his commanders not to bring on any engagement or "carry any entrenchments until we are prepared." He wanted "a heavy reconnaissance to the southeast and the enemy's rear if practicable." Such a move, in conjunction with the Helena operation, would further divert the attention of Confederate commanders, forcing them to deal with threats on both flanks and the front.

The plan began working when the Helena expedition forced Rebel commanders to look southwest. Brigadier General Alvin P. Hovey commanded some 7,000 men, and Brigadier General Cadwallader C. Washburn commanded a cavalry detachment. Washburn had orders to make "a dash upon the railroad near Grenada . . . , creating a diversion in favor of Grant's movement." Brushing aside Confederate pickets, the column traveled to Charleston, crossed the Tallahatchie, and Washburn's cavalry pushed ahead, damaging railroad branches above Grenada.[5]

Washburn, whose connections, via his politician brother Elihu, with Lincoln and Grant were his major attributes, led his cavalry toward Grenada and attacked railroad bridges on the Yalobusha. He arrived too late to attack a morning train to Memphis. The horsemen cut telegraph wires and destroyed bridges along the Mississippi and Tennessee, but they had to abandon plans to destroy Mississippi Central track because of "the character of the country to be passed over." Washburn abandoned plans to ride all the way to Grenada for fear of being trapped. On Monday morning, December 1, Washburn's riders reached Mitchell's Crossroads and rejoined the rest of Hovey's force, which had been skirmishing with Rebel cavalry. Washburn wanted to move to Coffeeville the next day, but he decided first to check reports of Rebels at Panola and Belmont, where none were found.

Next day, the concentrated Union force defeated Confederates at Oakland in a brief but bloody fight. Though only fifteen miles from

Coffeeville, Washburn decided to bivouac for the night in Oakland, and there he heard from Steele via Hovey that the mission had been accomplished, and the column should return to Helena. The withdrawal came in a hard rain, which exacerbated the difficulties of getting heavy artillery safely away over land that was "an alluvial formation filled with ponds, sloughs, and bayou, and subject to annual overflow, and the roads are impassable as soon as . . . rains begin."[6]

Once word passed among Confederates that the Union threat had subsided, Earl Van Dorn ordered Colonel John Griffith's Texas cavalry to pursue. On November 30, the Rebels reached Oakland and located and skirmished with Washburn's riders. Yankee artillery shelled Griffith's men with "grape and canister at a fearful rate." Griffith's horsemen charged and then retreated to avoid being flanked. The Federals rode on, and the brisk fight and the foul weather made Griffith glad to see them go.[7]

The Helena gambit had mixed results. Confederates had been unnerved, but not enough to take their eyes off Grant. Rugged terrain, unfamiliarity with the Grenada area, and bad weather all hampered Washburn's operation and limited his success. Work details quickly rebuilt bridges; rail traffic behind Confederate lines continued unabated; and Griffith's aggression kept the Federals from further damaging the vital Mississippi Central. Yet the campaign had a major impact on Pemberton's thinking, for he realized how vulnerable his left and rear had become, and he ordered his troops to march south. There had not been a significant battle; and though the operation had caused the Rebels to retreat, U. S. Grant continued to be frustrated by his inability to deliver a telling blow.[8]

In the meantime, Grant worried about his rear, though not because of a Confederate threat. John McClernand had continued recruiting troops and sending them downriver for his Vicksburg expedition. On December 1, he wired Secretary of War Stanton: "I trust it will meet with your views to order me forward to Memphis, or such other rendezvous as you may think preferable, in order that I may enter upon the more advanced work of organizing, drilling, and disciplining my command, preparatory to an early and successful movement, having for its object the important end of liberating the navigation of the Mississippi River." With a seasoned politician's flair, he continued, "Having worked early, assiduously, and zealously in this great enterprise, having it at heart, and the Governors and people of the northwest having pronounced favorably upon it and, so far as I can hear, upon me as the executor of it, I trust that the honorable Secretary of War will continue to encourage me by his sympathy and support."

Though earlier reassured by Washington that McClernand's machinations would not interfere with his operations, Grant wanted to solve the Vicksburg problem before McClernand arrived. To speed things up, he considered sending Sherman back to Memphis to organize an amphibious operation against Vicksburg. Grant later recalled, "I feared that delay might bring McClernand, who was his [Sherman's] senior and who had authority from the President and Secretary of War to exercise that particular command, — and independently. I doubted McClernand's fitness; and I had good reason to believe that in forestalling him I was by no means giving offence to those whose authority to command was above both him and me." It is unclear how much Grant trusted Halleck, though the two had a rocky past. Equally unclear is the role, if any, Halleck played in McClernand's attempt to take the river campaign away from Grant, although it is evident that Halleck did not speak out against McClernand's plans. Halleck understood politics, too; if Lincoln and Stanton signed off on something, Halleck would not stand in the way.[9]

The course of the campaign forced Grant's decision. In early December he had not made up his mind about sending Sherman downriver. When he heard the Rebels had abandoned the Tallahatchie line, Grant urged his commanders to go to Abbeville, forcing Pemberton to give battle or continue retreating. The Confederates kept pulling back, and on December 2 Grant notified Sherman that Union forces had occupied Abbeville, and the cavalry advance had pushed to Oxford. By the third, most of Pemberton's army had moved south of Oxford, and Grant paused. He realized he had to make up his mind about sending Sherman downriver, but he hesitated on account of reports of Rebels coming from Arkansas into central Mississippi. If true, Sherman could run into trouble.[10]

Meanwhile, Pemberton's army, its morale rapidly deteriorating, saw many sad faces among Oxford residents as they retreated to Grenada. A Louisiana soldier recalled "long columns of troops, tired, wet and soiled," pouring through the streets, "accompanied by carriages, buggies, and even carts, filled with terror-stricken, delicate ladies—whole families carrying with them their household goods and Negroes. The scene was one of indescribable confusion and excitement—one of those gloomy pictures of war so distressing in all its circumstances." On they marched in the rain, finally arriving at Grenada and camping along the south bank of the Yalobusha.[11]

Grant's soldiers followed through the bleak landscape, foraging for animal grain, wondering now why they had so carelessly burned civilian grain stores. As they settled in to wait on Grant's decision, men built shelters from the cold, and listened, sometimes with annoyance, at the "everlasting tum-tum of the Nigger's banjo." Others enjoyed the "nigger-dance. It would make you laugh yourself blind almost if you could see a lot of 'ebonies' congregated by moonlight or candlelight, one fiddling, another 'patting' . . . and four or five dancing in their native style." Destruction of houses, cotton gins, and other private property continued, despite warnings. The vandalism troubled some soldiers because of the poverty and the teary-eyed women they saw, and they were glad their families back home did not have to cope with war.[12]

Sherman's trip to rendezvous with Grant had been trying. He complained, "The roads are cut up terribly. This country is simply impracticable in rainy weather." Sherman's words underscored Grant's fears that weather, or Rebels, or both could destroy supply lines. Grant asked Halleck on December 5, "How far south would you like me to go?" Troops could cut the Mobile and Ohio Railroad at Tupelo, but on the other hand it would be better to hold Pemberton south of Grenada and send forces from Memphis and Helena to attack Vicksburg. Grant knew that "with my present force it would not be safe to go beyond Grenada and attempt to hold present lines of communication." The Helena expedition had forced Pemberton to retreat; those troops could reinforce Sherman's detachment for a river expedition that should "secure Vicksburg and the State of Mississippi."[13]

Halleck generally agreed, and he believed that by December 20 there would be enough troops for an amphibious strike at Vicksburg, continual pressure against Pemberton, and holding the Memphis-Corinth line. Halleck, as he did with other generals, gave Grant the latitude to change plans depending on circumstances. If Grenada should fall, the campaign against Vicksburg should be reevaluated. Grant was free to "move your troops as you may deem best," and retain any of Curtis's troops that remained in his department. Halleck had been mad because he had not authorized the Helena expedition, but the plan had worked. Still, Halleck wanted Grant and Curtis to stay focused on Vicksburg, rather than use men for tactical forays and limited results.[14]

Halleck had trouble controlling operations in the Washington political atmosphere. He pointedly told Curtis, "The movements on the Western rivers are frequently determined on by the joint action of the War and Navy Departments, and it sometimes happens that I can give no answer to the proposed plans of our generals in the West." Regarding the expedition downriver, Halleck advised, "I have been informed that the President has selected a special commander, and that instructions have been or will be given to him by the War Department. If so they have not been communicated to me, and until I receive them I shall consider the officer of the highest rank as the commander, whoever he may be. Probably the whole matter will be decided on in a few days, but how I do not know."[15]

While Sherman waited for word on the amphibious operation, he addressed an old problem, lashing out at the destruction wrought by his army. Belying his later reputation, Sherman gave notice that "indiscriminate and extensive plundering by our men calls for a summary and speedy change." He claimed that the army's mission "is to maintain, not to violate, all laws, human and divine." Plundering damaged the Union cause and the honor of the nation. Sherman reissued warnings to regimental commanders that they would be responsible for violations, and he ordered that Articles of War be read to each regiment once a month as a reminder of proper and orderly behavior.[16]

Despite Sherman's outburst, troops writing home indicated little discipline regarding foraging and plundering. An Iowan told his parents, "We pressed mules and horses into service to draw our knapsacks, provisions and fresh meat. We burned a good many rail fences, buildings and corn ports, sugar, molasses and cotton we could not use. We showed no mercy to the chickens, turkeys, geese, hogs, ducks, and every thing we could eat. I got a nice Negro. I made him carry my knapsack. That night he left me." Guilty veterans often blamed damages on new soldiers. Some men were "arrested & tied by the thumbs for unlawful killing," though how much such punishment deterred vandalism is uncertain. Many harbored such hatred for Rebels that they willingly ran the risk of consequences. One Federal wrote of exchanged Confederate prisoners: "They were the most horrible looking mortals that I ever saw. I Just felt as though I could Have torn the very hart out of them." Yet Grant's and Sherman's warnings did have a sobering effect on many men in the ranks.[17]

Mississippi citizens who felt the brunt of Union wrath often got the same treatment from Southern guerrillas who committed depredations, and regular Confederate soldiers who burned cotton according to government policy, leaving civilians unsure of whom to trust and blame. Perhaps observing Rebel soldiers vandalize their own people encouraged Union soldiers to do likewise. A disgusted resident spoke for many when he noted, "Between the two forces I have suffered heavily." No matter which cause they supported, people felt obliged to move their valuables and goods out of harm's way.[18]

Federals saw reasons for the growing civilian anger as the army moved farther south, for as they marched, they passed over territory already stripped by Pemberton's soldiers. Grant's men found mostly women representing the white population, males having gone to war or into hiding. Older slave men, as well as female slaves and their children, were more common sights. At Holly Springs, which soldiers uniformly thought a beautiful town, citizens scowled at the invaders, and some ladies warned that Price would make them pay.[19]

Attitudes of Federal soldiers also hardened, as they saw more of slavery. Most cared little for blacks, for they had clearly come south to restore the Union, not end slavery. Many saw little difference between abolitionists and secessionists, yet their experiences with slaves and masters sometimes proved enlightening. Wrote one Iowan, "I had an opportunity of seeing some of the beauties of the Peculiar Institution, which made an impression on my mind which can never be erased. one of which I will relate. On the first night of our return march [to Helena from a raid into Mississippi] we encamped on the farm of one of the Mississippi chivalry. Soon after we got fires built a little darkey came along, and we questioned him in regard to his master & the Slaves, and he told us that his master the day before had sent about thirty into the cane brakes to keep us from stealing them." A detachment went out to hunt them and "returned with 27 of the most wretched looking creatures I ever beheld, all women and children, half starved, filthy looking objects." Few had sufficient clothing to withstand the winter elements; for one soldier, the scene produced "a thirst in my heart for vengeance when I looked upon the master." Disgust became greater when the men learned that the owner had chained his slaves and drove them into the swamp. The Iowans freed them and encouraged others to flee plantations, leaving many owners "in almost a helpless condition."

The mix of civilian disgust at the Yankee invaders and Union soldiers' revulsion at slavery, plus the capture of Confederate soldiers, created intense friction as Grant's army moved into Lafayette County and neared the town of Oxford, another place that the Northerners thought quite beautiful, especially the grounds of the University of Mississippi. High regard for the looks of the place did not translate into civil relations with local residents. Many civilians harbored long-term bitterness rooted in encounters with Grant's army.[20]

One woman said of Union soldiers: "I never heard such profanity in all my life & so *impudent*, they would walk around the house & look up at the windows & say, 'I wonder how many *dam Secesh* gals they got up there.' " This woman, quite young at the time, stood up to a few soldiers and earned their respect, and her family escaped physical harm. Others in the area encountered rougher treatment, especially from members of the 7th Kansas Cavalry, who tore earrings off women's ears, ripped off rings and broaches, and pulled hair. The Kansans came to be hated by Confederate civilians and soldiers, as well as by many fellow Union soldiers.

A young girl named Ella recalled her mother returning home after the Union army had passed by and finding "everything in a state of confusion. Bonfires had been made of books, most of the family china had been trampled under foot, carriage and horses taken, provisions confiscated." Her little brother later yelled at the Federals in Oxford, "Old Yankee dogs!" Fortunately, the soldiers laughed the comment off, knowing full well the child was only repeating what he had heard adults say.

Oxford residents coped with the situation as best they could. They hid valuables in attics, cisterns, and underground, though Union soldiers found some items, digging up ground that looked as if things had been recently buried. With the help of slave labor that could still be controlled, women and older men and children tried to protect winter crops by splitting rails and putting up fences, though soldiers seemed to specialize in taking rails for firewood and raiding gardens. Salt became so scarce that people boiled dirt taken from smoke house floors in order to extract what they could. Portions of Oxford and environs quickly became a scene of devastation, leaving residents wondering if their beloved town would ever again have its charm and beauty.

Interaction between soldier and civilian produced memorable moments. One lady forced to play and sing Southern songs hoped soldiers would not find her silverware hidden in the piano. Young white children sometimes went to enemy camps and sang defiant anti-Yankee songs. One of the favorite songs of young girls, sung to agitate Yankee soldiers, but actually having the opposite effect, was to the tune of the "Bonnie Blue Flag":

> Oh, Yes, I am a southern girl
>   and glory in the name,
> And count it of far greater worth
>   than glitt'ring gems or fame.
> We envy not the northern girl
>   her robes of beauty rare.

Though diamonds grace her snowy neck,
   and pearls bedeck her hair.
CHORUS
Hurrah! Hurrah! For the sunny south so dear!
Three cheers for the homespun dress
   The southern ladies wear.

Children liked another song that rang of defiance:

Jeff Davis was our President
and Lincoln was a fool;
Jeff Davis rode a big, black horse
and Lincoln rode a mule![21]

Union soldiers smirked or smiled, but they learned quickly that Confederate women, who lived with fear fed by vulnerability, were far more bitter enemies than most Rebel soldiers. One man on guard duty in Oxford watched as "secesh cows" broke a small flagpole and threw the U.S. flag to the ground. A nearby officer made one of the women put it back up. The seething hatred between civilian and Federal soldier came close to boiling over on more than one occasion. A lady once rushed out into the yard of her mansion and waved wildly at the 8th Wisconsin's mascot, a bald eagle named "Old Abe," shouting, "Oh! See that *Yankee Buzzard!*" Foul responses from men in the 8th sent her scurrying back into her home.

A local physician named Bowles arranged for his family, his daughter and his niece, to escape via the Tallahatchie River bottom, astride a lame horse guided by a slave named Frank. His home was torched, but Sherman came along and ordered the blaze extinguished and established his headquarters there. Sherman ordered Mrs. Bowles and her small children to occupy a downstairs room with the door barricaded for their own privacy and safety. A black servant smuggled food to them via a hole in the floor.

Sometimes bored Union troops got creative at the expense of their comrades. One evening, a few dressed in clothing confiscated from Confederates surrounded a home where their officers were attending a local reception. They shouted the dreaded cry, "Guerrillas!" and rushed in, captured the officers, forced them to beg for their lives, and then issued paroles. Next day, the officers had wonderful stories to tell, highlighting their heroism, not mentioning paroles. On another occasion, some men of the 8th Wisconsin broke into a town drugstore, looking for alcoholic beverages. In the darkness they found a jar, smelled an aroma somewhat like alcohol, and imbibed. Later they opened the shutters, the light revealing that the jar contained a deformed black child's body, "preserved for embryological purposes," and the soldiers had drunk the preservation liquid, which was mostly alcohol.[22]

While his men improvised, imbibed, and endured, Grant decided to send Sherman down the Mississippi. Sherman would return his troops to Memphis and add reinforcements from Helena. Grant would keep Pemberton busy; and if Pemberton were to retreat, Grant would follow and link with Sherman in Vicksburg. Sherman later claimed that at this point he did not know of McClernand's activities; this is impossible to believe, given the effectiveness of military rumor mills and Sherman's close relationship with Grant. Likely Sherman wanted to give the impression that campaign discussions had been based on sounder reasoning than merely beating McClernand in a race to Vicksburg.

Grant insisted in his memoirs that he knew "an expedition down the Mississippi was inevitable," either under his control or McClernand's, and he wanted "to have a competent commander in charge." So, on December 8, he issued orders to Sherman and advised cooperation with David Porter's fleet to take Vicksburg. Sherman should cut the railroad opposite Vicksburg to make it hard for Confederates to send reinforcements from North Louisiana. Grant informed Halleck that Sherman was going downriver with a force of some 40,000. His own movements, Grant advised Halleck, would depend "on those of the enemy." Grant informed the commander at Helena, Frederick Steele, that he had "just received authority to retain all General Curtis' forces now within my department until further orders."[23]

Excited by his prospects, Sherman wired Porter in Cairo, Illinois, on December 8: "Time now is the great object. We must not give time for new combinations. I know you will promptly cooperate. It will not be necessary to engage their Vicksburg batteries until I have broken all their inland communication. Then Vicksburg must be attacked by land and water. In this I will defer much to you. My Purpose is to cut the [rail]road to Monroe, La., to Jackson, Miss., and then appear up the Yazoo, threatening the Mississippi Central road [Southern Railroad of Mississippi] where it crosses the Big Black." The expedition had to get under way before winter rains ruined roads in North Mississippi and forced Grant to halt. On the ninth, Sherman notified Grant that he was leaving for Memphis to get the expedition going.

Manpower requirements and logistical support for Sherman's mission fell into place. Steele advised Sherman with regard to landing down at the lower end of Milliken's Bend and cautioned about Rebel defenses on the Yazoo bluffs. Porter had six ironclads, four light wooden boats, and two rams available for the operation. Sherman could take 7,000 men and two batteries of the 16,700 troops and five batteries currently at Helena. If he decided he needed more, Willis Gorman, in command of Eastern Arkansas and headquartered at Helena, promised to cooperate.

Sherman contacted Grant at Oxford and reported that Morgan L. Smith's and George Morgan's divisions numbered about 20,000, or 10,000 fewer men than Grant thought. Thus, Sherman explained, he would need "as large an accession from Helena as possible." After all, he argued, "a feeble demonstration on Vicksburg would do harm rather than good."

Putting together a detached force while maintaining the North Mississippi front posed a challenge for Grant. Steele whined about giving up Helena troops, but Grant was confident that Sherman could handle the problem. Gorman, meanwhile, advised that the 10,000 troops Sherman had initially requested would be ready, meaning that Sherman would have 30,000 troops rather than the 40,000 originally projected, still a sizable force. Grant, still concerned about the vulnerability of his supply line in North Mississippi and assuming Sherman's success, asked Sherman to send small boats from Vicksburg up the Yazoo to bring supplies to the North Mississippi army. In the meantime, transports from Cairo were herded downriver to take Sherman's men to Vicksburg.[24]

While waiting for Sherman to get under way, Grant, hoping to reduce discipline problems, tightened restrictions on his troops, echoing Sherman's earlier order: "Women and children are hereafter to be excluded from the army in the field." All should be sent to Holly Springs or points farther north. He permitted some exceptions, such as "authorized laundresses, hospital nurses, or officers' servants, of which wing and division commanders are empowered to judge of the expediency of retaining."

Then came disturbing news from Nashville that Confederate cavalry, led by the intrepid Tennessean Nathan Bedford Forrest, had left Bragg's army and headed west, across the Tennessee, toward Grant's supply and communications lines. This news, combined with another Rebel cavalry venture, would haunt Grant's future. For the present, he sent cavalry to protect Corinth and asked Porter for gunboat assistance on the Tennessee.

Despite campaign pressures, Grant took time to correct illegal trading activity in the lower Mississippi Valley, involving mostly cotton. Exemplifying prevailing prejudices, Grant especially blamed Jews for the problem. He urged the War Department to buy cotton at a fixed rate and send it north to be sold, and then he would expel all traders, "a curse to the army." Grant also issued General Orders No. 11, which stated bluntly: "The Jews, as a class violating every regulation of trade established by the Treasury Department and also department orders, are hereby expelled from the department within twenty-four hours from the receipt of this order." Grant, in addition to his stated justification, doubtless remembered his father being betrayed in a trading deal that included Jews. In any event, President Lincoln later revoked the order because, in Halleck's words, Grant had singled out "an entire religious class, some of whom are fighting in our ranks."[25]

Grant also took time to set up a rather remarkable local welfare system. On December 12, he issued Special Field Orders No. 21, which acknowledged the "Distress and almost famine having been brought on many of the inhabitants of Mississippi by the march of the two armies through the land, and humanity dictating that in a land of plenty no one should suffer the pangs of hunger." His remedy included several facets. Loyalists would sell provisions, through area military posts, to local families based on need. A fund, composed of levies on disloyal persons, taxes on cotton, or other unspecified means, would be created to provide for free provisions to destitute families. Inspectors general would check accounts for accuracy and honesty.

Aside from humanitarian considerations, Grant considered pro-Union sentiment in North Mississippi worth cultivating, and, so far, too many of his men had done a poor job of reaping sympathy for the Union. Three days after Grant issued his order, a resident of Marshall County wrote Abraham Lincoln about miserable conditions. Admitting his prosecession past, the writer said he had since taken an oath of allegiance to the Union. He asked that his home area "be permanently considered in the lines of the United States Army," and in effect be allowed back into the Union. Though the letter, which implies much about morale among local civilians, made it to the White House, it got the writer in trouble with civilian and military authorities in Mississippi, and whether Lincoln ever saw it or responded in any way is unknown.[26]

While Grant busied himself, John McClernand wired Abraham Lincoln that around 40,000 troops had been raised for the river expedition. McClernand wanted to proceed and asked Lincoln's permission to do so. McClernand also wired Stanton, requesting Union soldiers available after a recent Union victory at Prairie Grove, Arkansas. "I am anxiously awaiting your order sending me forward for duty in connection with the Mississippi expedition," McClernand wrote. Stanton said he thought Halleck had already issued orders, and McClernand wired Halleck to "beg" that he be allowed to proceed. A suspicious McClernand then fired off telegrams to Lincoln and Stanton saying that he believed he had been "superceded" and wanted an explanation. Stanton immediately expressed surprise and said he would check on the situation.

Stanton followed up with a masterpiece of bureaucratic double-talk that must have infuriated McClernand, who understood the art all too well. "There has been," wrote Stanton, "as I am informed by General Halleck, no order superseding you. It was designed, as you know, to organize the troops for your expedition after they should reach Memphis or the place designated as their rendezvous. The troops having been sent forward they are not to be organized. The operations being in General Grant's department, it is designed to organize all the troops of that department in three army corps, the First Army Corps to be commanded by you, and assigned to the operations on the Mississippi under the general supervision of the general commanding the department. General Halleck is to issue the order immediately."

Stanton's statement was dishonest, for McClernand had been told that he would be in overall command of the campaign. On the eighteenth, Grant wired McClernand orders giving the latter command of a two-division corps, to be part of the Vicksburg expedition. Sherman would likewise command a corps. Grant hoped, he said, that McClernand could arrive soon, for "there should be no delay in starting"; but if he could not, he should let Grant know at once. McClernand also must send "a field return of your entire command — that is, of the river expedition — before starting." Grant must have smiled as he wrote; he knew McClernand could not possibly arrive before Sherman left. McClernand received his orders to go south on December 23, the day he married his deceased wife's sister.[27]

While Grant and his lieutenants revamped the Vicksburg campaign, John Pemberton felt helpless as his outnumbered troops waited to see what happened next. On November 13, he complained to Richmond that he had seen neither the unarmed Texans promised him nor the weapons with which to arm them. In fact he had nearly 5,000 unarmed men. Muskets of about that number had been sent to Brierfield Arsenal in Columbus to be repaired, and he had rounded up fifty gunsmiths to help. He also had shortages of small-arms ammunition and heavy artillery for Snyder's and Haynes's bluffs on the Yazoo. In addition to all that, his army needed clothing, shoes, and blankets.

Pemberton reviewed reports about heavy Union activity along the

Mississippi and the concentration of troops in Helena, obviously intended to continue threatening the Confederate left. With all the pressures on the Confederate front and the threat on the Mississippi, Pemberton chose this time to inspect Port Hudson, and he promised a disconcerted Earl Van Dorn that he would return quickly if needed. Pemberton, as he often did, acted as if his command were insulated from reality. He seemed not to grasp his army's morale problems or the gravity of Grant's actions.[28]

Pemberton also had a tendency to be sidetracked by insignificant issues, though poor Confederate intelligence gathering sometimes made discernment difficult. He almost panicked when he heard of a Union expedition from Helena down the Mississippi to the vicinity of Fort Hindman on the Arkansas River. The campaign had been canceled because of Sherman's concentration at Helena. Nevertheless, Pemberton begged Richmond for help, and the War Department asked Braxton Bragg to send assistance. Samuel Cooper also "requested" Theophilus Holmes to provide aid, while telling Pemberton that Holmes had been "ordered" to do so. Holmes had not and did not, and cemented his position by reminding Davis that sending troops to Vicksburg would likely mean the loss of Little Rock. Holmes knew Davis would do nothing to antagonize Confederate support in Arkansas. Bragg, meanwhile, shipped 3,000 small arms to Pemberton, though he complained that his command responsibilities did not include Pemberton.[29]

At this point, like Grant, Pemberton attended to administrative matters. Worried about the official designation of his troops, Pemberton managed to get Cooper to come up with the "First and Second Army Corps of the Department of the Mississippi." The title sounded as if Cooper made it up just to quiet Pemberton. Pemberton also had to settle the Sterling Price issue. Price complained to Richmond that he and his division had not been transferred to Missouri as promised. They could be spared now, he argued, though how, in light of Grant's threat, Price did not say. He mourned the loss of many of his men "by the casualties of war and the pestilential atmosphere of the Mississippi swamps," but he argued in vain. Richmond asked Pemberton if he would trade the Missourians to Holmes for a like number from Arkansas. Pemberton had no interest in giving up those crack Missouri troops.

Another development, which had long-range ramifications for Pemberton and the Vicksburg campaign, came on November 24 when Joseph E. Johnston received command of an enormous geographical area, which included most of the Confederacy outside Virginia and west of the lower East Coast states and extending to the Mississippi River. The

War Department apparently envisioned Johnston as a floating commander, establishing his headquarters where he could best communicate with his commanders, and the department expected him to "repair in person to any part of said command whenever his presence may for the time be necessary or desirable." Johnston reacted to his new duties with a strategic philosophy that Jefferson Davis and his government never accepted. Since his troops were outnumbered, Johnston advised concentrations of forces from both sides of the Mississippi. This army could go on the offensive against Grant, and the "defeat of Major-General Grant would enable us to hold the Mississippi and permit Lieutenant-General Holmes to move into Missouri. As our troops are now distributed Vicksburg is in danger." Beauregard had made similar arguments months earlier, and now, as then, they fell on deaf ears in Richmond.[30]

The change in command had no immediate impact in Mississippi. Johnston needed time to assume his new duties, and when he realized Davis would not accept his advice, he seemed to lose interest in doing anything. Anxious Confederates in North Mississippi had to fend for themselves, and the War Department encouraged Pemberton to report directly to Richmond, making Johnston's assignment rather superfluous. Pemberton continued monitoring enemy activity at Helena and accepted manpower limitations exacerbated by Holmes's refusal to cooperate. Due to the lull in North Mississippi, Pemberton weakened the Abbeville front to build up strength at Vicksburg.

Finally, after more badgering from Cooper, Holmes offered Pemberton a cavalry brigade from Texas, but Pemberton did not need cavalry, though ironically, within a few months he would be begging for horsemen. The army needed infantry and artillery to hold the line in North Mississippi, to counter enemy pressure on their center and both flanks. Rumors indicated McClernand was leading an expedition to Vicksburg, and other reports suggested Port Hudson might be in danger. If succor did not come soon, Pemberton might have to abandon North Mississippi.

A frustrated Cooper sent Holmes, via Pemberton, a strongly worded message. Since Pemberton did not need cavalry, "send to Vicksburg without delay the infantry force which you have been twice telegraphed for. The case is urgent and will not admit of delay." Holmes refused to budge. John Forney, meanwhile, sent a brigade from Mobile to Meridian, and Bragg sent a brigade for use at Vicksburg or Mobile. Pemberton welcomed the support, but he still worried about his flanks and suggested that the Brierfield Arsenal at Columbus be moved. Johnston agreed and ordered the arsenal sent to Selma in southern Alabama. Pemberton informed Bragg about retreating to Grenada: "You see my situation; it is for you to decide how far you can help me."[31]

As his army retreated, Pemberton ordered the army to destroy equipment that could not be carried. Pemberton wired Vicksburg, ordering M. L. Smith to burn steamboats that might fall into Union hands. Pemberton's commissary staff began building up supplies in Vicksburg to last for a five- to six-month period. Ideally, commissary officials needed supplies to subsist 10,000 men at both Vicksburg and Port Hudson, a goal beyond their reach.[32]

The effort to find Pemberton additional help at times seemed elusive. Cooper notified Johnston that Holmes had been "peremptorily" ordered to send support, but admitted that if troops came, they would arrive too late. Cooper pressured Johnston to send more men from Bragg's army. Pemberton reported to Bragg and Johnston that 21,000 men held the Yalobusha front, while 6,000 defended Vicksburg and 4,500 held Port Hudson. Johnston knew little about the overall situation in his new command area, but he assumed Pemberton would retreat to Vicksburg and rendezvous with Holmes. Maps and troop locations indicated that Holmes could get support to Pemberton much quicker than Bragg. Johnston pointedly told Cooper that Holmes must "be urged to the utmost expedition." If the enemy took Vicksburg, the Confederates could not "dislodge him."

Johnston pressed Pemberton: "Let me know by express which way you are moving and what your plans are. Urge General Holmes to quick movement. I am without the necessary information. Give it." Johnston agreed that Bragg should send cavalry to disrupt Grant's communications, but offered nothing concrete. Pemberton's reply that he was ready to fight Grant along the Yalobusha shattered Johnston's illusion that Pemberton and Holmes would concentrate at Vicksburg.

With Pemberton reporting directly to Richmond, Johnston had continual trouble communicating with Mississippi, especially from Bragg's Tennessee headquarters. It became readily apparent that it was absurd for the government to send a commander to take charge of an extensive area without allowing him to coordinate operations as he saw fit.[33]

Holmes, meanwhile, bombarded Richmond with arguments about why he could not do anything for Pemberton. The Yankees were demonstrating in force in Arkansas, and if he sent men to Vicksburg, Little Rock would be defenseless. If that happened, "the whole valley of the Arkansas will be stampeded, and the political party which has constantly cried out that the country is deserted by the Government will pave the way to dangerous disloyalty and disgust." Also, if Arkansas went, all the area west of the Mississippi would go with it, meaning no more supplies from that area for the East. Therefore, Holmes concluded, "with the greatest reluctance, I hesitate to obey your last order, because it presupposes the safety of the river." He could not reach Vicksburg in less than thirty days anyway, and it seemed obvious Vicksburg would not be attacked until Grant swept aside Pemberton's army in North Mississippi. Holmes thus made clear he intended to do nothing, and Cooper backed off: "It is impossible at this distance to judge your necessities, but . . . if you could give aid it was hoped you would do so." Holmes had won the debate, for Davis would not risk more controversy in Arkansas.[34]

In the meantime, Pemberton sent Johnston the requested assessment of the situation in Mississippi. He faced some 60,000 Federals pushing south, plus a smaller force threatening his rear. Scouting reports indicated Grant was sending troops downriver, and Union troops were demonstrating against Port Hudson. Since he only had 22,000, Pemberton said, he had been forced to retreat to the Yalobusha, where he would make a stand unless flanked. Heavy rains should slow enemy pursuit.[35]

Pemberton's tired soldiers also had to endure the bad weather as they settled into defensive positions behind the Yalobusha. They camped on high ground south of the river, which provided both scenic views and security, and "levied" slaves from local owners to help dig new defensive lines. Slaves also provided entertainment, sometimes dancing and sometimes playing a tamboo, a stringed instrument. Wood from nearby sawmills provided shanties for the soldiers, while the slaves stayed in a large warehouse. The men entertained themselves by playing cards and watching cockfights, and they, like defenders at Vicksburg, found locals a bit harsh, especially in the prices they charged for food and other goods. Confederate practitioners of free enterprise in Mississippi did not mind taking advantage of their own soldiers. Grenada also gained a reputation for immorality, characterized by drunkards, outlaws, gamblers, and "abandoned women." Law-abiding citizens would be relieved when the army left.[36]

North of the Yalobusha, Confederate detachments skirmished with Grant's slowly advancing columns. On December 5, fighting broke out about a mile from Coffeeville when a portion of a Rebel brigade tried to drive off Yankee cavalry. A spirited artillery duel ensued. Confederates attacked Union flanks, forcing a retreat called off at dark, disappointing the pursuers, who were Fort Donelson veterans recently returned from captivity after being taken prisoner at Donelson. These men, "notwith-standing the severe duties and deprivations of the last week, seemed to forget everything but the desire showed by all to repay the injuries suffered by them during their long imprisonment at the North." The fight had been decisive enough to secure Pemberton's Yalobusha line for the moment.[37]

After the fight, Confederates found the corpse of one of the hated Kansans, who had reputedly bragged that he would one day catch a Rebel and put him in a cage and take him around on an exhibition tour. During the battle, Mississippians perforated this Union soldier with twenty-seven bullets. Such incidents indicated the rising level of hard-line attitudes permeating both armies.

Despite their satisfaction, Pemberton's soldiers noticed that the people of Coffeeville seemed depressed and destitute. Wrote one, "The silence of death and of the grave seemed to partake of the general air of gloom that rested on the place." Some blamed Pemberton's retreat for the deteriorating morale of civilians and soldiers, one noting sarcas-tically, "If left to his own impulses [he] will [not] fight a battle or make a stand this side of the Gulf of Mexico." Obviously, Pemberton fooled himself when he assured Richmond his men were in good spirits. Of course, having spent little time at the front, how could he know?[38]

In any event, Pemberton's worries suddenly shifted to the Yazoo, where Isaac Brown had been ordered by the Navy Department to stop work on gunboats at the Yazoo City, Mississippi, naval yard until, and unless, adequate river defenses could be constructed. The defensive batteries currently consisted of nine heavy guns plus lighter field artil-lery but needed a 10-inch piece to be effective. The raft across the Yazoo north of Vicksburg was in place and strong, but possibly not strong enough. Brown warned that without a big gun other artillery might be unable to stop Union boats.

In addition to military problems, political dissatisfaction in Mis-sissippi was building against Pemberton. James Phelan, senator from Mississippi in the Confederate Congress, complained to Jefferson Davis about military concerns and declining morale, the latter largely due to a lack of faith in Pemberton on the part of both the army and civilians. An abler commander in North Mississippi might not have been outflanked, said Phelan. Resulting retreats had been a "staggering blow" to those expecting more of Pemberton. Since he was relatively unknown, "his want of prominence of itself at such a crisis depresses the spirit of the people." Many still referred to the Mississippi force as Van Dorn's army, and Van Dorn's image had been remarkably tarnished. Talk of his "negligence, whoring, and drunkenness" and "as the source of all our woes" was common. Phelan mourned, "Enthusiasm has expired to a cold pile of damp ashes." All the military setbacks were compounded by the "conviction that our army is in the hands of ignorant and feeble commanders." Phelan wanted Davis to come home and personally lead the army, and though that would never happen, Davis soon would be traveling to Mississippi to calm fears.[39]

With controversy swirling around him, Pemberton sought refuge in his Jackson office, where he buried himself in administrative details. Assured by M. L. Smith that Vicksburg was secure, Pemberton sent reinforcements to Grenada and Columbus. He also ordered supplies on the Mobile and Ohio Railroad moved south out of harm's way. Pemberton was no battlefield commander, but he understood troop deployment and logistical issues. In effect, he could make contributions behind a desk that he could not make leading an army into battle.

U. S. Grant caused Pemberton's increased concern about the Mobile and Ohio. He ordered a cavalry detachment to strike the railroad as far south "as practicable" and destroy Confederate property. To cover the raid, Grant ordered a demonstration toward Grenada. On December 15, the cavalry reached Tupelo unimpeded, except for rain and muddy roads. There they destroyed supplies and bridges and dismantled the railroad to the north and south. While retracing their route, they spied a large Rebel cavalry force headed north on the Pontotoc-Ripley road. After harassing the Confederate flanks for a time, they gave up trying to make the Confederates stand and fight. Rather than risk an attack, the Federals, mystified at the enemy horsemen's timidity, rode on to Oxford and spread the word of Confederate riders in the area. The Federal raiders had destroyed thirty-four miles of track and captured some 150 prisoners.[40]

After the raid, things momentarily quieted in North Mississippi, though those mysterious Confederate horsemen would change that. More immediate news came from Vicksburg and indicated the Union navy on the prowl. On December 11, two Union boats entered the Yazoo and ascended some twenty miles. In late summer, Confederates had littered the channel with obstructions and torpedoes (akin to modern-day mines). Two of the torpedoes exploded, hurting neither vessel, and both retreated back to the Mississippi. Next day, they came up again, supported by three additional warships, including the ironclad *Cairo*. Two mines exploded under the *Cairo*, and the ironclad went down in about twelve minutes, with only its smokestacks and flagstaff showing above water. The crew escaped, forced to abandon personal and military items on board. Confederates celebrated this, the first such sinking of a vessel in naval history, but the Union navy would not be so easily dissuaded.[41]

While he monitored the situation, Pemberton received new officers into his department. On December 14, Bragg ordered troops commanded by Franklin Gardner, Samuel Maxey, and Carter Stevenson from the Army of Tennessee to Pemberton's headquarters in Jackson. The transfer improved Pemberton's quantity of troops but, in the case of Stevenson's division, not necessarily the quality. Gardner eventually moved on to Louisiana to take command at Port Hudson.[42]

At this point came a turn in the campaign, unexpected by Pemberton and emanating from an unexpected source — Lieutenant Colonel John Griffith, 6th Texas Cavalry. Griffith and other officers in the First Texas Cavalry Brigade believed that a cavalry raid in the Union rear could force Grant to retreat. In a message to Pemberton, Griffith elaborated diplomatically: "We are the more bold to do so, and have less fear of the misconstruction of our motives, when we remember that you have been so recently placed in command over us; and that the multitudinous cares incidental to your responsible position have necessarily, thus far, precluded an examination of the position of the enemy, and to what is the best employment in which the cavalry, under your command, can be engaged. We, therefore, respectfully submit, if you will fit up a cavalry expedition, comprising three or four thousand men, and give us Major-General Earl Van Dorn, than whom no braver man lives, to command us, we will penetrate the rear of the enemy, capture Holly Springs, Memphis, and other points, and, perhaps, force him to retreat from Coffeeville."[43]

Griffith wrote carefully regarding Pemberton's ignorance of tactical possibilities on the Grenada front, but clearly the colonel did not appreciate the general's obsession with paperwork. Pemberton ignored the implication, talked personally with Griffith, but delayed a decision in order to check out more, this time unfounded, rumors of Union naval adventures on the Yazoo. Pemberton then issued orders implementing the Griffith proposal.

A troubled Earl Van Dorn must have viewed the operation as a godsend, a chance to recoup his reputation. About the same time, a Confederate officer wrote his wife of Van Dorn: "He says, and he is too proud a man to tell a lie, that all the reports in circulation about his

conduct towards the ladies is as false as the very blackness of hell."
Van Dorn insisted that he had never betrayed any woman's trust, was
neither devil nor saint, and had never "trifled with *untarnished virtue.*"
The general's comments did not stand against the facts of his personal
life.[44]

Pemberton assigned some 2,500 men to Van Dorn, and, in the early
morning hours of December 16, the Mississippian led his troops north.
The cavalry consisted of Texans, Missourians, Tennesseans, and Mississippians, all ignorant of where they were going or why. Pemberton
and Van Dorn had decided to hit Holly Springs to destroy the huge
stores of enemy supplies at the railroad depot. To prevent the details
from slipping out to Union scouts and spies, Van Dorn did a remarkable
job of keeping this information from his men.[45]

Rainy skies hovered over the column as horses splashed across the
Yalobusha at Graysport and veered northeast toward Houston, an indirect route to Holly Springs. Foul weather and muddy roads hampered
progress. At Houston, Van Dorn turned toward Pontotoc, confusing
Union scouts, who likely suspected that the Confederates would patrol
the Mobile and Ohio Railroad. In Pontotoc, residents cheered and
handed up food, milk, and wine as the men rode by. Van Dorn pushed
his men hard, because scouts reported Yankee cavalry in the area, and
he did not want to be seen.

The Yankee cavalry proved to be Grant's raiders returning from the
Mobile and Ohio, and the Rebel riders just missed bumping into detached Federal horsemen demonstrating toward Grenada. The Federal
commander, T. Lyle Dickey, had recoiled from forcing a fight, so he sent
scouts to sound the alarm. Dickey's efforts to warn Grant went awry
when confused couriers failed to find army headquarters until long
after Van Dorn's column had been spotted.

Van Dorn issued orders to ignore any Yankee scouts or skirmishers
and keep riding, and the column moved on to New Albany and crossed
the Tallahatchie, camping in a downpour near the river. On a cold,
clear December 19, the Confederates continued to Ripley; now deep
behind Union lines, Van Dorn beefed up security. Scouts found a
swampy, rugged trail leading to Holly Springs, and Van Dorn believed
the little-used lane provided good cover, so the column turned and
endured a rough ride. He worried because he did not know how much
the Yankees knew of his whereabouts. He briefed his officers on attack
plans, and word filtered quickly through the ranks that the men would
soon have an abundance of rations.

That night Van Dorn countermarched the column, leading his bewildered men, in columns of twos, back to the Holly Springs–Ripley main road. From there, they traveled west to within about five miles of Holly Springs. Van Dorn rested the men, waited for scouting reports, and sent riders ahead to warn civilians to keep quiet. Some locals proved their loyalty was questionable when they mistook Van Dorn's men for Federals and warned them of Rebel cavalry in the area. Others played it safe and pretended support no matter what their real sentiments might have been; true feelings were always hard to ascertain, especially in areas where both armies were operating. Van Dorn's scouts secured Federal passes and rode into Holly Springs and found no indication that enemy troops were on the alert. In fact Union soldiers planned a ball for the next evening.[46]

The scouts mentally noted the disposition of enemy troops. Detachments of Illinois Infantry camped near the railroad depot and on the city square. Six companies of Illinois cavalry bivouacked on local fairgrounds north of downtown. Other Federal troops were in supporting distance, but likely too far away to interfere. Hoping to strike swiftly without scattering his command and risking loss of coordination, Van Dorn decided to assign target areas and attack with most of his troops — Mississippians the fairgrounds, Missourians the depot, and Texans the town square. A few men picketed the periphery to sound the alarm if Federal reinforcements approached.

To the south a shocked U. S. Grant finally learned on the nineteenth that a large enemy cavalry force had gotten in his rear. The thoroughly disgusted commanding general immediately ordered cavalry pursuit. Union telegraph operators flashed the news to points north and northeast. Grant operated blindly since he had no idea where Van Dorn might be, though he suspected the Rebels were farther south than Holly Springs.

Union pursuit got off to a bad start. Commanders John Mizner and Benjamin Grierson, ordered to rendezvous, missed connections. Grant, worried about the Holly Springs supplies, wired Colonel Robert Murphy, 8th Wisconsin, commanding, to send out scouts. Murphy, an inexperienced citizen-soldier with influential friends, seemed unmoved and did nothing more than alert his cavalry. Grant sensed Murphy's complacency when Murphy replied that scouts would not ride until dawn.

South of Holly Springs, a black man informed Illinois troops that a large force of Confederate cavalry had ridden into the area. Two soldiers escorted the man to Murphy, who, disgruntled at having been awakened at 5:00 A.M., said this was old news and dismissed the intruders. He did notify Grant of the sighting, again promised to send out scouts, and said he would concentrate troops scattered about the area. Incredibly, Murphy then went back to bed without sounding any alarm.

Just before dawn, Van Dorn ordered his troops to resume the march, halting after a time to wait for dawn. At the first streaks of light, a rider appeared and detailed the location of Federal pickets. The column moved again toward Holly Springs and cheers broke out as Van Dorn suddenly and silently pointed his sword toward the enemy. The cavalry spurred their horses and rushed into town.

"Holly Springs is the handsomest place we have seen yet on our southward march. It is beautifully laid out, with wide streets, planted on each side with rows of shade-trees. Many of the residences are large and tastefully built. It has half a dozen churches, one of which, the Episcopal Church, is a little architectural gem. The town once had six or seven thousand inhabitants, but now has probably not more than one third of that number. Every store was of course closed; some of the merchants, who had any stock left, carried it out of town as soon as they heard of the approach of the army." Thus one Missouri journalist described the town about to be the scene of a memorable day.[47]

Federal troops heard cheers and the dreaded Rebel yells, high-pitched sounds of exultation that had already become legendary in the war. Illinois infantry scattered, chased by Missouri cavalry. A Mobile reporter observed "Yankees running, tents burning, torches flaming, Confederates shouting, guns popping, sabers clanking, abolitionists begging for mercy, Rebels shouting exultantly, women en dishabille clapping their hands, frantic with joy, crying 'kill them.' "[48]

Texans hit downtown with a roar, firing as much to amuse themselves as to kill the enemy. Federals fled in various stages of dress, forgetting all dignity. Mississippi Cavalry charged Illinois Cavalry at the fairgrounds, the Illinoisans taking the charge just as they assembled for roll call. With swords flashing on both sides, a general melee ensued. The Confederates got the best of it and soon bagged a large number of prisoners. Some Federals escaped and ran toward Memphis.

Victorious Confederates hurrahed all across town, cheering Van Dorn, the Confederacy, and Jefferson Davis. Women in bedclothes and robes joined in the celebration. By 8:00 A.M., Van Dorn's raiders had secured Holly Springs, and he ordered his men to reform and hold their positions. Then came mass destruction of Federal supplies, while patrols, guided by local women, found scattered Union fugitives hiding about town. Confederates found Grant's wife, Julia, in the Walter house. Van Dorn issued strict orders for her protection and posted guards around the home, but her carriage got burned during the excitement.

Colonel Murphy, still in his nightclothes, surrendered, and was taken to Van Dorn. Murphy later claimed to have been captured while trying to escape.

A curious turn of events came when Van Dorn learned that soldiers of the 109th Illinois, stationed south of town, wanted to surrender and be paroled. The unit consisted mostly of Southern sympathizers from southern Illinois, but Van Dorn refused to accommodate them. After all, "a disloyal regiment in the Union Army was a much greater asset to the Confederacy than even a larger number of prisoners who would be shortly paroled."[49]

In Holly Springs, things got out of hand as both Rebel victors and Yankee captives assaulted containers of whiskey. Local slaves ransacked the post office, looking for money among the mail, and the looting spread. Smart Confederates scrounged the town for fresh horses. Van Dorn knew he had to get his men under control and leave before Union cavalry arrived. To speed things along, he offered to parole prisoners, and Murphy agreed. The raiders continued destroying warehouses, shops, machinery, depot stores, track, and telegraph lines. Van Dorn knew dead telegraph lines would pinpoint his location, and he urged the men to hurry. Meanwhile, ammunition exploded, cracking windows and spreading fires that consumed homes and a hospital.[50]

By 4:00 P.M., the jubilant Rebels had remounted and left the town engulfed in flames and thick smoke. Destruction had been great; Van Dorn estimated $1.5 million worth, though the actual amount is unknown. Neither side documented casualties, though losses in killed and wounded must have been light. Confederates took along as much booty as their horses could bear and rode north up the Mississippi Central, cutting telegraph lines and tearing up rails as they went. At Davis' Mill (present-day Michigan City), they attempted capturing well-entrenched Indiana infantry guarding the Wolf River bridge. After three hours, Van Dorn gave up the fight and found another river crossing.

In Tennessee, the Rebels tore up track on the Memphis and Charleston, and on December 23 turned east and then south, striking near Bolivar to distract Federals from Nathan Bedford Forrest and his cavalry wrecking Grant's lines of communications in West Tennessee. Van Dorn diluted enemy pursuit by giving Federals two columns to hunt. While Van Dorn moved back toward Grenada, he feinted and created diversions, hoping to draw Union cavalry after him. Finding Grierson in pursuit, Van Dorn reunified the command for the final stretch run to safety.

After putting some distance between his troops and Grierson's, Van Dorn allowed a brief encampment on Christmas Eve, but continued on after midnight, leaving smoldering campfires. A rearguard detachment dropped off at Ripley forced a temporary Federal retreat. Christmas night, the raiders rested in New Albany and reached the safety of Confederate lines on the twenty-eighth. The rear guard rode in the next day. Forrest also escaped Federal pursuit, though losing much booty in a hard fight at Parker's Crossroads in Tennessee.

U. S. Grant's attempts to capture Van Dorn failed largely as a result of the lack of cooperation and coordination among his cavalry commanders. Meanwhile, with his supply stockpile gone, Grant ordered his army to withdraw to the Tallahatchie and cut rations until the dimensions of the disaster could be determined. He soon sent messages to Memphis and to Sherman regarding the debacle, and reported that the army must abandon the North Mississippi campaign.

In the Oxford area, white civilians looked on with "joy and *triumph*" as sullen Union troops, some blaming Grant for the disaster, marched north. Many slaves, dressed in their Sunday best and doubtless hoping to remain free and protected, now feared being left behind. Oxford suffered the consequences of Union anger. Soldiers raided many homes, and soon streets became littered with papers, books, and furniture. Someone set off an explosion in a bank, starting a fire that melted gold and silver coins, which were claimed by looters.

A silver statue of Jesus disappeared from a Catholic church, and a Union soldier shook his head sadly at the goings-on. He later wrote, "Every portion of the *fated* city seemed given over to *pillage* and destruction and no hand was raised to save anything from the general *sack and ruin*." Women and children at first glad to see the enemy leaving now stood tearfully watching the bedlam. The scenes reminded an observer "how the innocent shall suffer in the cause of treason and rebellion." Eventually, the men drifted away "in the dense dark wilderness of uncertainty and the silver lining of the dark cloud of war is not visible."[51]

Ironically, Pemberton had not closely tracked the successful raid, for he was preparing for important visitors. Jefferson Davis headed west in December to visit Bragg and Johnston, hoping to remedy lack of command coordination. Davis and Johnston arrived in Jackson on December 19, while Van Dorn's raiders were en route to Holly Springs. First they went to Vicksburg to inspect defenses, then returned to Jackson and went to Grenada to confer with Pemberton. The army passed in review, and all celebrated breaking news of Van Dorn's raid. But ominous reports of a large enemy force heading down the Mississippi loomed over the event. Pemberton shifted his attention from victory in North Mississippi to a threat at Vicksburg.[52]

Union soldiers, embarrassed and angered, retreated back into Memphis, guzzled liquor, and prowled sidewalks, some carrying bricks. They profanely declared the walkways for whites only, "not for any d——d niggers." Federals reoccupying Holly Springs brought the town more destruction. Jeered as they passed through after Van Dorn's raid, they burned homes, many getting caught and punished, many others getting away with arson. One soldier sadly noted that Holly Springs "is changed from one of the prettiest places I ever saw to a heap of ruins." In early January at night, "several houses were burning pretty close to camp. Soon houses were burning in every direction and continued so near all night. Double guards were put on around camp & Rolls called to see if any were absent. Guards were put all over town but still the fire raged." The town paid a high price for Van Dorn's visit.[53]

One Iowan noted that the Confederate raid and reaction to it underscored what the war in Mississippi had wrought: "The wholesale destruction of all species of property in the country—by friends and foes—had so exasperated the inhabitants throughout the section, who composed the membership of the partisan organizations, that a most wanton destruction of human life was inaugurated by both sides. Murders and cowardly assassinations were of daily occurrence, and the destruction of palatial plantations, in retaliation, was prosecuted relentlessly, and that in spite of the most stringent orders to the contrary."[54]

Grant's North Mississippi campaign ended without a major battle being fought. He maneuvered, and Pemberton and Van Dorn reacted. Grant's concern about his supply line, plus geography and weather factors, worked in the Confederates' favor, slowed the pace to a crawl, and gave Pemberton time to avoid risking his army while waiting for an opportunity to turn things around. That opportunity came, and though Van Dorn's raid was an obvious tactical choice, the fact that Pemberton did not think of it demonstrated his tactical ineptness. At least he had the foresight to approve it.

The chaos that followed the raid symbolized the coming of hard war to interior Mississippi. Relations between soldiers and civilians proved much more combative than conflict between armies. By the time Grant withdrew, guerrilla activity and hard war, factors that increasingly characterized the Vicksburg campaign, had expanded and intensified. Indeed, they seemed to take on a life of their own, beyond the reach of concerned commanders and soldiers. War's hell became a way of life to noncombatants caught between and among opposing armies.

It was hell for Grant, too. Later in the war, Sherman, with his special flair, stated that while he was smarter than Grant and knew more about army administration and logistics, there was an area where Grant always surpassed him: "He don't care a damn for what the enemy does out of his sight . . . ; he issues his orders and does his level best to carry them out without much reference to what is going on about him." That quality may have been true of Grant after the Vicksburg campaign but certainly not during it. He had been concerned about what the enemy was doing during the North Mississippi campaign and, as things turned out, with good reason. Not knowing what the enemy was up to had cost him dearly.[55]

Meanwhile, William T. Sherman carried on his operation downriver. He was determined, even after hearing of the Holly Springs disaster, to carry out his attack at Vicksburg. The decision proved to be a costly one for his army and Union momentum.

5

~~ Bloody Bayou & the Wild Goose

William T. Sherman arrived in Helena on December 20, the same day that Earl Van Dorn's cavalry effectively ended Grant's North Mississippi campaign. Sherman conferred with his generals and ordered a detachment from Friar's Point to the Tallahatchie to open direct communications with Grant. Sherman knew he had fallen two days behind Grant's schedule because of delays in getting transports to Helena, but he promised that the expedition would reach Milliken's Bend by the twenty-third and the mouth of the Yazoo two days later. Sherman learned the morning of the twenty-first that Union soldiers arriving in Memphis were reporting the Rebel capture of Holly Springs. Sherman assumed that, regardless of the veracity of these reports, Grant could handle things.[1]

In his zeal, Sherman determined to get downriver and make his attack as quickly as river transportation allowed. In the process, he made a key error; he led his men into a campaign without securing adequate reports of conditions and terrain. Apparently Sherman thought he could overpower Confederate defenses, but he would find that a Confederate force well led and possessing high ground could magnify its effective combat numbers. Also, Grant's retreat, which Sherman should have anticipated if the news of Holly Springs was true, allowed Pemberton to send reinforcements to Vicksburg from the Grenada front. A sober look at such possibilities should have convinced Sherman to call off or at least postpone the operation until he knew more about Grant's situation. But with the specter of McClernand on the river, with Grant counting on him, and with the news of a major repulse of the Union Army of the Potomac at Fredericksburg, Virginia, by Robert E. Lee, Sherman chose to proceed.

Sherman's expedition, some 30,000 men, arrived at Milliken's Bend a day earlier than planned. One soldier recalled how the troops went down the Mississippi: "Crowded with men, what seemed like an endless flotilla of steamers moved in a single line, and close together, gracefully curving around the bends, and presenting a spectacle more beautiful and imposing than anything I have ever seen in the nature of a military movement."[2]

When the troops disembarked, Sherman sent Stephen Burbridge's brigade of A. J. Smith's division to destroy a portion of the Texas, Shreveport, and Vicksburg Railroad near the Tensas River. Burbridge, a Kentucky Unionist, did his job well; in addition to tearing up track, his men burned Confederate cotton, corn, and cloth, leaving privately owned cotton undisturbed. Detachments destroyed the Lake Providence and Tallulah telegraph, and captured horses, cattle, and prisoners. Confederate cavalry hovered in the distance but made no move to intervene. The Federals wrought considerable destruction at the town of Delhi, burning the depot, cloth, medicine, drugs, machinery, bridges, trestles, and sawmills, along with capturing mail. Burbridge reported that the countryside offered an abundance of forage, corn, and cotton, and unless a large force came through could "afford a source of supply for a long time to come."

Burbridge's unimpeded expedition resulted in local charges of Confederate incompetence. District of Western Louisiana commander Richard Taylor, at the War Department's behest, conducted an investigation and concluded that his orders regarding combating enemy attacks had been either ignored or poorly executed, and he relieved two commanders. "The whole affair," Taylor wrote Secretary of War James Seddon, "was disgraceful to the service in the extreme." Taylor's wrath seemed harsh, given that Burbridge's troops heavily outnumbered Confederates.[3]

On Christmas Day, Sherman moved his army downriver, leaving A. J. Smith's division behind to wait on Burbridge. The expedition arrived along the west bank of the Mississippi directly across from the mouth of the Yazoo. Sherman sent another detachment to hit the Vicksburg-Shreveport railroad, this time closer to its terminus on the shore across from Vicksburg. Sherman believed that putting that railroad out of commission, if done right, would make it "useless to our enemy" for months to come.

Also on Christmas, Sherman talked with David Porter, and the two decided to land the army at a point on the Yazoo twelve miles upriver in the midst of "a system of bayous or old channels." The expedition moved up the Yazoo on the 26th, with gunboats providing cover from Rebel sharpshooters. From the head of the fleet to the rear, the transports carried, respectively, George Morgan's, Frederick Steele's, and

Morgan Smith's divisions. A. J. Smith's troops, waiting for Burbridge, did not arrive until the 27th.

After the transports docked, Morgan's division marched in a southerly direction toward Vicksburg for about three miles. On the twenty-seventh, Sherman ordered his whole force forward in four columns. From the Union left to right, Steele's division marched above and to the left of Chickasaw Bayou, which branched southeast off the Yazoo, and George Morgan, accompanied by Frank Blair's brigade of Steele's division, moved below, right of the stream. Morgan Smith took the road from a place called Johnson's plantation that led toward Vicksburg, bearing to his left, south of where Morgan crossed the bayou. Picket fire erupted as the army marched inland.[4]

John Pemberton and the Vicksburg troops reacted quickly to the news of Sherman's arrival. Continual reports of Union transports headed downriver led Pemberton on Christmas Eve to order a Columbus regiment and troops from the Yalobusha front to Vicksburg. Pemberton traveled with his guests, Joe Johnston and President Davis to Jackson, left them there, and headed for Vicksburg. If Sherman attacked from the north, Pemberton and his troops would be ready. Defensive works had been built to defend the Walnut Hills line, which followed the base of bluffs on Vicksburg's north perimeter at an angle to the northeast, terminating atop high ground overlooking the Yazoo.[5]

Until Sherman's arrival, the most recent excitement in Vicksburg had been prisoner exchanges. Refugees fleeing from enemy invasion to the north or destructive Union forays along the Mississippi had also swelled the population. River traffic had increased to the point that one Confederate physician described the Mississippi as "one continuous line of smoke." The earlier arrival of Johnston and Davis had also drawn sightseers. Most residents and visitors had a false sense of security based on the withdrawal of the Union navy during the past summer. Now that same navy was bringing trouble.[6]

The Confederate defenders of Vicksburg had a warning system consisting of a telegraph connection with Point Lookout, some eleven miles south of Lake Providence upstream. There on Christmas Eve night, spotters saw Sherman's armada and clicked off an urgent message to Martin L. Smith in Vicksburg. Philip Fall received first word of the armada from L. L. Daniel, whose exaggerated report shocked Fall: "Good God, Phil, eighty-one transports loaded with Yankees, and gunboats galore, passing down the river, and many more behind moving on, . . . I can see lights as far as the eye can reach up the river." Fall, stationed on the Louisiana side of the Mississippi across from Vicksburg, boarded a skiff and took off across the river. He flashed his red light signal to keep the Vicksburg batteries from firing at him as he approached the docks.

Many officers in the city were enjoying themselves at the Balfours, home of William, a prominent Vicksburg physician, and his wife, Emma, who would gain notoriety as a diarist. A muddy and disheveled Fall arrived at the mansion and pushed his way through the dancers until he found a scowling General Smith, who demanded to know what this intruder wanted. When he heard the news, Smith's complexion whitened to "ashy pale," and he declared, "This ball is hereby at an end." The enemy had arrived at the gates and would be in the area by morning, and noncombatants should leave the city.[7]

On Christmas Day, Smith ordered his men into the defensive works and placed Stephen D. Lee, a talented young South Carolina officer and artillerist who had served well in Virginia, in command of the Walnut Hills front. Engineers had supervised construction of trenches where the plain met the bluffs, and at the foot of the bluffs along the River road, which connected Vicksburg to Yazoo City. A parallel road ran along the top of the bluffs and provided excellent tactical options for shifting troops. The bottomland fronted by the bluffs formed a rough triangle between the bluffs and the Yazoo. Chickasaw Bayou bisected the triangle; landmarks west of the stream included the Annie E. Lake and W. A. Johnson plantations. East of the stream lay Thompson Lake and north and east of the lake was Benson Blake's plantation. From McNutt Lake, the source of the bayou to the southwest, the bayou followed the base of the bluffs for about a mile, then meandered northeast and northwest, emptying into the Yazoo. Further upriver a creek, swamps, and two lakes combined to make approaches to the bluffs in that area difficult.

Stephen Lee liked what he saw. He concentrated his defensive positions at five spots along the bayou where Sherman most likely would cross. Beginning from the southwest and following the bayou northeast along the base of the bluffs, these areas included a local racetrack on the Johnson plantation road; an Indian mound, some four miles above Vicksburg where the bayou was very shallow; a place a half mile north of the Indian mound where the road from the Lake plantation crossed the Bayou on a corduroy bridge; a levee near the Blake plantation on the east side of Thompson Lake that accessed the River road; and the end of Lee's right flank at Snyder's Bluff. Lee was not concerned about Snyder's, where several big guns could hold off the enemy, nor did he worry about the Johnson plantation road near the racetrack, protected by abatis (sharpened poles with points thrust toward the enemy). His assumptions proved correct; the racetrack area and the bluffs were never seriously threatened. Lee's soldiers improved trenches and felled trees to protect other possible crossings. Lee placed one regiment and artillery at the Indian mound, four infantry regiments and artillery near the Lake plantation road, and one regiment in between. On the morning of December 26, news arrived that the enemy had landed at Johnson's plantation.

Martin L. Smith's veterans went into the fight with confidence. Although his infantry had been mostly observers during the summer campaign, the experience had hardened them, and they likely looked forward to this unexpected opportunity to shoot at Yankees. They had seen enough war to understand that Sherman's choice of a battlefield favored the defensive.

Now that he had committed his army, Sherman learned from scouts that geography faced by the troops was "as difficult as it could possibly be from nature and art. Immediately in our front was a bayou passable only at two points — on a narrow levee and on a sand bar, which was perfectly commanded by the enemy's sharpshooters that line the levee or parapet on its opposite bank. Behind this was an irregular strip of bench or table land, on which was constructed a series of rifle pits and batteries, and behind that a high, abrupt range of hills, whose scarred sides were marked all the way up with rifle-trenches, and the crowns of the principal hills presented heavy batteries." Sherman realized his men faced a daunting task, but he remained confident.[8]

As December 27 dawned, Sherman's army moved along the bottomland north of Lee's deployed army. On the Union left, Morgan marched his troops down the road past Mrs. Lake's home; he had instructions to follow this road to Chickasaw Bayou and use pontoons to cross the stream, turn on to the River road and gain a foothold on the bluffs. Steele's division moved past Morgan's left toward the hills, while Morgan Smith deployed on the right to block the River road. A detachment from Steele's division went ashore near the mouth of the bayou at Blake's Levee to prevent Confederates from detonating torpedoes on the Yazoo. Steele advanced down the east side of what he thought was the bayou to cooperate with Morgan, who also received support on his right from Frank Blair's brigade. Unfortunately for the plan, Sherman, or one of his staff, had mixed up Thompson Lake with Chickasaw Bayou. Confusion soon reigned on Sherman's left.[9]

David Porter's fleet shelled Snyder's Bluff as a diversion, while the army marched. Steele's troops cut their way from the Yazoo to the levee. Porter asked Steele's help in protecting troops still disembarking from transports. Confederate snipers had turned the unloading process into a dangerous business, but Federal infantry chased them away. Steele ordered his troops to advance, and his lead brigade soon clashed with Confederate pickets. By then, Steele realized he was in the wrong place; once his advance troops chased away outnumbered Rebels, he ordered his soldiers to bivouac for the night on the levee, without fires. Despite the cold, Steele did not want to advertise his strength to the enemy.[10]

Morgan's men also had a frustrating day. Concerned about artillery fire his men had received the day before north of the Lake plantation, he ordered a battery to provide cover. The division moved cautiously, searching for signs of the main Confederate line. In the same area, Frank Blair's troops sought a good position on Morgan's right west of the Lake place. Blair's and Morgan's movements had not gone unnoticed by Confederate observers. One of Lee's brigades, headquartered at Mrs. Lake's, realized enemy troops were approaching from two directions—north (Morgan) and east (Blair). Louisiana infantry and two cannon resisted Morgan's advance, while Mississippi infantry blocked Blair. Though the Confederates were heavily outnumbered, their token resistance gave Stephen Lee more time to solidify his main line. Superior Union firepower forced Lee's advance troops at Mrs. Lake's back to a line of trees bordering the property, the men still between the enemy and the main defensive line.

Morgan saw the Rebels retreat and resumed his advance; a four-gun battery provided cover by shelling the vulnerable Confederates, whose commander, fearing the shells meant a major assault, ordered his exposed artillery to cease fire and withdraw. Rebel infantry resorted to tactics of flanking and enfilading fire to exaggerate their numbers and slow Morgan's advance.[11]

On George Morgan's right, Morgan L. Smith's troops followed Blair's. After pausing for a brief artillery duel, scouts rode forward to check bayou crossings. Rebels could be seen ahead near an Indian mound, and Blair sent two regiments wading across deep water to check the enemy's strength. The Federals soon encountered Louisiana infantry deployed to protect a work party piling obstructions in front of the Indian mound. The Louisianans offered fierce resistance, and more Union troops came up. Confederates fell back into well-constructed rifle pits, where they kept superior numbers at bay until nightfall. During the night Union volunteers removed some Rebel obstructions, and in the predawn hours an artillery exchange forced outgunned Confederates to retreat again.[12]

George Morgan had a frustrating day. As his troops formed to attack Lee's Confederates at Mrs. Lake's, Wisconsin cannoneers blasted Confederates with 20-pound Parrott shells; a Louisiana detachment across the bayou shot at the artillerymen; and John De Courcy's brigade fired back, as did Wisconsin gunners. The Louisianans left quickly, but they had stalled many times their number until daylight passed, giving the Confederates more time to shore up their main lines and to bring up reinforcements.

During the first day's fighting, Lee's small advance unit had slowed a large enemy force across a wide front. Assisted by terrain, the Rebels had used effective tactics in moving infantry and artillery around just enough to frustrate practically every move Union officers made. These unsung troops bought Lee precious time, and with every tick of the clock reinforcements from Grenada got closer and Sherman's odds grew longer.

On the Yazoo, Porter likewise accomplished little in his efforts to provide cover for small vessels looking for mines. Louisiana infantry, manning big guns on the Yazoo bluffs, and assisted by gusty winds and a narrow channel, bested Porter's navy. The *Benton* especially took a pounding, and the flotilla retreated back downstream.

As night fell, more troops arrived on both sides. A. J. Smith's division finally reached the general campaign area at 1:00 P.M. on December 27. The troops took several hours to disembark and then marched into the night, reaching Johnson's plantation and camping in the area earlier occupied by Morgan Smith and Blair.[13]

John Pemberton rushed to the front two brigades from Grenada and a Georgia brigade from Bragg's army. Lee held John Gregg's Grenada brigade in reserve, while the other, John Vaughn's, deployed near the racetrack. Georgians commanded by Seth Barton reinforced the Louisianans at the Indian mound. Pemberton's line now consisted of Vaughn on the left, Barton in the center, and Stephen Lee's brigade on the right, with Gregg in reserve. Back in Grenada, Dabney Maury's two crack brigades, commanded by Louisianan Louis Hébert and Tennessean John Moore, entrained for Vicksburg. While Pemberton was counting on brigades to hold off Sherman's divisions, able Confederate commanders, good soldiers, and geographic advantages made the army a potent force.

December 28 dawned, and Sherman reviewed scouting reports and pondered strategic and tactical possibilities. The two best routes across

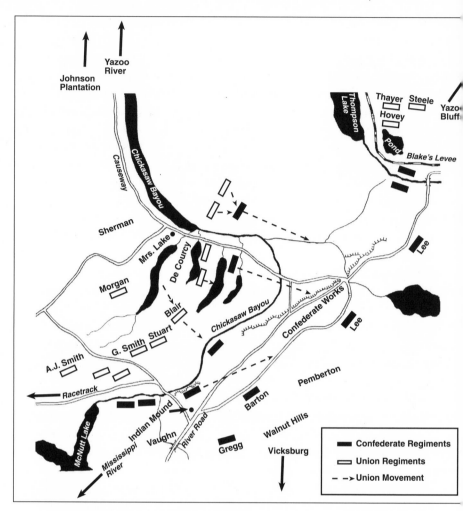

The Battle of Chickasaw Bayou: Action of
December 28, 1862. Map by Becky Smith.

troublesome Chickasaw Bayou, one at the Indian mound and the other
near Mrs. Lake's, remained formidable. The fortified River road gave
the Confederates a broad field of fire and also provided an interior line
for shifting troops. Sherman realized that he would have to break the
Confederate line before his men could climb the hills and fight their
way into Vicksburg. He needed the rail line that ran east in order to
block enemy reinforcements and to clear the way for Grant's expected
approach. Sherman clung to the illusion that Grant was still pushing
toward their planned rendezvous. Sherman could hear sounds of trains
in Vicksburg and cheering echoing among the ravines as more enemy

troops arrived, sounds that meant Grant was not in the Jackson-Vicksburg corridor.[14]

As Sherman grew anxious, Stephen Lee coolly adjusted his line, assigning troops to hold Blake's Levee on the Confederate right flank. At the River road, the levee turned sharply at a right angle and ran into a steep slope near a creek. A shallow pool lay within the angle, and the entire area had been obstructed. Confederates felt optimistic that eight infantry companies, consisting of Mississippians and Louisianans, and five pieces of 1st Mississippi Light Artillery could do the job.

While the small Rebel force dug in, Frederick Steele's troops across the way stirred in the early morning fog and advanced at 8:00 A.M. The advance soon ran into the Confederate infantry, which stopped Steele cold. The general personally examined the obstructed terrain and ordered a detachment to clear the way. Confederate fire cut down several Union soldiers, and a frustrated Steele brought up the 2nd Missouri Light Artillery; but Mississippi gunners held their own, though they slacked off because of dwindling ammunition.[15]

Steele thought the enemy guns had been disabled, and he ordered a charge. The narrow lane created by the lake and levee forced the Federals into a tight, massed formation, giving the Confederates a dense target they could hardly miss. As Steele's troops moved into the open, Lee's infantry and artillery sent rifle bullets and canister flying. Union troops dove for cover; when Steele received word that his casualties were mounting rapidly, he called off the attack. His men salvaged something by digging in beyond their starting point, which forced the small band of Rebels to hold where they were.

Steele's troops endured a sporadic artillery duel while the general waited for instructions from Sherman. An Iowan observed, "We could do nothing with them with the infantry," so ground troops kept their heads down during the shelling. Steele sent for more guns, and the increased firepower forced artillerists under the command of Colonel William T. Withers, one of Lee's talented brigade commanders, to take cover. Union artillery won the exchange but could not break the stalemate. Sherman ordered a withdrawal that evening, and Steele took his division back downriver to Johnson's plantation, where he was assigned to support Morgan. Withers's troops welcomed reinforcements and celebrated Steele's departure.[16]

Morgan accomplished no more than Steele did on the twenty-eighth. Early that morning, Morgan ordered artillery to soften Rebel defenses at the River road roadblock. As gunners prepared, the fog dissipated, and Louisiana infantry greeted the batteries with several volleys. The bemused artillerists had taken positions out of rifle range, however, and they poured shot and shell at obstructions where Mrs. Lake's property met the River road, prompting a response from Mississippi gunners. Morgan decided his guns would prevail, so he formed infantry to take the offensive. John De Courcy's brigade led the way, and Louisianans rose from their position in a "shallow ravine" to fire into De Courcy's flank. The Union advance came to a stop until De Courcy's right wing outflanked the Confederate position, but Lee's men counterattacked, though, being heavily outnumbered, they soon had to retire. Their resistance, however, deflated the attack on Morgan's front.[17]

The Louisianans re-formed and waited for expected reinforcements, but help failed to arrive, and the Louisianans pulled back across Chickasaw Bayou. Encouraged, De Courcy ordered his troops forward, supported by two additional brigades.

While troop movements continued, artillery exchanges made life dangerous for both sides. The small area of operations continued to negate Federal superiority in numbers and quality of guns. After the Louisianans retreated, concentrated Rebel artillery slowed Union advances. Though Federal gunners produced limited tactical gains, advantageous fields of fire allowed Mississippi artillerists to stand firmly by their guns. Confederate strategic withdrawals brought Pemberton's men closer to their main defensive lines along the bluffs, where their fire would be even more effective. Thus Federal divisions making progress would ultimately expose themselves to massed enemy firepower.[18]

Unfortunately for Morgan, his infantry accomplished little after the Louisianans withdrew. De Courcy's men closed in on a strong line of Rebel rifle pits and stopped for unclear reasons, though probably out of an instinct for survival. Elsewhere Morgan's reserves and a detachment on his left fared slightly better. Union troops on the east side of the bayou chased a Louisiana brigade from its forward position, but Confederate artillery stopped the Yankees, ending fighting on Morgan's front for the day. The two lines in some sections were close, and conversations ensued. Confederates tossed cornbread over the no-man's land to hungry, appreciative Federals.

Frank Blair's brigade had been held in reserve at the beginning of the day. At midmorning, it moved to the front, without artillery on account of the rugged terrain, and deployed on Morgan Smith's right. Blair advanced, his men exchanging fire with Georgians across the bayou. A few hours of fighting accomplished nothing, and Blair attempted to withdraw to support De Courcy. However, when Blair's men tried to disengage, they found themselves caught in artillery crossfire, and they had to stay put. Blair then tried to provide support across the bayou, but by the time his men got beyond the stream night had fallen, and, like the rest of the army, they camped in the cold without fires, which would have given away their position.[19]

On the Union right, December 28 brought similar frustrations. Detachments had managed to clear many obstructions around the Indian mound, but Confederate sniping slowed the removal of big felled trees across the ford. Louisianans in the area expertly picked off blue-coated soldiers who got in the line of fire. Powder and smoke from continual firing blacked the faces of the men from the Bayou State, causing some Union soldiers to think they were fighting slaves. Morgan Smith, ordered to coordinate his division's advance with George Morgan's, rode forward to observe and was felled by a sniper's bullet. David Stuart took over and sent for reinforcements.

Across the way, Seth Barton liked the Louisianans' position, supported by a Tennessee regiment and artillery, covering the ford. Barton placed his Georgia troops among the slopes of the Walnut Hills and warned his officers to be ready to shift quickly. The Confederate shuffle soon began, as Lee maneuvered to meet various threats. Barton sent Tennesseans to Lee and shifted Georgians to cover the vacated spot. Several Confederate companies shifted to help each other hold off Union thrusts. Lee, Barton, and John Gregg moved Georgians and Tennesseans to defend the Indian mound against De Courcy. The Confederates stood firm, despite Union cannon barrages.[20]

The fighting ebbed and flowed, each side absorbing casualties and refusing to give. The crack of musketry, according to one Confederate, almost drowned out "the thunder of the artillery." Erroneous news from Sherman that Morgan had crossed the bayou forced Stuart to send a brigade in support, though he warned that a crossing was "utterly impracticable." He called for volunteers to clear remaining obstructions, but guns of the 14th Mississippi Light Artillery ended the effort and by dark nothing had changed. While the fighting sputtered to an end on December 28, more Confederate reinforcements arrived.

A. J. Smith had quite a day directing traffic. He sent support to Morgan Smith's right and to the junction of Mrs. Lake's lane and the Vicksburg road. Other dispositions included sending a brigade to shore up Giles Smith's right and a battery to the road junction. Federal shifting to solidify the front posed no threat to Confederates whose dispositions commanded all approaches to the hills.[21]

During the twenty-eighth, Porter's fleet, supporting Sherman's troops, shelled Rebel positions while infantry officers tried to maneuver to better locations. Ironclads lobbed shells at Drumgould's Bluff to pin Rebel troops there. The shelling accomplished that, but did little else other than irritating Confederates setting up another battery.[22]

Although action on the twenty-eighth had brought some Union tactical successes, in truth Sherman's army had succeeded at little more than forcing Confederate units back into their strong defensive lines at the foot of the Walnut Hills bluffs. The day's events ensured that any further assaults by Sherman's army would meet with powerful resistance, growing ever stronger as reinforcements continued strengthening formidable Rebel works.

Two days of fighting had produced a stalemate and nothing more, and on the twenty-ninth Sherman planned to hit the Confederates with overwhelming numbers. He could not stay indefinitely where he was, and he realized that success required breaking through the enemy so that he could enter Vicksburg. He knew more Rebel troops were flooding into town, but he had no idea of Pemberton's strength. No additional Union troops were coming, since the hope of Grant's showing up was gone. With Pemberton controlling most railroads in the state, enemy troop strength could continue to grow unless Grant — and William Rosecrans in Tennessee — accomplished something dramatic. Sherman had heard nothing directly from Grant and had no news of Rosecrans, nor had there been any word from Nathaniel Banks, commanding Union troops to the south in Louisiana and supposedly on his way north. For the moment, Sherman was isolated.[23]

Sherman's plan to break the stalemate seemed simple, but deceptively so. George Morgan would march his division past Mrs. Lake's across Chickasaw Bayou, brush aside entrenched Confederates and take control of the Walnut Hills. Steele's division would provide support and occupy the River road. A. J. Smith, commanding his and Morgan Smith's divisions would cross the bayou at the Indian mound and overwhelm Confederate works covering the River road. If these goals could be achieved as easily as the plan sounded, they would have already been accomplished. Sherman mistakenly believed that coordinated sheer force could overcome the difficult geography and a well-positioned enemy.

Morgan spent the night of December 28–29 preparing for the assault as per Sherman's orders. Between the Indian mound and where the road from Mrs. Lake's crossed the bayou on a corduroy bridge, there appeared to be a weak spot not occupied by Rebels. Confederate commanders felt the Bayou there was barrier enough. Morgan ordered his men to bridge the water during the night. If all went well, Union troops could pour across and take the heights before Lee's Confederates reacted. Sherman approved.[24]

In the darkness, Morgan's engineers and volunteers bridged the wrong stream and had to start over. Engineering problems produced more delays, and as morning light filtered through the trees, Confederate scouts sounded the alarm. Mississippi artillery boomed, and the bridge crew scattered. A Federal regiment rushed forward to provide cover; Lee heard the commotion and immediately shifted troops, and Morgan's hope for surprise was gone. Lee sent Louisianans and Georgians rushing to the scene, later reinforced by Mississippians. The rest of the morning blue and gray fired at each other across the bayou. Rebel artillery was too high on the hills for gunners to effectively depress, or push down, cannon muzzles, but shells knocked tree limbs into Union ranks.

Morgan feared the reinforced Rebel line foretold an attack on the Union right, and he ordered Blair to back up De Courcy. Then Morgan changed his mind and sent Blair left to assault the Confederate right. While moving left, Blair's troops had to cross a bayou branch and go up a high bank. Cleverly constructed Rebel obstructions, natural geographic features, and double enemy lines of infantry supported by artillery made the task daunting.[25]

Blair sent an Illinois regiment forward, and they found empty trenches. Lee had pulled the Louisianans back, hoping to lure an attack, and had further told his men to stay low and hold their fire until Blair's advance got close. About this time an artillery duel erupted on Blair's right, and shot and shell rained on both sides of the bayou. Union shells destroyed a Rebel caisson coming up the River road. Lee's artillerists watched with disgust as much needed ammunition disappeared in a series of explosions.

By now, George Morgan had changed his mind, canceled the attack and so notified Sherman. A disgusted Sherman rode from his headquarters at Mrs. Lake's to look at Morgan's front. He saw the corduroy bridge, and the Confederate-infested bluffs beyond, pointed, and said simply, "That is the route to take!" and rode back to his headquarters. He then sent back a message, "Tell Morgan to give the signal for assault; that we will lose 5,000 men before we take Vicksburg, and may as well lose them here as anywhere else." Morgan passed the word to Blair and De Courcy. De Courcy could not believe what he heard and personally confronted Morgan, who confirmed the attack. De Courcy blurted, "My poor brigade!" and promised to do as ordered.[26]

Blair's comments are not recorded; he immediately massed his brigade in a double-line formation, fifty yards apart. Blair told his commanders to charge on a given signal; De Courcy likewise formed for the attack. The assault must be made, according to Sherman's orders, regardless of the bridge's condition. John Thayer's brigade, from Steele's division, provided support. Morgan's plan of attack called for Blair, Thayer, and De Courcy to slam headlong into the Confederate lines, while two other brigades crossed the bayou and attempted to get between Lee's and Barton's troops.

On the Confederate side, soldiers tensed, because they knew what all the Union movements meant. Pemberton arrived at the front to see for himself what was going on. After being briefed, he ordered two Louisiana regiments and a cannon to Lee from the Blake's Levee detachment. The Confederates would still be outnumbered, but high ground and a concentrated target remained on their side. The troops left at Blake's had to hold Steele in place. Every move was a gamble.[27]

Around noon, eighteen Union cannon boomed the attack signal. Blair's men crashed through obstacles to their front, crossed the stream, and scaled the opposite bank. The Confederate advance line melted away as outnumbered Rebels retreated in good order. On Lee's main line, three Tennessee brigades waited. Many blue-coated soldiers fell during the initial action, but Blair must have felt good, for his men had kept a steady forward pace, and over to his right De Courcy had also made good progress.

The initial success on Blair and De Courcy's front turned out to be the only highlight of their day. As Blair's men neared the Tennesseans, rifles roared, and Federal dead and wounded quickly littered the landscape. Blair urged his men on, but it soon became apparent to both Blair and De Courcy that to continue would result in unjustified slaughter. On the right, the brigades that attempted to push between Lee and Barton met similar fates, and they too pulled back. A Georgian rejoiced, but was repelled by "the feeling it put into me to see men shot down like hogs, and to see a man dead, all torn to pieces from shell fire."[28]

In his support role, Thayer experienced much frustration. Two Iowa regiments of his brigade moved to De Courcy's right after crossing the bayou. One moved forward, urged on by Thayer toward the Confederate left, but there were no troops to provide support. The attack stalled, and a survivor wrote, "At once the hills in front seemed a sheet of flame and smoke! Cannon and musket 'volleyed and thundered.' Still our lines swept on and on, floundering through mud and water, at times above their knees, their ranks being rapidly decimated by the destructive fire of the enemy." Finally, being the only unit left south of the bayou, the Iowans retreated. Lee, seeing success all along the line, sent two Louisiana regiments on a sortie that resulted in the capture of prisoners, guns, and flags. Confederates rushed severely wounded Federals to Vicksburg hospitals, where they received better care than they expected.

Despite surprisingly high morale among survivors, Morgan decided against renewing the assaults and went to see Sherman. They talked about the repulse, and Morgan proposed a truce to bury the dead and retrieve the wounded between the lines. Sherman at first refused, for a truce would be an admission of defeat. As daylight faded, he changed his mind, and Morgan wrote a note to Pemberton. A truce party attempting to deliver the message in growing darkness had to retreat when Confederates, unable to see the white flag, began shooting.[29]

On the Union far right, A. J. Smith sent his troops in early on the twenty-ninth. He ordered Giles Smith to charge across the Indian mound ford of the bayou and capture the hills beyond. Work details cut a ramp into the steep bank on the other side of the bayou to facilitate the assault. A Missouri regiment led the work party, followed by the three remaining brigade regiments, plus Illinois artillery. David Stuart's brigade from Morgan Smith's division (which Stuart now led) and William Landram's troops moved to the right to the racetrack to occupy Confederates and expand the Union front. Two Tennessee regiments watched and waited.

Seth Barton's soldiers on the Confederate left endured heavy shelling early in the morning; then Union guns quieted until around 11:00 A.M. The Rebels used the time to build up defenses; then Morgan's signal volley erupted, and A. J. Smith's advance raced forward. At the front, the attempt to cut into the opposite bank did not work, so engineers began mining operations. Four Mississippi guns, positioned only about forty yards away, made the task perilous. Giles Smith saw a path to the left and ordered the Missourians to shift and cross there. These soldiers managed to get across the bayou and take cover under the high bank. Louisianans fired effectively into Union workers attempting to cut another passage, and Georgians arrived on the scene to support hard-pressed Tennesseans. Confederates used their cover well, sometimes raising their guns above their heads and firing blindly in the direction of the enemy. Union troops had become so compressed that Rebel infantry succeeded without aiming.[30]

John Thayer, fresh from being repulsed at the causeway, and the remainder of his regiments arrived to cover Morgan's right, but their presence did not change the situation. Charles Hovey's brigade of

Steele's division prepared an assault where Blair's men had been poised earlier in the day; but then word came that Blair had withdrawn, and Sherman vetoed further attacks. Missourians still pinned down on the wrong side of the bayou finally got out with the help of cover fire from their brigade and darkness. Across the way, a Tennessee regiment arrived to support Barton's position. With the failure at the Indian mound, the Union attack of the twenty-ninth ended all along the battle line.

Sherman shouldered the blame for the day's failures. He thought his men had done the best they could and expressed himself "generally satisfied with the high spirit manifested" by the troops. That night he conferred with Porter; Porter's fleet had failed again to do any damage to Confederate positions on the Yazoo bluffs. Porter sent a boat to Memphis to get more small-arms ammunition, for Sherman decided to continue the fight. First he pulled the troops back out of artillery range and ordered them to camp, while a detachment conducted a reconnaissance.[31]

In Vicksburg that evening, Carter Stevenson's division from Bragg's army and a portion of Dabney Maury's brigade from Grenada arrived. Stevenson led an untested division, but for the moment numbers mattered more than experience. Joseph Johnston, still in Jackson, thought Stevenson's men should be held in reserve, but he rushed the division to Vicksburg after receiving a Pemberton wire: "I want all the troops I can get." A cold rain fell that night; Rebel cannoneers amused themselves by shooting at every noise across the bayou, noise mostly made by work parties trying to retrieve pontoons.

Maury marched his men to the front in the inky darkness; the distant rustling of the enemy was punctuated by haunting groans of wounded. Many Confederates shuddered at the sight of "lanterns of the surgeons and hospital men" that illuminated "a weird and fearful picture of the night." Maury found Lee and reported that he had 400 men with him now; the rest should arrive by morning. Maury frankly told Lee that even though they had equal rank, Lee should tell him where to deploy. "I will be responsible for all the failures if any occur, and you shall have all the glory. I know you are going to win," Maury assured an appreciative Lee.[32]

Union soldiers heard the trains and knew what they meant. They also saw slaves in the distance working to strengthen Rebel works. Soldiers tried to overcome miserable conditions by making beds of leaves and brush, which provided little relief from the rain. Most suffered through the stormy night without cover. One soldier wrote, "When daylight [of the thirtieth] *at last* dawned upon the pitiful scene we found ourselves in a swamp—(every inch of which stood under water) stiff blue and teeth rattling, scarcely able to walk, and many totally unable to speak!" Indeed large segments of the Union lines lay segmented among watery swamps, their plight made worse by the cold and the fire ban. An Illinoisan spoke for many, "I thought I would freeze to death." Other soldiers complained that Confederates had poisoned the spring water, and that several men died from drinking it. Perhaps, but it is more likely the men consumed naturally polluted swamp water.[33]

By the morning of December 30, Sherman had concluded that the Confederate line along the bluffs could not be broken. He told Porter that the army and navy should jointly assault the Yazoo bluffs, with 10,000 army troops assigned to the attack. Sherman thought the almost perpendicular terrain might provide good cover; if successful, the army might still make it into Vicksburg. Porter agreed to try. While Alfred Ellet's boats scouted for more water mines, Porter selected transports with the quietest engines to shift troops. If the Confederates got wind of what Sherman had in mind, they would immediately move to counter the attack.[34]

While Sherman and Porter plotted, skirmishing continued along the previous days' battlefronts, until a truce allowed Federals to retrieve dead and wounded. Soldiers on both sides had heard enough of the haunting sounds of Union wounded: "Oh boys! Come & help me," "Oh God, I am dying." Sherman's men had been frustrated at watching helplessly while comrades crawled about the battlefield in search of succor. Many grew angry when they found dead bodies stripped of clothing and shoes, and among the dead several appeared to have been initially wounded, then bayoneted or shot in the head to finish them off. Others no doubt died from lack of treatment and exposure to the weather. The dead had begun to smell in spite of low temperatures, thus adding to the distasteful task of retrieving wounded. Transporting survivors complicated the Union retreat to the Yazoo and shifting fronts.[35]

On December 31, the movement began. Porter sent Ellet with a team of volunteers to blow up a Confederate raft on the Yazoo at Snyder's Bluff; then he organized the loading of troops onto transports under cover of darkness. Union soldiers overheard Confederates in the area talking, rather loudly no doubt, of how many "damned niggers" would be freed the next day when Abraham Lincoln's Emancipation Proclamation went into effect. Many soldiers in blue, fighting to hold the

Union together but not sympathetic to black freedom, also opposed the proclamation.[36]

In Vicksburg, as the momentous year of 1862 drifted to a close, a resident named Mahala Roach penned her thoughts about its impact. "My life this year formed a great contrast to last year; then, I was in my home surrounded by all that could make life desirable; the dreadful war had not then affected *me*, and I lead [led] a gay, rather careless life. Now, I am an exile, and may soon be homeless. The tide of war has rolled to our very doors and a battle is now raging only a few miles from our home." She spoke for many who continued to endure at Vicksburg.[37]

Citizens and defenders of Vicksburg had indeed experienced quite a year, highlighted by two large-scale attacks. Thus far, the city remained safe, if somewhat scarred, but realities of war had invaded the town, and its residents could no longer pretend to be insulated from the conflict. This second attempt by Sherman's army, after Farragut and Davis had failed, served notice that Vicksburg's fate remained uncertain. Lincoln still aimed to get the key in his pocket, and U. S. Grant and his generals would not go away until the job was done.

January 1, 1863, dawned with a thick fog blanketing the Yazoo, symbolic of the city's gloomy new year. With visibility limited to a few feet, the Union expedition could not get under way. Porter told Sherman that conditions and delays made a daylight landing at the bluff necessary and very hazardous. Sherman now faced the reality that a large portion of the army waited aboard boats that could not maneuver in the fog; the rest remained in a low area that additional rains could flood more severely. These circumstances, coupled with the seemingly nonstop sounds of additional Rebel troops arriving at the train station, plus a message from Grant that the North Mississippi front had been abandoned, convinced Sherman to give up the campaign. He had lost 208 killed, 1,005 wounded, and 563 missing; enemy losses, on the other hand, were only 57 killed, 120 wounded, and 10 missing. Union wounded filled six hospital boats. Men lay about the decks with "every conceivable character of wound that your imagination can paint, contused, lacerated, gunshot," and "many of the poor fellows have been laying with wounds undressed and dangling limbs unamputated."[38]

An Ohioan recalled band music on January 1. Union musicians played "Dixie" as if saluting the victorious Rebels. A Confederate band struck up "Get Out of the Wilderness," as the Federal army left Chickasaw Bayou swampland. Sherman's soldiers criticized the leaders of their doomed efforts. One Iowan saw the campaign as "the useless, and seemingly senseless slaughter connected with Sherman's assaults upon those impregnable hills." A veteran wrote his family of rumors Sherman had been arrested for attacking without orders. Another bitter Union soldier wrote, "Sherman or Grant or both had made a bad blunder to say the least of it." Sherman had not been arrested, of course, but failure fueled such talk. The Federals had, in the words of a Confederate doctor, simply found Vicksburg "a hard nut to crack."[39]

A Missouri journalist made no effort to hide his disgust at the outcome. People would demand answers, he wrote, and when questions "are answered, the causes will be found in the mismanagement, incompetence, and probable insanity of the commanding general, and the intemperance, negligence, and general inefficiency of nearly the whole of the line and field-officers of his command." The newsman concluded that the whole operation seemed poorly planned and haphazardly executed.[40]

Confederates celebrated, one writing elatedly: "Vicksburg has made a name. It will be a green feather in any man's cap to have it said he was a defender of the Hill City." Stephen Lee remained concerned that another assault might be forthcoming. He sent troops to harass the Union withdrawal, just to be sure the enemy had given up the fight. Union gunboats kept the Confederates at bay, while one nervous boat pilot had to be forced at gunpoint not to pull away from the landing until his vessel was full. On January 2, the entire Federal force steamed downstream into the Mississippi, and up to Milliken's Bend, where John McClernand awaited.[41]

McClernand had finally arrived to take over the Mississippi River expedition. Disappointed that Grant had not been in Memphis to greet him, McClernand left the city on December 30 and proceeded downriver to Helena and conferred with General Gorman. The subject of Arkansas Post came up.

A settlement on the Arkansas River, Arkansas Post had at one time been the capital of Arkansas Territory. In 1862, Theophilus Holmes sent an officer to select defensive sites that protected access to the state's capital, Little Rock, as well as the Arkansas River Valley. Arkansas Post made the list, and the resulting fortification there became known as Fort Hindman in honor of General Thomas Hindman, Holmes's predecessor. The fort was designed as a defensive military position and as a base from which Confederate vessels could operate against Union shipping on the Mississippi.[42]

Federal general Alvin Hovey recognized the strategic significance of

Fort Hindman; hence his earlier expedition. The importance of the place had been further underscored when Rebel troops operating from the Post area forced a Union supply boat, the *Blue Wing*, to surrender on December 29 near the mouth of the White River. Despite this, Union officers debated whether the fort was worth a large campaign. McClernand soon insisted that it was, but did the idea originate with McClernand or Sherman?

During a conference aboard Porter's flagship on the stormy night of January 2, Sherman learned of McClernand's arrival. Porter later claimed that during their conversation he and Sherman discussed an attack on Arkansas Post. Porter perhaps first heard mention of it from Sherman, and Sherman later insisted it was his idea, not McClernand's. Sherman made no mention of the idea in his post–Chickasaw Bayou campaign report to Grant. Porter, known for creative reporting of events, could possibly have intended to steal thunder from McClernand. It is just as likely, perhaps more so, that Sherman and McClernand both had the idea, but it seems certain that McClernand made a decision to act after his Helena conference with Gorman. Sherman, no doubt miffed at having to surrender immediate command of his force to McClernand, insisted afterward that the latter had no definite ideas about the campaign. Perhaps so, perhaps not, but the controversy portended future problems. McClernand's mere presence seemed to agitate fellow officers.[43]

McClernand and Sherman met on January 3 aboard the *Tigress*. McClernand's version of the meeting is not recorded, so Sherman's written account must be viewed with care. Sherman said that they discussed the *Blue Wing*, that McClernand had no plans except to open the Mississippi to the Gulf, and that McClernand opposed taking Arkansas Post, contradicting McClernand's documented endorsement of the campaign. They all agreed that Sherman must forget about operating on the Yazoo. McClernand suggested, according to Sherman, that future options should be discussed with Porter.

The three met the next night, apparently in an atmosphere of ill will. Despite his initial favorable opinion of McClernand's non–West Point background, Porter now detested the Illinois politician, though the exact cause of his feelings is not known. McClernand's perceived rudeness to Sherman, whom Porter liked, only exacerbated the situation, at least in Porter's eyes. Porter told McClernand that if Sherman led the expedition, he and his fleet would participate in the capture of Arkansas Post. McClernand supposedly masked his anger, but Sherman pulled Porter aside and asked him to cool off, warning him that McClernand did not like Sherman anyway and that such comments would only make matters worse. Porter refused to back down, but tempers moderated, and McClernand and Porter apparently agreed that each could tolerate the other's coming along on the expedition. Porter wrote shortly afterward that he much preferred serving under Sherman, who was smarter than McClernand.[44]

McClernand took personal command of Sherman's army on January 4. In doing so on his own, he ignored the fact that Grant commanded all river operations. McClernand called his force of some 32,000 the Army of the Mississippi, to consist of Sherman's XV Corps and the XIII Corps commanded by George Morgan, whom Sherman blamed in part, and unjustly, for the failure at Chickasaw Bayou. McClernand's objective was to erase a threat to Union communications. Attacking Vicksburg at the moment was out of the question since the hill city had been heavily reinforced. There had been no word from Nathaniel Banks, and McClernand thought his army too large to be sitting around doing nothing. With the Union navy dominating the Mississippi, taking Fort Hindman might seem no more significant than swatting a fly. Yet militarily the campaign seemed justified, and Sherman later claimed it was, as did Grant, once he found out Sherman approved. Despite officer politics and infighting, the campaign seemed likely to raise troop morale, if nothing else.

McClernand showed good judgment in planning the strike at Fort Hindman. He understood, perhaps from what he had learned of Sherman's experience, that he should consider geographic factors in the Arkansas Post area. He briefed both corps commanders on the river route to the Post region, gave them instructions for troop deployment, and urged them to exercise initiative. Sherman would take the lead and advance on the right, with Morgan following on Sherman's left. Troop transports would go up the White River and turn into a connecting waterway to the Arkansas; hopefully, this indirect approach would confuse the Confederates. McClernand informed other commanders in the region about the campaign, including Samuel Curtis, who commanded the department. Curtis could coordinate his own operations against Little Rock with McClernand's campaign, thus diluting enemy resistance.[45]

Unfortunately for McClernand, his big mouth and natural abrasiveness went out of control about this time, agitating those whose power was greater than his. Still irked about his earlier treatment by Henry Halleck, McClernand requested that President Lincoln relieve Halleck, who doled out preferential treatment to West Pointers. McClernand also failed to notify Grant in timely fashion of the Post campaign. Grant, still having communications problems thanks to Van Dorn and Forrest, had not received messages of any kind from McClernand until his arrival in Memphis on January 10.

On January 11, in response to McClernand's letter detailing the Post operation, Grant angrily said that the expedition was a waste of time while Vicksburg remained in enemy hands. He did not absolutely forbid it but made clear it should not be done unless "absolutely necessary" for the reduction of Vicksburg. In Grant's view, the inability of the Confederates in Arkansas to transfer men to Pemberton made capturing Arkansas Post superfluous. The move, he wrote to McClernand, "might answer some of the purposes you suggest, but certainly not as a Military movement looking to the accomplishment of the one great result, the capture of Vicksburg." Grant concluded that, unless there were considerations he did not know about, McClernand should wait at Milliken's Bend for Banks and other reinforcements. Grant then notified Halleck of McClernand's "wild-goose chase." Grant's message arrived downstream too late to halt the expedition, and his language gave McClernand a loophole to proceed anyway.[46]

McClernand's wild-goose chase concerned Confederates. Brigadier General Thomas Churchill, a prewar Little Rock postmaster, commanded 5,000 men at Fort Hindman, and on January 8 he received reports of the enemy's approach. Scouts watched the Union fleet enter the White and then the Arkansas. The misdirection did not fool anybody, and Churchill knew he faced a severe challenge. With only three brigades and four unattached units, which included one six-gun Arkansas battery, it would take a miracle to hold off two Union corps and Porter's gunboats. River obstructions might slow and aggravate the Yankees but could hardly accomplish more than that.[47]

As Union transports steamed along, sights along the banks captured the attention of troops aboard. One soldier saw "several women and children all huddled together, and they were the hardest looking set of women that my eyes ever rested on. Never have I seen astonishment so well depicted. If the ghastly phantom Death had stood before them with all his terrors they could not have been more so. Their eyes started from their sockets as they strained forward for a better view of our coming." Like noncombatants in Vicksburg and in North Mississippi, Arkansans found war on their doorstep startling and frightening. McClernand's troops landed during the night of January 9 at a farm east of Fort Hindman on the north bank of the Arkansas. One brigade from Peter

Osterhaus's division of Morgan's corps disembarked to block Confederate attempts to send reinforcements from Little Rock.[48]

Churchill's pickets sounded the alarm, and his commanders nervously prepared to meet the Federals. Two of the three brigades rushed to outer rifle pits one and a half miles below Hindman. This proved to be an imprudent move, for Porter's boats immediately began shelling exposed Rebel flanks. The Confederates fell back to less-exposed works adjacent to the fort. Churchill's artillery, outnumbered and hampered by defective powder, responded ineffectively to Porter's shelling.

The Confederate retreat from outer works allowed Union commanders to advance their infantry to a plateau north of the fort where troops could shoot down at the Rebels. The fort's squared logs covered with railroad iron could be hit by arching shots from artillery, and the plateau gave Federal infantry the opportunity to compound Churchill's problems. Porter sent three gunboats — the *Louisville*, the *Baron De Kalb*, and the *Cincinnati* — upriver to shell the fort. Two lighter vessels, the *Black Hawk* and the *Lexington*, followed, firing into the Confederates, while the *Rattler* steamed into position to shoot into the enemy in the trenches near the fort. Confederate gunners temporarily disabled the *Rattler*, managing to keep up a spirited duel well into the evening in spite of the powder problem. The night scenes on the Arkansas impressed an Iowan: "Lying in the river is the fleet with their signal lights of various colors, mingling their different hues with the reflection of the beautiful bright stars in the water, while a shell would pass like a fiery meteor through the air, leaving a line of splendor in the water and forming one of the grandest sights the eye ever beheld." Meanwhile, Union infantry deployed for the next day's assault.

Churchill's line stretched from the fort to Post Bayou. That night an ominous message from General Holmes arrived; Churchill should hold out until the last man or until relief arrived, whichever came first. Churchill told his officers to take the orders literally. Men in the ranks no doubt scoffed at Holmes's hyperbole; they had no intention of voluntarily being slaughtered.[49]

January 11 dawned bright and sunny, bringing relief to men who had shivered through a cold night. McClernand and his officers spent the early daylight hours finalizing assault plans. Porter opened the fight when his gunboats began shelling Confederate lines around 1:00 P.M. When Rebel artillery responded weakly, Sherman did not wait until the scheduled attack time of 1:30. Perhaps hoping to steal thunder from McClernand, he sent his men forward in a massed attack. Porter saw

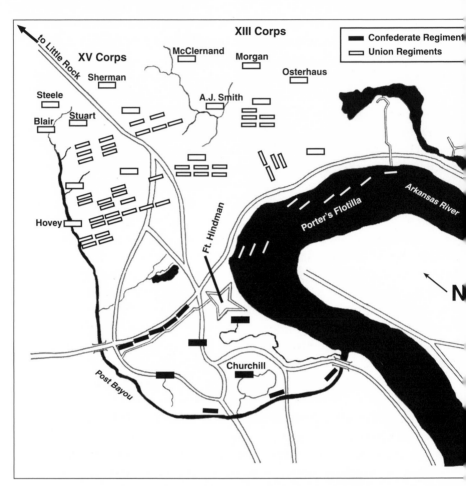

The Battle of Arkansas Post, January 10–11, 1863. Map by Becky Smith.

the charge, moved his boats closer to the fort, and gave Sherman cover fire.

Rebel resistance proved strong despite the numerical disparities. One Illinois soldier remembered how he and his comrades, already uncomfortable from being "wet up to our knees," had to endure a storm of artillery shot and "thousands of musket balls." Union soldiers dropped down, rolled over on their backs, put the butts of their rifles between their legs and loaded, rolled back over, and fired. This procedure allowed them to stay low, and they kept shooting as they crawled ever closer to enemy lines.[50]

The Confederates fought ferociously, but they were too few and had too many artillery deficiencies to challenge the Federal juggernaut for

long. By 3:00 P.M., white flags—adapted from underwear, shirts, hand-
kerchiefs, and anything else the right color—fluttered along Rebel
lines. Churchill had not authorized surrender, but apparently some of
his men quickly decided on their own that it made no sense to continue,
Holmes's message notwithstanding. When Union soldiers charged,
most Confederates threw down their arms and threw up their hands. A
Union soldier observed that the Rebels, though stout and hardy looking, were mostly ragged and dirty, and only a few seemed bitter about
the surrender.[51]

Victorious Federals recaptured boxes of new Enfield rifles, and many
exchanged their guns for the captured pieces. They also found among
the dead, wounded, and prisoners pieces of Federal mail that could at
last be sent north. Churchill had known he could not hold out indefinitely, but he had hoped to continue until dark, when he could extricate as many men as possible. Of course with McClernand's army widely
spread out, escape would have been problematical at best. In any event,
surrender flags torpedoed that hope, and Churchill ordered all his men
to lay down their arms. The men who surrendered soon boarded Federal boats bound for St. Louis, where they would be held until exchanged. Aside from some 60 killed and 80 wounded, Churchill surrendered 4,793; McClernand's losses included 134 killed, 898 wounded,
and 29 missing, and Porter reported 30 killed and wounded. The figures demonstrated that Churchill's men had given a good account of
themselves.[52]

The carnage impressed Union soldiers. An Indianan wrote his family
about numerous dead Rebels and sounds of the wounded "groaning
and struggling for aid." Then he changed the subject with "but enough
of that." Another Hoosier noted, "I went into the old fort, the sight was
sickening, the gunners and their assistants were all shot and torn, their
blood being splattered against the walls. Some had had their clothing
burned almost all off of them." Outside the fort, "men lay torn and
bleeding and dying. The pits were full of dead and wounded. Fire had
broken out in the buildings connected with the fort which had driven
them out of their breast works, causing them to be exposed to our rifle
and cannon shot."[53]

As Union troops leveled what was left of Fort Hindman, more of
them saw the ravages of war. One soldier described "guns dismounted,
men all killed and torn in fragments, not a whole carcass to be seen;
while along the line of works men and horses lay in piles." An Iowan
described in graphic detail the scenes of horror: "We saw the gaping
mouth and glaring eye over which the dull color of the butternut uni-

form cast its sickly hue. But here a still worse picture met the eye in face contortions; in brainless skulls; in limbless and headless bodies; here an arm, there a leg and close by, two booted and stockinged feet, still standing in their place but from which had crawled away the mangled body, leaving the red stains as the life blood gushed out." Some Confederates had hurriedly disposed of their own dead by pitching the corpses into gullies and pushing in banks of dirt on top. Rain later washed away the dirt, leaving bodies exposed.[54]

The cleanup proved daunting. Burial parties interred Confederates in trenches six feet wide and three to four feet deep. They placed corpses so that heads were near the fort and feet faced south toward the river. Union dead were taken to a spot in the woods northwest of the fort and placed in separate graves, their bodies covered with rubber blankets. Rare, heavy snow fell the next day, compounding burial tasks. The experience touched many, including a Wisconsin soldier who warned his wife: "I am A thousand times meaner A hundred times Harder and A damed sight wors Looking than I Ever was so you can form some sort of an idea what sort of A Looking man you have now for A Husband if this kind of Buisness wont make men hard I should like to know what will it is Every one for himself and dam the one that pulls the hind tit."[55]

The Arkansas Post campaign opened river approaches to Little Rock and undercut already shaky morale in Confederate Arkansas. A Little Rock newspaper editor wrote, "The taking of the Post is an unexpected blow to our people, and one which will be felt throughout our length and breadth." The Union victory helped restore the morale of most of Sherman's men, who wanted to forget Chickasaw Bayou. Still, an Ohio soldier wrote his parents that after Arkansas Post many men deserted, weather and camp conditions continued to be bad, and many soldiers suffered from various illnesses. An Illinoisan disagreed, however, when he wrote home that while Chickasaw Bayou had greatly discouraged the boys, the Arkansas Post campaign helped renew fighting spirits. Another veteran wrote that the boys yelled themselves "hoarse," because "this was our first victory and we had allmost become discouraged." Despite muddy, wet conditions, many no doubt saw Arkansas Post as a great victory at a small cost.[56]

The Chickasaw Bayou and Arkansas Post campaigns left the overall military picture in the Vicksburg campaign area much as it had been. Confederates held Vicksburg, and Union forces still posed a threat to the river city. Van Dorn's raid had embarrassed U. S. Grant, and his friend Cump Sherman had been humiliated at Chickasaw Bayou. Although the Arkansas Post operation had boosted Union morale somewhat, it had done little to enhance Grant's goal of taking Vicksburg. It did, however, demonstrate the value of joint Union navy/army operations. Together they did not succeed at Chickasaw Bayou because Sherman had made a poor choice of terrain on which to fight, in effect taking the navy out of the picture. The strategy at the Post allowed both branches of the service to contribute, and the results had been quite different. More than anything else, the campaigns added to Grant's and Lincoln's frustrations, and bought time for Pemberton and Davis. That situation remained unchanged for the next several months, as the 1863 campaign began with Grant continuing his search for a solution to the Vicksburg dilemma.

6

~~ Disputes, Diversions, Failures

As January 1863 dawned, Union prospects for taking Vicksburg seemed dim. Like Sherman, Grant took heat in the press and among the powerful for the failures in North Mississippi and at Chickasaw Bayou. Many speculated as to who Grant's successor might be. Clearly his future seemed to rest on shaky ground, yet he did not get fired, or even reprimanded. There were several reasons why Abraham Lincoln stood by this general. Grant had not always succeeded, but he had in fact not been defeated until the end of 1862. He was persistent, and Stanton's emissary, Charles Dana, sent positive reports that certainly helped Grant's image in distant Washington. John McClernand's bellicosity also aided his immediate superior. McClernand sent a bitter attack on Halleck to Lincoln on January 7, accusing Halleck of all sorts of things, mostly of undermining the Mississippi expedition that McClernand had planned. Lincoln, in no mood for such haranguing, responded in part: "You are now doing well—well for the country, and well for yourself—much better than you could possibly be, if engaged in open war with Gen. Halleck." Compared to McClernand, Grant must have seemed a blessing indeed to Lincoln, Halleck, and Stanton.

Grant must have sensed the support, and he immediately went to work, trying all sorts of things to take Vicksburg. From January to March, he implemented several plans, and time after time met with frustration, as did the thousands of men who tried to turn their general's ideas into success. While the Federal high command struggled to find solutions, men in the ranks wrestled with issues of emancipation, horrible conditions along the river, desertions, guerrillas, antiwar sentiments back home, and campaigns along rivers in the Mississippi Delta that tested them to their limits. Somehow the soldiers managed to maintain their focus on the task at hand, and for that U. S. Grant and his generals deserved much credit.

John Pemberton and his lieutenants knew that a continuing Union presence along the river meant that Confederates could not waste time celebrating Chickasaw Bayou. Pemberton experienced his own frustrations during the first three months of the new year. He did not have Grant's numbers, and he did not have Porter's fleet, which meant he could not go on the offensive, even had he been so inclined, and he was not. Pemberton's lack of tactical expertise caused him frequently to misread the enemy's intentions. Pemberton persisted in remaining at his Jackson office, rather than staying on top of things by moving his headquarters to Vicksburg. He and his men watched, reacted when they had to, and hoped that somehow they could continue their good fortunes in countering Grant's operations.

In North Mississippi, Grant worked to recover from Van Dorn's and Forrest's Holly Springs and West Tennessee raids. He mobilized his troops to repair and reopen railroad supply lines, while many of his men ate bleak holiday meals. Grant issued orders to clear out families between the Hatchie and Coldwater rivers and to deport south disloyal citizens from Memphis to slow the destruction of bridges and supplies by guerrillas. The situation gradually improved, but for a time, quartermaster officers had to depend on foraging from the depleted countryside.

Grant determined to get more troops downriver, while at the same time trying to stabilize West Tennessee and North Mississippi. He completely gave up the Tallahatchie line to focus on protecting Corinth. He learned that Nathaniel Banks, expected to move north from New Orleans and join in operations against Vicksburg, had not moved at all. News also came that William Rosecrans had defeated Braxton Bragg at Stones River in Murfreesboro, Tennessee. Grant feared that Van Dorn might now try to reinforce Bragg — and who knew what Bragg might do next?[1]

On January 13, Grant decided to take personal field command of operations against Vicksburg. He opted to take John Logan's and John McArthur's divisions with him downriver to join McClernand's force at Milliken's Bend. While he waited for Porter's fleet to refit, he intended to meet with Porter, Sherman, and McClernand to get "a better understanding of matters than I now have."

When Grant reached Milliken's Bend, he held a series of meetings with his commanders and Porter. On learning that the Rebels had solid fortifications on the bluffs from the south bank of the Yazoo River into the city itself, Grant determined to renew the Williams canal project that had failed in the summer of 1862. Initial efforts did not produce promising results, so Grant and his engineers tried relocating the canal entrance to enhance the water flow from the river. Grant informed Halleck: "The old canal left the river in an eddy and in a line purpendicular to the stream and also to the crest of the hills oposite with a battery directed against the outlet. This new canal will debouch below the bluffs on the oposite side of the river and give our gunboats a fare chance against any fortifications that may be placed to oppose them." Grant abandoned efforts to cut roads along the Yazoo to outflank the Confederates, because of "the intolerable rains . . . which have filled all the swamps and Bayou so that they cannot dry up again this Winter."[2]

Grant reminded Halleck that since he only controlled "troops in a limited Department, and can only draw reinforcements from elswhere by making application through Washington, and as a demonstration made upon any part of the old District of West Tennessee might force me to withdraw a large part of the force from the vicinity of Vicksburg, I would respectfully ask if it would not be [better] policy to combine the four Departments in the West under one commander." Despite being senior commander in the area, Grant insisted he had "no desire whatever for such combined command but would prefer the command I now have to any other that can be given." Grant noted that neither the navy nor the army had confidence in McClernand's ability, and he shared that opinion only because "it was forced upon me" by others. He intended to command in person and cautioned Halleck, "There is no special necessity of mentioning this matter."

While waiting for a response, Grant turned to another departmental matter that had infuriated him. The 7th Kansas Cavalry's bad behavior had surfaced once again during the pursuit of Van Dorn's raiders. During the chase, the Kansans had stopped to plunder New Albany. Grant deplored their "outragious conduct," and told General Hamilton, "All the laurels won by the Regiment and their Commander on the pursuit of the enemy from Holly Springs to Coffeeville have been more than counterbalanced by their bad conduct since. Their present course may serve to frighten women and children and helpless old men but will never drive out an armed enemy." Any further trouble would result in officers being arrested and the regiment dismounted and disarmed.[3]

Grant welcomed good news from Halleck; he now had command of all Arkansas "as you may desire to control," that is, troops within the reach of his orders. Halleck warned, however, that Rebel resistance at Port Hudson could delay help from Banks and the navy on the lower Mississippi. Grant welcomed the expansion of his authority, and he was additionally pleased to learn that President Lincoln endorsed the canal project. Grant ordered troops in Arkansas to protect his flank and rear by operating along the Arkansas and White rivers. A January 24 Union expedition up the White cleared the enemy from the river, but reports indicated Confederate threats against Helena.

Grant assured McClernand that shovels would be arriving at the Vicksburg front soon and asked for news from Banks. McClernand reported high water in the old canal, but there had been no impact on the main channel of the Mississippi. Rebels had concentrated along the railroad leading to Shreveport and downriver at Grand Gulf. Happily, Banks reportedly had reoccupied Baton Rouge, but, ominously, Vicksburg papers indicated that more reinforcements were pouring into Vicksburg.[4]

In faraway Washington, President Lincoln had confidence in Grant's ability, but he was concerned about the lack of information coming from the Vicksburg area. Halleck kept the president informed, but Lincoln hungered for more news. He scoured Richmond papers when he could get them, hoping to learn Confederate views about the situation on the Mississippi. Virginia editors, like the Confederate government, focused more on the eastern campaigns, and Lincoln's curiosity often went unsatisfied. Clearly he understood, perhaps better than Jefferson Davis, that the Union setback at Chickasaw Bayou had been temporary, and much remained to be decided on the Mississippi. Until Federal forces took control of the river, political pressures would keep Lincoln anxious about the situation on the lower Mississippi.

Union soldiers, meanwhile, reflected on the campaign, the war, Lincoln's Emancipation Proclamation (which went into effect on January 1, 1863), loyalty to the cause, and many other issues. Most were veterans now and felt qualified and confident enough to express their opinions bluntly to family and friends. They felt the same frustrations as their leaders, for most had thought that the war would be short and that by now they would be home. Instead, they faced inhospitable Southern weather and residents, and some did desert and go north. Most endured, however, out of devotion to the Union.

Soldiers working on the canal, which most thought was a waste of time, were concerned about the impressive works they saw along the hills across the river. One member of the 13th Illinois wrote his sister that the "coveted city" would "cost the ... lives of many a brave and true soldier." "To comprehend the strength of this strong hold," he continued, "one has to view its vastness himself and even then the mind will fail to do it justice." Rebels had "rifle pits behind which they can lay in safety and pick off our men at lesure." He saw cannon "which can be brought to bear on any point. look where you will you will see the ugly

mug of the iron monsters on the whole range of bluffs as one continuous fortification and . . . we can see the rebels busily at work strengthening their works." The general opinion among the men, he said, was
that the city had to be the most fortified place in the Confederacy, but
"she must and will come down."[5]

Whether they were veterans of Sherman's and McClernand's campaigns or newly arrived reinforcements, Federal soldiers were not
impressed by the countryside north and east of Vicksburg. Because
flooding and intentional crop destruction limited foraging, the men
welcomed food from home, some delivered by emissaries from as far
away as Wisconsin. One Indianan observed, "As we glide down the river
nothing but a Godforsaken country can be seen[;] houses where once a
happy family dwelled are now vacant[.] Plantations where the wealthy
planter loved enjoying all the luxuries that wealth could afford are now
a barren waste[.] Villages that once were prosperous and flour[i]shing
are now desolate and the whole country on eather side of the river looks
like some dreary waste where God in His wisdom has seen fit to wreek
his vengeance upon a wicked people." A Michigander wrote similarly:
"Plantations were burning far and near, down the river and inland from
the river. Hundreds of colored people had taken refuge under the
riverbank with their little bundles, and were in mortal fear for their
lives." Men on the transports drew guerrilla fire, and landing parties
retaliated by burning everything in sight.[6]

Sickness proved to be a more direct threat to Union soldiers than
Confederate partisans. Many developed what became known as the
Louisiana, sometimes called Arkansas, quickstep, which was diarrhea,
"the universal plague," caused no doubt by bad drinking water and
tainted food, usually a steady diet of hard bread and sowbelly. One
Illinois soldier said he would welcome what his sister fed her dogs.
Measles, typhoid fever, consumption, mumps, small pox, and malarial-
type fevers infested troops exposed to mosquitoes and other insects,
and burial details stayed busy. An Iowan complained to his wife that "it
is awful to see the suffering this war causes and the end is out of sight."
When men got sick, "they are not as mutch cared for as a sick hog is in
Iowa." A Wisconsin soldier begged his parents to send pain medicine
not available locally. Unhealthy places to sleep added to the misery. Dry
ground was rare; dried bean vines became bedding, and vacant slave
cabins provided slight protection from rain and cold.[7]

Some men sought relief in creative leisure time. Soldiers made small-
scale gunboats by nailing sideboards to rafts, armed with small cannon
made from melted lead. The one-man rafts, given colorful nicknames

such as "Destroyer" and "Terror" were rowed into combat on myriad waterways. Occasionally someone got carried away and fired live ammunition, but there were no casualties. Other soldiers read religious tracts, fished, and traded hurrahs with Confederate pickets for the respective presidents.[8]

Soldiers began questioning slavery's relevance to the war effort and openly opposed Lincoln's emancipation plan. An Illinoisan wrote his wife, "I am as far from being in favor of freeing the negro as any man tho I donte care what becomes of the negro if we can have peace." An Iowan decried the sending of "stinking niggers" north. An Ohioan noted "a great deal of dissatisfaction and political clamor among Soldiers which portends that Something will have to be done shortly to put a Stop to this, or Something *else* will take place. I look for an *Order* to be issued prohibiting the discussing of politics among the Soldiers Subject to the penalty of death." Another Federal wrote home, "If I had thot that it was the idea to set the Negroes all free they would not have got me to act the part of a Soldier in this war," but added, "I am in for anything that will cause Union and peace." Yet his hatred of blacks grew, and he soon expressed the hope for a proclamation allowing Union soldiers to shoot down slaves. Others felt the same way. Letters home included such comments as "I am union when union is our aim. But when It gets on the nigga. I am not"; "I would now rather have the union divided and let slavery alone where it is than to have the union restored and abolished"; and "I don't think a white man was ever calculated to be shot at for the sake of a nigger." Some blamed abolitionists and politicians for politicizing slavery, thereby encouraging Southern resistance.[9]

Other Federals found slavery abhorrent and its destruction a noble enterprise. The scenes of elderly blacks left behind by fleeing plantation owners led an Iowan to observe, "There was no money in these poor old worn out slaves and the cruel and barbarous master had abandoned them to their *fate*[.] As I looked at their worn out hands and fingers and bodies I thought of the long cruel years of bondage while under burning suns and in cold and heat they had labored for this *hellish* system of human slavery," and now they had been left to fend for themselves. When another soldier heard that a white owner classed his own mixed-blood children as slaves, he exclaimed, "*By G–d I'll fight till hell freezes over and then I'll cut the ice and fight on.*" Soldiers who by their mere presence became deliverers were touched when slaves offered gifts, cooking skills, and other free labor as enticements for a trip north. A Michigander found the freed slaves' plight both humorous and profound. "They presented a very comical appearance. Some dressed in cast off soldiers clothes[,] others in their plantation suits while the women were dressed in the coarsest field suits to the gaudy silks[,] laces & velvets of their mistress." All "wore the glad, cheerful expression of the liberated Slave." These sights and the reports of owner brutality transformed the prejudices of many soldiers in blue.[10]

Union soldiers had equally mixed opinions about slaves joining the army. Initiated in the summer of 1862, the Federal government's policy of enlisting black regiments did not meet with universal acclaim. Grant's troops thought it fine for blacks to dig trenches, but the idea of putting them into uniform caused worry. A disgusted Iowan wrote: "The idea of arming and equipping Negro Regiments for the purpose of making them soldiers is, to my mind, worse than ridiculous nonsense. Niggers will *work if you make them do so*. I do not believe you could pick out one thousand Negroes out of 50,000 who would *fight* with *loaded* guns, or who would not run at the first appearance of danger. . . . We are all going to the devil." An Illinoisan had "no objection to Sambo's doing my fighting[;] if there is fight in Sambo lets have it." Others thought it only just that blacks fight for their freedom.[11]

Dissatisfaction with the proclamation and other issues bred desertion, always a problem in idle armies, but not a critical one for Grant, who drew a steady stream of reinforcements from the Midwest. Although exact numbers will never be known, many Federal soldiers headed north. Most deserters were new recruits who disliked river travel, lived a harsh existence, and tired of bad food. Public punishments for captured deserters had limited effect. Surrounded by illness and death, men grew depressed, one writing mournfully, "I have been detailed ever since the 4th of October to make coffins until the 6th of January when I was appointed color bearer." A Wisconsin soldier grumbled, "Nearly one half of our Army are no better than Jefferson Davis and I honestly mean what I say." An Indianan confessed, "I am tired of the way things are going at Washington. It appears that nothing but the nigger can enjoy their attention there. The proclamation and other things have demoralized this army until it is worthless." He claimed that soldiers were deserting "every day and thousands say they will go and give themselves to the rebels as prisoners to be paroled rather than remain in the army." An Iowan reported that many soldiers supported controversial Northern peace politician Clement Vallandingham's public stand against war.[12]

Yet loyalty to the war effort remained firm. The fight for the Union became a matter of honor, as well as justice for those who had already died for the cause. Indeed, one Illinoisan declared that deserters had neither honor nor justice. He feared discontent back home was fueling Southern resolve and foretold a ruined country if the North did not unite. Vallandingham pleased some, but not everyone. An Iowa soldier commented, "The men are extremely bitter in denouncing the '*Peace*' men of the north, and indeed for my part I cannot see how any intelligent honest patriotic man can do otherwise." A Missourian unionist agreed: "I hate these northern trators worse and wors[.] I would rather this day take up my gun and blow one of their brains out than to kill two of those who like men are in arms against us. In our front many of the latter are their from circumstance[;] many are forsed to arms[;] they all have a better excuse than those in our rear." One soldier cheered his mother for slapping a prosecession woman, and an Indianan concluded: "I would rather sacrifice my life than to have one single star or stripe erased and if I was confident that my Life would be sufficient I would gladly lay that down[,] for it would procure liberty for that Boy of mine that I hope may never desert the way his father has marked out for him."[13]

Embracing the cause could be difficult within the milieu of hard war, but a Wisconsin soldier was "perfectly disgusted the way the war is carried on and it never will be Settled till they arm the blacks and confiscate rebbel property, lay the towns in ashes, etc." Still, troops like the 5th Kansas, accused of executing guerrillas, produced disgust with their actions. An Iowan concluded that "the name of the 5th Kansas grates harshly on the ears of the butternuts in Ark. and Missouri [and] well it may, for the Sabre, and Carbine, and Revolver has brought down many a one. . . . I have no pity, no mercy for the cowardly Scoundrels. i would rather put a Minnie Ball through the brain of one of them renegades than the . . . rebel down here. I want nothing to do with them. they are my deadly enemyes." Yet partisan counterstrokes, such as tossing a Union prisoner into a well, minimized Federal sympathy.[14]

Guerrilla activities in the Memphis-Helena area especially triggered Union backlashes. An angry Federal noted, "The Guerilas around heer are getting very troublesome[;] scarecely a night passing that they do not fire on our pickets and very often they will surprise an outpost and capture every man in it. The other evening they killed two and wounded fifteen out of twenty five men belong[ing] to the sixth Missouri." Across from Memphis, Federals burned a village in retaliation and had little compassion for those left homeless and huddled around an open fire. A recently widowed local man admitted that the place had been "a harbor for guerilas" and was not surprised at the retribution.[15]

Cramped and miserable conditions in the Memphis-Helena staging area also created problems for Union soldiers. Helena, said one, became infested with bad-tempered men and was "fuller of damnation than any place this side the regions of dark despair." Strange eating habits developed. "I eat a great deal of peper, Spice, Cayene peper, mustard and any thing hot," one soldier said, as "I find it is the only way to get through down here. That is to pickle ones self much as possible, and by the time Summer comes the musquities nor the wolves would care to fool with" him, nor perhaps people.

At Helena in March, a brawl erupted between Illinoisans on a boat and shore guards ordered to keep them there, and more violence erupted when other Illinois troops went ashore to forage. The provost guard drove them back, and missiles of stone, boards, coal, and dried mud filled the air. Threats of cannon fire forced the angry soldiers to withdraw. Troops with time on their hands could cause problems.[16]

Some soldiers blamed officers for army unrest. A Federal soldier wrote, "I am not going to tell any body that I am afraid there is too many Generals that would rather the war would continue for them to feather their nests a little better, it would be wrong for me to express myself that way, however I cant help but think it pretty strongly, and then we have some traitors holding high positions yet. I mean I think so. Those things I only think but one thing I know and that is that the officers of the Western department from Major Gens. down to second Lieuts are a desperately poor trifling ignorant low flung set of men some brave exceptions of course."[17]

Grant understood his army's discontent; he knew he had to combat idleness — hence the canal project and other "make-work" operations. Grant was also aware of criticism of him in the Northern press, along with the variously exaggerated and true stories about the negative conditions in which the army found itself. He later claimed, perhaps rationalizing, that he did not expect efforts against Vicksburg in early 1863 to succeed, but the men needed to be active until lower water levels allowed implementation of a workable plan.[18]

Confederates also found the early 1863 lull a test of endurance and commitment. Impressed by the enemy's sea of white tents across the river, plus all the gunboats and transports, they sensed that if Grant ever unleashed his masses, the town would be lost. That knowledge and the occasional gunboat shell fueled uncertainty and dread among citizens and soldiers and fed female curiosity. When missiles filled the air above the bluffs, "the hills were covered with crinoline to look at the flying monsters as their noise indicated the direction to which they were coming." The city's defenders could see the canal and applauded Confederate shells that scattered Yankees. Otherwise they complained about the food, the weather, illness, high prices, vices, and the army, and wondered about the future of slavery. Union deserters, arriving singly and in groups, provided some excitement and some hope.

Many soldiers struggled to balance duty with reality. A Louisianan wrote his wife, "If in after years when my children have had children and they as old men will gather together around a cheerful warm fire of a winter's night and will talk of the war that the Southern Confederacy gained her independence, they will tell of their father who stood amidst flame and smoke on their battlefield, if not more, and contributed his might for freedom." Another Confederate penned, "I am getting very, very tired of this war. The more I see of it the more I dislike it. . . . An officer, unless he is very high in command, is a dog who has to bow and bend to persons whom you would not notice in social life." He prayed, not appreciating the irony, for peace to free him "from this slavery, for truly a soldier or an officer in the army is nothing more than a slave . . . of some higher functionary." Soldiers tired quickly of pointless marches, such as a rainy night march of four miles to a railroad bridge. They "took possession of . . . Negro cabins and made fires and dried out our clothes as well as possible, but our blankets were wet and there was but little chance to sleep."[19]

Confederates from states other than Mississippi hated duty outside Vicksburg, away from action or excitement. Georgians in Jackson complained about poor food, illness, swampy terrain, and especially local attitudes. One soldier recorded that Jacksonians came within one vote of passing an ordinance to keep soldiers off city sidewalks. The idea of having to walk muddy streets angered men and hurt morale. One Confederate wrote bluntly, "The soldiers are all getting very tired of this war and if it is not stopt shortly they will stop it themselves by throughing down their muskets and going home. I am going to stay here till July[.] Then if they do not let me come home on fair terms I am coming on foul terms."[20]

Troops assigned to the Big Black River area east of Vicksburg pondered the war during their leisure time. A Missouri Confederate wrote his father: "I might not have pleased you in leaving home and coming to the Southern army, but I feel that I have done my duty as a man that would wish to live free." "Are we going to let the vandal hords of the north make us slaves in order to free the Negro? Are we going to allow the Lincoln dynasty to trample upon our rights as free men, violate our constitution, imprison our offending citizens without a trial by jury?"

Others grumbled about more mundane issues of inaction, mud, worthless officers, few newspapers, and noble Southern women. One noted, "The women and the private soldier have made this war theirs, coming generations will be unable to account for the tenacity with which we have fought this war unless they shall have some means of ascertaining the part woman has acted, and as history has no means by which to transmit a full account of this influence, our tenacity and persistence will ever remain a mystery to those who shall come after us."[21]

Low morale and homesickness induced desertion, though contemporary accounts rarely mention it, and Confederate rates in early 1863 did not match the Union's. Nevertheless, Grant could afford to lose men, and Pemberton could not. Now and then Pemberton had to divert manpower to clear out nests of deserters turned outlaws. Certain areas of Mississippi became havens for those wishing to escape the army. Most were probably Mississippians, though malcontents from elsewhere no doubt joined their ranks. Escaping from Mississippi to the east could be dangerous, given the military control of railroads, local militia, and cavalry patrols.

While soldiers coped, politicians and citizens worried about the Trans-Mississippi being severed from the rest of the Confederacy. Arkansans pressured Jefferson Davis to name Edmund Kirby Smith commander of the entire area. Louisianans complained to Davis about Union cavalry depredations. Federals burned houses and freed slaves who prowled about, and women felt especially vulnerable. The situation demonstrated clearly that no matter how often the Federals tried and failed, Confederates clinging to the lower Mississippi Valley could not hope for counteroffensives to drive out the enemy.[22]

In this atmosphere of uncertainty, John Pemberton and his staff busied themselves with strengthening defensive works. The Confederate mind-set continued to be that of digging in while waiting for Grant's next move. Cattle and hogs from surrounding areas filled commissary storehouses. Pemberton and Governor Pettus cooperated in procuring slave labor for digging fortifications and maintaining the railroad. Slave labor at Greenwood built defensive positions where the Tallahatchie and Yalobusha merged to form the Yazoo and worked at the government-run mill and warehouses in Vicksburg. Widespread demands for labor strained relations between the military and plantation owners. Confederate soldiers approved, for black workers did the hardest jobs and provided musical entertainment.[23]

Pemberton realized the difficulties he faced because of multiple enemy army and navy activities scattered across the lower Mississippi Valley. Reports of Union scouts reconnoitering Yazoo Pass forced him to send Confederate cavalry there. Federal activity along the Memphis-Corinth corridor kept Sterling Price's and William Loring's divisions on the alert. Pemberton sent Loring north up the Mississippi Central Railroad to regain territory lost to Grant. Loring advanced unimpeded to Coffeeville and Panola (present-day Batesville). Loring, an experienced officer and troublemaker who had been sent west to get him out of Virginia, proved to be a divisive force in Mississippi.[24]

Though the repulse of Sherman and Grant's retreat had been good news, Joseph Johnston decided to maintain forces in the Grenada area rather than take the offensive. Johnston and Pemberton knew that if Grant suddenly changed his mind and came down the Mississippi Central again, the 11,000 troops around Grenada and Van Dorn's cavalry could not stop him. Johnston also worried that Grant might concentrate at Vicksburg and besiege the city. Since no one expected help from Holmes in Arkansas, Johnston asked for troops from Robert E. Lee's army, recently victorious at Fredericksburg, Virginia. Johnston knew Pemberton could not hold off Grant indefinitely.

Jefferson Davis promised additional heavy guns to defend Vicksburg but offered nothing else. He instructed Johnston and Pemberton to keep communications open with Holmes; but Holmes's attitude was unchanged, and Davis still refused to overrule him. Pemberton wrote optimistically to Davis that Vicksburg defenses were getting stronger and the city would be held.[25]

Despite Pemberton's assurances, disturbing news multiplied. Federals returning from Arkansas Post had massed along the western side of the Mississippi and probably would make another assault — but where? Pemberton ordered Carter Stevenson, commanding in Vicksburg, to speed up construction of works, and he warned Franklin Gardner at Port Hudson to be alert. In Vicksburg, Stevenson impressed additional slaves, and commissary officers gathered a two-month supply of food. Stevenson reported Federals landing at Young's Point and asked for reserves from Jackson to protect Warrenton. Meanwhile, Pemberton read from papers taken from a dead Federal officer that Sherman had 21,000 men. Other reports indicated that the total enemy force was about 35,000, and that Grant and Banks would be coordinating operations.[26]

With intelligence indicating a continuing Federal buildup, Pemberton mobilized Price's division; but whatever Grant had in mind, it did not involve another advance into North Mississippi. Soon Pemberton transferred Thomas Waul's Texas Legion of Loring's division to Snyder's Bluff, and Price's division, led by John Bowen in Price's absence, entrained for Jackson, followed later by more troops from Loring. None of this concentration proved easy, on account of train transportation problems and bad weather. The result of the redeployment left Lloyd Tilghman's brigade of Loring's division as the only sizable force on the Grenada front, and then Loring sent another brigade to Port Hudson. Johnston approved Pemberton's adjustments to meet the latest perceived threats.

Pemberton's defensive line at Vicksburg now consisted of Dabney Maury's division, plus Waul's legion, holding Snyder's Bluff to the Indian mound; Seth Barton between the mound and the racetrack; Martin L. Smith's troops along the riverfront and in town; A. W. Reynolds's brigade deployed from Smith's left to Warrenton; and two other brigades held in reserve, with one regiment detached to guard railroad bridges.

Confederate concerns about protecting Vicksburg covered an expansive area. Defensive works at Snyder's Bluff had fallen into disrepair, and fluctuations in the Yazoo River's depth threatened raft barricades across the Yazoo. When the Federal vessel *Queen of the West* successfully passed Vicksburg, the failure of river batteries to sink it troubled Vicksburg's defenders, who naively thought their guns should have easily wrecked an enemy ship. They seemed to forget the experiences of the previous summer.[27]

The batteries looked impressive. From north of Vicksburg, south to Warrenton, gun emplacements included the Water Battery, positioned to fire at the head of De Soto Point. Next came the Louisiana and Wyman's Hill batteries. On the waterfront sat the Whig Office Battery, and the Depot Battery was near the railroad station. Farther south, Durreve's Battery and Todd's Battery protected the Warrenton flank. Rounding out the river artillery were Butler's, Caper's, and Gibbs's batteries, plus the Blakely battery (which included the storied "Widow Blakely" — a "widow" because of its uniqueness among Vicksburg's artillery) and one gun near a local home. All told, the Confederates had twenty-five big guns and one mortar to keep the river clear of Yankee boats.

A few guns had been improperly mounted on carriages, however, and the overall commander, Colonel Edward Higgins, complained about the lack of rifled guns in the Water Battery. Higgins received more, but it took weeks to deploy the big guns. As February dragged on, Pemberton continued worrying about the guns' effectiveness, especially after the *Indianola* also ran past unscathed on February 13.[28] Pemberton begged

Richmond for additional firepower, and finally Pemberton's emissary to the capital, George Mayo, secured promises of rifled weapons from the Selma, Alabama, and Tredegar (Richmond) foundries.[29]

Pemberton's attention turned north when he learned that Federals had destroyed the Yazoo Pass levee and enemy ships had reached the Coldwater River. Winfield S. Featherston took his brigade from the Big Black River bridge to Yazoo City, and John Bowen's division moved from Jackson to protect the bridge, as Pemberton continued shifting troops in response to Grant's actions. (Bowen had received a permanent command when Price left Mississippi for the Trans-Mississippi theater.) Price had been assured that his Missouri troops would follow when circumstances permitted, but those circumstances never developed.[30]

Meanwhile, Joseph Johnston, having returned to his headquarters with Bragg's army, complained loudly to Richmond about Pemberton's poor generalship. Johnston was disgruntled that Pemberton reported directly to the War Department, but Pemberton had been instructed to do so. Pemberton understood that Jefferson Davis expected direct correspondence; thus Johnston's control over the Mississippi army was more apparent than real.

Whether Johnston's dissatisfaction with Pemberton was more personal than professional is unclear, but Johnston's wife was blunt: "No one trusts him or has confidence in him. . . . Pemberton's opinion of himself is charming, if the country only had half as good a one, it would be well for all of us." Theophilus Holmes had similar feelings, once commenting that Pemberton had "many ways of making people hate him and none to inspire confidence." To others, it appeared that "his own Staff hate him and every man that goes near him is treated with rudeness and incivility." Pemberton's prewar service had hardened him into a martinet.

Whatever Johnston's personal feelings, he did not think the Confederacy had enough men to maintain a large army in Tennessee and save Vicksburg. Johnston argued that Pemberton needed 20,000 more men and that Davis had known this as recently as December. Troops could not be easily shifted between Middle Tennessee and Mississippi to meet enemy threats, Johnston said. He also refused to shift any of Bragg's cavalry force to help Pemberton, arguing that to weaken the one army to help the other solved nothing.[31]

The lack of effective communication between Pemberton and Johnston hurt Pemberton, who could have benefited from the advice, not to mention cooperation, of a more experienced soldier. Since Johnston's views often conflicted with Davis's, however, Pemberton might have been caught in the middle earlier than he eventually was. Johnston never changed his mind about the strategic insignificance of Vicksburg, and Davis clung to the view that the place must be saved.

The flawed command system in the Western Theater left Pemberton to deal alone with a morass of departmental issues in early 1863 that included obtaining Kirby Smith's cooperation; Smith now commanded the Trans-Mississippi. Grand Gulf needed to be better fortified in order to protect the extreme southern flank of Vicksburg. Pemberton wanted to link Port Gibson and Grand Gulf by telegraph. Port Hudson had been attacked, and it looked as if the Yankees intended to continue operations at Yazoo Pass.

Port Hudson proved to be a particular thorn in Pemberton's side, for in addition to countering Grant's intentions north of Vicksburg, the beleaguered Rebel general had to help protect the fortress to the south. Nathaniel Banks had replaced Benjamin Butler in New Orleans, and scouting reports indicated that Banks, another political general, was pushing north up the Mississippi. If the Confederates had to abandon Port Hudson, Banks could reinforce Grant, adding to the Federal advantage. Pemberton sent John Gregg's brigade to reinforce Port Hudson's commander, Franklin Gardner. Pemberton reported his actions to Johnston, who, uncharacteristically, praised Pemberton for his "activity and vigor in the defense of the Mississippi."[32]

An unexpected, ominous issue arose when Pemberton learned that David Porter had threatened to execute partisans caught firing on unarmed river vessels or burning cotton. (The burning of cotton was authorized by Confederate law to prevent it from falling into Union hands.) Pemberton stated that if Porter followed through, the Confederate response would be to execute Federal prisoners. Pemberton reminded Porter that Union troops had shot at unarmed Confederate vessels. If Porter persisted, Confederates would show no quarter to Union soldiers caught burning private property. Guerrilla activity obviously was threatening to promote hard war.[33]

Adequate supplies continued to be a critical problem. Pemberton's staff sent out the word: "Vicksburg must be fed before anything else." Wagons created a supply line from Vicksburg to Yazoo City. Food and forage came to Vicksburg from North Mississippi via rail and the Tallahatchie and Yalobusha rivers. A supply boat shortage hampered efforts to get the supplies on into Vicksburg. While Pemberton was drowning in administrative details, he wondered what Grant would do next; having learned nothing from Holly Springs, Pemberton continued to react rather than initiate.[34]

Grant wanted to keep Pemberton guessing; he had no intention of giving up the initiative. Yet things were not going well. He had tired of partisan activities in Memphis and warned, "If the proper government of the city requires it I will not oppose driving out every man[,] woman and child who will not live strictly up to all requirements." He wondered about the canal and complained to Halleck, "Since leaving there one week ago, I have not heard one word from them [his commanders]." He admitted that "constant rains and tremendous rise in the river may operate against us for the time being," but he wanted to be kept informed. Before leaving Memphis to return downriver in late January, Grant placed Stephen Hurlbut in command of the city and warned his commanders along the Tennessee-Mississippi border to be on the watch for another raid.

Halleck pressed Grant on the canal project: "Direct your attention particularly to the canal proposed across the point. The President attaches much importance to this." Grant arrived at Young's Point the evening of January 28, and after hearing reports he began losing hope that the canal would ever work. On the twenty-ninth, he advised Halleck that he was thinking of sending engineers to cut the levee blocking Yazoo Pass, since the canal project showed little promise. Grant assured Washington: "I am pushing everything to gain a passage, avoiding Vicksburg. Prospects not flattering by the canal of last summer." Yet men struggled with the ditch while he investigated other routes. In addition to Yazoo Pass, Grant examined the possibilities of getting Union boats below Vicksburg via Lake Providence to the Red River. He also looked over his shoulder to North Mississippi, ordering cavalry as far south as the Tallahatchie River to scout and to destroy bridges and rail lines.

Then Grant suddenly found himself in a confrontation with John McClernand. McClernand challenged Grant's authority to send orders directly to corps commanders rather than through McClernand's headquarters. McClernand clung to the illusion that the secretary of war and the president had given him command of "all the forces operating the Mississippi River." He could not, therefore, tolerate Grant's behavior, "otherwise I must lose a knowledge of current business and dangerous confusion ensue." The issue must be settled, McClernand said, for "one thing is certain, two generals cannot command this army."[35]

Grant understood the reality of the Stanton-Lincoln-Halleck duplicity involving McClernand, and on January 31 he pointed out that since he took command of the river expedition, McClernand had been limited to command of the XIII Corps. While McClernand had some leeway in corps command, all directives regarding its operations must come from Grant's headquarters. Grant emphasized that the president was commander in chief and that any order he issued would be obeyed, but Grant had been given authority, via Halleck, to take over field command of the army. McClernand's protests fell on deaf ears in Washington, and Grant was not surprised. Authorities there had no intention of risking the river campaign in McClernand's hands, regardless of his abilities, connections, and influence.[36]

All the while, work on the doomed canal continued. Grant refused to give it up altogether, for he knew he was being scrutinized from Washington. Regiments shouldering picks and shovels worked on 160-foot sections designed to be six feet deep and sixty feet wide. The men camped on levees and suffered in the wet, soggy, unhealthy lowlands. Despite Grant's determination, the work went slowly, heavy rains fell, sick lists grew longer, and the levees turned into graveyards. Supplies had to remain on boats, and trails inland became bottomless tracts of mud through which mules, rather than wagons, struggled to get to camps. High water caused continual breaks in levees, which exacerbated efforts to dig out the canal. Confederate cannon made the work even more dangerous.[37]

By early February, Grant had forced Pemberton to spread Confederate forces thinly over a long stretch of river, but he had accomplished little else. Constant high water and illness led William Sherman to comment that the canal simply did not "amount to much." The main river channel ignored man's feeble attempts to change its course. After the war, it eventually did what Grant had wanted; the Mississippi had a mind of its own and would not be rushed.

Through February completion of the canal continued to be elusive, and in early March Grant increased the work schedule to around the clock. The pace increased and another dredge arrived, but then the river broke through the levee on the new entrance, setting back work. The breakthrough caused such flooding that Sherman had to move his XV Corps to the levees at Young's Point, while McClernand's men went upriver to Milliken's Bend. By late March, Grant had had enough. Even if the canal could be used as a waterway, troop transports would have to pass through at night to avoid exposure to enemy fire, which had been so effective against dredging operations. When news reached Washington that the canal was functioning, and Union soldiers had boarded vessels to take advantage of it, Lincoln, monitoring the Halleck-Grant correspondence, dismissed the news as "humbuggery," which was an appropriate word to sum up the canal project.[38]

Grant turned his attention to crescent-shaped Lake Providence, located on the Louisiana side of the Mississippi some seventy-five river miles north of Vicksburg. Engineers thought Lake Providence could be linked to other waterways south to the Red River. From the point where the Red emptied into the Mississippi, Grant could send troops and supplies to assist Banks at Port Hudson, and transport troops upriver to assault Vicksburg from the south. From Lake Providence, the potential route would be to Bayou Baxter, Bayou Macon, the Tensas and Black rivers, and into the Red. To raise Bayou Baxter to a depth sufficient to float heavily laden boats, engineers would have to cut through the Lake Providence levee.

James McPherson's corps drew the work assignment, and John Logan's and John McArthur's divisions concentrated in the Lake Providence area. Advance work parties completed a ditch connecting the lake and the Mississippi, and other ditches connected Bayou Baxter with Bayou Macon. Confederate sympathizers attempted and failed to sabotage it by cutting a levee upriver to lower the Mississippi's water level. McPherson, a skilled engineer, recommended that the nearby Mississippi levee be cut to raise the water level in Bayou Baxter. McPherson also ordered the levee cut at a town called Ashton, above Lake Providence, to facilitate access to Bayou Macon. The resulting flooding would cause some homes to float away "like eggshells," but citizens would be warned ahead of time. McPherson's other division, Isaac Quinby's, provided security for the Providence operations.

Union soldiers found Lake Providence to be a pleasant place before some of their compatriots vandalized the area. A fire burned part of the town, and an Indiana soldier admitted, "They say it caught fire acidental but there is to many of such acidents in our army." An Iowan commented, "Lake Providence *has been* a very pretty village, a number of neat cottage residences surrounded by the evergreens peculiar to a southern clime gave it a very inviting aspect, two drug stores, a large hotel, three churches, etc." Men amused themselves hunting, fishing, and "pitching horse shoes and boating on the lake, everything that will float is used to ride on." Guerrilla activity often rudely interrupted such leisure. An ugly incident occurred when partisans gunned down a hated Kansan, who was hit four times and then received a second, lethal, volley when he tried to rise.[39]

The presence of partisans did not make McPherson's soldiers shy about foraging, and sometimes they appropriated goods, without compensation, from Jewish peddlers, excusing their behavior by recalling Grant's attitude toward Jews. Others went on expeditions, and Illinoisan William Lorimer had an adventure as he led a detachment of some twenty-five men, along with two wagons, into the countryside around Lake Providence. At a plantation, Lorimer rode to the main house, and four women came out to greet him. They were alone, except for black servants, and had few provisions left. One woman admitted her husband was at Vicksburg in Pemberton's army, two women were unmarried, and one was visiting from the North. Lorimer sympathized and moved on, but on subsequent trips, he developed a friendship with the women and often stopped to visit. On one such occasion, the women saved him from Confederate guerrillas by hustling him into a closet, where he almost suffocated among numerous dresses before the guerrillas rode off. Lorimer only stopped to see the women one more time. The episode revealed both the realities of fraternization, much to the disgust of guerrillas, and how precarious things could get away from camp.[40]

Also in the Providence area, cotton trading increased as fortune hunters from the north came down to buy cotton often confiscated by officers. Deals between buyers and the military caused a cynical Union soldier to note, "this war will never end[,] tha dont try to end it[,] the dam officers are making to much money[,] it is dam money makin war and if thare would com a Earthquake and sink all of the offcrs it would Brake up." Thus it was no surprise that officers allowed local slaves to pick cotton before the breached levee flooded the fields. Obviously, wherever armies assembled, opportunists joined guerrillas and vandals as part of the landscape.[41]

Grant soon decided the Providence venture had been a waste of time. The waterway connections, overflowing and full of trees, made it impractical as a boat passage south. Floodwaters had not sufficiently raised water levels to float large, loaded boats. McPherson refused to give up, but ultimately an impatient Grant ended the project. Nevertheless, the flooding later protected the Union left flank, after Grant decided to send his army down the Louisiana side of the river to cross the Mississippi below Vicksburg. For now, Grant decided to gamble on two other projects: the Yazoo Pass expedition and a campaign on Steele's Bayou and Deer Creek north of the Yazoo above Vicksburg.[42]

≋ Despite previous disappointments, Grant strongly believed in the Yazoo Pass expedition, an attempt to use inland waterways to get to the Yazoo and flank Confederate positions along the bluffs (Snyder's, Drumgould's, and Haynes's) on the Yazoo. The Pass campaign required joint army-navy operations, for the army required boats to move through the watery flatland of northwest Mississippi called the Delta. The navy also provided Grant additional firepower and essential logistical support. The Yazoo Pass episode demonstrated how much Union army operations depended on the navy during the Vicksburg campaign.

The campaign had many potential risks. As Union forces moved south into the Delta, their supply line would be long and vulnerable, as in December. The flooded Delta lowlands meant that local foraging would be limited. Levees protected some plantations, but the breach in Yazoo Pass would raise water levels everywhere. In many places, troops and boats would be isolated from dry ground. If they confronted Confederate works blocking their path, infantry would have difficulty maneuvering. Grant understood these factors, but potential success was worth the risks.

The Yazoo Pass, a small bayou several miles below Helena, Arkansas, located on the east side of the Mississippi, connected via Moon Lake to the Coldwater River. The Coldwater ran south into the Tallahatchie, which met the Yalobusha at Greenwood, Mississippi, to form the Yazoo. A substantial levee kept the Mississippi out of the mouth of Yazoo Pass. Once Union engineers breached it, the power of the Mississippi should do the rest, deepening the water passage to the Coldwater. Boats entering the Pass would immediately steam into Moon Lake and then into the relatively narrow channel that led to the Coldwater. The channel's heavy undergrowth and trees presented problems high water could not solve.[43]

Confederates understood the tactical possibilities the Pass offered the Yankees. Confederate work details began chopping trees in the connecting channel to complement obstructions previously prepared by Isaac Brown's naval crew in 1862. John Pemberton did not take the Pass threat seriously, though President Davis was concerned. In early February, when Grant focused on the area, Confederates could do little more than cut trees, and their efforts ultimately proved to be futile.[44]

On February 3, Federal explosives produced an opening in the levee that increased as the Mississippi roared into the Pass. Planter James Alcorn, former general of Mississippi State Troops, and an old Whig with Union sympathies, ordered his slaves to bring food, and he told Union officers that their boats should have little trouble getting to the Yazoo. Grant heard the news and wired Halleck that he hoped to clear the Yazoo and to use the Yalobusha to flank Grenada and destroy railroads.[45]

The blowing of the levee affected water levels well downstream into central Mississippi. Slaves rushed to build levees to protect crops, but it proved to be a losing battle. Farmers quickly shipped corn to the hills, and people all along the Yazoo rushed to high ground. Snakes invaded homes as the water rose, and people as far south as Yazoo City sought refuge with relatives in the Jackson area. As the Yazoo roared downstream, "it was a weird scene," "a wild and noisy time, waters roaring, men shouting, cows lowing, pigs squealing." When the water went down, debris marked flooded areas, fences were gone, dead livestock spotted the landscape, cabins and homes were wrecked or severely damaged, crops lay flat, and everything seemed to be coated with mud and slime. Sickness became a serious problem among people trying to salvage their losses.[46]

Grant relied on David Porter to get the operation moving. Porter outlined his plan for descending into the Delta and commented to one of his commanders: "If this duty is performed as I expect it to be, we will strike a terrible blow at the enemy, who do not anticipate an attack from such a quarter." His prediction proved to be hollow.

On February 7, six hundred infantry assigned to marine duty traveled by steamer from Young's Point to Helena, where they awaited a gunboat squadron commanded by Watson Smith. Benjamin Prentiss of Shiloh fame commanded army forces in the campaign. Meanwhile, Union officers, army and navy, reconnoitered the area and found the felled trees choking the connecting channel. Iowans and Indianans who had rafting and lumbering experience worked in damp, chilly, rainy weather and mud to clear the mess.[47]

Traveling by boat through the levee breach proved adventurous. One Union soldier long remembered how "our boat was whirled round and round like a toy skiff in a washtub. We all held our breath as the steamer was hurled among floating logs and against overhanging trees." Then the "rushing torrent carried us, backward down into the little lake. Not a soul of the five hundred on board the boat in this crazy ride was lost. Once in the lake we stopped, and with amazement watched other boats." Another soldier agreed that the ride "was very exciting, the limbs of trees would strike across the steamer and we had to run from one side to the other to keep from being brushed into the water." The "crazy ride" convinced the soldiers that "it was luck, not management, that half the little army was not drowned."[48]

By February 12, Watson Smith's fleet reached Helena. The next day, Smith inspected the Pass and seemed stunned to learn that Rebels had been seen around the Coldwater and that it might take as many as 30,000 men to successfully reach the Yazoo. Already worn down by previous campaigning, Smith felt discouraged about the prospects. Yet he resolved to proceed, and Porter added an ironclad, the *Baron De Kalb*, to the flotilla.

On February 15, General Prentiss arrived and lost interest in the Pass campaign when his officers suggested that a thrust up the Arkansas River might be more productive. John McClernand, still wanting an independent command, jumped on the bandwagon and asked for 21,000 men to attack Holmes at Pine Bluff. Grant quickly said no, pointing out, as he had before, that nothing could hinder his one great goal: opening the Mississippi. To Grant's way of thinking, Yazoo Pass offered more potential.[49]

Work continued on clearing the path to the Coldwater, while skirmishing broke out in the area. On the evening of February 21, the advance work party safely reached the Coldwater. Grant sent Leonard Ross's division to the Pass; Ross's assignment was to go up the Yalobusha from Greenwood to Grenada and destroy railroads.

Union activity at the Pass set off a flurry of correspondence at Pemberton's Jackson headquarters. On February 9, Pemberton received a report from Brown on the levee breach and Grant's probable intentions. Brown advised that artillery be sent to Greenwood and, though flooding would negate Yankee infantry, some sort of plan should be developed because the obstructions would not hold up Federal boats for long. Pemberton, with his usual lack of discernment, insisted there was no great threat.[50]

Pemberton found out soon enough that he could not ignore Brown's warnings. Enemy vessels continued to enter Moon Lake, and Confederates fought a losing battle trying to obstruct waterways. Mississippi state troops harassed the Federals, but their lack of numbers and firepower made them no real threat. A February 17 message from Brown startled Pemberton. The Yankees had broken through to the Coldwater, and it would take quickly constructed obstructions and a strong body of troops to save Yazoo City.

Brown rushed to meet the threat with two boats, the *Mary Keene* and the *Star of the West*. Carter Stevenson sent volunteers from Vicksburg to help man the vessels. Pemberton rushed back to Jackson from a Vicksburg inspection trip, and Loring left quickly for Yazoo City. With little hope of getting additional artillery, Stevenson sent two large-caliber rifled cannon from Vicksburg to Yazoo City. Pemberton advised Loring to hold Thomas Waul's Texans in reserve at Yazoo City in case a suggestion by Brown to establish a defensive position at Greenwood did not work.[51]

The Federals had made slower progress than Pemberton had been led to believe, which gave the Confederates precious time. A line of defense at the Coldwater was a possibility, but not a good one, and Brown had a more logical plan. He proposed building defensive works on the narrow strip of land between the Tallahatchie and the Yazoo west of Greenwood. Where the Tallahatchie and Yalobusha merged at Greenwood to form the Yazoo, the Yazoo from that point turned sharply west and then southwest to Yazoo City and beyond to the Mississippi. Where the Yazoo flowed west, its channel at one point was only about 500 yards south of the Tallahatchie channel, which turned east by southeast on its way to meet the Yalobusha. That 500-yard strip became the location of Fort Pemberton.

Loring traveled from Yazoo City to Greenwood to inspect the site, and he approved fortifications already under construction by slaves and soldiers. He especially liked the high ground on the right (south) bank of the Tallahatchie, from which heavy artillery could shoot at depressed angles directly at enemy boats. Loring had the option of making a stand at Yazoo City or Greenwood, but the possibilities offered by Fort Pemberton convinced him to concentrate there. Waul's Texas Legion arrived and deployed in a line of newly built trenches, and Pemberton also transferred Lloyd Tilghman's brigade from Jackson. Troops constructed rafts to block the Tallahatchie, and Loring decided to sink the *Star of the West* as an obstruction if necessary. He confiscated local steamboats and padded their decks with cotton bales. These so-called cottonclads would be armed and used to attack enemy boats if Fort Pemberton did not stop the Yankees. Loring set up an indirect communications line to Pemberton's Jackson office, by horse to the Mississippi Central and by rail to Jackson.[52]

On February 22, Pemberton learned that enemy boats had steamed into the Coldwater the day before. High water negated hastily built obstructions, and the Federal flotilla would soon be concentrated and heading south. Pemberton notified Loring, who at the time was on the Tallahatchie north of Greenwood, checking for signs of the enemy. Meanwhile, Thomas Waul, left in charge of construction at Fort Pemberton, requested and received more heavy artillery from Vicksburg.

Following his reconnaissance, Loring asked Pemberton for more reinforcements from Yazoo City and Grenada and two additional rifled guns from Yazoo City. Though he had received news of some 30,000 Union troops descending the Coldwater, more than seven times the actual number, Pemberton, who until now had cooperated with Loring, refused to weaken Grenada further. Loring had to be satisfied with Tilghman's brigade, still in Yazoo City. Pemberton wrote frankly, "I think you have as much infantry and field artillery as you can advantageously use at your present position." Though Pemberton's logic was sound, his refusal angered Loring.[53]

Joseph Johnston had seen newspaper reports regarding the Federals and Yazoo Pass, and he wired Pemberton for the facts. Pemberton curtly admitted that the enemy had broken through to the Coldwater, but he pointed out that Confederate defenses dominated the Greenwood area. Writing with more confidence than he likely felt, he told Johnston: "I do not think he [the enemy] can effect anything very serious." Johnston, given Pemberton's silence and attitude, probably was not convinced.

On March 6, Loring received word that enemy boats had reached the Tallahatchie, so he notified Pemberton, again requesting more heavy guns and infantry. Loring did not say so, but with the enemy closing fast, he seemed to be losing faith in Fort Pemberton. Isaac Brown traveled · up the Tallahatchie in search of cotton to pad more steamboats. The loaded steamer *Parallel* ran aground on its way back to Greenwood and had to be burned. Meanwhile, scouting reports indicated that enemy boats were getting closer, and Brown hurried back to Greenwood.

As the pace of the campaign quickened, it became apparent that Pemberton had not only ignored Johnston but had also failed to keep Richmond informed. A War Department message demanded information, and Pemberton reported that Union vessels had reached the Tallahatchie. Pemberton's silence no doubt concerned Jefferson Davis, but fortunately for the Confederates, the Federal flotilla's slow descent gave the Confederates time to make Fort Pemberton formidable.[54]

The fort, constructed of dirt, sand, and cotton, had been built so that its right flank rested on the Tallahatchie and its left on the Yazoo. Eight cannon, ranging in size from a 6-pounder to a 32-pounder, anchored the defenses. The line of earthworks, nearly 1,000 yards long, according to a Mississippi soldier, ran along a slant from the northeast on the Tallahatchie to the southwest on the Yazoo. The 32-pounder placed on the Yazoo had an unimpeded line of fire right up the Tallahatchie channel, which flowed from due north before turning east. Due to the slant in the line, other artillery would have a similar open field of fire at Union boats. Aside from cannon, Loring had 2,000 infantry, consisting of Waul's Texas Legion, the 2nd Texas, and the 20th Mississippi. Since the Union flotilla was getting closer, Loring ordered a raft placed diagonally across the Tallahatchie channel where it elbow-turned to the east. Right behind it, near the right flank of the Confederate line, the *Star of the West* was sunk, an ignoble end to a ship that gained fame when it was used in a failed attempt to get supplies to Union defenders of Fort Sumter. Loring notified Pemberton that he anticipated an enemy force of some nine gunboats, twenty-seven transports, and 5,000 infantry.[55]

The large number of Federal vessels negotiating the narrow channel from Moon Lake to the Coldwater caused the delay getting downstream. Watson Smith's naval detachment consisted of seven boats, plus fourteen transports bringing infantry from Helena. Smaller boats scouted the area. During the tedious passage through the channel—one boat at a time—snags, obstructions, and engine problems plagued pilots, and overhanging large limbs threatened everything on deck. While scouting parties looked for cotton to protect decks from enemy fire, two rams and a tinclad arrived to bolster Smith's naval armada, further congesting the waterways.[56]

On March 3, Smith's flotilla at last headed down the Coldwater, a wide stream with a slow current and a very crooked channel. The snail's pace made boats more vulnerable to wind gusts, which sent cumbersome hulls banging into trees along riverbanks. Mechanical problems on any boat brought them all to a halt while repairs were made. An Illinoisan observed, "The steamers that made the trip were a sorry looking lot, every thing was broken off of them that could be, the smoke stacks were thrown down and pilot houses riddled, paddle wheels were half destroyed and rudders many times broken. The fleet was little else than so many dismantled hulls." Men grew impatient at the pace; not until March 5 did the advance notice a wider channel as the flotilla neared the Tallahatchie. Men aboard felt some relief at the sight of plantations, which offered foraging prospects. Slaves ran to the riverbanks, staring in awe at the big boats that, in their minds, made the freedom promised by the great Lincoln a reality.[57]

As the ascent continued, guerrilla fire kept the armada alert. A witness recalled, "A guerrilla shot into our steamer and wounded one man, the first man to be wounded in our regiment. The Colonel went ashore with a small force and burned every building on the plantation from which the shot was fired." On March 6, Smith halted the flotilla some twelve miles into the Tallahatchie for a boat inspection, and little damage was found.

As plantation owners set their cotton fields afire on either side of the river, smoke began filling the air. Landing parties rescued some of the white fiber and tried to get accurate information from locals. They heard stories about massive fortifications being thrown up in Yazoo City and also in Greenwood. Smith rejected the notion that he might find trouble at the latter. Bored soldiers began shooting at livestock from the bank and going ashore to raid everything in sight. The long days and cramped quarters created an increasing number of discipline problems.[58]

Back on the Mississippi, Grant sent reinforcements. Isaac Quinby's division of James McPherson's XVII Corps embarked, and Quinby carried orders to take command of the expedition from Ross. Quinby did not realize the campaign had lagged, for he had been misleadingly told that he could land anywhere he wanted on the Yazoo, as if that would be easy, and that Smith had already reached Haynes's Bluff. Grant extolled to Halleck the success of the expedition, and he promised that when McPherson's whole corps reached the bluffs on the Yazoo, Vicksburg would be neutralized.

Quinby established contact with Ross and warned against getting into a fight unless one could be sure of winning it. A repulse would throw the whole campaign into jeopardy. Quinby did not know that rotting rations had further slowed the flotilla on the Tallahatchie, forcing men to go ashore foraging, and that low coal supplies forced stops for collecting wood. Ross, who thought he could occupy Greenwood by March 10, grew impatient, and blamed Smith for snail-like progress. Ross dismissed tales of large enemy numbers waiting near Greenwood. When Smith saw the *Parallel* burning, he slowed even more and sent the ironclads *Chillicothe* and *De Kalb* to investigate. On the evening of March 10, just over thirty miles above Greenwood, local blacks confirmed to ironclad crews that a large enemy fortification and raft obstructions lay ahead and that the *Star of the West* had been sunk in the channel.[59]

On March 11, Federal navy and army commanders aboard the *Chillicothe* saw Fort Pemberton frowning ominously a half mile downriver. Confederate gunners opened fire, striking the ironclad's hull twice. One shell damaged the wheelhouse; the other bounced off the armored hull. The boat's captain ordered reverse engines, and the boat backed up until partly out of view of the Rebels and then returned fire before heading upstream. The exchange of fire had been brief and indecisive, a portent of things to come.

General Ross decided to use his infantry to get a feel for the extent of the fort. He sent two Indiana regiments scouting along the Tallahatchie's west bank at Shell Mound Plantation, where the rest of the fleet had docked to wait on the *Chillicothe*. The Indianans moved within a few hundred yards of Fort Pemberton before running into a detachment of Waul's Texans. Each side fired a few shots, and the Indianans fell back, convinced that the flooded land around the fort made an infantry assault impossible.

William Loring kept Pemberton informed and asked for more of everything to be sent to Yazoo City in case the Yankees got by the fort. Meanwhile, Loring ordered Tilghman to send a regiment and battery to the Yalobusha from Grenada and to take the rest of his brigade to Yazoo City. Loring also ordered cattle and equipment from the fort to safer locations, causing the Federals to think the fort was being abandoned. When the two ironclads and a ram went downriver again, however, they drew enough fire to confirm that the Confederates had gone nowhere. During the exchange, the *Chillicothe* suffered major damage when a Confederate shell hit a gun that was being loaded; the resulting explosion damaged two gun ports and set afire cotton bales on deck. Smith lost four men killed and nine wounded.[60]

The campaign now settled into limited tactical maneuvering that kept both sides alert. Federal infantry foraged and wrecked area homes and outbuildings. They constructed a land battery of two 30-pounder rifled Parrott guns, which everyone expected would knock out the Rebel gun. Decks were reinforced with cotton, and the *Chillicothe* was repaired. Confederate artillerists kept silent to preserve ammunition. Loring's engineers built additional fortifications, and the Confederate supply line, in a safe zone to the rear of the fort, remained secure.

On March 13, the war of nerves continued. The two ironclads went downstream again, reinforced by a 13-inch mortar on a scow. The boats stopped side by side, and crews strapped them to two tinclads in the rear that could provide towing power if needed. The unfortunate *Chillicothe* took a number of hits, and the combined crews suffered eighteen casualties. A mortar crew lobbed forty-nine rounds into the fort, one of which hit a container of rifle cartridges, resulting in a fire that burned sixteen Confederate firefighters. Otherwise, Loring had only three killed and wounded.

That evening, both sides took stock, the Confederates rebuilding damaged mud-wall fortifications and Federal sailors repairing ironclads. A welcome supply vessel replenished Fort Pemberton's stores. Across the way, Union army commanders fumed at the navy's incompetence. Engineer James Wilson wrote John Rawlins of Grant's staff that one good gunboat could get the job done. Until the fort capitulated, Grant need not send more army troops.[61]

The artillery duels continued, both sides added an 8-inch gun to their batteries, and the stalemate lingered on. Union officers worried about dwindling artillery supplies, while Confederates added artillery to their left flank to enfilade Union troops in the unlikely event they would try storming the fort.

Wilson continued complaining to Rawlins about Smith: "I don't regard [him] as the equal of Lord Nelson." A breakthrough now, he said, would require more ironclads and more big guns, though just how many was unclear. Wilson seemed to forget that clogging the waterways would limit mobility without broadening the field of fire. An attempt by Union boats on March 16 to fire grapeshot (large shot banded together to give a shotgun effect when fired) while infantry tried to land close to the fort's bank ended when a Rebel shot sealed the *Chillicothe*'s gun ports.[62]

Loring felt confident until news came that Quinby's division was on the way. Loring called up three more regiments from Yazoo City and ordered construction of a back-up fortress south of Fort Pemberton on the right (north) bank of the Yazoo, dubbed Fort Loring. Confederates placed more rafts around Fort Pemberton, and Loring sent messages to partisans in the north Delta to try to slow Quinby's ascent.[63]

Meanwhile, Colonel Wilson, noting that Fort Pemberton did not rise very far above the Tallahatchie's water level, suggested widening the Yazoo Pass levee breach, letting in more water to flood the Rebel fort. It sounded good, and Union engineers tried the tactic, but the expanded breach failed to produce the desired result.

Wilson rejoiced anyway when he learned that Smith, on account of deteriorating health, was leaving and that James Foster now commanded. Foster called a council of war, and the officers voted to return to Helena. The navy could not take the fort alone, and the flooded countryside made the army's presence superfluous. General Ross urged Foster to wait for Quinby before ordering the withdrawal, but Ross changed his mind when he heard reports of Confederate attempts to blockade the Coldwater in the Union rear.[64]

Union scouts continued to search in vain for approaches to the fort other than the Tallahatchie. At the same time, Federal troops loaded supplies, armaments, and other equipment for the return trip; rumors of being cut off created a sense of urgency. As the flotilla turned and steamed upstream, Ross did not know that Quinby was already close at hand. Loring realized too late that the Yankees had withdrawn; patrols sent to harass the boats were disappointed to see the Federals fading from sight upstream.

Isaac Quinby, meanwhile, continued under the illusion that Ross had taken, or was in the process of capturing, Greenwood. He tried to get word to Ross that the latter should wait at Greenwood for Quinby's reinforcements before the flotilla moved down the Yazoo. Quinby, however, experienced all sorts of delays, so lead elements of his division did not reach the Coldwater until March 17.

Earlier, McPherson notified Grant that, given the shortage of transports, it could take two weeks to get the rest of his corps to Moon Lake. The delay concerned McPherson because he feared Quinby might need reinforcements. Grant replied that the operation had moved too slowly and that, based on Wilson's dispatches, Smith might be the problem. Whatever the case, Grant clearly wanted Quinby to move at once with as many men as possible, and the rest of the division could follow later.[65]

While military results of the campaign remained nebulous, the war had come home to Delta civilians, creating a horde of refugees and more Mississippi morale problems for Pemberton and Jefferson Davis. James Lusk Alcorn, the Union sympathizer, saw many neighbors and other Deltans headed across the Tallahatchie to the east when Union gunboats entered the area. Alcorn concluded that only military miracles could save the South; the day would come when slaves would be "ashes in our hands, our lands valueless without them." Alcorn blamed Jefferson Davis, whom he characterized as "the miserable, stupid, one-eyed, dyspeptic, arrogant, tyrant who now occupies his cushioned seat at Richmond." The Delta invasion no doubt produced anti–Confederate government sentiments among those who thought of themselves as immune to the war. A Federal retreat might boost morale, but it would not replace lost crops, repair vandalized homes, or undo flood damage.

Despite optimism at Fort Pemberton, the Yazoo Pass campaign had not ended. Grant was tired of it and began canceling orders for reinforcements, but, still casting about for solutions, he had yet another inspiration. He believed that waterways south and west of Greenwood could be used by Porter to cut Pemberton's supply line on the Yazoo. Porter could ascend Steele's Bayou into the Yazoo, and Loring would have to evacuate Fort Pemberton.[66]

The Steele's Bayou–Deer Creek operation originated with Porter, who saw it as at worst a creative diversion and at best a way to flank Fort Pemberton and gain a foothold on the Yazoo bluffs. His plan included taking a flotilla up the Yazoo from the Mississippi, turning north into Steele's Bayou to avoid Confederate artillery on the bluffs, and then moving via Black Bayou, Deer Creek, and the Rolling Fork and Big Sunflower rivers into the Yazoo between the bluffs and Yazoo City. Porter could then go upriver and cut Fort Pemberton's supply line or go downriver and flank the bluffs. The very threat should keep Pemberton from reinforcing Loring. Porter's plan did not take into account treacherous, narrow inland waterways.

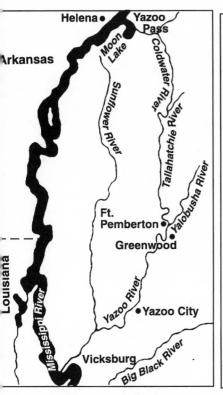
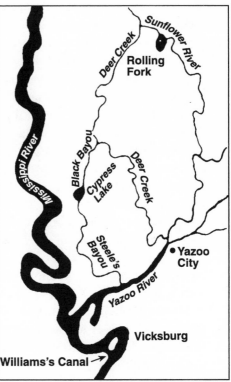

The Yazoo Pass Campaign, February 3–April 10, 1863. Map by Becky Smith.
Porter's Steele's Bayou Campaign, March 14–27, 1863. Map by Becky Smith.

On March 12, Porter checked the route and liked what he saw. He recommended the plan to Grant, who said yes in spite of having observed tree and limb obstructions during a personal tour. To augment Porter's five ironclads — the *Louisville, Cincinnati, Carondelet, Mound City,* and *Pittsburg* — Grant called on Sherman and McPherson for infantry and artillery support. An impatient Porter did not wait for the army; he set out on the sixteenth, leaving the *Louisville* to wait for Sherman.

Porter's boats struggled through Black Bayou, pushing aside trees and finally reaching a plantation near the confluence of Black Bayou and Deer Creek. Sherman arrived that evening, and he and Porter reconnoitered Deer Creek. Sherman frowned; his infantry and artillery needed dry land, and he did not see much of that. Sherman suggested going south down Deer Creek and fortifying its confluence with the Yazoo, or coming up the Yazoo and assaulting the bluffs directly. Porter insisted on continuing as planned, and Sherman acquiesced.[67]

Once the flotilla got into wider and deeper Deer Creek, the going was easier; but soon the landscape changed, and willow trees slowed the boats to a crawl. Plantation slaves flocked to the boats and begged for supplies, while burning cotton fouled the air. What planters did not destroy, Union soldiers and sailors took or burned.

News of the invasion sped ahead of Porter's boats, reaching the ears of Samuel Ferguson, commanding Confederate cavalry in the area. Ferguson's horsemen rode to the Rolling Fork and felled trees into Deer Creek. Porter sent ahead an armed tug to shell Ferguson's men, but with little effect. The campaign became a race, with the Confederates trying to obstruct the waterways ahead of the boats. Porter ordered a patrol to chase off Ferguson, and he sent messages to Sherman for help.

Sherman set up a staging area and waited for David Stuart's division, currently on its way down the Mississippi. Stuart had orders to land at Eagle Bend and march his troops overland to Steele's Bayou, and then go by boat to Sherman's camp. A lack of bridges slowed Stuart, and his troops did not arrive until the twentieth.

Ferguson's scouts, meanwhile, found a large sawdust pile above water level on Deer Creek and set up a base camp. Ferguson and his troops, charged with defending the lower Delta, had never expected to confront a naval force. Ferguson realized that he needed better defensive ground and sent news of his predicament to Vicksburg. Carter Stevenson responded by sending Winfield Featherston's brigade. Featherston brought his men to the front by boat and wading to Ferguson's camp.

Pemberton reported Porter's actions to Richmond and considered transferring men from Fort Pemberton to the new front. Assured by Vicksburg citizens familiar with the area that enemy gunboats could not make it through Deer Creek, Pemberton nevertheless sent cannon and two armed boats to the creek's mouth on the Yazoo. Pemberton never seemed to grasp his golden opportunity: trap Porter and take his ironclads—and suddenly the whole picture of the Vicksburg campaign would change. Yet Pemberton acted tentatively, debating whether to take troops from Loring to fight Porter.

On March 20, Ferguson heard that the *Carondelet*, Porter's lead vessel, was near the Rolling Fork. Obviously the obstructions had accomplished little. Ferguson decided to attack, and he sent an Arkansas regiment and artillery to attack Yankee patrols. The Confederates advanced to near the confluence of Deer Creek and the Rolling Fork and attacked a Federal battery deployed on Indian mounds. Porter's gunboats drove them off.

Featherston arrived, and he and Ferguson decided to renew the attack. Artillery would provide cover for infantry to board and capture the Union flotilla. After the Rebel artillery opened fire, the Federals abandoned the Indian mounds. Arkansas infantry prepared to attack, but Featherston's Mississippi troops did not show up. Their commander had decided his men could not wade the deep water, and he did not bother to tell Ferguson, who found Featherston eating supper. Featherston apparently smoothed things over and assured Ferguson that the next day would bring success. During the night, Confederates felled trees behind Porter's boats to prevent the Yankees from backing out the way they had come. Featherston's infantry would assault at dawn.

Porter, aware of the tree cutting and still without Sherman's troops, decided to give up the campaign; what had looked promising on maps simply had not worked. Porter notified Sherman, ordered his men to bathe the hulls in mud and slime to make it more difficult for the enemy to board, and instructed his pilots to drift the boats backward, ricocheting from bank to bank.

As the boats ran into obstacles, Porter prepared for the worst. His men plated the pilothouses with iron, drew half-rations, and readied to scuttle the boats if necessary. In such an event, every man would be on his own. Downstream, Confederates captured a note to Porter from Sherman that stated Sherman would try to protect the flotilla's rear.

On the twenty-first, Sherman sent troops east of Deer Creek. One of his generals, Giles Smith, rounded up black males to keep Rebels from using them to cut trees into the waterways. Smith also warned whites not to cooperate with Confederates if they wanted to keep their property intact. Sherman notified Grant of Porter's problems, and Grant ordered John Logan's division to reinforce Sherman.

At the same time, Porter's men worked feverishly to clear obstacles, while Confederates followed much too cautiously. Neither Ferguson nor Featherston seemed to grasp the opportunity at hand. The retreat quickly settled into sporadic skirmishing, and Federal detachments burned buildings that might provide cover for Confederate pursuers. Confederate commanders never made a serious rush at Porter's boats, and by 3:00 P.M. Porter got the welcome news that Giles Smith was nearby.[68]

While Porter breathed easier, Confederates argued among themselves about what to do next. Pemberton and Loring exchanged messages, Pemberton wanting help on Deer Creek, and Loring insisting that he could not weaken Fort Pemberton and that troops from Vicksburg should be sent to Ferguson. Stevenson wrote misleadingly to Pemberton that Porter would soon be captured, and Pemberton ordered reinforcements from Vicksburg. Many Confederates would have been glad to let Porter escape unscathed. A cavalryman complained: "You can have no idea of the condition of the roads—We march sometimes in water up to our saddle skirts for two miles and the mud is from one and half to two feet deep in places—it is a gloomy country—and full of mosketoes—& snakes."[69]

While Confederates bungled, Sherman brought up more troops, and Smith's infantry kept the lagging Rebels at bay. On March 22, Sherman, whose troops used candles to light their way during a hurried night march, arrived and kidded Porter about the near disaster. Porter did not mind; he was too relieved.

The campaign thus ended with a whimper. Porter's boats backed downstream into Black Bayou, the Yazoo, and the safety of the Mississippi. Featherston lamely blamed ammunition and food shortages for feeble efforts to capture the ironclads. Pemberton put a good face on inept Confederate actions by happily informing Richmond that the threat had ended. He made no mention of the destruction of crops and property wrought by Porter's men. An Alabama Confederate wrote, "One of the richest portions of Mississippi was laid waste and made desolate."[70]

The Steele's Bayou campaign underscored the Confederate handicap of not having a navy. Pemberton's forces, with the help of geography, checked two combined enemy army-navy operations at one time, but they could not take advantage of the situation in the absence of comparable naval help.

As if to further emphasize the point, David Farragut led a flotilla unimpeded up the Mississippi from New Orleans. Farragut wanted to block the Red River supply line, and he counted on Nathaniel Banks to produce diversions. At Port Hudson, three of Farragut's vessels were crippled by Rebel fire, but two went on upriver. On March 19, Farragut's *Hartford* and the *Albatross* ran easily by Confederate batteries at Grand Gulf, steaming on to Vicksburg to attack the Warrenton batteries on the twenty-third. Farragut managed to get past Grand Gulf on the thirty-first and safely back downriver. There his vessels effectively prevented Confederates from using the Red to transport supplies and the Mississippi to transport troops between Vicksburg, Grand Gulf, and Port Hudson. His brief excursion again showed the inadequacy of Confederate naval forces and Vicksburg batteries.[71]

Meanwhile, the Yazoo Pass campaign wound down. On the twenty-first, Quinby and his men steaming south met Ross and his expedition heading north. After much debate, Quinby persuaded other officers that the combined armada should return to Fort Pemberton. The big boats struggled to make U-turns, and locals watched in disbelief and anger as the hated Yankees returned. By the twenty-third, the flotilla stopped north of Fort Pemberton, and Quinby sent out patrols and the ironclads to scout.[72]

At Fort Pemberton, Loring had established second lines of defense, and he now had the rest of Tilghman's brigade on hand. Porter's retreat and the return of enemy forces to the Tallahatchie gave Pemberton no choice but to send additional guns and men to Loring, but he warned there would be no more available. Loring persisted, Pemberton relented, and by April 1 Loring had more troops than the Union forces he faced.[73]

Quinby got no more help, other than the rest of his division, the arrival of which swung total numbers back in Quinby's favor — but they arrived too late. Grant decided to abandon the Pass campaign. Reports about Fort Pemberton's strength and the flood conditions convinced him he had wasted enough time and troops there. He gave Quinby time to make an effort, and Quinby tried to get in the rear of the fort, but Loring had anticipated such a move and had constructed works to meet the threat. Foster had already told Quinby that he intended to take the flotilla back to Helena on April 1, so, with that deadline and little potential for success, Quinby abandoned the operation. The stalemate remained firmly in place.[74]

An Indiana soldier echoed Grant's conclusion that Fort Pemberton could not be taken. Infantry could do nothing in high water, and in any event the competition was fierce. Remembering the easy victory at Arkansas Post, he noted, "We are not contending with Arkansas Soldiers but the full Blood Johney Rebs[,] Mississippians and Texans Who don't know any thing else but fight." Another Hoosier told his father that the only reason the expedition had not gotten into the Yazoo was simply because it could not; the impudent Rebels blocked the way.[75]

Grant at last ordered Quinby to withdraw, and on April 4–5 Quinby's soldiers boarded transports for the Mississippi. Loring let them go with little more than a few artillery shells as a parting gift. By April 10, the convoy had docked at Helena, and the men rejoiced at being back on the wide Mississippi. Crowded, unhealthy conditions had plagued them, and they had nothing to show for it except additions to casualty lists. A soldier who saw the Yazoo Pass veterans wrote, "The men were a sorry looking set I can tell you. More than one third of them were sick and the rest so dirty as to be hard[ly] recognizable."[76]

John Pemberton did not press Loring to pursue. Lack of aggressiveness characterized both generals; and, while the enemy departure from Fort Pemberton could be called a victory, the setback did not bother Grant, for he quickly moved on to another plan. His three months of operations had kept Confederates guessing, widely spread their thin manpower, and depleted the countryside of supplies. Nothing had been settled, but Grant had damaged Pemberton's resources and, just as importantly, had affected the beleaguered commander's psyche. Pemberton had a false sense of security; the victory at Chickasaw Bayou and the repulses at Fort Pemberton and Steele's Bayou had to mean the enemy had abandoned efforts to bypass Vicksburg. Pemberton began to delude himself that Grant might give up on Vicksburg. He should have known better.

7

Turning Point

U. S. Grant finally made the right move with an operation he later claimed he "had had in contemplation the whole winter." He understood that failures would not be tolerated indefinitely. He had to take Vicksburg and clear the river, and until he accomplished that, the war in the Western Theater would drag on, and political pressure, especially on Lincoln, would persist. Grant dismissed a couple of obvious options, namely, a frontal assault from the river and a new drive down the Mississippi Central Railroad. He understood that an attack up the bluffs would produce nothing more than unacceptable casualty lists. The drive down the railroad had been tried and had failed, mainly because of the vulnerability of his supply line, and that would still be a problem. Sherman liked the railroad idea, but Grant feared reinstituting an old plan that would be unacceptable in Washington and would depress Union morale.[1]

The option he claimed to have postponed until better, dryer weather had come into focus as Grant analyzed maps and discussed strategy with his staff. By marching his army south on the western side of the river to a spot across from either Warrenton or Grand Gulf, he could, with Porter's cooperation, ferry his army into Mississippi. Grand Gulf made more sense, since it was out of range of Warrenton cannon, but it had also been fortified. In any event, once the army marched inland, with the navy controlling the river, Pemberton could be beaten, penned up, or chased off. Vicksburg would be in Union hands, forcing the ultimate surrender of Port Hudson, and the Mississippi would at last be opened to the Gulf. The plan meant that steamers had to run the gauntlet of Confederate artillery at Vicksburg to get downriver to transport troops across. Several vessels had made it past those batteries, however, so the risk was not as great as once thought. Logistics could be handled by setting up supply depots along the river to the south, where Porter's navy would provide protection. Grant kept the plan to himself for a while; in fact he did not mention it to Charles Dana. Dana heard gossip, however, and confronted Grant, but he made no effort to argue about the plan's merits with the general. Stanton had instructed Dana to observe, not to interfere with, Grant's operations.[2]

An additional angle regarding the supply situation concerned Nathaniel Banks, who was campaigning against Port Hudson. If Grant got his army south of Vicksburg, he could help Banks force Franklin Gardner to surrender, thereby opening an unimpeded Union supply line from New Orleans to Grand Gulf.

Grant misleadingly advised Banks on March 22 that he was leaning toward an all-out assault on Snyder's Bluff. Grant had not abandoned the idea of making such an attack, but the march down the Louisiana side of the river was a higher priority. If Banks had already taken Port Hudson, he could come upriver and join McPherson, still at Lake Providence at the time. If he had not, then he should pressure Gardner to keep reinforcements from Pemberton. About this time, Grant received a reminder from Halleck, "The great object on your line now is the opening of the Mississippi River, and everything else must tend to that purpose. The eyes and ears of the whole country are now directed to your army. In my opinion, the opening of the Mississippi River will be to us of more advantage than the capture of forty Richmonds."[3]

In his reply to Halleck, Grant noted his frustrations. Though he had forced the dispersal of Pemberton's troops, in the process he had scattered his own. The defenses at Vicksburg along the river had not been affected, so Grant obviously could not attack there. Halleck responded that Grant should simply concentrate his forces; and if Banks could not come to Vicksburg, then Grant should send help south or destroy enemy batteries at Grand Gulf.

Grant and his staff worked on details of the downstream venture. Several linked inland streams on the Louisiana side of the Mississippi would provide water passage for sending supplies south. A breach in the Mississippi levee around Milliken's Bend should raise water levels in those streams high enough to float supply boats. Grant chose New Carthage, a Louisiana community about thirty-five miles downstream from Milliken's Bend, as a staging area. It lay beyond the range of Confederate guns in the Warrenton area and was located between Warrenton and Grand Gulf, so the army could move upriver or down from there. On March 29, Grant gave the order that set the Vicksburg campaign on a course that produced long-sought results. John McClernand led the way, marching his XIII Corps from Milliken's Bend to New Carthage. It is worth noting that on this major turn in the campaign, Grant entrusted the advance to a man he often criticized. Grant's actions at this point, and later, proved that, while he might detest McClernand personally, he had a high regard for his generalship.[4]

After being reminded by Halleck that he was still expected to cooperate with Banks, Grant told McClernand that once his corps got ashore at Grand Gulf, they should move south to reinforce Banks. Once Port Hudson surrendered, then Banks and McClernand could march north to help take Vicksburg. It is doubtful that Grant seriously considered following through with such a plan, for he was much more concerned about Vicksburg than Port Hudson. Still, he could honestly tell Halleck that he had made arrangements to help Banks.

Grant had one last canal project in mind, a plan to connect the Duckport Landing on the Mississippi with Walnut Bayou; such a canal would theoretically allow flatboats to carry supplies from Milliken's Bend to New Carthage. Grant's enthusiasm soon waned. From March 31 to April 6 work went forward to a halfway point, and by the eleventh neared completion. Grant's thinking changed when he learned that enough boats were available in St. Louis to provide transportation and establish a supply line. He therefore abandoned the Duckport project; declining water levels made it unworkable anyway.[5]

Confederates across the river preferred the status quo. As long as Grant's army wallowed in the swamps, more bluecoats would desert, improving Confederate chances of holding Vicksburg. Artillerists enjoyed shooting at dredges, thereby contributing to disaffection among Grant's troops. Many Vicksburg defenders clung to the illusion that Yankees would massively reject "the nefarious designs of the Abolitionists" and the "cruelty and inhumanity" their war had wrought.[6]

John Pemberton, unsure of what Grant would try next, continued looking for additional slave labor, coping with his own desertion problems, and trying to stop civilian cooperation with the enemy. He assured Governor Pettus that slave owners would be reimbursed and that competent local overseers could supervise projects. As for deserters, Pemberton promised that those committing depredations would be "taken dead or alive." Regarding illegal trading with the enemy, Pemberton explained to Richmond, "citizens for the most part do not seem to perceive the wrong that is done in obtaining from an enemy articles which they think they greatly need." He ordered aid for destitute families north of the Yazoo and alerted guards at the Big Black River railroad bridge to watch for saboteurs. Despite these myriad concerns, plus the larger issue of a significant enemy presence across from Vicksburg,

Pemberton decided he needed to go to Richmond to consult with government officials. "I think," he wrote, "affairs here will admit of it." Pemberton would not make such a trip any time soon.[7]

Jefferson Davis continued to defend critics of his Vicksburg policy by insisting that he considered defense of the Mississippi along both banks "of primary importance." Further, he "deemed the defense of Vicksburg and Port Hudson as indispensable." In his April 10 message to the people of the Confederate states, Davis noted that the enemy had failed "to storm Vicksburg and Port Hudson." Obviously Davis felt comfortable with the situation at Vicksburg, an optimistic attitude reinforced by Robert E. Lee's successes in Virginia. Things were about to change in the West.

John McClernand's corps began moving south on March 31, with advance patrols reporting muddy roads and numerous streams that required pontoon bridges. As the scouts prepared to cross Roundaway Bayou, the last water obstacle before reaching the town of Richmond, Confederate cavalry fired a few rounds at the Yankees. Thomas Bennett, commanding the Union point, ordered his men across the bayou, where they chased away the Rebels.

McClernand and one of his officers, Peter Osterhaus, a native Prussian, rode down the next morning to find Bennett camped on the north side of the bayou. Osterhaus organized and rode with a scouting party that found a Confederate supply route connecting the area to the Mississippi. Osterhaus advised McClernand to leave an occupation force in Richmond to keep the route closed to the enemy. Other reports indicated that a decent road connecting Richmond and New Carthage had been located. The advance continued, with work details assisting with transportation and scouts sporadically firing at Confederate cavalry.[8]

McClernand's soldiers noted contrasts along the countryside as they marched. Trees "in full foliage and roses in full bloom" surrounded a plantation home in the Milliken's Bend area. As the columns moved further south, they observed the realities of war's impact. They encountered white people's "sullen eyes" and blacks greeting them "with joy and tears." One soldier described slaves left behind by fleeing owners as "a few wenches with swarms of young'uns and a few wind broken knock-need old Bucks," who "alone remain to represent the great institution which hitherto flourished like a green bay tree." At a plantation further down, they found the ruins of a mansion fired by the owner before he fled. Families unable to leave trembled at their possible fates, "but they can rest easy, for we did not come South to fight Women," claimed an Ohioan. "We want to whip Rebels not insult women — to capture guns &

equipments not household furniture, to take Vicksburg and not to burn a few deserted buildings." Another Federal, responding to his parents' admonitions, reminded them that soldiers "lay violent hands on anything we find to eat," but only took what was needed. One soldier blamed destruction on "instigation by abolition devils."[9]

While his troops marched south, Grant talked with David Porter about the navy's role in the campaign. Porter agreed to help set up a supply base at New Carthage and to coordinate the movement of troop transport boats past the Vicksburg batteries. Grant wanted a couple of Porter's ironclads to go below Vicksburg to disrupt any Confederate river traffic and neutralize Rebel land batteries. Porter agreed but told Grant that once the ironclads went down they might not be able to steam back upriver against the strong spring currents for some time. So if Grant still had notions of attacking the bluffs north of Vicksburg, he had better make up his mind now.

To settle the issue, Grant decided to go with Porter and Sherman up the Yazoo to reconnoiter. High water, cleared approaches to Confederate works, strong enemy defensive lines, and scattered artillery emplacements convinced Grant to abandon the idea of attacking the place. Grant assured Porter that the operation down the Louisiana side was his top priority. Grant believed that McClernand's corps and Porter's ironclads could successfully attack and hold Grand Gulf until the rest of the army arrived downriver.[10]

Few officers endorsed Grant's plan, the primary exception being McClernand, an ironic twist considering their tense past and even more confrontational future. Most of Grant's officers and confidants did not like McClernand having such a key role in the operation, but Grant was unmoved. Sherman likely protested; in a letter written home in early April, he stated bluntly, "McClernand is a dirty dog." Sherman still preferred campaigning in North Mississippi, but he yielded to Grant's wishes. A cynic might suggest that Grant purposely put McClernand in this position, because if he failed, Grant would have a good excuse to get rid of him. Given the disappointments Grant had already suffered, it seems unlikely he had any such thing in mind. Grant's personal feelings could be strong, but they were not petty enough to risk losing a campaign.[11]

The move south gained momentum, as more of Osterhaus's troops arrived in New Carthage. The mosquito population worsened, one man complaining that constant swatting of insects interfered with his writing a letter home. Flies and gnats contributed to the misery as did the ever-present, rather large snakes. One soldier put his hand on a serpent, "by accident of course. but I concluded both of us could not stay in the same vicinity together[;] as his snakeship did not show any disposition to leave why I left." Abandoned pantries and shipments from sanitation organizations back home enhanced rations. While soldiers foraged for food, they wryly noted how many locals "are anxious to come back into the Union & be loyal citizens."

Confederate Louisiana cavalry continued shooting, punching holes in levees and destroying local boats to slow Federal progress. Osterhaus sent patrols to screen the army against elusive Rebel horsemen, but they were only partially effective. Osterhaus and McClernand, while scouting, had to hit the dirt when pesky Confederates suddenly appeared in the distance and fired. Refusing to be intimidated, Osterhaus ordered his men to halt and set up camp and a staging area at Pointe Clear.[12]

On April 8, the continuing Abraham Lincoln campaign to arm former slaves caught up with the army as it snaked south. Logan and McPherson made supporting speeches that produced enthusiastic responses. General John McArthur also urged the men to accept the concept, commenting, "I have heard the opinion expressed in some portions of the army, that we could not whip the south; now I want to know the reason why; we have men enough, we have rations enough, we have guns enough, we have greenbacks enough, and . . . *we have greybacks enough.*" The men cheered; with active campaigning under away again and morale on the rise, many forgot their prejudices and welcomed, at least in theory, the addition of black soldiers.[13]

On the Mississippi side of the river, John Bowen, commanding at Grand Gulf, received scouting reports about the enemy's push south. Bowen secured the services of a couple of steamers and on April 4 sent Francis Cockrell and his Missourians across the river to Hard Times. When Bowen heard about Federals settling in at Pointe Clear, he immediately fired off a message to Pemberton, who seemed unconcerned.

Meanwhile, McClernand's troops continued fighting geography and Rebel cavalry. Some of the men found a scow, armed it with a howitzer, dubbed it the *Opossum*, and used it to drive off Confederates beyond New Carthage at Ione Plantation. Osterhaus learned from the owner that the main body of Confederate cavalry had retreated to Lake St. Joseph on April 5. Meanwhile, scouting reports indicated that flat boats could navigate bayous and sawmills could provide lumber for boat construction. Osterhaus increased the advance force to hold off Confederates until Porter's boats arrived. Slaves reported that Cockrell's Missourians had crossed the Mississippi, and Federal officers carefully chose camp locations to avoid shelling from Confederate boats. Osterhaus assigned two brigades to protect the long communications line from Milliken's Bend to New Carthage. Confederates watched, their numbers too thin to attack.[14]

At Milliken's Bend, McClernand discussed future movements with Grant. Grant decided to send Eugene Carr's division down, now that Osterhaus and his men had cleared the way. Carr's troops, freshly arrived from St. Genevieve, Missouri, were added to McClernand's corps. While in Milliken's Bend, Grant and McClernand reviewed Carr's and A. J. Smith's divisions. On April 12, Carr marched south.

An Illinoisan remembered the trip: "We marched most of the time, day and night with about one hours stop at noon and midnight to make some coffee and eat some hardtack and sow belly. We would stop occasionally for about fifteen minutes to rest and snatch a little sleep." The weather did not cooperate: "It rained about half the time and everywhere was water, mud, and slush. Sometimes we could not get water enough on our marches, but this time we got more than we could drink and we did not have anyplace to put the overplus."[15]

Federal foot soldiers reflected on the variety of native Louisianans they encountered. Some were struck by "how everything betokened an inveterate hatred of the soldier with the blue uniform." Soldiers in blue who sought drinking water at private residences met embittered resistance or grudging assent. Few white men could be seen, and the abandoned plantations offered such sights as "a long train of carts and wagons loaded with old grey headed decrepit Negroes and wenches accompanied with little darkeys from 9 days to five or 6 years old." These slaves had been left to fend for themselves.[16]

Soldiers continued to marvel at the countryside. "A certain degree of desolation & destruction," wrote one, "necessarily marks the passage of a large army through an enemy country, which here as elsewhere is greatly increased by the carelessness & wantonness of the troops. If the angel of destruction had passed over this region the blight would not have been more complete." Another veteran put it more succinctly when he wrote that everywhere they saw "the desolating scourge of demon *war*."[17]

Francis Cockrell hoped to at least stall the Yankee march by whipping the enemy advance. He attacked with one regiment at Ione Plantation, but the strength of three Union regiments forced him to retreat. Cockrell withdrew to safety, but his action alerted Grant to concentrate McClernand's troops, while McClernand sent the rest of Osterhaus's division to keep Cockrell quiet. McClernand notified Grant that Sherman or McPherson must protect the Milliken's Bend to Richmond segment of the line, now that the XIII Corps had moved south of Richmond.[18]

While McClernand's corps solidified Union control of New Carthage, David Porter had to push forward Grant's timetable, since Gideon Welles had instructed Porter to relieve Farragut at Port Hudson. Porter notified Grant that he would have to assemble the flotilla and run past the batteries as soon as possible, regardless of whether troops at New Carthage were ready to cross. Grant agreed and told Porter to proceed.

Porter tried to keep his mission secret. His men worked quickly at the staging area just above the mouth of the Yazoo. An unexpected guest, Jacob Thompson, once secretary of the interior to President James Buchanan, came by on a small boat with several other Southerners. Quickly captured, the prisoners were taken to Grant, who greeted them and, satisfied that these all too obvious spies really knew nothing of value, let them go. Union soldiers were also in the dark, one commenting in a letter written the sixteenth: we "do not know hardly anything[,] only what we see and do our selves." Grant, meanwhile, sent word downriver to McClernand that the passing of the batteries would probably take place at night, on April 14 or 15.

Bad weather delayed the attempted passage until April 16. Porter reviewed tactical considerations; the navy's experience with the *Arkansas* had shown that ironclads close to the Mississippi side of the river could stop and do battle with limited damage from Vicksburg batteries. Other tactical ploys included packing decks with cotton and hay bales, and diverting exhaust steam into the paddle wheel housing in order to muffle engine noise. Porter hoped to get past the batteries without the Confederates even noticing. Crews tied barges to the sides of the transports facing Vicksburg to help shield the thin-skinned vessels from artillery fire. They also lashed barges carrying valuable equipment to the starboard, or right, sides of the ironclads, and on the other side they attached barges of coal, both for protection of hulls and for refueling. Finally, they tied logs and otherwise useless boats to the sides of some vessels as additional padding.[19]

Circumstances in Vicksburg were much the same as when the garrison had been caught off guard the past December. Residents and soldiers went about business as usual, and officers like Carter Stevenson ignored reports of increased activity on the river above the Yazoo. Pemberton should have warned his officers and men in Vicksburg to be ever vigilant as long as the enemy remained in the region, but there is no evidence he did. As in December, a ball planned for the night of the sixteenth occupied many people, and this ball would also be interrupted by news from the river. The weather seemed to be on Porter's side when it held up the passage for a couple of nights.

Upstream, Porter's men fired up boilers in the afternoon, to ready engines for the evening's adventure and to cut down on smoke once the parade started. As a further precaution, Porter ordered lights out aboard all boats and slow speed so as not to draw attention. He distributed tactical instructions, which called for pilots to stay close to the Louisiana shoreline once the fleet rounded the tip of De Soto Point. Trees along the shore helped hide boat shadows and gave gunboats more shooting range. However, if the enemy started firing, all vessels should cross the river and steer close to the Mississippi shore to create difficult shooting angles for Confederate artillerists along the bluffs. Two Union batteries on De Soto Point would provide cover fire.

The flotilla moved out around 9:15 as planned, with Porter's flagship, the *Benton*, in the lead. Porter's seven armed boats contained a combined total of seventy-nine guns. Three transports trailed behind six of the armed vessels; the seventh took up the rear. An ammunition barge was allowed to drift down behind the fleet; if the barge got hit and exploded, the damage would, it was hoped, be confined.[20]

Along the Vicksburg shore and bluffs, the Confederates had thirty-seven large-caliber cannon (twenty smoothbore and seventeen rifled) and thirteen smaller field pieces. Four of the so-called big guns were barely so; they could be called field pieces, but they had high-velocity firepower. Edward Higgins's command consisted of upper batteries at Mint Spring Bayou to Glass Bayou, waterfront guns, and lower batteries south of town. The big guns were not placed atop the high city bluffs where their impact would be minimal. The most effective batteries, dubbed the Water, Wyman's Hill, and Marine Hospital, were some thirty to forty feet above the river. This location moderated, but did not solve, the problem of depressing muzzles to hit boats close to the Vicksburg shoreline. Of course, the effectiveness of the guns also depended on vigilant artillerists, and there were few on duty the night of April 16.[21]

At least Porter reached that conclusion as his fleet rounded De Soto Point with no sign of enemy recognition. Confederate pickets watched the whole show, too far away to sound effective alarms. They did the best they could. Detachments from Vicksburg had been alternately going to the Point for just such an eventuality, and this night a company of Louisianans landed on home soil and saw the boats. Some rowed back across to spread the word, while others set buildings afire, including the

Vicksburg, Shreveport and Texas Railroad terminus depot, both to sound the alarm in Vicksburg and to illuminate the river to alert Confederate gunners.

Grant's son, Fred, watching the action with his father and others on board the *Henry Von Phul*, Grant's floating headquarters, recalled how things livened up. "Suddenly a rocket went up from the shore. Then a cannon burst forth from Warrenton, and a shot passed directly in front of our boat. We stopped; a flame sprang lurid from a house at De Soto (not the point, but a little town opposite Vicksburg); then another on the river front, and soon fires were burning all along the shore, in front of the city, and the water was illumined as by day's brightest sun. There in front of us, steaming down the river, were six gunboats, which looked to me like great black turtles, followed closely by three fragile transports, moving directly toward the batteries of the doomed city." As for his father, he "was smoking; but I noticed an intense light in his eyes." One observer counted some 525 shots, and after the noise died down, Grant, assuming Porter had made out all right, ordered his boat back to Milliken's Bend.[22]

Porter's adventure proved more exciting than Grant may have realized. As the alarm spread, Confederates lit tar barrels to brighten the night and the river. The 14th Mississippi Light Artillery fired from atop Fort Hill, and Confederate infantry joined in with little effect. The ball at the William Watts home continued uninterrupted, and the few people in the streets seemed oblivious to flickering reflections of light along De Soto Point. Music drowned out sounds of battle from upriver, but the artillery noise soon penetrated the Vicksburg night. Many thought what they heard was only the shenanigans of bored cannoneers; but then a deep boom from a bigger caliber gun thundered, followed by more deep roars, and military personnel at the ball stampeded for the door.

Aboard the Union boats, sailors exchanged glances, surprised at the slow response of Confederate artillerists. But initial slow-paced booms quickly gained speed, and soon the Vicksburg batteries thundered up and down the waterfront. The flotilla quickly headed to the Mississippi shore as ordered, and Porter signaled his guns to answer. The fires, smoke, shadows, and noise caused the formation to break up. Ironclads became difficult to steer because of the cumbersome barges strapped to their sides and variants in currents close to shore added to the problem. Several spun around in circles as pilots desperately tried to maintain control.[23]

As the boats got close to the riverbank, Porter's heavy guns fired point blank into shoreline buildings, blowing them apart. Confederate guns scored hits too, though many batteries, thanks to Porter's tactics, overshot their targets. Rebel fire knocked a hole in a coal barge, forcing Union crews to cut it loose. The crew of the *General Price*, captured from the Confederates, had to cut its strapping to the *Lafayette*, after being hit by the *Louisville*. The *Louisville* also hit another friendly vessel and lost its coal barge.

One of Porter's pilots said that "it was the supreme moment of his life when the roar of the guns reached his ears. The enemy . . . in a moment were sending Minnie balls plenteous as rain drops in a summer shower. Shot and shell flew thick and swift as the lurid lightning's flash. With one hand on the pilot wheel, the other on the line connecting with the engine room, and as the fearful roar of bursting shells filled the trembling air, he rang continuously for more steam. When his boat had swept past the batteries and into the swirling waters below, she was throbbing, pulsating and quivering like a thing of life."[24]

Most Confederate infantry, lured into complacency by their commanders' false belief that the enemy had pulled out of the Vicksburg area, looked on, somewhat bemused by the show. Deafening sounds echoed through the bluffs, and a Georgian wrote afterward, "I have read in some book of fiction that distance lends enchantment to the view, but think the expression can never be so forcibly felt as when gun boats are throwing shell at the Regiment." If Pemberton remained slow to realize that the fight for Vicksburg had not ended, his men now had no such illusions. Porter's run convinced many that the war would go on and on. Wrote one Confederate, "We have given up all ideas of peace soon and are making our calculations in feeling to meet the worst yet."[25]

One steamboat, the *Henry Clay*, turned and started back upstream. Perhaps captain and crew panicked and hoped to find safety there. A Confederate shell hit the *Clay* and set it on fire. The crew left the boat, but the captain stayed aboard until several more shells slammed into the hull, and he too had to abandon ship. The crippled boat drew the attention of shore gunners, who concentrated their fire to make sure it did not escape. In doing so, some batteries allowed other vessels in the flotilla to steam by unscathed. The *Tuscumbia* and *Forest Queen* ran into misfortune when the former grounded and hit the latter while trying to back into deeper water. The two took multiple hits, but finally drifted downstream and to shore out of harm's way. The flotilla had one more stretch run to make before reaching safety. The boats passed and exchanged shots with Pemberton's southernmost battery at Warrenton. The shooting proved harmless to both sides, and Porter led the flotilla out of range where pilots assessed damage.[26]

Emotions fluctuated along the river that night. Farther downstream, McClernand's soldiers waited and worried when they saw the remains of the *Henry Clay* float by. Then the rest of the boats came in sight, shouts of joy rang out, and soldiers began dancing and imbibing. Back upstream, the Confederates consoled themselves with exaggerated accounts of the damage they had done to the Yankee navy. In truth a slow rate of fire, caused in part by the danger of cannoneers exposing themselves to Porter's return fire, and the location of batteries minimized Confederate effectiveness.

An enthusiastic Grant convinced Porter to run more boats south; the more available downriver, the faster the transfer of troops from Louisiana to Mississippi would be. The next expedition consisted of twelve barges, five stern-wheel (rear-wheel) steamers, and one side-wheeler. Crews prepared them as before, though a shortage of cotton bales forced the use of barrels of beef to protect bulwarks. This second wave carried over 600,000 rations for the XIII Corps. The boats would be practically defenseless, so Union details attempted to burn buildings still standing at De Soto to cover the river with a veil of smoke. Confederates fought desperately to keep the Yankees away, and with the help of the Wyman's Hill battery on the Mississippi side, plus high water and abatis, they drove off the enemy. Civilian crews refused to take the boats downstream, so experienced boatmen in Missouri and Illinois regiments volunteered; and by the night of April 22, the flotilla was ready. The trip downstream began, with high Union hopes of more success.[27]

The Confederates acted quickly this time. Signal guns on Fort Hill boomed as soon as the boats rounded De Soto Point. The Rebels fired the De Soto buildings and tar barrels to light up the river and make better targets of the flotilla. The vessels went full speed ahead; the smoke from guns and burning structures provided cover; and by the time the shooting ended, five transports had made it by and six of twelve barges had been undamaged. Despite all the Rebel firepower, the boats had combined casualties of two mortally and six slightly wounded.

The second passing of the batteries again demonstrated unrealistic Confederate expectations of artillery on the riverfront. The unarmed armada posed no threat of return fire, and the Confederate rate of fire increased, yet big guns still proved largely ineffective. Also, despite the best efforts of the government in Richmond, Vicksburg gunners simply did not have enough pieces to cover the long stretch in front of the city.

The artillery pieces had, therefore, been spread thinly to cover a wide range. The inability to depress guns enough to hit boats as they hugged the eastern shoreline continued to hamper the frustrated gunners. Thick parapets built to protect the guns from heavy naval ordnance contributed to compression angle problems and complicated the task of artillerists in loading and firing muzzle-loaded guns. The risks these cannoneers faced from exposure to enemy shells slowed the rate of fire. Finally, the position of shore batteries prevented converging fire on enemy boats; shooting from the east side of the river, they could not fire up and down lines of boats from end to end. Such fire normally reduced range problems, since overshots or undershots might still hit vessels to the front or rear of a target. The stationary batteries and Porter's plan of moving the boats from one side of the river to the other made such a tactic impossible.[28]

John Pemberton's reaction to April events prior to Porter's passage had been predictable, given his penchant to see good news where it did not exist. Along with several of his subordinates, he constantly misread Grant. Having seen Grant's efforts in early 1863 end in failures, Pemberton convinced himself that boats coming south from Memphis indicated a transfer of Grant's forces to Rosecrans in Tennessee. Pemberton reported the news to Johnston, who replied that reinforcements should be sent to Bragg from Vicksburg. News of the Federals' abandonment of the Yazoo Pass campaign, as well as the reduction of Union forces in the immediate Port Hudson area, fueled the illusion that Grant had been transferred to Tennessee.

Pemberton hesitated, however, to gut his own forces too quickly. Reports had also come in that a Federal division had landed at Greenville on the Mississippi and was pushing south along Deer Creek. Other messages indicated Federal plans for a two-pronged offensive against Vicksburg. Pemberton responded by building up troop strength at Snyder's Bluff and in Yazoo City. Still, he did not reject the possibility of Grant's leaving; in fact he tried to bargain with the War Department to send him more cavalry in return for sending infantry to Bragg. All the while Pemberton ignored mounting evidence that Grant's army was up to something big in Louisiana.[29]

Confederates cut trees on Black Bayou near Deer Creek to prevent a repeat of Porter's foray. Pemberton and other officers had heard much from angry residents in that area about previous Federal depredations. One Confederate soldier wrote bitterly of the enemy: "They are worse than the Goths and Vandals of the middle ages. Killing horses and mules—cows and hogs—sometimes taking only a quarter of beef—at some places mere wanton destruction—no need of meat—burning houses—quarters, gins and everything. Stealing all—crockery, cooking utensils—all the axes. . . . Stealing negroes. Some would not go with them—all the women were ravished, the Yanks holding them whilst others were gratifying their hellish desires."[30]

News of another Deer Creek threat, skirmishes with McClernand's advance, and Bowen's transfer of Cockrell's troops to Louisiana, should have alarmed Pemberton, but he seemed convinced that Grant was leaving. When Bowen asked for instructions about countering the large enemy force across the river, Pemberton replied with a masterpiece of vagueness. "If you can occupy a position, which cannot be turned," he wrote, "and can cover a sufficient front to successfully resist an assault, having made ample arrangements to withdraw your troops, by telegraph and signals, in event of enemy's vessels returning [Farragut's flotilla], you can, after leaving adequate force for your batteries and their defenses [at Grand Gulf], move the remainder of your troops to risk his advance." Then Pemberton stated clearly his personal views: "I do not regard it of such importance as to risk your capture." Pemberton wrote similarly to Richmond regarding McClernand's alleged move south: "not yet confirmed" and "much doubt it."

Despite additional tidings from Bowen to the contrary, Pemberton persisted in his denials. Continual river traffic headed toward Memphis seemed to support Pemberton's transfer theory. Soldiers in the ranks believed it, too, and they anticipated leaving Vicksburg for Tennessee to fight Rosecrans. Actually the traffic on the Mississippi resulted from cancellations of the Yazoo Pass and Steele's Bayou expeditions, plus the transfer of Frederick Steele's division to Greenville for a special assignment. Also, Halleck told Grant that transports were needed elsewhere; hence the traffic north.[31]

Cockrell and Bowen continued sending ominous messages, and Pemberton continued ignoring them—and he promised Johnston 8,000 men for Bragg! Pemberton stated flatly to Johnston, "Am satisfied Rosecrans will be reinforced from Grant's army." Believing Port Hudson to be secure, Pemberton asked Franklin Gardner to send troops to Bragg via Mississippi. Gardner obliged, and 4,500 troops traveled by rail to Jackson. To reach the 8,000 figure, Pemberton determined to send Lloyd Tilghman's 3,500-man force from Grenada to Tennessee. To satisfy Johnston's continued requests for more men, Pemberton also designated John Vaughn's brigade in Vicksburg for transfer.

On April 15, Pemberton finally came to grips with reality. Messages from above Vicksburg reported Union transports heavily laden with troops moving down, not up, the river. Bowen correctly predicted that the Yankees intended to run the batteries; if that happened, Cockrell's detachment could be cut off and lost. Pemberton, still in his Jackson headquarters, notified Carter Stevenson in Vicksburg that the Union evacuation of the area had obviously been a ruse. It had not been an intentional ruse, but Pemberton had effectively made it one by misreading the chain of events.[32]

The next day, Pemberton notified Johnston that most of Grant's army obviously had not left and that he was canceling the transfer of Tilghman's and Vaughn's troops. Pemberton then learned that large numbers of enemy troops remained in the Port Hudson area, and that in fact Nathaniel Banks had begun an offensive west of the river. Edmund Kirby Smith, commander of the Trans-Mississippi, proposed evacuating Port Hudson and sending Gardner's force elsewhere. This might force Banks to end his campaign, thereby reducing the threat to the Red River supply line. Smith no doubt reasoned it might also reduce requests for him to send reinforcements east of the Mississippi. Pemberton, of course, facing the reality of Grant's army on the Louisiana side in the New Carthage area, could not send any more troops to Port Hudson.

The situation Pemberton had long ignored suddenly crystallized when Porter ran past the batteries on April 16. He asked Johnston to return Abraham Buford's brigade, formerly of Port Hudson. Johnston agreed and hoped Kirby Smith would attack Union lines of communication in Louisiana. Meanwhile, Pemberton reported the latest developments to President Davis and asked for more big cannon to defend points along the Mississippi and Yazoo. Davis emphasized that he had already shipped several, more were on the way, and the government simply did not have enough to satisfy all needs.[33]

While Pemberton and his generals reexamined their situation, Bowen recalled Cockrell's troops, leaving Louisiana cavalry to resist Grant's operations. Pemberton sent reinforcements to Bowen in case the Yankees crossed in force, a possibility that seemed quite likely. Bowen soon had 4,200 men to defend Grand Gulf and keep the Federals out of the Big Black River, which ascended northeast into Mississippi from above Grand Gulf and provided water access to land approaches south and east of Vicksburg. To facilitate troop movements, Confederates bridged Hankinson's Ferry, located about ten miles above where the Big Black emptied into the Mississippi.

Pemberton established Tilghman's brigade as a strategic reserve in Jackson. Confederates seemed to think that Grant might try to land, go north, and approach Vicksburg from the east. Reports from a scouting trip downriver to check on Porter's strength convinced Pemberton to keep at least 5,000 men in place to rush to Warrenton in case the Yankees came ashore there. This line of thought suggested that a reserve force along the Big Black, south of the Southern Railroad bridge, might be more effective than posting Tilghman at Jackson.[34]

Carter Stevenson realized Tilghman was too far away, and Pemberton agreed to send the brigade to the Big Black as soon as Abraham Buford's recalled troops arrived in Jackson. Buford could have already been in Jackson had not Pemberton inexplicably delayed bringing the brigade from Montgomery, Alabama, where its Tennessee trip had stopped. Pemberton shifted troops to other possible trouble spots, including Snyder's Bluff, Warrenton, and even to northwest Mississippi in case Union boats tried another Yazoo Pass–type operation. Pemberton exchanged messages with Kirby Smith, each asking for help on his side of the river that neither had the means to give. While Grant consumed Pemberton's attention, Nathaniel Banks occupied Smith's.

On April 23, Pemberton learned that more boats had passed Vicksburg. Stevenson expected an attack at any time, and he deployed his division between Warrenton and South Fort, the latter being the southern anchor of the interior Vicksburg defensive line. M. L. Smith's division, plus Edward Higgins's river batteries, guarded the waterfront in front of the city, and John Forney's troops occupied the Yazoo bluffs. Pemberton realized that whatever Grant did, it likely would be against the southern flank, so he advised Stevenson to keep troops in Vicksburg standing by to reinforce Warrenton and Grand Gulf. Unfortunately, no railroad connected the Vicksburg area with Grand Gulf, so rapid movement south required fast marching in increasingly warm weather. Stevenson did not like overemphasizing one sector, but Pemberton assured Stevenson that his directives were intended to address possibilities and did not require overcommitment.[35]

Pemberton's worries continued to mount. He received a report indicating that strong river currents had swept away the raft on the Yazoo intended to block Porter's boats. Stevenson ordered a raft from Yazoo City placed on the lower reaches of the river. Added to all this, Richmond chose to transfer Dabney Maury from Vicksburg to Tennessee, forcing Pemberton to reorganize his command structure in the face of enemy threats.

Increased Federal activities and negative reports kept Pemberton off balance, and he never adequately prioritized his responses to Union operations on the Louisiana side of the river. Federal cavalry activity, especially two interrelated raids, one by Benjamin Grierson through the heart of Mississippi and another by Abel Streight east into Alabama, greatly impacted the Vicksburg campaign by further diverting Confederate resources and disrupting supply lines, and, more particularly, John Pemberton's attention.

The raids grew out of proposals by Stephen Hurlbut, who commanded the XVI Corps in Memphis, and William Rosecrans in Tennessee. Hurlbut wanted to strike the Southern Railroad of Mississippi, the vital Rebel communications link from Vicksburg to the East, while Rosecrans proposed sending riders into northern Alabama and across to Georgia, thereby cutting the Western and Atlantic Railroad in northwest Georgia, connecting Atlanta and Chattanooga. Hurlbut realized his and Rosecrans's concepts complemented each other; the two raids would force Confederates to spread their thin cavalry resources, improving chances of success. Grant agreed and approved the plan.[36]

On April 11, Streight's troops rode south out of Nashville. By the twenty-sixth, he had reached Tuscumbia, Alabama, and turned toward Rome, Georgia. Once his men, mounted on sturdy mules for travel through mountainous country, moved east, things began to unravel. Nathan Bedford Forrest and his cavalry stayed on Streight's heels, rarely giving the Yankees time to catch their breath. Forrest ran Streight down at Cedar Bluff, Alabama, an apt name for a surrender site, for Forrest shifted his troops back and forth behind hills, bluffing Streight into thinking he was heavily outnumbered. Streight surrendered on May 3; but while Streight failed to carry out his mission to tear up the railroad, he did draw Forrest far from Vicksburg.[37]

Benjamin Grierson led a column of some 1,700 men out of La Grange, Tennessee, on April 17, beginning his trek through Mississippi. He angled to the southeast, sending detachments to hit the Mobile and Ohio Railroad and traveled west of the railroad deep into the central part of the state. Along the way, he sent patrols out to raid the surrounding countryside; his tactics confused Rebel cavalry trying to pin him down. Grierson even sent a detachment on a circuitous route back toward La Grange to confuse pursuers. A skirmish with Confederate cavalry convinced these Union riders to return to La Grange rather than risk possible capture.[38]

Grierson led his main column through Starkville; a town resident wrote that the raiders "done emense damage to the sitesans [citizens] [,] too evy horse mule and Negro fellow and destroyed all the guns amunition provision and indeed evry thing they found[;] fortunately they did not visit mee[;] one of my Negro fellows ran away and likely is with them." The raiders continued south by southwest through Louisville, Philadelphia, and Union.[39]

By April 24, Grierson had reached Newton Station between Jackson and Meridian on the Southern Railroad. Here his cavalry destroyed track and supplies and escaped Pemberton's attempts to thwart the raid. Pemberton sent infantry, commanded by Loring, toward Meridian in an effort to cut off and capture Grierson. The hard-riding bluecoats continued south by southwest and almost ran into a blockade near Union Church. Wirt Adams's cavalry had ridden over to keep Grierson away from Grand Gulf. Grierson gave some thought to meeting Grant's army as it crossed into Mississippi, but he was not sure where Grant would cross. Once he learned of Adams's presence, Grierson continued south and fought a brisk skirmish with Confederate horsemen at Wall's Bridge near the Louisiana-Mississippi state line. After chasing off the Rebels, Grierson's troopers raced for Baton Rouge, where they arrived safely on May 2.

The raid was a spectacular success. Grierson reported, with little exaggeration, that his men had captured and paroled some 500 prisoners, torn up fifty-sixty miles of railroad tracks and telegraph lines, captured or destroyed around 3,000 stands of arms, as well as horses and mules that the Confederates could ill afford to lose. Grierson only lost three killed, seven wounded, and a few stragglers. He had produced "a big scare" in Mississippi, and many citizens who had not seen the enemy before the raid became very paranoid. Grierson had given North Mississippians "the general impression that this portion of the state will be overrun with Yankees." Grant summed it up well when he agreed with many Southerners that it was "one of the most brilliant cavalry exploits of the war." More to the point, and with only slight exaggeration, a Union informant told Grant, who included the statement in a message to Henry Halleck, that "Grierson has knocked the heart out of the state." A disgruntled Confederate soldier regretted that Grierson had not captured Pemberton.[40]

Meanwhile, Union cavalry operations in northwest Mississippi increased. Federal horsemen operated along the Coldwater and the Tallahatchie in an attempt to box in James Chalmers's Confederate cavalry. They failed, but they kept Chalmers so occupied that Pemberton could not, or would not, call him to Vicksburg to assist against Grant's coming invasion.[41]

Frederick Steele's campaign in the Delta area also preoccupied Pemberton at a crucial time. Grant and Sherman concocted Steele's operation to further divert Confederate eyes from the march south. Sherman sent Steele's division to the Delta, to move inland at Greenville, "reconnoiter" to Deer Creek, and march to Deer Creek plantations. Once he established a base of operations, Steele was to send patrols to capture or chase away Confederate cavalry and partisans. If local planters behaved, they would be left alone, but abandoned plantations would be looted. All cotton bales marked "CSA" must be burned, though much was burned before he arrived.

Early on April 5, the troops explored Washington's landing south of Greenville. Patrols found approaches to Deer Creek flooded, while bored infantry gathered in a local family home and sang around a piano. From Greenville, the columns moved inland and passed Confederate general Samuel French's plantation and moved near the present-day town of Leland, the soldiers foraging at will. Steele learned that Samuel Ferguson's Confederates were camped to the south, and he urged his men on.[42]

Slaves gave accurate information about the area and came out in increasing numbers to watch bluecoats march by. Noted an Iowan, "They seemed to be struck dumb, dazed, mouths wide open, staring in wonder and amazement, as we are the first Union troops that ever trod this section." One black woman expressed shock that the Yankees "haint got no hons." Many of these people had taken literally Southern propaganda that Northerners were horned devils. The soldiers advanced across an open field, while Steele's artillery dropped shells into trees to discourage potential Rebel ambushes. When the big guns opened, frightened slaves ran away. "They strung out a distance of 150 to 200 yards and I never saw such high stepping and tall running." Yet many later followed the troops back to Greenville, their desire for freedom greater than their fear of guns.[43]

Ferguson knew the Yankees had landed. Still protecting Deer Creek approaches to Vicksburg, he alerted Stevenson, asked for instructions, and sent a patrol to cut a levee where Black Bayou met the Mississippi. He hoped high water would stop the Yankees and perhaps cut them off from Greenville. Ferguson also sent spies to infiltrate Steele's column; the rest of his troops retreated south. Stevenson sent Stephen Lee's brigade to Rolling Fork to get in the rear of enemy positions. Ferguson continued retreating to a plantation some thirty miles north of Rolling Fork and deployed. He intended to fight a delaying action until he heard from Stevenson.

When Steele's advance came into view, Confederates opened fire, momentarily stunning the Yankees. Steele quickly deployed however, and his artillery raked Ferguson's position. Steele poised his men for an attack, but Ferguson withdrew farther south. The Federals stopped for the night, and they found the body of a black man hanging in a corn-crib. Locals explained that the man mistook Ferguson's men for Union troops, offered to guide them, asked for a gun to kill his owner, and bragged that he would rape any white woman. Ferguson's enraged soldiers immediately hanged him.

Ferguson's troops fell back to another plantation and deployed the night of April 7. Informed that Lee was coming, Ferguson decided to hold his position unless Steele forced a retreat. He did not know that Steele, too, had received word about Lee, and Steele immediately worried about his supply line. He decided not to fight Ferguson and Lee so far from his Greenville base, and his division retreated back up Deer Creek. He ordered the troops to destroy what could not be carried, and to take all horses, mules, and cattle. Slaves continued to follow along, and Steele sent a message to Sherman wanting to know what should be done "with these poor creatures."

On the way back, artillery dispersed guerrillas, and Ferguson followed, though the now barren area afforded his men no food. Lee pushed his troops, trying to catch up. Meanwhile, Pemberton ordered William Loring to send John Moore's brigade from Fort Pemberton. On the tenth, Steele's rear guard clashed with Ferguson's men near their base on the Mississippi. Ferguson, outnumbered and outgunned, soon called off the attack. Steele's men destroyed a bridge to further frustrate Ferguson's pursuit.[44]

Now back in Greenville, Steele asked Grant for more boats to transfer his men and confiscated livestock to Young's Point. The problem of what to do about large numbers of slaves persisted, and, with no word from Sherman, Steele asked Grant's advice. To Steele's surprise, Grant ordered him to camp at Greenville and operate as a buffer against Confederate attempts to get supplies from there to Vicksburg. As for the blacks, Grant said that males of military age should be invited to join colored army units then being organized.[45]

Steele's presence brought devastation to Greenville and the area, and the town continued to suffer. In late May, an Illinois chaplain saw the town from the river and noted it had paid for the sins of guerrillas. He was impressed by the "charred remains of the once pleasant little village. . . . This is the point where the guerrillas have been committing depredations for some time past." He saw "blackened chimneys and the leaves of the trees seared by the recent fire"; these "bore testimony to the retribution which they have received." Few houses could be seen standing.[46]

To the south, Lee and his troops, never in position to attack Steele, camped at Rolling Fork. Lee's patrols scouted for defensive positions to prevent a recurrence of Steele's expedition. Ferguson's cavalry watched Steele from afar, especially in light of reports of a new offensive against Vicksburg. The rest of Ferguson's force withdrew to Rolling Fork to replace Lee's brigade, which returned to Snyder's Bluff.

Steele remained in Greenville until April 22. Sherman, satisfied that his division had done its job in stripping the area of its usefulness to the Vicksburg garrison, asked Grant to return the division to his corps. Steele asked permission to return some confiscated carriages and tools to local citizens. Sherman approved, noting, "War at best is barbarism, but to involve all — children, women, old and helpless — is more than can be justified. Our men will become absolutely lawless unless this can be checked. Inasmuch as Greenville was a point from which the enemy attacked our boats, we were perfectly justified in making the neighborhood feel the consequences."[47]

The expedition indeed left a legacy of hard feelings. Some of Steele's men politely requested young women to sing to them, but, feeling coerced, they launched into Confederate songs with lyrics such as "The foe must be silenced forever." Sometimes the Federals barricaded people in their homes while raiding the grounds. They arrested and later released several locals. One young woman doubtless spoke for many when she confided to her diary, "Oh! What bitter-hatred toward Yankees was in my heart!", "Rather than go back into a union with such people, I would have *every man, woman, and child* in the Confederacy killed," and "I am wearied by the sight of yanks."[48]

Steele fulfilled his primary purpose of diverting the attention of Confederate commanders from Louisiana operations, and he contributed, along with other factors, to Pemberton's belief that Grant was withdrawing. The campaign also demonstrated how Grant could use his superior numbers, with the help of the navy, to tie down Confederate forces Pemberton needed elsewhere. Steele's troops contributed to the evolution of civilian hatred toward everything Yankee, while at the same time eroding morale among a citizenry reminded of their vulnerabilities.

Civilian morale in Mississippi indeed sank low as Grant's soldiers thrashed about the Delta region, spreading destruction. The presence of so many of the enemy in unexpected areas had an unnerving effect. Obviously the Confederacy could not guarantee protection to civilians, and hardliners worried that citizens might stop supporting the cause. One man bluntly stated, "There never was a more willfully injuried a more fouly wronged people than we. There never was a more implacable enemy a more fiendish a more hellish one than this Yankee horde and yet there are those who are willing to back into a union with them. Such creatures are more abhorrent to me than the vile Yankees themselves." Such outbursts changed nothing.[49]

Confederate troops in the Vicksburg-Jackson corridor waited and wondered where they might go next. Men in the vicinity of Clinton had survived swamp duty north of the Yazoo and dreaded thoughts of going back. For the moment they worried about the impact the enemy invasion had on their food supplies. They no longer believed in King Cotton; "bread stuffs will be found sovereign over all." Hopes for victory had not totally faded. One soldier noted that they had earned the enemy's respect, but Confederates no longer talked about one of them being able to whip five to ten Yankees. He suspected that such braggarts had never joined the army.[50]

Unfortunately for Pemberton and his thin ranks, Grant's diversions had not ended. He had yet another in mind; he wanted Sherman's corps to demonstrate against Snyder's Bluff. If convincing, the tactic would force Pemberton to shift troops north of Vicksburg, far from Grand Gulf. Grant was hesitant to discuss the matter with Sherman. He thought the diversion would work, but, he admitted, "I am loath to order it, because it would be so hard to make our own troops understand that only a demonstration was intended, and our people at home would characterize it as a repulse," as had happened along Chickasaw Bayou. Grant left the details to Sherman, who said he would do it, regardless of possible public reaction.

Sherman still had little faith in Grant's overall plan. He told Frederick Steele that if the diversion worked, and Grant made it safely to Mississippi soil below Vicksburg, then the army could move on the Jackson road to capture the city. Until word came of Grant's success, however, it would not be good to make any kind of "foothold on the Yazoo." The corps should be ready to reinforce Grant, whatever happened downriver. In effect, Sherman thought he might have to save Grant.[51]

For the Confederates, Sherman's move up the Yazoo came at a bad time. The water level on the Mississippi was falling, which in turn gave the Yazoo current more impetus as it flowed down to the Mississippi. Debris of all sorts rushed downstream, hammering the raft below Snyder's Bluff. On April 26, chains holding the raft in place snapped under the tremendous pressure, and it fell apart. Nothing could be done to replace it in the swift current, so Pemberton had another problem to draw his attention away from the other side of the Mississippi.

Downriver, John Bowen insisted that the Confederates concentrate their energy and manpower around Grand Gulf, and Pemberton, though distracted, listened. He ordered Stevenson to keep 5,000 men ready to send to Grand Gulf, and Stevenson promised he would; but he at once began hedging. He assured Pemberton that Grand Gulf batteries could hold their own against Porter, and in any event transferring a large Union force to the east side of the Mississippi would be time consuming. Stevenson feared that enemy activities below Vicksburg were a feint, and that once the Confederates began shifting troops there, Grant would throw his army directly against Vicksburg. Stevenson ignored the big picture and focused on his area of responsibility. Even after the boom of guns to the south on April 29 indicated Bowen might be in trouble, Stevenson waited until ordered by Pemberton to send men to Bowen. As Stevenson complied, he reported Sherman's presence on the Yazoo.[52]

On April 30, a Federal naval squadron, including the ironclads *Choctaw* and *Baron De Kalb*, moved up the Yazoo and opened fire on the bluffs. General Louis Hébert, commanding the Confederate defenses, reported the action and prepared to receive an attack. He had sixteen big guns and strong lines of entrenchments. While artillerists fired at each other, Federal soldiers on river transports went ashore and rustled cattle. The task did not prove easy, the beasts stampeded, and four had to be shot to avoid injury to Sherman's troops.

That afternoon, Frank Blair's division disembarked and rushed to find cover from Rebel artillery. Gunboats again came upriver to provide cover fire. Sherman's troops did a poor job of selling their attack, and Confederates suspected a diversion. It did not matter. On April 30, as Sherman ordered more noise, he received an urgent note from Grant to send two divisions downriver quickly. Porter had passed Grand Gulf, and the operation was on. Sherman assigned one division to protect the road from Young's Point to Richmond, and Frank Blair took charge of the diversion, while Sherman rushed Steele's and James Tuttle's troops south. Sherman's diversion had had little impact on the Confederate deployment of troops. Reinforcements would reach Bowen late, but they would have been late regardless of Sherman's presence. Stevenson's and Pemberton's uncertainties ensured that Bowen would be shorthanded.[53]

A Federal breakthrough to the south had come despite delays and frustrations. McClernand's troops kept closing up on the advance until the entire corps was crowded into the staging area at New Carthage. There they waited for McPherson, boats, and supplies. Grant left Milliken's Bend the morning of April 17 and, with an escort, rode south to McClernand's headquarters at Pointe Clear. Grant found McClernand's men busily transferring supplies by boat and wagon from Richmond to embarkation points.[54]

Grant and his generals worked out the details of concentrating McClernand's and McPherson's corps. Grant's personal interactions with his commanders contrasted sharply with Pemberton's ineffective long-distance management. Grant developed a relationship with his lieutenants that Pemberton never mastered, and for the remainder of the Vicksburg campaign, the results underscored the advantages of Grant's team concept over Pemberton's loose command structure.

During Grant's meetings, McClernand said he did not trust Porter's boats to get the troops across the river quickly, mainly because Grant did not have control of the navy. Grant did not waste time defending Porter, whom he trusted. He agreed that speed was essential but cautioned against moving before everything was ready. He ordered the army's pontoon train sent to McClernand. McPherson's three divisions continued moving south from Lake Providence.

As the two corps crowded into and around New Carthage, men occupied slave quarters or whatever other shelter could be found. Porter realized that the operation must move forward to relieve congestion and boost morale. He sent a few boats to explore enemy strength at Grand Gulf, and his scouts were impressed. Fort Cobun, forty feet above the river at a spot called Point of Rock, looked especially formidable. Porter warned Grant that the longer they waited, the stronger Grand Gulf would become. Porter then took his entire fleet down to fire at the Confederates and evaluate their response.[55]

Porter informed McClernand of his intent to attack Grand Gulf on April 23, and he asked for a detachment of infantry to come along as a landing party after the navy pounded the place into submission. McClernand, with Grant's assent, agreed, but at the last minute Porter called everything off, mainly because he believed a false report from an area citizen that the Rebels had 12,000 men and twelve large cannon.

Unconvinced, McClernand and Osterhaus rode a warship downstream and decided after looking through field glasses that the Confederate works were not very impressive. McClernand assured Porter that there was little activity among the Confederates and that naval guns should shell Grand Gulf before an enemy buildup. Grant arrived on the twenty-third, and Porter, still unconvinced, recommended against a frontal assault at Grand Gulf and suggested that the army march to some spot below Grand Gulf and be ferried across from there. Also, the troops could board transports, covered by gunboats, and float past Grand Gulf. Grant refused to commit to anything until he saw Grand Gulf for himself.

On April 24, Grant viewed the Rebel works and decided that they were not as formidable as Porter thought. As time dragged on, Porter wired Gideon Welles that he could not patrol the river to the south until Grant got his troops across. Grant finally sent an expedition to check for an appropriate landing place between Warrenton and the mouth of the Big Black above Grand Gulf. The scouts found nothing suitable, except possibly for Thompson's Bluff, an eminence south of the Big Black. Grant asked Porter to send a boat up the Big Black to close the river as a supply line to Bowen from central Mississippi, but Porter refused to send his boats into another small stream.[56]

On April 24, McClernand, still concerned about lack of space, sent Osterhaus with a patrol to a point opposite the mouth of Bayou Pierre, which emptied into the Mississippi below Grand Gulf. Federal troops and Louisiana cavalry skirmished as Osterhaus's troops pushed toward St. Joseph. In the midst of swamps and bayous and pesky Confederates, the men found an unobstructed road to Hard Times, a hamlet on the Mississippi, and reported to Osterhaus that a new base of operations had been found.[57]

The concentration of Federal troops continued in checkerslike fashion, as men moved from one point to another, regiments trailing regiments, enduring hard, dusty, forced marches. An Illinoisan remembered the endless walking: "I felt my feet smarting very badly, the regiment stopped for a short time and I took my shoes off and when I removed my socks the skin on my toes of both feet came off with them. Oh! but they were sore. I threw my socks away, put my shoes on without them. I tell you it was a hard thing to march with such feet."[58]

Carr's and Osterhaus's divisions finally boarded transports for the move downstream, though McClernand argued, without success, that he would like to wait for the rest of A. J. Smith's division so his whole corps could move at once. When Grant said no, McClernand procrastinated to buy time. He spent it predictably, allowing his political pal, Governor Richard Yates of Illinois, to make a stump speech. Adjutant General Lorenzo Thomas, accompanied by Grant, joined in with remarks supporting black troops in the Army of the Tennessee. A. J. Smith, who was present, declared firmly, but not officially, that he hated abolitionists worse than the devil. "If Jesus Christ," said Smith, "was to come down" and ask Smith to become an abolitionist to guarantee a trip to heaven, he would refuse. He probably said what many more were thinking.[59]

After the grandstanding, Grant returned later to McClernand's head-quarters and, finding the troops still ashore, wrote a strong reprimand, but he tossed the paper away when he saw how much McClernand had accomplished in organizing the embarkation point. Grant instead ordered McClernand to send the troops downstream to a point opposite Grand Gulf. Porter would attack, silence enemy batteries, and then land McClernand's troops at Point of Rock to establish a base of operations. As a contingency, if the landing could not be achieved, the transports would go further downstream to Rodney.

Troops complained about the poor conditions of the transports. Some barges had to be constantly pumped to keep them afloat. By the morning of April 28, McClernand reported that a large portion of his command had boarded. There were not enough boats to transport A. P. Hovey's division; and after a discussion with Porter and Grant, McClernand agreed that when the expedition reached Hard Times, Carr would disembark his people and the boats would come back to pick up Hovey's. Hovey's troops hit the road south, arriving at Hard Times on the morning of April 29.[60]

Upriver, James McPherson hurried to catch up; McPherson himself arrived at Pointe Clear and Grant's headquarters the night of the twenty-sixth. Grant told McPherson to send Logan's and Sanborn's divisions on ahead, while McArthur stayed behind to watch the road from Richmond to Pointe Clear. Rainy weather on the twenty-seventh held up things, but the sun came out, and McPherson's advance headed for Hard Times.

Cump Sherman and his three divisions remained far upriver. Grant decided not to increase congestion by hurrying Sherman's men; they were more valuable as guards along the Milliken's Bend–Richmond road. Sherman opened up a second line of communications along the ill-fated Duckport Canal. When it came time for Sherman's corps to join the rest, his men could travel two roads south.[61]

While the Union army poised to strike, John Bowen continued to plead with Pemberton. Pemberton had sent Wirt Adams's cavalry after Grierson, depriving Bowen of much-needed scouts. Even without Adams, Bowen figured out what Grant intended. He wrote Pemberton that the enemy would likely be ferried across the Mississippi, possibly at Rodney, and he urged a concentration of troops to meet the threat. Bowen felt he could handle a frontal assault at Grand Gulf; however, if Grant turned his far left flank and captured Port Gibson, Grand Gulf would have to be abandoned.

On April 28, Pemberton wired Davis about Grierson and mentioned

Union troops in the Hard Times area, but then he received another message from Bowen about "an immense force opposite me." Pemberton asked if Bowen had enough troops, and if not, what would be the smallest number of reinforcements needed. Obviously Pemberton still did not grasp what was happening, or he would not have quibbled over numbers. Bowen answered, "I advise that every man and gun that can be spared from other points be sent here."

Pemberton at this point told Stevenson to get Vicksburg troops ready to march, but he also told Bowen not to send for any more than he absolutely needed. Pemberton indicated that more men could be sent from Jackson if necessary. While Bowen thus dealt with his unrealistic superior, his men were ready for battle. The works at Grand Gulf were strong, and Bowen felt comfortable that he could repel attacks.[62]

John Bowen had the personality of a taskmaster who always had his men prepared. He had had no patience for the incompetence of a Van Dorn, and he did not care to be bothered with amenities when work was to be done. John Forney had found that out earlier when he traveled from Vicksburg to Grand Gulf to see Bowen. One of Forney's staff members described Bowen as tall, good looking, with a "ruddy complexion, long red moustache & goatee — pleasant voice, a little quick spoken, prominent features." Bowen seemed intelligent, but he could be "a selfish and Hypocritical man — one that would use sinister means for his own advancement," perhaps a reference to his charges against Van Dorn after Corinth. In the eyes of Forney's aide, Bowen did not pay sufficient homage and entertain the visitors; but Bowen had known for several weeks that trouble was coming, and he had no time to engage in formalities.[63]

Forts Cobun and Wade dominated Bowen's defenses. A company of the 1st Louisiana Heavy Artillery manned Cobun's four guns. Covered ways and rifle pits to the south connected Cobun and Fort Wade. Wade had been placed on a rise some twenty feet above the river and a quarter mile from the water's edge. Wade also had four guns in the capable hands of Missouri artillerists commanded by William Wade (Bowen's artillery chief) and Henry Guibor. Secondary rifle pits and more artillery lined the upper bluff, and Bowen had troops and guns on the Big Black guarding his right flank and rear and farther up the channel at Thompson's Bluff. Bowen had two crack infantry regiments under Martin Green and Francis M. Cockrell in reserve. Though Bowen had a few big guns, most of his cannon were smaller field pieces, ineffective against ironclads.[64]

Upriver, David Porter explained his battle plans to his officers. At

7:00 A.M. on the twenty-ninth, the *Pittsburg* would lead the way, followed by her sister ironclads *Louisville, Carondelet,* and *Mound City.* Everything went as planned, and by 8:15 these vessels had all opened fire at Confederate works. The ironclads first assaulted Cobun, then moved down to hit Wade. Then they turned their bows upstream, maintaining the line of battle, and settled in to batter Wade. The ironclads *Benton, Tuscumbia,* and *Lafayette* followed and also turned; these vessels concentrated on Cobun.[65]

A Union soldier described the fight: "The circling shells, the deafening and ceaseless detonations, the black, diminutive fleet, the batteries covering the face of the bluff, tier upon tier, belching forth streams of flame. Sometimes the gun-boats seemed to lie close alongside the shore batteries, within grappling distance. But most of the enemy's guns were too elevated, and the fortifications too strong, to be taken in this manner. The whole range of hills was lined with rifle-pits, and the field artillery could be moved to any point where a landing could be attempted." An Ohioan noted, "The boom of the guns was almost incessant, while the air around the boats and forts was filled with dense volumes of white smoke from the guns and exploding shells. Every shot from the enemy could be distinctly seen whenever they struck the water, dashing the spray high in the air."[66]

On the Confederate side, a Missourian atop the bluff overlooking the forts watched the show. He recalled forgetting "my danger in the rugged grandeur of the scene. Huge shells would strike the surface of the high banks above our feeble batteries, explode, and cover guns and gunners with piles of sand, out of which the latter would work themselves like moles or gophers, and cheerily clear their pieces again for action."

The shelling went on for some time and eventually had a telling effect on Fort Wade, damaging the works and killing the fort's namesake. Louisiana gunners at Cobun kept firing after the action at Wade waned. Porter's flagship, the *Benton,* received a Cobun shell that came into the pilothouse and destroyed the wheel. The boat spun out of control but soon grounded, in a defilade position, which meant Rebel shot and shell could not hit it. The heavy firing had a haunting effect: "Above all and around all hangs and looms the smoke of the conflict like a cloud, hiding almost every object from view," a truly "grand and impressive" sight.[67]

With the Wade guns falling silent, the ironclads focused on Cobun, but the well-constructed fort held up to hammering that continued into a fifth hour. The fighting lasted until nearly 1:00 P.M., when Cobun gunners had to slacken firing because of an ammunition shortage. Nevertheless, Confederate resistance convinced Porter and Grant not to attempt to land troops at Grand Gulf. Grant went to his backup plans and ordered McClernand's troops to move across the base of Coffee's Point, located across the river from Grand Gulf, and then on to Disharoon's plantation on the banks of the river. By the time the battle ended, the shooting had gone on for about five and a half hours. Porter's vessels, with the exception of the *Tuscumbia*, which had engine damage, managed to get back to Hard Times by half past two that afternoon.[68]

Porter had lost eighteen killed and fifty-seven wounded. Fred Grant grew sick at the sights aboard Porter's flagship *Benton*. "The deck was covered with blood and pieces of flesh; several dead men, torn and lacerated, lay about us. Some of the gunners, with still bleeding wounds, were standing firmly by their guns. Admiral Porter had been struck with a piece of shell on the back of his head; his face was colorless and expressed great agony; he leaned forward, using his sword as a cane for support. General Grant told him that he did not believe the transports could land in front of the batteries. The admiral agreed with him on this point." The two decided to attack again with gunboats late that afternoon, providing cover for the transports to run past.[69]

Bowen's men hurried to repair the parapets and other works that suffered heavy damage. Bowen lost three dead and nineteen wounded. He fired off a message to Pemberton asking for additional supplies, especially artillery munitions. Bowen had had only thirteen guns in the fight, eight of which were 30-pounders or less, and yet his men had fought to a standstill a naval flotilla that had eighty-one guns, most of them 42-pounders. Porter sent a gunboat down in the late afternoon to shell Confederates attempting to shore up their works.[70]

Taking advantage of the late afternoon sun to blind Confederate gunners, Porter led his boats in a screening action to get transports and barges past Grand Gulf to ferry Grant's troops across downstream. Once again artillery thundered over the river. As soon as the flotilla got safely by, the ironclads and gunboats went downriver some four miles below Grand Gulf and anchored. Porter lost one man killed and Bowen none.[71]

The battle of Grand Gulf had ended in a draw, but Grant was not deterred as he merely shifted his landing point downstream. He intended to get his troops across the Mississippi into Mississippi, and John Bowen would be forced to throw together a hurried and heavily outnumbered defense, thanks to John Pemberton's slow grasp of reality. Pemberton's failure to study maps and make calm, cool decisions caused him to ignore the greatest point of danger. On the other side, once Grant made his turning-point decision, his masterful April diversions and co-operative subordinates kept his plan viable and ultimately made it work. Pemberton's failure to understand Grant's tactics and tenacity lulled him into a false sense of security that now was about to erupt into a rude awakening.

8

~~~ Port Gibson

After being stymied at Grand Gulf, U. S. Grant could not have been as confident as his memoirs make him sound. He must have wondered if he had chosen yet another plan that might fall apart, or stall, or cause him to step back and rethink strategic options. He had made a major commitment, and if he indeed failed again, Abraham Lincoln might be compelled to place another general in command. Whatever he felt, Grant maintained a positive attitude, adjusted, and moved on. Grant considered crossing at Rodney downriver, the choice Bowen had guessed. He also looked at Bruinsburg, an old landing site between Rodney and Grand Gulf where, according to locals, two roads led inland. A black man, perhaps the same black man named Bob who volunteered to serve as a guide, assured Grant's scouts that a good road connected the place with the town of Port Gibson, and Grant made his choice.[1]

John McClernand moved his corps south to a point across from Bruinsburg, and on April 30 his men began boarding a hodgepodge of vessels to go to Mississippi. By 8:00 A.M., boats steamed across the river to the airs of patriotic band music and loud cheers, unusual behavior for an army that was supposed to be trying to keep the enemy in the dark about its intentions. The noise says much about the confidence of Grant's army. The ferrying went uneventfully, and Indiana troops stepped on Mississippi soil first. A local man watched the Union hordes filing ashore, but Federal soldiers detained him to keep Bowen from getting the word. Soldiers found Bruinsburg, founded in 1796 by Peter Bruin, to consist of a deserted house and a few slave shacks. Other dwellings had been burned. By war's end, Bruinsburg would be totally extinct, but remembered in the annals of the Vicksburg campaign.[2]

Within a few hours, most of McClernand's corps had made it ashore. Officers worried about men milling about in the open along the shore-

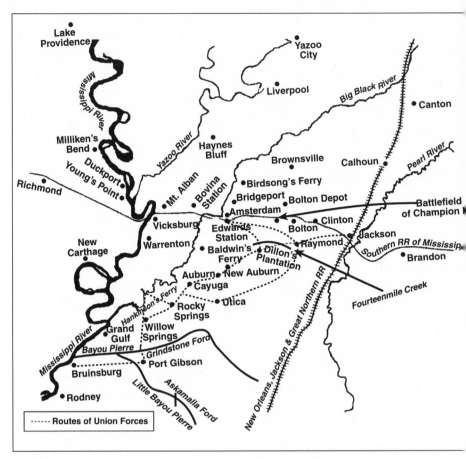

Grant's Inland Campaign, May 1–July 17, 1863. Map by Becky Smith.

line; bluffs lay a mile or so to the east, and the army needed to get there quickly, ahead of any Confederate troops that might by now be rushing to the area. Indicative of uncertainties that surrounded the last few days, the men had not been given their standard three-day rations for campaigning, and this and other delays kept the army stationary until late afternoon. Around 4:00 P.M., McClernand's men marched, some in the advance still without food. A shortage of horses and mules meant that many officers had to walk or scrounge up inferior mounts. The good animals went to artillerists, who had some steep inclines ahead to negotiate.

With cavalry not yet on hand, Eugene Carr's division took the lead, relying on Wisconsin troops in the van to ferret out Rebels that might be lurking among the hills. These men made it atop the bluffs and found themselves on the scenic grounds of the Windsor plantation, highlighted by a spectacular mansion bordered with colossal Corinthian pillars. McClernand determined to keep his troops moving in spite of the overwhelming view. Surely the alarm had been sounded by now, and the general wanted to reach Port Gibson before Confederates destroyed bridges across Bayou Pierre, which Union intelligence indicated ran east to west on the north side of Port Gibson. The Federals moved south and at Bethel Church turned left to the east on the Rodney–Port Gibson road. Some undisciplined soldiers took turns firing at the church steeple, their shots sounding a warning to Confederate scouts.[3]

Soldiers who had food carried it in unconventional ways. An Iowan recalled having more than

> could be stowed away in the haversack. What should we do? A detail was made of two men who placed their guns so a box of crackers could be placed across them, and they marched along the side of the company, and were frequently relieved by a new detail. What should they do with the extra meat? The bayonets were placed on their guns and run through the meat; so each man had his extra ration of meat fixed on his bayonet. Then at a right shoulder shift, we proceeded on our march. When others saw how we had arranged to carry our extra rations they adopted the same plan, so that the whole army could be seen for miles worming its way over that vast flat country with the bayonets gleaming in the sunshine, and the ration of meat in its place. It was picturesque and beautiful to behold.[4]

Soon the soldiers found themselves tramping through a region marked by high bluffs and steep hollows, crisscrossed by countless ridges that intersected at all sorts of angles. A variety of vegetation and forests of hardwood and cane clogged ravines. The only clearings consisted of tilled soil on small farms that dotted flat ridges. As night fell, a detached patrol took the lead, replacing skirmishers. An Illinois soldier recorded: "The moon is shining above us and the road is romantic in the extreme," and "The green foliage on the great trees around us, and its denseness through which here and there steals the silvery rays of the moon, reminds us of the stories of fairyland." An Indianan thought the hills and hollows had not been trod upon "since the panther and the Bear had evacuated them." Their black guide led the way, and the men wound through rugged terrain eastward toward Port Gibson.[5]

Indeed, the countryside had changed little from the early days of settlement in the late 1700s. The rugged landscape limited farming opportunities and population growth. Mississippi citizens in this area must have surely thought the war would never find them. They soon discovered that they, like North Mississippians, were not immune. They fled and later returned, and the area, except for lead and iron buried in the ground, and bloodstained floors on homes occupied by wounded soldiers, changed very little. Some of the 1863 homes still stand, in varying conditions. The land is now occupied mostly by animals and hunting clubs and is occasionally invaded by timber companies. It is fit for nothing else, other than its historical significance.

None of the Union common soldiers and officers realized just how significant a role terrain would play when they ran into Bowen's Confederates. Geography in fact proved to be an equalizer, giving outnumbered Confederates a great advantage in holding up Grant's march inland. It took more than geographic factors, however, to make a stand indefinitely against numbers more than three to one in the Union's favor. Pemberton's failure to act in a timely manner ultimately negated geographic advantages. Frantic efforts to get reinforcements to the area proved futile.

Back on the river, James McPherson's XVII Corps reached Disharoon's plantation and were ferried across. Late in the day on April 30, McPherson's lead elements, two brigades of John Logan's division, stepped ashore and moved toward the bluffs to support McClernand. Transports worked through the night; at one point two collided, and one sank. The debacle caused the loss of two lives, plus guns, horses, and artillery equipment, delaying the completion of Logan's crossing until the early morning hours of May 1. Still, Grant and Porter managed in a short time to get 22,000 troops across from Louisiana to Mississippi, accomplishing "the greatest amphibious operation in American history up to that time." Yet the staggered troop crossings demonstrated that if Pemberton had listened to Bowen, the Confederates might have contested the landing and forced Grant to make a perilous retreat back across. Now Grant had the advantage, a foothold, and he made the most of it. He later wrote, "I felt a degree of relief scarcely ever equaled since." Much work remained to be done, but at last he was "on dry ground on the same side of the river with the enemy."[6]

John Bowen knew he was in trouble once Union boats got safely past Grand Gulf. Wherever they might land downstream, he would be flanked and thus be forced to turn his defensive posture to the south. Bowen knew, too, that he did not have enough men to force the Yankees back across the river once they established a position on the Mississippi side. He could not fight them in a pitched land battle either, at least not for long, but he knew he must do something while waiting for reinforcements. Bowen ordered Brigadier General Martin Green to send an advance force to Port Gibson to scout roads from there toward Natchez and Rodney. Bowen promised Green additional infantry and artillery as soon as possible.[7]

More troops arrived from Vicksburg, including Brigadier General Edward Tracy's brigade of Alabamians and the Virginia Botetourt Artillery. Tracy reported to Green for deployment instructions, and the generals realized that, despite their small numbers, they would have to divide forces to defend two roads. A main road heading west from Port Gibson toward the river forked about a mile out of town. The left fork led to Rodney, the right to Bruinsburg. Green recommended to Bowen, who had just ridden in from Grand Gulf, that their soldiers dig in near Magnolia Church, located on a ridge on the Rodney road. Scouts and local citizens reported Yankees coming down both the Rodney and Bruinsburg roads, and Green believed that the advantages of high ground and rugged terrain around the church would both help him delay Grant's march and give any reinforcements on the way more time to reach the battlefield. Green placed a small detachment on the Bruinsburg road, while the bulk of his command moved southwest on the Rodney road.

Green worried about his vulnerable right, because false reports indicated Yankees were on the Bruinsburg road. Green had no way of knowing the truth, so he sent Tracy's entire force down the Bruinsburg road. William Baldwin's brigade arrived later in the morning after a hard march from north of Vicksburg and reinforced Green on the Rodney road. Separating the two roads were deep ravines covered in junglelike vines and brush and drained by Centers Creek. Each wing would have trouble reinforcing the other, because, given the tangled terrain, they would have to backtrack over the roads to their rear. Tracy's men, exhausted by their long march from Vicksburg, collapsed to the ground to rest and sleep. Green could only hope he would not need them for a few hours.[8]

Aside from the enemy presence somewhere west of Port Gibson, John Bowen had concerns about reports of Federal gunboats ascending Bayou Pierre. If true, the enemy could sever communications between Grand Gulf and Port Gibson. The Confederates had put a raft in the bayou to block traffic, but Bowen knew that it would not hold up gunboats, at least not for long. He sent the 1st Missouri and a six-gun battery to reinforce a detachment already watching Bayou Pierre. Bowen also kept troops at Grand Gulf, in case Union boats renewed shelling, and on bluffs commanding the Big Black River, to watch for enemy vessels. Already heavily outnumbered, Bowen was now left with a long, segmented, paper-thin line of defense.[9]

In making plans and deploying troops, Bowen and his generals had to keep several factors in mind. Why not concentrate where the Bruinsburg and Rodney roads merged near Port Gibson, rather than divide the army? The Confederate leadership had no idea how many men Grant had, because Francis Cockrell had abandoned Louisiana to prevent being trapped, and the Louisiana cavalry left behind had not been able, owing to a flooded countryside and lack of numbers, to get beyond the Union advance to make a count of the enemy. Ascertaining numbers would have been difficult anyway, since the Federal corps were strung out over several miles. So Bowen could not risk making a stand against possibly overwhelming numbers with Bayou Pierre so near to his right flank and rear. If flanked on his left, his men would be trapped between the whole Union army and Bayou Pierre. On the other hand, if he pulled his line to the south, Grant could push by him, take Grand Gulf, and have an open road to the north and Vicksburg. The overriding strategic concept that guided Pemberton and his generals was protecting Vicksburg. Fighting a divided army offered the Confederates better prospects. The tangled terrain that made communications difficult for Bowen's army would have the same effect on Union troops traveling down different roads. If Bowen and his lieutenants wanted to make the most of geographic advantages, they had to contest Grant's advance down each road and hope Pemberton could get more men to the front.

In Jackson, John Pemberton examined the situation that his failure to listen to Bowen had largely created. He sent Bowen more reinforcements, though they would not arrive in time for the coming fight near Port Gibson. Pemberton wondered if Grant might be planning a two-pronged attack, for reports indicated a major enemy presence north of Vicksburg along the Yazoo. If Pemberton sent too many men south, the Yankees might break through to the north. The force that flustered Pemberton, William T. Sherman's, had not been very effective, but the ruse worked, in that Pemberton paid more attention to it than he should have, losing valuable time in the process. Reports from Bowen soon left no doubt where the main Union attack would come, and Pemberton ordered troops from Grenada, Columbus, Meridian, and other scattered locations to Jackson. The commanding general, meanwhile, boarded a train for Vicksburg, where he should have been all along, instead of evaluating Grant's river movements from afar. Had Pemberton personally seen the passage of batteries by Porter's fleet, and had he paid attention to Bowen's warnings, he might have put two and two together and avoided the crisis his miscalculations caused.[10]

As darkness consumed the last daylight on April 30, General Green's Confederates rested behind the cover of a fencerow near Magnolia Church. Green walked out to check his pickets and, according to family legend, soon came to the A. K. Shaifer home, where occupants were hurriedly packing a wagon for a quick getaway to Port Gibson. All the talk of Yankees on the way had terrified the family. Green assured them there would be no danger, certainly not until morning. By now, clocks had passed the midnight hour, and with the arrival of May 1 had come a volley of musketry, fired by Confederate pickets and the Union advance, the 21st Iowa. Minié balls struck home, wagon, and furniture. The ladies fled quickly, forgetting valuables left behind. The wagon clattered through Confederate lines. Green smiled at the wild retreat and ordered his outposts to hold up the Union van as long as possible.[11]

The shots that initiated the battle of Port Gibson brought the rest of the 21st Iowa to the front. However, one of the Iowans noted, "the ground was so broken with ravines and obstructed with underbrush and cane, or was so washed into ditches with rains" that the troops gave up trying to do anything until they reached the plateau where the Shaifer home sat. All seemed quiet, and Union commanders assumed that shots fired from the house had been strays. Federal scouts slowly continued forward into the darkness; nothing happened, so the main column, held up until all seemed clear, swung into motion. Green's soldiers, alerted by the burst of gunfire, waited silently for the enemy to come into view. They could hear officers shouting orders and the shuffling of hundreds of feet, the sounds echoing eerily among the steep ravines. They heard assurances that all was clear, and still they waited, until the blue advance got within some fifty yards of the Magnolia Church line. Then they pulled triggers and lanyards, and flashes of light and the crack and boom of rifles and artillery swept over the plateau.[12]

Iowans hit the dirt and sought cover, while artillerymen rushed one 12-pounder cannon forward to shell the Rebels. Green's artillery responded from some 300 yards away, and more Union guns were pushed forward to support the exposed gun. Colonel William Stone, commanding the Yankee advance, ordered the Iowans to feel out the Confederate line. They took cover in ravines except for two Iowa regiments sent beyond the battery, and another Iowa and a Wisconsin regiment formed a second line behind the artillery. Indiana artillerymen rushed up to provide support.

Shooting continued in the darkness, and survivors were left with

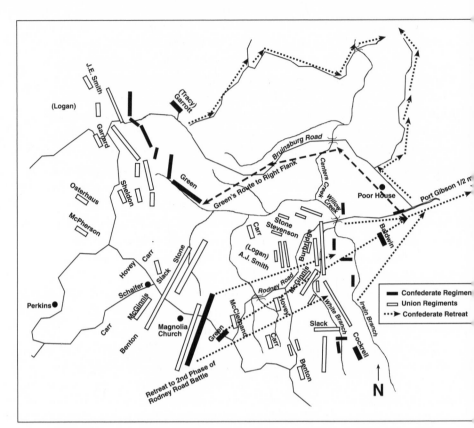

The Battle of Port Gibson, May 1, 1863. Map by Becky Smith, adapted from Michael B. Ballard, The Campaign for Vicksburg *(Conshohocken, Pa.: Eastern National Park and Monument Association, 1996).*

memories of shell and canister providing a dangerous fireworks display, screams of the wounded, yells of the combatants, and pitiful sounds of wounded horses. The echoes bounced across the landscape; it was an event to remember, one that men on both sides would have preferred passing up. A few hours before daylight, both sides stopped firing, as if by mutual consent. There could be no winner in such a fight, because neither side could exploit advantages in the dark, when they had no idea what the advantages might be.[13]

Union troops struggled to get to the front, but the black night and tricky terrain slowed marching to a staggered walk. The only good landmark turned out to be lights at the Caleb Perkins home, turned into a field hospital by Federal surgeons. Soldiers moving toward the sound of guns may have had second thoughts as they passed by the sounds and smells of bodies undergoing repair. Eugene Carr decided to halt his men near the Shaifer house and wait for light before deploying.[14]

When dawn broke, the sun's rays "dance[d] about on the treetops," bringing with it canister, "hurtling, whistling, whizzing above us, around us." Union officers and soldiers looked about incredulously. They found themselves in the midst of a landscape worse than what they had passed through earlier. Nobody really knew how a battle could be fought here without losing all sense of organization, not to mention direction. John McClernand and his staff rode up, and a black man told them that a road that led northeast (off to the left) from the Shaifer house intersected the Bruinsburg road where Confederates had set up defensive positions. McClernand could see evidence of battle lines in that direction, and he knew he had to advance his corps along both roads to keep the Rebels from attacking his left flank. The connecting road proved to be a key tactical feature of the battlefield. The Confederates had to fight on two fronts as they had figured, but they still had to return to the road junction to reinforce either front, while Grant's generals used the closer connecting road to reinforce each wing as needed.[15]

Most of Tracy's Alabamians occupying the Bruinsburg roadblock slept soundly until awakened by battle sounds to the south. Tracy ordered his men to turn in that direction, just in case enemy troops tried to hit their left flank. At dawn, Tracy learned that Green needed support to hold his position at the church. If he pulled back, Green would leave Tracy vulnerable, and possibly the two Rebel wings would be cut off from each other, which might result in total disaster. Tracy sent a regiment and two guns from the Botetourt Artillery via the road junction to Green's aid.[16]

Tracy adjusted his line, placing two remaining Botetourt guns in the center, flanked on either side by Alabama regiments. The artillerists noted nearby slaves joining in the exodus of civilians from the battlefield. A Botetourt artillerist later criticized Tracy for putting the guns in an exposed position rather than deploying them behind the infantry. Union bullets soon wrought havoc among horses and men. Tracy realized that the road to the Shaifer house gave the Yankees a straight shot at his right, so he ordered infantry forward as skirmishers to watch for a Federal advance. Meanwhile, Tracy, like Green, no doubt kept looking to the rear for reinforcements, because combined they had only 2,500 men, not enough, even with the aid of geography, to hold very long.[17]

More troops were coming, and they, like Tracy's soldiers, were worn out from little sleep and long marches — but they would have no time to rest. The reinforcements consisted of William E. Baldwin's brigade and Colonel Francis Marion Cockrell's Missourians. Cockrell, an inspirational field commander, had waited with his men at Grand Gulf, left there by Bowen in case the Bruinsburg landing was a feint. As a result, the Missouri troops, trained by Bowen and without doubt his best soldiers, did not get into the battle at Port Gibson until late in the day. When Baldwin marched his troops through Port Gibson, local women cheered and cried, pleading with them to save the day, but they too would arrive after the battle had raged for hours.[18]

On the battlefield, Tracy's men watched and waited. Soon they spotted Yankees coming from the direction of the Shaifer house. McClernand wasted no time sending troops to his left; he ordered Carr to push forward a detachment to block any Confederate flanking maneuver. Illinois troops changed fronts and raced toward Tracy's position; Alabamians saw them coming and opened fire. The Illinoisans responded, artillery from both sides joined in, and morning light slowly revealed the battleground. Federals received instructions to stay low to avoid enemy artillery shot. The resulting stalemate made McClernand aware that he had to fight a two-front battle, so he sent Peter Osterhaus's division to clear the connecting road, freeing Carr to concentrate on the Magnolia Church line. Federal manpower advantages became apparent as Union divisions attacked Confederate brigades.[19]

Theophilus T. Garrard's brigade led Osterhaus's division into battle, joined by Illinoisans who had made initial contact with Tracy's troops. A brief artillery exchange settled nothing, and Garrard decided to test Rebel strength. He sent one regiment to the left and two to the right and held two more in reserve. One of Garrard's Indianans later complained of cane twenty to thirty feet high, the horrible visibility causing two incidents of friendly fire. The Midwesterners charged both the enemy and the terrain, but they soon faltered at resistance from determined Alabamians and Virginia artillerists. Lionel Sheldon's brigade of Ohioans and Kentuckians supported Garrard's line. Osterhaus planned to turn Tracy's left, but trying to align his troops in the tricky ravines, all the while under Confederate fire, proved difficult and necessitated shuffling regiments to protect exposed flanks. At 8:15 A.M., the assault went forward, and the Federals moved some 400 yards before hitting the main Rebel line. Seeing that the Confederate left extended farther than he thought, Osterhaus shifted troops to his right. He soon realized that geography had created gaps in his front that maneuvering could not easily overcome. Osterhaus and his officers worked quickly to reconnect their line, while the troops continued fighting.[20]

On the Confederate side, General Tracy saw with much relief an additional Alabama unit rapidly moving toward the fighting. While Osterhaus sent in brigades, Tracy had to be content with a regiment just arrived from Vicksburg. The additional regiment plugged the gap created by the advance of more Alabamians to set up a strong skirmish line, which was being forced back. Union fire concentrated on the Confederate center, and Tracy moved into harm's way to get a better view. The general soon fell mortally wounded, struck by a Union sharpshooter's bullet. One witness said the general fell hard on his face, crying, "O Lord!" on the way down and dying quickly. Perhaps Tracy had known his time was nigh. Slightly less than a month before he had written a friend: "Life is very short and I think we should waste as little of it *as possible* in separation from those we love." Colonel Ishom Garrott of the 20th Alabama suddenly found himself in command, and he had not been privy to Tracy's plans, if indeed Tracy had any, other than holding his position. Garrott notified Green that Tracy was dead and asked for instructions, and received the simple reply that Garrott's troops must hold.[21]

Though demoralized by Tracy's death, his men felt somewhat rejuvenated when the other two guns of the Botetourt Artillery rumbled up from Vicksburg. The extra guns stabilized the Confederate line only briefly, and by 10:00 A.M. Union pressure forced Garrott to pull his cannon back to avoid capture. Two badly damaged guns had to be left behind. An hour later, the entire Confederate line became heavily engaged as the Yankees increased pressure. Soldiers began running out of ammunition, and Garrott shifted troops to his heavily threatened right flank, where deep ravines and thick underbrush helped the Rebels hang on for several hours.[22]

Osterhaus tried to maintain a semblance of alignment, and finally decided to make his main attack on the enemy center, where the road and adjacent fields offered better terrain for a charge. Though he had momentum and the firepower to do the job, Osterhaus at this point suddenly lost his nerve and refused to attack until reinforced. The Alabamians' stubborn defense and the poor visibility convinced him that he had to have more men, when in reality he had more than he needed. His men could have easily cleared the field of Confederates, but he did nothing. Help eventually came when lead elements of John Logan's division arrived at the Shaifer house in the early afternoon. Osterhaus received John E. Smith's brigade and placed the Illinoisans and Indianans on the left of the battle line. Some of these troops battling underbrush and terrain encountered a black bear that had been disturbed by all the noise. Fortunately, "the bear seemed to be worse scared than the men," and beat a hasty retreat.[23]

John Bowen did not have enough manpower, but he did his best to counter the increasing pressure on his two wings. In the face of the enemy buildup, Green had been forced to pull back from the Magnolia Church line. Baldwin's brigade and Cockrell's Missourians, the latter having finally reached the battlefield from Grand Gulf, arrived to stabilize the Rodney road situation. Bowen used this opportunity to shift Green's battle-weary troops to the right wing in support of Garrott. Unfortunately Green and Garrott did not communicate, and Garrott moaned when he saw that Green, unfamiliar with the battlefield situation, deployed on the Confederate left rather than the threatened right.[24]

Garrott tried to rectify the situation by transferring a regiment from the left to reinforce the threatened portions of his line. About that time Osterhaus's assault hit Garrott's right, and the lone Alabama regiment there, thinly stretched and heavily outnumbered, recoiled quickly and fell back, with many taken prisoner. Garrott ordered a regiment to stem the breakthrough, and with the help of the survivors of the enemy assault, they managed to stabilize the right momentarily. Other reinforcements from the Confederate left and center came up, and Garrott ordered forward the two remaining working guns of the Botetourt Artillery. The Botetourt's officers lay dead or wounded, so a sergeant, Francis Obenchain, took command and ordered the shelling of Osterhaus's attack force. Green's six regiments entered the fray, temporarily shoring up Garrott's bruised and fractured line.[25]

Osterhaus now ordered another assault, this time with the added firepower of John Smith, an Illinois friend of Grant's, and his brigade. Geography continued dictating tactics as battle lines became disconnected and the fight evolved into a vicious series of small, close-up battles along ridges and in ravines. Numbers soon told, and the Confederates began pulling back. Most of the fighting took place along the Confederate center and right. Green commanded the left, and his men saw little action because the approach to their front required Union troops to move across a clear ridge.[26]

Missourians newly arrived from Cockrell's brigade provided some Confederate hope by countercharging to relieve the pressure on Garrott's Alabamians. In the process, they recaptured two disabled Botetourt guns. But when the Missourians encountered an Indiana regiment posted behind a fencerow, they came to a halt, suddenly finding themselves alone beyond the Confederate line. Colonel Eugene Erwin appealed to Garrott to attack, but Garrott could not take the risk. So for the remainder of the afternoon, both sides peppered away, and the stalemate persisted. The Union lines continued to be strengthened by troops from Bruinsburg, while Garrott and Green tried to hold their ground. Around 5:00 P.M., Green received word from Bowen to hold until sunset. If an advance was not possible, then the right wing should retire. Green decided not to wait, especially since Confederate defenders were on the verge of being overwhelmed; for unknown reasons he had not officially taken command of the wing, but he finally did assert himself and order a retreat. The left led the way while the center and right tried to hold off Osterhaus's legions.[27]

John Smith, more aggressive than Osterhaus, recognized that the Rebels seemed to be giving way, and he immediately ordered an advance. Terrain and a stout Rebel defense forced caution. On account of poor Confederate communication about the withdrawal, the Missourians found themselves very much alone amid masses of bluecoats. The regiment's colonel decided to fake an assault from where the Confederate left had been, and for a time the ruse worked as Union commanders halted to prepare to meet an expected charge on their right. Federal troops did, however, capture forty-six Missourians; thanks to Obenchain and the Botetourt guns, the rest got away. Survivors of the Confederate right wing escaped across Bayou Pierre. As night was coming on, John Smith, satisfied with possessing ground held by the enemy, halted for the evening.

Federals on Grant's left were ecstatic because "flag after flag floated over the rebels position just as the setting sun tinged the still smoking hills with gold." Osterhaus had won the day with only 246 casualties, 232 from his division and 14 from Smith's brigade. He might have lost fewer men had he made a more determined effort and ended the stalemate sooner. Confederate losses are difficult to ascertain, since Green's troops fought on two fronts. Total losses for Tracy and Garrott's brigade numbered 272. Green lost 160 in the day's fighting.[28]

The Confederate left wing ultimately suffered the same fate as their comrades on the right, though they too put up a hard fight and on two different fronts. John McClernand personally commanded Union troops in the battle along the Rodney Road, and he had a much tougher time than Osterhaus. When McClernand heard fighting begin on Osterhaus's front early that morning, he ordered Carr to clear the Confederates from Magnolia Church ridge. William Benton's brigade of Illinoisans and Indianans led the advance on the right, while William Stone's brigade of Iowans and Wisconsinites formed on the left. Carr instructed Benton to take the church ridge, from where he should be able to enfilade the Confederate line that slanted from southwest to northeast across the Rodney road. Stone supported Benton by keeping pressure on the Rebel right.[29]

Union cannon signaled the launching of the attack. Things went according to plan as Benton's brigade pushed Rebels off the church ridge. Federals grabbed dense cane to pull themselves up steep inclines, all the while dodging bullets and wooden splinters airborne from enfiladed fences. The main Confederate front lay some 200 yards away, and Benton tried to shore up his line before moving on. Thanks to heavily vegetated ravines, his right flank drifted off to the right, leaving a gap filled by an alert Illinois regiment. Carr's strategy surprised Green, who thought the Yankees would approach over relatively even ground on his right. Green, as he later demonstrated on the Bruinsburg road front, seemed unprepared when the enemy did not do the expected. He realized quickly that a full brigade was pressing his left; so he sent word to Tracy for reinforcements, and an Alabama regiment and two Botetourt guns arrived. By that time, Green had lost the services of part of his artillery because of a lack of ammunition; cannoneers soon found a few additional rounds.[30]

A bullet knocked out a Mississippi officer, and by the time he regained consciousness his face and hair were covered with blood and mud. He turned over his company to his second in command and then tried on his own to find a doctor. Still dizzy, he fell down one of the steep inclines so prevalent on the battlefield and landed in a water-filled hole. He might have drowned had not a comrade seen his fall and rushed to his aid. Dodging dust and rocks kicked up by the ongoing fighting, he finally found an available horse, which was soon struck and killed. He eventually made it to a field hospital, where he was greeted with the ear-splitting screams of a young man having his leg amputated. He "thanked God that I had been hit in the head!"

Alabamians, covered by artillery fire, charged Benton's line and ran into withering enemy fire on the church ridge. A Mississippi regiment and one from Alabama rushed into the teeth of Stone's infantry and artillery. Union firepower proved too much, and the Confederates ground to a halt. Over to the left, a regiment of Arkansans could not move forward and pulled back from Magnolia Church ridge. Bowen rode to the rear to find General Baldwin; before leaving he told Green to try holding another hour at least.[31]

Benton, meanwhile, reformed his left to keep the Confederates from pushing through the space between his and Stone's brigades. Alvin P.

Hovey's division arrived on the scene and occupied ridges south of the road; Hovey received orders to hold back until Andrew J. Smith's division came up. As Smith's troops approached, McClernand ordered them onto a narrow, short ridge, which immediately became congested. Portions of Smith's troops moved north of the road to find room. Little wonder that one soldier recalled that he rarely saw "two [men] of one regiment together," so confusing was the terrain. One of Landrum's Illinois regiments wound up holding the left flank of the Federal Rodney road line. With Smith's men preparing to charge, Hovey sent his division to assist Benton; Brigadier General George McGinnis sent his brigade to Benton's left while a fellow Indianan, Colonel James Slack, placed his four regiments on Stone's right.

Battlefield adjustments went on continually, as Federals tried to maintain a solid front to assault Green in spite of terrain and Confederate fire. By now, McClernand realized that he had enough power to break the Rebel center, so he canceled his plan to turn Green's left. McClernand preferred direct assault to maneuver, and, given the nature of the terrain, his decision seemed sound. Why waste time maneuvering when he had numbers to smash the enemy? The troops would not get much artillery support, owing to terrain problems, but they should not need it.[32]

Hovey tired of waiting for an attack signal and ordered two regiments to charge Green's artillery. A rail fence and Rebel crossfire, plus canister at close range from Confederate guns, halted the Indianans and Ohioans who made the charge, and they quickly fell back to the shelter of ravines. All of Stone's brigade plus an Illinois regiment rushed forward and outflanked the Confederate right. Hovey yelled for a general advance, and a massive wave of blue-clad soldiers pushed toward Green's artillery, and the two Botetourt guns fell into Union hands. Indianans turned the guns eastward and sent a canister charge into fleeing Rebels. Federal troops later spent much time arguing about who got to the guns first — and, thanks to battle confusion, to this day the answer is elusive. Besides the guns, Green lost three caissons and three ammunition wagons, 200 men captured, and regimental colors.

While Union soldiers celebrated capturing the guns, fellow troops routed Alabamians, taking prisoners and flags, on Green's right. Far on the Federal right, Benton's men continued on, driving two Arkansas regiments east into ravine-infested terrain. The retreating Rebels finally saw Baldwin's brigade forming along the road to their rear. Bowen stood there too, and Green reported that he had been overpowered; his men needed to be re-formed and given a breather. At this point, Bowen sent

Green and his men over to the Bruinsburg road, where they spent the rest of the battle.[33]

As they hurried to the front, Baldwin's men realized the severity of war's impact on Port Gibson's civilians: the whole town was in a state of pandemonium. Then Baldwin's men encountered a sweaty, desperate Bowen who urged them on. Beyond Baldwin, back toward Port Gibson, Bowen saw much to his relief Cockrell rushing his Missourians forward. Bowen then sent one Missouri regiment to aid Garrott and Green and attached two Missouri regiments, plus artillery, to Baldwin's brigade.

Bowen realized that while Green's position atop Magnolia Church ridge provided a clear field of fire, it also made his troops easy targets, especially when the well-hidden Yankees suddenly emerged from ravines. So Bowen organized his second line of defense to provide more cover. He set up a line in the bottomland of Willow Creek (east of where the Rodney road turned north toward its junction with the Bruinsburg road) in the area where the stream forked, separated by a thickly wooded ridge. The White branch ran east of the ridge, and the Irwin branch flowed on the west side. Louisiana troops occupied the center of the line, while two Missouri artillery pieces were parked on the tip of the ridge, where the creek divided into the two branches. From this position, the guns could enfilade Yankee flanks as the enemy came into the valley. Mississippians held the left for a time and had the advantage of cover in the bottomland growth, plus a field of fire that gradually arose from the creek bottom to a cleared crest. Union troops on that crest would be easy targets. Cockrell positioned his troops on the left where cane and other thick foliage concealed the Missourians. Bowen thus intentionally strengthened Baldwin's left, where he surmised the next major enemy attack would come.

Louisiana troops deployed on a high ridge north of the Rodney road, and additional Mississippi infantry waited in reserve on another ridge south of the road, several hundred yards to the rear of the battle line, providing support for two pieces of artillery. The capable John Landis commanded a four-gun Missouri battery on a ridge 300 yards behind the Mississippians. And Baldwin set up a skirmish line in the White Branch bottom and a roadblock. Meanwhile, Bowen ordered Missouri infantry and cavalry regiments to abandon their now superfluous positions near waterways and hurry to the battlefield.[34]

The fighting grew hot and bitter as McClernand's troops advanced. One of Baldwin's soldiers never forget "the screaming and bursting of shells, the whistling of shot, the *ping* of bullets, the shrieks of the wounded and the groans of the dying," all seemingly "calculated to strike terror to ears unused to such scenes. I frankly confess that I was badly demoralized." This same soldier later wrote that he thought General Baldwin too drunk to ride (a common complaint against officers by enlisted men), and that he also saw a surgeon who seemed to be intoxicated as well as a lieutenant who was shaking, either from ague or fright. As for the outcome, "*some men had already begun to suspect the motives as well as doubt the judgment of Gen. Pemberton.*"[35]

At Magnolia Church, Union soldiers continued celebrating the Rebel retreat as if the battle were over. McClernand and Governor Richard Yates of Illinois made speeches; Yates and Illinois congressman Elihu Washburne traveled with the army as observers and to politic, given the large number of Illinois troops in Grant's army. Both Yates and Washburne helped tend the wounded, shouted encouragement, and dodged bullets by falling flat when volleys erupted. McClernand claimed the victory as a "great day for the northwest," and Grant sat quietly, only for a few moments, before pointing out that the enemy had not been routed but merely had retreated and should be pursued.

The tired Federal soldiers got a brief water break, and commanders took time to re-form commands. One Illinois soldier later complained, "This day was the hardest days work for me that I ever experienced in my life. Our Regiment was on the reserve line that day and we were double-quicked or ran from point to point back and forth and wherever our line was wavering or giving back. we were rushed into help them hold the line. when darkness came I felt more dead than alive."[36]

The troops advanced around noon, with George McGinnis's in the lead, followed by Benton's. Scouts looked for signs of Rebels, and James Slack's brigade, on McGinnis's left, descended into the hollows and ran into the Rodney road ahead, where it turned north toward Port Gibson. Brigades from A. J. Smith's and John Logan's divisions followed in the rear. On the far left, William Stone's brigade soon reached an open plateau above Centers Creek and received Confederate fire. As the fighting developed, Slack's men came up on the right of Stone's, and McGinnis's followed, aligning on Slack's right. En route they found wounded Rebels "trying vainly to extricate themselves from the living and dead — the human weight that held them down."

McClernand and his officers decided to pause until Rebel positions could be identified. This proved difficult because huge gaps seemed to exist in the enemy line, and McClernand suspected a trap. He decided to make sure there were no gaps at all in his front line of attack. Raw power had worked once and should again. Stephen Burbridge of A. J. Smith's division formed two regiments of his brigade at a refused angle (slanting away from the front) on the right to hold off any possible Confederate flank attack. Scattered shots rang out from the woods to Burbridge's front; but an Ohio battery came up and fired a few rounds, and things quickly quieted.[37]

Still unsure about what lay concealed in the long creek bottom to his front, McClernand ordered skirmishers forward. Brigades followed, and the thick undergrowth soon forced a gap in the line; but most of the troops made it to the ridge beyond the White branch and found themselves subject to flanking fire from Rebel artillery. Landis's 24-pounder shells sent Union troops diving for cover; from the ragged terrain they fired back at Confederate infantry, which joined in to make the ridge a no-man's land. For about an hour and a half the fighting went on until McClernand decided that he must make a strong move to end the stalemate.

Using power tactics, McClernand deployed additional troops along the center of his line to bludgeon the Rebels. He sent James Slack's brigade to the far right, placed Burbridge in the center and ordered John Stevenson's brigade to fill the gap left by Stone's struggle with terrain. Burbridge further strengthened his position by asking Stevenson for a regiment; Stevenson complied and also brought up two additional regiments. McClernand now had twenty-one regiments packed into a line that extended end to end less than half a mile, in effect daring the Rebels to stop him.[38]

General Bowen observed the Yankee dispositions, and, though concerned, for the moment he feared more for his left flank than the masses to his front. If the Federals figured out that the Natchez–Port Gibson road ran near that flank, Union troops could not only turn the Confederate flank but also get into the Rebel rear — and Bowen would likely be forced to surrender. To forestall such a disaster, Bowen turned to men he trusted, the Missourians, to drive back the Union right. As these troops marched down the Irwin Branch hollow, they caught the attention of Alvin Hovey.

Hovey realized that Bowen was strengthening the Confederate left, and he at once issued orders concentrating four artillery batteries. By the time the guns deployed and began firing, the Missourians had already passed the impact zone. Cockrell quickly got his hard fighters into position and ordered a charge; the Missourians poured over the ridge and hammered Slack's right, killing and scattering Union soldiers. Hovey's massed artillery tried to stop the wave, but could not. One of McGinnis's regiments turned to meet the charge, slowing the Missourians while Indianans from Benton's brigade rushed to the fight.

Illinois and Missouri (Union) artillerists saw infantry support melt away, and Confederate Missourians continued pushing, slugging it out with a Wisconsin regiment from McGinnis's brigade. Some of Slack's battered survivors reformed and pitched in to help, and one of McGinnis's reserve regiments came up to assist. Two Benton regiments joined in, followed by Burbridge's reserve, a McGinnis Indiana regiment, an Ohio battery, and more Federals, all joining to repel Cockrell's assault.

Cockrell's men, becoming more outgunned with every passing minute, finally retreated back over the ridge and re-formed, supported by a Mississippi regiment. Three Indiana regiments followed and produced a sweeping fire that forced back the Rebel left. Bowen's Missourians had shown a flash of brilliance, but the lack of reinforcements to follow up an advantage haunted the Confederates and not for the last time. The battle now settled into another standoff.[39]

Bowen likely never realized he had sent the Missourians against McClernand's center rather than the Union right. The men who attacked knew soon enough that they had taken on more than they could handle. A survivor recorded, "A charge at double-quick was ordered; and through the iron hail, with even alignment and the steady tread of the drill ground, the two regiments threw themselves into the stunted shrubbery and the bed of the little stream. Instead of one brigade, we now found that two confronted us—either one quadrupling our numbers—and the continuous roll of small guns was appalling, almost drowning the fierce discharge of the artillery. The noise was so incessant that no orders could be heard; and the bullets flew so thick that hardly a leaf or twig was left on the bare poles of what had been a diminutive forest when we entered it."[40]

Congratulating his Missourians on their effort, Bowen admitted that he did not think many of them would survive, but he explained that the charge had to be made to save the army. McClernand, upset that he had been forced to use so many reserves to beat off Cockrell's attack, seemed stunned. Bowen worried about the ensuing lull, for he still feared a flank and rear attack, perhaps via the Natchez–Port Gibson road. To get a feel for what the Yankees might have in mind, Bowen ordered Baldwin to launch an attack down the Rodney road. Baldwin's men moved forward at 4:00 P.M., preceded by blasts from Confederate artillery. Mississippi and Louisiana troops made little progress before retreating in the face of massed Union fire from several regiments. Bowen now knew that McClernand's force had not been divided for a flank attack. The main body of the Union army remained concentrated.[41]

Finally, the ponderous enemy line showed signs of life, pressing Cockrell until he had to retreat to the left rear of Baldwin's left, creating a vulnerable angle exploited by oncoming Federals. Missouri gunners tried to stall the charge, but their guns did more damage to friendly troops than Union soldiers. Pressure on Baldwin's Louisianans increased as Burbridge's and John Stevenson's masses moved forward. An artillery duel broke out between Landis's Missourians and Samuel De Golyer's 8th Michigan Light Artillery along the ridges overlooking Willow Creek bottom. De Golyer fired canister into Louisianans on the ridge crest, causing many casualties. Bowen realized the day had been lost and ordered a retreat.[42]

The Missouri Confederates headed toward the Bayou Pierre suspension bridge. Cockrell deployed some troops as a rear guard while the rest of the army crossed. Some got away clean, but others had trouble because of pressure from elements of Stone's, McGinnis's, and Stevenson's brigades. When news spread that the Grand Gulf road had been blocked, Confederate officers jammed the road into Port Gibson with their troops, all hurrying to escape capture. Things might have gotten ugly, for John Stevenson was poised to attack the congested Confederates until he noticed that his brigade was isolated. Burbridge and all the troops on the Union right had been ordered to pull back and make camp. McClernand, perhaps relieved to have won the day after such hard fighting, allowed Bowen to escape. An aggressive Union pursuit could have resulted in the capture of many of Bowen's soldiers. By letting them go, Grant and his generals lost an opportunity to cripple Pemberton's ability to defend Vicksburg. While Confederate soldiers made their way through Port Gibson to cross Bayou Pierre, chaos erupted in the town. Families fled through streets and down roads, and women begged for protection. A blazing bridge, fired by retreating Rebels, added to the surreal scenes of the night.[43]

As May 2 dawned, U. S. Grant ordered McClernand to prepare his troops for more combat. By 6:00 A.M., Union brigades aligned, and skirmishers probed for the enemy. Men in the ranks no doubt felt great relief when they realized that the Confederates had left the area. All that remained along Rebel paths were dead soldiers and varieties of equipment. The army marched into Port Gibson and found public buildings filled with enemy wounded. McClernand sent an officer to inform Grant; but by the time the messenger caught up with the commanding general, Grant had already ridden into town, where the determined courier superfluously informed the commanding general that Port Gibson had been taken. Most of the army rested while a few worked to bridge Little Bayou Pierre.[44]

Port Gibson was a thriving town even before the founding of Vicksburg. At that time closer to the Mississippi River than it is today, the place had been named for Samuel Gibson, an early settler. Area residents had been enthusiastic about the war, and ten companies of citizen-soldiers were organized and sent to the Confederate army in 1861. Now Federal troops occupied streets and homes; businessmen closed their stores or at least tried to; a local woman's college was converted to a hospital; and townspeople who did not flee feared what the Yankees might do to them. The small town in fact fared rather well; according to a story that is probably apocryphal, Grant said the town was too beautiful to burn.

Certainly it did not burn, but houses and stores were ransacked, homes damaged, and supplies confiscated, which caused local hardships for months to come. The entrance of Union troops into the streets brought a mood of fearful uncertainty that did not go away until the war ended. Federal forces would continue to occasionally show up, either on cavalry raids or to take hostages for exchange with Confederates who forced Northern-born schoolteachers to do menial tasks in their camps. War had come to stay in Port Gibson.

Union soldiers admired the town and enjoyed a time of rest. Some took pleasure in sorting through discarded Rebel knapsacks, but they had to find places downwind of the stench of decaying human corpses and slain horses. One small slave girl made an impression. A Illinoisan noted that the child had plenty of questions and told them "about a Yankee schoolmiss who hated us. The little darkey was nearer a secesh than any negro I had seen." Federals rarely interacted with locals, since so many townspeople had run away and those left rarely made themselves visible.[45]

An Illinois doctor watched his Confederate counterparts perform surgery, and he thought their ineptness "more certainly destructive to the confederate cause than Yankee bullets. It was this: a rebel soldier had been wounded by a buck shot or pistol ball penetrating the thigh bone about two inches above the knee joint, directly in front. The wound was very simple and did not fracture the bone. They decided to amputate the thigh and placed the patient on the table." The Union physician tried to tell the Confederates the amputation was not necessary, but the latter insisted that it must be done, botched the procedure, and the soldier bled to death.[46]

Meanwhile, poorly clad Confederate captives, escorted by heavily armed Federals, began a long trek to the Mississippi and beyond. Union soldiers likewise dealt with Confederate wounded and dead left behind as a result of Bowen's hasty retreat. One Iowan found the butternut-colored uniforms that most Confederate prisoners wore to be unattractive, but much more suited to field duty than Federal blue, for they made Rebels harder to see. The Rebels looked healthy enough, and most of the captives seemed "quite gay and festive." But "the better dressed and most intelligent looked sad and gloomy." These may have been officers from upper-class Southern society, the sort who had pressed for war and had the most to lose.[47]

The Federals could not believe that in their haste, the Confederates had, in lieu of burial, used the tops of felled trees to cover bodies piled in heaps. Fred Grant watched with horror the gathering of corpses from both armies. The burial details "would take a body, carry it back a short distance, and then place it with others upon the ground. They had arranged two lines of dead bodies, one of Union soldiers and one of the enemy's men. This ghastly sight was so frightful to me that I started off and joined another party who were collecting the wounded, and followed them a distance of about a quarter of a mile, to a small log house which had been taken and arranged for a hospital."[48]

An impatient General Grant tried to get things moving. Tired of waiting for a new bridge across Bayou Pierre, he ordered James McPherson to send John Smith's brigade up Little Bayou Pierre to check Askamalla Ford. From there Smith should cross and march to Grindstone Ford on Bayou Pierre and hopefully hit the retreating Rebels in their flank and rear. For security, McPherson added General Elias Dennis's brigade to the flank march. The men crossed at Askamalla without incident and soon marched onto the Port Gibson–Vicksburg road. They captured a supply depot containing several thousand pounds of bacon, surprisingly not destroyed by Bowen's troops, and halted to await the rest of the XVII Corps.[49]

John Stevenson's brigade approached Bayou Pierre west of Port Gibson and found bridges wrecked. Across the bayou, Francis Marion Cockrell's Missourians waited, supported by artillery. Ironically, Stevenson sent the 7th Missouri (Union) to check enemy intentions. A fight broke out between the Missourians, a stark reminder of the tragedy of civil war. Cockrell received reinforcements around noon, and Confederate fire increased. Missourians in blue began slipping back away from the firing line, but Stevenson abandoned his plans to break off the fight when division commander John Logan came on the scene. Logan brought up two batteries to shell Cockrell's position. The fighting continued until news came that a bridge had been constructed in Port Gibson. Stevenson disengaged and his men marched for the crossing.[50]

The XVII Corps crossed Little Bayou Pierre and rushed to reach Grindstone Ford before the bridge there could be destroyed. Smith's and Elias Dennis's brigades rejoined their comrades, and the lead brigade, Marcellus Crocker's, reached the ford at 7:30 P.M., too late to keep the bridge from being set ablaze by Confederates. With the help of a few local ex-slaves, a detachment put out the fire. Infantry could use the ford itself to cross, but the bridge would have to be rebuilt for the passage of horses and artillery. Engineers set to work, and by shifting boards, confiscating lumber from nearby dwellings, and creative use of ropes, the new bridge was ready for use by the early morning of May 3. McPherson's corps crossed and camped. McClernand's XIII Corps, worn down by the hard fighting on May 1, remained in Port Gibson, resting and refitting.[51]

While Grant considered his next move, John Pemberton worked desperately to salvage the disastrous situation south of Vicksburg. On May 1, at his headquarters in Vicksburg, he received messages detailing Bowen's defeat at Port Gibson. Pemberton passed along some of the reports to Richmond, to Johnston in Chattanooga, and to Edmund Kirby Smith, commanding the Trans-Mississippi area. Also on May 1, Johnston sent a message to Pemberton, suggesting a concentration of all forces to prevent Grant from landing on the east side of the Mississippi. Johnston repeated the gist of the message the next day, assuring Pemberton, "Success will give back what was abandoned to win it."

Johnston's advice came too late to be of any consequence to Pemberton. Whatever Johnston intended Pemberton to abandon, and later exchanges indicated he probably meant Port Hudson and Vicksburg, especially the latter, his attempts to direct operations from afar were ill advised and ineffective. If Johnston read the signs of Grant's activities better than Pemberton, and if he suspected prior to May 1 that Grant had decided to attempt a landing below Vicksburg, then certainly he should have warned Pemberton earlier. Johnston's insinuation that Pemberton should be the aggressor and go after Grant, regardless of the consequences, went against Pemberton's, and for that matter Johnston's, strategic philosophy. Johnston might preach concentration and attack, but he rarely practiced either.[52]

As for Pemberton, he fired off instructions north, south, and east to bring men from Grenada, Port Hudson, and Meridian. William Loring, who had hurried from Meridian to Jackson, took the train to Big Black Bridge and assumed command of Lloyd Tilghman's force, consisting of two regiments and a battery, and headed quickly to Port Gibson. The haste and panic at Pemberton's headquarters surfaced in initial instructions to Loring, which said that he should "proceed at once," without telling him where to proceed. Tilghman, an old West Point friend of Pemberton who had developed a feud with the Pennsylvanian after Pemberton accused him of disobeying orders in North Mississippi the previous fall, had not forgiven the commanding general even though Pemberton had acknowledged his error and apologized. Tension between the two arose again when Tilghman got word to send his men on south, but to wait for Loring at the Big Black. Pemberton's vague messages left both Tilghman and Loring miffed, wondering, and hesitant, and Pemberton grew angry at their inaction. He told Loring to "obey" and to do so "at once." Tilghman received a reminder that his orders had been "peremptory, and will be obeyed at once." Surely, neither general felt very confident that Pemberton and his staff had a strong grip on things. Neither did the many common soldiers who understood that the enemy would now try to cut the railroad to Jackson and starve Vicksburg. One commented that the commanding general, that "imbecile in Jackson," held the fate of Mississippi in his hands, and "a halter is almost too good for him."[53]

Pemberton had already grown impatient with Loring, both for the latter's constant complaining at Fort Pemberton and for his attempt to usurp Pemberton's authority by issuing departmental orders intended to counter Federal cavalry activity in North Mississippi. Pemberton reminded everyone that he still commanded the department, and that "all orders [are] to be issued in my name." Pemberton had concerns about the situation to the north, but without Earl Van Dorn's cavalry, which had been transferred to Braxton Bragg, Pemberton had to deal with the more immediate threat posed by Grant.[54]

While he rushed to get Loring and Tilghman to Bowen's aid, Pemberton sent messages to Carter Stevenson, commanding the Vicksburg defenses. Stevenson must send a brigade to Bowen at once, and Pemberton wanted to know if Stevenson had enough rifles in the city to arm some 600 exchanged prisoners. Stevenson sent Alexander Reynolds's Tennessee brigade south and said, no, he did not have spare guns for that many men. Stevenson may well have been hoarding guns in Vicksburg and simply did not want them leaving the city. Frustrated, Pemberton sent word to General John Adams in Jackson to secure rifles there if possible and to send them to Vicksburg detachments guarding bridges around Jackson.

Meanwhile, Pemberton decided to keep cavalry posted at Meridian to protect the railroad there in the hope that more reinforcements would be coming from the east. Benjamin Grierson's raid convinced

Pemberton that he must use his cavalry to protect supply and communications lines. Pemberton later changed his mind and ordered Abraham Buford's cavalry to Vicksburg from Meridian. Buford left a detachment to guard a railroad bridge west of Meridian.

Concentration of Confederate troops continued. Winfield S. Featherston entrained his brigade in Grenada for Vicksburg, while Carter Stevenson asked Pemberton to allow him to head south with two brigades. Pemberton said okay and placed John Forney in charge of the Second Military District, which included city defenses, until Stevenson's return. John Moore's brigade moved from Chickasaw Bayou south to Warrenton.[55]

Pemberton sounded the alarm elsewhere. He wired Governor John Pettus that Grant had crossed the river; all state archives, the Jackson Arsenal's machinery, and all army records should be transferred to points east. Clearly Pemberton had little confidence that he could protect both Vicksburg and Jackson, and Vicksburg was his top priority.

Ordnance chief George Mayo transferred available guns and ammunition from Jackson to Vicksburg, and subsistence chief Theodore Johnson received instructions to make sure the hill city had plenty of supplies. Rations would be cut at once. Pemberton's narrowly focused determination to save Vicksburg became more and more evident. At no time did he imply that he intended to take the offensive against Grant. Pemberton's defensive mind-set made Grant's job much easier.[56]

Pemberton's immediate response got under way when Loring left Jackson on May 1 with a company of artillery. He met Tilghman at the Big Black River bridge, and the two headed south with the latter's troops, leaving another artillery company at the bridge. The next day, Tilghman and Loring learned details of Bowen's defeat and heard that Union soldiers had been seen heading toward Grindstone Ford. Loring feared that if the enemy got across Bayou Pierre, Bowen could be trapped in an area bordered by the Big Black to the north, Bayou Pierre to the south, and the Mississippi to the west. Loring ordered Arthur E. Reynolds's brigade to the ford, and Loring and Tilghman rode off to find Bowen. Reynolds found a Federal detachment trying to repair the bridge, and he decided not to do anything in the dark other than deploy his men along the bluffs north of the stream.[57]

Bowen received Pemberton's message the evening of the lost battle; no doubt Bowen must have smirked at news of reinforcements, two brigades, on the way, with no indication of when they might arrive. Despite any disgust he felt about Pemberton's slothfulness, Bowen remained a soldier, and he did his best to recoup Confederate fortunes.

Assured of more men, Bowen decided to make a stand against Grant along Bayou Pierre. When Loring's men arrived, Bowen planned to put them on his left and give battle. He soon learned, however, that reinforcements were too far away and too few to mount any kind of resistance. Bowen knew he could not remain south of the Big Black. The news that Grant's army had crossed Little Bayou Pierre confirmed the necessity to retreat. Bowen also had to consider the possibility of Union gunboats coming up the Big Black and limiting his possible retreat routes.[58]

The night of May 2, Bowen met with Loring and Tilghman and summarized his situation. Bowen exaggerated Grant's numbers, but he rightly stated that even with reinforcements they could not hope to stop Grant here. Bowen offered to turn over command to Loring, his senior, but Loring refused and agreed that the army must move north to safety. Bowen ordered the retreat and sent a brigade of Tennesseans to help hold the Yankees at Grindstone Ford. Bowen's evacuation route included crossing the Big Black at Hankinson's Ferry on a makeshift bridge. Bowen received word from Pemberton to destroy everything of military value at Grand Gulf, but Bowen decided to save supplies for his own hungry army. The lone Confederate regiment still at Grand Gulf destroyed ammunition and spiked guns.[59]

By the morning of May 3, Grand Gulf had been disarmed, and Confederate columns headed north. Loring now took command, and as the soldiers marched they heard sounds of battle at Grindstone Ford. Unfortunately, Alexander W. Reynolds's Tennessee brigade had been wandering aimlessly in a futile search for the place. Arthur E. Reynolds's Mississippi troops had gotten into a fight without support. Loring ordered Tilghman to take Tracy's Alabama brigade, now commanded by Stephen D. Lee, to help the Mississippians. Cockrell's Missourians stood ready to reinforce Reynolds and Lee if needed.[60]

The rest of the Confederates proceeded to a flatboat transformed into a bridge at the Big Black. While the soldiers crossed, Carter Stevenson came on the scene, with two brigades from Warrenton. With a beefed-up force now on the north side of the river, and with adequate supplies and a large contingent making up what amounted to a rear guard back at Grindstone Ford, Loring paused, wrote a message to Pemberton asking what to do next, and ordered the army to camp while he awaited a reply. Loring chose to cross the Big Black quickly rather than assault the advance of James McPherson's XVII Corps, which was isolated from the rest of Grant's army. Perhaps Pemberton's tentativeness had rubbed off on his subordinates. More likely, Loring feared risking a battle when he did not know the exact locations of Grant's troops. Loring understandably did not want to take the offensive without knowing more.[61]

Back at the Grindstone Ford area, John Logan's division crossed and encountered weak resistance from Reynolds. After a brief flurry of artillery fire that scattered Yankees, the Rebels fell back, and Stephen Lee's and Lloyd Tilghman's brigades joined them. The sounds of guns alerted McPherson to push more men across the ford, and as the reinforced Yankee line surged forward, the Confederates continued retreating up roads leading to Big Black ferries. McPherson ordered a two-pronged pursuit, skirmishing increased, and the Rebels pulled back again. Cockrell's troops got drawn into the sporadic fighting, and they put up a strong stand on a high bank bordering a creek; but the danger of being flanked soon forced them to retire, and at last Loring's rear guard made it across the Big Black. Efforts by Confederates to destroy the flatboat bridge failed when Ohio troops arrived and chased the Rebels away.[62]

In the Union rear, Grant tried to reinforce McPherson. McClernand left behind Eugene Carr's division to occupy Port Gibson, to protect communication lines with the Mississippi, to parole wounded Rebels, and to care for Union wounded. The other three divisions marched toward McPherson's front, their way hampered by supply wagons, heat, and narrow roads. The XIII Corps still managed to make good time, reaching the Willow Springs area by evening. McClernand spent the night in the Alfred Ingraham house and learned that Mrs. Ingraham ironically was a sister of Union general George Meade and that an Ingraham son had been killed at Corinth. Apparently, McClernand and his staff experienced little hospitality from the family, despite the Union army connection. McClernand sent foragers to scour the countryside that night for supplies; the men confiscated buggies and mules in addition to large supplies of food. They found slaves who had been abandoned by masters; many of the freedmen and Union soldiers feasted on bacon and hams left behind by Bowen's forces.[63]

The afternoon of May 3, U. S. Grant rode with his escort to check out Grand Gulf, which they saw had been abandoned by the Confederates. Porter and his sailors had heard loud explosions from the Grand Gulf area earlier, and they correctly surmised that the Rebels were destroying ammunition before pulling out. Porter took most of his fleet to check and found the town and its defenses deserted. Grant's army now had a measure of security, and Porter moved on with his flotilla to take over the Red River blockade.[64]

Downriver, Nathaniel Banks and David Farragut had been operating against Port Hudson in order to relieve pressure on Grant. Grant had promised to get troops to Banks if transportation could be found, but that had not happened. Banks, meanwhile, infuriated Washington with his diversionary campaigns (Halleck called them "eccentric") rather than focusing on clearing the Mississippi. Communications between Grant and Banks had been very slow, and ultimately Grant, while sitting at Grand Gulf and planning future movements, decided that he must continue without worrying about Banks. Grant's army had the initiative, and it would be foolish to mark time while trying to work out joint operations. Banks eventually besieged Port Hudson, which denied Pemberton desperately needed troops at Vicksburg.[65]

Grant notified Halleck of his intentions and assured the general in chief that a solid position had been established on the east side of the Mississippi. Grant intended to move inland, his direction uncertain, but obviously keeping in mind his target—Vicksburg. In later years, Grant claimed that he decided to cut his army off from the base of operations being established at Grand Gulf. On May 3, 1863, he wrote in this vein to Halleck, "The country will supply all the forage required for anything like an active campaign, and the necessary fresh beef. Other supplies will have to be drawn from Milliken's Bend. This is a long and precarious route, but I have every confidence in succeeding in doing it." But, clearly, Grant did not intend to sever his army from its base, nor did he do so.[66]

A tug and barges loaded with supplies had already passed Vicksburg batteries, and more such shipments were being prepared. The generally ineffective Confederate artillery scored an occasional hit but could not stop the flow of supplies. Union details collected available wheeled vehicles in the Port Gibson–Grand Gulf area and loaded them down with ammunition. The strange-looking assembly of wagons and carriages followed the army into interior Mississippi. A Union soldier wrote home on May 5 that a train of 100 wagons, filled with provisions, had left Grand Gulf en route to the army. Sherman received word to round up 120 wagons at Milliken's Bend for transporting supplies. On May 11, an Iowan recorded in his diary that he and his comrades were "guarding an immense wagon train loaded with provisions" heading for the army, which by then was closing in on the capital city of Jackson. Grant, thinking ahead, issued orders to establish a supply base on the west bank of the Mississippi below Warrenton. This shortened the long supply line from Milliken's Bend. Until things fell into place, the troops depended on foraging and wagon trains from Grand Gulf. One Indianan noted approvingly, "We live principally on the produce of the planter — think it excellent 'war policy' to quarter a hungry army on the produce of the enemy and on his own land."[67]

With the victory at Port Gibson and successful efforts to drive Confederates farther into the interior of Mississippi, Grant had more than a secure foothold. John Pemberton's inability to understand Grant's intentions resulted in an open door into central Mississippi. Bowen's men had proved that Pemberton had an army of very capable fighters. Bowen's aggressive use of terrain had served him well, but Pemberton did not have Bowen's warrior mentality or his tactical insights. Pemberton had shown that he was incapable of divining the enemy's intentions, and he had let Bowen's men be heavily outnumbered as a result. Pemberton's limitations as a tactician, strategist, motivator, team builder, and battlefield leader, already suspect, would be sharply defined in the next two weeks.

Yet many factors shaped Pemberton's dilemma. He did not have consistently reliable information about Union activities on the other side of the Mississippi. He also could not afford to ignore Sherman's threat north of Vicksburg, although the Chickasaw Bayou experience should have made it apparent that a comparatively few Confederates could hold off many times their number as long as they held the high ground. Pemberton should have been more willing to gamble sending troops from Vicksburg to Bowen. Pemberton's delay in moving his headquarters to Vicksburg also deprived him of getting a feel for what was going on along the river. For that he had no one to blame but himself. His previous experience in South Carolina lurked in the back of his mind; he would not make the mistake of stripping Vicksburg defenses to make a stand downriver, especially when he could not know with certainty exactly where Grant would land. When he had suggested abandoning Charleston, he had suffered a severe public relations backlash, and he would not risk doing the same at Vicksburg.

Even had he concentrated all he had at Bruinsburg, as Joe Johnston later suggested, success would not have been guaranteed. Pemberton would have had to be clairvoyant to know where Grant would land in time to get the Confederate army there into position. In Porter's navy, Grant had an advantage that Pemberton could do nothing about. The ironclads would have shelled a Confederate force anywhere close to the Bruinsburg landing. Finally, placing an army south of the Big Black and Bayou Pierre to stop Grant would have provided Porter an opportunity to use his fleet to hit the Confederate right flank and perhaps cut off the army from Vicksburg. Pemberton would show time and again that he had no intention of risking the uncovering of Vicksburg. So, while Pemberton did move slowly, did isolate himself from the front at a critical time, did get too preoccupied with Grierson's raid, and did react in contradictory ways to Grant's crossing, the circumstances of those days and hours were much more complicated than most of his critics have noted.[68]

By contrast, Grant played out his hand brilliantly. The diversions and the movement down the Louisiana side, plus the flexibility Porter's presence provided, gave Grant options that allowed him to succeed despite the uncertainties he faced. He likely never envisioned his various operations prior to April, and then his diversions during that month, as part of a grand strategy to unnerve Pemberton into scattering his troops. But taken all together, everything Grant had tried, the failures and the successes, had worked together to steal a march on a frustrated and discombobulated foe. The successful strategy had practically ensured that once Grant got past Vicksburg, and Grand Gulf, in a position to cross the Mississippi, there would be no opposition.

At that point, it was too late for Pemberton to undo the damage caused by his misreading of Grant's intentions. With no rail links between Vicksburg and Port Gibson, Pemberton would have to rely on hard marching by his troops, and they could not march fast enough to get to Bowen in sufficient numbers to stop Grant's march inland. Pemberton's only viable option would have been to abandon Vicksburg and send all he had to meet Grant, and Jefferson Davis would never have tolerated that.

Grant's tenacity and patience had been remarkable ever since he started his campaign to take Vicksburg. Now as his army moved inland, he would continue his style of weighing options, maintaining flexibility, and keeping Pemberton guessing. Grant recognized, too, that his target had to be not just Vicksburg but Pemberton's army itself. What good would Vicksburg be if, after being captured, it required a large occupation force to hold it against a Confederate army still on the prowl? Taking the city and allowing Pemberton to escape would be a victory, but a hollow one; Grant had come too far and suffered too many frustrations to settle for less. Before he faced that issue, however, Grant and his army would experience much more campaigning and hard fighting.

9

Raymond & Jackson

As he paced the floor in his Vicksburg headquarters, John Pemberton knew that U. S. Grant's string of failed operations had ended. The Union army was marching inland somewhere to the south, and Pemberton could only guess Grant's exact target. The idea of concentrating and attacking Grant did not dominate Pemberton's thinking. He rarely thought in terms of attack, but this was a good time to draw inspiration from Holly Springs and launch a campaign against Grant's supply base at Grand Gulf. Yet Grand Gulf had enemy gunboats within reach, a problem Van Dorn had not faced in North Mississippi. Pemberton never considered such an option anyway; his overriding concern had been and remained how to defend Vicksburg, and the answer to that question got more elusive by the minute.

On May 3, Pemberton notified Jefferson Davis that his forces to the south had retreated to north of the Big Black. Pemberton cited "subsistence and proximity to base, and the necessity of supporting Vicksburg," as reasons for the withdrawal. Pemberton's words indicated his determination to take no risks that threatened the safety of the hill city. He built up his reserve force near the Big Black River where the Southern Railroad crossed. Acting quickly on Loring's reports of Union troops advancing north, Pemberton ordered troops to dig in around the bridge and stationed troops in Jackson as reserves for the inland campaign. Cavalry returned from their futile efforts to catch Grierson and camped in Raymond to watch for enemy approaches up the road from Port Gibson.[1]

While shifting men, Pemberton and his staff worked feverishly to prepare Vicksburg for battle. Procurement of bacon and beef north of the Yazoo became a top priority, as well as transfers of supplies from the Grenada area to Vicksburg. Slave workers increased the pace of building defenses at Jackson. Work details packed digging tools in the Yazoo

City area and sent them downriver to Snyder's Bluff. Pemberton ordered tightened security along the railroad from Jackson to Vicksburg to protect ordnance shipped to the latter. Reports of supply shortages in Vicksburg meant that matériel intended for the Trans-Mississippi might have to be retained.[2]

These decisions having been made, Pemberton looked for more troops to defend Vicksburg. He wired Franklin Gardner at Port Hudson, demanding that Gardner come north and bring 5,000 troops with him. Pemberton's staff instructed Texas politician Thomas Waul, now commanding at Fort Pemberton, to leave a token force there and bring the rest of his Texas Legion to Snyder's Bluff. Troops in Jackson left for Edwards Station, east of the bridge over the Big Black. Desperately needed cavalry in North Mississippi had been tied down by Union forays in areas ravaged by the December campaign of the past year. While Pemberton and his staff searched for troops, Illinois riders burned a courthouse in the town of Hernando. Such developments put more pressure on Pemberton and the Confederate government to protect local citizens. Pemberton should have transferred most of the North Mississippi cavalry to the Vicksburg front, but he dared not risk the probable public outcry.[3]

Pemberton ordered Loring to bring his troops north to the Big Black bridge. Loring feared retreating in the face of the enemy, which he knew had a strong presence at Hankinson's Ferry. He could be forced to fight, and he reminded Pemberton that the Yankees might move on Warrenton by water rather than land. He reported that three brigades of his command were currently marching north. Pemberton gave Loring permission to do what he thought best, but by the time Loring got the message he had already evacuated the Hankinson's Ferry area.

Thus far, Pemberton and his staff had done a relatively good job of concentrating troops, but then, seized by another notion of trying to cover all bases with limited resources, Pemberton decided to break up Loring's command. The deteriorating military situation seemed occasionally to throw Pemberton and those around him into fits of confusion when they had to be calm and rational. To replace Loring's soldiers, Carter Stevenson marched his troops to near Warrenton to guard Vicksburg's southern flank. Pemberton instructed James Baldwin to bring his brigade back to Vicksburg, while Loring, Tilghman, and Tilghman's troops came to the Big Black railroad crossing. Bowen's brigade also marched for the bridge, and Stephen Lee's Alabama troops, supported by a Bowen regiment, screened the rear, keeping John Logan's division at bay. The shifting of troops did not always seem logical, and men marched long distances to satisfy the demands resulting from the tactical inexperience of Pemberton and his staff.

Fortunately for Pemberton and the Confederates south of the Big Black bridge, Union forces showed no inclination to pursue the troops on the move. Grant decided that he would hold the XIII and XVII corps in place and wait for Sherman and his XV Corps to arrive from Milliken's Bend. On May 4, as he issued orders, Grant had decided to move directly on Edwards Station. To keep Pemberton guessing, Grant sent a detachment in another direction, toward Warrenton. Grant intended to continue doing what had worked so well. He sent out patrols and detachments to force Pemberton to keep his soldiers scattered, leaving their ranks too thin to attack. Some of Seth Barton's Georgians, for example, breathed a sigh of relief when Federals north of the Big Black saw them and decided to pull back.[4]

McClernand, at Grant's behest, ordered patrols to check roads leading to ferries. A Rebel deserter told Peter Osterhaus that Rebel steamboats had docked at Hall's Ferry, so on May 5 Osterhaus took his division east between the Big Black and Bayou Pierre. Illinois cavalry on the point had a sharp skirmish with Confederates near Big Sand Creek, reminding the Federals that Confederate forces had not completely evacuated the area. Scouting reports brought to Grant indicated an enemy buildup in the Edwards area. Meanwhile, Eugene Carr left Port Gibson and brought his division to the front, reaching McClernand's corps on the fifth. Port Gibson did not matter now that Grant had secured his supply base at Grand Gulf.

Grant sent word up the Mississippi that reinforcements would be needed as the campaign progressed. He ordered a division of the XVI Corps to come downriver from Memphis, filling the gap there with reinforcements from Helena and Columbus, Ohio. Grant asked the navy to help protect his supply line from Milliken's Bend to Hard Times. He advised that no more river supply runs should be made at night under a full moon; he did not want to lose any more tugs, and he figured that a connecting road across De Soto Point would soon alleviate supply-line security problems. Grant's ability to get more troops without weakening other fronts, along with the cooperation he had from the navy, contrasted sharply with Pemberton's options.[5]

On May 6, McClernand marched his corps to Rocky Springs. To solidify his front and perhaps force Pemberton's hand, Grant decided to penetrate further into the interior of Mississippi, and that evening he issued marching orders. The more he distanced the army from his supply base at Grand Gulf, the more perilous would be the journey. He lost five supply wagons coming from Port Gibson when Wirt Adams's Confederate cavalry attacked, but the damage did not compare with Van Dorn's feat.

The men welcomed other wagons that arrived safely on the ninth. Grant and McClernand had reviewed the men the day before, and several confident soldiers, in the midst of washing clothes, had turned out in formation without shirts. Nobody—neither the men nor the officers—cared. The troops were cocky and enjoying the consternation of Mississippians. A Missouri soldier in blue noted, "The old planters flea at our approch like the chased deer before the hounds leaving everything behind that they cant take along[,] most of the old niggers woman & children[,] corn & thousands of lbs. of bacon and molasses[,] sweat potatoes etc." Risks remained, however, and Grant would not feel the confidence reflected by his men until Sherman reached the front.[6]

Sherman had not yet crossed the Mississippi. Since May 1, his army had been on the move, by land and water. He left Frank Blair's division on guard duty at Milliken's Bend and Young's Point and took his other two divisions to Richmond via Hard Times. By March 5, the column approached the Somerset plantation. The march proved pleasant enough, though at times the picturesque scenery was marred by destroyed property. Iowa soldiers who had spent time in Confederate prisons burned some homes, no doubt angering Sherman, who still detested such lack of discipline. To reduce pillaging, he ordered guards to protect some residences. Sherman's advance began crossing the Mississippi the evening of May 6, the same evening that Grant decided to continue his march north. As Grant moved forward, only a small portion of one of Sherman's divisions had set foot on Mississippi soil.[7]

Grant knew of potential Rebel threats in the Warrenton and Big Black bridge areas, and scouting reports and rumors indicated that Confederates were concentrating more troops in Jackson. As the army moved northeast up the Big Black valley, Grant sent patrols to sound the alarm if Rebels tried to get into the rear or on the left flank. Grant certainly had not forgotten Holly Springs. McClernand marched his corps on the left, nearest to Big Black, while McPherson marched to the right toward the Raymond community southwest of Jackson. Once again, McClernand took the route of greatest danger, shielding the army from Pemberton's entire force. When Sherman arrived, he was to pass McClernand and move north between the other two corps. Grant's general plan called for all corps to advance toward the Southern Railroad, covering a front that extended from Edwards east to Bolton. Once on the rail line, Grant would turn his army west and march straight for Vicksburg.

As Grant continued north, Abraham Lincoln waited anxiously for some word of what had happened to the Union army in Mississippi. On May 11, he wired an officer in the Washington area to inquire if Richmond papers had printed anything about events around Vicksburg, and he received a negative reply. Whatever Grant was up to, he was in no position to send messages, and official Washington had to wait for news — and hope that it would be tidings of victory.[8]

John Pemberton, still short on cavalry and not using what he had very effectively, remained in the dark about Grant's intentions. Confederate intelligence gathering in Mississippi had never been very good, and it proved to be especially poor during Grant's inland campaign. Various Federal feints convinced Pemberton that the major blow would come at Warrenton, so Pemberton sent Loring's troops to cover the area between Warrenton and the Big Black bridge. He instructed Bowen to march his tired men to an area south by southeast of the bridge. A more sensible disposition, given their locations, would have been to send Bowen where Loring went and vice versa. Perhaps Pemberton thought of Bowen as Grant did McClernand. Bowen could be trusted to fight, so why not put him at a point to block Grant from reaching the railroad in case Warrenton turned out not to be the main target? Yet Pemberton and his staff did not show much sympathy for the men in the ranks who had to make long marches.

On May 5, Pemberton's line of defense consisted of Stevenson's division on the far right, Loring's (with the addition of Baldwin's brigade) in the center, and Bowen on the left. Other troops included a brigade each at the old Chickasaw Bayou battlefield, in reserve north of Vicksburg, and supporting Colonel Edward Higgin's river defense troops watching the city waterfront.

Soon Pemberton had to reconsider his dispositions even as his troops marched to assigned locations. When Peter Osterhaus's division crossed Big Sand Creek, Pemberton decided that the Yankees were not headed to Warrenton after all. He ordered Loring to bring Tilghman's brigade to the Big Black bridge. Loring did as he was told but realized on his arrival that the Union threat remained miles away. By the afternoon of May 6, Bowen's division arrived, and Loring proceeded back south. Once again, Pemberton's weak tactical experience and poor intelligence wearied his troops for no good reason.[9]

Confederate soldiers and slaves turned their attention to digging defensive works along either side and in front of the line from the Big Black railroad bridge to Warrenton, along riverbanks, and in Vicksburg. Obstructions filled all roads approaching from east of the river. A detail moored the steamer *Dot* crossways in the stream near the railroad crossing as a footbridge to facilitate rotating work details on both sides. To the south, Stevenson thought his segment of the defensive line too long for his men to hold, and he asked that Martin Smith bring his division from Vicksburg to help. Pemberton, paranoid about further weakening the city's defenses, refused.

Meanwhile, reports poured in about a heavy enemy presence along the east bank of the Big Black below the railroad. Faulty Confederate intelligence remained true to form; all of the reports were false, but they kept Pemberton and his generals nervous and active. Bad news from Richmond indicated that General P. G. T. Beauregard, now commanding in Pemberton's old post in South Carolina, had insisted that he could not send more than 5,000 reinforcements to Mississippi. Jefferson Davis promised Pemberton that some 3,000 men captured at Arkansas Post, about to be exchanged, would be sent to him and that 4,000 rifles would soon be on the way. Davis cautioned Pemberton with advice that became an albatross around the already conservative Pennsylvanian's neck: "To hold both Vicksburg and Port Hudson is necessary to a connection with Trans-Mississippi." These instructions dominated Pemberton's thinking for the next several days.[10]

Should Pemberton have embraced Davis's position, or should he have favored Johnston's advice to attack Grant without worrying about Vicksburg? That historical question has been long debated, but in considering the situation several things must be kept in mind. Davis had stood by Pemberton while Pemberton was being vilified in South Carolina. True, Davis had removed Pemberton from command there, but, given the circumstances, he had done Pemberton a favor. Then Davis had given the beleaguered officer a more significant command and a promotion to lieutenant general. In Pemberton's mind, he owed the president, and he would obey Davis, regardless of what Johnston might think.

While Pemberton manipulated his troops, he received ill tidings from Port Hudson. Franklin Gardner, like Pemberton a Yankee who had married into a Southern family, said he could not send 5,000 men to the Big Black, at least not quickly, because he did not have enough train cars. He sent John Gregg's brigade to Osyka in southern Mississippi to go by rail north to Jackson, but Gregg's men had to walk several miles to reach the train that took them the rest of the way.

Pemberton needed more than a brigade, but since Davis, who tended to disperse his Western forces, wanted both Port Hudson and Vicksburg held, Gardner had to stay with the remainder of his troops.

Concerned that the Yankees had something in mind besides Warrenton, Pemberton tried to anticipate Grant's moves. Messages to Jackson urged Governor Pettus to send all army food and weapons there east to safer locations. Pemberton reassured Pettus that men from Beauregard's command and from Port Hudson would soon arrive in Jackson to shore up defenses. Meanwhile, a small contingent of state troops, men Pettus wanted in Jackson, came from Columbus to reinforce Pemberton's right at Warrenton.[11]

U. S. Grant wanted to keep moving and maintain pressure on Pemberton, but circumstances continued delaying his army's progress. Sherman's troops did not finish crossing the Mississippi until May 7, and Grant did not want the three corps spread out over a wide area, so he held up. McClernand used the delays to get a three-day ration supply distributed to his men. Supply wagons continued coming up from Grand Gulf, unloading, and making return trips. Grant counted on Sherman's presence in the rear of McPherson's and McClernand's corps to protect the supply line. Even so, distribution of goods occasionally broke down, as on one occasion when some twenty-eight wagons got stuck in mud, causing scattered anger among hungry soldiers.[12]

Reports from Confederate deserters confirmed that the Rebels were strengthening their lines, especially around Edwards, so Grant pushed his army slowly northeast away from the Confederates to give Sherman time to catch up. Sherman's XV Corps reached Willow Springs, while McClernand faced further delays due to supply problems. Wirt Adams's Mississippi troopers clashed periodically with the Yankees as Adams tried to get a fix on where Grant intended to strike, a tough task since Grant's thinking remained in flux, even as his army moved.

Grant wanted to hit the railroad, but his frustrations mounted as he waited to mobilize his three corps into a coordinated movement. Sherman sent word to Grant that the supply situation at Grand Gulf would not be adequate until properly organized. Grant responded that he did not expect the depot to supply the army all it needed; supplements would have to be found in the countryside. Of course, with troops scattered from Grand Gulf to the northeast, those in the advance had first chance at foraging, leaving little for their comrades who followed. Grant told Sherman the obvious: the more time the Union army took to get going, the more time the Confederates had to build up defenses and bring in more troops.

McClernand's XIII Corps pressed on northeast to Fivemile Creek near a crossroads village named Cayuga. A local woman expressed concerns about losing her home and property. She insisted that her family had no interest in the Confederacy, and Grant ordered her place left unharmed. Her property's salvation proved to be an exception. Grant set up headquarters at Cayuga and ordered McClernand to halt at Fivemile Creek on May 11 so that the XV Corps could pass. McClernand sent patrols north by northeast to secure the area. Grant maintained his plan for Sherman to take the center between McClernand and McPherson, who reached Utica on May 10 with the XV Corps.[13]

Logistics also concerned Grant's men, who took what food they pleased from locals, wherever they could find it. Some fared well with local cattle, sheep, and hogs. Pemberton's refusal to bring in cavalry from North Mississippi to strip the area of food before Grant's soldiers arrived helped the Union cause. The march inland produced ravenous scavenging that disturbed some of the men, mainly because soldiers raided houses and destroyed things for the pure fun of it. The pretty countryside became spotted with wrecked houses, one soldier noting that such things as dishes, women's clothes, and quilts littered many yards. This Indianan saw everything as "peaceful except the hostile army around me and the troubled occupants of ransacked homes." As the army moved north, they found more abandoned homes.[14]

McClernand's scouts continued probing the countryside ahead. Cavalry checked out the Telegraph road, which ran west toward Edwards, and, finding stiff resistance, retreated. A detachment went east toward Raymond and reported a shortage of water. Otherwise, McClernand's men spent May 11 in camp, cleaning clothes and enjoying the weather. Bad news came from Virginia, where Union troops had been defeated by Robert E. Lee at Chancellorsville, and from Georgia, where Bedford Forrest captured Abel Streight and his cavalry.

Along the Big Black, skirmishing broke out between Tilghman's Confederates and advance elements of Sherman's corps, an Ohio regiment sent to protect the corps's left flank and secure Hall's Ferry. The Ohioans wound up at Baldwin's Ferry, where Tilghman's men were camped, and Tilghman, acting as timidly as other Pemberton generals, ordered his troops to retreat across the Big Black. Meanwhile, the rest of the XV Corps advanced, passing among the ranks of the XIII. A holiday mood prevailed, though deprivations still caused many a soldier to complain.[15]

Grant, to restore discipline, order, and coordination, issued detailed marching instructions for the three corps on May 12. McClernand on the left would march his men to the community of Auburn, northeast of

Cayuga and several miles due south of Edwards. From there he would turn west along the Telegraph road, putting one division south of the road to cover his flank; the XIII Corps would go as far as Fourteenmile Creek. Sherman in the center was to take the bridge spanning the creek near Dillon's plantation. On the right, McPherson targeted the community of Raymond. With the supply situation looking up, thanks to a wagon train of supplies at Cayuga and another on the way from Grand Gulf, Grant's army at last seemed ready to make decisive moves.

McClernand's and Sherman's corps moved in a northerly direction, not encountering opposition until Sherman's advance received fire from Wirt Adams's horsemen at the Fourteenmile Creek bridge. Sherman rode to the sound of battle, and once Adams's cavalry had been chased away, he ordered a new bridge built where the old had been burned. By the evening of May 12, the XV Corps had made its way to Dillon's plantation and camped, and Grant set up headquarters in the Dillon home.

McClernand's XIII Corps moved north along the Telegraph road, with Illinois cavalry on the point skirmishing with dismounted Missouri Confederates. Again, numbers told, as McClernand rushed two infantry regiments to scatter the Confederates. An Ohio regiment pursued the retreating Rebels until they ran into Bowen's Missourians. By the time fighting ended for the day, McClernand's forces had control of a strategic ford and bridge. The successful maneuvers by the XIII and XV corps put Grant in a position to move quickly to the Southern Railroad.[16]

At Confederate headquarters, Pemberton wrestled with the situation facing him. He sent John Gregg's brigade, having arrived at Jackson, to Raymond to report on enemy movements. The timid general refused to risk hitting Grant's left flank, for if he failed, Pemberton feared that Grant might take Vicksburg quickly; and President Davis's dictum to hold Vicksburg and Port Hudson never stopped ringing in Pemberton's ears. In addition to deploying Gregg's unit, Pemberton put Wirt Adams in charge of all cavalry in the area with orders to harass, patrol, and cut lines of communications where possible. Adams's reports convinced Bowen that the time for a big fight had drawn near. Bowen asked Pemberton if the Confederates should make a stand at Edwards or pull back to the Big Black bridge area; Pemberton chose withdrawal to the Big Black if Grant advanced west with his whole force. In the back of Pemberton's mind was the notion that the heights along the west bank of the Big Black would make a strong defensive position.

Pemberton's lack of rapport with his commanders and his tactical deficiencies continued to cripple his efforts to prepare for Grant's offensive. Loring responded to an order to move southeast by marching his men to Baldwin's Ferry. Pemberton only intended for Loring to travel within supporting distance of Bowen at Edwards. Pemberton lost his temper, and an equally angry Loring had to adjust his deployment. Meanwhile, Pemberton shifted troops over long distances as he vainly tried to anticipate Grant's moves. Waul's Texas Legion, for example, marched from Chickasaw Bayou south to Warrenton.[17]

To counter Grant's possible attack on the Big Black bridge, Pemberton ordered Loring to send two brigades west of the bridge, and be on the alert, and to keep his remaining brigade, Tilghman's, at Baldwin's Ferry. Stevenson left three brigades in Warrenton and marched his remaining four to Loring's right. Pemberton decided that if Grant should wheel east, he would attack the Union rear; but it is unlikely he would have done so, for an attack carried the risk of defeat. He also decided that, once Loring neared Bovina west of the bridge, Bowen could advance to Edwards. Once Bowen moved, Loring would cross the Big Black and occupy the vacated trenches.

Having made tactical decisions from his Vicksburg headquarters, Pemberton now decided to go to the front and take personal command of the army. He left John Forney in charge of his and M. L. Smith's divisions in Vicksburg, and told Forney to send a brigade to Mount Alban, between Vicksburg and Bovina, to support either the Big Black front or Chickasaw Bayou, depending on developments. Thus the nervous Pemberton, rather than massing his army to meet Grant, continued a dispersal policy that ensured he would have fewer men on hand than Grant, if and when the two clashed. By contrast, Grant kept his three corps moving in concert, all within supporting distance of each other, detailing only a few men to protect the wagon supply line to Grand Gulf.

The decisive confrontation of the campaign turned out not to be where Pemberton anticipated. Gregg, still at Raymond watching for the enemy, had been told not to bring on a general engagement if heavily outnumbered. He could attack the flank and rear of Grant's army if the opportunity arose. Gregg disobeyed those orders, admittedly on account of his ignorance of the situation in his front, thereby setting in motion events beyond Pemberton's reach and control.

When Gregg and his men arrived in Raymond, they received a warm welcome, but Gregg could not enjoy it because he did not see Wirt Adams's cavalry as expected. Gregg found instead some forty Mississippi state troops scouting to the south. These, plus five of Adams's cavalry in Raymond on detached patrol duty, turned out to be all Gregg could count on for information about enemy troops coming up the Utica road from the south. Pemberton expected Adams to assist Gregg, but his badly written message to Adams created confusion. The wording, either by Pemberton or by one of his staff, told Adams to "direct your cavalry there to scout thoroughly." Adams took "there" to mean Raymond and that Pemberton meant only the five troopers already in Raymond. Pemberton actually meant that Adams should take his cavalry "there," to Raymond, and scout. The misunderstanding would be costly to Gregg's brigade and cause U. S. Grant to make a decision significantly affecting the campaign.[18]

Despite his erroneous interpretation of Pemberton's instructions, Adams realized that Raymond was vulnerable, so he sent a fifty-man detachment from Edwards to Raymond. These troopers had to take a roundabout route because of the presence of Yankees between Edwards and Raymond and did not reach the latter until late on the evening of May 11. They told Gregg about encountering the enemy, and Gregg feared the Federals might be moving between Edwards and Raymond, which of course was true. If the enemy penetrated far enough, Gregg's brigade would be isolated from Edwards and Jackson. He sent the fifty troopers to scout to the north and west.

Meanwhile, Pemberton decided that any Union move eastward must be a feint, that Grant intended to keep moving north to the railroad, and that Gregg should stay put and hit Grant's right flank when the opportunity arose. Gregg did not have enough men to make much of an attack, and though Pemberton had ordered a brigade from Jackson to help out, it might not arrive in time, and might not be enough even if it did.

Before daylight on May 12, Gregg was awakened and informed that the enemy had been spotted close by on the Utica road, but state troops could not get close enough for an accurate count. Gregg made an ill-fated decision to attack. Perhaps Gregg, knowing that Pemberton considered Union movements to the east a feint, jumped to the conclusion that a feint should not involve very many troops, certainly not more than a brigade. Perhaps, too, cavalry screened the brigade, kicking up enough dust to make a small force seem large. When reports indicated around 3,000 of the enemy at most, Gregg decided to take the offensive. Gregg had no idea how erroneous those reports were. He reasoned that if he could scatter the Yankees, he would have more room to harass Grant's true right flank. Gregg thus aimed to sweep aside what he believed to be a beatable enemy force. His scouts had seen McPherson's ad-

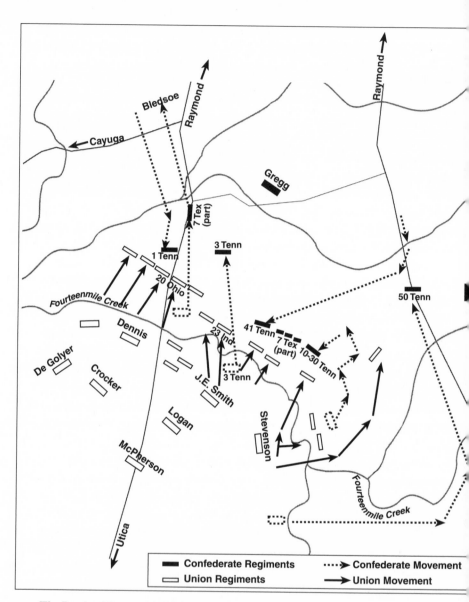

The Battle of Raymond, May 12, 1863. Map by Becky Smith, adapted from Michael B. Ballard, The Campaign for Vicksburg (Conshohocken, Pa.: Eastern National Park and Monument Association, 1996).

vance; behind that advance came the rest of the XVII Corps. Gregg unknowingly had chosen to send his lone brigade against two divisions.[19]

Gregg's battle preparations included deploying the 7th Texas at the junction of the Port Gibson and Utica roads, southwest of Raymond on the west side of the Utica road. The 50th Tennessee took position across the Gallatin road at right angles to the road itself. The 10th/30th Tennessee Consolidated regiment filed in behind the 50th to provide support as needed to their fellow Tennesseans or to the Texans via a connecting road to the south. The 3rd Tennessee deployed near the city cemetery with orders to support both flanks. On a rise northwest of the junction of the Port Gibson and Utica roads, Gregg placed Hiram Bledsoe's three-gun battery, supported by the 1st Tennessee Battalion. These guns had orders to shell a bridge that crossed Fourteenmile Creek on the Utica road, should the enemy try to use it. The 41st Tennessee remained in Raymond to watch the brigade's flanks and rear, and to provide support. Gregg thus deployed his brigade to cover approaches to Raymond, while at the same time keeping them close enough together to operate as a unit.[20]

The battle of Raymond opened when Texas colonel (and future general) Hiram Granbury sent skirmishers from his 7th Texas forward to cover the Fourteenmile Creek bridge. Union skirmishers fronting McPherson's corps exchanged shots with the Texans from some 100 yards away. McPherson had been ordered to convince the Rebels that he had designs on Jackson. McPherson had encountered little resistance along his march other than home guards, who scattered quickly, as did regular Confederate cavalry. Along the way, Union Missouri cavalry had thrown a scare into locals with a raid on the New Orleans, Jackson and Great Northern Railroad south of Jackson. The night of May 11, Grant ordered McPherson to occupy Raymond and stock up on supplies. Neither Grant nor McPherson anticipated any resistance.

The crack of musketry on the early morning of May 12 caught the Yankees by surprise, especially when the shooting continued. As the men marched by an old lady puffing on a corncob pipe, they laughed when she warned them that Pemberton's boys waited up ahead. An Ohioan noted, "The whole country was still with the stillness which you only see . . . after a hard day's work in the fields. The grass where we lay was sweet with clover, and a few wild flowers showed their heads here and there. In the woods not very far away a mocking bird was singing. Near where I was an old dead tree had fallen over on to the big arms of one of its neighbors, and on one of its decaying branches a red squirrel popped up its head, looking down at us along the brownish street that marked his usual highway to the ground." Rifle fire in the distance intruded on the serenity.[21]

By 9:00 A.M., McPherson decided that he was encountering more than just token skirmishers, so he ordered his cavalry to guard the corps's flanks while Ohio infantry from Elias Dennis's brigade of John

Logan's division came up to disperse the pesky Rebels. Around 10:00 A.M., Federal skirmishers moved down an incline through open fields toward trees that lined the banks of Fourteenmile Creek two miles southwest of Raymond. Within about 100 yards of the trees, the Federals ran into heavy Confederate infantry fire. Union soldiers hit the ground, some dead, some wounded, most getting out of harm's way, as three shells from Bledsoe's battery exploded in their midst. McPherson hurried forward to the sounds of battle and quickly overestimated the numbers he faced. Certainly he did not expect a mere regiment to give battle.

Samuel De Golyer's 8th Michigan Battery rushed up to duel Bledsoe's. Meanwhile, more infantry support arrived as Dennis's remaining three regiments took position along the battle line. Dennis ordered a charge, and his brigade surged forward, bolted a fence, and stormed into the trees. There, most of the troops stopped to catch their breaths while a strong Union skirmish line waded the shallow creek and pushed the Rebels some 200 yards beyond.

General Logan, meanwhile, sent John Smith's brigade to the right of the Utica road. These troops moved across open terrain and then entered a tangled mass of undergrowth, where the brigade lost all organization among vines, bushes, and briars. Indianans had some success crossing the creek, but three Illinois regiments became thoroughly entangled and bogged down before reaching the water.

John Gregg watched as the battle unfolded, still unaware of his peril. He apparently sent no scouts around either Union flank in order to determine the size of the force he faced. With no thought of retreat, he quickly developed a plan to win the fight, a plan based on the false assumption that he faced either a weaker force than his own or at most one about the same size. He knew that the creek flowed north northwest from the southeast toward the battlefield and then turned sharply west as it went under the Utica road. If he could pin down the Yankees along the road and then swing his left against the bowed, refused enemy line he might force their right flank into the rest of their line and capture the whole force. Around noon he sent the 50th Tennessee west and south to get beyond the Federal right with the 10th/30th providing support. The 3rd Tennessee occupied the gap left by the 50th's departure, and the 7th Texas covered the 3rd on the left. The 41st Tennessee came up to provide support as needed. Gregg ordered the Texans to begin the attack, which spread from the Confederate right to the left. The Tennesseans on the far left had orders to capture De Golyer's battery if possible.[22]

The 7th Texas advanced as Gregg waved his sword, and the Union skirmish line broke and ran to the rear. Dennis's main force quickly moved up and took cover in the creek bed and poured a telling fire into the oncoming Rebels. The Texans on the right of the line sputtered to a halt, but the left kept coming toward the men of the 20th Ohio, who were in a precarious position because another Ohio regiment had retreated, leaving the 20th vulnerable to a flank attack.

Like the 20th Ohio, the 23rd Indiana found itself in a ticklish situation. It had become separated from other regiments in Smith's brigade and now bore the brunt of the 3rd Tennessee's attack. The surprised men of the 23rd fired one round and then became submerged in hand-to-hand combat with the cheering Tennesseans. The Indianans soon broke and fled, not rallying until they came up on the right of an Illinois regiment, which had also gotten isolated during the forward movement.

Meanwhile, the 20th Ohio came close to breaking. With Texans bearing hard on their right, and Tennesseans charging Hoosiers, the Ohioans stepped back, on the verge of turning and running. General Logan now rode up and, with sheer force of will, rallied the 20th. The Texans wrapped around their right, but the beleaguered 20th held on, partly owing to their firepower and even more to geography. The creek turned on their right, and the high creek bank, trees, and underbrush blocked the Texans' line of fire.[23]

One of the Ohioans noted that the Texans "didn't scare worth a cent." Their tactics including "jumping up, pushing back[,] forward a step, and then falling back into the same place, just as you may see a lot of dead leaves in a gale of wind, eddying to and fro under a bank, often rising up as if to fly away, but never able to advance a peg. It was a question of life or death with us to hold them, for we knew very well that we would go to Libby [Prison in Richmond] — those that were left of us — if we could not stand against the scorching rifle fire which beat into our faces in that first hour." The astonished Ohioans saw a Rebel officer calmly stop firing, light his pipe, and resume firing "as leisurely as if he had been shooting rats. Why that fellow didn't get shot I don't know," wrote Henry Dwight of the 20th. At last relief came, forcing the Texans back, leaving piles of dead and wounded.[24]

Despite impressive tactical maneuvers, Gregg's brigade soon reeled under McPherson's superior firepower. John Stevenson halted his brigade in an effort to protect his men from the blinding dust storm raised by Smith's troops. However, as the battle developed, Stevenson led his regiments to the rear of De Golyer's guns. McPherson, seeing his forward troops having trouble maintaining organization, held Stevenson back. When the Union right suddenly became vulnerable to flanking fire, McPherson sent Stevenson in that direction to extend the line. Urgent pleas from the front forced Stevenson to break up his division. One Illinois regiment hurried to shore up Smith's left, while another ran to slow down the Texans on the right. His remaining two deployed on the right of one of Logan's Illinois regiments, thus extending McPherson's line to the right along the bend of the creek bed.[25]

On the Confederate side, Gregg decided that, largely because of successes on the field so far, he faced relatively even numbers. The smoke and dust of the battlefield kept him from seeing McPherson's additional troops shoring up the battle line, and he had received no reports to contradict his underestimate of enemy forces. The absence of Adams's cavalry seduced him into continuing the struggle and kept him in the dark. In truth, Gregg's men had had close contact with only two Federal brigades; McPherson now had thirteen on the battlefield ready to join the fight. Gregg continued pressuring the Federal right, with the 50th Tennessee moving far to the left in close proximity to the 10th/30th Consolidated. Colonel Thomas Beaumont's 50th lost the element of surprise when his skirmish line foolishly fired a few rounds. As Beaumont surveyed his front, he realized to his horror that there must be at least a division up ahead. He immediately dispatched a rider to tell Gregg, but the messenger could not find the general. Disgusted and alarmed, Beaumont drew his men up in a defensive position, leaving Colonel Randall MacGavock and the Consolidated regiment wondering what was going on. On the Confederate right, the 7th Texas lost ground on account of a determined counterattack by the 20th Illinois.[26]

Now the battlefield looked very different from when the fighting started. Along the creek bed, Union forces held the line for some 125 yards east of the bridge, their field of fire to the north. Rebels held the creek bed for some 100 yards beyond the east end of the Union line, and they fired south at the Yankees. A curve in the creek separated the two battle lines. It remained to be seen how long these positions would hold.

Colonel C. H. Walker's 3rd Tennessee, positioned between the Texans's left and the 50th Tennessee further to the left, went into action. Walker assumed that the 50th would support his left. As his troops departed from a wooded area and ran into a clearing, they received heavy fire on their left flank. Obviously the 50th was not there, but Walker remained convinced that the regiment would show up and ordered his men to find cover and wait. The Tennesseans had been shot at by a wandering Illinois regiment that happened to see enemy troops and opened fire. As more Federal forces came into the fight, along with additional artillery, Gregg, hearing very little from his Texans and the 3rd Tennessee, realized that something had gone wrong. He ordered up the 41st Tennessee from its reserve position, but they were a long march away.

Meanwhile, John Smith sent his troops charging into the 3rd Tennessee. Assaulted by four regiments, Walker's men held for nearly an hour before pulling back. Several fell into Union hands as the regiment retreated. Most made it to a ravine where they rallied, and the 41st Tennessee arrived just in time to stem the Union attack. Hiram Granbury watched as the big 3rd Tennessee fell back, and he should have realized that the enemy had much more than a brigade. However, it took an attack on his men by fresh enemy troops to convince him.

The 20th Ohio came up out of the creek bed and drove the proud Texans from the field. The 7th fragmented, part of it finding refuge with MacGavock's Consolidated infantry, and the rest being covered by the 1st Tennessee Battalion. Things continued to go badly for Gregg when Bledsoe lost one rifled gun that overheated and burst from continuous firing, leaving the Confederates with only two smoothbore cannon.[27]

While Gregg pondered his situation, McPherson continued shuffling troops, first sending a brigade from Marcellus Crocker's division to the far left, then, when the Texans gave way, shifting two Indiana regiments from the same division to support Smith and Stevenson. Rebuffed by an Illinois colonel, who insisted his regiment had things under control, the Indianans took a reserve position farther to the right and waited for an opportunity to get into the fight.

Across from the Union right, Gregg's left flank had been slowly pulling back, unaware of the beating inflicted on the center and right. The 50th Tennessee, yielding to enemy pressure, recrossed the creek and moved east to the Gallatin road, then north to the ridge, where it had started out early in the day. Here, they ran off a few Union skirmishers and formed a line facing south. MacGavock's Consolidated Tennesseans lost touch with the 50th and now received word from Gregg that they must move right to reinforce the center of the line. The gap in the Confederate line between MacGavock and the 41st Tennessee was considerable, some 400 yards. Across the way, additional Union regiments jockeyed for position to protect the Union right. Ohioans crossed the creek, swung left and eventually ran into the 50th Tennessee as the Rebels moved north along the Gallatin road.

A Missouri Union regiment waded the creek and moved toward Rebels deployed on a hill. There, MacGavock's men received artillery fire thanks to their visible position. Sensing that to fall back would further rupture the Confederate line and to stay would invite casualties, MacGavock ordered a charge. He wore a scarlet-lined gray cloak, making him an easy target for Union gunmen, and he fell dead soon after giving the order to advance. His men nonetheless ran down the hill, scattering the Missourians, who retreated to the creek and cover fire of nearby Illinois troops. MacGavock's regiment, now commanded by Colonel J. J. Turner, pulled slowly back up the hill and held firm when the Missourians counterattacked. Then the 41st Tennessee, in position to the right of Turner's men, suddenly pulled out as if retreating. Actually, they had been ordered to the far left by Gregg, who seemed unaware that the 50th Tennessee was already there, and there was no threat there anyway. The Texans moved into the spot held by the 41st.

On the Federal side of the line, Crocker's division deployed, making the Union line even more formidable. Massed artillery battered Confederate positions but did remarkably little damage. The smoke and dusty conditions may have contributed, for cannoneers could not always tell where their own men were. Nevertheless, McPherson showed surprising complacency by not having his gunners fight more aggressively. The battle ended with all of the Union artillery still south of the creek.

Gregg now realized that he must pull out; his right wing had been broken, and if he tarried his center and left would be scattered. He ordered the 1st Tennessee Battalion to bluff a charge at one of Crocker's regiments on the Federal left. The move bought time, and the 1st Tennessee quietly shifted to cover the retreat of the 7th Texas. The 3rd Tennessee, no longer in condition to fight, received orders to pull out. Gregg's instructions proved to be the last that provided any coordination for the withdrawal.[28]

A comical episode on the Rebel left illustrated how much the battle had gotten beyond the control of Gregg and his commanders. The 41st Tennessee was moving to the left as ordered when Beaumont's 50th Tennessee suddenly began moving west to the sound of guns. The regiments passed each other without speaking and soon each occupied the former position of the other, accomplishing absolutely nothing in the process.

Colonel Turner, informed by scouts that Yankees were about to get in his rear, pulled his men back, without telling any fellow commanders, and then charged into and stampeded an Ohio regiment. Turner's men in turn had to pull back in the face of fire from Indianans. Beaumont realized that he might be flanked, so he led the 50th Tennessee north, taking positions on either side of the Utica road. Several companies of the mounted infantry from Jackson came up unexpectedly to offer help.

With good cover fire available, Gregg led his regiment back through Raymond and onto the Jackson road. Soon the worn-out Confederates went into camp. They were no doubt relieved that the enemy did not press them. McPherson's men were glad to see them go. An Ohioan summed up the battle well: "The fight was fought with loaded guns, bayonets, & fists & clubs, butt end of muskets[.] [O]h! dear but the men fought desperately on both sides." Portions of brigades from Logan's and Crocker's divisions followed, but they stopped in Raymond, where they feasted on food prepared by local ladies for Gregg's victorious soldiers. Gregg's men did not have time to stop and eat.[29]

In Raymond, the Federals found a hospital inside the stately Hinds County courthouse where some eighty Rebel wounded were being tended. Federal wounded were taken to St. Marks Episcopal Church and the Methodist Church. Surgeons endured long hours, for the battlefield contained many wounded, many piled with the dead. Much soil had been dyed red. One Iowan described the battlefield as a scene of "wreckage of all arms of the service, broken wagons, scarred trees, newly made graves." Gregg's miscalculation had cost him 73 killed, 252 wounded, and 190 missing. McPherson had lost 66 killed, 339 wounded and 37 missing. According to these numbers, as reported by each side, Confederate casualties had outnumbered Union ones by 515 to 442. Yet McPherson insisted that his men buried 103 Confederates and had captured 720 including many seriously wounded. Either way, Gregg and his men, heavily outnumbered, had been beaten badly, though they put up a good fight, all things considered.[30]

The battle had shown that a poorly managed larger force could be held up for some time by an inferior one. McPherson's tentativeness caused him to feed units into the battle piecemeal; regiments with little understanding of terrain merely plugged gaps and reacted to trouble spots. Most Union soldiers did not know where the enemy lines were and what plans had been formed. None had, for McPherson just kept troops coming, leaving decisions to commanders who felt their way along. McPherson won because he had superior numbers, not because he exhibited superior generalship.

For most of the battle, Gregg seemed at a loss as to what his men were doing. He deployed well, but once the shooting started and dust and smoke blanketed the landscape, he never understood the course of the fighting. Like McPherson's commanders, Gregg and his lieutenants reacted to what they could see, sending regiments hither and yon, trying to hit enemy flanks, trying to bludgeon much larger numbers. Had Gregg been told he had taken on a corps, surely he would have disengaged; but battlefield conditions and lack of scouting reports masked the disparity in numbers. Little wonder that the battle developed into uncoordinated attacks that kept everyone confused.

As Union troops marched into town, they received a cold reception amid "the horrors of war." Wounded from both sides forced the use of homes and additional public buildings as hospitals. Local ladies moved "around among the suffering and dying with words of comfort and consolation," and some Federal troops felt moved by the scene. An Illinoisan, however, "witnessed the extreme astonishment and disgust possessed by southern *ladies* for the Yankee army. Poor beings." One local woman thought the soldiers in blue to be "very common looking men." Logan's staff told citizens there would be no pillaging, and McPherson convinced one family that if allowed to pitch his headquarters tent in their yard, he would see to it they were not bothered.

Then townspeople watched in dismay as Raymond became inundated with "aid[e]s, officers of all kinds, guards, niggers and horses." Despite officers' assurances of protection, looting of homes and slave quarters broke out all over town. One disgusted resident noted, without any sense of irony, "It's the meanest thing a white man can do, stealing from a nigger." Soon the entire corps marched in, waving flags, singing patriotic Union songs, and creating consternation when they launched into the Union version of "Bonnie Blue Flag," a popular Confederate ditty.[31]

One woman, Letitia Miller, watched Union troops march in front of her father's house, then stop, and set up camp. The troops took down a fence for firewood, emptied the smokehouse of food, took chickens, and drove off a cow and calf, despite pleas that her sister, suffering from typhoid fever, needed milk. The town's transformation into a large field hospital created a surrealistic atmosphere. Letitia summed up the state of the wounded: "Just a little wound in hand or foot—gangrene—death." Wounded and healthy soldiers borrowed family books, never to return them.[32]

An Indianan thought there were certain limits: "I noticed that where the people stayed at home and asked protection their property was protected. The other homes were sacked and nearly all valuables were destroyed." He was amused that some East Tennessee prisoners voluntarily took the oath of loyalty, angering captured Texans. Also, some locals seemed to suddenly switch sides. "It is astonishing to hear the loyal citizens talk[;] they are loyal[,] always have been — were only waiting for an opportunity — where they had protection to declare themselves — had always voted the *Linkun* ticket, etc., but such talk has long since played out." Other soldiers wanted no constraints. A few days prior to the battle at Raymond, a Union soldier frankly wrote his wife: "Had the Feds always done as they are now doing — fight with sword in one hand, and the torch in the other! — I believe the war would have been over long ago."[33]

The battle of Raymond settled nothing, but it gave Grant food for thought and in that respect altered the course of the campaign. As the battle wound down, Grant rested at his evening headquarters, the Dillon home, and there he received news of the fight. Though McPherson inflated the size of Gregg's force, Grant now realized that turning his back on Jackson and moving west might be risky. Scouting reports indicated that trains were bringing additional Rebel troops into the capital, and Joseph E. Johnston allegedly had arrived to take command of Rebel troops. Other reports convinced Grant that Confederates were concentrating at Edwards. His army had skirmished with Rebel cavalry (Wirt Adams's troops) and infantry (part of Bowen's division), and now McPherson had been in a hard fight on the Union right flank.

Grant did not feel comfortable dealing with the enemy at Edwards and at the same time worrying about an attack on his right or to his rear. He decided that Pemberton's timidity meant a Federal thrust at Jackson to chase Johnston away and to destroy enemy supplies and the railroad would be a safe move. Then Grant could wheel his army back to the west and take care of Pemberton. He understood his opponents, and thus he had no doubt that the plan would work. Information received from local pro-Union informants and planted Union agents regarding the disposition of Confederate forces also convinced him that his plan would succeed.[34]

Grant steered his army east by northeast. He ordered McPherson to Clinton, where his XVII Corps would turn right toward Jackson. Sherman took the XV Corps northeast, traveling via Raymond to enter Jackson from the southwest. McClernand deployed three divisions of his XIII Corps at Raymond, while his fourth, A. J. Smith's, waited at Fourteenmile Creek for Frank Blair's division of Sherman's Corps, which was escorting a wagon supply train from Grand Gulf. McClernand would, in effect, be the reserve force for the campaign against Jackson. Grant counted on Pemberton's staying at Edwards; if that did not happen, Grant wanted to be sure he had troops in place to protect the wagon train.

Despite the risk, and because they had faith in Grant rather than an understanding of the tactical situation, Union troops marched confidently in new directions on May 13. Grant had gotten them this far, and they saw no reason to doubt his judgment, whatever he might be up to. Wirt Adams's cavalry skirmished with McPherson's advance, but otherwise the XVII Corps's march to Clinton proved uneventful. They saw few people, most having fled the area, and found few supplies, departing Confederates having finally stripped the area in the path of the enemy army. After his corps camped for the night, McPherson sent engineers and infantry to tear up track west of Clinton. The men did their jobs well, destroying nearly two miles of track, but they got no sleep that night, returning to Clinton just as the rest of the corps marched toward Jackson.³⁵

Sherman's corps also had a relatively peaceful march, though the men had a brief scare. After lead elements passed through Raymond, Minnesotans received enemy fire on the Mississippi Springs road. The resistance proved to be nothing more than a small scouting party of Rebel Kentucky mounted infantry. James Tuttle's division led the way, followed by Steele's. The corps camped for the night a short distance from Raymond on the road to Jackson.

Meanwhile, John McClernand, whose men frequently engaged in sharp skirmishing with some of Pemberton's troops from Edwards, had to devise a way for his army to do an about-face and march toward Raymond. He ordered A. J. Hovey's division to bluff an attack on Edwards to cover Eugene Carr's and Peter Osterhaus's divisions while they turned toward Raymond. Hovey carried out the feint, then began withdrawing his troops, one regiment at a time, to march east and rejoin the corps. Confederates briefly attacked but were quickly driven off by Hovey's strong rear guard. Carr and Osterhaus spent the night of the thirteenth in Raymond, while Hovey camped at Dillon's plantation.³⁶

While most of Grant's army moved east, A. J. Smith's troops headed south to New Auburn, burning a bridge across Fourteenmile Creek to protect their rear. At New Auburn, they camped on a local plantation, China Grove, and waited for Frank Blair. Blair's division had had quite an odyssey in trying to catch up to the rest of the army.

During Blair's march down the Louisiana side of the Mississippi, his men had endured gnats, hot weather, poorly constructed bridges that had cost them some wagons, and problems getting boats for transportation from Hard Times to Grand Gulf. On May 12, having arrived at Grand Gulf, Blair moved his division out with the 200 wagons of supplies for the front. Blistering heat and water shortages plagued the march, and the men had to pass on the narrow road hordes of freed black men headed for Grand Gulf to enlist. By early May 14, Blair's column reached Cayuga, where a heavy rainstorm provided welcome relief from the heat but produced much mud. By the night of the fourteenth, Blair reached (Old) Auburn, where Smith's men welcomed them. So far, anyway, the supply train was safe, but much depended on Grant's success.[37]

Grant's decision to attack Jackson left Pemberton in a quandary about manpower. Gregg contributed to Pemberton's problems with his ill-advised attack and retreat from Raymond. Now Grant's move toward Jackson effectively blocked reinforcements going from Jackson to Vicksburg. Gregg had been reinforced on May 13 by part of W. H. T. Walker's brigade from Savannah, Georgia, one of the units ordered to Mississippi by Jefferson Davis. From Charleston, South Carolina, came a brigade led by a Palmetto State general with the unlikely, but appropriate, name of States Rights Gist. All told, the two brigades meant that Pemberton would have 5,000 additional troops to battle Grant rather than the 8,000 to 10,000 that Davis had pledged but could not supply. Poor railroad conditions between South Carolina and Jackson had forced Gist's troops into several detours and even a steamboat ride. Walker had been the first to arrive, on May 11; Gist's advance reached Jackson the evening of the thirteenth.

Gregg welcomed Walker's troops, but he soon made another error in judgment that cost the Confederates. Assuming that skirmishing on the road between Raymond and Jackson merely indicated enemy screening of McPherson's concentration at Clinton, Gregg quickly withdrew back into Jackson, giving Sherman an unfettered road to the capital. Pemberton, forced to depend on Gregg's decision making, approved the withdrawal, noting again that there should be no attack on a superior force but rather a concentration to protect Jackson. Obviously, Pemberton believed contesting enemy advances produced more risks than opportunities. Gregg's men found much chaos and panic among local citizens in Jackson on the evening of the thirteenth. Government records and offices had already been evacuated, as the state government, except for Governor Pettus, who tried to rally the citizenry, fled eastward to temporary residence in Enterprise. Many months passed before lawmakers could return to business as usual in Jackson.[38]

As Grant had been told, Joseph E. Johnston had arrived in Jackson, traveling with some of Gist's troops. Johnston had been with Braxton Bragg's army since leaving Mississippi back in December, but Jefferson Davis's concern about the deteriorating situation in Mississippi led Secretary of War James Seddon to order Johnston to hurry to the state and "take chief command of the forces," which Davis promised to augment. Johnston himself should arrange to have 3,000 sent from Bragg's army; Bragg would be replenished with exchanged prisoners from Arkansas Post.

Before reaching Jackson, Johnston read a May 12 telegram from Pemberton, who warned that Federal forces were moving toward Edwards along the railroad. Pemberton said he would fight if he thought his force at Edwards was sufficient, but, no matter what happened, he had determined to leave two divisions in Vicksburg. Pemberton complained that reinforcements were arriving slowly and that he desperately needed 3,000 cavalry — "a positive necessity" — to screen his position. He figured on being heavily outnumbered, but he hoped to stop Grant at the Big Black. At the time, Pemberton actually had more troops than Grant, but Grant's successes had apparently convinced Pemberton otherwise. Also, Grant's pressure along the Big Black convinced Pemberton that an attack was imminent. Pemberton's thinking meant that the Union thrust at Jackson was a safe move, as Grant anticipated. During these critical hours, Pemberton never considered the offensive.[39]

After reaching Jackson on the thirteenth, Johnston went to the Bowman House hotel where he received a report from Gregg. Gregg told him Pemberton's location and then commented, erroneously, about Sherman being at Clinton with four divisions. Actually, McPherson had two divisions at Clinton, while Sherman approached from the southwest with two, and the Confederates remained in the dark about Sherman's real location. Whose troops these were did not matter to Johnston. He had a notion of joining forces with Pemberton, but now the enemy was obviously in the way.

Johnston learned that he had about 6,000 men in the Jackson area, and he figured that number might double after the rest arrived from the East, plus Texan Samuel Maxey's brigade from Port Hudson, expected within a few hours. Johnston sent a message to Pemberton by three different riders. He urged Pemberton to open communications between Jackson and Vicksburg, a rather difficult task since Grant's army was in the way, and he also wanted to organize an attack, having Pemberton move east toward Clinton, while Johnston moved west. Johnston's words and deeds soon proved he never intended to do any such thing, for he knew Union troops were between Confederate forces, and a pincer movement meant risks that he would not take.

After looking over incomplete and poorly located earthworks thrown together around Jackson by black laborers and white citizens, Johnston convinced himself that Grant would launch an attack, one that he could not fend off, and so the city must be evacuated. Johnston still did not know of Sherman's proximity, and he certainly did not know for sure what Grant intended. He had stated clearly his true attitude in a May 13 message to Richmond, written after he sent instructions to Pemberton. His wire stated plainly, "I am too late." Despite Jefferson Davis's directive that Vicksburg must be held, Johnston gave up that notion quickly. Grant could have the place; Johnston merely wanted Richmond to know that he had come to Mississippi "too late" to do anything about it.[40]

The evacuation of Jackson began the rainy night of March 13–14. Johnston assigned troops to carry Confederate property to the small town of Canton, some thirty miles northeast of Jackson. Gregg took charge of Gist's and Walker's troops; Johnston ordered Gregg to buy time for the evacuation, fighting a rear-guard action if necessary. Gregg deployed three miles northwest of downtown, placing a brigade and battery astride the Jackson-Clinton road, with Walker in reserve. Gregg's brigade, commanded temporarily by Robert Farquharson, remained in Jackson for the moment, also in reserve. Gregg filled trenches with state troops who serviced seventeen artillery pieces.[41]

That same night, Grant ordered McPherson and Sherman to move toward Jackson early on the morning of May 14. McClernand provided support, sending one division to Clinton, one to Raymond, and another northeast of Raymond. McPherson and Sherman exchanged messages in an attempt to coordinate their arrival on the outskirts of Jackson at about the same time. McPherson heard gossip about Johnston's presence in Jackson, but he dismissed rumors that the Confederates had 20,000 men there. Nevertheless, he warned his men to anticipate resistance.

When McPherson's corps moved east at 5:00 A.M., his advance brigades struggled in muddy roads brought on by the heavy rain. By 9:00 A.M., a patrol saw Confederate troops on high ground in the distance, and soon Rebel shells began exploding all around. Union artillerists rushed to duel the Confederates. McPherson's commanders extended the right of the Union line, with two regiments held in reserve, both having to shift positions to avoid enemy shot and shell. As more Union brigades arrived and deployed, McPherson urged John Logan forward to support, but as he readied to signal a general assault, light rain

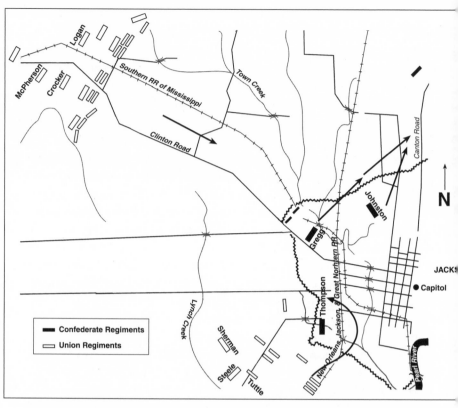

The Battle of Jackson, May 14, 1863. Map by Becky Smith, adapted from Michael B. Ballard, The Campaign for Vicksburg *(Conshohocken, Pa.: Eastern National Park and Monument Association, 1996).*

suddenly turned into a major storm. To keep ammunition dry, McPherson waited.[42]

Sherman's XV Corps also moved out at 5:00 A.M. Grant rode with his friend Sherman as the corps swept toward Jackson. Grant had visited with Sherman in Raymond, and while there he ordered the arrest of the publisher of the Vicksburg *Whig*, whom he planned to hold hostage until Confederates freed a New York *Tribune* correspondent captured at Vicksburg. The Vicksburg editor was ill, so Grant allowed him to remain in Raymond. The editor's daughter thought Grant "to be a vain old fellow. He kept telling us that he looked so rough because he had been marching so much." He claimed, she said, that the *Whig* editor had been more troublesome than Rebel generals. Sadly for Confederate hopes, Grant, if he said such a thing, exaggerated only a little. Patriotic editorials probably inspired Confederate troops more than Pemberton and most of his generals.

On their approach to Jackson, Sherman's troops heard cannonading off to the west. As the advance neared rain-swollen Lynch Creek, they found Confederates dug in on the other side. Rebel scouts had finally figured out that Sherman had not gone to Clinton, and Gregg realized he had to stall the enemy on two fronts. He quickly assembled a small force of infantry and artillery, commanded by Kentucky colonel A. P. Thompson, to hold up Sherman's corps.[43]

These Confederates had just reached Lynch Creek and deployed when Sherman's advance came up. Confederate artillery opened, and Sherman, riding to the front, ordered an attack. At about that time, 11:00 A.M., the rain slackened, and Union artillery soon silenced Rebel cannon. Massed Union artillery drove Confederates back from the bridge and into trenches designed to protect the southwestern approaches to Jackson. By retreating from the bridge, and not making any effort to destroy it with cannon fire, Thompson's force gave up their only opportunity to delay Sherman's advance. The bridge gave Sherman his only immediate chance to cross the creek; and though its narrow breadth slowed his men, no bridge at all would have caused a much greater delay.

James Tuttle's division led the way through woods and up a hill, beyond which they could see open ground to a line of trees where Confederates waited. Federal soldiers rushed forward, but outnumbered Confederate infantry and artillery fired away from their trenches. Tuttle, frustrated by the resistance, called up his reserve; but the fresh brigade found canister from enemy guns, manned both by state troops and citizen volunteers, too much to deal with, and they retreated to the woods.[44]

When Sherman consulted with Grant, he pointed out that Rebel works ran off to the left as far as he could see, but he could not tell the length of trenches to the right. Sherman sent an engineer and an Ohio regiment on a roundabout route to check in that direction. The scouting trip led to the discovery that works on the enemy left had been abandoned. About this time, as Frederick Steele's division arrived, Union troops, guided by a local black man, swept through the empty entrenchments and came up behind unsuspecting Rebel gunners confronting Tuttle. Tuttle's brigades heard the commotion and charged, and Sherman's pincer forced a quick Rebel surrender. Most regular Confederate troops had already left to support their comrades fighting McPherson on the Clinton road.[45]

Gregg's delaying tactics against McPherson had not worked well. He sent a brigade toward Clinton to feint a flank attack. McPherson ignored the threat; he felt confident that when the harsh weather lightened up, he could move east without difficulty. He felt especially confident when John Logan's full division deployed to support Marcellus Crocker's. When the rain ended around 11:00 A.M., McPherson ordered Crocker forward, and the Federals quickly ran into a hail of rifle bullets and artillery fire. The line reached shelter some 500 yards from the Rebels and closed ranks for what they hoped would be a decisive charge. Advance patrols could not break through the Confederate line, but Crocker judged that he did not face a major force.

Crocker ordered a charge, his soldiers cheered, and a Federal wave hit the Confederate line, driving into quick retreat a South Carolina regiment, whose colonel fell wounded. Yankees and Rebels struggled hand to hand, and numbers soon told, with surviving Confederates pulling back into earthworks. Other Confederates moved east toward the Canton road, and Crocker ordered a battery to shell the retreating enemy, while Union infantry regrouped. An Indianan recalled the initial charge: "The order was given, we went with a Hoosier yell that was heard three miles. Cannon balls boomed through the air, shells screached and bullets whistled, but on we went." The charge had been about as brief as his description.[46]

As McPherson's corps continued toward Jackson, Union cannoneers shelled Confederate trenches, which his advance patrols found empty. Around 2:00 P.M., Gregg had received word that supply wagons were safely out of Jackson on the Canton road. Having accomplished his mission, Gregg ordered his troops to follow the wagons north; he left behind just enough men and cannon to keep the enemy cautious. The Confederates camped some seven miles north of Jackson the night of May 14; they had escaped without incident, though a Union brigade's attempts to block the retreat route had almost succeeded. Union troops turned their attention to the occupation of Mississippi's capital city and putting out fires that the Confederates had set to destroy food and equipment that could not be evacuated.[47]

Fred Grant almost became a prisoner of war when, thinking the battle had ended, he rode into town and suddenly found himself observing Confederate troops passing north. The soldiers moved rapidly and, fortunately for Fred, paid no attention to the diminutive, blue-coated, dirty boy sitting astride his horse and watching. Young Grant recalled, "I was very small, very wet, much splashed with mud, and altogether unattractive. I was the only 'Yankee' around." He breathed a sigh of relief when he saw a rider coming in the distance carrying a U.S. flag.[48]

Grant, Sherman, and McPherson met at the Bowman House to congratulate each other and discuss future operations. They reviewed battle reports that stated the two corps had lost 41 killed, 251 wounded, and 7 missing. Their estimates of Confederate dead, wounded, and captured totaled 845. Seventeen cannon had fallen into Union hands, guns John Pemberton would desperately need. McPherson also had good news for Grant. It seemed that a Union spy, planted by Stephen Hurlbut (still commanding in Memphis), had been one of Joe Johnston's couriers to Pemberton. In addition to loyal U.S. citizens and slaves, Grant used infiltrators frequently to glean information in enemy territory. The spy, possibly an adept operative named Charles Bell of Illinois, brought his copy of Johnston's message to McPherson, so Grant now understood that Johnston wanted to get the Jackson Confederates to cooperate with Pemberton's army. Grant talked with the spy and realized he must move at once.

For all Grant knew, Johnston would turn southwest and try to catch the Union army in between the two Confederate armies. McPherson headed his corps toward Bolton on the Southern Railroad, the point Grant figured Johnston would target. McClernand also received orders to march his corps to Bolton. Sherman and his corps spent May 15 destroying railroad equipment and Confederate supplies in Jackson.[49]

As for the Confederate military situation, Johnston's precipitous withdrawal from Jackson meant that reinforcements for Vicksburg still east and south of the capital city could not get to their destination by rail. Some indeed had to stop and find Johnston the best way they could; troops coming from the south returned to Port Hudson. Johnston's decision proved fatal to whatever hopes the Confederacy had of saving Vicksburg. While the upcoming showdown between Grant and Pemberton on May 16 at Champion Hill usually is defined as the turning point of Grant's inland campaign, Johnston's abandonment of Jackson proved in some ways to be an equal disaster. Had Johnston held out to give reinforcements hurrying to Jackson time to arrive, he might have bogged down Grant's march and given Pemberton time to execute the pincer movement Johnston claimed to envision. By giving up quickly on Jackson, and for that matter Vicksburg, Johnston robbed Pemberton of thousands of troops and numerous cannon, munitions, and equipment. When Johnston moved to Canton, he took himself and the troops with him out of the Vicksburg campaign, for, once there, he became almost frozen in place in the Canton area, and later in the Jackson area (after the Union troops evacuated the place), leaving Pemberton to stand or fall on his own.[50]

Grant's decision to move on Jackson thus proved to be a brilliant one, mainly thanks to the cooperation of Joseph Johnston. The Union excursion to the capital also contributed to the progressive rending of civilian life and the institution of slavery in Mississippi. In the southern part of the state, streams of fearful refugees moved east. One witness claimed that some 500 slaves passed by the Taylorsville area in a period of two to three days just prior to the Confederate evacuation of Jackson. Most came from river plantations that had been raided or threatened by Union troops and were being sent along with a few white families to safer territory. Grant's relentless inland campaign no doubt drove off many hardliners who realized that safety could only be found where Union troops were not.[51]

On May 15, Sherman set his men to work heating and twisting railroad rails into "Sherman's neckties." The Yankees also torched the Pearl River bridge and a textile factory that had manufactured items for the Confederate army. Other destruction included an arsenal, an iron foundry, a carriage factory (which had been making artillery carriages, limbers, and caissons), and assorted shops that might contribute to the Rebel cause. The state penitentiary, converted to a munitions factory, also went up in flames, though not at the hands of Union soldiers. Sherman believed that former convicts, taking advantage of the chaos, torched their erstwhile prison. Union soldiers got rowdy, thanks to supplies of whiskey found in the city, and they committed overt acts of arson. Buildings falling victim to the chaotic situation included a Catholic church, hospitals, railroad depots, banks, and other buildings downtown. The state capitol survived.

Sherman did his best to stop random looting and destruction, noting angrily that such "injure the morals of the troops, and bring disgrace on our cause." In the midst of destructive activities, an Illinoisan admitted, "All is confusion and tumult. The confiscated whiskey is suffering severely and three fourths of the men are drunk." While Union soldiers plundered, they also gave food to "poor white women & children, who followed . . . all over town mixed all up in a crowd together unmolested by the troops." A Confederate earlier took note of "women, old men & children & in one profuse mass . . . rushing in every direction."[52]

The Confederate Hotel—once the United States Hotel, the imprint of that name being still visible on the front facade—received special attention from Sherman's forces. The owner had supposedly mistreated Union prisoners sent south after Shiloh. The owner asked Sherman for protection, claiming Union sympathies, but Sherman was suspicious. He assured the man he had no plans to burn the property, but as he rode out of town he saw it in flames. An Iowan recalled, "His hotel was made of wood, and was large and high, so that it made a fine fire." Sherman did not rebuke those responsible.[53]

While Sherman finished up at Jackson, Grant rode ahead with his staff to Clinton and stopped for the night. The next morning, May 16, Grant notified Sherman that Pemberton apparently was moving east from Edwards and that Sherman should send a division to Bolton, and bring the other on as soon as possible. Around 10:00 A.M., Sherman sent Steele's division east, and Tuttle's followed a couple of hours later. Details paroled prisoners, and severely wounded Union soldiers remained in Jackson under the care of a Union doctor. Sherman's soldiers marched out of Jackson, leaving the state capital useless to the Confederacy in general and John Pemberton in particular.[54]

Thus far, all that could go wrong for Pemberton had gone wrong. Gregg's ill-fated decision to fight had cost Pemberton a brigade and more. Johnston's arrival had confused Confederate options, and now Pemberton had to deal with the conflicting views of Davis and Johnston. Logistical links with the east via railroad were now gone, thanks to Johnston's evacuation of Jackson. Grant's army between Pemberton and Jackson meant that troops coming west to reinforce Pemberton would be blocked and forced to join Johnston's small army retreating to the northeast from Jackson. The countryside south and east of Vicksburg, which had been a source of supplies for the Confederate army, had been stripped by Grant's troops. These were the facts; Pemberton had to deal with them, and given his lack of confidence in himself and the absence of rapport with his generals and his men, he had extraordinary difficulties to overcome. Whatever decisions he made would be both guided by, and exacerbated by, his pledge to Jefferson Davis to defend Vicksburg and Johnston's view that Vicksburg was not worth risking an army to defend. The situation would have been daunting to a general with greater capabilities than Pemberton. He would do the best he could, but circumstances and his own shortcomings doomed his efforts.

10

~~~ Champion Hill & the Big Black

While U. S. Grant neutralized Jackson and turned west to move in for the kill, John Pemberton did nothing other than send a large portion of his army from the west bank of the Big Black east to Edwards Station. John Bowen's division turned south at Edwards and deployed on high ground north of Mount Moriah. Ohio soldiers from John McClernand's corps camped a mile or so farther south. Loring's division came next and divided, with one brigade going to Bowen's left and the other to his right. After settling in, the troops began building defensive works. Later, Carter Stevenson's division arrived, and all but one brigade, deployed near Bowen's left, camped in the rear for reserve duty. Pemberton set up headquarters at Bovina between the Big Black and Vicksburg, leaving Loring in field command. He ordered Loring to make a forced reconnaissance to determine Grant's location. If the Federals turned toward Jackson, Pemberton wanted to go after Grant's supply line.[1]

Pemberton should have acted sooner and with more élan. McClernand's corps had skirmished with Confederate outposts during the battle at Raymond, and the Union advance had gotten as far west as four miles from Edwards. Then Grant's instructions reached McClernand about the attack on Jackson. When McClernand turned his corps east, Alvin Hovey feinted, and his troops repulsed a Rebel reconnaissance patrol. Arkansas troops rushed back to the main Confederate line with reports of Yankees in force across Fourteenmile Creek. Scouts later reported McClernand's move east.[2]

Loring did nothing at first, and then he notified Pemberton that the Federals were marching on Jackson. Pemberton had some 22,000 men confronting McClernand's corps of about 13,000. Aggressive leadership might have resulted in McClernand's being attacked before Grant could send help. Such a move would have left Grant in a quandary, but thanks to Pemberton's unyielding defensive mentality, shared by Loring, another opportunity to disrupt Grant's campaign slipped away.

Pemberton remained idle, refusing to concentrate all his forces, as Johnston had advised him to do, and during the lull there seemed to be confusion at Pemberton's headquarters. John Forney, commanding in Vicksburg, did not know the location of troops assigned to guard the Big Black, men he might need. Forney knew Union reinforcements had landed at Young's Point, and he feared an attack on Vicksburg's southern flank, perhaps in conjunction with Grant's maneuvering to the east. Pemberton sent the information requested, but admitted he did not know the whereabouts of Thomas Waul's Texas Legion, an astonishing indictment of incompetent staff work.[3]

Finally, on May 14, Pemberton moved his headquarters to Edwards. About the time he mounted his horse to leave, a courier delivered a message from Johnston dated the thirteenth, the one ordering Pemberton to head for Clinton in an attempt to execute a pincer movement, the same one a spy had delivered to Grant. Pemberton did not know that the order meant nothing, since Johnston had given up Jackson and retreated to Canton. Pemberton immediately replied, stating his intent to move his whole available force of 16,000 east; he had some 6,000 more than that, another indication that his staff had not kept him well informed. He intended to leave one brigade to guard the bridge over the Big Black, and Forney's and M. L. Smith's divisions would stay in Vicksburg. He told Johnston, "In directing this move, I do not think you fully comprehend the position that Vicksburg will be left in, but I comply at once with your order." Pemberton did not yet understand that Johnston attached no importance to the city.[4]

After a courier departed with Pemberton's message, Pemberton and his staff composed marching instructions, sent word to Forney to rush supplies to Edwards, and mounted up to ride east. Along the way, Pemberton had serious second thoughts about Johnston's order. Pemberton did not have correct figures, but, based on what he knew, he suspected there might be at Clinton some 20,000 enemy troops (actually McPherson's two divisions, attacking Jackson as Pemberton rode). Pemberton had a good idea where McClernand was, and he calculated that if he moved east from Edwards toward Clinton, the Yankees could get around his right flank and thus between his army and Vicksburg. When he reached Edwards, he did what an insecure commander, torn between conflicting orders from his immediate superior and his president, would be inclined to do. He called a council of war and reminded his officers that the army's main duty was to defend Vicksburg; doing what Johnston ordered would make that duty difficult, perhaps impossible. The majority of his lieutenants endorsed Johnston's order anyway, but Loring put another proposal on the table.

Loring called for a movement toward Raymond to the home of a Mrs. Sarah Ellison, where the army would turn south to Dillon's plantation on the Raymond–Port Gibson road, Grant's main supply route. Loring believed that A. J. Smith's division could be beaten before the Yankees sent reinforcements. Several officers endorsed Loring's idea, accepting the premise that if Grant lost his supply line, he would be forced to withdraw to the south. Though Grant had decided on May 12 to shut down the supply line, some 200 loaded wagons still rolled toward the army, and their loss would strain Grant's logistical situation.[5]

Pemberton at first rejected Loring's proposal, and he insisted that the best option was to have the army dig in on the high west bank of the Big Black. He maintained that he could not support any operation that took the army farther from Vicksburg. Pemberton believed that Grant could not break through the defensive line he envisioned, and that, once repulsed, the Union army would be in a precarious situation. Then the Confederates could take the offensive. Pemberton's weakness as a leader suddenly emerged again, for when he saw that his officers wanted to fight, he caved in and agreed to Loring's plan.

Johnston, with the benefit of hindsight, and ignoring his own ill-advised behavior, later criticized Pemberton's vacillation, especially since the outcome of the war council meant disobeying Johnston's orders. In fact, Pemberton rightly resisted Johnston's directive, for to advance on Clinton, when Johnston had moved northeast toward Canton, would have placed Pemberton's troops in jeopardy of being flanked and routed. Moreover, if Pemberton had made a unilateral decision to dig in on the west bank of the Big Black, he would indeed have presented Grant with a formidable obstacle. That possibility is one of the great "what ifs" of the campaign. The decision having been made, Pemberton sent a courier with a message to Johnston, pointing out he had adopted strategy that would give him the option of choosing a battleground. Pemberton also detached troops to secure the Big Black bridge and ferries, and ordered Forney to send additional rations.[6]

Pemberton's second message, detailing the council of war, reached Johnston as he rode with John Gregg along the road to Canton. The earlier message, stating his adherence to Johnston's instructions, arrived shortly afterward, an indication of worsening communications problems. Johnston, choosing to ignore any culpability on his part, had already become angry at Pemberton's slow response, all the more so when he realized that his order had been disobeyed. Of course, Pemberton's going southeast meant that the armies would be farther apart, but Johnston had destroyed opportunities for cooperation when he abandoned Jackson and moved northeast. If Johnston wanted to concentrate the two commands, as he had indicated, then he had chosen a strange direction for retreat. Johnston quickly wrote a reply, telling Pemberton that Jackson had been evacuated and thus Pemberton's thrust at Grant's supply line was impractical. Pemberton must move toward Clinton, and Johnston would meet him. When he wrote these lines, Johnston was still moving away from Clinton.

While Johnston traveled farther from the rendezvous point he had chosen, and while Pemberton prepared to cut Grant's supply line, Grant, with Johnston's May 13 message in hand and unaware that Pemberton was not obeying the order, prepared to find and attack Pemberton quickly, before he could join forces with Johnston. Grant did not realize that Confederate commanders working at cross purposes gave him more time, and he would soon be handed a golden opportunity to whip Pemberton.[7]

Raymond, still coping with hundreds of wounded soldiers, received unwelcome visitors as a portion of McClernand's corps pushed through town after the Union victory at Jackson. Blue-coated soldiers invaded homes, taking food and forcing ladies to keep their shutters closed to ensure privacy from troops in their yards. Looting went on unabated this time, and McClernand and his officers seemed unconcerned about the breaking of Grant's rules regarding protection of private property. One resident noted with disgust that a mixed-blood female slave, a "fancy yellow girl, an especial pet of one of the subordinate officers," joined in the thievery without fear of retribution. Citizens along the Vicksburg-Jackson corridor learned the hard way that war had come for a long visit.

McClernand's officers finally posted guards to protect homes, but stores were cleaned out. People outside the city limits, far away from officers, had little protection at all. Livestock stolen or slaughtered, fences trampled and used for firewood, the stench of animal waste — from "rotten chickens, turkeys, pieces of beef" — left behind by soldiers, plus human waste, all left conditions in Raymond "almost unendurable." One Union soldier protected a family that gave him overnight lodging by pretending to be a provost guard, but even he stole a watch. Illinois troops took fine china, silverware, and other valuables and shipped them north to their homes.

During all the chaos, black women taunted former owners, and a young white boy shot one of the women. At that point, several black men came up and threatened to kill the boy if he did not call them "master." He refused, but the infuriated slaves backed down. One white woman did not see the coming of the Yankee army as a day of jubilee for the slaves. Of all the people who suffered from the military campaigning, she wrote, "I pity the Negroes. They flocked in . . . expecting to experience freedom. Well, the women were put to washing for the hospital. They wash from daylight until dark." They were not paid or given lodging, receiving nothing but daily food rations. Soldiers hired them to make shirts but rarely paid for the finished product. Though many Federals treated these women in the manner of their white Southern owners, the owners seemed to think they occupied the moral high ground. That hypocritical attitude was reinforced when many slave women returned to their owners after the Federals had cleared out of the area. A Raymond resident thought Midwestern soldiers held "Negroes in the greatest detestation." Black and white people in Raymond welcomed or endured the enemy's presence until Vicksburg surrendered, their worlds forever changed.[8]

Most of the troops soon passed on through, as McClernand pushed his troops west on May 15. Peter Osterhaus's division left Raymond at around 4:00 A.M. and reached Bolton at 8:00 A.M., capturing a few Rebel scouts along the way. Osterhaus's soldiers seized Confederate supplies and burned railroad and other bridges that might be of use to the enemy. To avoid a traffic jam on the Jackson-Vicksburg road, McClernand shifted Osterhaus south to a trail called the Middle road, thus giving both Hovey's division and McPherson's corps more room. Hovey's troops arrived in Bolton as the last of Osterhaus's troops marched south.

Meanwhile, other McClernand troops made their way toward the new front. Carr marched his division west from Raymond and took position behind Osterhaus. A. J. Smith's and Frank Blair's divisions (Blair was in Sherman's corps but in the coming battle he would be attached to McClernand's) marched from Old Auburn to Raymond. Blair camped west of Raymond on May 15, and Smith moved his division closer to Edwards. Thus, on the fifteenth, McClernand had his corps, plus Blair's division, in a position to move forward against Pemberton.[9]

McPherson's troops made good progress. The XVII Corps took the Jackson-Clinton road west, with Logan's division followed by Marcellus Crocker's. Logan's advance reached Bolton around 4:00 P.M. and took position on Hovey's right flank. Crocker followed close behind and his brigades camped between Bolton and Clinton.

Grant reached Clinton shortly before 5:00 P.M. and wrote instructions for the next day's advance. McClernand would move slowly toward Edwards and make contact with the Confederates, but he must avoid starting a fight unless he knew he could win. McClernand asked that McPherson be directed to cooperate in the move toward Edwards, a request that must have made Grant smirk, for he never welcomed advice from McClernand. Grant had his men positioned to move on a broad front, down three roads: Jackson, Middle, and Raymond. Grant did not know the best news for his cause; despite a landscape dotted with enemy campfires, Pemberton had no idea that two enemy corps were poised close to his army the night of May 15.[10]

Pemberton proceeded with plans for his march against Grant's supply line without giving any thought to being attacked. Why he felt he could roam freely in proximity to Grant's army is inexplicable. Pemberton obviously had no comprehension of the tactical situation he faced as his army moved southeast. Wirt Adams's cavalry led the way, trailed, in order, by Loring's, Bowen's, and Stevenson's divisions. Supply wagons followed, and a cavalry detachment took up the rear to prevent straggling. In the coming battle, which Pemberton would not be prepared to fight, his deployment would be Loring on the right, Bowen in the center, and Stevenson on the left, a battle alignment not by design but forced by circumstances. Pemberton intended to follow Loring's suggested line of march: the Raymond road to Mrs. Ellison's, then to Dillon's. There, the army should find Smith's and Blair's divisions guarding the target, Grant's wagon train. Pemberton intended to get under way early on May 15, but supplies from Vicksburg had not arrived, another example of poor staff work. Despite incompetent leadership at the top, the Confederate army seemed anxious to get on with it. According to a staff officer, the men looked and marched like soldiers hungry for battle. Other problems lay in the offing.[11]

Adams's cavalry did not thoroughly scout the route ahead. When Loring's advance reached a crossing at swollen Bakers Creek, the bridge was gone, washed away earlier, and the creek was still flooded from the heavy rain that had also hit Jackson. The relationship between Adams and Pemberton and Pemberton's staff is a curious one; they had trouble communicating, as in the Raymond debacle, and Adams neglected basic cavalry scouting duties. Pemberton long claimed that his lack of cavalry created problems, exemplified by his having to send infantry in a vain attempt to stop Grierson, which exacerbated his efforts to concentrate forces at Port Gibson. Yet, given Pemberton's inability to make good use of the cavalry he did have, one has to wonder whether more horsemen would have made a difference. In any event, Loring could not ford the creek, and Pemberton ultimately was responsible; but clearly Adams's cavalry had botched their job.

Loring tired of waiting for water levels to go down and suggested that the army cross an intact bridge to the north on the Jackson road, turn east, and then take the Ratliff road (named after a local family) to the Raymond road. Pemberton agreed and the army turned north, but the new route made maintaining division formation difficult. A patrol rode ahead to make sure that the column turned onto the correct road after crossing the creek. The roads could be confusing, for, beyond Bakers Creek, the Jackson road turned sharply left and passed over an eminence known locally as Champion Hill, named after the family that owned the property. Another road continued east off the Jackson road, the so-called Middle road. The Ratliff road forked off to the southwest to the Raymond road. The junction of all these roads formed a crossroads that would be crucial to the maneuvering of forces on both sides during the coming fight.

As Loring's soldiers reached the Raymond road, Adams reported that his scouts had made contact with a large force of Yankees north of the road in the Bolton area. Rather than risk a fight in the dark, Pemberton told Loring to halt where he was, near Mrs. Ellison's place, and camp for the night. Loring sent two regiments a mile east of the Ellison place to set up a roadblock in case the enemy wandered too close. Pemberton and Loring established evening quarters in the Ellison home.

Back along the line, Bowen did not halt his troops until around 10:00 P.M. He could see campfires to the east, and he understood what they meant. Bowen deployed his men in line of battle where they camped and posted pickets to the east to watch for Federals. Stevenson, farther behind, did not get his large division out of Edwards until 5:00 P.M., and his advance did not reach the rear of Bowen's division until dawn on May 16. In contrast to Bowen, and indicative of the gap between their leadership skills, Stevenson ordered his men to camp where they stood, not posting any guards to protect his position. Farther back, the wagon train caught up around dawn.[12]

Despite the almost comedic mismanagement of the march, Confederates in the ranks maintained high morale. A Tennessean recorded, "These are effective men, Men that are fighting for their property of their families for their rights. Thousands now driven from their homes[;] such men can't be subjugated, unconquerable with too much hatred to even wish for peace, all joyful and full of glee marching perhaps right into the jaws of death. Ah, will the GOD of battles give this splendid army to Lincolns hords who have robbed the defenseless women and children the staff of life . . . setting fire to their homes and leaving all to shift for themselves." The soldiers found it took more than confidence and rhetorical motivation to win a fight that their commanders stumbled into.[13]

Unlike the precise mobilization that Grant and his generals had carried out on May 15, the undisciplined planning by Pemberton and his staff and miserable scouting led to many wasted hours and resulted in the army being in a position where it would be difficult to repulse an attack. Scores of soldiers in the rear got little sleep and would not be as alert as their well-rested enemy. A lieutenant in Pemberton's army did not think Pemberton "knew either the number, intentions either real or probable of the Enemy and more than that—not even his exact whereabouts." Pemberton's lack of experience and ability as a field general were never more evident than on May 15, 1863.[14]

U. S. Grant had too much on his mind to spend a peaceful night at Clinton. Then around 5:00 a.m. on the sixteenth, he received from two Southern Railroad employees a mostly accurate accounting of the troops Pemberton had and a report on Confederate plans to hit the Union supply line. At that point, Grant sent word to Sherman to hurry the XV Corps to Bolton. Grant ordered McClernand to push Smith's and Blair's divisions west on the Raymond road, while Osterhaus and Carr advanced on the Middle road. McPherson should follow Hovey's division down the Jackson road. Grant then mounted and rode with his staff and young son toward the anticipated battle.

By the time McClernand received Grant's instructions, the XIII Corps was already marching, for McClernand had decided on his own to send his divisions forward in the arrangement Grant had in mind. McClernand visited McPherson early and urged that the XVII Corps support Hovey. McClernand, in his condescending manner, assured McPherson that the XVII Corps could mop up after the XIII Corps defeated the Rebels. McPherson ignored McClernand's arrogance and agreed to the sound proposal; Hovey might need help. Logan, followed by Crocker, followed Hovey's line of march. As the Union columns snaked forward along three roads, patrols screened the advance.[15]

Though the coming battle in the Champion Hill area gave the Confederates their first opportunity to fight Grant on anything approaching equal terms, Pemberton's neglect in preparing his army for a possible fight gave Grant great advantage. Once the shooting started, Pemberton and his army would have to make quick adjustments in the midst of battle. Grant, on the other hand, had maneuvered his army into a battle that must be won. A defeat might cut him off from Grand Gulf; most certainly, it would set back future campaigning against Vicksburg for months. Such a turn of events could mean Grant's dismissal from command, boost Southern morale, and be devastating to the North. Grant likely gave no thought to losing, for, since landing at Bruinsburg, his men had been successful in three battles; he realized by now that the Confederate leadership was not aggressive and not to be feared, and he made plans accordingly. He was gambling, but the odds seemed very much on his side.

As in most battles, geography played a key role at Champion Hill. The hill itself stood higher in 1863 than it does today (because the crest was the site of gravel operations in the 1930s), and around it in all directions ran ridges and deep ravines similar to the terrain at the Port Gibson battle site. On the east side of the high ground ran Jackson Creek; on the west side flowed Bakers Creek. Troops would at times march blindly in ravines owing to the high ridges all around, and the angles of the ridges forced advantageous or difficult alignments, depending on the circumstances. Narrow roads further limited maneuverability. The day was hot, and running up and down steep ravines tested the physical condition of men on both sides. The geography and the lengthy battle lines dictated potential communications problems between upper and lower levels of command. Officers at company, regiment, and brigade levels often had to make decisions on their own, on the spur of the moment.

The battle began early on the Raymond road, where opposing forces were in closest proximity, when a detachment of Indiana cavalry exchanged fire with a patrol from Wirt Adams's unit. A. J. Smith brought up Stephen Burbridge's brigade, and soldiers at Loring's roadblock prepared for a fight, while Adams rode to warn Pemberton. An Ohio battery shelled the roadblock, and A. J. Smith cautioned Burbridge to ascertain the strength of the Rebel position, but not to bring on an engagement until the rest of the division arrived. Alabama sharpshooters went forward to contest the Union advance, and for an hour and a half infantry fire raged along both lines, buying time for Pemberton.[16]

As Adams briefed Pemberton, a courier arrived with a message from Johnston. Pemberton learned for the first time that Jackson had been abandoned and that Johnston wanted to rendezvous north of the Southern Railroad in the Clinton area. Pemberton, perhaps because he knew now that continuing southeast meant having to fight, decided to obey basically the same order he had previously rejected. His decision is

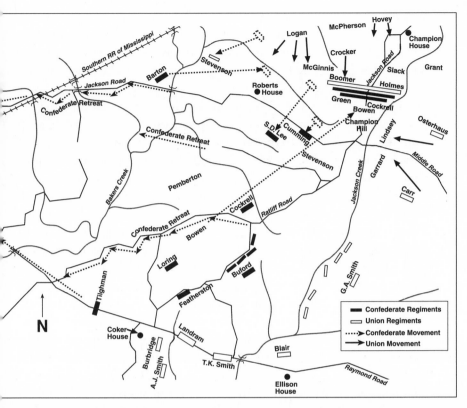

The Battle of Champion Hill, May 16, 1863. Map by Becky Smith, adapted from Michael B. Ballard, The Campaign for Vicksburg *(Conshohocken, Pa.: Eastern National Park and Monument Association, 1996).*

difficult to understand, given his determination to keep his army between Grant and Vicksburg. Perhaps Johnston's reiterating the order jolted Pemberton into obedience. But even at this hour, he did not fully appreciate what lay to the east. Compounding his situation, he had his army strung out in a way that made moving north and east to meet Johnston very difficult, for his wagon train would now be the advance, unless Loring looped back northwest, with Bowen and Stevenson falling into line. With two Union corps, plus Blair's division of Sherman's corps, moving to the attack, such a maneuver simply could not be accomplished. Nevertheless, Pemberton wrote a quick note to Johnston saying that he would do as ordered: his army would travel back to Edwards and take the Brownsville road to reach Clinton. Pemberton had the presence of mind to order the wagon train to get out of the way of the countermarch.

Meanwhile, sounds of combat down the Raymond road continued, and a worried Loring suggested forming a battle line. Pemberton agreed, and Tilghman's brigade, at the head of the column, deployed on either side of the road in front of the Ellison house. Federal artillery soon demonstrated that this was an exposed site, and Loring withdrew west of the Ellison place to a ridge that overlooked the Jackson Creek valley. There, he deployed Abraham Buford on the left, Winfield S. Featherston in the center, south of the road, and Tilghman on the right from the ridge down into the creek bottom.[17]

Portending trouble with his subordinates at an inopportune time, Pemberton argued with Loring about retreating to join Johnston. Details of the dispute are unknown, but one of Featherston's staff noticed words were "warm — and no good feeling was evinced by either party. There was ill-will and that too displayed in a manner that was a credit of neither party. That there was no harmony — no unity of action, no clear understanding of the aims and designs of our army was clearly apparent — and instead of there existing mutual confidence on the part of the Commanding General and his subordinates — there was just the opposite."

As the sounds of battle spread, John Bowen deployed on the Middle road. He placed Martin Green's brigade on a ridge near the Ratliff house, while Francis Cockrell's troops filed in on Green's right. Green's men had an extensive field of fire to their front, but trees blocked their vision on the left. Bowen sent a patrol to set up a roadblock.

At the rear of the Confederate column, now the left wing, Carter Stevenson sent an escort to protect the wagon train's retreat and to patrol the strategic crossroads. By 9:30, the 400 wagons were safely on the road, and Pemberton's troops had room to march to a junction with Johnston. By 9:30, however, joining Johnston was a moot point. In retrospect, Pemberton made a serious mistake in not rescinding his order to send the train away from Champion Hill. Once it became obvious that a battle must be fought, supplies needed to be relatively close to the army.[18]

While Confederates tried to sort out an increasingly bad situation, the Federal advance continued along the Middle and Jackson roads. Carr and Osterhaus moved their divisions unimpeded on the Middle road. They heard sounds of battle to the south on the Raymond road. McClernand sent word to both to advance quickly but "cautiously." Osterhaus's advance ran into resistance where the Middle road ran into a heavily wooded area, and on either side of the road lay hills and deep ravines. Gunfire up ahead between his van and the Confederates quickened Osterhaus's pulse, and he immediately ordered up Theophilus T.

Garrard's and Daniel Lindsay's brigades. Farther behind, Carr's division deployed to support Osterhaus.

Osterhaus's reinforced advance chased away Rebel pickets and pushed unimpeded for about a mile before stalling in front of Confederates massed east of the crossroads. Because of the open landscape, Osterhaus held back his cavalry and deployed infantry and artillery to break through the position, held by Colonel Alexander W. Reynolds's Tennesseans of Stevenson's division. With cannon providing cover fire, Osterhaus's Kentuckians on the right and Indianans on the left tried to advance, but Alfred Cumming's Georgia brigade rushed up to support Reynolds. Garrard's four regiments could not break the Confederate line, and Osterhaus pulled his troops back.[19]

Pemberton moved his headquarters around 9:00 A.M. from the Ellison house to the Isaac Roberts home several hundred yards south of the crossroads. This put him near the center of the Confederate battle line, but he did not see it that way. He felt that his men had effectively stalled enemy advances, and, with the wagon train out of the way, the army could continue withdrawing to join Johnston. His line that morning now ran at a slant from the southwest to the northeast; later a portion of the left flank hooked, or refused, at a ninety-degree angle back to the northwest. So far, the main Union threats seemed to be on the Raymond and Middle roads, and the terrain being in favor of the Confederates, who held the high ground, Pemberton felt he could hold back the Yankees long enough to withdraw his entire army from the field. At some point, he had obviously decided that a junction with Johnston was more important than protecting Vicksburg, a complete reversal of his previous thinking. Clearly, the sequence of events that day in May had rattled Pemberton. He did wonder if Grant would get by him and move on Vicksburg; he knew it would happen if he left to concentrate with Johnston at Clinton. He did not know, since he had not sent cavalry to patrol roads to the east, that more than two Union corps would not let him withdraw.[20]

Confederate efforts to leave the area proceeded. Stephen D. Lee, commanding one of Stevenson's brigades, received word that Reynolds believed he could lead the way. Reynolds ordered his troops to leave Cumming's Georgians at the roadblock and cross Bakers Creek, get to the Brownsville road, and guard the wagon train a few miles northeast of Edwards. Lee's brigade moved left to the crossroads, becoming the left flank of the Confederate line, and he did what Pemberton had not, sending a patrol up the Jackson road toward Champion Hill, near the Sid Champion home.[21]

On the other end of the Rebel line, William Loring stabilized his position and recalled his roadblock detachment, and on their way back the troops destroyed the Jackson Creek bridge. Loring, meanwhile, decided that a ridge to his rear, where the Coker family home sat, would be more easily defended and provide better cover. His division would be in position to keep the Ratliff road open, thus preserving a line of communication with the rest of the army. Wirt Adams pulled his cavalry back to Bakers Creek for rearguard duty.

A. J. Smith's division followed Loring's retreat at a slow pace, lest they march into a trap. The Federals halted when they saw the creek bridge wrecked, and Confederate artillery challenged them to rebuild it. However, Confederate batteries' smoothbore ammunition could not stand up to Union rifled guns in the ensuing exchange. A Missouri Confederate described the action as "the most splendid artillery duel . . . that I have ever witnessed in open fields, when both parties were in full view; this lasted for thirty minutes, during which time the guns on both sides were handled in the most skillful and scientific manner." Many Union shells "fell in and around the battery, while others struck the ground in our front, and, ricocheting, burst over our heads or beyond, near the guns; the fragments scattered and fell in every direction." After their cannon prevailed, a Union detachment repaired the bridge. By 11:00 A.M., Burbridge's brigade reached the ridge west of Jackson Creek bottom. The artillery duel then heated up again, and A. J. Smith decided to push no farther until all of his division and Blair's reached the ridge.[22]

On the Confederate left, circumstances dashed Pemberton's hopes of avoiding a battle. Stephen Lee's patrol at the Champion home reported a large Union column coming west along the Jackson road. Lee understood the gravity of this threat; if the left flank did not hold, the entire army would be cut off from Vicksburg and unable to join Johnston. Also, the two divisions still in Vicksburg would be hard pressed to hold off Grant. Lee at once began shifting his brigade more to the left along the 140-foot-high crest of Champion Hill. Lee notified Cumming, on his right, and Stevenson of the situation. Hovey's division, followed by McPherson's XVII Corps, was closing fast.

This new development forced Pemberton to rethink his strategy. On the Middle road, his troops had stalled Osterhaus and Carr, and on the Raymond road Loring was holding his own against A. J. Smith and Blair. His men faced east, but now, with Lee forced to change fronts, the left flank was refused to the northwest. The fairly straight line fronts on both sides had been compromised by Union troops coming down the Jackson road. Because he had initially focused on the middle and right of his line, Pemberton had been taken completely by surprise, though an earlier routine reconnaissance would have informed him of the Jackson road threat. If Lee on his own initiative had not sent a scouting patrol, the situation could have been much worse. Even so, Pemberton had no time to shore up his left before fighting broke out there.[23]

Hovey realized that he was closing on Carter Stevenson's division, and he sent word to McClernand that if the division kept going on the Jackson road, the men would have to fight, especially on his right flank. The question was, should he move forward and engage? Hovey also notified McPherson about the strong force of Rebels up ahead. Given the circumstances, the prudent thing for Grant to have done would have been to attach Hovey's division to McPherson's corps, so McPherson could make the call. McClernand, told that Grant was with troops on the Jackson road, did the right thing by referring Hovey to the commanding general, and asking for instructions for his front.

Interestingly, Grant rode with McPherson's corps; for most of the campaign since Port Gibson, the commanding general had chosen to be with Sherman. His choices indicated that though he had no desire to be in McClernand's company, he also trusted McClernand enough not to have to keep an eye on him. This was another sign that Grant's personal preferences did not bias his opinion of McClernand's abilities.

Grant urged McPherson to keep his soldiers moving. He fretted when he found the advance halted while workers repaired the bridge, unfortunately destroyed by Osterhaus's men earlier. Then he saw Hovey's wagon train blocking the road and ordered it to one side. The confusing situation also kept Grant from receiving McClernand's 9:45 A.M. message until nearly noon, and he ordered McClernand to attack with his whole force at the first opportunity. McClernand did not get the reply until midafternoon. Grant's earlier directions to be cautious, and the delayed delivery of this message, kept his center and left from moving in force until late in the day.

If Grant had set up his headquarters along the Middle road, with a system of couriers connecting him to his flanks, more equal pressure might have been exerted on the Confederate line. He could see successes on the Union right and issued aggressive instructions accordingly. Despite the tricky terrain, couriers riding north and south from a central command position on the Middle road would have had less ground to cover than those riding from the right to the center to the left and back again. Despite the absence of equal pressure on the enemy, things worked out well, for by spreading his front along three roads, Grant kept Pemberton from concentrating on any one sector; and the initial contact on the Confederate center and right so focused Pemberton's attention that he gave the Federals an opportunity to deliver a hard blow where he did not expect it.[24]

On the left, Confederate generals Stevenson, Lee, and Cumming watched the threat to their front rapidly increase. Yankees pressured their outposts, and they hurriedly deployed a line of defense facing north northeast. Stevenson sent Pemberton urgent messages for help, but, as had happened in the past, Pemberton seemed slow to grasp the danger. He understood the potential disaster much too late.[25]

The advance of Hovey's division, George McGinnis's brigade, reached the Champion home shortly before 10:00 A.M. McGinnis looked ahead at the slopes leading to the crest of Champion Hill and saw a heavily wooded area and large numbers of enemy troops beyond. McGinnis deployed his brigade in two lines, and his skirmishers drove off the Confederate patrol. McGinnis conducted a personal reconnaissance to within a couple of hundred yards of the crest without being fired on, and rode back to the Champion home where Grant and Hovey had arrived.

Before McGinnis returned, Hovey placed James Slack's veteran brigade on the left. Slack also deployed in two parallel lines and took position in a rye field. While Federal soldiers lined up and awaited orders, McGinnis reported to Grant that the Rebels had a good position, and the terrain of plowed fields, slopes, underbrush, and heavy timber ahead would be challenging. Nevertheless, McGinnis urged an attack, but Grant refused until McPherson's XVII Corps could join in.[26]

John Logan's lead division arrived at the Champion house by 10:00, and McPherson directed Logan to McGinnis's right. Logan positioned his men at ninety-degree angles to McGinnis's troops; this gave Logan a straight shot at flanking Carter Stevenson's left. Logan ordered two brigades to make the attack, while the third, John Stevenson's, waited in reserve. Three batteries deployed to provide support. McPherson and Grant decided not to wait on Crocker to deploy; so, at around 10:30, McPherson gave the signal, and some 10,000 soldiers of Logan's and Hovey's commands charged the Confederate line atop Champion Hill. An Indianan claimed that orders to keep as quiet as possible seemed effective, for when the charge came, the first volleys felled many battery horses and soldiers in the Confederate ranks. The intense fighting led one Union soldier to later call the area "a charnel house." Another complained that his regiment's colonel got so excited his men became confused and fired into another Union unit.[27]

To say the Confederates were unready to receive an attack would be a gross understatement. A gap existed in their line after Lee extended the left flank. Cumming's left moved to Lee's right, but Cumming's right had been forced to remain where it was to protect an Alabama battery at the crossroads. As the Union forces came on, the longer Union line forced Lee to send his men even farther left, which increased his distance from Cumming. With his five Alabama regiments stretched slightly less than a mile, Lee waited behind a rail fence.

Cumming tried to remedy the situation, though it seemed hopeless. He kept two of his Georgia regiments at the crossroads with the Alabama artillery, all facing east. He led the rest of his command up the Jackson road to find Lee, and he soon saw that Lee had moved. He sent one regiment and part of another to follow Lee and cover the latter's right. Cumming then posted another regiment, plus four companies, along the Jackson road itself. The new deployment meant a gap of some 300 yards existed between Cumming's forward position and the crossroads. To make matters worse, the Confederate line on Champion Hill formed a right angle with three of Cumming's Georgia regiments, all shorthanded, defending Carter Stevenson's right wing. In their awkward defensive position, they could not deploy effectively to fight off the enemy, for they could easily be flanked on their right. Stevenson, meanwhile, further weakened his position by sending a regiment from Seth Barton's brigade and a company of artillery to the rear to secure the bridge across Bakers Creek.[28]

Aided by steep ravines and vegetation, Lee's men managed to stall John Logan's advance brigades for a time. One Illinoisan recalled ground "very broken[,] most of it densely timbered[,] some of the hills we had to fight over were so steep that we had to pull ourselves up by the bushes[.]" The fighting soon revealed a key weakness in Lee's deployment; his left flank, like Cumming's right but more so, was vulnerable to a flank attack. Logan saw the opportunity, and he sent for John Stevenson's reserve brigade to hit the exposed Rebel flank and get in the enemy's rear on the Jackson road.[29]

From the crest of Champion Hill, Carter Stevenson saw what was happening and again begged Pemberton for reinforcements. Then Stevenson ordered Seth Barton, deployed on Cumming's right on the right of the crossroads, to hurry to the left, extending the Confederate line down into the bottomland of Bakers Creek. Barton rushed three of his regiments, less the one guarding the bridge, more than a mile. The Georgians barely took time to deploy before they assaulted John Stevenson's skirmish line, driving the Union advance back into the brigade. Stevenson's men fired volleys in return, and the Georgians came to a halt. A Georgia battery attached to Barton, plus Mississippi artillerists, shelled Logan's line from their position near the G. W. Roberts home (this Roberts was the brother of Isaac Roberts, whose nearby dwelling was also a battlefield landmark), but the same terrain that made life difficult for charging Union infantry provided shelter.[30]

When McPherson received word that Logan and Hovey had reached the main Confederate line, he decided to overpower the Rebels. He ordered both division commanders to attack in force. On the Jackson road, McGinnis's brigade of Hovey's division headed toward the crest of Champion Hill, the battle line in somewhat of an arc as the Federals approached Cumming's line. Conquering the terrain, Hovey's and Logan's soldiers came like a wave toward the Confederate line, weathering a storm of canister, finding shelter among the ravines, and preparing for a final rush.

McGinnis used a tactic to keep casualties low and momentum strong. After his men stood to charge, he lowered his sword, and they hugged the ground as a volley of Rebel bullets passed harmlessly overhead. While the Confederates reloaded, the Yankees rose and stormed straight at the enemy. The west side of the Georgians' salient caved in, and Georgians in two regiments had to fight for their lives and position. Finally, they gave way to superior numbers, leaving behind many comrades captured, killed, and wounded, as well as losing four cannon. Two remaining Georgia regiments faced east with their flank totally exposed, and they had to bail out quickly to avoid being overwhelmed.[31]

Alfred Cumming later attributed the Georgians' shaky performance to several factors. He said no pickets had been posted, though he did not blame himself for that. Overwhelming enemy numbers, inexperience in battle, and the lack of cohesion due to Cumming's recent assignment to command all contributed to the debacle. Pemberton criticized the Georgians in his postbattle report, and on that point Cumming wrote, "If he shall . . . have derived any satisfaction therefrom, let him have it."

Other Federals now shifted right and Stephen Lee's brigade got hit in the right flank and in the front, and a sortie to capture enemy cannon failed. Two of Lee's Alabama regiments fell back to the Jackson road, leaving a gap along the main line that forced a general withdrawal. Confederate cannon at the crossroads shifted their field of fire from the Middle road to the Jackson road to meet the Union threat.[32]

It was now about 1:30, and the battle along Champion Hill ridge had been raging for about an hour and a half. The Confederates had been driven from the hill, and Lee redeployed, with his line on either side of the Jackson road, west by northwest of the crossroads. Stevenson's overall line ran from the crossroads to the bridge at Bakers Creek, but it could not hold for long. On the right, two Georgia regiments felt the brunt of an assault by James Slack's brigade, which had walked, climbed, and crawled through rough ravines before coming up on the left of the Union line along the Jackson road. During their charge, Slack's Iowans captured four cannon and shot down teams of horses while overwhelming Georgia infantry. A Virginia Botetourt artillerist complained later that Confederate gunners got little infantry support. One artillerist begged the Yankees not to shoot down the men as if they were horses. Pemberton and his staff found many of these demoralized troops near the Roberts house and tried to rally them back into the fight.[33]

The lack of coordination between Lee's and Cumming's brigades created segmented defensive lines and threatened the survival of Carter Stevenson's whole division. Seth Barton called up two more Georgia regiments, but these were not enough to hold off John Stevenson's brigade. Confederate soldiers fell back in disarray, while artillerists fired double loads of canister in a vain effort to stem the Yankee tide. Captain Samuel Ridley of the 1st Mississippi Light Artillery fell fatally wounded, having refused to leave his guns. One Mississippi cannoneer claimed later that only eight men out of eighty-two in the battery escaped from the battered left wing.

John Stevenson's men drove a gap between Barton and the rest of Carter Stevenson's line, and the Georgians fell back, rallied, and set up a roadblock on the west side of Bakers Creek. John Stevenson's troops controlled the Jackson road, and if Pemberton had to retreat, and it looked like he would soon have no choice, his staff would have to find another route back to Edwards. A pleased General Grant sent via courier an oral message to Logan, lauding the Illinoisan for making history this day.

The Confederate left had been routed, sixteen artillery pieces had been lost, and Carter Stevenson's division had to retreat to near the Bakers Creek bridge. Hovey's division now controlled the all-important crossroads. Pemberton had desperately called for help from his other two division commanders, Bowen and Loring, but both refused, insisting that enemy forces in their fronts were too strong, though they had not been pressured like the left. By ignoring Pemberton's orders, they underscored the uncooperative relationship the commanding general had with his subordinates. Grant came to Champion Hill with an army that was very much a team; Pemberton fought him with a loosely coordinated group, anarchical in nature.[34]

When the situation on the left became critical, Bowen responded to Pemberton that he could not reinforce Stevenson unless ordered to do so. A rider returning from Loring rode up about that time with the same story, and Pemberton knew it would be risky if he weakened the center or right to save Stevenson. Yet Pemberton soon realized that the situation on the left had deteriorated to the point that risks must be taken. Bowen would soon be forced to do something anyway, because a gap already existed between his left and Stevenson's right, and the collapse of Stevenson's forward line left Bowen's left flank more vulnerable.

Pemberton insisted that Bowen rush one brigade to the left and bring the other as quickly as possible. Pemberton by now had become quite discombobulated, both by Stevenson's collapse and the reluctance of Bowen and Loring to help. A private noticed that the general had trouble mounting his horse, so much so that a staff officer had to help. Pemberton became so impatient that he personally rode to Cockrell's brigade and ordered the Missourian to support Barton, then changed his mind and sent him to the crossroads to attack Slack's Iowans.

Cockrell's men double-timed their way across planted fields of corn and rye, encountering groups of beaten soldiers from Carter Stevenson's division. Cockrell's troops suffered from flanking fire because none of Stevenson's routed troops provided cover. Bowen arrived with Green's Brigade of Arkansans who deployed on Cockrell's right. Cockrell ordered a charge, and Bowen's division surged forward. Pemberton and his staff tried to get demoralized soldiers back into the battle, and women singing "Dixie" in the yard of the Isaac Roberts home urged the men on. To inspire his troops, Cockrell rode among his men with a magnolia flower in one hand and a sword in the other.[35]

The veterans from Missouri and Arkansas charged around 2:30 P.M., slashing into Slack's brigade, which they had demolished at Port Gibson. Under the generalship of three outstanding officers — Cockrell, Green, and Bowen — the Confederate wave slammed into the Iowans, who broke ranks and fled, leaving behind four previously captured cannon. McGinnis watched from the heights of Champion Hill and sent a message to Hovey. Ohio artillerists tried to slow down the Rebels. Despite casualties, Bowen's men kept going as if meeting no resistance. In short order, the division cleared Champion Hill of the enemy, in the process recapturing four more cannon and pushing the Federal line back nearly a mile. Carter Stevenson's blunder of sending supply trains too far from the battlefield cost the Confederates dearly. Bowen's men nearly expended their ammunition and could find no more. A magnificent charge that had nearly split the Union army ground to a halt in view of the Champion home a few hundred yards ahead.[36]

An Arkansan long remembered Bowen's thrust. "With a forward march we passed those troops that were falling back, and then we were ordered to charge. We had caught the enemy with empty guns, and they gave way easily. We were charging up the long slope from the Negro quarters to the highest peak of champion hill and almost parallel with the public road to Bolton. At the top of the hill we met another long line of blues climbing the steep hill. They were within eight feet of us when we gained the top of the hill, and without orders it seemed as if every man in our ranks fired at once. Never before nor since have I ever witnessed such a sight. The whole line seemed to fall and tumble head-long to the bottom of the hill. In a moment they came again, and we were ready and again repulsed them."[37]

An Iowan in George Boomer's brigade, which Cockrell's men hit head on, recalled, "It was surrender or try to get past them [to the rear]. I ran like a racehorse, — so did the left of the regiment, amid a storm of bullets and yells and curses. I saved my musket anyway. I think all did that, — but that half-mile race through a hot Mississippi sun, with bullets and cannonballs plowing the fields behinds us, will never be forgotten. My lungs seemed to be burning up." As the intensity of the battle increased, the Iowan was left to "wonder that a man on either side was left alive. Biting the ends off my cartridges, my mouth was filled with gunpowder; the thirst was intolerable. Every soldier's face was black as a Negro's, and, with some, blood from wounds trickled down over the blackness, giving them a horrible look." An Illinoisan in the fight recol-lected, "We could see the rebs just in front of us, I was loading and firing as fast as I could, I made a step back and to the left and fell into a ditch that I had not seen." This soldier survived, but his brother did not.[38]

Bowen worked to keep the drive going. Pemberton had managed to get battered Georgia regiments regrouped and back to the front, where they entered the fighting between Cockrell's and Green's brigades. Ste-phen Lee tried to help by sending two Alabama regiments to Cockrell's left. The Alabamians seemed uninterested until they saw the Missou-rians fly by; then they aligned and charged. The Alabamians ran into trouble trying to negotiate a fence, and Samuel De Golyer's Michigan gunners drove them back to the shelter of trees. One of De Golyer's men recalled, "We ran up the hill, where bullets, shot, shell and other missiles of death were flying thick as hail. Captain De Golyer waved his hat and exclaimed, 'Come on boys!' " The artillerists joined the infantry in a surge through the hilly terrain.[39]

Meanwhile, Union commanders quickly organized a counterattack. Crocker's division of McPherson's corps had gotten into action by supporting the assault on Carter Stevenson's left. One of Crocker's brigades, George Boomer's, had been shifting to the right when news arrived about Bowen's charge. Grant wanted Boomer to mend the crack in the Union center. Boomer pushed his men into the breach, and soon they felt the wrath of Cockrell's Missourians on their front and Green's Arkansans on their exposed left flank. Hovey came to the rescue by massing sixteen guns southeast of the Champion home that blasted Green's brigade. The guns and the timely arrival of Samuel Holmes's brigade on Boomer's left brought Green's men to a halt. The fresh forces of Boomer and Holmes held up the Confederate tide while Hovey re-formed his men. Grant brought over another brigade from the right to align on Boomer's right and recalled John Stevenson to support the Union center.[40]

As a result, Bowen's brilliant charge ended, and his tired men reluctantly pulled back in the face of the Federal buildup. Georgia regiments, briefly rallying to shore up Bowen's left, fell apart and scattered, putting two Alabama regiments in jeopardy. Most of the 46th Alabama got cut off and had to surrender. Bowen received a report that the Yankees were sending more troops to his right in a flanking maneuver. He correctly assumed that these were soldiers he had faced on the Middle road earlier in the day. If he got flanked and cut off from the crossroads to the rear, Bowen feared he could lose his whole division and what was left of Stevenson's.

Because he had been caught up in the heat of battle, Bowen did not know about developments on the Confederate right. John McClernand sent a brigade to plug the gap between Union forces on the Middle and the Raymond roads. When McClernand got word from Grant in the afternoon to press forward if the opportunity came, he issued orders for an attack; A. J. Smith and Osterhaus led the way, supported by Blair and Carr. Theophilus Garrard's brigade charged down the Middle road, brushing aside a Rebel roadblock and pushed to within a third of a mile of the crossroads. Osterhaus rode with the brigade, and he halted when he saw large numbers of Confederates ahead.[41]

Bowen also called for reinforcements when he saw the Osterhaus threat on his right. None came, largely owing to the situation on the Confederate right and William Loring. Loring had been forced to shift his troops left, or north, when Bowen pulled out his division in the attempt to salvage Stevenson's collapse. Loring deployed Abraham Buford on the left, Winfield Featherston in the center, and Lloyd Tilghman on the right, covering the Raymond road about a third of a mile west of the Coker home. Loring and his generals nervously kept an eye to their front, somewhat amazed by McClernand's lack of aggression.

Pemberton and others later criticized Loring for not sending help to the left, but if Loring had pulled many of his troops to support Stevenson, the Raymond road would have been left open. True, McClernand procrastinated, as he had been ordered to do early in the day before receiving Grant's message, but Loring could not know that would happen. Loring did know that leaving the Raymond road unprotected would be inviting disaster. The strained relationship between Loring and Pemberton no doubt came into play. Pemberton refused to believe Loring had potential trouble on his front. Hearing no sounds of heavy fighting, Pemberton obviously thought Loring was being his usual obstinate and obnoxious self. Loring thought Pemberton out of touch with reality if he believed that the right flank could be weakened or abandoned without dire consequences. After exchanging messages that settled nothing, Pemberton insisted that the situation on the left had so deteriorated that he must have Loring's two closest brigades. Still, nothing happened, and finally Pemberton, in a fury, rode off to find the brigades.[42]

As Pemberton rode south, he encountered Buford's brigade, and ordered two regiments to the crossroads to reinforce Green, who was in danger of being flanked. Buford took the rest of his men west of the crossroads to keep the Jackson road open. Pemberton rode on, searching for Loring, and Buford's regiments reported to Green, who sent detachments to block the Middle road and to protect artillery northeast of the crossroads.

It soon became obvious that two regiments could not save the day. Bowen's division continued falling back before superior numbers, abandoning the top of Champion Hill and leaving four captured cannon behind. With the Yankees showing no signs of letting up, and knowing that more Union forces were coming down the Middle road threatening his ability to retreat, Bowen ordered a general withdrawal, and many Confederates gave up and raced from the battlefield. Confederate Missouri cannoneers opened up with great effect on Osterhaus's advance, giving the division more time to backtrack.[43]

An Arkansan remembered the retreat turning into a stampede. As he ran to keep up with his Arkansas unit, he saw a man shot through the stomach. The wounded Confederate begged for help and grabbed him, streaking his pants legs with blood. But the Arkansan broke loose and again ran, the desire to escape being greater than compassion. Hours later, he was captured, escorted to Port Gibson, and imprisoned. An Indianan observing the retreat noted, "It was hard to tell who was the best man for about two hours, but at last we got too hard for them and they run, like the Devil was after them."[44]

As Buford reached the area with the rest of his brigade, he watched in horror as Bowen's hard-fighting division streamed backward with the enemy hot on its heels. Buford could not save the Jackson road, and the Confederates there fled, leaving a battery behind. Finally the hot weather did what Pemberton's efforts to halt the blue wave could not, forcing the hard-driving, but panting, Federal divisions to halt and take a well-deserved rest at the crossroads. Rather than wasting men in an attack, Buford deployed his troops along high ground south of the crossroads, giving retreating Confederates a thin shield behind which they could re-form. The two Buford regiments sent to Green now rejoined the brigade. The fight ended on the Rebel left and center.[45]

Pemberton never found Loring. After riding farther along the plantation road, Pemberton gave up and came back to the Isaac Roberts home, where he learned of the disastrous situation his army now faced. Pemberton felt he had no choice but to retreat toward Vicksburg by way of Bakers Creek. Then a courier rode up and said that Loring had arrived and was deploying Featherston on Buford's left. It turned out that Loring had not taken the plantation road, but had used an obscure trail, without informing Pemberton. Along the way, Loring and his men had seen defeat in the faces of downtrodden men who could not be rallied. They realized that whatever hope there was for saving the army seemed to be in their hands.

In his usual way of taking charge without first checking with his commanding officer, Loring not only placed Featherston's men in position, but he also re-formed the remnants of Lee's brigade and prepared to attack the crossroads. At that moment, a rider delivered Pemberton's retreat order. Again, in typical fashion, Loring decided to take matters into his own hands and ordered the army to attack anyway. Then Thomas Taylor of Pemberton's staff rode up and demanded on behalf of Pemberton that Loring obey the order and fall back to Edwards. Loring's men, most of whom had escaped heavy combat, would be the rear guard for Stevenson's and Bowen's retreating survivors.[46]

The onus of shielding the army fell to Lloyd Tilghman's brigade, still fronting the enemy on the Raymond road. Since the course of the battle had given the Federals control of the Jackson road, Pemberton had no choice but to steer his army to Edwards via the Raymond road. Thankfully for the Confederates, Bakers Creek waters had gone down considerably during the day, and Pemberton's engineers had constructed a bridge; so the army could use both the ford and bridge to escape. If Tilghman should be overwhelmed, however, the retreat could turn into a disaster very quickly. Loring simply told Tilghman the Raymond road must be held.[47]

Much of the action on the Raymond road during the late afternoon had been an artillery duel between Tilghman's artillery and Burbridge's guns. A. J. Smith, perhaps fearing a repulse, ordered Burbridge to stay in place; Burbridge thought, probably correctly, that he could have swept the Confederates aside and reached Edwards ahead of the rest of the Union army. Smith, usually a very competent officer, had a conservative nature, and he refused this day to take risks. McClernand had ordered an attack, but Smith either felt free to exercise battlefield judgment, or he did not receive the order.

As the artillery standoff continued late into the afternoon, Lloyd Tilghman helped with the sighting of a 12-pound cannon, and an enemy shell fragment hit him in the upper torso, ripping open his chest and killing him instantly. A Confederate soldier claimed the shell almost cut Tilghman in two. The slain general's son, on a sortie to drive off enemy sharpshooters, just missed the gory scene. Arthur Reynolds took command of the brigade and asked Loring for instructions.[48]

To Reynolds's rear, the Confederate retreat continued, sometimes in an orderly way, and sometimes in a disorganized mob fashion. Bowen's division and Lee's brigade went down the road that Loring had used in his trek north, and, covered by Loring's regiments, they made it safely down the Raymond road across Bakers Creek. Pemberton ordered Bowen to deploy on the other side of the creek and cover Loring's retreat. Pemberton and his staff rode on to the Big Black bridge to check defenses in case the enemy continued pressing.[49]

Federal soldiers rejoiced in their obvious victory, but they had little time to enjoy it. One noted that throughout the fighting the men had been run "from one hill to another until I was pretty near gone up the spout." Harsh remnants of battle met the victors' eyes. An Iowan observed of the remains of a Confederate battery: "Never in any battle had I seen such a picture of complete annihilation of men, animals, and material as was the wreck of this battery, once the pride of some Southern town." An Illinoisan "saw piled up against a Small house about a dozen awfully mangled bodies of men, my blood ran Cold at the Sight. others was in the hospital haveing their legs and arms taken off by the Surgeon." A wounded Confederate was missing one arm and one ear, and yet he brought water to a comrade with a terrible stomach wound.

Of all the brave deeds he witnessed during the war, wrote one Federal, "I can think of nothing to equal that." Another Illinoisan summed up the landscape: "I never before saw such a sight as this battlefield presented. Friend and foe lay together dead & dying and such sickening wounds—some with an arm some with a leg torn off and some with their bodies literally torn to pieces by shell."[50]

Indianans had a poignant encounter with another wounded Rebel. The man spoke up, "Where is the Yanks?" A Union soldier replied, "We are the Yanks!" The battered Confederate replied, "Well, I can't help it." A musket ball had hit him in the face, knocking both his eyes from their sockets. A sympathetic Federal wrote, "They were hanging down on each side of his nose, and thick, glossy blood covered his entire breast. He could hear plainly, and seemed to be in his right mind."[51]

The battle barged into the lives of area families. The Champion family home became a heavily used hospital occupied with over twenty makeshift operating tables. Recuperating Federals regained their strength from food cooked in the house. On another part of the field, as Union soldiers marched past a home, they saw on the front porch a lady dressed in black. She seemed unmoved by all the turmoil of battle; "a scornful smile played on her features," but she could not hold back tears.[52]

While Pemberton used Loring's relatively fresh troops to cover his retreat, Grant did much the same in putting together a pursuit. Since most of McClernand's men had escaped heavy combat, Eugene Carr's division led the chase. John Stevenson, unaware of the XIII Corps's assignment, sent a regiment to harass Loring's rear while two regiments and a battery traveled a roundabout route to hit Confederates at the Jackson road bridge. Carr's advance came up and harassed Loring's troops. Buford's brigade made enough noise to force Carr's and Stevenson's soldiers to deploy. Buford left behind a company of artillery to keep the Yankees honest while the rest of his troops headed for the Raymond road. Union officers decided to call off pursuit, as it seemed obvious the Rebels were too far ahead and moving too rapidly to be caught from behind. But the chase was not over.

On the Brownsville road, Alexander W. Reynolds, still guarding the wagon train, received word at midafternoon of disastrous Confederate fortunes. Orders directed him to take the wagons west of the Big Black and to help Seth Barton's beleaguered brigade. Reynolds left two regiments with the train and searched for Barton in the Jackson road area. Barton, meanwhile, learned he was cut off from the main line of retreat and managed to get his Georgians back to Edwards over the Bakers Creek bridge on Jackson road.[53]

McClernand sensed that Pemberton's army could be destroyed if the Federals kept up the pressure. Notified by scouts of Reynolds's approach, he asked Stevenson to see to these Rebel troops. Federal cannon fired a few rounds in Reynolds's direction, primarily as a warning. Reynolds did not know that Barton had left the area, but he smelled a trap and turned back to catch up with wagon train, which crossed the Big Black on a pontoon bridge at Bridgeport.

Things got a bit hectic when Union cavalry caught up with some of Wirt Adams's men, covering Reynolds's rear. Some 150 Rebels surrendered, and the Confederates lost a couple of wagons and several mules. Once Reynolds got his men and the wagons across the river, a detachment destroyed the pontoon and the column moved on to Bovina.

Carter Stevenson tried to secure his retreat by sending Stephen Lee and his battered brigade to the Jackson road to slow Federal pursuit. Lee saw a large Union brigade, William Benton's, coming, and, knowing his men had had enough for one day, he veered toward the Big Black bridge, arriving at about ten o'clock that evening. Federal pursuit followed toward the Raymond road, and Indiana artillery lobbed shells into Confederates who could be seen moving west.

Benton's threat to his flank forced Bowen to abandon his position protecting the creek crossings. Just one of Loring's regiments had crossed, so Loring now had to get the rest of his division to Edwards or the Big Black as best he could. Bowen moved south of Edwards to keep out of artillery range, and his worn division did not reach the Big Black bridge until around midnight.[54]

After Bowen left, Union forces took over Edwards the night of May 16. Benton's men found a cotton gin, railroad cars filled with ammunition, and supplies all ablaze at the hands of Confederate troops. Federals finally extinguished the fires before they spread, and they bandied about wild rumors that Pemberton had been killed. By late evening, large numbers of Grant's army camped in Edwards and beyond, all the way back to Champion Hill, some sleeping among the dead. Crews spent the night searching for survivors and sending them either to the makeshift Union hospital at the Champion home or to the designated Confederate facility at the Roberts house. Every home in the area, no matter how humble, became a hospital for men from both armies. Grant and his staff spent the night on the porch of a local home, likely Isaac Roberts's.[55]

The evening proved to be especially long for William Loring and his division. When the Yankees gave up pursuit, Buford's and Featherston's brigades made it to the Raymond road without incident. A. E. Reynolds, commanding Tilghman's brigade, pulled back his troops to the west, basically turning his back on A. J. Smith, who showed no signs of pursuing. Reynolds soon fell in behind Featherston, and then came news that Bowen had abandoned the crossing. Loring initially decided to force his way across the creek, but after one regiment made it, he had second thoughts. He knew that Grant had troops on his right and that A. J. Smith was behind and might attack. Also, Loring did not relish trying to maneuver in the darkness among so many hostile forces. A local doctor guided the division across another Bakers Creek ford to the south. Onward to the Big Black bridge, Loring led his men, including the recalled regiment that had crossed the creek and a dismounted Missouri cavalry unit separated from Bowen's division on its nighttime odyssey.

Delays and detours brought the troops close to the Coker home where A. J. Smith camped, and Loring lost men who wandered into Union lines and were captured. Muddy trails forced abandonment of twelve cannon and seven wagons, five filled with artillery ammunition and the other two with rifle and pistol bullets. Finally, the tired men reached a ford near Mount Moriah. As the men marched, they praised Loring for trying to save them and complained about Pemberton's bungling, though a few defended the commanding general.

Off in the distance to the northwest, they saw the sky glowing around Edwards, which told Loring the enemy had taken the town. He looked for a ford on Fourteenmile Creek, which would allow his troops to get around Edwards and make it to the Big Black bridge. After talking with locals, however, Loring decided he would have to fight his way through to the Big Black. The frustrated general called a council of war, and all agreed that the division could not reach the rest of the army. The only viable option was to go southeast and then try to join Johnston, which was accomplished on May 19 at Jackson.

Union soldiers later claimed they saw a large body of troops moving to the south, but McClernand dismissed them as unfounded rumors. Had McClernand been more receptive, the fight at Champion Hill might have had an even more devastating ending for the Confederates.[56]

The struggle at Champion Hill had been decisive, for Grant's ultimate success now seemed, if not assured, highly likely. Casualties had been severe. The Union army had lost 410 killed, 1,844 wounded, and 187 missing, while the Confederates reported 381 killed, 1,018 wounded, and 2,441 missing. Actual Confederate figures were probably higher. Loring arrived in Jackson with some 3,000 fewer men than he led into battle on the sixteenth.

What Pemberton would do remained to be seen. He could retreat into Vicksburg, or he, too, could join Johnston. If he did the latter, Grant would march to Vicksburg and have the two Confederate divisions there heavily outnumbered. If Pemberton chose to retreat to Vicksburg with his surviving troops, then Grant could storm the works; and if such tactics failed, he could reestablish contact with the river and receive thousands of reinforcements. He would have Johnston at his back, but Grant had seen enough of Johnston's timidity not to be overly concerned. Whatever Pemberton decided, Grant had the upper hand.

In his memoirs, Grant criticized Pemberton for not escaping to concentrate with Johnston. Grant understood that this would have opened the door wide for him to take Vicksburg, but he still thought it the appropriate move. He implied that he would have let Pemberton go in peace, at least for the moment. Given Grant's nature, and the need to secure Vicksburg, he would have eventually gone after Pemberton and Johnston, but he might have had a hard time catching them. The outcome of the campaign would certainly have been the same. Clearly, Grant never lost his focus on his main goal, the capture of Vicksburg. In Virginia in 1864, he would forego real estate for the capture or destruction of Robert E. Lee's army. In Mississippi, however, Vicksburg took precedence over enemy armies in Grant's mind, for he understood the political necessity to clear the Mississippi. Ultimately, he bagged the town and an army, the latter being a gift due to Pemberton's poor judgment.

Grant later blamed McClernand for not being aggressive enough to make Champion Hill the decisive battle. Grant's comments clearly stemmed from the old feud. McClernand followed orders, which, for most of the battle, encouraged caution. Once he received orders to move aggressively on the Raymond road, most of his troops did. Grant had the turning-point victory he required; he did not need scapegoats.[57]

As Grant paused to rest his army, hoards of reinforcements rode transports downriver. These men must have wondered what lay ahead as they saw the results of the hard hand of war along the Mississippi. Ever-present guerrillas continued to fire on boats, and Federals continued going ashore to retaliate. Even slave cabins fell victim to the torch, but soldiers had little regret for the ever-expanding landscape of solitary chimneys lining the banks. Grant's move inland had not relieved the tensions and realities of war on the river. And when he returned to the river, help would be waiting.[58]

Pemberton had no reinforcements coming, though a significant Confederate force sat idle in the Canton-Jackson area. Pemberton's immediate concern was to get his army reorganized. He rode through works constructed east of the Big Black the evening of the sixteenth and ordered John Vaughn to file his Tennesseans into the rifle pits. Later, he added Bowen's battered division to the front line to hold off the Federals until Loring arrived. Pemberton then rode on to Bovina to set up headquarters. Stevenson's disorganized, depleted, and distraught brigades convinced Pemberton and his staff to send these men on to Mount Alban out of harm's way. The men were so worn down, however, that Stevenson camped close to Bovina. At the front, Bowen deployed Green's Arkansans on Vaughn's left, and Cockrell's Missourians filed on his right.

The night drifted by, the Edwards fires dimmed and died, and Loring's division did not come. Pemberton waited anxiously; if Loring came, the army would be reunited and could perhaps dig in on the west bank bluffs and challenge Grant to cross. May 17 dawned and still no Loring. But rather than pull his army across to the west bank, Pemberton chose to wait longer, a decision that cost him heavily in men and matériel.[59]

When daylight came, Pemberton shored up his defensive position on the Big Black. One of John Forney's brigades, William Baldwin's, had been guarding Hall's Ferry and then Mount Alban. As news of the battle at Champion Hill drifted west the next day, Baldwin sent portions of his brigade east to the Big Black. Pemberton posted these men on the west bank bluffs on the seventeenth, and Baldwin sent pickets to scout the river above and below the bridge in case the enemy conducted flanking movements.[60]

John Bowen took charge of the bridge defenses; he thought the works adequate but too expansive. He had about 5,000 soldiers, and the ranks would be thin if he stretched them to cover all the lines of entrenchments. Pemberton's chief engineer, Samuel Lockett, placed the main line of works west of a bayou that flowed from south of the railroad to north of the tracks. The water formed a moat of sorts in front of the trenches, and abatis further enhanced the position. Bowen's right rested on Gin Lake, a body of water shaped somewhat like a fishhook, which lay east of the bridge and south of the railroad. Cockrell's flank rested near the base of the shank of the hook. The Jackson road, the likely Union approach route, came toward Cockrell's position. From there, the line ran north to and beyond the railroad, stopping on the banks of the Big Black, where the channel turned north and east from the bridge. On this left flank, a line angled east of the bayou to provide

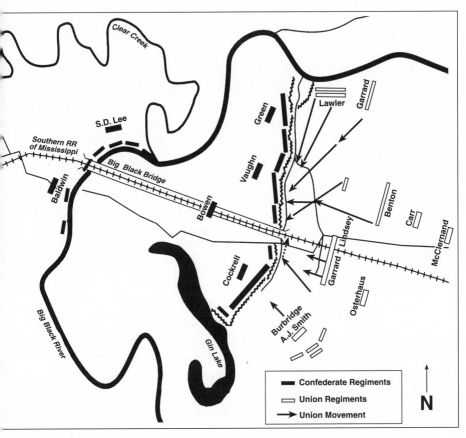

The Battle of the Big Black, May 17, 1863. Map by Becky Smith, adapted from Michael B. Ballard, The Campaign for Vicksburg *(Conshohocken, Pa.: Eastern National Park and Monument Association, 1996).*

Confederate riflemen a position not only to reinforce the left but also to deliver flanking fire into attackers along the main line.

Other landmarks included a blockhouse on either side of the track east of the bridge, previously used for defensive purposes against cavalry. Just south of the bridge, the steamer *Dot* remained moored west to east to provide a floating bridge for traffic the railroad bridge could not accommodate. Happily for the Confederates, the boat was one of four trapped in the interior of the Big Black channel by the loss of Grand Gulf.[61]

In the center of the line, Vaughn's brigade consisted largely of East Tennesseans, whose Confederate sympathies, as indicated by the timid behavior of Gregg's Tennesseans at Raymond, were suspect. Aside from their questionable loyalties, most were conscripts and thus were not fighting voluntarily for the Confederacy. These men, reinforced by a Mississippi regiment, should not feel the brunt of an attack anyway, so Bowen, despite misgivings, kept his concerns silent.

On the left, Bowen had another problem. Martin Green seethed about the lack of leadership at Champion Hill, and he blamed Pemberton most of all. Supposedly, he told a young woman who lived on a nearby plantation that he hoped the Yankees captured Pemberton. If Bowen knew about Green's feelings, and it seems Green made no secret of his anger, he must have wondered how effective Green's leadership might be. Bowen knew the Arkansans could fight; they had proven their worth on several occasions. So he likely felt that once the shooting started, Green and his soldiers would do their duty.[62]

Pemberton worried more about being flanked than facing an enemy breakthrough at the bridge. He trusted Bowen to hold until Loring arrived, and he had confidence that his defensive works were strong. In Bovina early on the seventeenth, he heard artillery rumbling in the east, and he advised Forney to send more train cars to Bovina. Pemberton obviously knew he could not hold Grant for an extended period. He scribbled a message to Johnston that detailed his being forced to fall back on the Big Black after the battle at Champion Hill. Pemberton confessed that he expected to retreat into Vicksburg. If that happened, he would have to give up Snyder's Bluff. He noted that supplies of food in Vicksburg might last sixty days, and he asked for instructions.

Johnston, John Gregg, and their troops had spent May 16 lounging around a place called Calhoun Station. Johnston made little effort to communicate with Pemberton or to learn of Grant's whereabouts. Pemberton's message about turning the army and moving via the Brownsville road to Clinton arrived late in the day, but Johnston did not get his troops on the road until the seventeenth. Even then, he did not send scouts to look for Pemberton; he assumed the latter's route would be as stated in the message. But given a normal day's marching, there was no way Johnston could reach Clinton the same time as Pemberton. Johnston's lethargy remained evident; he simply had no stomach for fighting. He did not hear of Champion Hill and the aftermath until the evening of the seventeenth, while camped on the road to meet Pemberton. He urged Pemberton to evacuate Vicksburg and save the army if it was not too late.[63]

Grant, meanwhile, determined to maintain his momentum. After a restful night, most of Grant's soldiers also had an urge to finish the job. They had won a great victory with only two of their three corps, and now the third, Sherman's, had come up after spending the night of the sixteenth at Bolton. Grant ordered Sherman to take his troops to Bridgeport north of the railroad, cross the Big Black, and move west in order to threaten Pemberton's flank and rear. Sherman ordered Blair's division to lay down a pontoon bridge, which was accomplished by evening, and Union troops began crossing the Big Black after Pemberton's troops had been defeated again on the seventeenth.[64]

Sherman's other brigade, Ewing's, still guarded the supply wagons near Old Auburn. On the seventeenth, Ewing's men and the wagons moved toward the front and picked up a few stragglers from Loring's division. A fighting general would have sent out scouts, been aware of Ewing and the supply wagons, and attacked. Loring probably never knew what an opportunity he missed. Ewing reached Blair's old campground near the Coker house by evening of the seventeenth.

James McPherson's corps moved slowly, portions of it passing through Edwards on the seventeenth and camping west of Edwards. Because of mopping-up duties on the Champion Hill battlefield, some of McPherson's men did not start for Vicksburg until the eighteenth. Hovey's division attended to the dead and wounded and salvaged supplies scattered over the field. They built shelters for the wounded and, assisted by blacks from surrounding plantations, spent hours digging graves for the dead.

John McClernand's troops did not get the seventeenth off. Displaying his usual tendency to beat other corps to the punch, he had his troops on the road in early morning darkness. His divisions tramped through Edwards at 3:30 A.M., Carr in the lead. The soldiers saw few signs of life, even after hints of dawn lightened the landscape; a few dazed Rebels drifted by, perhaps hoping to be captured and spared more fighting. The Federals moved on through and some four miles west of Edwards, and McClernand's skirmishers drew fire from Confederates. Illinois regiments rushed ahead, looking for a quick victory, only to draw back in awe as they spotted the long line of Rebel entrenchments, extending far in both directions. Troops in the van went into the woods north of the railroad and sent word to Carr, who quickly deployed on either side of the railroad.[65]

The battle at the Big Black developed very quickly. Bowen did not expect fighting to break out along the center of his line, where his defenses were strongest. He ordered Green to bring a regiment from the river's west side to provide support. Carr observed the commotion and worried about his exposed right flank. He immediately ordered Mike Lawler, in reserve behind Carr's right, to fill the gap that extended from the right over to the river. By now, Osterhaus's division had arrived, and McClernand sent these brigades south of the railroad.

Acting quickly, Colonel Daniel Lindsey, brigade commander on Osterhaus's right, ordered an advance through a storm of cannon and small-arms fire to within about 300 yards of Bowen's line. There, Lindsey waited for the rest of the Union line to come up. T. T. Garrard's brigade was to have followed behind Lindsey, but word came that Lawler needed help on the right. A portion of Garrard's troops veered off in that direction while the rest deployed on Lindsey's left.

During exchanges of artillery fire, a shell fragment wounded Osterhaus in the leg, and Albert Lee took over the division. The shelling continued, with cannoneers from Wisconsin, Indiana, and Michigan dueling the Missourians and Mississippians across the way. Grant watched and decided that McClernand would break through without any help. Grant most wanted to keep the Confederates from destroying the rail bridge.[66]

Low morale covered Confederate trenches like a blanket of fog. Soldiers knew they faced only a portion of Grant's army, and as soon as more came up, the game would be over. Green worried because with the Big Black looping so close to his rear, a breakthrough at Bowen's center by the enemy might cut off Green's troops from Cockrell's. Artillerists knew that without horses, which had been herded to the rear, they would have to abandon their guns if Bowen's line broke. Deserters began drifting back out of the line to avoid the expected debacle. Officers' attitudes that led to open defiance of Pemberton and derision of his orders at Champion Hill had no doubt spread, and, after the beating of the sixteenth, Pemberton should not have expected his men to fight so soon, especially in such a poorly chosen location.

The absence of a fighting spirit worried Samuel Lockett into asking permission to prepare for destruction of the railroad and floating bridges. Lockett obviously thought Bowen's line would not hold long. Pemberton approved, and Lockett ordered the distribution of turpentine-soaked wood and cotton along the railroad bridge and barrels of turpentine loaded onto the steamer. Men with lit torches took their places at points where they could set fires quickly. Yet Pemberton waited in vain for Loring. By waiting, Pemberton risked losing more men and matériel, especially cannon, than he could afford to. Yet he did not want to give up, for he needed Loring's men; with them he could take a stand on the west bank; without them he could not. So he made his risky, though understandable, decision. Pemberton secured the position as best he could. West of the river, Stephen Lee deployed on bluffs north of the railroad, and Baldwin's troops took position to the south. If the army had to escape, their presence would be vital.[67]

Union battle plans evolved on the battlefield, and as they did it became apparent that Pemberton's army could not hold. Bowen remained convinced that the attack would come across open ground, while Federal commanders, impressed by Bowen's line around the railroad, looked to turn the Rebel left. Mike Lawler learned that a swale near the Big Black could shield an entire brigade. Though close to the Rebel line, Lawler's men had to sprint from there across open ground into fire from the diagonal line of Confederate trenches near the riverbank. Lawler thought the risk worth possible gain, and his men occupied the swale. Soon his regiments were ready to charge, protected by cannon he ordered to enfilade the detached diagonal line. Lawler also posted sharpshooters to keep the enemy low and provide cover for his left.

While Lawler and Carr deployed, McClernand brought up Burbridge's brigade on the left. Other regiments came up on the right, solidifying McClernand's line. Lawler continued his preparations, ordering trees cut to make room for one more cannon, sending two Indiana regiments to provide diversions, and arranging his troops in a tight, narrow alignment, two regiments across and two deep. Because of the massed formation, Lawler told his men to hold their fire until upon the Rebel line. Giving the order to fix bayonets, the 250-pound, heavily perspiring officer rode up out of the swale and took a deep breath to bellow the order to charge.[68]

Grant observed all the activity and was satisfied that the moment of decision was near. A member of his staff rode to the general's side and handed him a note dated May 11 from Henry Halleck, who wanted Grant to pull the army back to Grand Gulf and cooperate with Banks at Port Hudson. Smiling to himself, Grant folded the note and pocketed it, commenting that he did not think he could obey just now.[69]

Mike Lawler yelled, and his men rose up and charged. He had the affection of his troops; he insisted on discipline, but he often left his uniform coat rolled up and strapped to his saddle. He went into battle in short sleeves and wearing a straw hat, his appearance revealing his down-to-earth character. As Lawler's men, Iowans and Wisconsinites, surged, Bowen's dismounted cavalry, caught totally by surprise, disappeared after minimum resistance. The Missourians could have waved and done as much damage. A few Iowans, including two colonels, fell on the front lines, but rear regiments passed by unscathed while shocked Missourians tried to reload.

As the blue wave rolled, Lawler ordered Indiana skirmishers to change fronts and join the attack. Charging at an angle across Green's front, the Yankees hit the portion of Bowen's line held by the 61st Tennessee. At the abatis, Lawler's men stopped, delivered a volley, and then thrashed their way through water and timber, while the Indianans came up on the left and shot into the Confederate line before assaulting the obstructions. Meanwhile, cannoneers on Lawler's left kept up a constant fire at Missourians who survived the initial shock.

When Lawler's yelling soldiers swamped the line, the Tennesseans demonstrated just how little devotion they had to the Southern cause. Most threw away their weapons and ran as fast as possible to the bridges. Those who did not feel like running stayed behind and waved white cotton, pulled from defensive works and wrapped around their weapons. The Union charge caused the utter disintegration of the Rebel line as far south as the railroad. The collapse of the center isolated Green's brigade, and he ordered a withdrawal.[70]

Lawler won such a quick and easy victory that he had to deal with a multitude of prisoners. Meanwhile, he sent troops to cut off Confederate retreats, though some desperate Rebels jumped into the Big Black, many drowning in the swirling currents. Some ninety Missourians surrendered.

Francis Cockrell's fierce fighters never had a chance. When Cockrell heard the commotion north of the railroad, he quickly made his way there and saw the disaster. Cockrell knew he was flanked and yelled to his men to fall back quickly to the river. They obeyed, though not with the character he would have wished. Chaos spread like a rabid fever; men forgot military discipline and thought only of escape. One Confederate confessed, "We all had to make our way out the best way we could," as he and his comrades ran along amid a shower of bullets. One soldier was "too timid to raise up and expose himself enough to shoot toward the federal line."[71]

Lawler's breakthrough likewise surprised the rest of McClernand's corps as blue-clad soldiers down the line realized they had no enemy to fight. An Illinois private, Jimmy Atkins, climbed on an abandoned Confederate gun, "clapped his elbows on his side and crowed like a game cock." The gun was aimed east along the Jackson road, and Atkins, thinking it was unloaded, pulled the lanyard, sending a shell flying just over the heads of his comrades in arms. Luckily, no one was hurt, though Atkins was shaken up. Other Federals turned Rebel guns and fired them at their previous owners. Fred Grant, the general's twelve-year-old son, strayed too near the river and received a slight wound in the leg. Fred insisted he "had been killed," but he recovered quickly enough; his reassured father showed little concern. Young Grant's experience served as a reminder that the enemy was still close by and dangerous.[72]

Samuel Lockett saw the debacle from atop the west bank bluffs and felt relieved that Lee and Baldwin were deployed to slow the Union thrust. Supported by Landis's Missouri battery, these men stood firm while the masses of their disorganized comrades got across the river and swept by. Lockett patiently waited before signaling the torchbearers, though some Confederates were still on the east bank when the fires started. The railroad bridge and the floating bridge quickly became engulfed in flames. A rear guard consisting of several of Cockrell's men, still on the east side and unseen by Lockett, had to swim across. Crews of three Rebel steamers south of the bridges torched their vessels and joined in the retreat to Vicksburg. Detachments also set ablaze supplies between the Big Black and Vicksburg that might fall into enemy hands, disappointing straggling soldiers who found their baggage and knapsacks in ashes.[73]

Pemberton rode east when he got word of the rout, thinking he might rally the men and make a stand on the west bank of the Big Black. When he saw the dispirited mob headed west, however, he knew he could not. He had finally accepted that Loring was not coming, and without Loring he could not make a stand. Inevitably he would be flanked, and if that precipitated another shattering of his line, the army might be well cut off from Vicksburg and captured. So he sent the surviving troops into the city's defenses, where Forney's and Smith's divisions awaited. Pemberton spoke, more to himself than to those around him, "Just thirty years ago I began my military career by receiving my appointment to a cadetship at the U.S. Military Academy, and to-day . . . that career is ended in disaster and disgrace." Lockett tried to encourage Pemberton by pointing out that the two fresh divisions in Vicksburg would bolster the army, and Vicksburg might be saved. Pemberton did not think so; as he and Lockett boarded a train at Bovina for Vicksburg, Pemberton had little hope.[74]

News of the disasters reached Vicksburg ahead of the army. Townspeople heard that, during the battles, "for some reason our men would not fight and we were utterly routed." Rumors flew about that the Northern-born Pemberton had sold out the city, and "many believe it." One resident confessed to his diary, "We are lost," and "Things look very gloomy," in fact "things look too dark for even me to be hopeful." As more and more of Pemberton's troops came into town, however, spirits rose, though for many only Joseph Johnston could offer the promise of succor. Vicksburgians and Pemberton's soldiers found out soon enough that Johnston offered no hope at all.[75]

Behind the Confederates, McClernand waited too late to get men to the river to save the bridges. He saw Confederate supplies exploding and burning on an abandoned train torched by the Rebels. Still the victory had been impressive. His officers counted 1,751 prisoners and 18 cannon and assorted equipment and ammunition, including 1,525 rounds of artillery shot and 1,421 small arms. McClernand had lost 39 killed, 237 wounded, and 3 missing; Confederate returns were barely reported, so one can only be sure that most of their casualties were in the "missing" category.

General Grant, as usual, was thinking ahead. He told McPherson to cross near Amsterdam, just north of the railroad and south of Bridgeport, where Sherman was to cross. Clearly Grant thought Pemberton might turn north, and Sherman and McPherson would be able to cut him off. McClernand's men, once they had mopped up the battlefield, cut trees and planked a floating raft bridge, constructed by McPherson in part from wood that survived Confederate blazes. Sherman's corps crossed that evening at Bridgeport. Meanwhile, Grant got in touch with Nathaniel Banks. Obviously Grant's successes in Mississippi suggested that Banks should send help rather than ask for any. As things worked out, each soon began their own sieges, Banks at Port Hudson and Grant at Vicksburg. The fate of Port Hudson, however, depended on what happened at Vicksburg.[76]

The Confederates' lack of coordination and communication, and thus their working at cross-purposes, had allowed Grant to conquer a divided enemy. Johnston took himself out of the campaign; indeed, he had never been, nor ever would be, in it. Pemberton, trying to please Jefferson Davis, who insisted that Vicksburg and Port Hudson must be held, and to please Johnston, who thought both places worthless militarily, had been caught in the middle, a victim of a convoluted command system and his own indecisiveness. Too dispirited to think clearly, he chose to back his bedraggled army into Vicksburg rather than evacuate the city and head north where he might have escaped to campaign again. When he chose to take his army into Vicksburg, Pemberton sealed the fate of his troops and the city he had been determined to defend.

11

Assaulting Vicksburg

John Forney and Martin L. Smith missed the action at Champion Hill and the Big Black, but messages and sounds of artillery indicated the fighting was rapidly approaching. Forney had commanded the Second Military District, which meant the city defenses, since Pemberton left for the front, but Pemberton ordered his return to division command on Sunday, May 17, before the debacle at the Big Black. Forney's and Smith's deployments around town included Louis Hébert's brigade to the north on the Yazoo bluffs, John Moore's (plus some Mississippi state troops) around Warrenton to the south, Francis Shoup's brigade (Smith's division) in Vicksburg, and Edward Higgins's heavy artillery units along the waterfront. Smith's other brigades and Thomas Waul's Texas Legion had been sent as reserves to the west side of the Big Black. Samuel Ferguson's troops harassed Union vessels around Greenville, but he reported to Forney in Vicksburg.

On the seventeenth, Pemberton sent several messages to Forney as the long day marked by the short battle at the Big Black wore on. Hébert should evacuate the Yazoo bluffs and bring all supplies there back to Vicksburg. When Forney got word of the army's retreat from the Big Black, he ordered his men into defensive works. He also instructed that supplies not immediately deliverable to the city, and all Yazoo steamboats, be evacuated north of the Yazoo out of harm's way. Scouts rode east to report on Pemberton's situation, and Yazoo artillerists destroyed heavy guns on the bluffs rather than risk their falling into enemy hands. Hébert's troops marched into town early on the morning of the eighteenth, bringing along lighter artillery. Forney deployed them into the left-center of the Confederate line, north of, and including, a work called the Great Redoubt.

Hébert did not like what he saw. "In spite of the previously vaunted report that Vicksburg had been surrounded by fortifications that were impregnable, we found a very feeble line," he later wrote, "and very weakly thrown up with little redoubts here and there." Obviously, much work had to be done and quickly. Joseph Johnston's previous comments back in December about inadequate defenses seemingly had been ignored. Insufficient works possibly reflected Pemberton's problems in securing slave labor.[1]

John Moore's brigade deployed on Hébert's right; Moore's right extended to the Southern Railroad. A single Alabama regiment was on Moore's right, and the 2nd Texas took position in a lunette, which eventually bore the regiment's name, that blocked approaches to Vicksburg from the Baldwin's Ferry road. The lines here were "too narrow and shallow," and Moore's soldiers spent hours digging.[2]

To the east, Carter Stevenson commanded the retreat march back into Vicksburg. William Baldwin's and Stephen Lee's troops served as the rear guard, and these two brigades eventually entered Vicksburg on the Confederate right with the rest of Stevenson's depleted division. Pemberton figured that Grant would attack the Confederate center, and he knew Stevenson's men needed time to regroup. One of Lee's Alabama regiments got left behind and, with no orders, stayed close to the Big Black and shot at Union bridge builders. Their commander finally led his men to Vicksburg, the foul-up perhaps having bought Pemberton a little time to rest his army.[3]

Waul's Texans and a battalion of Louisiana Zouaves soon arrived from picketing duty at Big Black ferries and deployed in reserve positions south of the railroad in a deep ravine. At the time, Waul's force consisted of twelve companies of infantry, organized into two battalions, plus one battalion each of cavalry and artillery. These tough Texans made their presence felt during the coming struggle for Vicksburg. Forney placed Waul's artillery along the right center of the defensive line. Bowen's exhausted division arrived, and Pemberton placed the troops in reserve behind the left center of his line.

Panic disassembled many units during the race for Vicksburg and sorting out troops took much precious time. The army's turmoil fed civilian fears, and a chaotic atmosphere prevailed around town. Many civilians living outside the city, between Vicksburg and the Big Black, came streaming into the perceived safety of ever-receding Confederate lines. Fatigued soldiers fell into the trenches and slept, while the fresh soldiers of Forney and Smith positioned artillery in strategic locations.[4]

The scenes of Pemberton's army streaming into Vicksburg made lasting impressions. One diarist wrote on the seventeenth: "About three o'clock the rush began. I shall never forget that woeful sight of a beaten, demoralized army that came rushing back, humanity in the last throes of endurance. Wan, hollow-eyed, ragged, footsore, bloody, the men limped along unarmed, but followed by siege guns, ambulances, gun carriages, and wagons in aimless confusion. At twilight, two or three bands began playing Dixie, Bonnie Blue Flag, and so on, and drums began to beat all about; I suppose they were rallying the scattered army." Emma Balfour described her town as being "*jammed* with wagons, cannons, horses, men, mules, stock, sheep."

Disgruntled soldiers and civilians blamed Pemberton for it all, to the point that Bowen advised Pemberton to make a statement of his determination to fight for Vicksburg. Pemberton agreed and issued a proclamation: "You have heard that I was incompetent, and a traitor; and that it was my intention to sell Vicksburg. Follow me, and you will see the cost at which I will sell Vicksburg. When the last pound of beef, bacon, and flour, the last grain of corn, the last cow and hog and horse and dog shall have been consumed, and the last man shall have perished in the trenches, then and only then will I sell Vicksburg." Despite the obvious hyperbole, the words boosted morale.[5]

On May 18, Pemberton and his staff continued positioning troops. Stevenson occupied the area between the railroad and South Fort, a defensive work south of town overlooking the Mississippi. Georgians and Tennesseans who had not done well at Champion Hill and the Big Black, respectively, constructed many of their own lines to replace the poorly dug and poorly placed. Stephen Lee's impressive brigade occupied Stevenson's left, where they were more likely to see action than the rest of the division.

Bowen's division received instructions to be ready to move wherever needed. Cockrell camped near the city graveyard, while Martin Green took position behind John Moore's brigade. These men would redeem themselves for the panicky retreat at the Big Black.

Martin Smith's position on the left included high ridges north of town and Mint Spring Bayou, where Baldwin's brigade deployed. Francis Shoup was on Baldwin's right, with his right connecting with Forney's left at Stockade Redan, which blocked the Graveyard road entrance to Vicksburg. To Baldwin's rear, John Vaughn's Tennesseans, who had been cowardly at the Big Black, occupied the prominent ridge known as Fort Hill, which overlooked the Mississippi. Vaughn received a few men from Loring's division who, having been cut off from their comrades, had made it safely to Vicksburg. This position had such natural strength that Pemberton no doubt believed Grant would never try to attack there; hence, untrustworthy fighters perhaps could hold it.

Pemberton left his cavalry outside the city, where they could attack the enemy's rear. Pemberton sent word to Wirt Adams, whose troopers were slowing Grant's advance, to get behind the enemy and harass and destroy supply wagons, and do whatever else he could to hurt the Federals.[6]

While waiting for Grant, Confederates continued strengthening their works. Samuel Lockett had supervised construction of the long irregular line that formed a crescent from north to south. Lockett had created many variations of military fortifications, including redoubts, lunettes, redans, ramparts, parapets, and various artillery positions, all connected by infantry trenches. Many of the works had not been used for some time, and rain had washed dirt into previously dug lines, accounting in part for their poor condition. Many outer works simply had not been completed, a situation that had to be rectified quickly. Missourians had to fix stretches of lines that would subject them to enfilading fire, and reposition logs placed in the open, where flying splinters, resulting from enemy bullets, could be hazardous.[7]

The defensive line had several key points. The far left of the line north of Vicksburg was anchored on the Mississippi River. From that point inland to the work called Stockade Redan, workers had constructed two lines: the outer on a ridge north of Mint Spring Bayou and the inner along Fort Hill ridge. At Stockade Redan, these lines merged where the ridges came together a mile and a half east of the river. From that point, the exterior line turned south along a ridge for about a mile, a ridge cut by Glass Bayou, to where the Jackson road entered Vicksburg. The line continued south along a ridge between a bayou and a creek and crossed the Baldwin's Ferry road and the railroad. The works turned southwest at Square Fort (later known as Fort Garrott), the fort defending the angle in the line. Near where the Hall's Ferry road came into Vicksburg was a place called Salient Work, and here the ridge became more level, turned to the southwest, and continued along another ridge between streams. A few hundred yards east of South Fort, the works crossed Stouts Bayou and went to South Fort. From that point, a line of trenches went north, following the riverbank; this line was intended to cover the lowland between the bluff and the river.

Lockett and his fellow engineers faced challenges in constructing strong works to block roads and the railroad that entered Vicksburg. The River road north to Yazoo City came into Vicksburg where the left flank came up to the river. The heights of Fort Hill commanded the road. The Stockade Redan works on the Graveyard road included the redan itself south of the road and the 27th Louisiana Lunette on the north side. Between the two, the Confederates built a stockade of poplar logs. To the south of Stockade Redan, the smaller Green's Redan provided works for flanking fire against attackers. Ditches and obstructions fronted these works. Traverses, or banks of dirt, were built to deflect ricochets, and embrasured parapets, walls of dirt with openings for cannon to shoot at the enemy, were built at the lunette and Stockade Redan.

At the Jackson road entrance loomed the 3rd Louisiana Redan north of the road and the Great Redoubt to the south. The 3rd Louisiana work had no ditch to its front and could accommodate two cannon. The Great Redoubt was about a hundred yards long and consisted of three separate but connected works divided by curtains, or flat walls of earth. The redoubt contained three cannon and was considered the strongest position on the line.

A mile or so south of the Great Redoubt stood the 2nd Texas Lunette, built to block the Baldwin's Ferry road; a lunette normally consists of four faces and three salient angles, with a ditch to the front and open in the rear. The 2nd Texas work was somewhat irregular in shape and had no rifle trenches on its left flank to connect with the rest of the line in that direction. A deep ditch fronted the lunette. To the south, the railroad entered Vicksburg through a cut in the bluff, and on the south bank of the bluff was the Railroad Redoubt, which contained traverses to protect flanks. The redoubt had embrasures for three cannon and rifle pits to the rear to thwart attacks from the gorge behind the work.

On down the line stood Square Fort, a redoubt built where a ridge ran into the main line of works. The fort contained three cannon, and a mile to the south stood the Salient Work, which had two big guns guarding the Halls Ferry Road. The final key work was South Fort on the far right. This work had a ditch in front, as well as a 10-inch rifled gun and a 10-inch mortar and was designed to shell the Warrenton road and the Mississippi.

Beyond the exterior line in the center and right center areas, the Confederates had cut down trees to make a thick obstruction of abatis (interlocked poles with sharpened points positioned to face enemy approaches). Also, cannon were placed wherever ridges had approaches that might tempt attackers. The guns served two purposes: protection against frontal attacks and protection from flanking fire. Rifle pits some five feet deep, with steps to access the crest, ran all along the line, connecting the key works. In front of these lines lay abatis, cane, and tangles of telegraph wire, plus any other obstructions the defenders could dream up. Grant's army would find that Pemberton's troops, with decent positions and behind defensive works, could be formidable.[8]

〰 The Union army moved steadily toward Vicksburg, but Grant ordered his corps commanders to step up the pace. Once across the Big Black, McClernand's XIII Corps marched west on the Jackson road to Mount Alban and looked for an access road to the Baldwin's Ferry road. To increase speed, Grant ordered supply wagons held back and guarded at the rear of the army. By nightfall, McClernand's men camped on the Baldwin's Ferry road about four miles east of Vicksburg. Patrols reported flags flying above the enemy's works, an indication that the Rebels intended to make a stand.

As the army moved toward the long-sought prize, Grant and his entourage stopped at a home and asked for water. The lady of the house, supposing that these were the only Yankees in the area, warned that they could never take Vicksburg. Grant assured her that he expected to do so if it took thirty years. As they talked, a vast sea of blue appeared on the crest of the hill to the rear, "and the lady retired, much chagrined."[9]

While McClernand continued to be the left wing of Grant's army, Cump Sherman's corps became the right. His troops marched west on the Bridgeport road to a road junction where their presence controlled links between Vicksburg and the Yazoo bluffs. After securing the junction, Sherman led his corps to the fork of the Jackson and Graveyard roads. Like McClernand, Sherman had closed to within about four miles of Vicksburg. Grant rode up and informed Sherman of the basic deployment he had in mind: Sherman on the right, McPherson in the center, and McClernand on the left. Sherman congratulated Grant on the campaign, calling it "one of the greatest" ever waged, and he urged Grant to report on it at once to Washington. Vicksburg should fall, but even if it did not, the campaign had been brilliant. Sherman admitted that he had opposed crossing below Vicksburg and gave all the credit to Grant. After their brief conversation, Sherman sent his troops down the Graveyard road, leaving a regiment to guard the Jackson road until McPherson's corps, the army's center, arrived.

Grant decided to storm the Vicksburg works. He believed Confederate morale was low, and so far, with the exception of Bowen, they had not shown him much. Too, he knew his men wanted to finish the job. Their victories had been brilliant, and to stop them now and settle for an investment without giving them the opportunity to end the campaign quickly did not seem prudent. How many of Grant's soldiers actually looked forward to attacking a well-entrenched enemy is not known, but certainly most wanted a quick end to the campaign. If a siege became necessary, his soldiers needed to know that it was necessary, and that could only be determined by assaulting Pemberton's lines. There were other considerations, too. If he had to besiege Vicksburg, Grant would need more men and matériel, both of which Washington might wish to send elsewhere, especially to Tennessee and Virginia. On the other hand, a quick victory would free up men and equipment to be sent to other trouble spots. Grant also had concerns about Johnston, who would likely be sent reinforcements, and the longer Pemberton held out, the more time Richmond would have to send Johnston troops. Finishing the campaign rapidly would ease a lot of concerns.[10]

As Grant closed in, Pemberton spent May 18 inspecting his defensive works. In the course of his tour, Pemberton received a May 17 message in which Johnston ordered the evacuation of Vicksburg. Pemberton stared at the paper dumbfounded; had not all the fighting and killing been about saving Vicksburg? Johnston had never thought so, and Jefferson Davis had never thought anything else. Pemberton sided with Davis and reflected that an evacuation would have dire consequences: "It meant the loss of the valuable stores and munitions of war collected for its defense; the fall of Port Hudson; the surrender of the Mississippi River, and the severance of the Confederacy," he wrote. "These were mighty interests, which, had I deemed the evacuation practicable in the sense in which I interpreted General Johnston's instructions, might well have made me hesitate to execute them."

The facts dictated that Pemberton would have had trouble evacuating anyway. His most viable chance of escaping occurred on the night of May 17–18 when he could have marched north along the Big Black, crossed the river and linked with Johnston, which is what Johnston had in mind. That would not have been a certainty, however, because Sherman and McPherson were in position to either hit Confederate flanks or give chase. Since Pemberton rejected Johnston's position that Vicksburg was not worth losing an army, he never considered making such a move.[11]

As a gesture to appease Johnston, Pemberton called a council of war, read Johnston's order, and asked his generals if they thought the army could evacuate Vicksburg. All endorsed the opinion that, given the army's low morale, it would be impossible to get the army out and preserve it as a fighting force. Then the assembled heard a few cannon reports, indicating that the Yankees were closing in northeast of Vicksburg. This meant that Pemberton's most feasible route of escape had been closed. The Confederates must fight or surrender. Pemberton penned an explanation to Johnston, declaring he would defend "the most important point in the Confederacy" until the end.[12]

Joseph Johnston had little notion of what was going on with Pemberton's army, but he understood from his visit to Vicksburg that Pemberton would have to go northeast to get away. Johnston thus guided his troops to be in position to help Pemberton escape up the Mechanicsburg corridor, the land mass between the Big Black and the Yazoo. As he rode along on the eighteenth, he first received a message from Pemberton about the battle at the Big Black and its aftermath. Next morning, he heard again from Pemberton about the council of war and the decision to stay in Vicksburg. Johnston, filled with contempt for his subordinate, promised to try to get reinforcements and returned his army to Canton.[13]

Back in Vicksburg on the eighteenth, Pemberton worked to block Sherman's threat northeast of town. General Shoup's Louisianans sounded the alarm to Hébert in Stockade Redan to shift troops left to meet Sherman's corps. Two regiments rushed up, and M. L. Smith, aware of the threat, sent another from his division on the Confederate left to fill the gap between Shoup and Baldwin's brigade. Across the way, Frank Blair, with the 13th U.S. troops leading the way, moved to within a third of a mile of Stockade Redan. Thomas Kilby Smith's brigade and Illinois light artillery deployed and fired at the Rebels from north of the Graveyard road.

Sherman rode up and ordered troops down into the Yazoo bottom to establish communications with Porter's fleet, and Steele's division moved off the hills and downward, encountering resistance from Baldwin. Yankee firepower kept the heads of Baldwin's troops low; artillery exchanges erupted, further cowering the Confederates. Since battle lines were not well established, bullets flew randomly in several directions; a soldier, standing near where Sherman and Grant stood talking, fell dead, underscoring the danger. The Confederates continued to reinforce their left with Cockrell's men coming across the Mint Spring ravine to Baldwin's left. Opposing forces exchanged volleys until dark. McPherson's corps arrived and deployed on either side of the Jackson road.

The results of troop movements on the eighteenth had Sherman's corps contacting Confederates on the Union right, while both McClernand and McPherson encamped near the Confederate lines. Now the showdown began, with Grant in position to establish contact with the navy, the key to getting reinforcements. Pemberton, on the other hand, was minus Loring's division, and his only nearby succor was a general who did not like to fight and did not think Vicksburg worth fighting for. Clearly, the downward spiral of Pemberton's fortunes seemed destined to continue.[14]

Pemberton, no matter how burdened or depressed he may have felt, did not shrink from the job at hand. He continued analyzing defenses and decided late on the eighteenth to pull his defensive line on the left back from north of Mint Spring Bayou to Fort Hill. One of his engineers had pointed out the obvious: whatever the advantages of the forward position, having a deep ravine between that line and Fort Hill was too dangerous. Early on the nineteenth, Baldwin and Cockrell withdrew to Fort Hill. Artillerists set up twelve guns, Cockrell's Missourians camped behind Baldwin's right, and Shoup's Louisianans filed in on Baldwin's right. Some of Loring's stray troops formed a reserve unit.[15]

When Union commanders realized what had happened, Steele's troops marched in and occupied the trenches vacated by the Rebels. Steele had orders to dig in and make contact with Porter, which was accomplished. Plans were drawn up to establish a supply base on the Yazoo.

Steele then prepared for battle. On a given signal, his men swept through the valley, picked up Rebel stragglers, and came up on the edge of the bluff, where they saw the enemy line, accented by heavy gun barrels sticking through embrasures, not a reassuring sight. On Steele's left, Frank Blair's division was about 500 yards northeast of Stockade Redan; to their front they could see dreaded abatis. Blair sent out skirmishers, and around 9:45 his artillery opened. A brigade of Tuttle's division was behind Blair's line, having wasted time on a trip to the Chickasaw Bayou bottom to contact Porter, who had already been contacted by Steele. The incident underscored just how anxious Grant was to link with Porter.[16]

The other two Union corps likewise moved toward Pemberton's line. One of McPherson's brigades, Thomas Ransom's of John McArthur's division (McArthur with his other brigade had been sent to Snyder's Bluff), fought its way through dense hollows to northwest of the Jackson road before occupying a ridge above the north branch of Glass Bayou. John Logan's division went west along the Jackson road until his advance was within about three-quarters of a mile of the 3rd Louisiana Redan. George Boomer's brigade, the only one from Isaac Quinby's division on hand, was on Logan's left.

McClernand formed his corps behind the ridge above a creek, with

A. J. Smith north of Baldwin's Ferry road, and Peter Osterhaus to the south. Carr's only available brigade was held in reserve. At 10:00 A.M., McClernand's batteries opened fire; the Confederates, hamstrung by limited ammunition, did not respond. The Union skirmish line drove in Texas pickets, thereby gaining control of creek crossings. The Federals then deployed for an advance into a creek ravine, a half-mile east of Confederate works, but Rebel artillery lobbed shells among them, forcing men to seek cover among the rugged hollows and swales. Additional broken ground still separated them from the Confederates and forced Osterhaus to plug a gap between his and Smith's divisions.[17]

Grant had been kept informed, and, while he might have preferred waiting for more preparation, he acted quickly. Surely a grand assault now would finish off Pemberton's army. Grant instructed his corps commanders to get as close to the Rebel line as possible. At 2:00 P.M., there would be a three-shot artillery signal, and the assault would begin. Tactical maneuvers would be up to the commanders.

There was a complication that Grant may or may not have been aware of. Sherman's corps was the only one close to the Confederate line. Sherman ordered Blair to attack Stockade Redan from the east and north. Most of McPherson's troops were better than 1,000 yards away from the Confederates, and McClernand still had to cope with very rugged terrain to make contact. Unless the Confederates panicked the way they had at the Big Black, progress would be difficult and very uncoordinated. When 2:00 P.M. arrived and the signal guns were fired, the grand assault quickly fragmented.[18]

Frank Blair, relatively close to the enemy line, had to deal with Green's and Hébert's troops, plus Cockrell's Missourians called up to support. Increased activity on Sherman's front had alerted the Confederates; Blair's men crossed a deep ravine, where scattered sinkholes awaited, screened by high grass and cane and cut timber.

To the left, Kilby Smith's brigade of Blair's division pushed ahead on both sides of the Graveyard road, but the terrain destroyed alignment. While Confederate bullets swarmed all around, Smith had to call several halts to re-form. Finally the men got to within 150 yards of Stockade Redan and paused. The three regiments on the left had some protection behind a ridge, but the two on the right of the road had no cover other than a ditch fronting the redan. Smith notified Sherman, who replied simply that the brigade should get as close as possible and take advantage of opportunities.[19]

Giles Smith, to Kilby Smith's right, had similar terrain problems. One regiment provided cover fire for the advance and then the whole brigade changed into a ravine and up to the north face of Stockade Redan. The Confederates kept up a constant fire, and many blue-clad soldiers went down wounded or dead. The rest climbed up the ridge into the face of the works. Smith's Illinoisans and Missourians faced such a withering fire that they had to stop the charge and seek shelter.

The 13th U.S. Infantry took heavy casualties as they came up from a ravine and crossed a hill. "Onward to the charge was the motto, and most gallantly did we charge," wrote one. At times subject to crossfire from Stockade Redan and the 27th Louisiana Lunette, these army regulars struggled to within a stone's throw of the redan before being forced to take cover "to keep from being annihilated." Survivors counted some fifty-five holes in their regimental flag, and one noted, "Just after dark the rebels set a house on fire to keep us from getting our killed and wounded off the battlefield." Sherman authorized placing the words "First at Vicksburg" on their colors.[20]

Hugh Ewing's brigade had a similar fate at the 27th Louisiana Lunette. Charging with miraculous speed through abatis and felled trees, two regiments, one from Ohio and the other from West Virginia, surged close to a ditch fronting the works, but the combined fire of two Louisiana regiments stopped them cold. Ewing's other regiments got bogged down and could not provide support. The Ohioans and West Virginians kept trying and failing, repulsed by Confederate fire from houses, taking heavy losses and going nowhere. Sherman and Blair finally had to admit failure. Sherman decided on two contingencies: if the attacks stalled into the evening, there would be a general withdrawal under cover of night; if the Confederates broke, reserves would come up to take advantage.[21]

A Confederate penned a picturesque description of Sherman's May 19 charge to his wife:

Under cover of heavy artillery fire, they wind through the valleys until they come within a short distance of our works. In perfect order they form in a solid body, six deep — They begin their advance — They think of their late successes and on they rush with flying banners and glittering arms. Their numerous sharpshooters cover their advance. On they come! Our cannon pours forth the deadly grape into their ranks — They fill up the vacant gaps without pausing a moment — They come now in startling proximity to our works — Not a musket yet has been fired by our men — They have received orders to wait until they can see the whites of their eyes — Not a single head is seen above the works, except now and then a solitary sentinel who stands ready to give the fatal signal — They come now within seventy yards of our lines — Now a thousand heads are above the earthworks — A thousand deadly guns are aimed and the whole lines are lighted up with a continuous flash of firearms and even the hill seems to be a burning smoking volcano. The enemy's solid columns reel and totter before this galling fire — like grass before the mowing scythe they fall. For awhile they pause and tremble before this deadly storm of death and then in confusion and dismay they fall back.[22]

The rush to charge fueled poor planning. The brigades trying to break the Rebel line went into battle without ladders that might have facilitated scaling embankments. The glitch was brought to Kilby Smith's attention when he considered ordering an all-out assault by two of his regiments and the 13th U.S. Infantry. Trying to take such works from the ditch without ladders would be futile, and Smith canceled the attack.

The Confederates ironically could do very little harm to enemy soldiers trapped closely beneath their guns. Every time Rebel infantry rose to shoot down at the Federals, a Union volley blasted away, thus providing cover fire for the bluecoats stuck in no-man's land. The Confederates fired many rounds anyway but with little effect. The shooting continued into the evening, and Sherman's infantry ran low on ammunition, forcing runners to brave the shooting to replenish supplies. A fourteen-year-old drummer boy in the 55th Illinois named Orion Howe earned a Medal of Honor for his work in fetching the vital rounds. Though suffering a leg wound and bleeding, Howe got news of the problem to Sherman, and soon a company of Iowans pitched in to help.

As the fighting continued, Confederates unable to shoot down on the attackers began lighting cannonball fuses and rolling the balls down the banks into Federal ranks. Often the intended victims extinguished the fuses or quickly grabbed the balls and threw them back into the Rebel works. Confederates nevertheless made good use of these improvised hand grenades, as did Union troops later during the siege.[23]

As darkness cloaked the battlefield, withdrawal orders came, and Union soldiers trapped for several hours began the tedious task of returning to the safety of friendly lines. Many of Sherman's men had to wait for fires set by Confederates to die down before running for cover.

On the Union far right, Steele's troops dug in, and Federal artillery came across a cleared ridge, traversing a gauntlet of Confederate fire. Clemens Landgraeber commanded these Missouri cannoneers, and their rapid run across open ground earned Landgraeber the sobriquet the "Flying Dutchman." Snipers tormented the battery and forced Steele to send a patrol to chase them away from nearby buildings. The Federal patrol then fired down on Higgins's Water Battery, forcing Confederate gunners to abandon their pieces. Higgins's artillerists later built protective traverses.

John Thayer led his brigade into a ravine to within about 300 yards of the Rebel line. Around 2:00 P.M., his men ran out into the Mint Spring hollow and began climbing the steep high slope toward the 26th Louisiana Redoubt. Confederate fire contested the advance of Thayer's Iowans until they reached the foot of Fort Hill ridge. Here, a sharp terrain angle gave Thayer's men protection from guns that could not be depressed enough to be effective. Rebel resistance and the terrain, however, convinced Thayer to forget about storming the hill, and at nightfall he withdrew.[24]

On Sherman's left, Thomas Ransom's brigade of McPherson's corps, in position to attack at the appointed hour, 2:00 P.M., ran into trouble because of a lack of coordination. A Wisconsin regiment attacked prematurely, drawing Illinoisans on their right into the fray. These two regiments left three behind; then the Wisconsin troops got bogged down in obstructions. The Illinoisans kept going, reaching a ridge about 100 yards from enemy lines, where they halted in the face of several volleys from two Mississippi regiments, plus flanking fire from Louisianans in the 3rd Louisiana Redan; the Louisiana troops were too far away to do much damage, but the isolated Illinoisans had to dig in and stay put.

To Ransom's left, Logan pushed his division forward along the Jackson road and swept to within about 400 yards of the Confederate line. John Smith's skirmishers made it to the Shirley house, even closer to the Rebel works. Nevertheless, Logan made little headway on the nineteenth. His artillery support was not within range, and only his left flank made significant progress.[25]

On the Union left, McClernand's artillery hammered away at enemy lines. The XIII Corps infantry charged en masse toward Confederate lines less than a half mile away. Despite drawing crossfire from Rebel artillery, the Union front crossed a small branch, but then encountered typically rugged countryside and heavy Confederate fire that broke formations. During the advance, McClernand's flanks began pushing toward the middle, creating a mass of disorganized men that made easy targets for Vicksburg's defenders. Such uncoordinated concentrations accomplished nothing. McClernand and his generals decided to halt and realign to get ready for the next day. The corps had gained valuable real estate to within some 400 yards of the Rebel line. Skirmish lines held the forward position while the rest of the troops pulled to the safety of the hollow immediately to the rear.

Grant had to accept failure, but his men had gained enough ground that he thought a renewed assault might succeed. The spirited Confederate defense by proven veterans, and even suspect Georgians and East Tennesseans, plus Smith's and Forney's rested divisions, had shown that the relatively easy string of Union victories in recent days had ended. Grant's losses on May 19 included 157 killed, 777 wounded, and 8 missing. Confederate losses are uncertain, but probably totaled 200.[26]

〰️ While Grant and his lieutenants considered a second assault, he may well have been thinking of siege possibilities. Despite the awful terrain and losses already suffered, the men who understood siege tactics likely did not want to be a part of one. That kind of warfare required hard work, exposure, and lots of time and patience. Grant's men were used to hard marching and fighting, and they were on a roll; Joseph Johnston was still somewhere in Grant's rear, and the best solution to Johnston was a quick victory at Vicksburg. Then Grant could send troops to dispose of Johnston's army. Grant worried more about Johnston than he should have; perhaps the ghosts of Shiloh and Holly Springs still haunted him. Another fruit of quick victory would be the freeing up of thousands of men to help Banks at Port Hudson. But if a siege became necessary, and dragged on for days and weeks, Grant would still worry about taking reinforcements that could be aiding the Union cause in other vital operations. Juggling all these aspects of the situation led Grant to conclude that he must renew the attack.

Apparently, McPherson and Sherman shared Grant's hesitancy, although they certainly supported his decision. McClernand thought another attack was a good idea, though he may have been reflecting the mood of his men rather than a careful analysis of the situation. It was curious and "ironic that the decision to assault the second time was in accord with the judgment of the one man whose military opinions Grant most distrusted."[27]

Before he ordered another charge, Grant made sure troops that had not been available on May 19 were in place and ready. He wanted to give Pemberton the whole load. Part of Hovey's division had been slowed by escorting to the Mississippi some 4,408 prisoners (including 2,500 captured at Champion Hill) that Pemberton had lost since May 1. Brigades continued coming in, and by the evening of the nineteenth, seventeen of twenty-six had arrived. Jacob Lauman's division had stayed in Grand Gulf to guard supplies. Meanwhile, Grant told his engineers to coordinate the supply base on and routes to the Yazoo with access to the rear of the army. By the twenty-first, wagons loaded with supplies were rolling from the Yazoo behind Union lines via various roads and newly constructed bridges north of the city. As supplies arrived at camps, one soldier said, "Hardtack!" as Grant rode by, and comrades took up the cry. Grant reined in and promised that variety in their diets was at hand, and the men cheered.[28]

Along the front, commanders assessed the results of May 19. Sherman ordered his men to build additional gun emplacements and clear new approach paths. Confederate artillerists did their best to make the work hazardous. The shelling set off big-gun duels all along the lines. Soon Confederate cotton along parapets was on fire, and a Union defensive dugout was demolished. During these exchanges, Union Missouri infantry chased away Confederates near the mouth of Mint Spring Bayou, a key tactical move that blocked a path for Rebel couriers to get in and out of Vicksburg.[29]

Sherman's officers tried to strengthen the corps's position. Blair provided picket cover fire, while Tuttle's troops dug earthworks and gun positions. By May 22, Blair had some twenty-seven cannon flanking the Graveyard road, all within easy range of Stockade Redan. Inside the redan, Francis Shoup complained that his cannon could not respond effectively to concentrated Union fire. Without adequate tools, Shoup's men spent much time repairing their defensive works.

To Sherman's left, McPherson's corps inched along the Jackson road toward the 3rd Louisiana Redan. John Logan, whose division deployed on either side of the road, saw a deep ravine ahead, with strong Confederate trenches along the ridge beyond that ran northwest and ended in a refused position overlooking Glass Bayou. This meant that the enemy line would be difficult to flank, and that attempts to cross the hollow would be devastating. John Smith's brigade deployed between the road and the bayou to participate in the attack expected against the northeast slope of the 3rd Louisiana position.

Close by, Mrs. James Shirley cowered near a chimney. She was pro-Union, but her home was so situated that Union forces could not guarantee her safety. McPherson finally talked her into moving to a cave located well to the rear of the home. The white Shirley house quickly became a landmark.[30]

South of the Jackson road, John Stevenson deployed on a ridge about

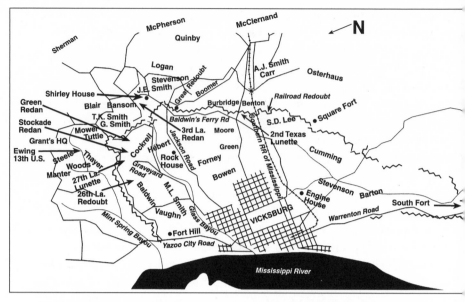

The Vicksburg Assault, May 22, 1863. The positions of the armies on this map remained basically the same during the siege. Map by Becky Smith.

400 yards east of the 3rd Louisiana Redan. Cannoneers deployed as terrain permitted, their guns ranging from close to the redan to 600 yards out. Shells from Union rifled guns kept redan Confederates busy repairing defensive works. Forney recommended that dead mules and horses be skinned and the hides used to wrap cotton bales in the defensive works. The tough hide would stand up better against enemy missiles.

Other problems addressed by Union officers included enemy trenches that ran west from the 3rd Louisiana Redan to Great Redoubt, 200 yards away. Ravines along this line ran into the Rebel works at right angles, which made coordinated attacks impossible. Geography forced George Boomer of Isaac Quinby's division to deploy on the same ridge as Logan, but in a way that neither could easily support the other. While Samuel Lockett had had time to choose his ground, Union officers had to make the best of what was available. There seemed to be no way to coordinate an all-out assault. Quinby's position underscored the difficulties; his left was more than twice as far from the Confederates as his right. He sent skirmishers to find symmetrical paths of advance, but they could not. McPherson tried to overcome terrain problems by massing artillery behind Quinby, some thirty guns separated by only a few yards in between.[31]

Maneuvering artillery proved difficult. An Illinois gunner noted the problems with moving a battery down into a gully, up a hill with a forty-degree ascent angle, and then getting into position, all in the face of the enemy. Infantry details often rushed to assist, carrying shells by hand or pushing and pulling gun carriages. After the batteries fired for a time and received orders to move again, great care had to be taken to avoid touching hot tubes. Later, when the army settled in for a siege, artillerists welcomed setting up in one position and for the most part staying there.[32]

On the Union left, many of John McClernand's troops spent the night of the nineteenth building works around cannon emplacements. McClernand was pleased with the effectiveness of his artillery against Rebel positions. His deployments in preparation for the next assault included A. J. Smith's division east of the Railroad Redoubt, Osterhaus's troops along ridges east and southeast of Square Fort, and Carr in reserve on the Baldwin's Ferry road. From his observations, McClernand concluded that the 2nd Texas Lunette north of the railroad made it possible for Rebels there to pour a flanking fire at any Federal attack on the Railroad Redoubt. To counter this, he must apply sufficient pressure to lunette defenders to prevent their helping anyone, but getting close to the lunette could be a deadly undertaking.

A. J. Smith drew that unenviable job. His division deployed about a third of a mile southeast of the lunette, with Stephen Burbridge's brigade in the lead. McClernand feared Smith's right might be exposed when the division wheeled in the direction of the lunette, so he asked McPherson for help; but McPherson's left was over a half mile from Smith and the terrain in between made support impossible. Nevertheless, on May 20, Smith ordered his men forward, and two regiments advanced to a ridge fronting the lunette and there met a storm of fire. They managed to go further, but then they discovered that both flanks were exposed on account of vine-riddled, undergrowth-laden hollows breaking up the brigade's formation. Burbridge decided to secure the line near where the advance stopped, his right in a position to fire at the east side of the lunette.

That evening, Carr's troops relieved Smith's. After a night of digging in, the Union troops felt more secure, and the shocked Texans could not believe McClernand had gotten so close. McClernand, of course, trumpeted the accomplishment and stirred hard feelings by implying that his men had done more hard fighting than the other corps. His bombast presaged more serious problems in his relationship with Grant.

Beginning on May 21, McClernand's artillery hammered the lunette, disabling two Confederate guns and knocking down large clumps of earthworks. The Texans repaired the damage and added revetments, structures that supported the walls of the lunette. Two guns from a company of Mississippi Light Artillery took the place of the rifled pieces wrecked by the Yankees.[33]

While military action ebbed and flowed, another incident intensified the Grant-McClernand feud. Without telling McClernand, Grant ordered Hovey to watch for Johnston at the Big Black. It is doubtful Grant would have bypassed Sherman or McPherson in such a manner. Quite naturally, McClernand wanted his entire corps at the front before the next attack, so he ordered Hovey to Vicksburg. Hovey did not question the order, but he worried about leaving the area; so he asked Grant's advice, since the original order had come from the commanding general. Grant fumed when he received Hovey's message; if Johnston should come to Pemberton's relief, the Union rear would be unprotected. Grant sent a rider to McClernand to stop Hovey, who had already ridden ahead to McClernand's headquarters. Hovey reported that he had left two infantry companies at the bridge, and that scouts sent east had seen no signs of Rebels. Grant felt better and told McClernand that he could keep one of Hovey's brigades (George McGinnis's), but the other would have to go back.[34]

Though Pemberton and his generals did not think the army could escape from Vicksburg, Union forces had not yet blocked access to the outside world. Grant did not immediately secure the Confederate right, perhaps because he hoped to end the campaign without the bother. So the road leading south to Warrenton remained open, but Pemberton still gave it no thought. To retreat in that direction would mean crossing the Big Black at some point, and with Porter's navy capable of ascending that stream, plus Grant's likely posting of guards at all crossings, escape would be problematical at best. Grant left forces in Grand Gulf and sent others to the Yazoo bluffs, remaining confident that Pemberton would not attempt to leave via Warrenton.

Then Grant changed his mind, though not because he wanted to block the route south. He sent a brigade there as a diversion to keep Confederates busy, busy enough that when the next major assault came, Pemberton could not draw troops from his right to reinforce the rest of his line. If Pemberton should risk pulling troops from the Warrenton road, the brigade would march into Vicksburg, or at least try to. This was the last major step Grant took before planning his second assault. His troops had pushed within a reasonable distance of the Rebel works, and artillery had been strategically placed. He notified Porter that he wanted the navy to bombard the city's river defenses in conjunction with the assault, and to also shell South Fort to support the tactical operation on the enemy's right. Grant scheduled the attack for 10:00 A.M. on May 22.[35]

The Confederates suspected that Grant would try again. Pemberton's men worked day and night to shore up their defensive works. Traverses went up all along the lines at major defensive positions in order to minimize the effects of Union artillery. Officers and their staffs attempted to streamline communications and drew up emergency plans. Pemberton did not think his army could indefinitely withstand enemy assaults; he sent word to Johnston that he needed rifled musket caps and wondered when a relief army would show up. Until he heard something from Johnston, Pemberton realized he would have to make . do with what he had. He moved his headquarters to a home on Crawford Street that was thus far undamaged; there, he would be more equidistant from the ends of his battle line.

The beleaguered general also had to deal with troublesome internal issues during these trying days. John Bowen wanted a place in the battle line and wanted each division to provide its own reserve. He tired of his men doing dirty work for others and being subjected to Union artillery without the luxury of shelter in reasonably well-built frontline works. Pemberton refused because he did not want to make major adjustments to his line with the enemy so close. Not only that, he liked having Bowen's crack fighters in reserve to reinforce trouble spots. Pemberton also worried about pro-Union elements in the city, people that might resort to sabotage. Stevenson employed known loyalists to help guard ammunition and food supplies, both of which had to be conserved. Another concern had to do with taking care of food on the hoof, and details moved cattle and swine to places deemed safe from Federal artillery.[36]

Grant's officers and men stayed busy; he wanted their lines strengthened in case a siege became necessary. Each corps received a large supply of ladders for use in the coming assault. Soldiers cleared buildings within Union lines for their potential use as hospitals. Families who had not escaped before Grant's army arrived found themselves without bedding, mattresses, and other supplies needed by physicians and their patients. Surgeons laid out their instruments, preparing for the grim business to come, and they would be very busy. After the nineteenth, Union troops better understood the task of taking Rebel works. One soldier noted, "But of what use is it for men to charge where birds could not fly. The like of these fortifications are not in the United States."[37]

While Federal troops prepared for the second assault, McClernand endeared himself to Grant once again by protesting a broad attack on all fronts. McClernand favored the overpowering moves on selected points that had served him well in the past, but the difficult terrain had already proven that such tactics were almost impossible to carry out. McClernand, curiously enough, did not practice what he preached. He spread his corps thinly over a mile. He did, however, demonstrate sound tactical thinking when he sent cavalry to demonstrate at South Fort to convince the Rebels that there was more than one brigade along the southern approaches.

In the spirit of McClernand's proposal, though he certainly was not intentionally endorsing it, Sherman formed his troops into a sledge-hammer formation, a long column with regiment following regiment. The approach to Stockade Redan was the one place on the Confederate perimeter where McClernand's power tactics might work. Sherman hoped to avoid spreading his line thin and getting men entangled in the kinds of ravines and obstructions that had plagued his offensive on the nineteenth. He also ordered more cover fire to force Confederates to keep their heads down during the charge.[38]

When May 22 dawned, Federal infantry and artillery spoke loudly. On Sherman's front, Frank Blair put together a detachment of volunteers, some 150 strong, to lead the way. These men expected a high casualty rate, for they would be out front, facing initial Confederate fire. Blair's three brigades would move forward one after the other, as Sherman had dictated. Tuttle's division, similarly aligned, would follow Blair's.

At 10:00 A.M., the appointed hour, the Forlorn Hope detachment, a term used to describe a hopeless action, charged down the Graveyard road, an appropriate avenue for this day's events. They could not return fire because they carried planks and ladders to be used by those that followed. Friendly artillery pounded the Confederates while the 150 charged. As the men closed on the Rebel line, Union cannoneers shifted fire to either side of their flanks. The seemingly doomed volunteers advanced within 150 yards of Stockade Redan, and Confederates remained ominously quiet.

At that point, the road went through a swale before emerging into the open, and as the Forlorn Hope burst into the clearing, three Confederate regiments aligned two deep in the redan arose as one and fired a devastating volley that sent surviving Federals diving for cover. A few managed to get into the ditch and tried to climb up the slope fronting the redan. One planted a flag that several Confederates unsuccessfully tried to retrieve. One Yankee carried a banner and shouted, "You sons of bitches surrender this fort." He raised the flag, and in a moment bullets shredded it into a mass of strings. The experience convinced the men in blue that the road was "a very unhealthy thoroughfare."[39]

Blair's brigades fared no better. Ewing's led the way, sweeping up the road and, near where the passageway emerged into the open, getting bogged down. Bodies from the Forlorn Hope clogged the way, and more men fell. Two Ohio regiments in the lead refused to go any farther, forcing the two regiments following to veer south of the road to a high point east of the redan. There they provided cover fire so that the Ohioans could pull back. Blair called off the attack.

Sherman's other troops experienced similar results. Giles Smith and Kilby Smith led their respective brigades into a ravine south of the Graveyard road. Giles Smith's troops scrambled to a ridge barely 100 yards from Green's Redan, the fortification that formed the left (from the Federal viewpoint) of Stockade Redan. Kilby Smith's troops deployed on Giles Smith's left, and the two brigades poured heavy fire into Rebel works. Tuttle's troops remained on the Graveyard road, awaiting the signal for their turn at charging into the Rebel maelstrom of fire. On Sherman's right, Steele's division spent the morning just getting into position via the Mint Spring Bayou ravine.[40]

On Sherman's left, McPherson's right flank likewise spent the morning moving rather than shooting. Thomas Ransom's brigade advanced to within 100 yards of the enemy line, but Ransom saw that if he charged, his men would be vulnerable to flanking fire from a Rebel salient in Green's Redan. So he held his position until Giles Smith's troops showed up on his right. By then, it was nearly midafternoon.[41]

On McPherson's left, John Logan had the unenviable task of taking the 3rd Louisiana Redan and the Great Redoubt. Logan assigned John Smith to the former and John Stevenson to the latter, leaving his third brigade in reserve. At 10:00 A.M., Smith's brigade charged, moving out of a hollow behind the Shirley house and running down the Jackson Road toward the redan. Four abreast, they got within about 100 yards of the work when the lead regiment panicked and veered off the road. Smith sent another regiment, which made it to the slope of the redan. They remained there until dark, dodging Confederate grenades. Smith canceled his operation.[42]

Stevenson's men went down into a hollow that sheltered them from enemy fire southeast of the redoubt. Forming two assaulting columns and carrying ladders, they had orders not to fire until they reached the Confederate works. When the initial artillery barrage stopped, Stevenson's soldiers climbed out of the ravine and raced toward the redoubt. The Louisiana defenders fired rapidly, and still the blue wave came on. The Federals made remarkable progress, but Stevenson lost momentum and men when he stopped to redeploy the two wings into a line of battle. Soldiers hit the dirt while friendly artillery pounded the Rebels. Confederate fire slackened, and Stevenson ordered a charge. As the men rose with a cheer, two Confederate cannon raked them with canister. A Union Missouri regiment reached the redoubt ditch and found their ladders were too short. Casualties mounted, and Stevenson withdrew; within thirty minutes, he had lost 272 men.[43]

Isaac Quinby's division moved out from behind a ridge about 500 yards east of the enemy line defended by John Moore's brigade of Forney's division. The Federals ran across an exposed ridge and in their front saw a hollow choked with obstructions. Quinby called a quick council of war. George Boomer said his brigade could not penetrate enemy lines, so Quinby gave him an extra regiment; but Boomer did not order the attack. The confusion kept Quinby's troops idle for several hours.[44]

On McClernand's front, his twenty-two pieces of artillery roared from daybreak until 10:00 A.M., knocking holes in Confederate works. McClernand assigned Eugene Carr's division to capture the Railroad Redoubt and the 2nd Texas Lunette, while Peter Osterhaus advanced against Square Fort.

Mike Lawler's brigade of Carr's division led the attack on the redoubt, with William Landram's, of A. J. Smith's division, in support. Lawler's troops came up out of a ravine about 150 yards east of the redoubt, the men formed in a double battle line. They ran into heavy Confederate fire, but, as at the Big Black, they kept going — though the fire here was more concentrated and determined. One lone Confederate regiment held the redoubt, and part of it was detailed with another regiment to protect the gorge to the rear. Stephen Lee notified Thomas Waul that he should have his Texans ready for action; and when McClernand's guns fell silent, Waul sent troops to reinforce the redoubt on the west and south. Two Iowa regiments advanced to the ditch in front of the redoubt, and some entered through a hole made by Union artillery. Most defenders fled, and more Iowans piled into the ditch. Those inside, subject to flanking fire from other Confederates, climbed back into the ditch, leaving behind several Confederates hidden behind a traverse.[45]

A soldier in the 22nd Iowa described the attack:

At once the Confederates opened with grape and canister, plowing grape through our ranks. Steadily, we pushed on up the slope into the ditch and over the parapet, placed the flag on the fort, and kept it there for some time. Thirteen prisoners were taken out of the fort, only a few of our boys got into the fort and they had to come out of it, and remained in the ditch outside. By this time the Confederates that fled or were driven away returned with re-enforcements, so we now had to protect ourselves the best we could. That was done by all kinds of devices. On the open [area] we dug holes for our bodies in the ground, or in the wall of the ditch with our bayonets, or maybe a friendly stump protected us. As the regiment moved forward, it was met with a torrent of shot and shell and minnie balls. The rebels for a moment stood on the top of their rifle pits, pouring their deadly shot into us.

Union sharpshooters shot down Confederates who foolishly exposed themselves.[46]

South of this point, a Wisconsin regiment, along with a few Iowans separated from their regiments, and one of Landram's brigades came over a ridge and found a ravine filled with abatis separating them from the Rebel line. These troops leapt bravely, but foolhardily, into the pit below, and the obstructions, plus Confederate fire, quickly created a bloody mess. The Federals sought cover and fired back at Alabamians and Texans. The defenders stuck "their guns over the works without raising up and fir[ed], so that we could not see them to shoot. They would run their bayonets over into our men who were laying in the ditch and could not get out."[47]

The remainder of Landram's brigade came up to support Lawler. Lawler could tell that more Confederates were rushing from other points to shore up their line, and he urged his troops to hold while he appealed for help. Meanwhile, Lawler's casualty lists grew and included two Iowa regimental commanders. Inside the redoubt, the Confederates in hiding had to surrender after a rescue attempt failed. They were taken to Osterhaus and eventually north to the Johnson's Island prison. The fight for the redoubt settled into a stalemate.

Several Union soldiers fell into Confederate hands, including an Illinoisan who recalled that the defenders' fire "convinced us that instead of them all being dead they were entirely too much alive." Trapped in the ditch in front of the Railroad Redoubt, the men waited until dusk, when the Rebels began rolling lighted shells down among them, killing a couple of men instantly "and nearly paralyzing the rest of us." The beleaguered attackers agreed to surrender and were marched downtown into an enclosure at the jail and courthouse. Their captors treated them "very kindly, which convinced us that they were good citizens in time of peace and brave soldiers in time of war."[48]

William Benton's brigade of Carr's division, meanwhile, led the attack on the 2nd Texas Lunette. Benton's troops charged from a ravine near the Baldwin's Ferry road toward the left front of the lunette. An Illinois soldier never forgot "balls and shells . . . ripping across" their front "like storm-driven hail." His unit "was practically destroyed for the time as a regimental organization," as it charged "under a tremendous fire of grape, cannister and bullets, which cut down many of our men." Leaping on the shooting steps inside the lunette, the 2nd Texas poured volleys into the onrushing Yankees. The one working Confederate cannon in the works belched out load after load of canister, cutting wide holes in blue ranks. The attackers veered to the left and rushed the southwest rifle pits held by an Alabama regiment and part of the 2nd Texas. The attack failed, though a few Indianans made it to the ditch in front of the lunette. They could not return fire but were in a relatively safe position. One Illinois soldier fell into Confederate hands and was taken to General Pemberton who questioned him; the soldier later declared, however, that "I never told him one word of the truth." He was jailed in a "nigger-pen" for one night and then paroled.[49]

Burbridge supported Benton, and his brigade came on the run to within a few yards of the works before pausing to stabilize his right flank. A. J. Smith told Burbridge to send help to Benton between the lunette and the railroad. Burbridge protested, but Smith retorted that the order came from Carr and had to be obeyed. Burbridge again protested, arguing that he could not hold his position if he gave up half his command. Smith relented, and soon one of Carr's staff arrived, angrily demanding an explanation. Burbridge reported the situation to McClernand, who simply told him that Carr's decisions must be obeyed. Carr refused to change his mind, and Burbridge gave in.

Burbridge sent two regiments against the face of the lunette. The Confederates could not depress their cannon enough to shoot into the Yankees, and the close infantry fighting ignited cotton bales. Confederate volunteers rushed up and shot several Federals almost at point-blank range, sending bodies rolling down the incline. Burbridge's assault came to a standstill, and Confederates again rolled lit cannon balls into the Federal ranks. Momentum shifted to the Rebels, and Burbridge, without permission, ordered a withdrawal in order to reunite his brigade. Fortunately for his military career, Burbridge about that time received Carr's permission to use his own discretion.

With his brigade now at full strength, Burbridge brought in artillery support, a 6-pounder cannon hauled up a slope by the Chicago Mercantile Battery. From only about ten yards away from the Confederate embrasure, the cannon shot canister into the lunette. Union fire continued to ignite cotton bales, and the defenders had to toss bales aside, thereby exposing themselves to more canister fire.[50]

Martin Green with his reserve brigade was on the way to the front and John Moore's position when he heard from Stephen Lee that defenses at the Railroad Redoubt were in trouble. By the time Green and his troops arrived there, the situation had been contained. Green left a sharpshooter battalion at the redoubt and moved the remainder of his force toward the 2nd Texas Lunette. Green's arrival stabilized Confederate defenses, and both sides settled down for an afternoon of continual shooting.[51]

Osterhaus ran into a similar stalemate when he attacked Square Fort with his division, supported by one of Hovey's brigades. The men crossed through obstructed and deep ravines to within 200 yards of the enemy line. A member of the 114th Ohio recalled the wicked sounds of missiles flying from the Confederate lines. "We move on, and amid all the din and confusion, and rising high above the roar of the battle, can be heard the voices of the brave boys of the 69th Indiana singing, 'We'll rally round the flag, boys.' " Osterhaus's left had to cross an exposed ridge and took heavy casualties, and he decided that all he could do was hold. Hovey's brigade, commanded by William Spicely, never got into the fight. Perhaps these troops would have been better used in support of near breakthroughs at the Railroad Redoubt and the 2nd Texas Lunette.[52]

The second great assault had fizzled thus far. Only on McClernand's front had there been a breakthrough, and it was temporary. Other works had been approached, and a few flags had been planted; but hopes of overwhelming the Confederates and marching into Vicksburg on the twenty-second faded by 11:00 A.M. Positioned where he could see the general assault up and down the line, Grant could tell that his troops had gotten bogged down and nothing more could be accomplished. Then he received a message from McClernand.

Friction and rancor between McClernand and Grant came into play once more. McClernand stated that he was heavily engaged, that the Confederates were being reinforced, and that he needed a diversion on his right from McPherson to relieve the pressure. McPherson's corps had done very little fighting, with only seven of his thirty-two regiments making much of an effort. Too, Isaac Quinby's division was so positioned that it could move quickly to the area of the 2nd Texas Lunette. Grant responded that McClernand should seek reinforcements from his own reserve and from his own units that were not under fire. Grant implied that all of McClernand's troops were not heavily engaged, but, with the exception of one brigade, this was not so. As in other instances, Grant would have reacted differently to pleas from McPherson or Sherman.

McClernand refused to be ignored. He sent another message that contained some truth, but was misleading. He claimed that his corps had partial possession of two forts, that U.S. flags were flying over both, that the fighting was hot, and that a "vigorous push ought to be made all along the line." McClernand magnified the successes of his troops, for only at the Railroad Redoubt had there been anything like partial possession of a work, and if flags implied capture, that part of the message was untrue.

Grant again tried to brush McClernand off. He told his corps commander to send for John McArthur's troops, currently on McClernand's far left at Warrenton. Grant had to know that McArthur was too far away to give immediate help. Grant shared McClernand's note with Sherman, and, to his credit, Sherman ordered a renewed attack by his corps. Grant, having second thoughts, told McPherson to do likewise.

At his observation post, dubbed "Battery McPherson," Grant received yet another message from his left. This time McClernand claimed that his men had gained Rebel entrenchments at several points, that a stalemate had occurred, and that he had sent word to McArthur and wanted advice on whether to use all or a portion of McArthur's troops. He also told Grant that he could not draw from his reserves because all his troops were engaged, though the idle brigade still was not engaged. Unconvinced that McClernand was telling a straight story, Grant ordered McPherson to send Quinby's division to McClernand.[53]

At 2:00 P.M., Sherman ordered Giles Smith and Ransom to send their brigades forward. At 2:15, they moved, with the same results as before. As soon as the soldiers in blue came up out of the swale into the open, Missourians and Mississippians rose and picked them off. Sherman's casualty list mounted, and the assault did nothing to ease pressure on McClernand. One of Ransom's soldiers recorded, "As our line of battle started and before our yell had died upon the air the confederate fortifications in our front were completely crowded with the enemy, who with an answering cry of defiance, poured into our ranks, one continuous fire of musketry, and the forts and batteries in our front and both sides, were pouring in to our line, an unceasing fire of shot and shell, with fearful results, as this storm of fire sent us, intermixed with the bursting shells and that devilish rebel yell, I could compare it to nothing but one of Dante's pictures of Hell, a something too fearful to describe."[54]

For some reason, Sherman, perhaps too proud to have McClernand best him, refused to give up. So he ordered Tuttle to attack Stockade Redan again. Around 3:00 P.M., Tuttle's troops formed on the Grave-yard road. One of his brigades was supporting artillery, so he deployed the two remaining to the right and left of the road. The men were to charge and get as close as they could to the redan, and then wait for help.

After an artillery bombardment, the brigades charged. In addition to the soldiers, "Old Abe," the eagle mascot of the 8th Wisconsin, went into the fight sitting on his perch next to the regimental flag. As could have been predicted, the roadway became piled with dead and wounded men as lead regiments emerged into the open. A few made it to the ditch, where survivors of earlier attacks still huddled, and made the meaningless gesture of planting flags. Again, Rebels rolled shells down the slope, adding to the Yankee casualty list. Sherman told Tuttle the obvious: "This is murder; order those troops back." His order probably saved Old Abe and many of the 8th Wisconsin, who were not sent into the meat grinder. It took Sherman three failures to accept reality.[55]

On Sherman's right up to that point, practically nothing had happened. Thayer held his brigade south of Mint Spring Bayou waiting on Steele to come up with the rest of the division. Geography protected Thayer's men from the 26th Louisiana Redoubt. When Steele's advance finally arrived, the men raced across an open ridge where many fell, hit by missiles from Confederate artillery on Fort Hill. Steele ordered his men to form south of the bayou, where they would be out of harm's way. At 4:00 P.M., Steele gave the order to charge.

An Iowan described his experience. "At the bottom of the hill there is a little creek and I am running at such speed the first thing I know one leg is mired in the mud but I manage to draw it out . . . quick for the balls are plowing the mud all around me. We climb another hill and run down that. So far we have not lost a man in our company. The third hill is more dangerous still, for we have to run plainly exposed to a line of rifle pits probably a mile long. This line is a curve or circle and we are advancing toward the center, consequently the rebels have an enfilading fire on us, but they are a good way off, probably ¼ of a mile, and they can not fire with precision, but they fire at squads." The Iowans continued on to the third hill along a top of a ridge, and from there they descended a ravine, advanced to a mound of dirt they called "sugar loaf," and fell back in the face of a Confederate sortie. A captain of the 9th Iowa noted that during the offensive "the men fell so fast that the other regiments refused to follow and support us." The survivors laid low until dark and slid down an embankment to safety.

Their comrades in arms from Thayer's and Charles Woods's brigades had similar adventures, initially climbing up a steep slope to their front. Over the course of a 200-yard span, the hill inclined upward for 110 feet of rough, obstructed terrain. A few made it to the slope of the 26th Louisiana Redoubt, but those who tried to climb its fifteen-foot heights quickly gave up. The attackers made no headway, and Steele did not bother calling up his reserve brigade; after dark, he recalled the survivors.

Sherman's corps never operated as one; all his attacks were delivered separately, giving the Confederates plenty of time to shift reserves where needed. The works were so strong that not many had to shift. However, if all attacks had been delivered at once, certainly Sherman would have had a better chance of a breakthrough. As things developed, he had no chance at all.[56]

Sherman's soldiers settled in, digging works where Confederate fire could not reach them. Troops in advance positions, like Giles Smith's and Hugh Ewing's of Blair's division, held where they were, giving Grant solid lines within a hundred yards or so of Stockade Redan. Soldiers built covered paths connecting trenches to the rear. Grant had not made a formal decision about siege operations, but clearly Sherman and his officers were settling down for a long haul.[57]

In the Federal center, McPherson also accomplished little, though Pemberton and his generals expected a major thrust there. Reinforcements from Bowen's and M. L. Smith's divisions had been called to the rear of Hébert's position to support the 3rd Louisiana Redan and the Great Redoubt. Logan's division made a halfhearted thrust down the Jackson road at around 2:00 P.M., but after his lead brigades met heavy losses, Logan called things off, leaving some men stranded southeast of the redan, and they soon pulled back. John Stevenson's troops remained in a hollow in the same area.

At midafternoon, McPherson's other division, Quinby's, left to help McClernand. One brigade stayed behind to give the illusion that the front was still at full strength. Quinby apparently did not figure that dust clouds raised by his moving troops would alert the Confederates. Pemberton, having already reinforced his right, was not overly concerned. McClernand, delighted with the reinforcements from McArthur and

Quinby, promised Grant an all-out assault, "and doubt not that I will force my way through." After Quinby arrived, however, McClernand divided the command, sending a part to Carr and another to Osterhaus. Carr then proceeded to divide the men once again, part to the 2nd Texas Lunette and part to the Railroad Redoubt.

When these reinforcements arrived at the lunette, Burbridge, perhaps understandably, but astonishingly since he had received no orders, decided that these new troops had come not to join but to relieve him. So he pulled out, except for one regiment that did not get the word. When General Green saw Federal troops departing, he sent dismounted cavalry on a sortie, disrupting the Union push by Quinby's troops toward a gap between the lunette and rifle pits to the north. With Burbridge gone, the officer in charge ordered a retreat.[58]

George Boomer's brigade, sent to Carr, had orders to break through between the lunette and the redoubt. At 4:30, his men went forward, facing a blistering frontal and flanking fire before descending into an abatis-infested hollow. While Boomer re-formed his troops, fighting continued to rage at the redoubt, where Stephen Lee worked to rally troops to drive the Yankees out. He saw Boomer coming and feared the worst. More enemy colors appeared along the works, limiting the amount of shifting the Confederates could do. Finally, Lee turned to the fiery Thomas Waul, who welcomed the challenge.

Waul rushed to the front with one battalion of his Texas Legion, his men coming up on the west side of the gorge. Waul checked the situation and saw that his men would have the railroad cut on their left and Federal riflemen on their right as they advanced. So he asked his officers to select thirty-five men to make the charge. Three Alabama soldiers volunteered to join the Texans. At 5:30, led by an Alabama colonel and a Texas captain, the select group swept forward in one of the most remarkable charges of the Vicksburg campaign. Federal troops in the redoubt fled, and the banner of the 77th Illinois was torn down and captured.[59]

The charge added to what had already been a tough day at the redoubt; numbers of Federals fell ill or dead from sunstroke. Soldiers poured water on each other to counter the sun and battle heat. Murderous Rebel fire now caused an Illinoisan to react defensively. "I can remember pulling . . . pulling my hat over . . . my face, as if that would be any protection to me." Men clung to the ground, and when an officer called for them to charge, they refused rather than face annihilation. Until dark, men hid in ditches: "The hissing, howling and screeching of the shells and shots as they passed over our heads was awful. If the infernal regions are any worse, keep me out of them."[60]

With Federals still in the ditch, Waul called for two more of his companies to advance. Stephen Lee went with them, and this second wave mounted the works and shot into the Yankees. Rebels pulled triggers and rolled cannon balls, all the while facing Union rifle fire. Soon Waul's storming parties corralled several prisoners and more stands of colors. The Confederates got a reprieve of sorts when George Boomer fell dead while ordering his men to attack. His successor decided that with the Railroad Redoubt firmly in enemy hands, it would be pointless to continue. Carr agreed and ordered the men to hold until dark and then pull back. To the south, the day ended with a whimper when Quinby's other brigade prepared for an assault that was canceled by Osterhaus because of darkness. A disappointed McClernand kept his wits. Worried about the gap between his right and McPherson's left, he ordered Quinby to return to his original position.[61]

McArthur's troops did not reach McClernand that afternoon. Porter's boats occupied the attention of Confederate river batteries, while McArthur led his men north and east close to the river in their journey to pressure South Fort. The resulting artillery exchanges were spirited but produced few casualties. Porter's sailors cheered when they saw McArthur's troops racing north along the Warrenton road.

Seth Barton and his Georgians, still recovering from Champion Hill, stood in McArthur's way. Barton warned Pemberton, who merely replied that Barton must hold. With the other areas of his line threatened, Pemberton could not send help. McArthur, worried that enemy cannon at South Fort might wreak havoc among his troops, slowed on his own and at around 11:00 A.M. stopped, while sharpshooters crawled toward the fort.

Finally, McArthur prepared for an attack, but then came word that McClernand needed help. McArthur intended to ignore the request, since it contradicted his original orders, but a corroborating note from Grant convinced him to cancel the assault. McArthur led his troops east via a roundabout route and did not make contact with the XIII Corps until night. He did not reach McClernand's headquarters until midday of the twenty-third, and then he had to countermarch back to where he was. McArthur kept his troops on the Warrenton road until the twenty-sixth, when he received orders to report to McPherson.[62]

So ended the May 22 assault, in which Grant had committed over 40,000 troops. He had lost 502 killed, 2,550 wounded, and 147 missing, compared to Confederate estimates of around 500 total casualties. In repulsing Grant's attack, Pemberton had only used about half of the 28,000 men available to him. Grant, obviously a bit embarrassed, blamed McClernand for adding to the casualty list by sending out misleading reports that led to renewed attacks by Sherman and McPherson. McClernand later wrote a detailed denial of Grant's accusation. McClernand's messages had indicated more success than he had attained, and in that sense he had misled Grant. But McClernand had certainly come closer to a breakthrough than his two fellow corps commanders. Nevertheless, the long-standing feud between the two caused Grant to seize this opportunity to blame McClernand, and McClernand's later actions growing out of the assault would give Grant the opportunity to get rid of his nemesis.[63]

Meanwhile, Grant and Pemberton faced the distasteful task of dealing with hundreds of corpses decaying in the hot summer sun. Pemberton's officers pleaded with him to initiate contact with Grant in order to get the dead buried. Most bodies lay close to Confederate works, and the stench quickly became unbearable. Grant refused to initiate anything, so on the twenty-fifth Pemberton sent a message through the line in which he noted Grant's silence and added that "in the name of humanity I have the honor to propose a cessation of hostilities for two hours and a half, that you may be enabled to remove your dead and dying men." Grant agreed and named 6:00 P.M. as the starting time, with the truce to last for two and a half hours as proposed by Pemberton. At the appointed hour, silence enveloped the city as details buried the dead and recovered the wounded for treatment.[64]

The burial work haunted many men who saw the grisly business firsthand. An Illinois soldier recorded in his diary: "The men [corpses] were as black as a Negro and swelled as tight as their clothes would hold, and the maggots were working on them as on any dead animal. Awful! Awful! Not civilized warfare." Another noted pointedly, "The effluvia from their Corpses are stifling." An Indianan wrote home, "I saw sights that I pray God I may never see again." Some of the bodies had become so disfigured from decomposition they could not be identified. Others had been stacked "alternately cross-wise" in front of Confederate works; the Confederates claimed that they did not think it "prudent" to risk burial details until a truce was declared.[65]

Men on both sides who could not bear the scenes visited with each other and exchanged good-natured greetings and gibes. Soldiers traded tobacco and coffee and other items. A Confederate noted, "A large number of our soldiers went into the federal camps taking dinner with them in some cases. It was a common sight to witness the meeting of father and son and brothers, as well as other relatives, serving in the two contending armies." Many Missourians from both sides took the opportunity to have brief reunions. One observed, "There was not much crying, but much mingling and men on each side seemed to size opponents up." Overall, the Rebels looked rough to the Yankees, but the latter "had great respect for their ability to shoot straight."

As the wounded were brought in, surgeons and their assistants went to work. A Union surgeon summed up the carnage well in a letter home. He noted that he had just amputated a lieutenant's leg, had 300 badly wounded awaiting attention, and had amputated so many limbs he had sickened of life. "I am now all covered with blood & yet I must cut, cut, cut yet tonight."[66]

In the aftermath, U. S. Grant decided on a different strategy, one that he had hoped would not be necessary. He had attempted to overwhelm a foe already beaten several times in battle, but his optimism faded owing to uncoordinated attacks and strong defensive positions held by an outnumbered but determined band of Rebels. A siege would take time, but in the end, barring unexpected problems, must be successful. A siege also required more men, men that would be needed elsewhere, but, with victory within the Union's grasp, Grant knew Washington would support his needs. While he remained concerned about Johnston lurking behind the Union lines, Johnston's performance at Jackson had indicated that it was unlikely Grant had anything to worry about. In any event, Grant and Porter now controlled the lower Mississippi, and Grant could easily receive reinforcements.[67]

Porter returned to Vicksburg with a portion of his fleet, because he had grown restless prowling the Red River. He left vessels to support Banks at Port Hudson and came back upriver against a current not as challenging as it had been before, and by late May Porter would be positioned to shell Vicksburg and patrol the river to secure supply bases. Grant no doubt was much relieved and pleased to have Porter on hand.

While Grant plotted new strategy, Abraham Lincoln on May 22 sent a wire to Memphis. Richmond papers indicated that Grant had defeated Pemberton near Edwards, and there were other signs of Grant's successes. Lincoln obviously wanted corroboration and, even more, additional news. Stephen Hurlbut, commanding in Memphis, replied that a wire just received from Grant's headquarters, written on May 20, detailed victories at Port Gibson, Raymond, Jackson, Bakers Creek, and the Big Black bridge. Though Lincoln did not yet know of the repulsed assaults at Vicksburg, he must have smiled broadly at the long-awaited word from Mississippi of Grant's victorious sweep through the state. Lincoln felt a measure of satisfaction that he had stuck with Grant and many of Grant's lieutenants when they had been criticized. Lincoln's judgment and patience had been vindicated, and he wrote to one acquaintance that Grant's campaign in Mississippi "is one of the most brilliant in the world." The fact that it would take a siege to force Vicksburg's surrender did not change Lincoln's assessment.[68]

The May 19 and 22 assaults had likewise vindicated to a degree Pemberton's Confederates. They could still fight, especially since strong works and rugged terrain equalized their disproportionate numbers. Yet repulsing the attacks had at times been tenuous work, and, while victorious, the Rebels could hardly feel secure about the future. They depended on Johnston to bail them out, but as the days and weeks passed, those hopes would fade. While Federal reinforcements streamed into Vicksburg, Pemberton and his men had no such prospects of additional support, except for Johnston. Richmond would send Johnston more men, but time proved that he did not intend to use them on Vicksburg's behalf. In the end, Pemberton's army could not endure a lengthy siege. Johnston, lacking interest in the matter, did nothing, and an impotent Confederate government could do nothing about it. Pemberton and his army were on their own.

Railroad Redoubt looking northwest from Union lines
(Vicksburg National Military Park)

Approach to Stockade Redan along the Graveyard road
(Vicksburg National Military Park)

Fort Hill, an eminence that anchored the left flank of the Confederate line (Vicksburg National Military Park)

John M. Thayer's Approach to the 26th Louisiana Redoubt (Author's Collection)

Sap roller (large cane-woven cylinder) and gabions (smaller cylinders) on exhibit at Vicksburg National Military Park (Author's Collection)

Shebangs of Illinois soldiers with the Shirley house in the background (Vicksburg National Military Park)

Siege cave entrance (Vicksburg National Military Park)

Original members of the Vicksburg National Military Park Association, including William T. Rigby, seated second from left, and Stephen D. Lee, standing in the center (Vicksburg National Military Park)

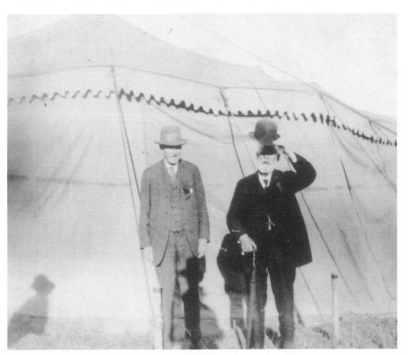

Scenes from the 1917 Veterans Reunion
(Vicksburg National Military Park)

12

~~~ Siege Operations

Federals and Confederates accepted the reality of a siege and changed their mind-set from campaigning in the open to trench warfare. Union troops by the thousands continued steaming downriver from points north, and Grant's engineers planned approach works to narrow gaps between lines. Grant only had four engineer officers on hand, so he mobilized all his West Point–educated officers to assist. Point cadets had exposure to engineering studies, and they would see how much they remembered.

Additional men allowed Grant to secure his position, especially north of Vicksburg in the Mechanicsburg corridor, where he expected Johnston to try to force an opening for Pemberton to escape. Reinforcements also gave Grant the ability to rotate men in and out of the front lines, thereby resting his soldiers in a manner that Pemberton could not.

The waiting game produced an expected casualty among Grant's officer corps. With time to focus on house cleaning, Grant got rid of his nemesis, John McClernand. Ironically, and perhaps predictably, McClernand handed his commanding general the ammunition needed to send him packing. Earlier in the campaign, Grant might have hesitated to act, but with Pemberton's army trapped, and Johnston seemingly inert, Grant no longer needed McClernand.

The final episode involving the two protagonists began when McClernand and his staff sent a "congratulatory order," dated May 30, to his men and newspapers, and no doubt to political friends in Illinois and Washington. Most of the order reviewed the XIII Corps's role in the campaign, from its march down the Louisiana side of the river up through the Vicksburg assaults. McClernand had a right to be proud; his corps had established an exemplary combat record. What set off alarms, and steamed both Sherman and McPherson, as well as Grant, were comments about the May 22 assault. McClernand stated: "How and why the general assault failed, it would be useless now to explain. The Thirteenth Army Corps, acknowledging the good intentions of all, would scorn indulgence in weak regrets and idle criminations. According justice to all, it would only defend itself. If, while the enemy was massing to crush it, assistance was asked for by a diversion at other points, or by re-enforcement, it only asked what in one case Major-General Grant had specifically and peremptorily ordered, namely, simultaneous and persistent attack all along our lines until the enemy's outer works should be carried, and what, in the other, by massing a strong force in time upon a weakened point, would have probably assured success."

Sherman saw the order for the first time in a Memphis newspaper handed to him by Frank Blair. Sherman vented his anger in a lengthy letter to Grant's headquarters, condemning the statement as political in nature and questioning its authenticity. If it was authentic, then McClernand had violated an order, published in 1862, that forbade the publication of official military reports and correspondence, with a penalty of dismissal from the service. McPherson also wrote a long missive to Grant, complaining of McClernand's self-serving tone at the expense of the rest of the army. Grant demanded an explanation from McClernand, who replied that the order was correct as printed, and he apologized for Grant's not receiving a copy, an oversight he blamed on his adjutant.

McClernand's honesty and his attempt to pass the blame on to a member of his own staff did not impress Grant. In an earlier message to Charles Dana, Edwin Stanton had made clear that if McClernand, or anyone for that matter, caused trouble, Grant had permission to act. Stanton said plainly, "General Grant has full and absolute authority to enforce his own commands, and to remove any persons who, by ignorance, inaction, or any cause, interfere with or delay his operations. He has the full confidence of the Government, is expected to enforce his authority, and will be firmly and heartily supported; but he will be responsible for any failure to exert his powers."

This strong statement of Washington's support, as well as the anger of his other two corps commanders, gave Grant the opportunity to take decisive action. He therefore issued an order, dated June 18, that stated succinctly: "Maj. Gen. John A. McClernand is hereby relieved from the command of the Thirteenth Army Corps. He will proceed to any point he may select in the state of Illinois, and report by letter to Headquarters of the Army for orders." Grant appointed E. O. C. Ord to take over the corps.

McClernand did not go quietly. In addition to sending strong, acerbic letters of protest to Grant, he appealed to Stanton, Halleck, and Abraham Lincoln, but to no avail. McClernand learned that whatever political power he possessed, it was not strong enough to keep the Lincoln government from supporting a successful general.[1]

On the military front, Grant instructed his commanders and engineers on May 25 to implement siege tactics, which meant mining operations and approach trenches. The labor was done by work parties of white Federal soldiers and freed black Southerners. Among other things, they built artillery emplacements and dug endless ditches. They employed a procedure called sapping, in ways that tightened the grip on Pemberton's army. "Sap" was a siege term for trench, and sap rollers, large cylindrical contraptions stuffed with cotton for protection from bullets and other missiles, were pushed ahead of digging parties as they shoveled their way toward Rebel lines. Pemberton's soldiers countered with fireballs made of flammable material, attempting, often successfully, to burn saps. In fact, both sides used the fireballs, usually made from compacted wet hay ignited by powder charges.[2]

An Ohioan explained siege jargon and trappings to his wife: "Gabions are made of stakes and grape vines, with which the woods hereabout are full, and are merely baskets two or three feet high, without top or bottom. They are set on end in rows, larger stakes driven through them, and then filled with earth. Sometimes the stakes of the gabions project a few inches at one end and are sharpened and driven into the ground. Gabions are used to make the inside facing of earthworks, called revetment, and to form the sides of embrasures for guns." He also described fascines as siege implements "made of canes, the same used at the north for fishing rods, and being cut into proper lengths are used for the same purposes as gabions."[3]

Grant manipulated his forces to secure the army's southern flank by fortifying the Warrenton and Hall's Ferry roads. Jacob Lauman's division marched around the rear of Union lines from the Yazoo bluffs to Warrenton. Lauman placed one of his brigades across the Warrenton road south of South Fort, and the other dug in astride the Hall's Ferry road. Some of Lauman's soldiers thought their officers failed "to show an exercise of common sense" by positioning troops too close to the river and thus within range of friendly gunboat shells that too often fell among Union ranks.[4]

Grant's action prompted Pemberton's engineer Samuel Lockett to send Seth Barton's troops onto the lowland between South Fort and the

Mississippi to construct abatis to protect the southern flank. Working at night, Barton's men captured more than a hundred unsuspecting Union pickets and made it safely back to their trenches. They failed, however, in their mission to build effective abatis.

Lockett turned to Carter Stevenson for help, and the latter sent work parties to construct a gun emplacement near South Fort. This battery impeded Federal attempts to squeeze between South Fort and the Mississippi and into the rear of Pemberton's army. This was good news and bad news for Confederate soldiers settling into the Vicksburg works. Grant's army might be blocked at key entrances for the moment, but the Yankees also had obstructed all exits. From late May forward, the capitulation of Pemberton's army became a matter of time. Many believed Johnston would come, but that one hope was ebbing.[5]

Grant focused much attention on the Mechanicsburg corridor, the approach to Vicksburg from the northeast between the Big Black and the Yazoo. He seemed overly worried about Johnston, especially since Johnston had done nothing to cause any concern. Despite his string of successes, memories of Shiloh and Holly Springs appeared to linger in Grant's mind. He seemed to perceive, despite evidence to the contrary, that the government's trust in him was tenuous. In any event, Johnston was a loose end, and loose ends had caused Grant trouble more than once in this war. As weeks passed, Union reinforcements built an impressive defensive line from north of Vicksburg along the Yazoo to the east and southeast, with the right flank anchored on the Big Black. In much of this area lay rich bottomland that could have provided much needed food for Pemberton's and Johnston's troops. Grant made sure they would not get it.

The siege became an active one for Grant's soldiers, and Pemberton's army could do little more than observe and shoot when opportunities arose. Over the coming weeks, Federal forces employed thirteen distinct approaches to Rebel lines in an attempt to crack the defensive perimeter. The work required long, hard hours as Grant and his subordinates constantly adjusted to take advantage of terrain. Moving artillery from hill to hill proved especially difficult; getting the heavy guns down into a deep ravine was easy enough, but getting them back up to the next ridge often required several teams of horses and much manpower.[6]

In Virginia, Jefferson Davis, his cabinet, and Robert E. Lee met to discuss the state of affairs at Vicksburg. Lee wanted to invade the north for a second time, in hopes of going all the way to Pennsylvania. He had several diplomatic and military reasons for wanting to make the march, among them the belief that such a move would reduce Union pressure on Pemberton by forcing Yankee strategists to send reinforcements from the Western Theater to the East. Such thinking seemed a stretch. The Union Army of the Potomac had more men than Lee's army already, so taking men from Grant to thwart Lee was not a probable scenario. Lee more than likely simply wanted to go north to convince Davis that Confederate troops in Virginia should stay in the East, where they would be needed. Lee convinced the cabinet and Davis, and Johnston would receive no troops from Lee. Lee usually got what he wanted, and Davis, though anxious about Vicksburg, would not go against his trusted general.

In Vicksburg, Union siege operations got under way. Beginning on Sherman's right, one of the most challenging approaches proved to be John Thayer's. Engineers had to find ways to approach the 26th Louisiana Redoubt, sitting high on a ridge west of Stockade Redan, with a broad field of fire looking down at Federal operations. To accomplish this, trenches had to be dug across Mint Spring Bayou and up the valley to the redoubt. The work began with the digging of a tunnel under the ridge that separated Thayer's troops from enemy fire on Fort Hill some 300 yards away. To get from the side of the ridge facing Rebel lines to a point close enough to the base of the Fort Hill ridge to be in defilade position (where enemy guns could not be depressed enough to fire at them), working parties had to cross a 150-yard open area.

The solution to the open-ground problem proved to be a trench, six by six feet, covered with fascines. This protected the workers from small-arms fire, though the Confederates could hit the origin of the trench with depressed cannon. To keep the Rebels from concentrating their attention in one area, engineers instructed work parties to dig to the right and to the left, on either side of a high ground spur in the valley. The two lines came together on June 9 at a point 100 yards from the redoubt.

To counter the Federals, Francis Shoup instructed his troops to erect a stockade fronting the redoubt, and between the two works they constructed trenches. Shoup's laborers completed the additional defenses on June 15, and the Confederates strung out abatis and wire entwined with brush between the redoubt and Stockade Redan.

The Yankees kept at it, and by June 26 Thayer's Approach was within sixty yards of the redoubt. Confederate sharpshooters made life uncomfortable for the burrowing fatigue parties, but they kept coming. By July 3, the day before Pemberton officially surrendered, the approach was at the palisade fronting the redoubt. Louisiana troops dug tunnels in an attempt to blow up the head of the works and a 24-pounder howitzer shot down into the approach. Union soldiers started digging a countermine.[7]

To Thayer's left, Union soldiers dug three approaches to the Stockade Redan defenses, though only one was potentially effective. The stockade complex provided a challenge; it was flanked by Green's Redan on the south and the 27th Louisiana Lunette on the west, with a log wall filling the gap between Stockade Redan and the lunette. The Graveyard road penetrated the defenses through a gate fronting the northwest slope of the stockade, a gate permanently closed during the siege. Around the complex of works, as on other portions of the battlefield, the ridges had been cleared before the war by cultivation, while the myriad ravines and hollows had been timbered and filled with undergrowth. Confederates chopped trees to build abatis and other obstructions. Loess, while firm, was a soil that was easy to dig and facilitated Union approaches.

The three approaches were Ewing's (the major one, named after Brigadier General Hugh Ewing of Blair's division), Buckland's (after Brigadier General Ralph Buckland of Tuttle's division), and Lightburn's (after Brigadier General J. J. Lightburn of Blair's division). Ewing's was begun on May 23 and was designed to provide a covered path along the Graveyard road to the entrenchments where troops had dug in about 100 yards east of Stockade Redan after the May 22 failure. Buckland's Approach was begun on May 30 and ran down into a ravine from a ridge some 150 yards north of the Graveyard road and ascended Fort Hill ridge. The approach got to within about twenty-five yards of the Rebel defenses, and mining operations then began.

Ewing's Approach advanced to within 150 yards of the stockade by June 3. Since most of the digging was done at night, the Confederates found themselves at a disadvantage, for they did not have extra powder or flares to light areas fronting their works. To slow the enemy, Confederates went out at night to dig trenches in front of the works. This provided a better field of fire and buffered the main defensive walls. They also buried booby-traps of explosives around the entire complex, to be detonated in case evacuation became necessary. Confederate officers ruled out sorties (the sending out of patrols) at night because they could not afford to risk having troops captured. As it was, they had to be careful not to stick their heads carelessly above the top of earthworks, for such recklessness could be fatal. The soldiers also had to be vigilant about removing cotton bales set on fire by Union artillery. Federal marksmen during the day and Union artillery at night kept pressure on the Confederates. There was a brief respite on June 10 when heavy rains shut down everything.

On June 14, artillerists in the Arkansas Appeal Battery, who had their one gun knocked out by Federal fire, ignored the sortie policy and went out that night armed with powder barrels and small shells, which they lobbed into Federal working parties, inflicting several casualties. A 10-inch mortar, transferred from South Fort, also proved effective for Confederates. Its 90-pound shells made life interesting for Union soldiers digging along the Graveyard road. Nevertheless, the approaches got ever closer. By the middle of June, Missouri soldiers on both sides were close enough to visit, exchanging insults and news and coffee for tobacco.

By June 20, Ewing's Approach was within a remarkable twenty feet of the outer front slope of Stockade Redan. The sap roller could be pushed no farther owing to obstructions and remained in place as a buffer against Confederate fire. From this forward point, the Federals moved right and left, building raised works high enough to allow riflemen to shoot down into the stockade. The Confederates began mining operations to undercut enemy structures, and the Yankees countermined. On June 24, the Confederates failed in an attempt to set off explosives. Two days later, they succeeded in setting off two explosions that stalled Federal mining operations.

Grant ordered the mining of the redan. Out of sight of most Confederates, Union soldiers dug a gallery to the north slope of the stockade. Much dirt had to be removed, and air holes dug to relieve the workers. The workers remained as silent as possible, avoiding use of tools that would make noises alerting the Rebels. Some 2,200 pounds of powder were packed into the mine for detonation.[8]

Giles Smith's brigade dug approaches to Green's Redan from the depths of a ravine up a ridge along different spurs, with each moving toward the redan. Hébert's Mississippi troops initially held this area, but in early June they were shifted to reinforce the Great Redoubt. Green's brigade came over from Fort Hill to take charge. The change did not thrill Green's Missourians and Arkansans because they had few digging tools, and the position was vulnerable to Union artillery fire. As a countermeasure, Confederates placed nearby a 20-pounder Parrott called "Crazy Jane" (so named because part of its barrel had been shot off, which gave shells fired from the gun erratic trajectories).

Smith's approach moved slowly until the Confederates succeeded in setting off mines in its vicinity. Smith sped up operations with cane sap rollers tied with wire and grapevines to divert enemy pressure. Green received a report of the increased activity from his hospital bed, where he was recovering from a wound received on June 25. He insisted on being released, returned to the redan, and, while looking at enemy lines through an embrasure, fell dead from a sniper's bullet. Thomas Dockery assumed command of the brigade. By July 2, the saps were close, and desperate Confederates threw shells and dug countermines.[9]

Southeast of Green's Redan, Thomas Ransom of McArthur's division, McPherson's corps, operated in June against Rebel works held by Mississippians of Forney's division. Union engineers thought this position important because, if breached, the rear of the Mississippians' position could be used by Union artillery to pin down Confederates and prevent counteroperations. With artillery support, the head of the approach got to within a few feet of the Confederate line by June 28. Mining operations were not suited to the terrain, so Ransom waited for Grant to issue orders to charge.[10]

The most significant approach in terms of location and effect proved to be John Logan's, dubbed "General Logan's canal" by some of the men, on the Jackson road. The target was the 3rd Louisiana Redan, confusingly referred to in Union reports and letters as Fort Hill. McPherson realized that taking the redan would fracture the Rebel line and cause the Confederates to give up their outer ring of defense. The path to the redan, the only feasible route, was a ridge, along which the Jackson road entered Vicksburg. From the redan, constructed on the north side of the road (across from the Great Redoubt), a span of open ground some 500 yards long spread to the east. Since Logan's division supplied most of the troops that worked on the approach, it bore his name.

Work began on May 26 about fifty yards southeast of the Shirley home, some 400 yards from the redan. The white Shirley structure became a siege landmark and survived the siege despite being pitted with bullets "like a man with smallpox." Logan's troops built a sap roller that had four wooden wheels and was three feet in diameter and one foot thick. The wheels were connected with wooden axles, pierced to allow propelling by wooden crowbars. The platform was so arranged that cotton bales surrounded the structure, protecting work details; some men operated the contraption, some dug, and others served as guards. The wheels made a racket when the thing moved, but the cotton and high banks on either side of the road provided good cover, and work proceeded quickly. Within three days, the approach, measuring eight feet wide by seven feet deep, had been extended well west of the Shirley home. Turpentine-soaked balls fired from Confederate guns occasionally started fires that were quickly extinguished.

On May 28, Confederate artillery fired at work details, but a Union battery at the Shirley house (dubbed the White House Battery) quieted the Rebels. During the exchange, McPherson lost a campaign veteran, the commander of the 8th Michigan battery, Captain Samuel De Golyer. By June 3, the approach had reached the crest of a knoll only 130 yards east of the redan. Andrew Hickenlooper, supervising the approach, ordered this position fortified and brought in cannon. Battery Hickenlooper contained three guns and prevented Rebel flanking fire.

Forney understood what was going on and requested reinforcements from Pemberton. Three regiments from Cockrell's Missouri brigade arrived, and one was given the job of holding Confederate lines flanking the road. The men watched nervously as the Yankee approach continued on past Battery Hickenlooper to within seventy-five yards of the redan. Hébert ordered his men to destroy the large sap roller that protected Federal workers. Wrapping turpentine-soaked cloth around their bullets, the Confederates fired hot missiles that soon set afire cotton bales on the roller. The tactic worked so well that the roller soon was nothing but a quartet of wheels. The Yankees quickly built another, five feet wide and ten feet long, and kept going.

As work proceeded, a strange structure emerged on the landscape south of Battery Hickenlooper. Built with railroad ties from the Southern Railroad, the structure was called Coonskin's Tower, after an Indiana sniper named Henry Foster, who wore a signature coonskin cap. By shooting from between the crossties, Foster and his comrades sent bullets down into the redan, making life miserable and tenuous for Hébert's troops. With Confederate artillery quieted by superior Union firepower, the Rebels had to rely on ineffective small-arms fire against the crossties.

By mid-June, the head of the approach was twenty-five feet from the face of the redan, near enough that Federal officers, fearing enemy night raids, canceled evening shifts. To protect workers, the fatigue parties dug infantry pits south and southwest of the main approach trench. The trenches were so close that Confederates discovered that when moonlight revealed their silhouettes, they could be subject to deadly Yankee fire. Meanwhile, Confederate bullets set afire another roller, again quickly replaced by Federal workers. By June 21, the new roller was just a few yards from the exterior slope of the redan, close enough for defenders to throw small shells into the midst of the Union work detail. As a countermeasure, Federals brought two 30-pound Parrotts to Battery Hickenlooper, and the guns soon knocked a hole in the redan, forcing the Louisianans to rebuild the wall at night. Lockett ordered a parapet built at the gorge of the redan to protect the rear. Near the redan's walls, Federals began mining preparations.

Volunteers, experienced coal and lead miners all, began driving a mining shaft underneath the redan's main wall. The entrance shaft extended into the earth for forty-five feet, and smaller openings were dug straight ahead and to either side of the main shaft for another fifteen feet. Digging was easy, and the firm earth did not require support beams. Engineers cut a hole in the bank along the side of the road so that diggers could dump dirt through the opening down into the ravine below. To counter Federal mines, Confederate defenders dug a shaft down through the flat ground within the redan. They could angle effectively in several directions because the ridge was so narrow. The countershaft frightened away Union work parties, but not for long. By June 25, the shafts underneath the Louisiana Redan had been completed.

The miners took 25-pound sacks of black gunpowder into the galleries and packed over two tons of powder, supplied by David Porter's fleet, into the main and side tunnels. After placing the explosives, workers packed dirt back into the shafts and filled the tunnels with heavy logs to keep the explosion impact from spreading too far, especially back into the approach works. Louisiana defenders suspected that something major was about to happen and threw lit shells to disrupt the Yankees.

McPherson informed Grant all was ready, and Grant ordered the detonation for 3:00 P.M. on June 25. Artillerists in proximity to the redan prepared to open fire as soon as they heard the explosion. Infantry poised to send volleys into enemy lines to hold back Confederate reinforcements while Union troops attacked through the breach. Meanwhile, Logan's troops waited for orders to launch a mass assault.

Since Union troops knew what was coming, silence fell over the redan area as clocks and watches approached 3:00. Jerome Dann of the 20th Illinois recalled: "I remember seeing birds fly over us and noted the unusual quiet. The dust lay thick and when stirred up hung in a thin cloud over us. The heat was intense." Hébert figured something was up, so he pulled all his troops, except the 43rd Mississippi, behind a traverse at the gorge. Three o'clock came and went and nothing happened, and Mississippians continued their vain efforts to find the enemy tunnels with a countermine.

Finally, at half past the hour, the earth around the redan raised upward like an oversized divot. One soldier penned a vivid description: "All at once a dead heavy roll, a hundred shouts, and you could see nothing but a black cloud of dirt and powder smoke, throwing the earth thirty or forty feet in the air, and about half of the wall rolled over the ditch as if turned by a ponderous plow. Instantaneous with this was the crack of a hundred cannon, as though they were all pulled off by one lanyard . . . while the infantry advanced with a yell that none but soldiers can give, rushed up the breastworks and a galling fire ensued between the rebs at the bottom and at the top. Our men tried hard to dislodge them and take possession of the fort, but it was too much." Through the haze created by dirt clouds, Illinois troops led the way up the remnants of the redan wall toward the breach. They found themselves in a crater about twelve feet deep and forty to fifty feet wide, shaped somewhat like a bowl. Hébert's troops, firing from behind the traverse, poured volley after volley into the blue wave, slowing the Union advance.

A soldier in the 20th Illinois described the charge: "The up-heaved earth was soft, and our feet sank deep into the loose dirt as we rushed over the dead and dying up the incline to the foot-wide crest of undisturbed earth, which, fortunately for the defenders of the Fort, remained to obstruct the on-slaught of the union forces. As many of the 20th as could fill the circular space at this narrow divide rushed forward ready to leap into the Fort, but we were met by the . . . ranks of Pemberton's veterans, with fixed bayonets and loaded muskets. The fighting at first was of the hand-to-hand order, and I recollect that the color-bearer of our Regiment forced his way to the summit in the midst of the fiercest of the conflict and stuck the foot of the flag pole in the dirt."

An Illinois regiment ran into the saucer-shaped hole, where on the west side dirt had piled high on the rim. From that direction, Confederate defenders poured continuous volleys and thrust bayonets at the closest Yankees. Federals snuggled up to the bank for protection. Timbers were brought in to build up the defensive position. Casualties mounted, and Logan wailed, "My God, they are killing my bravest men in that hole."

Union attacks came in shifts as infantry climbed traverse walls trying to get to Hébert's men, who in turn rolled lit shells down the incline. Federal soldiers "were torn and mangled in a manner seldom seen even in war." Logan's troops threw a few shells of their own, while men alternately loaded and fired over the crest that divided the opposing forces. Confederate cannon burst logs intended to protect Union infantry, and a mixture of splinters and shrapnel whirled through the air, causing numerous casualties.

While the maelstrom continued, a Missouri regiment rushed to the scene, and its colonel foolishly climbed the wall of the parapet, shouting encouragement to his men for a counterattack. He fell dead, and the defenders lost interest in exposing themselves to a similar fate. Louisianans and Missourians rolled more shells down among the Yankees with great effect. The Federals responded in kind, and the fight settled into a stalemate, with neither side anxious to take a risk. As evening came, Union commanders continued rotating regiments in and out of the crater, dividing men into small teams of shooters and loaders in order to keep up the onslaught. Rebel defenders likewise took turns in perpetuating the struggle.

During the night, the fighting continued unabated. Grant thought that if he could get his men into the rifle pits on the north side of the crater, a breakthrough on the Jackson road would be at hand. Hickenlooper received instructions to get two cannon inside the crater, from where they could blast Hébert's troops at the gorge. Heated fighting in the crater doomed that notion, and Grant decided that McPherson must recall his men. The Confederate line had not broken, but Federals could at least say they had pushed back the Rebel front. During the fighting, Grant lost 34 killed and 209 wounded, compared to 21 Rebels killed and 73 wounded, small numbers considering the bitter fighting. The circumstances dictated wild shooting over careful aiming, and lives were spared.

On June 27, McPherson told Hickenlooper to dig another shaft to the right of the crater, and work began the next day. Lockett ordered defenders to roll a barrel of powder forward and ignite it to break up earthworks protecting the miners. The resulting explosion did not work as Lockett hoped, and the digging continued. The Confederates settled for countermining, using black labor this time to prevent further loss of soldiers.

When McPherson heard that sounds of digging in the countermine were getting louder, he ordered workers to set explosives and notified Logan to get ready for more action. On July 1 at 3:00 P.M., the Federals detonated nearly two tons of powder. The explosion caused more damage than the first, severely impairing the left front, the right face, and the terreplein of the redan, leaving a thirty-foot-deep crater in its wake. The blast killed all but one of the black counterminers, the lone survivor landing inside Union lines, and Federal soldiers delighted in telling his story. When asked how high he went, he allegedly responded, "Dunno, massa, but t'ink about t'ree mile." Along the gorge line, falling dirt buried several Rebels. Many Confederates fell backward down the steep ravine to the rear of the redan, but most quickly recovered, grabbed the nearest rifle, and climbed back up, expecting to meet a blue wave coming their way.

As before, Union artillery boomed at the sound of the blast, and shells blew holes in the remaining walls, forcing Confederates to improvise with bags of dirt to keep openings plugged. Federal mortar fire added to Rebel problems, and Cockrell lost 8 killed and 48 wounded. As night fell, Union artillery fell silent, except for the mortars. The fighting continued until July 3 when flags of truce quieted action all along the lines. Cockrell's Missouri regiments had taken turns manning the trenches to keep the line intact. The Rebels suffered greatly from the mortar fire, losing 21 killed and 72 wounded between July 1 and July 3.[11]

On McClernand's front, the XIII Corps tried five approaches. Confederates had four major works fronting McClernand's lines from north to south: the 2nd Texas Lunette, the Railroad Redoubt, Square Fort, and the Salient Work. During planning stages, Federals prepared gabions and fascines and, before starting approaches, strengthened their own lines, paying special attention to parapets fronting artillery emplacements. Federal cannon on McClernand's front proved to be quite effective against Rebel works. Soldiers defending the 2nd Texas Lunette had to add a couple of feet of dirt to blunt the penetrating power of 30-pound Parrott shells.

To provide infantry protection for work parties, engineers supervised the construction of parallel lines running across the front of enemy works, as well as direct approaches. The fatigue detachments persevered through stifling heat and Confederate fire, and by June 19, when E. O. C. Ord replaced the sacked McClernand, the works along the corps's front were "constantly approaching the enemy." Ord, however, was not pleased.

When he arrived on the scene, Ord found shallow, narrow rifle pits and artillery pieces mostly where they had been in place on May 22. To cover himself, Ord blamed McClernand for not seeing to it that engineering standards for siege operations were followed. By June 25, Edwin Stanton's spy, Charles Dana, reported that trenches had been dug wider, connected up, and made more accessible for moving both artillery and men closer to Rebel works. Dana believed that within a week Ord would be able to "crown the Rebel lines with his artillery."

Serious approach work on the XIII Corp's front began when a work party started digging the A. J. Smith Approach at a point about 100 yards from the 2nd Texas Lunette. Within a few days, a second line was started about fifty yards south of the first and within the same ravine. The second line aimed at the salient, the angle of the lunette that jutted out at the Federals. Problems included rugged terrain that made sap rollers useless and ground harder than that found in other spots along the Rebel front. Eventually, workmen got the lines close enough to have them be connected, and Smith's sharpshooters made life uncomfortable for the Texans. Lockett ordered countermining measures that were ineffective.

By June 18, more level ground had been reached, and two sap rollers were employed to facilitate the approach. Most previous work had been at night, but, with smooth terrain ahead, the men now needed more protection. Rebel gunners tried, with limited success, to blow apart the rollers. Countermining continued, and by June 28 the Texans thought their tunnel was under the rollers, which were within three yards of the outer lunette bank. When the explosion came, however, the closest sap remained unharmed.

On July 1, the right approach neared a rise across the Baldwin's Ferry road from the lunette, and the other reached the crater caused by the explosion. A Mississippi artillerist picked up a smoothbore rifle, stuffed an artillery fuse down its barrel, and fired at the sap roller on the Union right approach, causing a fire that destroyed the roller. Yankee firefighting frustrated similar attempts to burn the other roller. The Rebels then tossed out an 18-pound shell that exploded against the roller, killing one Federal, and convincing others to let it burn. Mining and countermining continued as the Federals moved ever closer to the lunette walls, and the defenders continued rolling shells into the midst of the Yankees. Union officers prepared to counter with mortars.

An approach named after Eugene Carr targeted the Railroad Redoubt. As in the case of Smith's, this operation was two-pronged. The right approach began north of the railroad cut on June 2, to the east of the redoubt, while the left originated in a ravine southeast of the first. By mid-June, the ditches had been connected: the right trench was within 150 yards of the target; the left zigzagged down into a timber-choked ravine and up along a ridge, having progressed to within eighty yards of the redoubt. Pickets on both sides had a gentlemen's agreement not to fire at each other after dark, and this helped Federals working on a parallel connecting trench. One story went that an "inquisitive reb wishing to see what our men were doing, looked over the wall [of dirt], when one of [our] men gave him a spat on the head with a spade, and told him to keep on his own side of the fence." Actually, lackadaisical attitudes of the Confederates permitted the Union approach to get within 180 feet of the salient. Spreading out from the connecting trench to each side, the Federal parallel stretched for about 1,000 yards.

On June 25, attackers utilized a sap roller to move toward the salient. Rebels began countermining, and Yankees reacted with two guns of the 17th Ohio Battery. Small-arms fire however forced the Ohioans back. The night of July 2, Confederates detonated underground explosives, but the blast did little damage.

A third approach was undertaken in James Slack's sector on June 30 and bore his name. Designed to branch to the right of a parallel connecting trench, it was part of another approach named in honor of A. P. Hovey. Slack's approach targeted the portion of the Confederate line defended by the 23rd Alabama. The work parties reached to within thirty feet of enemy trenches. Union pickets suckered Alabama pickets into conversation as a cover for the operations, and when the Alabamians figured out the ruse, they started a firefight that lasted about two hours.

The approach against Square Fort did not get under way until late June because available engineers were preoccupied with other projects. This approach, too, involved two trenches, right and left lines that began southeast and south of the fort and came together some ninety feet southeast of target. On June 17, during the fighting on this front, Colonel Isham Garrott of the 20th Alabama, who had been thrown into the breach at Port Gibson, was killed, dying unaware that he had been promoted to brigadier general, effective May 28. The Confederates renamed the fort in his honor.

Hovey's approach got under way on June 23; on the twenty-eighth, Alabama pickets warned the lead diggers to pull back, but Union workers in turn warned of artillery bombardments to follow if they did. That threat kept the area quiet for a time. On July 1, Fort Garrott's defenders began countermining, and by July 3, when the digging stopped, the Yankees, using a sap roller, got to within sixty feet of the fort's face.[12]

The one approach that produced Confederate sorties was named for Lauman, whose division remained attached to the XIII Corps during the siege. Lauman's approach originated in the Hall's Ferry road area. Engineers decided that a ridge several hundred yards east of, and parallel to, the Salient Work provided the most feasible approach. Two artillery emplacements of two guns each provided cover for diggers. Confederates returned fire, but with little success. At that point, Rebel officers decided to try a sortie composed of volunteers. The men went out the night of June 1 and were beaten back by Union canister fire.

To secure the guns, Lauman ordered rifle pits constructed 200 yards to their front. He then ordered an attack to clear the ridge of Rebels. With the governor of Iowa and other dignitaries from that state looking on, Lauman sent the 3rd Iowa to lead the way and had a Wisconsin regiment provide support. Alfred Cumming's Georgians returned fire and contested the advance. Federal gunners quieted a Confederate battery, and the Georgians fled, giving Lauman's work details more security. Soon a parallel line extended to the sector of the Confederate line held by the 56th Georgia.

Cumming tried additional sorties, resulting in a pattern of firefights and nothing accomplished by his men other than bagging a few Federal prisoners taken by surprise. Federal lines drew ever closer; Union guns continued pounding down Rebel works; and Georgians and Tennesseans spent many hours rebuilding their battered defenses. Union infantry at one point set up an ambush, which Rebels managed to avoid; but the increasingly aggressive tactics by both sides led to an end of the sorties, for the Confederates were losing men and gaining nothing.[13]

The final approach on the far Union left was Herron's, named after General Francis J. Herron, whose division from the Department of the Missouri arrived at Warrenton on June 13. The chief engineer in that sector planned approaches against Confederates blocking the Warrenton road. Tableland sliced by ravines lay in front of Confederate works, ravines that provided the only cover for Federal digging parties. Approaches were developed on either side of Stout's Bayou, with artillery exchanges occasionally livening things up. On June 25, Herron's Missourians pushed forward to new trenches some 500 yards closer than from where they had started. Pemberton, alerted by Seth Barton, sent a portion of Cockrell's Missourians to help hold the line.[14]

Approach operations, all of which ended at whatever stage they were in on July 3 when surrender negotiations began, demonstrated the vigorous activities that defined the nature of the siege, from beginning to end. Soldiers did not merely sit behind defensive works and fire at each other until the Confederates ran out of food. Siege operations placed soldiers on both sides under stress and strain, as they worked in the hot Mississippi summer climate to approach enemy lines or repel attempts to break through defensive positions. Grant's army had the advantage from the beginning, since Federal reinforcements made it possible for Union workers to rotate and rest. Confederates had to tough it out as best they could, without any hope of help. Fraternization became common and provided refreshing breaks in the siege, especially for worn-out Confederates. Soldiers on picket duty visited at night, discussing all sorts of topics and swapping newspapers and food. Neither side found anything pleasing or romantic about that summer.

Pemberton's men and Vicksburg citizens endured and longed for an end to the shooting and suffering.[15]

Soldiers had varying reflections on their experiences. A Union infantryman described typical duties as "sharpshooting by day and picket duty by night, and digging in approaches and parallels all the time, while from dawn to dark balls and shells were going over us continually from both ways." Another declared, "We cannot call this fighting, it is merely artillery practice." Men improvised protection by placing timbers over trenches to keep out shells and hand grenades tossed by Confederate defenders. They also made woven baskets of grapevines to protect themselves while on picket duty.

The men accepted danger as a way of life. One soldier wrote, "One day is like another, firing is kept up all day and most of the night, with artillery and musketry, sometimes the artillery all opens along the line. I have no better way of expressing it than referring you to a thunderstorm. . . . Lots of our boys have stood close enough to the rebels to reach them with their bayonet, but instead of trying to do each other harm, they will talk to each other, swap knives and exchange chews of tobacco. Our officer says to him, 'Hello, old fellow, you will have to move your lines back, I have my men on that line.' 'All right,' said the rebel officer, and moved his men back without further words.' "

Shooting on the front line had many ramifications. Sore, bruised shoulders often resulted from extensive firing. Federals learned to shoot through holes in the works and then get out of the way quickly, for Confederate sharpshooters used the puff of smoke as a target. Team shooting involved men working in groups of three. One would shoot, another load, and the third slept, all rotating within each team's two-hour shift. They tired of it quickly. One Wisconsin soldier complained, "This going out once or twice a day to shoot at human beings like ourselves seems strong business for me." An Illinois sergeant wrote in his diary, "The weather is very warm and we keep under the shade as much as possible but our duties are so hard that we do not get to lie idle much. Fatigue duty, guard duty, and duty in the rifle pits all together give us enough to do." The men rested in "shebangs," which consisted of shelves "dug in the hill side, one foot deep and long enough to lie down, covered with a double roof of cane thatched."[16]

A Michigan soldier stationed along the Yazoo bluffs penned a description of soldiers digging earthworks. "Today we are throwing up a redou[b]t and constructing a covered road to it. Not covered over, I don't mean, but protected from the fire of an advancing enemy so that the redou[b]t and surrounding rifle pits are manned and relieved without compelling troops to pass under fire. In constructing these rifle pits every possible advantage is of course taken of the surface of the ground over which the enemy must pass. In the first place, a narrow ditch is cut with a jog [a notch or step] in one side and the dirt thrown out towards the foe, forming a sort of breastwork, so that the men may step up on the jog, take a deliberate aim over the bank which forms an excellent rest, fire and then step back into the deeper part of the ditch or rifle pit, completely under cover to reload."[17]

Some soldiers, bored to the point of acting stupidly, played absurd games of running along the top of works to see who could make it without being shot. A man might accept a dare to run out of the rifle pits, climb up and seize a clod of dirt, and run back to safety. On one such occasion, a soldier ran along high points around a Rebel fort and was descending to safety when a bullet thudded into his flesh, and he fell dead. A witness said in disgust, "A foolish sacrifice to adventure! Almost a suicide."[18]

Leisure time consisted of letter writing, playing chess, reading, studying the Bible and praying, playing cards (chuck luck was a popular game though it was hard to win and subject to frequent raids by officers), making camps more comfortable, and sending money home by the Adams Express Company, whose agents followed the army to offer their services. Occasional visits from governors and other dignitaries from home states offered pleasant diversions.

Most men embraced cleanliness, something that had been forsaken during the long weeks of campaigning prior to the siege. Lice, a common and persistent enemy, invaded their clothes, which had to be boiled to rid them of the pests. A soldier said that one of the cleanest men he knew got his clothes infected once by getting on a train crowded with soldiers in soiled uniforms. Men said they would rather fight Rebels than lice, which seemed more numerous.

Mosquitoes also invaded campsites, getting so bad inside tents at times that men exploded powder from cartridges in order to smoke out the insects. In a wry frame of mind, a soldier near Warrenton wrote his parents: "Last night one of them came into My tent & Attacked me. he grabed me by the throat & Began to knaw me, I got up Jumpt at my revolver And shot him through the head But did not fase him. So he Escaped carrying with him my Boots, hat, & 5,000 doll. In Green Backs."

Diet and sickness often went hand in hand. Soldiers in the area of blackberry bushes, which grew in abundance around Vicksburg, enjoyed cobblers, regrettably without cream. Too much fruit no doubt caused health problems familiar to the veterans. Fevers and diarrhea plagued most soldiers, who made occasional trips to hospitals, suffering not from wounds but from camp maladies. Their stays were not necessarily pleasant. One noted that when he was ill, and the sun shone in the tent, lice could be seen climbing onto the beds and holding dress parade. Hot days and humid night work increased sick rolls markedly. Water became precious; as time passed, river water became polluted "with ded horses muels and Cattle and all other kinds of filth."[19]

A few men actually found elements of romance in their siege experience. An Illinois chaplain remarked, "I know not how it is, but there is a strong fascination about the place of danger and it is singular to see with what an eager interest the pickets watch for the enemy; their eyes glisten, and they peep about with a stealthy movement like a cat." A Union artilleryman placed such thinking in perspective: "It seems strange how utterly indifferent men become to a shower of death."[20]

An Indianan living in "hoosier hollow," found mortar fire fascinating. "First we would see a dim flash as of distant lightning[,] then a ball of fire shoot up and commence flashing as the side in which the lighted fuse was turned toward us as the Shell turned over and over in ascending, it would turn slower and slower untill it had arrived at about an angle of 45 degrees from us, when it would commence descending, just at that moment we would hear the report of the Mortar and as the Shell was descending we would hear the buzzing noise it made, and usualy bursting near the ground and not far from our lines we would hear the report of the bursting Shell almost at the same instant it bursted."[21]

Other Union soldiers found that the sights and sounds of artillery "made every timid hair on our heads stand upright." The shelling wrought much tragedy, as shells and fragments dismembered even bystanders. One Iowan saw a female visitor to a Rebel fort lose most of one arm when a shell hit the area; he rationalized that the woman had no business being there. An Indianan, however, confided to his wife, "I fear that our shelling the city has killed many women & children. War is terrible enough without the sad work of destroying the innocent."

Their hearts had been touched in other ways earlier, as when Confederate prisoners taken during the May 19 assault had been marched to the river and ultimately transported to Northern prisons. Groups of worried local women and children watched, hoping for a glimpse of a loved one. Some Federals laughed, but others "felt they had a right to expect our sympathy, for we have mothers and sisters at home and God only knows how soon they may be weeping our loss." A soldier who visited an aged widow behind Union lines disapproved of taking the private property of such a person, who had no relations in the Confederate army. The siege produced much soul-searching among Union troops.[22]

In their letters, many Federals invoked patriotic themes and cast aside earlier worries about the Emancipation Proclamation to embrace Lincoln's vision of the war as a fight for black freedom. A Missourian wrote his mother: "I feast a great deal on the prospects of a future glory which is soon to pervade this land and make glad the heart of many thousands that have hither too been kept under bonds of oppression & misery." He delighted in seeing slaves who left their masters or were "sauntering round & kicking up their heels purficly unmanageable by their masters if they under take to correct or control them they either remonstrate or run away." He pitied the privations of average Southerners, blaming their troubles on slave owners who had prospered "by the sweat and toil & unrewarded labour of an oppressed race of humin beings whome they have treated as brute beasts depriveing them of every thing sacred or divined not only extorting from them all their unconditional labour but ringing from them every principal of justice, marriage virtue & even life its self all has been looked upon with impunity."[23]

Their military successes made most Union soldiers more intolerant than ever of peace advocates in the North. A frustrated Illinoisan wrote, "It is a great price the Country is paying to suppress this rebellion, and it makes the wickedness of all the history which has led to this rebellion and so to the necessity of this War seem very great. What hell can be punishment enough for [former U.S. president James] Buchanan? And, talking about hell, our Soldiers would like to kindle one for some people in Illinois and may one day do something towards it. Knowing as we do how the people down here have glossed over the treasonable utterances of [Clement] Vallandingham [sic], we don't admire the men who wish to make a fuss about the mild and inadequate punishment which has befallen him?"[24]

But Grant's string of victories had not turned Union soldiers who considered themselves Democrats into Republicans. A soldier from Lincoln's home state of Illinois said plainly, "Men Opposed to the Abe Lincon gang As I under stand all those who does not agree with Abe & his gang ar Cauled Coper Heads[.] if that is a Coper Head, 3 Fourths of the Men in the Army are Coperheads." Another soldier did not go quite that far: "I care nothing for the Negroes. I am for Union and that only, and if they [the abolitionists] was down here a while they would soon learn to care nothing for Slavery so the[y] could put down the Rebillion the easiest way that would soote them best."[25]

As young soldiers always do to relieve the stresses of war, many focused on humor and found it in creative ways. Members of the 49th Indiana intentionally cheered long and loudly one night, and soon the air was filled with zinging ramrods launched from Rebel rifles. Panicky Confederates, expecting a charge, had hurriedly fired a volley, sending ramrods still in rifle barrels on a fast trip into no-man's land. At other times, humor came from unexpected sources. When the governor of Iowa, Samuel Kirkwood, and other state dignitaries visited with constituent soldiers, the state's adjutant general, no doubt to impress the men, "crawled along trenches to a picket post where he borrowed a Springfield [rifle] and poking it under the head log, the muzzle pointed out over Vicksburg, pulled the trigger. As usual a quick response came from the other side, and a rebel bullet struck a tree with the well-known 'spat,' ten feet above the General's head. This caused the gallant Iowan to drop his gun, fall flat in the ditch, and with an: 'I tell you, boys, that was close wasn't it?' and make a hasty retreat on all fours." The soldiers got a hearty laugh and speculated on how this politician would later enhance the incident.[26]

The realities of war could also elicit callous racial humor. An Iowan described how, during an artillery duel on June 17, a Confederate shell came through a ravine and into a colonel's tent, crashing into a cracker box there and coming out underneath the colonel's tethered horse. A sick black servant occupied the tent at the time, and he rushed out "on all fours, he was too frightened to stand up. He looked wild and he was the whitest black nigger I ever saw. A dog bounded after him yelping from fright and the colonel's horse was trying to see how high he could kick with both feet. When I got through laughing I got behind a rock." Another Iowan documented a June 4 adventure: "One shell comes down and bursts right over our heads, one piece flying into the wash tub where our nigger was washing our clothes and cuting a hole in my shirt, and scaring the nigger till he almost turned white."[27]

Some soldiers monitored the activities of black soldiers in the army. One noted, "Yesterday a large number of negro soldiers were at work in the rifle pits close to the rebel forts. The rebels are always exasperated at the sight of negros in our employ." The Confederates began throwing shells by hand, and Union artillery answered. This Illinoisan admitted that he respected black soldiers more than he ever thought he would. Exhibiting prejudice in other regards, he went on, "They are superior to the Irish and far more likely to make useful citizens. Of course I refer to the well known *lower class*. The protestant Irish are . . . superior to the Scotch and English." Many whites appreciated blacks whose labor freed whites to fight: "They seem to thoroughly understand that on the success of the Union Armies depends the question of their freedom."[28]

Upriver at Federal bases on the Louisiana side, many blacks suffered greatly even as they were anxious to leave their familiar plantation world as a result of Grant's campaign. A Pennsylvania soldier, who arrived in June from the Eastern front, found a region "abounding in Negroes, vermin, reptiles and filth. There are thousands of escaped contrabands of all sexes, sizes and colors gathered here. It is very questionable if they have made much by running away. They appear to be less able to stand the camping out than the soldiers. Most of them have coughs or colds and nearly all the dysentery. There is a party of them engaged all the time in digging graves, and if they don't take better care and be more cleanly the place will soon be nothing but a graveyard. They are far better looking Negroes than the ones we have in the north and if they were fixed up and dressed as well, would be a very respectable looking people." The war for freedom had produced a large populace of new citizens whose future was quite uncertain.[29]

Others affected by the siege included Union soldiers who served on the periphery. Along the northern flank of Vicksburg, an Ohio artilleryman bragged to his family about the comfort he and his comrades enjoyed. They could "go to bed when we please and get up when we please; No roll calls to attend and we can go to the landing for a bath whenever the notion suits us. We are not in the least afraid of an attack, but even if they should come to[o] strong for us, we could limber up and retreat to the landing when we would be under the cover of the gunboats" along the Yazoo. He complained though about a "wild goose chase" sortie to the Big Black; sorties became a common source of complaint among soldiers sent to check on signs of Johnston's men. And plenty of discomfort was experienced in the Yazoo area. Bad water, mosquitoes, sand-flies, ticks, beetles, ants, and many varieties of worms combined to make for rough days and sleepless nights.[30]

The bluff area became almost barren of homes. Before the Yankees arrived, the area had been a landing for Confederate supplies and occupied by Rebel defenders. Now, as then, campsites covered most of the landscape; most homes were in ashes. New arrivals learned that house burning was an unwritten rule, adhered to with few exceptions. Whatever Grant or Sherman or other generals might think, "we confiscate everything and drive the people off before us farther into Dixie."

Residents who retained their homes were viewed with suspicion. They might claim pro-Union sympathies, and they might be short of clothing and food; but Federals suspected they would be pro-Confederate if Pemberton's men called the tune. Those with proven Northern connections were given more leeway, but not necessarily trusted. In areas they controlled, despite the presence of a trapped Rebel army and another Confederate force outside the works, the Federals felt comfortable with their situation, mainly because reinforcements and matériel arrived on a regular basis.[31]

To the east along the Big Black line, troops watching for Johnston were mostly bored. A soldier noted, "Two thirds of the time we have nothing to do. Of the rest, one third, we spend with gun in hand as videts watching the roads and bypaths leading towards Vicksburg. Our orders with regard to passengers are very strict. At night we strain our eyes upon every suspected path, each hoping to be so fortunate as to capture a rebel dispatch bearer." Some men sympathized with locals, for the army had stripped away food and much water. No doubt some shared their rations.[32]

South of Vicksburg, pickets far from the front sometimes experienced the ramifications of the siege thanks to the long-range capabilities of cannon and small arms. They captured stray Rebels and moved their camps around; but they complained that they were "nearly all the time engaged, at something and to keep us awake we have the music of shells, canister, grape, and musket balls all around and over us and some times right among us that is kept up all the time day and night." These men could see the enemy forts, which meant they could be seen — hence their efforts to keep moving. They had orders to keep locals from leaving the city, a policy based on the assumption that holding people in Vicksburg meant food supplies would be exhausted sooner.[33]

Some Union nurses and physicians experienced the siege from the river, occasionally traveling the waterfront with a yellow hospital flag flying above the boat. A nurse observed Rebel prisoners being transferred to Young's Point: "A more distressed lot of human being[s] I never saw. I felt sorry for them if they were rebels and I wished there was no such things as war." She also saw Grant's canal, "the celebrated ditch," and "a good many of our troops and also contrabands. All had nice beds of cotton strewed all over the camp. We looked through a glass and saw Vicksburg plainly. The streets are entirely deserted, as the people, we were told, were all burrowed in the sides of the hills and our army was shelling them, poor things." She wanted a cannon ball lying in the sand along the banks for a souvenir but learned it was too heavy for a war prize.[34]

Captured Union troops saw the siege from both sides of the lines. Confederates herded an Illinoisan and several comrades into Vicksburg near Pemberton's headquarters, and later fenced in an area around the jail downtown. An inmate recalled, "The jail was a good sized two story building very strongly built & composed of Brick[.] a small cook house of the same material filled one corner of the yard and from this important institution twice a day they gave us a piece of cornbread and a small piece of India Rubber Beef and what they call coffee could be made from the bran of the meal. A few Negroes performed the cooking operation." These men were soon paroled and sent across the river, where, left on their own, they crossed back into friendly lines.[35]

On the Louisiana side of the Mississippi River, many of Grant's troops guarded supply depots and staging areas, and also watched for Confederates who might try to escape across the river. Occasionally, they had to dodge Confederate shell fragments raining among them, but otherwise they had a much easier time of it than comrades conducting siege operations. One soldier admitted that "my conscious smites me when I think that I am laying here tough and harty."[36]

Union reinforcements arriving from the Eastern Theater drew mixed reviews and had varying opinions of the Vicksburg area. A Midwestern soldier observed: "They look well and are generally more intelligent than our western troops." Others found them arrogant. New Hampshire troops sweltered in the oppressive summer heat along the Yazoo bluffs; they just hoped to avoid illness and get out of this "*awful hole*" alive. Massachusetts soldiers worked on fortifications at Snyder's Bluff without too much complaint, but they did get nervous about having to dwell among numerous snakes, especially because "almost every day we heard of some soldier dying from the bite of a rattler."[37]

Within Confederate lines, the siege became a matter of endurance for Pemberton's men and Vicksburg's civilians. Most soldiers remained determined until the end; others reached their limit and simply gave up. Confederate desertions convinced Grant's men that victory was certain. As early as late May, one Union soldier wrote, "There is not a day but there is men coming into our lines from Vicksburg. And they all say that they are scarce of provisions. They will have to give it up soon." The 30th Iowa received the surrender of a Confederate captain and his company in mid-June, and as the news drifted along Union lines, Grant's soldiers were heartened at the prisoners' "most miserable account of the sufferings of the citizens and Soldiers inside of Vickburg[;] the [Confederate] Capt says his heart is as strong in the cause of the Confederacy as ever, but that he was not a going to stay in there to be starved to death. he says the men will all desert in a short time if the Commander does not surrender the place." Some Confederates asked Union soldiers across the way about the treatment of prisoners, and if they could go to Camp Chase prison in Ohio. Camp Chase was hardly a paradise, and men asking to be sent there had certainly reached the breaking point.[38]

Confederates who stuck it out most often thought and wrote about the lack of food, though they also touched on routine matters like sorties, the oppressive heat, and welcome rainstorms. Otherwise, they read and played cards and amused themselves as best they could, maintaining remarkable senses of humor under the circumstances. A Mississippian noted the only time he had plenty to eat was when an enemy shell hit a mule. Dead animal carcasses, though, created a stench described as "intolerable."

The human body's reaction to deprivation surprised soldiers. Cases of diarrhea seemed to decline as rations declined; in fact, some noticed victims of the disorder actually gained weight. One sarcastically noted that it just proved "we all eat too much." Some were fortunate enough to be camped near vegetable gardens, which they tried to keep productive. Fellow Confederates raided the gardens at night, often destroying plants rather than leaving them to produce more. As time went on, the men had to do without meat and then bread. Daily fare became small amounts of bacon, peas and sugar, pea bread, and corn and rice meal. Stories persisted that some Confederates and Vicksburg civilians ate rats, and it probably did happen, though the practice was not widespread. One diarist insisted that the price per rodent reached a dollar and that demand outpaced supply.[39]

The men especially remembered pea meal and pea bread. Corn, when available, was ground into meal for various purposes, usually cornbread, so someone came up with the idea of using more plentiful peas in the same manner. After a Vicksburg mill ground up the peas, the meal "was accordingly mixed with cold water and put through the form of baking; but the nature of it was such, that it never got done, and the longer it was cooked, the harder it became on the outside, which was natural, but, at the same time, it grew relatively softer on the inside, and, upon breaking it, you were sure to find raw pea-meal in the centre."[40]

Early in the siege, Rebels did not realize how rare supplies of meat would become, so following the two May assaults, and subsequent artillery barrages by the Federals, dead horses and mules abounding inside Confederate lines were not viewed as sustenance. Details gathered up carcasses and hauled them to the river, and soon Union troops on Grant's southern flank began reporting hundreds of dead animals floating south down the Mississippi. Later, mule meat became acceptable fare, a Vicksburg newspaper describing it as "sweet, savory and tender, and as long as we have a mule left we are satisfied our soldiers will be content to subsist on it." "Wharf-rats" (muskrats) also became a valuable delicacy. In addition to being a garbage dump, the river, upstream from dumping areas, provided drinking water for many Confederates. Details hauled the precious liquid from the river, and the torrid summer heat made it distasteful in a hurry. The men of necessity drank it quickly, before it could cause stomach ailments.[41]

While many of Pemberton's men knew they were fighting insurmountable odds, they remained surprisingly optimistic. Events like the successful smuggling of 200,000 percussion caps into the lines on June 16 raised hopes. Brave adventurers like Lamar Fontaine brought such supplies in, as well as messages from the outside world, which seemed far away to Pemberton's trapped soldiers. Fontaine traveled from Jackson to the Mississippi and rowed a dugout canoe along the east bank of the river until reaching the city safely. He informed Pemberton of Johnston's buildup, of Robert E. Lee's victory at Chancellorsville, and of Bragg's army coming to help. Such news, even if only partially true, led men to think that "evidently we are expected to hold on some time longer, but it is dangerous to depend on it. God alone can enable us to do so, & principally by keeping back the enemy."

Troops behind the front lines dug shebangs into the sides of the bluffs, but they had to be more careful than the enemy because shelling from the river in their rear could be even more dangerous than cannon fire from the front. They looked forward to evenings when fire usually slackened; they then carried on their good-natured banter with the Yankees. Many got so used to the noise that they could not sleep in the silence that followed the surrender. They also treasured transfers to the relatively safer right flank.[42]

As time passed, many Confederates who stayed the course battled their feelings as patriotism faded. The Richmond government seemed immensely distant and unconcerned. One soldier complained, "I feel that the President has shamefully neglected us in every particular." Those who feared they would not survive, but refused to consider surrender, instructed wives to rear their children in the "nurture of the Lord," and to discipline the little ones strongly, preparing them for a hard life. They would be inheriting a world "uncharitable, cold and unfeeling."[43]

Others observed scenes that stirred patriotic feelings and caused them to lash out at those willing to give up the fight. A Mississippi soldier became "heart sick to see the condition of the women and children in Vicksburg." Damaged homes, food shortages, and living underground brought great burdens, but their resolve was "enough to turn the hearts of true Southerners to steal [steel] against the savage horde doing this; but instead of this thousands of our people have gone to the enemy and are now aiding the enemy in their work of destruction. A great many more weak kneed patriots who are despairing and are willing to make peace on the enemies own term." He applauded those who remained "firm in their determination to drive the cruel invader from our soil."

The same soldier soon expressed despair, however, at a life "most miserable under the most tormenting suspense[;] we are compelled to remain in our rat holes all day, and what little exercise we get we take at night. It is not sufficient to keep us up." After breakfast, he and his fellow Confederates stayed low until supper, then came out and stretched. And on it went, men getting worn down by inactivity and rations "short and not good." Some men resorted to "cooking and eating young cane and various kinds of weeds." Siege realities often made patriotism tenuous at best.[44]

Religion provided solace to many depressed Confederates. A Missourian wrote in mid-June, "The birds are warbling their morning melodies and all nature seems to be happy. Man alone is arrayed against each other. It is one of those beautiful Sabbath mornings that makes the heart swell in gratitude to almighty God for his blessings on the human race, a portion of whom He is now punishing for their national and individual sins. May God's blessing abide with us through this day and soon deliver us from the foe, that is endeavoring to dispoil our homes and wrench from us those rights so dear to the human heart—freedom and independence." The soldier went on to say that he hoped the Confederates would soon be delivered from their "prison."[45]

The routines of the siege did not necessarily dull Confederate determination. One soldier insisted that "troops are in fine spirits and determined to hold Vicksburg or die in the trenches." Chances to fight back fueled adrenaline. When friendly artillery set cotton bales on fire in front of Federal works, Pemberton's men reveled in shooting at Yankees trying to extinguish the blazes. Sometimes generals wandered through the maze of trenches, offering the men encouragement or telling them to sleep on their arms in anticipation of an enemy assault.

The men took turns on guard duty but had orders not to leave the trenches, and not to dispose of clothes, since there were no replacements. Dead along the lines were buried in shallow graves with little or no ceremony. Examples of bravery abounded, perhaps none more poignant than that of the young teenager who volunteered to take canteens from one area of Confederate works to another where a man was suffering with a severe fever. The boy almost made it but fell, hit by several shots from Union lines. Some ill Confederates who refused to leave the trenches died at their post without suffering wounds; they succumbed to siege conditions. Common sacrifices created a camaraderie that strengthened morale.[46]

As June drifted by, shadows of hopelessness spread over Confederate lines. One Rebel noted that he almost regretted to hear of progress by Robert E. Lee's army, for if Mississippi fell, it did not matter what Lee did. Confederate leaders seemed to have gone "clean daft." Even if the city should be saved, this soldier would always blame Richmond for the suffering because in his view only Federal incompetence had kept Vicksburg from falling already. Staunch symbols of the besieged city were vulnerable to Union shelling; the imposing Warren County Courthouse, standing on a bluff overlooking the river, took a shell that smashed through the roof, doing considerable interior damage and cracking the floor. The courthouse survived, but the damage seemed to underscore the plight of Pemberton's army.

Civilians, too, experienced the downward spiral of the city's fortunes. Aside from horrendous wounds suffered from enemy artillery, Vicksburgians had to deal with food and supply shortages of all types. Scarcities caused prices to soar ever higher, and items that had once cost a few cents or a few dollars were priced beyond the means of most. In late June, flour sold for $600 a barrel, biscuits at $8 a dozen, and pies at $4 each. Daily rations for soldiers continued to shrink, consisting at one point of a quarter pound of bacon and of flour or rice flour, an eighth of a pound of sugar, one-twelfth of a quart of peas, and one-fiftieth of a gallon of molasses. Civilians likely subsisted on similar portions.[47]

Inside the city, available building and home space quickly was converted to hospital use, forcing interactions between soldiers and civilians. Large numbers of soldier patients suffered from battle wounds and illness because of exposure and food and water shortages. Using private homes as hospitals sometimes tested Pemberton's diplomatic talents, but most citizens cooperated, and those who did not were often coerced. The places stayed busy and were not immune to shelling. Doctors and civilian hospital workers occasionally suffered wounds.

Hospital scenes varied and were often gruesome. Surgeons were routinely covered with blood and wielded knives and saws as if on an assembly line. One soldier left a vivid description of common amputation surgery: "They were applying chloroform to his mouth and nose. He now becomes insensible and seems to rest in sweet sleep. The surgeon, whose duty it is to perform the bloody job, rolls up his sleeves and takes a drink of brandy to strengthen his nerves. A tight cord is passed around the leg — then the gleaming knife cuts through the flesh all around — a flap of skin and muscle is turned back — then with a strong stroke the knife cuts down to the bone and next the saw with quick stroke completes the job and the leg is removed — the artery having been tied with a small cord, the flap is then turned down over the stump and a few stitches complete the job." The leg was tossed onto a macabre pile in the yard.[48]

Women worked tirelessly in the hospitals: "They seemed to know no cessation in their days and nights of watchfulness and care. Without noise — without display — meekly and faithfully they went forth upon their pious and holy mission, like ministering angels, carrying balm and healing to the poor soldier, cheering his hope of recovery, or soothing the last moments of expiring life. These were 'Sisters of Mercy' — a sisterhood of the Catholic Church. Their noble and Christian devotion to the cause of suffering and humanity throughout the South, during the war, can never be forgotten." These observations, written by a Missourian after the war, demonstrated how women's war roles had special meaning in Southern memories.[49]

Similar tributes noted young women, "fearless of the storm of iron and lead, penetrating every portion of the city, as they attended to the necessities of their brave, wounded and dying protectors. The annals of history can furnish no more brilliant record than did the heroic women of Vicksburg during this fearful siege." Many soldiers "bade farewell to earth amid the thunder and din of the siege, feeling the soothing pressure of soft hands upon their clammy brows, and the glance of tender, pitying eyes gazing into the failing light of their glazing orbs, as these ministering angels hovered about the lowly cots of the dying soldiers."[50]

Civilians in general had memorable experiences during the siege. Most lived in caves, venturing out when the shelling lightened up to hasten to their homes and assess damage or obtain clothes and other items. Cave life and furnishings were not comfortable. A woman described her cave home as having "two entrances. Where it rounded at the back was an alcove; there my mother and the younger children could lie down at night. Three or four boards and a brown blanket made their bed, and every single morning the brown blanket had to be hung out to dry. My dress would be wet, our hands would be beaded with moisture. I slept in an old chair, my father in a broken-armed rocker." A nearby cistern provided water.[51]

Groups of citizens occupied "communal caves." One such complex "was shaped like the prongs of a garden rake, the five excavations from the street or road all terminating in a long central gallery, so that in case any one of them should collapse, escape could be made through the inner cave and its other branches. The entrance galleries at either end were reserved for servants and cooking purposes, and the intervening galleries and inner central gallery were occupied as family dormitories, separated from each other by such flimsy partition of boards, screens, and hangings as could be devised." Dangers "abolished the unwritten law of caste. The families of planters, overseers, slave-dealers, trades people, and professional men dwelt side by side, in peace if not in harmony. By common consent a narrow passageway was kept always open beside the tent-like dormitories, and in the main cave a central space was set apart as common meeting ground." On that ground, kids played, women sewed, men swapped news, and all prayed.[52]

Any day could prove adventurous, as when shells suddenly came down and exploded in or near homes. Shrapnel, glass, and wood sprayed all around, knocking down plaster on the inside walls. A woman who experienced such an event and survived it frantically wiped dust from her eyes and hair and then noticed fire. With the help of a servant, she managed to extinguish the blaze. Other incidents included a street vendor cut in half by a shell and a woman returning to her home from hospital duty being beheaded, her daughter dying a few weeks later from the shock. Such were the traumas that beset civilian Vicksburg.[53]

The siege prompted many adaptations and odd circumstances. A young woman recalled slaves being brought into town to prevent their capture. Wounded and healthy soldiers crowded around homes, some sleeping on the ground, and listened to families talking inside, doubtless wishing they were home with their families. Women made clothes from homespun material, cooked without flour, made sweet potato coffee from dried peels, and mostly lived on bacon and cornmeal. Many lived "like rats shut in a hole. Food became scarcer and harder to procure." Corn whiskey was the only medicine, and it was "frightful in strength and effect." A lady who tried to open a restaurant found quickly that hungry soldiers took what they wanted. Cannon reverberations broke windows and mirrors, and shells cut trees several centuries old. Dead bodies could be seen floating in the Mississippi, and fish could be seen gnawing at corpses. Some people who heard about this refused to eat fish caught in the river after the siege ended.[54]

The city of Vicksburg, battered off and on since the summer of 1862, deteriorated at an accelerated pace as the siege wore on. By late June, a

Louisiana soldier noted that the area seemed to have been "visited with a terrible scourge. Signs wrenched from their fastenings; houses dilapidated and in ruins, rent and torn by shot and shell; the streets barricaded with earth-works, and defended by artillery, over which lonely sentinels kept guard. The avenues were almost deserted, save by hunger-pinched, starving and wounded soldiers, or guards lying on the banquettes, indifferent to the screaming and exploding shells. The stores, the few that were open, looked like the ghost of more prosperous times, with their empty shelves and scant stock of goods, held at ruinous prices." In the finer parts of town, "palatial residences were crumbling into ruins, the walks torn up by mortar-shells, the flower-beds, once blooming in the regal beauty of spring loveliness, trodden down, the shrubbery neglected."[55]

John Pemberton, the general whose decisions had led to the siege, endured a growing sense of helplessness and loss of hope. He and his men had moments of cheer, as when Confederate artillery set on fire the Union ironclad *Cincinnati*. Never mind that the Federals salvaged the vessel and eventually had it back in service. The incident offered a glimmer of success. An increasingly despondent Pemberton knew that true relief could only come from beyond Vicksburg, and with every passing day only the occasional delivery of firing caps by intrepid couriers brought any contact with and news from the outside world. Jefferson Davis toyed with sending reinforcements from Robert E. Lee, but Lee resisted, insisting he could do more for Pemberton by applying pressure in the East; and so for that, and other reasons, he invaded Pennsylvania. The bottom line became apparent: Pemberton and his men had been left to their own devices, and Richmond could do little more than press the intransigent Johnston.

Jefferson Davis worried over the siege, the ultimate outcome of which was all too apparent. He wrote Lee that Johnston's refusal to attack Grant before Grant began receiving reinforcements had been a severe mistake, as Lee had predicted. All reports indicated that the Union lines were getting stronger daily, and any chance of a direct assault by Johnston had disappeared. Davis urged Bragg to send troops from Tennessee, for it seemed logical that some of the hordes going downriver to join Grant must be from William Rosecrans's army. Unlike the Confederates, however, Union officers could shift troops and raise and send more troops without materially weakening positions elsewhere. Davis realized, too, that no matter how many men he might find and send to Johnston, Johnston would not do anything with them. Like a physician waiting for a patient to die, Davis hoped for some kind of miracle and braced himself for the loss of Vicksburg.[56]

While the armies faced each other across siege works, military action elsewhere erupted frequently, both close by and miles away. Union troops at such places as Young's Point, an important supply base, kept pesky Louisiana Confederates at bay. In a June 15 skirmish near Richmond, Confederates retreated from an attack, leaving frustrated and angry Union pursuers behind. Federal soldiers complained that the enemy did a "cowardly act, which they had done once before," when they fired from windows and behind houses occupied by women and children, forcing the Yankees to charge rather than risk shooting civilians. After running off the Confederates, they sent the women and children back to Young's Point and burned the neighborhood.[57]

Memphis had to be kept secure to facilitate the transfer downriver of incoming reinforcements and supplies. Stephen Hurlbut, commanding the area, sent cavalry to check on enemy activities and to keep Confederate cavalry commander James Chalmers from interfering with the Memphis and Charleston Railroad, still a vital Union supply route. Chalmers was more concerned about protecting crops in North Mississippi than in conducting offensive operations. Perhaps hypocritically, however, Joseph Johnston encouraged Chalmers to disrupt Grant's Mississippi River supply line.

Chalmers sent a brigade to carry out this mission, and the Confederates coerced one steamer into surrendering. After emptying the vessel of cargo and passengers, they burned the boat. When boats from the Mississippi Marine Brigade came by, the Rebels held their fire since these vessels were armed. The marine brigade had been sent back to the Mississippi to escape the falling water level of the Tennessee. One of the marine brigade boats fell behind, and Chalmers's troops fired on it from above the river village of Austin. An angry Charles Ellet got the news, brought his flotilla back to Austin, and sent out patrols that killed three, wounded twelve, and captured three, while losing two killed and nineteen wounded. Ellet then ordered his men to burn the entire town. Taking charge personally, "Ellet sent the torchbearers ahead to burn the school, where books still lay open, and where problems in arithmetic, scratched upon blackboards, still waited to be solved. As the boats shoved off from the smoldering town, the academy burst into flames, belching smoke from every door and window." One of Ellet's officers called the incident an "unmilitary act" and said that "the sad scene of women and children left alone with their burning houses slowly eating away all hope" would forever be etched in his memory.[58]

Aside from protecting Memphis and Mississippi River bases, Grant worried most about Joseph E. Johnston. Reports indicated Johnston had around 24,000 men; he actually had 12,000 around Canton and 10,000 in Jackson. As the siege progressed, Grant paid close attention to securing his Big Black line to protect the rear of his army and to guard the Mechanicsburg corridor, where he expected Johnston to approach in order to help Pemberton break out. Union troops destroyed Confederate earthworks, bridges and trestles between the Big Black and Bolton, and track to the east toward Jackson. Federal cavalry occasionally skirmished with Rebel horsemen, but Union raids on the countryside east and northwest of Vicksburg kept supplies out of Johnston's hands; and Union engineers supervised the construction of rifle pits and artillery emplacements on the west bluffs of the Big Black near the old bridge. Grant even sent an ill-fated cavalry expedition into south-central Mississippi to attack the New Orleans, Jackson and Great Northern and the Mobile and Ohio railroads to frustrate Johnston's logistics. The raiders were captured, but the episode demonstrated to Confederates that Grant paid great attention to detail.[59]

Grant sent Frank Blair with an expeditionary force of six brigades along the Mechanicsburg corridor, and along the way Blair was alarmed to hear scouts report that A. P. Hill, from Robert E. Lee's Army of Northern Virginia, and his division had arrived to reinforce Johnston. Blair continued, but Grant had second thoughts. While looking at area maps, Grant concluded that if he were Johnston, he would cross the Big Black and fall on Blair's flank and rear. So he ordered Blair to return, no doubt pleasing the troops. During the trip, an Iowan noted: "Today was the hottest day I ever saw. Our whole days march was through a vast field of corn down the Yazoo bottom. We could get no water untill about 2 P.M. when we came to a large steam mill system where we rested about an hour. If thare ever is a man who will go to Hell by the private request-publicly expressed by a soldier[,] Genl Blair goes thare without a dissenting voice."[60]

Johnston received reports of Union activity and occasionally sent patrols to check their veracity, but the Confederates arrived too late to deal with Blair. Nevertheless, Rebel riders chased away Union cavalry sent to burn a railroad bridge on the Mississippi Central, one of Johnston's supply arteries. Meanwhile, John C. Breckinridge's division arrived in Jackson; Johnston now had 28,000 men. When added to Pemberton's 30,000, the total gave the Confederates a brief 7,000 man advantage over Grant, but Grant had many more on the way. Several miles and Grant's army separated the two Rebel forces, and Johnston had to be the catalyst if Confederates were to take advantage of this narrow window of opportunity. Admittedly, it would have been difficult to coordinate actions with Pemberton, but Johnston, despite reinforcements, seemed uninterested.[61]

Grant continued to send out patrols and then decided to check on the corridor himself; with Charles Dana and an escort, he went by steamer up the Yazoo. Grant soon became sick and retired to a room inside the boat's cabin. The incident seemed innocent enough; Grant had not been feeling well before the trip. The pressures of command, the unhealthy conditions around Vicksburg, a virus of some sort, any of these may have caused his illness. In later years, a newspaperman named Sylvanus Cadwallader, wrote that Grant was drunk. Tales of Grant's excessive drinking, attributed to a low tolerance of alcohol and some prewar disappointments, plagued him for many years. Though there were denials that Cadwallader was even present, another story, from a different source, surfaced that on a second trip Grant had become inebriated. The stories, written after Grant had become a national figure, and therefore vulnerable to slander, are unconvincing.

While Grant's concerns about Johnston never went away, he had other worries, such as reinforcing his positions at Young's Point and Milliken's Bend. Confederates under General John Walker attacked the latter position as part of Richard Taylor's plan to attack Milliken's Bend, Lake Providence, and Young's Point on June 7 to reduce pressure on Pemberton. U.S. Colored Troops and naval vessels beat off Walker's division after a fierce fight that produced accusations of atrocities by both sides, a rather common occurrence when black Union troops fought Confederates. The Louisiana offensives failed because Confederates could not combat the Federal navy, which provided firepower and mobility for the shifting of infantry and field artillery. The action at Milliken's Bend concerned Grant, who paid closer attention to protecting his broad perimeter, especially his supply bases.[62]

During this time, Joseph Johnston's forces dug in at Yazoo City and Benton, while his cavalry scouted the Mechanicsburg corridor and along the east bank of the Big Black to Baldwin's Ferry. Despite occasional skirmishing, Johnston had no inclination to roam; stalemate suited him, even after Bragg sent him a cavalry division. Johnston complained about a lack of artillery, though the record shows he had some seventy-eight guns, certainly enough to threaten Grant; but, in Johnston's mind, he did not have enough to risk an offensive.[63]

While Johnston dawdled, civilians within his limited sphere of influence suffered. In Madison County, north of Jackson, Federals frequently disrupted people's lives. Wrote one embittered Mississippian, "I think any man would prefer death to such a life as many of those live who are left within the enemies lines, every thing they have is taken from them before their eyes and given to their Negroes or taken by the soldiers, lades dresses are given to Negro women, Negro men are dressed in yankee uniform and formally mustered into the Service of the United States in the presence of their masters and those families who are thus stripped of every thing are limited to one suit of clothes and a daily ration which is issued to them by the federal commissary." Another commented, "Where the Federal Army has passed there is nothing left but desolation. I never believed that a civilized people could be so heartless." With the Federals raiding the country between the rivers, a country once rich in food became barren.[64]

Civilian anger sometimes turned toward Confederates. Johnston's soldiers in the Jackson area did not always find a warm welcome. An Alabama reporter observed,

The streets of Jackson present a lively appearance, although there is little or no business doings and little or no sympathy is felt by the troops passing through. Last year a rumor got afloat that the people of Jackson did not want soldiers to walk upon their sidewalks. It has gone through the entire army and is believed, although Mayor [Charles Henry] Manship gave an official denial through the columns of the [Jackson] *Mississippian*. The troops hoot at their comrades to 'come off the sidewalks.' 'The Yankees have burnt you town have they? glad of it — you are might[y] glad to see us ain't you? You'll let us walk on your sides walks won't you?' Jackson has a name hard enough without this unkind report, which appears to be generally believed by the troops who are very bitter."[65]

Grant's buildup continued, as Halleck called for help from Ambrose Burnside's Department of the Ohio, John Schofield's Department of the Missouri, and Rosecrans in Tennessee. Schofield promised several regiments and field artillery, while Rosecrans insisted he needed all he had to take the offensive against Bragg. Rosecrans appealed to Burnside for reinforcements, but Halleck insisted that Grant get first priority. Burnside sent some 8,000 men, designated the IX Corps and commanded by John Parke.[66]

Grant, cheered by Halleck's ability to get more troops to Vicksburg, wanted even more, and he advised Hurlbut in Memphis to keep just enough men to defend the city and send the rest to help with the siege. Grant was willing to vacate points in Kentucky and in West Tennessee.

He wanted all boats in Memphis to stay there to transport men down-river. Hurlbut was upset and, bypassing Grant, appealed directly to Halleck, warning that he would not have enough men left to patrol West Tennessee and North Mississippi. Halleck permitted Hurlbut to retain any essential troops.[67]

As subsequent events proved, Grant's worries about Johnston were mistaken. Johnston spent many hours sending reports to Richmond that understated his strength and offered numerous excuses. The War Department promised him no more troops, but asked if Bragg could do more. Johnston coyly said that taking more men from Bragg would mean losing Tennessee. The government had to decide between Mississippi and Tennessee, a political decision that Johnston knew no one in Richmond would make.

On June 15, Johnston wrote Richmond that saving Vicksburg was "hopeless." Secretary of War Seddon promptly replied that the city "must not be lost without a desperate struggle. The interest and honor of the Confederacy forbid it. I rely on you still to avert the loss. If better resources do not offer, you must hazard attack. It may be made in concert with the garrison, if practicable, but otherwise without, by day or night, as you think best." Johnston insisted he could not launch an attack because the Big Black protected Grant's rear and even if he crossed it, he would have trouble recrossing it.

Since nothing else worked, Seddon resorted to flattery: "I have great deference to your superior knowledge of the position, your judgment and military genius, but I feel it right to share, if need be to take, the responsibility, and leave you free to follow the most desperate course the occasion may demand." He homed in on honor: "Rely upon it, the eyes and hopes of the whole Confederacy are upon you, with the full confidence that you will act, and with the sentiment that it were better to fail nobly daring than through prudence even to be inactive."

Seddon suggested attacking Banks at Port Hudson to take pressure off Pemberton. Johnston insisted that such a campaign required surrendering Mississippi. In truth, Johnston's position had not changed since he arrived in Jackson and notified Richmond that he was too late. Pemberton had gotten boxed in, contrary to Johnston's orders, and as far as Johnston was concerned, he was not responsible for Pemberton's fate. Vicksburg was gone, and that was that.[68]

Initially, Johnston promised to march to Pemberton's aid as soon as Breckinridge arrived. He asked Pemberton's advice on how the two armies could cooperate and what route Johnston should take, and Pemberton suggested the Yazoo bluffs. Pemberton guessed it would take

30,000 to 35,000 men to make the plan work, and Johnston seized on Pemberton's figures as proof that he was "too weak to save Vicksburg." Johnston feebly wrote, "It will be impossible to extricate you, unless you cooperate, and we make mutually supporting movements. Communicate your plans and suggestions, if possible." Johnston placed the burden of planning a rescue on the back of his subordinate.[69]

At this point, with Grant tightening the siege lines, communications between Pemberton and Johnston became sparse, for messengers had great difficulty getting through the lines. Pemberton remained effectively cut off from the outside world. Soldiers in both armies listened in vain for cannon and musketry indicating Johnston was attempting a breakthrough. As time passed, the Federals relaxed. When the IX Corps arrived on the scene on June 17, Grant's strength grew to 77,000, sealing Pemberton's doom.[70]

Johnston nevertheless intended to put on a show. He ordered a few troops to help fortify Yazoo City, but Union gunboats had left nothing worth fortifying. On June 11, Johnston decided it was time to do something, so he concentrated two divisions on the Big Black some twenty miles west of Canton. Scouts located crossings along the Big Black, but then Johnston received news about Union reinforcements and backed off. After that, he organized his so-called Army of Relief into three divisions, two containing four brigades and the other five. This was a cumbersome framework, a departure from the usual three-brigade division. The structure demonstrated that Johnston was not interested in alacrity.[71]

Yet Grant persisted in his worry; when some of his cavalry were routed near Birdsong's Ferry on June 22, he responded quickly. Johnston might finally be on the move, so Grant ordered Sherman to take five brigades to stop Confederates from crossing the Big Black. Sherman soon had 34,000 men and seventy-two cannon deployed at strategic locations west of the river. The alarm proved false, but because he could not conceive that Johnston would remain idle, Grant left Sherman's detachment in place. Grant simply could not relax as long as Johnston remained a loose end.[72]

As time ticked away, John Pemberton grew more depressed, both by circumstances in Vicksburg and by Johnston's inaction. As before during certain periods of troubles in his life, Pemberton tried to get someone to step in and clean up his mess. This time he asked Johnston to contact Grant about negotiations. Pemberton actually stated that he thought Johnston could bluff Grant into allowing Pemberton and his army to leave Vicksburg with "all its arms and equipage." Johnston, of course, refused, noting that Pemberton must act on his own behalf. Johnston then suggested an equally absurd option; Pemberton should get across the Mississippi and unify his force with Kirby Smith's. How that could be done with Union boats patrolling the river, Johnston did not say. Pemberton did not contact Johnston again prior to July 4. That day became infamous in Vicksburg and in the Confederacy because Pemberton, the Pennsylvanian, with no hope of succor and no remaining options, surrendered to Grant.[73]

Given Pemberton's and Johnston's attitudes, Vicksburg and Pemberton's army had been doomed to surrender from the moment Pemberton chose to retreat into the city's defensive works. The Confederates gave a good account of themselves, but with no hope of reinforcements, and with food and ordnance supplies cut off, resistance could not go on indefinitely. They managed to strain Union manpower in areas far beyond the river city's borders, but the Federal army had the numbers to withstand such demands. The prize was worth the price, and Grant's persistence gained him well-deserved acclaim when the end came, though the timing of it heaped more controversy on Pemberton.

13

≋ Surrender & Second Jackson

The certainty of surrender weighed heavily on John Pemberton's shoulders. On June 28, he received a note signed "Many Soldiers."
The message, which perhaps was Union propaganda, encouraged Pemberton to feed or surrender his soldiers, for surrender would be better
than desertion. Pemberton left no written response to this curious letter, though certainly it must have unnerved him. On July 1, he polled
his generals on the question of the army fighting its way out of Vicksburg to the south. Not a viable option, it was the only remotely imagin-
able alternative to capitulation. The same problems that had kept Pemberton from considering escaping south weeks earlier still existed. To
the south and southeast flowed the Big Black with the Mississippi on the
west. The area was a cul-de-sac that could be contained by Grant with
the transfers of additional troops to various fords and by David Porter's
gunboats ascending the Big Black.

The generals quickly pointed out what Pemberton already knew: the
army could not force its way out, and Grant would not let them go in
peace. Carter Stevenson stated the obvious; if the soldiers had to march
south to escape, "the chances are a large number of them now in
the trenches could not succeed." John Bowen and Martin L. Smith
concurred, and both recommended surrender. Joseph Johnston responded to a Pemberton message suggesting that Johnston propose to
Grant the surrender of Vicksburg, but not of Pemberton's army. Pemberton had to know that Grant would accept no such terms. Johnston's
reply never reached Pemberton, but his words say much about his state
of mind. No help was forthcoming from the Trans-Mississippi, and Pemberton had Johnston's permission to initiate negotiations. "It would be
a confession of weakness on my part," Johnston wrote, "which I ought
not to make, to propose them."

On July 3, Pemberton sent a note to Grant requesting an armistice "with a view to arranging terms for the capitulation of Vicksburg." He proposed that he and Grant each name three commissioners to discuss details, and added a statement with defiant overtones: "I make this proposition to save the further effusion of blood, which must otherwise be shed to a frightful extent, feeling myself fully able to maintain my position for a yet indefinite period." Pemberton asked Bowen, a prewar acquaintance of Grant's, to deliver the proposal.

Grant refused to be intimidated and immediately responded with the same terms that brought him notoriety at Fort Donelson. He would consider no terms except the "unconditional surrender of the city and its garrison." He did offer a splinter of an olive branch: "Men who have shown so much endurance and courage as those now in Vicksburg will always challenge the respect of an adversary, and I can assure you will be treated with all the respect due to prisoners of war." Grant rejected Pemberton's commissioners' idea, for he considered his terms nonnegotiable.

Union messengers gave the news to Bowen, who reported Grant's response to Pemberton, and during their conversation misled Pemberton into thinking that Grant wanted a personal conference at 3:00 P.M. Bowen in fact had asked if Grant would agree to a 3:00 P.M. meeting, and Grant had said yes, but the idea was Bowen's. Grant had not wanted a meeting, and he certainly had no intention of continuing negotiations, his position having been made clear already. Bowen had also told Grant that Pemberton wanted to talk. Obviously, Bowen had lied to both to get them together, thinking the arrangements could thus be settled more quickly. Pemberton rode with Bowen and Louis Montgomery, a Pemberton aide, to the rendezvous. Surprised and angered when he learned that Grant had not asked for a conference, all the more so when Grant restated his unconditional terms, Pemberton said pointedly that the siege would continue. "I can assure you," he continued, "you will bury many more of your men before you will enter Vicksburg."

At this point, Bowen suggested to Pemberton and Grant that the two step aside and allow their representatives to discuss the situation in hope of finding a solution. Pemberton later claimed the suggestion came from Grant, but Grant insisted it came from Bowen. Grant had no doubt that Pemberton eventually would have to surrender, but he knew too that Pemberton's threat was not empty. If the fighting continued, more would die, and that seemed pointless. While the two talked, Bowen and Montgomery discussed surrender matters with James McPherson and A. J. Smith.[1]

The conference initially produced a cease-fire and an agreement to continue negotiations. The lateness of the hour meant that the actual surrender could not occur before the next day, July 4. This seemed accidental, though Pemberton later argued, perhaps in self-defense against widespread Southern criticism, that he chose the day because he thought he would get better terms on an important U.S. holiday. He buttressed his claim by arguing that, based on ration rates at the time of surrender, his army had enough food to go on for several more days. Pemberton's defensive stance on the issue implied he had planned all along to surrender on the fourth, but the facts make his claim suspicious.

Whatever the case, the final agreement called for a Federal division to march into Vicksburg on July 4 at 8:00 A.M. The Confederate officers and men would be paroled and allowed to leave the city to march east to a point where they would wait for the exchange process (paroled soldiers agreed to stay out of combat until exchanged on a one-to-one basis with prisoners on the other side). Grant had decided this would expedite the process of his sending reinforcements from his own army to others in need. Otherwise, he would have to retain many men to guard prisoners sent north to prison camps. Officers kept their "side-arms and clothing, and the field, staff, and cavalry officers one horse each." The rest retained only their clothing. A thirty-wagon supply train would be provided to feed the parolees. The seriously ill and wounded, once able to travel, would receive the same terms. Pemberton wanted to hold out for even better terms, but his officers voted to accept and he acquiesced.[2]

In Vicksburg, the surrender produced a wide range of emotions. Elated Union soldiers refuted a local newspaper's derision of rumors that Grant expected to dine in the city on July 4. The paper editorialized that a rabbit could not be cooked until caught. Several soldiers printed their own version of the newspaper after the surrender, commenting that Grant had "caught the rabbit," and the paper would no more eulogize mule meat and "fricasseed kitten."[3]

Union troops had taken much more than a rabbit. Estimates of the numbers of surrendered soldiers and matériel are extensive. Accepted figures regarding Pemberton's surrender totaled 29,491 men, plus 172 cannon of all types, 38,000 artillery shells, 58,000 pounds of black powder, 50,000 rifles, 600,000 rounds of ammunition, and 350,000 percussion caps. Captured food included 38,668 pounds of bacon (quite a haul of pork, considering how long Confederates had been resorting to mule meat), 5,000 bushels of peas, 51,241 pounds of rice, 92,234 pounds of sugar, 721 rations of flour, and 428,000 pounds of salt. On the battlefield, Grant had, since March 29, suffered 10,142 casualties in his own army, while the Confederates had lost 9,091, plus a surrendered army.[4]

Grant sent a brief announcement to Henry Halleck: "The enemy surrendered this morning. The only terms allowed is their parole as prisoners of war. This I regard as a great advantage to us at this moment. It saves, probably, several days in the capture, and leaves troops and transports ready for immediate service. Sherman, with a large force, moves immediately on Johnston, to drive him from the State. I will send troops to the relief of Banks, and return the 9th army corps to Burnside." Grant did hang on to the IX Corps for a while, assigning it to Sherman for his campaign against Johnston. In a message to an inquiring Ambrose Burnside, Lincoln defended Grant's delay in returning Burnside's men, noting that Grant was "a copious worker, and fighter, but a very meagre writer, or telegrapher," and had simply forgotten to tell Washington that he needed the IX Corps a little longer.[5]

After their ceremonial march into Vicksburg and an initial splurge of wild celebrations, Federal soldiers found themselves surprised and often shocked at the bedraggled look of Vicksburg survivors. Not uncommon were such comments as "they are a wretched looking set of men rag[g]ed dirty and half starved." One soldier wrote: "When we beheld the emaciated condition of the women and children at the entrance of their cave dwellings, along the roadside, on our way in, we didn't feel a bit like cheering. The boys emptied their haversacks for the little ones, and watched them devour the rations like starved animals." Another admitted, "We were much surprised at the wretched appearance of these men, whose clothing was not only filthy with dirt, but hanging in ragged festoons from their bodies—their feet bare, or wrapped about with rags, and their whole appearance denoting the sufferings which had been endured by them from an insufficient supply of rations." A Wisconsin soldier added: "Very few of them could walk without aid twenty rods. So completely emaciated were they, that one would believe them dead lying down. The hip bones of some of them had [come] through the skin, and their bodies were a mass of sores caused by vermin." The city's atmosphere was polluted by the stench of dead animals combined with the body odor of soldiers and citizens, who could not spare water for bathing.[6]

A Missouri Confederate corroborated the radically depleted condition of comrades: "Weakness from fatigue, short rations, and heat, had left thousands of the troops decrepid—six thousand [an exaggerated number] of them were in the hospitals, and many of them were crawling about in what should have been convalescent camps." He also noted the deteriorating morale of civilians, who had had lived so long "in daily terror of their lives, never being able to sleep a night in their homes, but crawling into caves, unable to move except in the few peaceful intervals in the heat of the day." Some Confederates now visited the hospitals for the first time to check on comrades in arms. The scenes were unforgettable: "Men with both legs off; some with an eye out, others without arms, and again, some who could once boast of manly beauty and personal attractions, rendered hideous by the loss of the nose or a portion of the face, so as to be unrecognizable by their nearest and dearest kindred."[7]

For the most part, blue and gray interacted in a civil manner. Many talked "as if they had been old friends; indeed many did recognize old acquaintances." Soldiers on the picket lines "have been together all along the lines *shaking hands*, trading pocket knives, exchanging papers, etc., etc." An Indiana soldier commented, "They have discovered that the Yankees are human beings and not the men they were represented to be." An Illinoisan recalled, "I leaned my rifle against the pits and went out in front and got two Johnnies, a Lieut. and one of his company, and took them back into a ravine where our cooking was done and we ate a harty meal of hard tack and coffee." A Louisianan confirmed that many Federals "brought haversacks filled with provisions," acknowledging that their former enemies must be "starved nearly to death."

Confederates enjoyed watching a Federal drill instructor giving black troops a hard time. The instructor carried a big stick and for punishment whacked men on the backside. Then he would look at the Rebels and wink, "and a rebel yell would be the result." Pemberton's soldiers rejoiced, too, while watching Yankees breaking into stores and taking food that had, during the siege, been available only at exorbitant prices. Rebel soldiers "felt as if a portion of their wrongs were avenged."

While there were many instances of friendly interaction among the soldiers, women who had endured the siege were not prepared to be so quickly forgiving. Having suffered privations and witnessed the destruction of their homes, many Vicksburg women had no intention of welcoming Grant's conquerors into their midst. A Union soldier commented about local women in a letter to his wife: "If there is any human being worth[y] of contempt & scorn, it is a rebel woman." He had noticed that no matter how aid had been offered, some Vicksburg women remained aloof and angry whenever Yankees wandered too close.[8]

As he completed a long letter begun on June 20, one Confederate took a romantic view of the siege, and in reflecting on its aftermath perhaps expressed the spirit of women bitter over the surrender:

How changed now the scene. Spread out before me are the splendid steamers of the enemy, exhibiting the riches and power of our strong and wealthy foe. As I looked upon the scene and reflected upon the mighty blow we had just received — upon a long protracted war that now awaited us — upon the streams of blood yet to be shed — upon the future strength of our young men and the carnage and desolation and destruction which should sweep over our beloved South, as I thought upon these things, tears of bitter anguish fell from my eyes and a cloud of darkness and gloom settled upon my mind. Farewell ye mighty hills, upon whose rugged peaks I have often stood and with solemn awe admired and adored the power of the Almighty, to whom belongs the strength of the hills. No more shall I roam over those lovely hills and deep valleys, for they are now in the possession of a hateful foe, desecrated by the vile footsteps of a heartless, cruel and unprincipled enemy who comes with the felonious purpose of desolating our homes, of spreading the shadow of death over our firesides and of enslaving a free and noble people. And thou great Father of Waters upon whose lovely banks I have stood as sentinel in the lonely watches of the night, looking with covert eyes across the dim and dark waters for the approach of the enemy's boats, no more shall I guard thy rolling waves nor walk up and down thy friendly banks. Thy proud waves, unguarded by Southerners, shall now roll on to the mighty ocean upon no friendly errand for us but beating upon thy placid bosom the power and wrath of our deadly foes."[9]

As news of the surrender spread, reaction in the North was predictable. Unionists had great cause to rejoice when they learned that Grant's victory had come the day after Robert E. Lee's defeat at Gettysburg. Newspapers in the Union states pronounced the victory with celebratory declarations. Vicksburg had at last returned to the Union; with its surrender, and that of Port Hudson on July 9, came free access along the Mississippi River. The Confederacy was now split, the Trans-Mississippi having been cut off. A Chicago editor intoned, "The Mississippi may bear its burdens of trade and commerce unchallenged beneath . . . frowning batteries." Many suspected that Pemberton's surrender, along with Lee's retreat from Pennsylvania, signaled the "winding up" of the rebellion. Missourians loyal to the Union saw the surrender as a sign that Confederate sympathizers might now leave the state alone, since neither the river nor its tributaries could be used by the Rebels for incursions into Missouri. Some Northerners voiced support for an embargo of Vicksburg to punish the town for its rebellious ways.[10]

In the South, the news of double defeats at Vicksburg and Gettysburg caused much consternation. There is considerable evidence that the Gettysburg loss, while certainly disappointing, did not have a long-lasting negative impact. Lee had lost many good soldiers, but his army was still intact and certainly able to regroup and fight again. Most Southerners did not view Lee's setback as something that doomed the Confederacy. The loss of Vicksburg and Pemberton's army brought a quite different reaction.[11]

A heavy sense of foreboding swept over the Confederacy as news of Vicksburg's loss gradually spread. In the city, a surrendered Louisiana Confederate noted that many of his fellow prisoners felt betrayed by the Richmond government and considered the cause lost. A Missourian called the event "a sad and almost paralyzing blow to the South." A Mississippi civilian moaned, "Well, our beloved Vicksburg has fallen, the city of a Southern heart's pride. Our own Mississippi is now invaded and what is to become of us?" In Texas, a refugee from Louisiana worried that the Yankees would now come west, that in fact Federal armies could invade from so many directions there would be no place to hide. In South Carolina, two diarists thought losing Vicksburg had severely crippled Southern hopes. Emma Holmes observed, "It is a terrible blow to our cause and will prolong the war indefinitely — oh, how much depended on its salvation." Mary Boykin Chesnut said of her reaction to the news: "I felt a hard blow struck on the top of my head, and my heart took one of its queer turns. I was utterly unconscious." Confederate ordnance chief Josiah Gorgas said of the loss of Vicksburg and Port Hudson in conjunction with Lee's repulse: "The Confederacy totters to its destruction."[12]

The Confederate press was generally unforgiving. Richmond papers blamed Jefferson Davis and his selection of generals, one declaring: "The country has suffered enough at the hands of his favorites." Confederate forces should be concentrated to meet threats, and men of proven ability should be put in command. Lee should go on the defensive, so more troops could be sent west to retake Vicksburg. Pemberton had caused the disaster, not Johnston. So went faultfinding and finger-pointing in the aftermath of the surrender. A few editors did call for unity, but they were in the minority.[13]

Amid recriminations and second guessing, Pemberton and his staff worked out the details of the surrender with James McPherson, who was appointed by Grant to administer the Federal occupation of Vicksburg. The main problem was paroling so many soldiers, but another matter seemed to cast a shadow of absurdity over the process. Confederate officers were concerned about keeping their black servants; Grant authorized McPherson to allow that, as long as the servants were willing to go with their masters. The coercion of servants by officers resulted in many blacks insisting that they wanted to leave Vicksburg with their erstwhile owners. The obvious subterfuge so angered McPherson that he canceled the policy, though he allowed a few exceptions. When at last it came time for Pemberton to lead his army east out of Vicksburg, McPherson no doubt watched the Confederates go with feelings of relief.[14]

Shortly after the terms of surrender were finalized, an irritable Pemberton had an interesting encounter with U. S. Grant that Fred Grant was to recall. The Union general was riding with his staff when

he reached a house of some pretentious appearance, partially built of stone. There was an assemblage of Confederate officers upon the porch. General Grant dismounted at this place and entered. No one met him at the gate or asked him to take a seat among them. General Pemberton was there, with his staff, but he received his conqueror in a most frigid, cold manner. After a moment General Grant said: 'I would like a drink of water; where can I find it?' One young officer more politely inclined than others pointed to the door of the house and said: 'I presume you will find a glass of water inside the house.' General Grant went back through the house and entered the kitchen. I followed him. There was an old Negress, who gave us the coveted drink. Perhaps our enemies assembled there did not realize that that same morning my father had interfered with any firing or saluting in exultation over the victory.[15]

Once his march east had been approved, Pemberton received instructions from McPherson. The Confederates who had not already slipped out of town, or were still too ill to move, would assemble and move east along the Jackson road to Edwards, then to Raymond, bypass Jackson, cross the Pearl, and continue on to Meridian via the Southern Railroad route. Rebel soldiers who refused to sign paroles would be sent north to Federal prison camps. On July 11, the march began, the Confederates maintaining a slow pace in the stifling summer heat. The army would stop in Enterprise, Mississippi, near Meridian, and wait out the thirty-day parole period before reassembling in Demopolis, Alabama. Along the way, Pemberton got in touch with Jefferson Davis and convinced the reluctant president to grant thirty-day furloughs to the men. Pemberton only had 1,600 men from Missouri who agreed to stay on and continue in the war, but he believed he could perhaps convince more by giving them time off. The Missourians, because of the realities of war in their state, could not easily go home and return within the thirty days. Davis later tried to renege, but Pemberton went ahead with the plan, though he did scale furlough time according to how far soldiers had to travel. By the time he worked out the details, the issue became a moot point, since most of the men had already left for home.[16]

While en route to Enterprise, Pemberton met briefly with Johnston, who had by then very tentatively led his army west, reaching the Big Black area about the time Pemberton surrendered. After hearing news of the fall of Vicksburg, Johnston had turned his troops around and marched for Jackson. Johnston pretended to be glad to see Pemberton, but Pemberton saluted coldly, snapped words to the effect that he was reporting as was his duty, turned, and walked away. There is no evidence the two ever saw each other again, though they would embark on a war of words over blame for the loss of Vicksburg, a war lasting well beyond the surrender and the end of the Civil War.

In Richmond, Jefferson Davis sadly tried to pick up the pieces of the disaster on the Mississippi. He admitted to Theophilus Holmes that cooperation between troops on both sides of the Mississippi had ended, an ironic admission in light of Davis's past refusal to make Holmes cooperate. Davis urged Holmes to "hold and give such security to the valley of the Arkansas as will ensure the production of sufficient food to maintain the army as well as the residents of the country." Other than that, Holmes could try to use Indian allies effectively and perhaps plan an invasion of Missouri. Davis's advice sounded as empty as it no doubt felt when he gave it.

Holmes had underscored Grant's victory in a negative manner for the Confederacy when on July 4 he attacked Helena, Arkansas, where his army was repulsed by Benjamin Prentiss's occupation troops. Regardless of what Holmes had intended by such a late move, he only brought to a predictable end the futile efforts of Trans-Mississippi forces to bring some sort of relief to Pemberton's situation. Their performance caused Grant to worry and produced nothing.

With the city of Vicksburg now securely in Union hands, Grant knew that to seal his victory, Sherman must either rout and capture Johnston and his army or at least chase them away. On June 28, Johnston had finally issued marching orders to his four division commanders—William Loring, W. H. T. Walker, Samuel French, and John C. Breckinridge—to advance toward the Big Black. The divisions had moved toward the Birdsong Ferry and Edwards Station areas, and patrols scouted Sherman's line. By July 4, Johnston was convinced that attacking Sherman north of where the railroad met the Big Black would be futile, so he decided to shift south, beginning the next day. Then came word that Pemberton had surrendered, and Johnston marched his army back to Jackson. Johnston later admitted that he only intended "to make such close and careful examination of the enemy's lines as might enable me to estimate the probability of our being able to break them; and, should the chances of success seem to justify it, attack in the hope of breaking them, and rescuing the army invested in Vicksburg. There was no hope of saving the place by raising the siege." Clearly, Johnston only moved to get Richmond off his back. Up until his brief move west, he had steadfastly refused to help Pemberton or Gardner at Port Hudson. His favorite excuse seemed to be "the want of field transportation."[17]

Sherman, already alerted by Grant to take the offensive against Johnston once Pemberton surrendered, received news of the capitulation while Grant was still working out surrender details. Grant bluntly told Sherman: "I want Johnston broken up as effectually as possible, and roads destroyed." Sherman responded that as soon as he received word that the surrender was official, he would "secure all the crossings of the Big Black" and move east; and he wanted six more divisions. Soon he had three corps ready to go after Johnston: the XIII, commanded by E. O. C. Ord, assigned to march toward Jackson along the Southern Railroad; the XV led by Frederick Steele, assigned to move north of the railroad; and the IX under John Parke, assigned to the Mechanicsburg corridor as the army's left flank. Despite harassment by Johnston's cavalry, all three corps made good initial progress.[18]

Sherman's troops had some memorable, and in some cases disturbing, experiences as they moved toward Jackson. Wanton destruction of private property seemed to escalate to new heights, while face-to-face encounters with local citizens produced soul-searching. Soldiers saw signs of previous fighting and everywhere the refuse of war left by thousands of men.

Iowa soldiers had a particularly gruesome experience when they camped in the Champion Hill area. They spent a routine evening, sitting around campfires singing and swapping stories, but all noticed a bad, strange odor that seemed to permeate the place. The next morning, one of the Iowans arose and scouted around, returning to tell his comrades, "Go over to that hollow, and you will see hell." Some accepted the dare, but they looked only once and hurried away. One

penned an account of the horror. After Champion Hill, some Confederates, probably cavalry details, returned to the battlefield and attempted
to bury bodies left behind by Pemberton's army. With enemy troops in
the area, they had to act quickly, and "in their haste had tossed hundreds of their dead into this little ravine and slightly covered them over
with earth, but the rains had come, and the earth was washed away, and
there stood or lay hundreds of half-decayed corpses. Some were grin-
ning skeletons, some were headless, some armless, some had their
clothes torn away, and some were mangled by dogs and wolves. The
horror of that spectacle followed us for weeks."[19]

Other troops also found corpses, both of men and animals. There
seemed to be "misery and destruction everywhere — cotton houses and
cotton gins in flames every where — ordered to stop it — can't be done —
the men keep at it. The countryside was desolated, stripped of food and
dwellings, few homes remained standing, no slaves in sight, no livestock
of any kind," other than carcasses that Confederates had driven into
ponds and then killed to spoil the water for Yankees. Acts of ruining
waterholes particularly incensed Sherman's troops and no doubt contributed to the wide swath of destruction along the way. Civilians too
must have suffered from the spoiling of water.[20]

Soldiers took special delight in assaulting Jefferson Davis's brother
Joe's property in Hinds County. The campaigning throughout the
county exacerbated damages already suffered. Many parts of the county
were stripped of the valuable and the worthless; homes were burned,
and food was taken, whether in smokehouses or on the hoof. Farmers
trying to start over after the war found the countryside bare. Grant was
quoted as commenting while riding through the county during the
army's earlier advance on Vicksburg: "What were the people of this
beautiful country thinking of to go to war?"[21] If they had supported the
war, they must have been having second thoughts now.

Many Federal soldiers and Mississippi civilians had memorable, often
harsh encounters. A scene at one home was typical: "A splendid piano
stood on the back stoop, a fine library was thrown open and the contents scattered all over the house, part of a nice set of dishes yet stood on
the table in the dining room, the looking glass was smashed and the
pieces scattered about and wreck and confusion were on every hand."
Near Edwards, Wisconsin troops found a home still standing and occupied by an elderly woman and several children. The dwellers begged
for food, and the soldiers shared. At another home, an aged woman had
died, supposedly from the shock of enemy troops coming, and several
soldiers took time out to construct a coffin for the funeral. At yet an-

other place, an attractive young woman was spiteful until she found out one of the men was a doctor, not a real Yankee soldier.

As the march reached the Jackson area, a woman who was supposedly ninety-five years old asked the same doctor and his staff why war was being waged on women, children, and sick people. "Gentlemen, look through my house; if you live to be as old as I am, pray never to see the like again as long as you live! Look into that room . . . ; see how the soldiers tore up my things! My daughter lay in there sick; and she has a sick little baby; yet they took the clothes off her bed; tore open the feather beds; broke up the furniture, as you can see!" The doctor was "ashamed" and "humiliated." A Pennsylvania soldier who had fought in the Eastern Theater probably had such things in mind when he observed, "War in this country is a very different thing. This is war in earnest. Destruction, misery, devastation and everything that can be added to them make the sum of it."[22]

Johnston's Confederates probably never realized — or gave much thought to the possibility — that their tactic of ruining drinking water would cause a backlash against civilians. The retreating army had had its own share of water problems, exacerbated by the July heat. Johnston and his soldiers doubtless supposed that the torrid weather and lack of water would at least slow Sherman down, and at best cause him to have second thoughts about attacking Jackson. On July 8, the Confederate army began occupying old earthworks in the capital city, setting up artillery positions and otherwise getting ready for Sherman's approach from the west.

Why Johnston decided to make a stand at Jackson is unclear. Perhaps he felt he must make a show of resistance somewhere to appease Davis and the War Department. The entrenchments defending the city from approaches west of Jackson were not strong, and the army had the Pearl River at its back. In effect, Johnston potentially could find himself in a situation similar to Pemberton's at Vicksburg. The big difference was that Johnston did not have the Union navy behind him on the Pearl. Nevertheless, Johnston believed that he could repel an attack by Sherman, while he also feared that Union siege tactics would force him to retreat.

The Confederate deployment included John Breckinridge on the left, south of downtown Jackson and in position to guard the southern approaches of the New Orleans railroad and the Terry road entrance into the city. The Pearl River protected Breckinridge's left flank, and Samuel French moved in on Breckinridge's right. Along French's front, the Raymond road, the Robinson road, the Clinton road, and the Southern Railroad from Vicksburg entered Jackson's west side. W. H. T. Walker's troops aligned northwest of downtown, covering the entrance into the city by the New Orleans rail line from the north. Between Walker and Loring, who occupied the right flank, the Livingston and Canton roads entered Jackson. Loring's right was somewhat protected by the meandering Pearl.

Though held up briefly by Confederate skirmishers and slowed by lack of water, Sherman's troops moved steadily toward Jackson. Ord approached along the Robinson road, fanning out his troops south of the road, with A. P. Hovey and Jacob Lauman swinging to the far right, moving toward Breckinridge's division. Ord's other three divisions deployed in front of French. Steele came down the Clinton road, his three divisions confronting French's right flank and Walker's division. Parke came in from the north, his four divisions marching toward Walker's right and Loring's division.[23]

Sherman initially planned to pressure Johnston all along the Confederate front, possibly attempting to turn Breckinridge's left. After getting a look at Rebel fortifications, Sherman did what Johnston had hoped he would not do; he set up artillery positions and lay siege to the city. Meanwhile, Johnston decided he could not attack without "risking the army," nor could the army, lacking supplies, stand a long siege. To avoid criticism from Richmond, Johnston did not withdraw at once but, for the second time, abandoned Jackson eventually. He suggested his intentions to Davis in a July 11 message, in which he detailed the weakness of his army's position and the lack of supplies, and said that siege tactics by the enemy would force him to withdraw.[24]

Sherman's troops settled into siege operations, with artillery thundering and infantry taking potshots at enemy heads. Sherman knew he had to wait until a shipment of more artillery shells arrived from Vicksburg before he could attack. Perhaps his experiences at Chickasaw Bayou and on May 19 and 22 at Vicksburg had also convinced Sherman that direct assaults were not preferable to pressing and maneuvering Johnston into retreating.

Sherman tried to keep his men active. Parke's troops advanced from the north, but the advance was merely a misunderstanding or mistake on someone's part, and the poorly coordinated operation never amounted to anything. To the south, Hovey and Lauman received orders from Ord to press closer to Breckinridge's front. This was similar to Grant's strategy at Vicksburg to narrow the distance between Federal and Confederate lines. While Hovey pressed forward west of the New Orleans railroad,

Lauman's troops advanced north on the east side. Portions of Lauman's division then launched an ill-advised attack against a strong Confederate position fronted by thick abatis that broke up the Union alignment. Lauman lost 68 killed and 302 wounded and 149 missing. Confederate losses totaled only 7. Lauman was despondent, mumbling to one of Sherman's aides, "I am cut all to pieces."[25]

The siege then settled into routine artillery exchanges until July 14, when Breckinridge complained to Johnston about the stench of dead Union bodies, casualties from Lauman's attack. Johnston contacted Sherman, who agreed to a truce to bury the remains, which, after lying in the hot sun, were in advanced states of decomposition. Following the truce, Johnston sent cavalry to look for Sherman's supply trains bringing artillery ammunition, which they attacked with mixed results that did not prevent most of the projectiles from reaching Union batteries. Otherwise, occasional sorties, plus bursts of cannon and musketry fire, broke the monotony but added few names to casualty lists.[26]

On learning that his cavalry had failed to capture or destroy most of Sherman's ordnance supplies and impressed by the Federals' artillery superiority, Johnston decided on July 16 to evacuate the city. Beginning that evening, and continuing until the early morning hours of the seventeenth, Johnston managed to get his entire army across the Pearl River without any harassment by Sherman's troops. Some Union soldiers heard wagon noises that implied the Rebels were pulling out, but nobody seemed to take the possibility seriously, least of all Sherman, who was convinced that Johnston was building up his defenses. Thus there was much surprise at dawn, when Sherman's army found the city empty of Confederates.

Johnston left the area after having suffered casualties of 71 killed, 504 wounded, and 25 missing. He also left behind over 23,000 artillery rounds, nearly 1,400 small arms, and three cannon plus large numbers of accoutrements. His departure also left much railroad rolling stock — engines and cars — north of Jackson in the Grenada area to the destructive forces of the enemy. Johnston had not seen to the repairs of a railroad bridge over the Pearl River, which would have allowed the transfer of railroad cars to safer places. His actions crippled the railroads in Mississippi not only for the remainder of the war but also for many years thereafter. Johnston would soon be relieved of his command and would then engage in sharp, bitter exchanges with Jefferson Davis over who was responsible for the loss of Vicksburg.[27]

A few days later, a disgusted Davis wrote Robert E. Lee about Johnston's latest failure. Johnston, "after evacuating Jackson, retreated to the east, to the pine woods of Mississippi, and if he has any other plan than that of watching the enemy it has not been communicated." Johnston clearly had no other plan, and Davis understood that. Johnston just wanted to be left alone.

Sherman decided that forcing Johnston to flee was enough, and he informed Grant that because of the hot weather and scarcity of water he would not pursue. After all, the Confederates would be consuming available water and spoiling the rest, as they had done en route to Jackson. Grant urged Sherman to at least send cavalry to keep Johnston from escaping unharried. Sherman did not have adequate cavalry in the area, so he ordered Steele to take a picked force and press Johnston. The Federals followed the Confederates to Brandon, and after exchanges of gunfire Johnston retreated east to Morton. Steele's troops burned and looted in Brandon, while Sherman, looking at reports of railroad and telegraph destruction, decided he had done enough. He issued orders for his army to return to Vicksburg, having lost 129 killed, 752 wounded, and 231 missing.[28]

Jackson suffered more destruction, as fires set by departing Confederates spread and Union troops went on another orgy of vandalism that often got out of hand. Many ignored orders to refrain from "destroying everything they came across"; they spread devastation "to every household in the town." Pennsylvania troops took women's clothing, and many of them donned the garments to spite their victims. Soldiers who had been instructed to tear down burning buildings to prevent blazes from spreading often carelessly tossed aside burning boards, fomenting what they had been detailed to stop. Some soldiers rationalized that in committing theft they were only following the crowd. One Federal experienced something that his fellow soldiers no doubt would never let him forget. Angry citizens standing on a Jackson lawn jeered Wisconsin troops as they passed. A woman tried to get some of the men to come over and talk, phrasing the invitation as almost a dare. One obliged and walked over to ask what she wanted. When he got within reach, she threw her long skirt over his head, "gathered it tight around his throat and hailed others to come and help choke a Yankee."[29]

Sherman's campaign provided a decisive and conclusive footnote to the campaign. On July 9, Franklin Gardner surrendered Port Hudson to Nathaniel Banks, in effect giving the United States control of the Mississippi from its source to its mouth, or, as Abraham Lincoln phrased it, letting the Father of Waters again roll "unvexed to the sea." With Vicksburg in Federal hands, Gardner knew it was pointless to hold out at Port Hudson, where his outnumbered troops had put up a deter-mined defense equal to Pemberton's at Vicksburg.[30]

 Henry Halleck had worried about Banks's fate, writing Grant on July 11 that he was "exceedingly anxious." He hoped Grant would act quickly to reinforce Banks and get the IX Corps to Rosecrans, who might now be facing a Bragg army about to be supplemented by John-ston's Jackson army. Halleck pronounced triumphantly: "The Missis-sippi should be the base of operations east and west." And, ever the bureaucrat, he looked to the future. What, he asked Grant, "is to be done with all the forces in the field? This is an important question, which should be carefully considered."

By the time Grant received Halleck's message and wrote an answer, Sherman had won at Jackson and Port Hudson had been surrendered. Grant responded, "My troops are very much exhausted, and entirely un-fit for any present duty requiring much marching." Yet Grant thought Mobile should be the next target, and he urged Halleck to approve an operation against the Alabama Gulf Coast port city. Grant asked for a leave of absence to visit New Orleans, in the hope of overseeing the Mobile operation. Halleck refused both requests; Grant commented in his memoirs, "So far as my experience with General Halleck went it was very much easier for him to refuse a favor than to grant one." Grant watched with disgust as Halleck dispersed the Vicksburg army, "as had been the case the year before after the fall of Corinth when the army was sent where it would do the least good."[31]

Abraham Lincoln rejoiced at Grant's success. On July 13, the presi-dent wrote his general, "I do not remember that you and I ever met personally. I write this now as a grateful acknowledgment for the almost inestimable service you have done the country." Later in the same note, Lincoln commented, "When you got below, and took Port-Gibson, Grand Gulf, and vicinity, I thought you should go down the river and join Gen. Banks; and when you turned Northward East of the Big Black, I feared it was a mistake. I now wish to make the personal acknowledg-ment that you were right, and I was wrong." Lincoln could not, however, go along with Grant's Mobile idea. In August, he sent word to Grant that while the Alabama expedition was tempting, the invasion of Mexico by France had led him to conclude that the U.S. government must be firmly established in western Texas to blunt any ideas of French activity there. He therefore sided with Halleck's proposal to disperse troops to that and other areas.[32]

Grant's disappointment would not last. Ahead lay the victory at Chattanooga and his appointment as general of all Federal armies, replacing Halleck. For the present, he could enjoy the fruits of a hard-fought, hard-won, very long campaign, fraught with disappointments, but ending with a great victory. As he later recalled with pride, "The capture of Vicksburg, with its garrison, ordnance and ordnance stores, and the successful battles fought in reaching them, gave new spirit to the loyal people of the North. New hopes for the final success of the cause of the Union were inspired. The victory gained at Gettysburg, upon the same day [actually a day earlier, on July 3] added to their hopes. Now the Mississippi River was entirely in the possession of the National troops."[33]

The loss of the Mississippi River, and with it the severance of the Trans-Mississippi from the rest of the Confederacy, brought about much soul-searching in Richmond. Grant's victory had been positive proof of the fallacy of restricting outnumbered Confederate armies to the defense of specific locations where they could be cut off and trapped. Despite his defeatist attitude, Johnston had been right about the necessity of giving up places so that Confederate armies could maneuver and pick their fights. Whether he would have aggressively gone after Grant if Pemberton had abandoned Vicksburg and brought his army to Canton is another matter. The word "aggressive" is not usually used in the same sentence with "Joseph Johnston."

Disgusted with Johnston's recalcitrance, Jefferson Davis remained firm in his support of Pemberton. He wrote the beleaguered general, "I thought, and still think, that you did right to risk an army for the purpose of keeping command" of a portion of the Mississippi. "Had you succeeded, none would have blamed; had you not made the attempt, few, if any, would have defended your course." Yet Davis felt Confederate generalship had simply failed. In a private letter written in August, he stated bluntly, "The disasters in Mississippi were both great and unexpected to me. I had thought that the troops sent to the State, added to those already there, made a force large enough to accomplish the destruction of Grant's army. That no such result followed may have been the effect of mismanagement, or it may have been that it was unattainable." An investigation would be made, but "it would afford me but little satisfaction to know that they resulted from bad Generalship and were not inevitable."[34]

As for John Pemberton, the ghosts of Vicksburg never left him. Strong criticism of his generalship and personal integrity became quite intense, to the point that in order to continue in the army he had to resign his rank and accept a lieutenant-colonelcy of artillery, as well as transfer to the Eastern Theater. Davis tried and failed to find him another command commensurate with his rank of lieutenant general. Attempts to place him in the Army of Tennessee officer corps led to threatened rebellion in the ranks by Confederate troops who thought he had deliberately lost Vicksburg to the Yankees.[35]

So the long Vicksburg campaign ended, but the numerous ramifications of its outcome lingered on. Vicksburg citizens had to endure enemy occupation while trying to rebuild their once proud town on the Mississippi. Commanders, both winners and losers, moved on to other duties, but officers and common soldiers on both sides long relived, and refought, the battles, the trials and tribulations, the triumphs and disappointments. What had begun with an attack from the river had ended with a siege that tested endurance and the human spirit. The Civil War never left Vicksburg, and the Union campaign to take the city never left the minds of civilians caught in the path of the campaign, or of combatants who survived the rigors and controversies of defending and capturing the Confederate Gibraltar. What happened at Vicksburg and in the surrounding region may not have been as dramatic as three July days in Gettysburg, but the results were more decisive. On July 4, 1863, the Confederacy lost more than an army, more than a town, and more than a river. Grant's victory irrevocably turned the tide of the war in the Western Theater in favor of the Union.

14
≈≥ Aftermath & Legacies

When the siege ended, Vicksburg citizens had to rebuild their personal lives, repair their homes, and refurbish a town scarred by Union shells and bullets. Contrary to the view expressed by a few Union soldiers, Vicksburg had suffered much damage. Any number of buildings were marred or worse, and streets had large gashes where heavy artillery and mortar shells landed. Structures not receiving direct hits showed signs of long neglect. Assessing the aftermath proved difficult at first, for the streets were filled with both Union and Confederate soldiers wobbling about in a drunken state, and much looting went on in houses, stores, and even cemetery vaults, until Grant issued orders to put a stop to such behavior. He was only partially successful at first, but eventually Federal authorities appointed a provost marshal, who managed to establish "good order and discipline."[1]

A particularly depressing aspect of postsiege Vicksburg was the lingering presence of putrid animal carcasses and unburied, or partially interred, human corpses, which acted as magnets for green flies and scavengers, such as buzzards. Federal details filled ditches, leveled some fortifications, and blocked entrances to caves, many of which had become garbage dumps, in an attempt to control the disposal of refuse and stop the spread of sickness caused by unsanitary conditions. Doors were pulled from dwellings in order to meet the need for stretchers to transport sick and wounded. Crudely marked graves dotted the city's landscape. Typical was an Illinois soldier's grave a few hundred yards north of the Southern Railroad. His friends laid railings around the interment spot and marked it with a "headboard with letters cut in it deep."[2]

Soldiers felt both justified and guilty regarding the manner in which they buried the dead. Union troops and Confederates alike were often interred where they fell. One Union soldier wrote his sister that a friend had been "buried the best he could be under the circumstances. He was buried in the clothes he had on with his blanket wrapped around him." Many corpses were not wrapped in blankets; conventional burial practices were not or could not be observed: "If you could see a battlefield once and the dead on it and see how they had to bury them you would think and find out to[o] that they can not be buried as they can at home." In the heat of battle, hasty and unmarked graves became commonplace. Confederates interred one Federal after shooting him down during siege action near their lines. After the surrender, the visible grave site had disappeared in ground pummeled by artillery. Union soldiers managed to track down a Rebel who had taken some letters off the body, and the Confederate pointed out the grave, which presumably was then marked.[3]

The campaign's dead lay scattered beyond Vicksburg itself, reminiscent of the macabre site near Champion Hill, but many—perhaps most—bodies would never be located. Poignant and unusual stories often surrounded those found. One Union soldier bemoaned his brother's fate of lying beneath the ground at Champion Hill. He wrote his uncle: "I know it seems hard to leave him buried in a traitorous land. But the blood of our fallen heroes will purify and place an indelible stamp of true patriotism upon this cursed soil." This soldier's anti-Rebel passion eventually cooled when counteracted by his marriage to a local Vicksburg woman. The widow of a Confederate received a message about her fallen husband from a woman who lived near Bolton: he was buried "nice and clean in a nice box on our place close to the road so that passers by could see who he was."[4]

Many dead, Union and Confederate, lay under the ground where they fell among the thousands of acres of farmland in the Vicksburg vicinity and beyond. Some plantation owners did not care that renewed cultivation of land after the siege might desecrate graves. A few weeks before the war ended, Union officials in Vicksburg issued an order to stop planters from encroaching "upon the grounds" occupied by the corpses of soldiers. The edict proclaimed that soil in which blue or gray were buried "will be held sacred to that purpose, and no cultivation of the soil will be permitted for a space of six feet on either side of any such grave, nor will any weeds or other rubbish be allowed to be thrown upon ground so occupied." The difficulty of enforcing such a decree over an expansive area was obvious.[5]

Three years after the war, even as the Vicksburg National Cemetery for Federal soldiers and the Confederate graveyard in the Vicksburg city cemetery were gradually being filled with remains from scattered grave sites, controversy arose over farmers continuing to abuse graves un-earthed on their land. They often instructed their field hands to take any plowed-up bones and set them aside on nearby stumps to get them out of the way. The workers were to tell officials asking questions about graves that the remains found on their boss's property had already been taken to Vicksburg. During one investigation, thirty-seven graves abused by farm implements were located, and officials expected to find more.[6]

The creation of the two cemeteries produced cooperation between Federal and local authorities. The city cemetery had been used during the siege to bury army and civilian dead. A few formal funeral cere-monies had been conducted, but such occasions could be dangerous. In one documented case, soldiers who had been killed when a Union shell penetrated the county courthouse were taken to the city ceme-tery; while the procession was en route, more shells fatally struck down some of the mourners. One observer noted that during the siege "the beautiful City Cemetery—was riddled by the plunging shot."[7]

Despite the problems of beaten-up ground and scattered bodies, the cemetery work continued. The Confederate Cemetery Association gave official thanks to a U.S. Army colonel whose early work in developing the national cemetery at Vicksburg resulted in the compilation of a lengthy list of some 3,000 locations of Confederate grave sites. The colonel presented the information in a bound volume to the associa-tion. Yet a local newspaper bemoaned in 1868 the differences between Vicksburg's Confederate resting place, "in a remote corner of the city cemetery," and the national cemetery created by those honoring the Union dead; "rich[,] prosperous and victorious," the North erected "splendid monuments to its heroic dead," while the "South, poor, suf-fering and vanquished, enshrines *its* dead in the *hearts* of its surviving children." Regardless of the rhetoric, both burial grounds embodied shared concerns over honoring the fallen, no matter what the color of their uniform was. The cemeteries today, only a few hundred yards apart, symbolize more a legacy of conciliation than one of conflict, and the Confederate site is not remote, but very prominent.[8]

Once the immediate shock of surrender waned, many and varied thoughts went through the minds of Vicksburgians as they coped with conquering Yankees, wrecked landscapes, casualties, filth, and disease. As one historian has noted with a romantic flair: "Late on the afternoon of July 3 Vicksburg had died. The hills and the houses still stood, and people still ate and slept in them; the river still flowed, and for the first time in almost three years the wharves were crowded with ships; some-where there was even a laugh and a song—but despite these things the city was a gutted shell. The heart and core of the city—its political, economic, and social structure—which was built and supported within the cradling framework of hills, homes, and river had ceased to exist." Politically, Confederate Vicksburg had indeed come to an end. It would be several days before Jefferson Davis heard of the surrender, and Mis-sissippi governor Pettus made himself scarce somewhere to the east. The state was still in the Confederacy, but more in name than in fact.[9]

Many citizens reacted cautiously to Union soldiers in their midst. A few residents who had expressed opposition to secession now felt bitter toward the Federals who wrought destruction and ruin. These people still held to the illusion that they could oppose going to war and avoid its impact when it came. Many firm secessionists lashed out at friends and neighbors who took loyalty oaths to the Union. Dedicated Unionists, despite the liberators among them, now and then made their senti-ments known, but overall kept quiet. They understood that the Union army would not always be there to protect them from angry Confeder-ate sympathizers. There were residents who openly expressed anti–Confederate government sentiments, for they felt betrayed by their local favorite son, Jefferson Davis. It is difficult to know the degree to which antigovernment expressions reflected anti-Confederate feelings. One could be disgusted with the Davis government and still be loyal to the Confederate cause.[10]

An observer named Armistead Burwell, a native Unionist who had left town for friendlier confines in Missouri, visited Vicksburg in August 1863 and on returning to St. Louis wrote to Abraham Lincoln. Burwell claimed to be a longtime resident of the city and assured Lincoln he was familiar with both the people of Mississippi and the residents of Loui-siana parishes across the river. In Burwell's opinion, there were thou-sands of Mississippians "who desire most ardently the restoration of the United States Government, who yet see no way, in which their senti-ments can be safely or beneficially expressed." Burwell insisted, "The majority of those who have not resolved upon taking sides with the Union when it is safe and expedient to do so, is bitter and unsparing in its denunciation of Jeff Davis & Co. This is their first step and a long one, upon the return path. If you wish to hear Jeff Davis, Wifgall, Toombs, Floyd &c &c cursed from the bottom of the heart, & with the whole soul, go disguised to Vicksburg, and converse with the men of Mississippi." Burwell went on to state, with much emotion and a dash of hyperbole, "I affirm, that there are more unconditionally Loyal or Union men in that state, proportion to population, than in the states of Ohio or New York. This is the great fact, which you as President ought to keep steadily in your view." He hoped that Lincoln would make positive overtures to Mississippi and Louisiana and thereby bring an end to the conflict in those states. Unfortunately for Burwell, and those who shared his views, the Federal presence in those two states was not strong enough to allow Lincoln to do much; given his tall, gangly stature, it would have been difficult, not to mention dangerous, for him to go disguised to Vicksburg and converse with local dissidents.[11]

Though usually not so vociferously expressed, such anti-Confederate and antiwar sentiments as Burwell's were hardly unique in Vicksburg after the surrender. The numbers of deserters, soldiers absent without permission, and stragglers tired of war, and just tired in general, increased dramatically during the latter stages of the campaign. Union officials in the Mississippi Valley worried that Rebel soldiers who had left the Confederate army would swell the ranks of guerrillas in Kansas and Missouri. Many others did not care about fighting anywhere, doubtless agreeing in principle with a woman who stated a prevailing sentiment: "The Yankees have ruined this country completely and I am afraid the Confederacy is gone also." The loss of Vicksburg did not induce large numbers of civilian men to rush into the ranks of the Confederate army to avenge defeat. Lacking confidence in Pemberton, and disgusted at the seeming absence of support from Richmond, many Rebel soldiers in Mississippi decided that enough was enough and simply refused to carry on the fight. Whether they were anti-Confederate in general or opposed to Pemberton and the Davis government in particular did not matter. The negative impact on morale and further participation in the war was the same.[12]

While postsurrender emotions ebbed and flowed, James McPherson, appointed by Grant to oversee the captured city, addressed economic problems. Praised by many citizens for his fairness and humanitarian acts, McPherson established a program to feed the hungry, and soon long lines stretched from distribution points down ravaged streets. The siege had caused many businesses to shut down, and finding capital and labor to repair damaged buildings and build up inventories took time. Local commerce fell victim to crippling inflation, caused by shortages of goods and currency. Blatant profiteering and reckless speculation further exacerbated the situation. Commercial disruption led to high unemployment, which further stalled restoration of the city's economic life. Vicksburg, once "growing, amoral, and unbridled," had been transformed by war into a "refugee haven, military enclave, and jumping-off point for adventurers who sought fortune." However, for "those persons who had an adequate income and were not lacking life's necessities, occupied Vicksburg was not an altogether unpleasant place in which to pass a year or two as an Army officer or would-be businessman or financier."[13]

Economic issues often had racial overtones, for freed slaves created issues that had to be addressed by Federal conquerors. Ex-slaves who did not join the Union army had basically two choices. They could go to contraband refugee camps, established by order of U. S. Grant, or they could go to work for profiteers trying to take advantage of confiscated farmland. Examples of the latter option included picking cotton for white businessmen who contracted with the Federal government; black field hands in this case usually were paid a penny a pound. The businessmen's share was in the range of sixty-seventy cents per pound, while the government received half the cotton. The U.S. Treasury Department had already established a lessee plan in the summer of 1862; the intent was to give loyalists control of farmland north and south of Vicksburg and adjacent to the Mississippi. The lessees hired black labor, and in many cases unscrupulous profiteers victimized these field hands in ways that mirrored slavery abuses. Some observers described lessees as men "whose highest thought is a greenback, whose God is a cotton bale, and whose devil is a guerrilla." Even after the surrender, guerrilla activities, especially in Louisiana, continued to haunt river environs around Vicksburg.

Though it was obvious that the Union government and military intended to reward local Unionists and to help blacks who needed work, halfhearted attempts to regulate all the various activities generally failed. After all, the siege was over, but the war was not; and controlling the shenanigans of those who took advantage of loose, often anarchical, programs was not a high priority.[14]

\~≋ Blacks, who for various reasons did not go back to the fields, often enjoyed the emotional high of freedom after the surrender and then later suffered from the demeaning conditions of the refugee camps. The presence of Union troops emboldened freedmen, who now made clear to local whites that the days of meek deference to masters were over. Black men voluntarily swelled the ranks of Union Colored troops, thereby, noted Abraham Lincoln, strengthening the Federal cause and weakening the Confederacy. Black women walked city streets arm in arm with white Federal soldier boyfriends. But those blacks who eventually found themselves in contraband camps came to realize that their newfound dignity could be fleeting.

Initially these camps, which had been set up in the Vicksburg region as early as November 1862, were "sinkholes of misery and degradation." Grant appointed Chaplain John Eaton of Ohio to superintend the camps and refugees, and Eaton managed to bring some order out of sordid chaos. Prior to the surrender, black refugees gathered at points along the river where they were subject to unhealthy camp conditions and ruthless raids by guerrilla bands. Hundreds, perhaps thousands, died in camps at places like Young's Point. After the surrender, the poor conditions persisted, and more died along the banks of the river that now symbolized their manumission.

Perhaps the most unusual and ironic development that grew out of Grant's efforts to deal with freedmen issues occurred at Davis Bend, on Brierfield, the former plantation of Jefferson Davis. There, the Union military tried to create a "negro paradise" by having former slaves colonize the place. Mismanagement ultimately doomed this wartime experiment. The failure to provide a better life for freed slaves in the Vicksburg vicinity, and for that matter in most of the defeated Confederacy, continued through the Reconstruction period until white "redeemers" reenslaved blacks with segregation laws.[15]

While freedmen's hopes for a better life gradually faded, Vicksburg fell short of its prewar promise. Local merchants were slow to respond to postsiege, postoccupation, and postwar opportunities. The war brought the outside world to Vicksburg in ways that citizens never envisioned. Aggressive opportunists grabbed control of various economic markets, for cotton and other products, as well as the lucrative shipping industry that blossomed throughout the Mississippi River Valley at war's end. As local businessmen did little more than watch, "merchants from the Memphis area were stealing trade all the way down to Yazoo City, and retailers from New Orleans, St. Louis, and even Cincinnati were moving into what formerly had been Vicksburg's exclusive business area." A willed shortsightedness and a self-imposed racial caste system, intended to recapture a mythical, elusive past, blighted the hopes of Vicksburg and the surrounding area that had suffered through the campaign and siege.[16]

For many years, a story has persisted that anti-Union feelings remained so strong in Vicksburg after the surrender that the Fourth of July was not celebrated there until the mid-twentieth century. However interesting that story may seem, there are a number of reasons for questioning it. First of all, Federal troops occupied Vicksburg for several years after the surrender, well into the Reconstruction era. Surely these troops celebrated the Fourth, and some citizens no doubt joined in. The fact that many Union soldiers courted, and occasionally married, local women made joint festivities even more likely. Also, anecdotes handed down through generations of Vicksburgians indicate that citizens celebrated the Fourth long after Federal troops had departed. Whether city officials sanctioned the Fourth as a day of celebration is not known, and perhaps the legend stems from ambiguity about the official status of observances. The implication has been that the Fourth was ignored, but it is conceivable that private citizens, or even businesses, observed the holiday. Southern observations of July 4 were for many years, before and after the war, characterized more by family picnics than by formal city or county activities. The Fourth story may play well to tourists, but it seems to have little foundation in fact.[17]

Vicksburg was not the only town forced to embark on a long, frustrating recovery period. The change in Union war policy "from pragmatism to hard war" during the campaign left physical and emotional scars. The impact of Federal destruction on towns like Jackson, Holly Springs, and Corinth was severe enough that returning to prewar conditions was not easy. The towns themselves, notably Jackson, bounced back in a rather surprisingly short time, though the political disruptions of Reconstruction slowed the recovery. The surrounding rural countryside, which had been chewed up by both armies, faced much greater challenges. Small farms and large plantations had been stripped of food, forage, horses and mules, buildings, and slave field hands. The loss of labor was especially significant because the state's agricultural economic base had depended on slaves. Hard war, as a policy, sometimes got out of hand, and there was much destruction for the sake of destruction — "sheer vandalism, but most had occurred in retaliation, deserved or otherwise, for bushwhacking and other partisan incidents." Confederates had done their part to contribute to the ravaging of the land, and Rebel guerrillas had exacerbated Union hard-war attitudes. As time passed, white Mississippians dared not point fingers at their own kind. The Yankee invader alone had caused it all. So, although the Confederacy may have lost Vicksburg, and ultimately the war, it won the hearts of those who conveniently forgot that their sufferings were attributable to many perpetrators, not all of them wearing blue.[18]

Grasping at the past, and reshaping it, proved to be a typical reaction among women who had experienced the campaign. Their accounts of deprivation, harassment, and physical abuse tended to blame vile Yankees. They cleansed their memories of depredations by Confederate soldiers, as well as neighboring whites, who took advantage of wartime conditions that left many areas lawless. War turned their lives upside down and forced them to assume roles they once would have shunned, and in any event were often ill prepared to assume. Someone had to be held responsible, and as time passed and the noble defenders of Vicksburg assumed their places in the pantheon of Confederate heroes, all the blame shifted to the obvious villains, the invaders from the North. An enshrined Vicksburg took the place of a lost Vicksburg, and women both within and outside the city played their part in seeing to it that the cause, if lost, remained glorious in the Southern white mind. Their views contradicted the disaffection from the Confederacy so clearly evident after Vicksburg fell. Over the intervening months and years, reality had been changed into illusion.[19]

Far beyond the geographical limits of the campaign, the capture of Vicksburg had a multifaceted impact on the remainder of the Civil War. While the story faded from newspaper headlines in favor of new battles, the military, political, and psychological ramifications of the Union victory and Confederate defeat resonated across the country. Aside from wanting to build a strong Union presence in Texas, Union strategists, especially Halleck and Lincoln, seemed unable to define and pursue a comprehensive campaign to follow up their successes on the Mississippi. Attempts to secure the Mississippi and campaigns in the Trans-Mississippi highlighted the months after July 1863. Sherman swept from Vicksburg to Meridian in February 1864 to make sure Confederates had few logistical tools to retake Vicksburg. His march was impressive, and it served as a prelude to the war-making philosophy Sherman used in Georgia and the Carolinas later in the war. The devastation wrought by his men did not prevent Confederates from talking about blockading the lower Mississippi again. The Rebels, however, had neither the navy nor the manpower to retake Vicksburg or create a similar bulwark against the Union.

Meanwhile, the Federals' preoccupation with the Trans-Mississippi produced nothing but embarrassment, as demonstrated by Nathaniel Banks's disastrous Red River campaign of 1864. As two military historians, Henry Hattaway and Archer Jones, have noted: "The immense geographical extent of the region made military successes and territorial conquests essentially illusory, as Price's late 1864 Missouri raid dramatically demonstrated. For a long time the trans-Mississippi constituted Lincoln and Halleck's strategic tar baby." In effect, the capture of Vicksburg left Washington wondering what to do next in the lower Mississippi Valley, a question never adequately answered.[20]

Vicksburg's lessons stayed with Grant when on his next assignment he went to Chattanooga to break up the Confederate entrapment of Rosecrans's army, a result of the Rebel victory at Chickamauga. Using proven tactics of maneuver and deception, Grant broke the siege, and his troops sent the Confederates fleeing into North Georgia. He was then promoted to replace Halleck as commander of the Union armies. Grant decided to steer the Army of the Potomac, which had long been throttled by Robert E. Lee. The setback at Gettysburg had not changed one important fact: Lee still had an able army and must be dealt with before the war in the East could be brought to an end. As at Vicksburg, Grant wanted to force the enemy to turn to meet him. In this case, he proposed moving into North Carolina, in Lee's rear, and cutting all railroad links between Virginia and points south. Lincoln, however, along with Halleck, who now worked for Grant, strongly objected, for they feared Lee would strike north and once more panic loyal Union citizens. So Grant backed off and settled for slugging it out with Lee.[21]

Yet Grant did not abandon his turning, flanking tactics. Many of his confrontations with Lee in 1864 resulted from his attempts to flank Lee and get in his rear, or, more to the point, to cut off the Confederate army from Richmond. Grant's Virginia campaign did not involve as much maneuvering as he used to capture Vicksburg, but he certainly continued to follow the principles that had worked before. As he had done in Mississippi and Louisiana, Grant also made sure his logistical line was secure. Sherman likewise relied on the tactical lessons learned around Vicksburg when he campaigned against Joseph Johnston in Georgia. Sherman continually forced Johnston to retreat by threatening the Confederate flanks. Sherman secured his logistical line back to Chattanooga by sending small armies into Mississippi to occupy Nathan Bedford Forrest, thus keeping Forrest from cutting the Union supply line.

Robert E. Lee and other Southerners understood the lessons of Vicksburg. When news came that Grant had been promoted, Northern newspapers gave various accounts of what Grant would do. He might stay in the West or come east. Robert E. Lee was not sure, but he remembered how Pemberton had been convinced that Grant was giving up on Vicksburg, even as Grant's army moved down the Louisiana side of the Mississippi. Lee warned Jefferson Davis that Grant might try to deceive the Confederates in Virginia, and they must be sure of true Federal intentions before making commitments. Clearly, Lee respected what

Grant had accomplished on the Mississippi and did not intend to make the mistake of taking his new opponent lightly. Others also feared imitations of Grant's success. Mary Chesnut, aware of how Grant had penned up Pemberton in Vicksburg, feared that the same Union strategy might doom Savannah in late 1864. The details of Grant's triumph penetrated the psyches of Southern soldier and civilian alike, and at Petersburg he turned their fears into reality.[22]

Tales of the siege were passed along beyond Vicksburg, both by word of mouth and in print. Published in New York in 1864, Mary Ann Loughborough's account, *My Cave Life in Vicksburg, with Letters of Trial and Travel*, told readers of the ordeal that the siege posed to civilians. The siege thus began to capture the public's imagination in ways that no other Civil War campaign or battle could. The specter of people living underground to escape the ravages of war gave Vicksburg a firm and unique place in the national imagination long after the particulars of the campaign faded from memory.

Songs and poems reflected Vicksburg's legacy. In 1863, "Cuffee's War Song" by L. B. Starkweather and the "Never Surrender Quick Step" celebrated Grant's victory, while the "Vicksburg Schottish" was dedicated to the women of Vicksburg. In 1864, "Elegy" was published as a memorial to Union general George Boomer, who had been killed during the siege, and "Grant's the Man" by C. L. Abdill praised the general's heroics. Other related works that came out before the war ended included "Vicksburg—A Ballad," "Bombardment of Vicksburg," and "The Cotton-Burners' Hymn." The campaign obviously attracted the attention of composers, North and South. Postwar writings continued to examine the mystique of the battles and siege that had brought the Mississippi back into the Union.[23]

≋ Perhaps no one felt the ramifications of Vicksburg's capitulation more deeply than Jefferson Davis. He had to cope with the Pemberton-Johnston feud and his own personal war with Johnston. Aware of the public charges and countercharges, people began taking sides about the responsibility for the loss of Vicksburg, and few blamed Johnston. Other Confederate generals argued about the failure of Trans-Mississippi officers to provide relief. Davis endured harsh political criticism, and he lost a measure of public confidence that he never regained. Some Southerners observed the July 4, 1864, anniversary of the surrender as a sad day "for the happiness of our Southern Confederacy." Others blamed Davis for the double loss of Vicksburg and Chattanooga, and eventually they would fault him for the debacle at Atlanta, another campaign that underscored Davis's testy relationship with Johnston.

Many Southerners rejected attempts by some of the Confederate press and Davis supporters to put a positive spin on Grant's victory. The idea that the surrender freed up Rebel armies to be more effective elsewhere was especially scorned by many, who found it impossible to "close our eyes upon the painful consequences of the downfall of this hope of the Confederacy." Southern newspapers that scalded Davis immediately after the surrender kept up their heated criticism, which came to be fueled by bad news from Chattanooga. One paper referred to the twin defeats at Vicksburg and Port Hudson as 1863's "greatest reverses." After Vicksburg, Southerners began to look away from Davis and focus on military leaders, especially Lee, as their only hope for salvation.[24]

After Vicksburg, Confederate military fortunes in the portion of the Western Theater west of Georgia were dismal or insignificant. Sherman's Meridian campaign showed how the loss of Pemberton's army had left the Vicksburg area of operations almost devoid of Rebel troop strength. In Louisiana, there would be a spark when Richard Taylor repulsed Banks's foray up the Red River, but the victory was hollow at best, for it had no impact on the outcome of the war. Everywhere, with the exception of Chickamauga, a Confederate victory that offered brief possibilities for reoccupying Chattanooga, Davis's troops had to stay on the defensive. When Braxton Bragg frittered away his victory, and Grant chased him away from Chattanooga, all the Confederates could do was try to protect Atlanta, which ultimately proved impossible. The last major offensive in the West, John Bell Hood's disastrous invasion of Tennessee in late 1864, led to the destruction of the only major Confederate force outside Virginia. Vicksburg set a downhill course in the West from which the Confederacy never recovered. The loss of an army and the fracturing of a nation proved too much for Davis and his limited resources to overcome.

For the main military personages who participated in the Vicksburg campaign, the future held a variety of experiences, ranging from surviving the campaign by only a few days to long, illustrious lives, from descending to ascending in military rank, from obscurity to fame. In personal terms, the campaign certainly proved to be a turning point.[25]

John Pemberton felt the sting of losing Vicksburg for the rest of the war and beyond. When Davis failed to find him a new position, he resigned from his rank of lieutenant general and accepted a lieutenant colonelcy of artillery. He served as an artillery inspector in Virginia and the Carolinas until the end of the war. Afterward, he tried unsuccessfully to establish a farm in Virginia and ultimately moved back to Pennsylvania, where he worked for his family until his death on July 13, 1881. He never saw Vicksburg again after leading his paroled army east, and he had no desire to. He is buried in Laurel Hill Cemetery in Philadelphia, Pennsylvania.

Among Pemberton's chief lieutenants, John Bowen died from dysentery on July 13, 1863, and was temporarily buried near Raymond. Later his remains were transferred to the Confederate section of the Vicksburg city cemetery, but the exact location of his grave is unknown. After Vicksburg, M. L. Smith became chief engineer of both the Army of Northern Virginia and the Army of Tennessee, and helped plan Mobile's defenses near the end of the war. He died on July 29, 1866, and is buried in Athens, Georgia, the hometown of his wife. John Forney served in the Trans-Mississippi region after the surrender, and during his postwar years he farmed and worked as a civil engineer in Alabama. He died on September 13, 1902, and is buried in Jacksonville, Alabama. Carter Stevenson served with the Army of Tennessee for the remainder of the war. In Virginia, his home state, after the war, Stevenson worked as a mining and civil engineer, passing away on August 15, 1888. He is buried in Fredericksburg. William Loring also received a command in the Army of Tennessee, and after the war soldiered in Egypt. Eventually, he returned to the United States; he died in New York City on December 30, 1886, and was interred in St. Augustine, Florida. After Vicksburg, Francis Marion Cockrell led his Missourians in the Army of Tennessee. Promoted to brigadier general, he served notably in the Atlanta and Tennessee campaigns, receiving a serious wound during the latter at Franklin. Returning to duty in 1865, he surrendered at Mobile; after the war, he practiced law in Missouri and represented that state for thirty years in the U.S. Senate. He also served on the Interstate Commerce Commission under President Theodore Roosevelt. Cockrell died on December 13, 1915, and is buried in Warrensburg, Missouri. Earl Van Dorn was killed by an allegedly jealous husband in Tennessee on May 7, 1863, and is buried in his hometown of Port Gibson, Mississippi.

Two other key Confederates during the campaign were Joseph E. Johnston and Isaac N. Brown. Johnston, in spite of his feud with Jefferson Davis, was appointed commander of the Army of Tennessee, was later relieved of the post, and toward the end of the war was reappointed to it, surrendering the army in North Carolina in 1865. He was elected to the U.S. House of Representatives from his native Virginia in 1879, and was U.S. commissioner of railroads for six years. He died of pneumonia on March 21, 1891, after marching bareheaded in bad weather in William T. Sherman's funeral procession in Washington, D.C. He is buried in Green Mount Cemetery, Baltimore, Maryland. Following his service in Mississippi, Isaac Brown took command of the ironclad *Charleston*, which participated in the defense of Charleston Harbor. His postwar years included working as a farmer in the Mississippi Delta and later moving to Texas, where he passed away on September 1, 1889.

U. S. Grant's star continued to rise, and, after a bloody overland campaign, he forced Lee to surrender on April 9, 1865. The successor of Andrew Johnson, Grant served as president of the United States for two terms (1869–1877); his presidential years were marked by corruption and betrayals by friends he thought could be trusted. His cigar smoking resulted in throat cancer, and he managed to complete his much-praised memoirs just before his death on July 23, 1885, at his home in Mount McGregor, New York. The city of New York offered the Grant family an excellent deal to have the general's remains interred in a proper tomb, so, belying his Midwestern character, Grant, along with his wife, rests in a mausoleum there.

Grant's number one lieutenant had a successful post-Vicksburg career. In addition to his Meridian jaunt and capture of Atlanta, William T. Sherman conducted his famous "march to the sea" from Atlanta to Savannah, Georgia, all in 1864. Thereafter, he led his army north through the Carolinas, where he accepted Johnston's surrender. In 1869, he became commanding general of U.S. armies and was a popular speaker at veterans' reunions. He died in New York City on February 14, 1891, and is buried in Calvary Cemetery, St. Louis, Missouri. Sherman remains a condemned figure among many self-ordained "Confederates" in the South for the destructive campaigns after Vicksburg.

John McClernand eventually got back command of the XIII Corps, but an illness in Texas forced him to resign. Despite his support for Lincoln and the war effort, McClernand remained active with the Democratic Party in postwar Illinois. He died on September 20, 1890, and is buried in Springfield. James McPherson, the postsurrender military governor of Vicksburg, eventually was appointed commander of the Army of the Tennessee, which he led during Sherman's Atlanta campaign. McPherson was killed in action near Atlanta on July 22, 1864, and is buried in his native Ohio near the town of Clyde. John Logan temporarily replaced McPherson, before reassuming command of the

XV Corps, which he led during the Atlanta and Carolina campaigns. He returned to Illinois after the war and was elected both U.S. congressman and U.S. senator from that state, and was an unsuccessful vice presidential candidate. He died on December 26, 1886, while serving in the Senate, and is buried in Washington, D.C., in the Soldiers Home National Cemetery. Benjamin Grierson continued cavalry service in Mississippi after his successful 1863 raid, and also participated in the campaign against Mobile. At the end of the war, he left the army with the rank of major general of volunteers; later, he was appointed colonel of the 10th Cavalry, serving mostly in Arizona, New Mexico, and Indian Territory. He retired as a brigadier general, and died on September 1, 1911; he is buried in Jacksonville, Illinois.

The two chief Union naval commanders during the campaign both continued their successes. David Porter experienced some frustration when he commanded a fleet supporting Nathaniel Banks's ill-fated Red River campaign in 1864. Low water thwarted Porter's boats in the Red. He later commanded the naval blockade near Wilmington, North Carolina, and assisted in forcing the surrender of Fort Fisher, a key Confederate supply base. Porter also aided in the capture of Richmond in 1865, when his boats ascended the James River. He became superintendent of the U.S. Naval Academy in 1869 and was promoted to admiral in 1870. He died on February 13, 1891, and is buried in Arlington National Cemetery. David Farragut, his foster brother, spent a good portion of his post-Vicksburg service trying to capture Mobile. During the fighting there, he issued his well-known statement, "Damn the torpedoes. Full steam ahead." After Mobile fell, Farragut turned down command of the North Atlantic Squadron, citing poor health as the reason. He went to New York, and later back down to Richmond to participate in the occupation of the Confederate capital. In 1866, he was promoted to admiral and toured Europe with the Mediterranean Squadron. He died on August 14, 1870, and was interred in Woodlawn Cemetery in New York City.

~~~ Two Vicksburg campaign veterans, one a well-known Confederate and the other a lesser-known Union officer, joined forces to lead the way for the establishment of the Vicksburg National Military Park in 1899.

Stephen D. Lee served as a cavalry commander after Vicksburg was surrendered. He later was appointed a lieutenant general, the youngest Confederate officer to attain that rank, and led John Bell Hood's old corps in the Army of Tennessee, surrendering with the remnants of that army in North Carolina in April 1865. After the war, he returned to his adopted state, Mississippi, and dabbled in farming and politics before becoming the first president of the Agricultural and Mechanical College of Mississippi (present-day Mississippi State University) in 1880. During that time, he became involved with the United Confederate Veterans and with the establishment of the Park. Lee died on May 28, 1908, and is buried in Friendship Cemetery in Columbus, Mississippi.

William T. Rigby was a lieutenant in the 24th Iowa during the Vicksburg campaign. Following the war, he earned a degree at Cornell College in Iowa and became a banker in the Iowa town of Mechanicsville. Like Lee, Rigby was active in veterans' affairs. He passed away on May 10, 1929, and is buried in the Vicksburg National Cemetery.

In 1895, Rigby was elected secretary of the Vicksburg National Military Park Association, of which Stephen D. Lee was a founding member. The association worked successfully to get the U.S. Congress to pass a bill establishing a national military park at Vicksburg. The bill became law in 1899, and Rigby, Lee, and Union veteran James G. Everest were named the initial commissioners of the Park, with Lee being elected by the two former Union soldiers as the chairman of the group. Rigby succeeded Lee as chairman after Lee's ill health forced him to resign in November 1901. The two old soldiers often fought over the wording of marker descriptions and other issues, but they reached compromises and together forged a solid foundational beginning for a park that comprises today some 1,800 acres and 1,328 markers and monuments, carefully preserved earthworks, and the remains of the *U.S.S. Cairo*, rescued from the muddy waters of the Yazoo. The Park is a remarkably scenic, majestic, and poignant memorial to Lee, Rigby, and the thousands of veterans on both sides who fought there.[26]

Like Rigby and Lee, blue and gray veterans were more inclined than civilians to mend fences. In October 1917, Vicksburg campaign veterans met for a "National Memorial Celebration and Peace Jubilee" in Vicksburg. Supervising officials prepared for 12,000 to 15,000, though only around 8,000 showed up. The reunion was peaceful, and Willard D. Newbill, the U.S. Army colonel in charge of the event, wrote in his report: "Their reunion is now only a memory, but they could not have encamped on more beautiful historic ground nor in a place they could have taken greater pride and delight. They looked upon this Park as their own and loved it as sacred soil; and to them it will remain, in keeping with their brave, loyal old spirits and declining years, a vision of rugged autumn beauty, and for them hereafter hold a double significance as a spot where once they struggled in bitter strife, but where they again met over half a century later in the brotherly love of restored confidence and in complete reunion under their original flag."[27]

As for the Vicksburg campaign and its place in history, it continues to languish in the shadows of the Eastern Theater in general and of Gettysburg in particular. Unless more historians are willing to change the paradigm of Civil War turning points from the Eastern to the Western Theater, Vicksburg is likely to remain overshadowed. The campaign is, in a sense, a victim of its length, scope, and complexity. It is much easier for historians and buffs alike to understand a campaign of a few weeks, culminating in a three-day battle, than to grasp intricate operations that lasted over a year and included several significant engagements. Besides full-scale battles, the struggle for Vicksburg consisted of cavalry raids, naval encounters, combined army-navy operations, subcampaigns affecting the final outcome, and a siege that included classic applications of military science. Professional soldiers continue to visit, study, and appreciate better than most the Vicksburg campaign areas and the significance of what happened there.[28]

The campaign's effect on the outcome of the war was profound, arguably more so than that of any other military event. After Gettysburg, Robert E. Lee's army continued fighting for nearly two more years. With the fall of Vicksburg, the Confederacy lost an army that never fought again. The Confederacy also lost thousands of square miles of territory and suffered a permanent disruption in logistical support, sporadic though it had been, that the Trans-Mississippi supplied to the rest of the Confederacy. Scattered military action continued in the region encompassing Louisiana, Arkansas, Mississippi, Alabama, and West Tennessee, but the loss of Vicksburg and the Mississippi in effect shrank the Western Confederacy from Texas to the Alabama-Georgia border. The ordnance lost when Pemberton surrendered could not be replaced. The impact of the surrender on Southern morale was considerably greater than that of Lee's withdrawal from Pennsylvania.[29] In fact, it is one of the unfortunate paradoxes of the Civil War that Vicksburg mattered more and is remembered less than many campaigns and battles of distinctly smaller consequence.

Soldiers and civilians who experienced the campaign seemed to grasp these truths to a greater degree than succeeding generations. They understood that a watershed had been reached on the rocky road back to reunion. Though the war dragged on, for many on both sides who saw the Stars and Stripes flying over the city of Vicksburg, the issue had been decided. When elderly campaign veterans gathered fifty-four years later "under their original flag," they no doubt felt that the camaraderie they shared had been made possible by their common legacy. Southern soldiers viewed the campaign from a perspective that hate-filled civilians, women and men, could not comprehend or understand.

The veterans of the campaign gained neither the attention nor the notoriety of their comrades in arms who carried on the struggle in the Eastern Theater. No doubt some bitterness remained among surviving veterans, for memories of comrades shot down by rifle fire or torn apart by artillery shells or bayoneted in close combat could not be totally submerged by the passage of time. The long campaign, with the destruction and guerrilla activity that accompanied it, had engendered and magnified strife and hatred. Yet examples of fellowship had been striking following the surrender.

As the years went by, veterans gained a better understanding of the war, beyond what they had personally seen and experienced. They perceived what had been decided among the hills and ravines of Vicksburg and developed greater appreciation of the bravery of comrades, and even foes, who struggled there. Certainly they could look back and see the decisiveness of the surrender, whether they had fought to prevent it or to bring it about. They remembered comrades left behind on the battlefields of Iuka and Corinth, among North Mississippi hills and streams, in Delta and Louisiana swamps, along and in rivers small and mighty, on blood-soaked ground at Chickasaw Bayou, Arkansas Post, Port Gibson, Raymond, Jackson, Champion Hill, the Big Black, and Vicksburg itself. In their minds and memories, regardless of the uniform they had worn, the Vicksburg National Military Park summed up the tragedies and heroism that characterized the momentous campaign they and the fallen had waged. For them, that knowledge secured their proper place in the history of their Civil War.

Notes

General biographical information on various persons involved in the Vicksburg campaign came from Ezra J. Warner's two classic volumes, *Generals in Gray: Lives of the Confederate Commanders* (Baton Rouge, La., 1959) and *Generals in Blue: Lives of the Union Commanders* (Baton Rouge, La., 1964); Mark M. Boatner III, *The Civil War Dictionary* (New York, 1959); Richard N. Current, ed., *Encyclopedia of the Confederacy*, 4 vols. (New York, 1993); and David S. Heidler and Jeanne T. Heidler, eds., *Encyclopedia of the American Civil War: A Political, Social, and Military History*, 5 vols. (Santa Barbara, Calif., 2000).

Abbreviations

DU	Duke University, Perkins Library, Durham, N.C.
ETSU	East Tennessee State University Library, Johnson City, Tenn.
IHS	Indiana Historical Society, Indianapolis, Ind.
ISHL	Illinois State Historical Library, Springfield, Ill.
ISL	Indiana State Library, Indianapolis, Ind.
LC	Library of Congress, Washington, D.C.
LSU	Louisiana State University, Hill Memorial Library, Baton Rouge, La.
MDAH	Mississippi Department of Archives and History, Jackson, Miss.
NA	National Archives, Washington, D.C.
OCHM	Old Court House Museum, Vicksburg, Miss.
OHS	Ohio Historical Society, Columbus, Ohio
OR	*The War of the Rebellion: A Compilation of the Official Records of the Union and Confederate Armies*, 128 vols. (Washington, D.C., 1880–1901). All citations of *OR* refer to series 1 unless otherwise indicated.
ORN	*Official Records of the Union and Confederate Navies in the War of the Rebellion*, 35 vols. (Washington, D.C., 1894–1927). All citations of *ORN* are to series 1 unless otherwise indicated.
RG	Record Group
TU	Tulane University, Special Collections Library, Jones Hall, New Orleans, La.
UI	University of Iowa Libraries, Special Collections Department, Iowa City, Iowa
UM	University of Michigan, Bentley Library, Ann Arbor, Mich.
UMC	University of Missouri–Columbia, Western Historical Manuscript Collections, Columbia, Mo.
UNCCH	University of North Carolina at Chapel Hill, Wilson Library, Southern Historical Collection, Chapel Hill, N.C.
USAMHI	United States Army Military History Institute, Carlisle Barracks, Pa.

UT   University of Texas at Austin, Barker Center for American History, Austin, Tex.
VNMP   Vicksburg National Military Park, Archives, Vicksburg, Miss. Unless otherwise noted, references are to the Regimental Files Subseries of the Vicksburg Campaign Series.
WHSA   Wisconsin Historical Society Archives, Madison, Wis.

CHAPTER 1

1. Morris, *Becoming Southern*, 108–9; Bette E. Barber, "Dickson, Sage of Walnuts Hills," *New Orleans Times-Picayune* clipping, ca. May 29, 1949, in Cockrell Papers, DU; Samuel H. Lockett, "The Siege of Vicksburg from an Engineering Point of View," Lockett Papers, UNCCH.

2. Morris, *Becoming Southern*, 109; Harrell, *Vicksburg and the River*, 13–14.

3. Morris, *Becoming Southern*, 109–10; Grabau, *Ninety-Eight Days*, 16–17.

4. Morris, *Becoming Southern*, 115, 121.

5. Ibid., 120; Grillis, *Vicksburg*, 41, 43.

6. Grillis, *Vicksburg*, 43, 44, 49.

7. Ibid., 53, 55; Morris, *Becoming Southern*, 115, 116.

8. Morris, *Becoming Southern*, 127–28, 174–75, 177.

9. Christ, *Papers of Davis*, 6: 668.

10. *Vicksburg Daily Whig*, November 8, 1860.

11. Walker, *Vicksburg*, 25, 26.

12. *Vicksburg Daily Whig*, November 13, 1860.

13. Ibid., November 17, 1860.

14. Ibid., November 30, 1860.

15. Walker, *Vicksburg*, 28–31, 31n; Morris, *Becoming Southern*, 178; G. Moore, "Separation from the Union," 1:443–44.

16. G. Moore, "Separation from the Union," 445; Walker, *Vicksburg*, 31, 33.

17. Hess, "Mississippi River, 187, 189, 203.

18. Ibid., 189; Winters, *Civil War*, 10–11.

19. Hess, "Mississippi River," 189; Dubay, *Pettus*, 95; D. Rowland, *Military History of Mississippi*, 35–36; Walker, *Vicksburg*, 35–36.

20. Dubay, *Pettus*, 29–30.

21. Ibid., 78–79, 83, 93, 95, 96, 103; Weinert, "Neglected Key to the Gulf Coast," 282; Winters, *Civil War*, 11.

22. Hess, "Mississippi River," 189, 190.

23. Ibid., 190, 191; *Chicago Daily Tribune*, January 15, 1861.

24. *Chicago Daily Tribune*, January 23, 1861; Lewis, *Sherman*, 144.

25. Hess, "Mississippi River," 192–94.

26. Ibid., 195–96, 199–203; Lewis, *Sherman*, 252.

27. Walker, *Vicksburg*, 35–38.

28. Ibid., 38; Grillis, *Vicksburg*, 62.

29. Walker, *Vicksburg*, 39.

30. Ibid.; Crist, *Davis*, 7:41.

31. Walker, *Vicksburg*, 40–41.

32. Ibid., 41; Crist, *Davis*, 7:59; Grillis, *Vicksburg*, 63.

33. Walker, *Vicksburg*, 42–43.

34. Ibid., 43, 44; Grillis, *Vicksburg*, 63, 64.

35. Walker, *Vicksburg*, 44–45.

36. B. Anderson, *By Sea and by River*, 33–34; Marszalek, "Where Did Winfield Scott Find His Anaconda?" 77, 80; Coombe, *Thunder*, 11.

37. Winters, *Civil War*, 45; *ORN*, 4:156–57.

38. *ORN*, 16:519–20.

39. Winters, *Civil War*, 45; Cooling, *Forts*, 5–6.

40. Winters, *Civil War*, 45–48.

41. *ORN*, 16:580–83, 677–79; Dubay, *Pettus*, 115–16.

42. Winters, *Civil War*, 49.

43. Ibid., 52–53; *ORN*, 16:696–97, 703–30.

44. Cooling, *Forts*, 5; Hattaway and Jones, *How the North Won*, 39, 51.

45. *OR*, 4:254.

46. *OR*, 4:385.

47. *OR*, 4:390; Daniel and Bock, *Island*, 1, 3, 4.

48. Daniel and Bock, *Island*, 8; Cooling, *Forts*, 11–12.

49. Cooling, *Forts*, 12.

50. *OR*, 4:405.

51. *OR*, 4:421, 422.

52. Walker, *Vicksburg*, 46.

53. Russell, *Diary*, 293, 296.

54. Walker, *Vicksburg*, 49; *Vicksburg Daily Whig*, April 24, 1861.

55. Russell, *Diary*, 295, 297.

56. The following discussion is based on Walker, *Vicksburg*, 49–50, 52–56, 58–60.

57. *OR*, 6:740, 746, 751.

58. *OR*, 6:753, 758, 760–61, 769.

59. *OR*, 3:783–84.

60. Hearn, *When the Devil Came Down to Dixie*, 40–42; Porter, *Incidents*, 95.

61. Porter, *Incidents*, 95–96.

62. See Connelly, "Vicksburg," 49–53.

63. *OR*, 6:684, 694–95.

64. Winters, *Civil War*, 78–79; *OR*, 6:823.

65. *OR*, 4:448, 481, 564, 565.

66. Hattaway and Jones, *How the North Won*, 62, 65, 66.

67. Evangeline ? to My Dear Love, February 9, 1862, Crutcher-Shannon Papers, MDAH.

68. On the battle of Shiloh (Pittsburg Landing), see Daniel, *Shiloh*, and Sword, *Shiloh*.

69. Coombe, *Thunder*, 18–21, 23, 26–28.

70. Daniel and Bock, *Island*, 101, 146–48.

71. On the battle of New Orleans, see Hearn, *Capture*.

72. Walker, *Vicksburg*, 68–69.

CHAPTER 2

1. Butler, *Correspondence*, 1:428; *ORN*, 18:245, 462, 528–30, 533.

2. *ORN*, 18:530–31; Bearss, *Rebel Victory*, 4; Winters, *Civil War*, 103.

3. *ORN*, 18:465, 473–78, 489–91, 494–95, 531–32, 782, 810; Still, *Iron Afloat*, 63; Bearss, *Rebel Victory*, 15, 20; *OR*, 15:423, 736; F. W. Curtenius Diary, May 15, 1862, Journals/Diaries/Letters Subseries of Vicksburg Campaign Series, VNMP.

4. *ORN*, 18:491–92, 533, 782–83, 810.

5. *OR*, 15:6–7; Still, *Iron Afloat*, 64.

6. William Y. Dixon Diary, vol. 1, May 2–4, 9, 12–13, 17, 1862 entries, Dixon Papers, and J. M. Doyle to Josiah Knighton, May 24, 1862, Josiah Knighton and Family Papers, LSU.

7. *OR*, 15:7; Charles K. Marshall letter, June 30, 1862, printed in Jackson *Daily Mississippian* [summer 1862], clipping, Marshall file, OCHM.

8. *ORN*, 18:493, 498–99, 502, 507, 704–5, 725, 810; *OR*, 15:23.

9. *ORN*, 18:507.

10. *ORN*, 18:519–22.

11. *ORN*, 18:508–10, 575–76.

12. *OR*, 15:22–23.

13. *OR*, 15:23–24; *ORN*, 18:534, 761; Hermann, *Pursuit of a Dream*, 40. In his splendid study, *Hard Hand of War*, Grimsley examines guerrilla categories; see especially p. 42.

14. *ORN*, 18:520, 535, 762; *OR*, 15:23–24.

15. *OR*, 15:23–24; *ORN*, 18:535; Winters, *Civil War*, 110–11.

16. *OR*, 15:7, 22, 24; *ORN*, 18:520, 535; Sydney Champion to Matilda Champion, [summer 1862], Champion Papers, DU.

17. *OR*, 15:8.

18. *OR*, 52(2):316–17; Bearss, *Rebel Victory*, 51.

19. *OR*, 15:741–42.

20. *OR*, 15:742, 746.

21. *OR*, 52(2):318–19, 15:746. See also *OR*, 6:652.

22. *ORN*, 18:783; Dixon Diary, vol. 1, May 30, 1862, LSU; Rowland Chambers Diaries, Diary 6, May 26–27, 1862, LSU; Mahala Roach Diary, May 28, 1862, UNCCH.

23. *OR*, 15:8.

24. *ORN*, 18:756, 783–84, 789, 797, 801–2, 815–16, 820.

25. *ORN*, 18:546–47, 785, 789–90, 797–98, 802, 816, 820; William Smith to brother, June 16, 1862, Smith Letters, LSU.

26. *ORN*, 18:547, 798, 802; Bearss, *Rebel Victory*, 61.

27. *ORN*, 18:552–53.

28. *OR*, 15:752 ; William Leroy Brown to wife, June 7, 1862, Brown Papers, USAMHI.

29. *OR*, 17(2):591.

30. *OR*, 15:752–53.

31. *OR*, 15:754, 756, 758; Dixon Diary, vol. 1, June 19, 1862, LSU.

32. *OR*, 17(2):612.

33. *OR*, 17(2):599, 606, 897, 52(2):325; 15:758; Emmie to Dearest Mother, June 8, July 2, 1862, Crutcher-Shannon Papers, MDAH.

34. *OR*, 15:761–63, 766, 770, 17(2):622.

35. *OR*, 52(2):324, 15:15, 767; Henry, *History*, 34; Chambers, "My Journal," 240; "During the First Siege," 11.

36. Spencer Bowen Talley Memoir, p. 15, USAMHI; W. E. Holloman Journal, July 4, 1862, 46th Mississippi file, VNMP; Richard and Richard, *Defense*, 56.

37. Richard and Richard, *Defense*, 51.

38. Ibid., 49, 55; Clippings Scrapbook, "Civil War Incidents in Vicksburg," OCHM.

39. *ORN*, 18:554, 562–65, 580–83.

40. *ORN*, 18:555–59; Hearn, *Admiral David Dixon Porter*, 124–25.

41. *ORN*, 18:561, 571–72, 664–66.

42. *ORN*, 18:582.

43. *ORN*, 18:586.

44. *ORN*, 18:639, 587, 727.

45. *ORN*, 18:639, 727, 750; *OR*, 15:8.

46. *ORN*, 18:584, 23:241; Slagle, *Ironclad Captain*, 249–50.

47. *ORN*, 18:584–85.

48. *ORN*, 23:242–43, 590–91.

49. *OR*, 15:27.

50. *ORN*, 18:640.

51. *OR*, 15:8; Marshall Letter, June 30, 1862, OCHM.

52. Joseph Quitman to Louise Lovell, June 29, 1863, Quitman Family Papers, UNCCH.

53. Carey Johnson Lee to sister, July 7, 1862, 27th Louisiana file, VNMP.

54. *ORN*, 18:585–86, 619–20, 623, 727, 751, 798, 640–41.

55. *OR*, 15:9; Jefferson Davis to John J. Pettus, February 3, 1862, and G. W. Freeman to John J. Pettus, August 9, 1862, Pettus Papers, RG 27, MDAH.

56. *ORN*, 18:589–90, 641.

57. *ORN*, 18:599–602.

58. *ORN*, 18:602–8; Duffy, *Lincoln's Admiral*, 139.

59. *ORN*, 18:593, 608.

60. "During the First Siege," 11; Richard and Richard, *Defense*, 57–58.

61. *ORN*, 18:610, 624–25; Slagle, *Ironclad Captain*, 249; Duffy, *Lincoln's Admiral*, 139, 141.

62. *ORN*, 18:626–32.

63. *ORN*, 18:632–36, 675, 23:235.

64. *ORN*, 23:244, 19:6.

65. *ORN*, 18:647–52; Still, *Iron Afloat*, 64–66.

66. *ORN*, 19:40–41, 68, 132–33.

67. *ORN*, 19:69, 133; I. E. Fiske to John Comstock, July 24, 1862, Comstock Papers, UNCCH.

68. *ORN*, 19:4–7, 9–10, 133–34.

69. *ORN*, 19:11, 13, 15, 40, 46, 60.

70. *ORN*, 19:18, 45–46, 50, 61; Slagle, *Ironclad Captain*, 277.

71. *ORN*, 19:17, 19, 59–60, 62.

72. *ORN*, 19:50–51, 52, 55; *OR*, 15:31–32; Dabney Maury Scales to father, July 31, 1862, C.S.S. *Arkansas* file, OCHM.

73. *ORN*, 19:53–54, 63–64.

74. *ORN*, 19:5–7.

75. *ORN*, 19:772; *OR*, 15:16; Sydney Champion to Matilda Champion, July 9, 1862, Champion Papers, DU; Bearss, *Rebel Victory*, 281.

CHAPTER 3

1. *OR*, 15:16, 746, 766, 778.

2. *OR*, 15:15, 54, 76, 330–31, 786.

3. Sydney Champion to Matilda Champion, [August 1, 1862], Champion Papers, DU; *OR*, 15:76–77, 791.

4. *ORN*, 19:130; *OR*, 15:17; I. N. Brown, "Confederate Gun-Boat 'Arkansas,'" 578–79; Read, "Reminiscences of the Confederate States Navy," 350; Gift, "Story of the Arkansas," 206.

5. I. N. Brown, "Confederate Gun-Boat 'Arkansas,'" 579.

6. *OR*, 15:54, 79, 82–83, 548; Davis, *Breckinridge*, 319–20.

7. *OR*, 15:80, 550–51; Gift, "Story of the Arkansas," 12:206–10.

8. *ORN*, 19:131, 135–36, 23:283–87.

9. Sydney Champion to Matilda Champion, September 26, 1862, Champion Papers, DU.

10. Samuel Lockett to Nelie Lockett, August 4, September 17, 1862, Lockett Papers, UNCCH; Samuel A. Whyte Diary, August 19, 2002, Whyte Papers, UNCCH; Alison Diary, December 26, 1862, UNCCH; Walker, *Vicksburg*, 116–26.

11. *OR*, 15:54, 77–78, 791.

12. Agnew Diary, August 2, 14, September 22, 28, October 17, 1862, UNCCH; David N. Holmes to parents, October 27, 1862, Holmes Papers, ISHL.

13. Thomas J. Blackwell Diary, October 28, 1862, 31st Mississippi file, VNMP.

14. William Woodward to Wife (Louise), July 4, 15, 19, Woodward Papers, USAMHI; Daniel Dinsmore to brother, September 4, 1862, Jasper Barny to brother, October 1862, Dinsmore Papers, ISHL.

15. *OR*, 17(2):150; U. S. Grant, *Memoirs*, 265; Badeau, *Military History of Grant*, 1:107–8.

16. *OR*, 17(2):178–79. For an analysis of Sherman's attitudes toward hard war during the Vicksburg campaign period, see Marszalek, *Sherman*, 188–231.

17. U. S. Grant, *Memoirs*, 265–66; *OR*, 17(2):160.

18. *ORN*, 23:286–87.

19. *ORN*, 23:294, 296, 302, 362, 388, 428–29; Robert H. Carnahan to wife, August 18, 1862, Carnahan Papers, USAMHI; Coombe, *Thunder*, 168; Gosnell, *Guns on the Western Waters*, 143; Soley, "Naval Operations," 559.

20. Hattaway and Jones, *How the North Won*, 205–6, 212–3; S. Marrett to Dear Companion, August 24, 1862, Marrett Papers, DU; H. H. Felton to Family, October 29, 1862, Felton Letters, LSU.

21. U. S. Grant, *Memoirs*, 262–64.

22. Hattaway and Jones, *How the North Won*, 206–8, 217–18.

23. *OR*, 17(2):655–57, 659, 662–64.

24. *OR*, 17(2):182, 189, 194, 197.

25. *OR*, 17(2):675–76, 678; Blackwell Diary, August 20, 1862, 31st Mississippi file, VNMP.

26. *OR*, 17(2):175, 182–83, 189; 16(2):333.

27. *OR*, 17(2):687, 690–95.

28. *OR*, 17(2):198, 200, 208, 696.

29. *OR*, 17(2):697–704.

30. *OR*, 17(2):706–7.

31. *OR*, 17(2):222, 227; *OR*, 17(1):65; *OR*, 17(1):67; Cozzens, *Darkest Days*, 126, 133.

32. *OR*, 17(2):710, 712, 717.

33. *OR*, 17(2):714–26.

34. *OR*, 17(2):717, 250; Blackwell Diary, September 12, 1862, 31st Mississippi, VNMP.

35. Cozzens, *Darkest Days*, 302–6; G. W. Giles to Dear Shoug, October 5, 1862, Giles Letters, LSU.

36. *OR*, 17(2):724–25.

37. *OR*, 17(2):237, 294, 296–97; U. S. Grant, *Memoirs*, 281; Bearss, *Vicksburg Campaign*, 1:22–23, 31. The specific titles of Bearss's volumes are *Vicksburg Is the Key* (vol. 1), *Grant Strikes a Fatal Blow* (vol. 2), and *Unvexed to the Sea* (vol. 3).

38. *OR*, 17(2):296, 308; Simpson, *Grant*, 155. See also *OR*, 13:778–79.

39. Kiper, *McClernand*, 129–31, 135–37.

40. Ibid., 132–43; *OR*, 17(2):274–75, 282.

41. *OR*, 17(2):312–13, 315–19.

42. Simon, *Grant Papers*, 6:243, 256, 261; *OR*, 17(2):338–40.

43. Barney, *Recollections*, 173.

44. Simon, *Grant Papers*, 6:262–63, 268, 278.

45. Senaca Thrall to wife, November 16, 1862, Thrall Papers, UI; Boyd, *Diary*, 84, 90–91.

46. Simon, *Grant Papers*, 6:288; *OR*, 17(1):469, 17(2):319.

47. "Journal of Company A, 14th Illinois Volunteer Infantry, May 25, 1861 to September 23, 1863," p. 35, Anthony and Smith Papers, ISHL; Seneca B. Thrall to wife, November 6, 1862, Thrall Papers, UI; Boyd, *Diary*, 82.

48. *OR*, 17(2):321; Simon, *Grant Papers*, 6:266–67.

49. John Given to home, November 13, 1862, Given Papers, ISHL; Grimsley and Miller, *Union Must Stand*, 66; John J. Barney to all at home, December 2, 1862, Barney Papers, WHSA.

50. *OR*, 13:778–79, 17(2):322.

51. *OR*, 17(2):322–24, 327, 328, 331.

52. Ballard, *Pemberton*, 1–113, examines the pre-Vicksburg life of Pemberton.

53. *OR*, 17(2):716–17, 724, 727.

54. *OR*, 17(2):715, 728–29, 733, 52(2):381.

55. *OR*, 52(2):382, 17(2):728.

56. *OR*, 17(2):717, 732, 734–36, 52(2) 377.

57. Tunnard, *Southern Record*, 211.

58. *OR*, 17(2):736–38; J. R. Waddy to John Gregg, November 4, 1862, RG 109, chap. 2, vol. 57, Letters and Telegrams Sent, Department of Mississippi and East Louisiana, NA.

59. *OR*, 17(2):738–42.

60. *OR*, 17(2):742–45.

61. *OR*, 17(2):745–47; Bearss, *Vicksburg Campaign*, 1:51.

62. Blackwell Diary, November 7, 10, 12, 17, 19, 23, December 1, 1862, 31st Mississippi file, VNMP.

63. *OR*, 17(2):336, 348.

CHAPTER 4

1. *OR*, 17(2):348, 356, 361, 362, 364, 17(1):471; George Marshall, "Civil War Reminiscences," p. 27, Marshall Papers, ISL.

2. *OR*, 17(2):365–68, 377–79. For an examination of Grant's staff during the Vicksburg campaign, see R. S. Jones, *Right Hand of Command*, 86–122.

3. "An Account of the Experiences of Lyman M. Baker in the Union Army and in Andersonville Prison," p. 3, Baker Papers, ISHL; George Hovey Cadman to Esther Cadman, November 23, December 14, 1862, Cadman Papers, UNCCH. As bad as the destruction was in 1862, it would be worse later in the war, during 1864 campaigning in North Mississippi. See Sobotka, *History of Lafayette County*, 33, 36.

4. Robert S. Finley to Mary A. Cabeen, December 18, 1862, Finley Papers, UNCCH; W. A. Rorer to Cousin Susan, November 28, 1862, Willcox Papers, DU; Rankin Poge McPheeters to Annie McPheeters, McPheeters Family Papers, USAMHI.

5. *OR*, 17(2):368–70, 17(1):528–29.

6. *OR*, 17(1):530, 533–37; W. A. Montgomery to sister, December 12, 1862, Bailey Papers, USAMHI.

7. *OR*, 17(1):539–40.

8. Montgomery to sister, December 12, 1862, Bailey Papers, USARMI.

9. *OR*, 17(2):372; U. S. Grant, *Memoirs*, 288.

10. *OR*, 17(2):374, 17(1):471–72;

David G. James to parents, December 4, 1862, James Papers, WHSA.

11. Tunnard, *Southern Record*, 215–16.

12. Sylvester W. Fairfield to Lizzie, December 1, 1862, Fairfield Papers, IHS; Nelson Diary, November 28, 1862, IHS; Bishop Diary, November 29, 1862, IHS; James Smith to Fair Friend Mattie, November 24, 1862, Smith Papers, ISHL; Metz Diary, November 26, 1862, DU.

13. *OR*, 17(2):374, 17(1):472.

14. *OR*, 17(1):423, 17(2):392–93.

15. *OR*, 17(2):382–84, 17(1):467, 471.

16. *OR*, 17(2)401–2.

17. *OR*, 17(2):390; Wright, *History of the Sixth Iowa Infantry*, 146–47.

18. Thomas Douglas to parents, December 1, 1862, Douglas Papers, USAMHI; Byers, *With Fire and Sword*, 44; James P. Boyd Diary, November 26, December 5, 6, 1862, Papers, ISHL; Daniel Harmon Brush Diary, November 23, 1862, Brush Papers, ISHL; William H. Nugen to sister, December 12, 1862, Nugen Papers, DU.

19. James Alcorn to Amelia, December 18, 1862, Alcorn Papers, UNCCH; Baker Diary, December 26, 1862, UNCCH; Katherine Polk Gale, "Recollections of Life in the Confederacy, 1861–1865," pp. 9–10, Gale and Polk Family Papers, UNCCH.

20. Seneca B. Thrall to wife, December 3, 1863?, Thrall Papers, UI; Boyd, *Diary*, 94; Adoniram J. Withrow to Lib, Cottoy, and Clara, December 8, 1862, Withrow Papers, UNCCH; Joseph Crider to Samuel Crider, November 29, 1862, and to William Crider, January 30, 1862, Crider Papers, UMC; Edward Rolfe letters in Lillibridge, *Hard Marches, Hard Crackers, and Hard Beds*, 45.

21. Seneca Thrall to wife, December 24, 1862?, Thrall Papers, UI; Maud Morrow Brown, "What Desolation! At Home in Lafayette County, 1860–1865," p. 107, Brown Papers, MDAH; Cornelia Lewis Scales to Loulie W. Irby, October 29, 1862, January 27, 1863, in Lumpkin, *"My Darling Loulie,"* 45–48, 60; Ella F. Pegues, "Recollections of the Civil War in Lafayette County," pp. 3–4, Brown Papers, MDAH; Mrs. Calvin [Maud Morrow] Brown, "Lafayette County, 1860–1865: A Narrative," pp. 28, 30 [29], 31 [30], 32 [31], 33 [32], Brown Papers, MDAH.

22. Brown, "What Desolation!," 102; James Vanderbilt to mother, December 15, 1862, Vanderbilt Papers, ISL; Non-commissioned Officer, *Opening of the Mississippi*, 37; Byers, *With Fire and Sword*, 46–47; "Incidents of the War of the Rebellion," p. 3, 8th Wisconsin Infantry Reunion Papers, WHSA.

23. Simon, *Grant Papers*, 6:404; *OR*, 17(2):392–94; Sherman, *Memoirs*, 210; U. S. Grant, *Memoirs*, 287–88; *OR*, 17(1):474, 601, 17(2):392–93.

24. *OR*, 17(2):392, 396–97, 402–3, 408–9, 412–15.

25. *OR*, 17(2):396, 400, 404, 415, 424; Simon, *Grant Papers*, 7:54.

26. *OR*, 17(2):405; Richard Phillips to Abraham Lincoln, December 15, 1862, Lincoln Papers, LC. The Phillips letter and other Lincoln papers are being transcribed by Knox College and are available on the Library of Congress's website, <http://memory.loc.gov/ammem/alhtml/malhome.html>.

27. *OR*, 17(2):401, 415, 420, 425; Kiper, *McClernand*, 153.

28. *OR*, 17(2):749–51; Bevier, *First and Second Missouri*, 165; E. McD. Anderson, *Memoirs*, 249.

29. *OR*, 13:359, 17(2):752–55.

30. *OR*, 17(2):756–57, 759–61.

31. *OR*, 17(2):757–59, 762–64, 766–68, 770–73; Ballard, *Pemberton*, 118; Gary Lancaster, "Brierfield Arsenal and Supply Depot," unpublished manuscript, courtesy of the author.

32. *OR*, 17(2):772, 774–76.

33. *OR*, 17(2):776–77, 782, 797–98, 800, 802.

34. *OR*, 17(2):777–82.

35. *OR*, 17(2):782–84.

36. *OR*, 17(2):784–85; E. McD. Anderson, *Memoirs*, 252–53; William Nichols to sister, December 10, 1862, Nichols Papers, UMC; *Mobile Register and Advertiser*, January 16, 1863.

37. *OR*, 17(1):494–96, 503–5.

38. Blackwell Diary, December 5–6, 1862, VNMP.

39. *OR*, 17(2):785–93; Christ, *Papers of Davis*, 8:539–41.

40. *OR*, 17(2):793–94, 796–99, 17(1):496–99.

41. Soley, "Naval Operations," 559.

42. Castel, *General Sterling Price*, 31–32; *OR*, 17(2):794–96, 800.

43. Barron, *Lone Star Defenders*, 131–33; Josephy P. Lesslie to wife and folks at home, December 25, 1862, 4th Indiana file, VNMP.

44. Barron, *Lone Star Defenders*, 133; Bears, *Decision in Mississippi*, 187–88; *OR*, 17(2):788, 792; Samuel Lockett to Nelie Lockett, December 17, 1862, Lockett Papers, UNCCH.

45. My discussion of Van Dorn's raid is based on Arthur B. Carter, *The Tarnished Cavalier*, 127–59, and Hartje, *Van Dorn*, 247–70.

46. Grimsley and Miller, *Union Must Stand*, 70.

47. F. Moore, *Rebellion Record*, 6:214.

48. *Mobile Advertiser and Register*, January 7, 1863, quoted in Carter, *Tarnished Cavalier*, 138.

49. Carter, *Tarnished Cavalier*, 142.

50. John Will Lindsey to Nancy, December 27, 1862, Lindsey Papers, ISHL.

51. Boyd, *Diary*, 95–99, 101.

52. Ballard, *Pemberton*, 227.

53. Boyd, *Diary*, 106; Charles Henry Brush Diary, January 6, 1863, Brush Papers, ISHL; Francis Marion Johnson Diary, January 8, 1863, Johnson Papers, ISHL; George Hovey Cadman to Esther, January 5, 1863, Cadman Papers, UNCCH; Andrew Bush to wife, January 17, 1863, Bush Letters, OCHM.

54. Wright, *History of Sixth Iowa*, 154–55.

55. Lewis, *Sherman*, 424.

CHAPTER 5

1. *OR*, 17(1):604–5.

2. Foster Memoirs, p. 43, WHSA.

3. *OR*, 17(1):629–30, 15:952–54, 962–63, 983–84.

4. *OR*, 17(1):605–6.

5. *OR*, 17(1): 656–66, 672–73, 17(2):803; Ballard, *Pemberton*, 128.

6. Alison Diary, December 26, 1862, UNCCH; Chambers, "My Journal," 253–54.

7. Lee, "Details of Important Work," 53–54; "What Telegraph Men Did for Vicksburg," 72; undated and unidentified clipping in scrapbook titled "How Telegraphs Saved Vicksburg: A True Story of the Civil War," M. J. Smith Papers, MDAH. Versions of General M. L. Smith's exact comments vary, but the gist is the same.

8. Bearss, *Vicksburg*, 1:152–54; *OR*, 17(1):606.

9. *OR*, 17(1):621–22; Bearss, *Vicksburg*, 1:164.

10. *OR*, 17(1):651; Bearss, *Vicksburg*, 1:166.

11. *OR*, 17(1):635, 642, 654, 686, 690, 695; Bearss, *Vicksburg*, 1:166–67.

12. *OR*, 17(1):635, 696; Committee of the Regiment, *Story of the Fifty-fifth*, 188–89.

13. *OR*, 17(1):627, 642, 648, 687; *ORN*, 23:573–73.

14. *OR*, 17(1):606, 666, (2):807; Sherman, *Memoirs*, 216–18.

15. *OR*, 17(1):651, 687, 690–91.

16. *OR*, 17(1):651, 690–91; David Palmer to Parents, January 3, 1863, Palmer Papers, UI.

17. *OR*, 17(1):647, 695. In the *OR*, the 29th Louisiana is mistakenly referred to as the 28th, and the 7th Kentucky is erroneously referred to as the 3rd.

18. *OR*, 17(1):641, 643–44, 647, 691, 696.

19. *OR*, 17(1):649, 654–55; Bearss, *Vicksburg*, 1:183; F. Moore, *Rebellion Record*, 6:316.

20. *OR*, 17(1):607, 635, 677.

21. *OR*, 17(1):627–28, 636, 677; Chambers, "My Journal," 255.

22. *ORN*, 23:581, 592.

23. *OR*, 17(1):607; Sherman, *Memoirs*, 218–19; Morgan, "Assault on Chickasaw Bluffs," 466.

24. *OR*, 17(1):607–8; Richard M. Hunt, "Battles of Chickasaw Bayou and Arkansas Post," n.p., Hunt Papers, USAMHI ; Morgan, "Assault," 464–65.

25. Morgan, "Assault," 464–65; *OR*, 17(1):655, 682, 695.

26. Morgan, "Assault," 466–67; *OR*, 17(1):655, 682.

27. *OR*, 17(1):646, 649, 652, 655–56, 688, 692.

28. *OR*, 17(1):649–50, 656, 682–83; Gary Ray Goodson Sr., *The Confederate Georgia 7,000: Part II, Letters and Diaries*, 1996, excerpts from writings of Henry W. Robinson, Georgia file, OCHM.

29. *OR*, 17(1):658–59, 682; William Marsh to parents and brother, Febru-

ary 17, 1863, Marsh Papers, ISHL; Black, *Soldier's Recollections*, 28; Morgan, "Assault," 3:469–70.

30. *OR*, 17(1):628, 633–34, 677–79, 697; Boyd Diary, December 28, 1862, ISHL.

31. *OR*, 17(2):608–9, 634, 661, 679; *ORN*, 23:585, 592.

32. Bearss, *Vicksburg*, 1:216; Maury, "Winter at Vicksburg."

33. Price F. Kellogg Journal, December 29, 1862, Kellogg Papers, ISHL; William Kennedy to wife, January 2, 1863, William J. Kennedy Papers, ISHL; Hunt, "Chickasaw Bayou"; Samuel Burdick Diary, December 28, 29, 31, 1862, WHSA; William R. Eddington Memoir, n.p., 97th Illinois file, VNMP.

34. *OR*, 17(1):609; *ORN*, 23:588.

35. George Marshall, "Civil War Reminiscences," p. 29, Marshall Papers, ISL; McGregor, "Chickasaw Bayou"; Andrew McCormack to parents and sisters, January 2, 1863, McCormack Letters, Wiley Sword Collection (used with permission); Sanders Diary, excerpt from *Louisiana Genealogical Exchange*, March 1970, OCHM; Andrew J. Sproul, Narrative, February 12, 1863, Sproul Papers, UNCCH; Maury, "Winter at Vicksburg"; Foster Memoirs, p. 46, WHSA.

36. *OR*, 17(1):662–63; Black, *Soldier's Recollections*, 29.

37. Roach Diary, December 31, 1862, UNCCH.

38. *OR*, 17(2):609–10, 625, 671.

39. James Hanna, "Nine Months of War, The Campaign and Capture of Grand Gulf and Vicksburg," 114th Ohio file, VNMP; *Thirty-fourth Iowa*, 9; Clark Whitten to wife and friends, January 8, 1863, Whitten Papers, USAMHI; Hunt, "Chickasaw Bayou"; Alison Diary, January 2, 1863, UNCCH.

40. F. Moore, *Rebellion Record*, 6:310, 314.

41. *OR*, 17(1):610, 684–85; Sydney Champion to Matilda Champion, [January, 1863], Champion Papers, DU; Marshall, "Civil War Reminiscences," 30.

42. *OR*, 17(1):701; Kiper, *McClernand*, 156–57.

43. *ORN*, 23:491–92, 604; Kiper, *McClernand*, 157–59; Sherman, *Memoirs*, 220.

44. Sherman, *Memoirs*, 220–21; Kiper, *McClernand*, 158; Porter, *Incidents*, 130–31.

45. *OR*, 17(1):701–2, 709, 17(2):546, 22(1):887; Kiper, *McClernand*, 161.

46. Kiper, *McClernand*, 167–68; Simon, *Grant Papers*, 7:209–11.

47. *OR*, 17(1):780; Bearss, *Vicksburg*, 1:418–19.

48. Kiper, *McClernand*, 170; *OR*, 17(1):704; R. R. Hall Diary, January 9, [1863], OCHM.

49. *OR*, 17(1):780–81; *ORN*, 24:107–8; Meyer, *Iowa Valor*, 169–71.

50. *ORN*, 24:108; *OR*, 17(1):707, 723; William Eddington Memoir, 6.

51. *OR*, 17(1):724, 781; Eddington Memoir, 6; David Holmes to parents, February 2, 1863, Holmes Papers, ISHL; Andrew McCormack to parents and sisters, January 18, 1863, Wiley Sword Collection.

52. *OR*, 17(1):708, 716–19, 781; Samuel Gordon to wife, January 10–12, 1863, Gordon Papers, ISHL.

53. Joseph P. Lesslie to wife and folks at home, January 20, 1863, 4th Indiana Cavalry file, VNMP; Marshall, "Reminiscences," 35–36.

54. Black, *Recollections*, 33–34; Abernethy, "Incidents," 410; John H. Ferree to brother, May 9, 1863, Ferree Papers, IHS.

55. Eddington Memoir, 6–7; Hunt, "Chickasaw Bayou"; Henry Clemons to wife, January 15, 1863, Clemons Letters, WHSA.

56. S. H. Stephenson to Parents, January 28, 1863, 48th Ohio file, VNMP; David Holmes to parents, January 8, 12, 1863, Holmes Papers, ISHL; Hunt, "Chickasaw Bayou"; Abernethy, "Incidents," 409–10.

CHAPTER 6

1. J. E. Smith, *Grant*, 230–31; Grant, *Memoirs*, 304–5; McFeely, *Grant*, 120–21; Basler, *Works of Lincoln*, 6:70–71; Simon, *Grant Papers*, 7:103, 105, 108, 121, 138, 158, 171, 189, 216.

2. Simon, *Grant Papers*, 7:223, 233–34.

3. Ibid., 7:234, 236, 273; *OR*, 17(2):575.

4. *OR*, 17(2):579, 24(1):9; Simon, *Grant Papers*, 7:239–43; Winters, *Civil War*, 174; Edward H. Ingraham to Aunt, March 18, 1863, Ingraham Papers, ISHL.

5. Basler, *Works of Lincoln*, 6:43, 83; M.(?) R. Adams to sister, January 31, 1863, 13th Illinois file, VNMP.

6. John G. Jones to parents, March 23, 1863, Jones Papers, WHSA; Joseph F. McCarthy to Seth, January 14, 1863, McCarthy Papers, IHS; Byron MacCutcheon Autobiography, "Down the Mississippi to Vicksburg," n.p., UM; John L. Matthews to father, January 24, 1863, Matthews Papers, ISHL.

7. Tillman Hartman to mother, March 27, 1863, 23rd Wisconsin file, VNMP; Adams to sister, January 21, 1863, 13th Illinois file, VNMP; Matthew R. Adams to sister, January 31, 1863, OCHM; Eugene McWayne to home, January 17, 21, 1863, Wiley Sword Collection; Price F. Kellogg Jour-nal, n.p., Kellogg Papers, ISHL; Duncan G. Ingraham to Anna, April 6, 1863, Ingraham Papers, ISHL; Uley Burk to wife and children, February 12, 1863, 30th Iowa file, VNMP; John G. Jones to parents, March 23, 1863, Jones Papers, WHSA; Luke Roberts to Mrs. C. M. Roberts, March 1, 1862 [3], Roberts Collection, Harrisburg Civil War Round Table Papers, USAMHI; Abner C. Hinman to ?, February 11, 1863, Hinman papers in Stone Collection, USAMHI; T. S. Seacord to Anna, January 8, 1863, Seacord Papers, ISHL; Bennet Grigsly to wife and children, January 30, 1863, Grigsly Papers, IHS; Black, *Recollections*, 37; David N. Holmes to parents, January 12, 1863, Holmes Papers, ISHL.

8. George Marshall, "Reminiscences," pp. 37–38, Marshall Papers, ISL; Andrew McCormack to home, February 27, 1863, McCormack Letters, Wiley Sword Collection.

9. Andrew J. Sproul to Fanny, January 26, 1863, Sproul Papers, UNCCH; William H. Clark to wife (Emaline) and children, February 20, 1863, Clark Papers, ISL; Townsend P. Heaton to John Heaton, February 11, 1863, Heaton Letters, OHS; James N. Stewart to friend, February 14, 1863, in Helen E. Livingston, comp., "Sing the Jubilee: Compiled from the Letters, Diaries, and Papers of David James Palmer," Palmer Papers, UI; Andrew Bush to Mary, February 11, March 26, 1863, Bush Letters, OCHM; Richard Hall to father and mother, February 24, 1863, Hall Letters, LSU; John Ruckman to John Kinsel, February 16, 1863, Ruckman Letters, Journals/Diaries/Letters Subseries of Vicksburg Campaign Series, VNMP; David Moreland to Henry Moreland, January 28, 1863, Moreland Papers, ISL.

10. Boyd, *Diary*, 120–21; Ephraim Brown to Drusilla Brown, January 25, 1863, Brown Papers, OHS; Jerome Robbins Journal, Number 7, pp. 44–45, Robbins Journals, UM.

11. McPherson, *The Negro's Civil War*, 165; Packard Diary, February 9, 1863, ISHL; David Holmes to parents, February 24, 1863, Holmes Papers, ISHL; Seneca Thrall to wife (Mollie), January 20, 1863, Thrall Papers, UI.

12. S. H. Stephenson to parents, January 28, 1863, 48th Ohio file, VNMP; Luke Roberts to Cassia, January 10, 1863, Roberts Collection, Harrisburg Civil War Round Table Collection, USAMHI; John J. Barney to Sam (brother), February 13, 1863, Barney Letters, WHSA; Richard and Richard, *Defense*, 112; George Chittenden to wife, February 8, 1863, Chittenden Papers, ISL; John Blasdell to wife, February 1, 1863, Blasdell Papers, ISL; S. H. Stephenson to parents, February 6, 1863, 48th Ohio file, VNMP; Robert W. Henry to wife, February 20, 1863, Henry Papers, UI.

13. William L. Dillon to brothers and sisters, January 25, 1863, Dillon Papers, ISHL; Daniel Buchwalter Diary, Feb? [1863], 120th Ohio file, VNMP; Seneca Thrall to wife, March 12, 1863, Thrall Papers, UI; John V. Boucher to mother, February 15, March 14, 1863, and Boucher to Mr. Sawyer, March 2, 1863, Boucher Papers, USAMHI; W. A. Montgomery to sister, March 7, 1863, Bailey Papers, USAMHI; Zacharia Dean to wife, April 6 [in letter dated March 21 at heading], 1863, Dean Papers, IHS; David Holmes to parents, February 2, 24, 1863, Holmes Papers, ISHL; Joseph Plessie to wife, February ?, 1863, 4th Indiana Cavalry file, VNMP; John M. Godown to Fannie, January 1, 1863, McLaughlin Papers,

ISL; W. A. Montgomery to sister, March 22, 1863, Bailey Papers, USAMHI.

14. Joel Norton to brother, February 5, 1863, Norton Letters, WHSA; Popchock, *Soldier Boy*, 53; Metz Diary, January 28, 1863, DU; David Palmer to parents, December 18, 1862, in Livingston, "Sing the Jubilee," Palmer Papers, UI.

15. John W. Burke to sister, Burke Papers, ISHL; C. S. Beath to Isaac Funk, February 19, 1863, Funk Papers, ISHL.

16. Clark Whitten to wife and friends, December 8, 16, 1862, Whitten Papers, USAMHI; John P. Davis Diary, March 15, 1863, Davis Papers, ISHL; William H. Van Meter, "A Condensed History of the 47th Regiment of Illinois Vol. Infantry," p. 10, Cromwell Papers, ISHL; W. A. Smith to father, February 17, 1863, Fox Papers, ISHL; Joseah H. Myers to Joe, February 8, 1863, Gebbart Papers, DU.

17. John Lindley Harris to father, April 6, 1863, Harris Papers, ISHL.

18. Grant, *Memoirs*, 295–96, 303–5.

19. Alison Diary, January 23–25, 30, 1863, UNCCH; Henry T. Morgan to Ellen, February 20, March 28, 1863, Morgan Papers, USAMHI; Alfred Bowman to mother and father, February 25, March 18, 1863, Bowman Family Papers, ETSU; R. A. Wilson to wife, February 21, 1863, Wilson file, OCHM; *Mobile Register and Advertiser*, February 25, 1863; Gerald Golden, unpublished history of 37th Alabama, p. 363, copy provided to author by T. Michael Parrish; Henry Wade to Margaret Wade, January 30, February 1, 3, March 1, 5, 1863, Wade Family Papers, TU; Thomas J. Rounsaville to Ma and sisters, February 23, 1863, Rounsaville Letters, Civil War Mis-

cellaneous Collection, USAMHI; Richard and Richard, *Defense*, 108–12, 115–22, 127–28, 132.

20. W. H. Baker to sister, January 1863 (two letters, specific days not indicated), Cherokee, Ga., Artillery file, VNMP; Matthias Murphy to R. Floyd, January 18, 1863, 40th Georgia file, VNMP; Benjamin Franklin Moore to Robert Moore, February 10, 20, 1863, 42nd Georgia file, VNMP; Fred Smith to parents, January 10, 1863, *Civil War Times Illustrated* Collection, USAMHI.

21. James Calvin Brown to father and mother, brother and sisters, February 9, 1863, 3rd Missouri (Confederate) file, VNMP; W. A. Rorer to Cousin Susan, January 15, February 16, 1863, Willcox Papers, DU.

22. Bettersworth, *Confederate Mississippi*, 217, 220, 236, 244; John C. Pemberton to Carter Stevenson, February 21, 1863, RG 109, chap. II, vol. 57, NA; Arkansas Delegation, R. W. Johnson et al., to Jefferson Davis, February 2, 1863, and Anna M. Farrar to Davis, June 20, 1863, Davis Papers, DU.

23. J. H. Morrison to Major Reed, January 27, 1863, RG 109, chap. II, vol. 57, NA; John C. Pemberton to John J. Pettus, February 3, 14 [19?], 1863, and Thomas B. Reed to Carter Stevenson, February 26, 1863, Pettus Papers, RG 27, MDAH; Fred Smith to parents, January 10, 1863, *Civil War Times Illustrated* Collection, USAMHI.

24. *OR*, 17(2):821, 824, 827, 835, 841.

25. *OR*, 17(2):823, 828, 52(2):203.

26. *OR*, 24(3):593–605.

27. *OR*, 24(3):597, 601–4, 613, 632.

28. The Confederates later captured both the *Queen of the West* and the *Indianola* near the Red River, though nei-

ther stayed in Rebel hands for long. The *Queen* was lost to the Federals; and, tricked by a blackened log that in the dark of night they took for an ironclad, the Confederates blew up the *Indianola* to prevent its recapture. Despite the ultimate outcome, the saga of each vessel demonstrated the vulnerability of Confederate batteries on the Vicksburg waterfront. *OR*, 24(2):18–19, 337–38, 342–43.

29. *OR*, 24(3):623, 632, 15:848–53.

30. *OR*, 24(3):638–40, 646.

31. *OR*, 24(3):665, 23(2):761, 13:888; Mrs. Johnston quoted in Bearss, *Vicksburg*, 1:465; Symonds, *Johnston*, 202; Govan and Livingood, *Different Valor*, 188–89. P. Ellis Jr. to brother, February 17, 1863, Munford-Ellis Family Papers, DU.

32. John C. Pemberton to Simon B. Buckner, March 18, 1863, RG 109, chap. II, vol. 60, Letters and Telegrams Sent, Department of Mississippi and East Louisiana, NA; Pemberton to Stephenson, February 21, RG 109, chap. II, vol. 57, NA.

33. Pemberton to Stephenson, February 21, 1863, RG 109, chap. II, vol. 57, NA; Duncan McKenzie to uncle (Duncan McLaurin), January 28, 1863, McLaurin Papers, DU.

34. Ballard, *Pemberton*, 120–21; Pemberton to Lloyd Tilghman, March 2, 1863, J. C. Taylor to L. Minco, March 12, 1863, J. L. Thompson to L. Lindsey, March 16, 1863, Pemberton to Loring, March 17, 1863, RG 109, chap. II, vol. 57, NA; Bearss, *Vicksburg*, 1:467.

35. Simon, *Grant Papers*, 7:245, 249, 251–53, 257–58, 260; *OR*, 24(1):10, 24(3):19; Grant, *Memoirs*, 294.

36. Simon, *Grant Papers*, 7:164.

37. *OR* 17(2):572, 24(3):7, 9, 13; *ORN*, 24:380–81; Bearss, *Vicksburg*,

1:436–38; William Murphy to John Murphy, January 30, 1863, Murphy Letters, OHS.

38. Committee of the Regiment, *Story of the Fifty-fifth*, 212; *OR*, 24(3):16–17, 38, 51, 90, 685, 24(1):18; *ORN*, 24:208; Bearss, *Vicksburg*, 1:447–48, 461; Grant, *Memoirs*, 298, 303; Sherman, *Memoirs*, 226, 229; Basler, *Works of Lincoln*, 6:155.

39. *OR*, 24(3):44, 78–79; Bearss, *Vicksburg*, 1:470, 472; J. K. Newton to father and mother, February 28, 1863, C. P. Alling, "Four Years with the Western Army in the Civil War of the United States, 1861–1865," p. 6, 11th Wisconsin file, VNMP; James C. Vanderbilt to mother, February 26, March 6, 1863, Vanderbilt Papers, ISL; Seneca Thrall to wife, February 14, 1863, Thrall Papers, UI; Lewis Trefftzs to brother, March 14, 1863, Trefftzs Papers, ISHL; Charles Thompkins to wife, February 10, 1863, Thompkins Papers, DU.

40. William C. Caldwell to mother, March 29, 1863, Caldwell Papers, UM; William A. Lorimer Memoir, n.p., 17th Illinois file, VNMP.

41. P. C. Bonney letter, March 3, 1863, excerpts from Winifred Keen Armstrong, ed., *The Civil War Letters of Pvt. P. C. Bonney*, Publication of the Lawrence County Historical Society, Lawrenceville, Ill., 1963, in 31st Illinois file, VNMP.

42. Bearss, *Vicksburg*, 1:477–78.

43. Ibid., 482–83.

44. *ORN*, 23:709, 24:294.

45. *OR*, 24(1):17, 373.

46. Katherine Polk Gale, "Reminiscences of Life in the Southern Confederacy, 1861–1865," pp. 10–11A, Gale and Polk Family Papers, UNCCH; L. C. Sheppard, "A Confederate Girlhood," pp. 25–27, Sheppard Memoir, UNCCH.

47. *ORN*, 24:244, 251, 255; *OR*, 24(1):374, 24(3):36.

48. Byers, *With Fire and Sword*, 50–51; "An Account of Lyman Baker in Union Army," p. 4, Baker Papers, ISHL.

49. *ORN*, (24):252–53; *OR*, 24(3):56–57.

50. *ORN*, 24:294; *OR*, 24(1):368, 378, 24(3):56.

51. *OR*, 24(3):622, 626, 629–30.

52. *OR*, 24(3):630, 638–39; *ORN*, 24:294, 296.

53. *ORN*, 24:297; *OR*, 24(3):630, 641, 643–46.

54. *OR*, 24(3):649, 652, 656–57; *ORN*, 24:299.

55. *OR*, 24(3):662, 721–22, 24(1):389, 415–17; *ORN*, 24:300; Francis Marion Baxter, "My Service in the Confederate Army from April, 1861 to May 22, 1865," Baxter Papers, MDAH.

56. Bearss, *Vicksburg*, 1:510–11; John V. Boucher to Mrs. J. V. Boucher, April 12, 1863, Boucher Papers, USAMHI; "An Account of Lyman Baker in Union Army," p. 4, Baker Papers, ISHL.

57. *ORN*, 24:246, 262–63; "An Account of Lyman Baker in Union Army," p. 5, Baker Papers, ISHL.

58. *ORN*, 24:246, 263; *OR*, 24(3):87; A. T. Mahan, *Gulf and Inland Waters*, 145.

59. *ORN*, 24:246, 264, 266; *OR*, 24(1):20, 393–94, 24(3):86–87, 94.

60. *ORN*, 24:268, 272; *OR*, 24(1):412–13, 415–16.

61. Bearss, *Vicksburg*, 1:521–23; *OR*, 24(1):412, 416; *ORN*, 24:247, 273–76; Karl Kreible to Wilhelmine, March 21, 1863, Kreible Letters, Journals/Diaries/Letters Subseries of Vicksburg Campaign Series, VNMP; Golden, unpublished history of 37th Alabama,

pp. 382–83, T. Michael Parrish Collection.

62. *OR*, 24(1):380–83, 396; Bearss, *Vicksburg*, 1:524–26.

63. *OR*, 24(1):413–14.

64. *OR*, 24(1):390, 396–98; *ORN*, 24:280–84.

65. *OR*, 24(1):398, 403, 405–6, 414–15, 24(3):98, 105, 112–14, 118, 123, 680.

66. James L. Alcorn to wife, March 16, 1863, Alcorn Papers, MDAH; *OR*, 24(1):21.

67. *ORN*, 24:474; *OR*, 24(1):474, 24(3):112–13.

68. *OR*, 24(1):21, 432–39, 455–59, 465–66, 24(3):112, 52(2):436; *ORN*, 24:474–77, 485, 487–48, 493–95, 688; Pemberton to commander, Yazoo City, March 19, 1863, RG 109, chap. II, vol. 60, NA; Porter, *Incidents*, 160–61; Sherman, *Memoirs*, 230–32.

69. *OR*, 24(3):680, 682, 684; Sidney Champion to Matilda Champion, March 29, 1863, Champion Papers, DU.

70. Bearss, Vicksburg, 1:566; *OR*, 24(1):435, 448, 460; Sherman, *Memoirs*, 232–33; Pemberton to Jefferson Davis, March 28, 1863, RG 109, chap. II, vol. 60, NA; Willett, *History of Company B*, 31.

71. For an account of Farragut's campaign, see Bearss, *Vicksburg*, 1:693–704.

72. *OR*, 24(1):407; *ORN*, 24:287; Bearss, *Vicksburg*, 1:537.

73. *OR*, 24(1):419–20, 24(3):669, 671, 677–80, 686–96; Bearss, *Vicksburg*, 1:545.

74. *OR* 24(3):127, 134, 24(1):407–9, 419–20.

75. Robert Shields to sister (Nellie Constant), March 29, 1863, Shields Papers, ISL; E. P. Stanfield to father, March 30, 1863, Stanfield Papers, IHS.

76. *OR*, 24(1):419–20; James K. Newton to father and mother, April 18, 1863, 14th Wisconsin file, VNMP.

CHAPTER 7

1. Grant, *Memoirs*, 295–96, 305; *OR*, 24(3):179–80.

2. Grant, *Memoirs*, 305–6; Simon, *Grant Papers*, 7:473, 475, 486; Dana, *Recollections*, 32–33.

3. *OR*, 24(3):104, 126, 24(1):19–22.

4. *OR*, 24(1):23–25, 46; Bearss, *Vicksburg*, 2:24–25.

5. On the canal project, see Bearss, *Vicksburg*, 2:43–51.

6. ? Coke to ? Starr, April 7, 1863, 1st Louisiana Artillery file, VNMP.

7. Pemberton to John J. Pettus, April 2, 1863, to M. R. Clark, April 5, 1863, to James Seddon, April 8, 1863, April 8, 1863, to Samuel Cooper, April 11, 1863, to H. C. Tupper, April 14, 1863, to Carter Stevenson, April 16, 1863, to C. A. Banks, April 21, 1863, and F. M. Stafford to John Adams, April 17, 1863, RG 109, chap. II, vol. 60, NA.

8. D. Rowland, *Jefferson Davis*, 5:466, 471; *OR*, 24(1):490–91, 495.

9. Crooke, *Twenty-first Iowa*, 49, 53; Daniel Buchwalter Diary, April 4, 1863, 120th Ohio file, S. H. Stephenson to brother, April 18, 1863, 48th Ohio file, W. H. Raynor Diary, April 16, 1863, 56th Ohio file, VNMP; W. L. Rand to parents, April 20, 1863, Rand Papers, ISHL.

10. *OR*, 24(1):26, 491, 24(3):151–52, 168; *ORN*, 24:520; Bearss, *Vicksburg*, 2:27.

11. *OR*, 24(1):74, 24(3):179–80; Badeau, *Military History of Grant*, 1:183; Simpson and Berlin, *Sherman's Civil War*, 439; Bearss, *Vicksburg*, 2:29–30.

12. Oran Perry, "Perry Tells the

Story of the Siege of Vicksburg," copy of article from *Vicksburg Evening Post*, June 16, 1926, in 69th Indiana file, VNMP; Clark, *Downing's Civil War Diary*, 108–9; John G. Jones to parents, April 16, 1863, Jones Papers, WHSA; George Chittenden to wife, April 17, 1863, Chittenden Papers, ISL; Seneca Thrall to wife, April 11, 1863, Thrall Papers, UI; Fred Starring to Will ?, April 24, 1863, Bailhache-Brayman Papers, ISHL.

13. C. Hunt Diary, April 8, 1863, 20th Ohio file, James Newton to parents, April 10, 1863, 14th Wisconsin file, VNMP.

14. *OR*, 24(3):713–14, 24(1):490–92; Perry, "Perry Tells Story," 69th Indiana file, VNMP; Bevier, *First and Second Missouri*, 171.

15. *OR*, 24(3):108, 122–23, 186; Eddington Memoir, p. 10, 97th Illinois file, VNMP; Bearss, *Vicksburg*, 2:39.

16. Asa E. Sample Diary, April 5, 9, 1863, Sample Papers, IHS.

17. Bernard Schermerhorn to wife, April 19, 1863, Schermerhorn Papers, IHS; Sample Diary, April 14, 1863, Sample Papers, IHS.

18. *OR*, 24(1):140, 494–97; Bevier, *First and Second Missouri*, 171–72.

19. *OR*, 24(3):132, 186, 188, 740, 24(1):70–77; Bearss, *Vicksburg*, 2:53; *ORN*, 24:555; Grant, *Memoirs*, 306–7; Porter, *Incidents*, 175; Nathan Dye to father and family, April 16, 1863, Dye Papers, DU.

20. *OR*, 24(3):740, 24(1):70, 75, 125; *ORN*, 24:682; Bearss, *Vicksburg*, 2:58–59.

21. *OR*, 24(2):336–37, 24(3):688; Bearss, *Vicksburg*, 2:60–61, 63–65.

22. Bearss, *Vicksburg*, 2:65; Richard and Richard, *Defense*, 133–34; F. Grant, "General Grant," *National Tribune*, January 20, 1887.

23. Bearss, *Vicksburg*, 2:66–68; Walker, *Vicksburg*, 151–52; *ORN*, 24:555–56.

24. *ORN*, 24:553, 556–58, 682, 697–98; A. B. Balch, "Memories of Soldiers by One of Them," Forrest Papers, ISHL.

25. A. L. Dorsey to father and mother, April 21, 1863, 43rd Georgia file, VNMP.

26. *ORN*, 24:563–64, 566, 704.

27. Bearss, *Vicksburg*, 2:73–74; *OR*, 24(1):78, 567–68, 24(3):212, 215–16.

28. Bearss, *Vicksburg*, 2:76–79, 80–82. My comments on Confederate artillery problems are based largely but not exclusively on Bearss's analysis, pp. 80–82.

29. Ballard, *Pemberton*, 134–35; *OR*, 24(3):716–20.

30. Sidney Champion to Matilda Champion, April 4, 1863, Champion Papers, DU.

31. *OR*, 24(3):724, 730, 733; George H. Chatfield to mother, April 15, 1863, Chatfield Papers, USAMHI.

32. Ballard, *Pemberton*, 136–40; *OR*, 24(3):744–45.

33. *OR*, 24(3):733, 747, 751–53, 760, 773–75.

34. *OR*, 24(3):733, 755–57, 761, 770, 772, 779–80; Bearss, *Vicksburg* 2:98.

35. *OR*, 24(3):761, 770, 775, 779–80, 783, 788, 15:1042, 1044.

36. *OR*, 24(3):743, 748, 753, 757, 761, 52(2):456; Bearss, *Vicksburg*, 2:129–32.

37. On Streight's raid, see Hurst, *Forrest*, 117–24.

38. An account of Grierson's raid is in Bearss, *Vicksburg*, 2:187–36. The standard monograph on the raid is D. A. Brown, *Grierson's Raid*.

39. H. M. Call to sister, July 5, 1863, J. R. Rust Papers, UNCCH.

40. Simons Diary, April 25, 1863, UT; Jason Niles Diary, no. 16, May 2, 1863, Niles Papers, UNCCH; Agnew Diary, vol. 7A, May 7, 13, 1863, UNCCH; *OR*, 24(1):34.

41. This cavalry action is detailed in Bearss, *Vicksburg*, 2:187–99.

42. Ibid., 109; *OR*, 24(3):158, 173.

43. Ainsworth Diary, pp. 28–31, UM.

44. *OR*, 24(1):502–9, 24(3):717, 719.

45. *OR*, 24(1):502, 24(3):186–87.

46. N. B. Baker Diary, May 24, 1863, 116th Illinois file, VNMP; J. W. Fitch-patrick Diary, May 18, 1863, 3rd Iowa file, VNMP; "Autobiography and Civil War Diary of Balzer Grebe," p. 18, Ehlers-Grebe Papers, ISHL.

47. *OR*, 24(1):503–6, 24(3):209, 762.

48. Worthington Diary, April 19, 23, 24, 28, 1863, UNCCH.

49. William H. to Ruffin Thompson, March 22, April ?, 1863, Thompson Papers, UNCCH.

50. W. A. Rorer to Cousin Susan, April 22, 1863, Willcox Papers, DU.

51. Sherman, *Memoirs*, 347; *OR*, 24(1):49, 24(3):240, 245.

52. Bearss, *Vicksburg*, 2:258; *OR*, 24(1):256, 678, 24 (3):797, 800, 804.

53. *ORN*, 24:589–600, 695; *OR*, 24(2):384, 24(3):246, 260–61; Bearss, *Vicksburg*, 2:263–65; Tunnard, *Southern Record*, 227.

54. Bearss, *Vicksburg*, 2:269–70; F. Grant, "General Grant," *National Tribune*, January 20, 1887.

55. *OR*, 24(3):204–5, 211; *ORN*, 24:704; Bearss, *Vicksburg*, 2:271–74, 277.

56. *OR*, 24(3):225–26, 228, 231,

24(1):27–28, 79–81, 663; *ORN*, 24:522, 606.

57. Bearss, *Vicksburg*, 2:285–89.

58. *OR*, 24(1):80; "An Account of Lyman Baker in the Union Army," p. 7, Baker Papers, ISHL.

59. *OR*, 24(1):80–81; James P. Boyd Diary, April 21, 1863, Boyd Papers, ISHL.

60. *OR*, 24(1):81, 593, 24(3):237–38, 242; Bearss, *Vicksburg*, 2:297.

61. McPherson's and Sherman's movements south to below Vicksburg are detailed in Bearss, *Vicksburg*, 2:297–304.

62. *OR*, 24(3):792–93, 797, 24(1):257.

63. Rogers, " 'Prospects of Our Country,' " 43–44.

64. *OR*, 24(1):663–64; *ORN*, 24:626–28.

65. *ORN*, 24:607–8, 610–11, 613, 615–23, 625–26.

66. Crooke, *Twenty-first Iowa*, 53–54; W. H. Raynor Diary, April 29, 1863, 56th Ohio file, VNMP.

67. Bevier, *First and Second Missouri*, 412; Charles A. Hobbs Diary, April 29? / 30?, 1863, 99th Illinois file, VNMP; Bearss, *Vicksburg*, 2:311.

68. Grant, *Memoirs*, 317; *OR*, 24(1):574–75.

69. F. Grant, "General Grant," *National Tribune*, January 20, 1887.

70. *OR*, 24(1):576; Bearss, *Vicksburg*, 2:314.

71. *ORN*, 24:615, 617–19, 623, 625.

CHAPTER 8

1. *OR*, 24(1):48; Grant, *Memoirs*, 317–18.

2. A. B. Hubbell to William T. Rigby, April 30, 1908, 42nd Ohio file, VNMP; F. Grant, "General Grant," *National Tribune*, January 27, 1887; Brieger, *Hometown Mississippi*, 83; Bearss, *Vicksburg*, 2:318.

3. *OR*, 24(1):143, 601, 615, 621, 628, 631.

4. S. C. Jones, *Reminiscences*, 29–30.

5. Charles A. Hobbs Diary, May 1, 1863, 99th Illinois file, VNMP; L. B. Jessup Diary, May 2?, 1863, excerpts in letter to William T. Rigby, June 10, 1902, 24th Indiana file, VNMP.

6. *OR*, 24(1):643; Bearss, *Vicksburg*, 2:346; Grant, *Memoirs*, 321.

7. *OR*, 24(1):663, 672.

8. *OR*, 24(1):663, 678, 672.

9. *OR*, 24(1):658, 663–64, 672.

10. *OR* 24(3):804–5; Greene, *The Mississippi*, 127.

11. Bearss, *Vicksburg*, 2:353; *OR*, 24(1):628, 631. Union reports indicate that Confederates fired the first shot.

12. Crooke, *Twenty-first Iowa*, 55; *OR*, 24(1):628.

13. *OR*, 24(1):615, 625, 629, 672; S. C. Jones, *Reminiscences*, 30–31.

14. *OR*, 24(1):615; Charles Hobbs Diary, May 1, 1863, 99th Illinois file, VNMP.

15. *OR*, 24(1):413; Hobbs Diary, May 1, 1863, 99th Illinois file, VNMP.

16. *OR*, 24(1):678.

17. *OR*, 24(1):679; Kelly, "Thirtieth Alabama," 138; Frances G. Obenchain to William T. Rigby, July 4, 1903, Virginia Botetourt Artillery file, VNMP.

18. *OR*, 24(1):668, 675; Chambers, *My Journal*, 263.

19. *OR*, 24(1):143, 615, 625; Samuel Gordon to wife, May 6, 1863, Gordon Papers, ISHL.

20. *OR*, 24(1):586–92, 664, 679; Minor Ellis to uncle (W. W. Thomas), June 2, 1863, Thomas Papers, IHS.

21. *OR*, 24(1):143, 679–80; Frances Obenchain to William Rigby, July 4, 1903, Virginia Botetourt Artillery file, VNMP; Edward Tracy to my sweet dear friend, April 4, 1863, Tracy Papers, UNCCH.

22. *OR*, 24(1):679–80; Kelly, "Thirtieth Alabama," 135.

23. *OR*, 24(1):680; Kelly, "Thirtieth Alabama," 135; "Journal of the 46th Regiment, 1861–1865," Sinks Papers, ISL.

24. *OR*, 24(1):668, 670, 673.

25. *OR*, 24(1):673, 680–81; Kelly, "Thirtieth Alabama," 136.

26. *OR*, 24(1):588, 643, 681.

27. *OR*, 24(1):643, 673, 681; Kelly, "Thirtieth Alabama," 135.

28. *OR*, 24(1):587, 668, 671, 673–74, 682; Joseph Bowker Diary, May 1, 1863, 42nd Ohio file, VNMP. See casualty breakdown in Bearss, *Vicksburg*, 2:402–7.

29. *OR*, 24(1):602, 615–16, 625.

30. *OR*, 24(1):672–73; Charles Hobbs Diary, May 1, 1863, 99th Illinois file, VNMP.

31. Howell, *Going to Meet the Yankees*, 156–57, 159–60; *OR*, 24(1):626, 664, 673.

32. *OR*, 24(1):144–45, 593, 599, 602, 606–7, 610–11, 626, 689; Bearss, *Vicksburg*, 2:379; Charles Hobbs Diary, May 1, 1863, 99th Illinois file, VNMP.

33. *OR*, 24(1):602–3, 607, 609, 614, 622, 626, 664, 673.

34. *OR*, 24(1):662, 664, 668, 675–76; Chambers, "My Journal," 264; Bevier, *First and Second Missouri*, 177–78.

35. Chambers, "My Journal," 264, 267.

36. Charles Hobbs Diary, May 1, 1863, 99th Illinois file, Joseph Bowker Diary, May 1, 1863, 42nd Ohio file, VNMP; William R. Eddington, "My Civil War Memoirs and Other Experiences," p. 8, Eddington Papers, ISHL; *OR*, 24(1):145, 603.

37. *OR*, 24(1):627, 629–30; Charles Hobbs Diary, May 1, 1863, 99th Illinois file, VNMP.

38. *OR*, 24(1):593, 603, 611, 627, 652.

39. *OR*, 24(1):603–4, 609, 611, 613, 664, 668, 688–89.

40. Bevier, *First and Second Missouri*, 416–17.

41. Ibid., 180–81; E. McD. Anderson, *Memoirs*, 298–99; Chambers, "My Journal," 264; *OR*, 24(1):676.

42. *OR*, 24(1):653, 666, 676.

43. *OR*, 24(1):653, 66, 677; Chambers, "My Journal," 265.

44. *OR*, 24(1):660, 24(3):260; Bearss, *Vicksburg*, 2:410; James B. Taylor Diary, May 2, 1863, 120th Ohio, VNMP.

45. Hawkins, "History of Port Gibson," 279, 281, 291; Headley, *Claiborne County*, 364–74; Charles Hobbs Diary, May 1, 1863, 99th Illinois file, VNMP; W. H. Raynor Diary, May 2, 1863, 56th Ohio, VNMP; Samuel Gordon to wife, May 6, 1863, Gordon Papers, ISHL; S. C. Jones, *Reminiscences*, 32.

46. Silas T. Trowbridge Autobiography, excerpts, pp. 119–21, OCHM.

47. Charles Cady to brother and sister, May 6, 1863, Cady Papers, UI; Seneca Thrall to wife, May 6, 1863, Thrall Papers, UI; John C. Francis to Mrs. Cassia Roberts, May 9, 1863, Roberts Collection, Harrisburg Civil War Round Table Papers, USAMHI.

48. John H. Ferree to brother, May 9, 1863, Ferree Papers, IHS; F. Grant, "General Grant," *National Tribune*, January 27, 1887.

49. *OR*, 24(3):262, 24(1):635, 653, 706.

50. *OR*, 24(1):653–54, 669.

51. *OR*, 24(1):129, 635, 727, 24(2):31.

52. *OR*, 24(3):808, 815, 24(1):658–61; Ballard, *Pemberton*, 141–42.

53. *OR*, 24(3):810–13; Ballard, *Pemberton*, 134, 144–45; Willis Herbert

Claiborne Diary, May 1, 1863, Claiborne Papers, UNCCH.

54. Ballard, *Pemberton*, 145.

55. *OR*, 24(3):810, 812, 815, 820, 24(2):385, 52(2):466.

56. *OR*, 24(3):819–21.

57. *OR*, 24(1):655–57.

58. *OR*, 24(1):660, 666.

59. *OR*, 24(1):655–57, 666, 677, 24(3):816.

60. *OR*, 24(1):656, 666, 669.

61. *OR*, 24(3):823, 24(1):656–57; Bearss, *Vicksburg*, 2:423.

62. *OR*, 24(3):225–26, 24(1):635–36, 645, 669, 683, 707, 722–23, 727, 774.

63. *OR*, 24(3):265–67; Bearss, *Vicksburg*, 2:428; Samuel Gordon to wife, May 6, 1863, Gordon Papers, ISHL; Joseph Bowker Diary, May 3, 1863, 42nd Ohio file, VNMP.

64. *OR*, 24(1):49, 755; *ORN*, 24:627, 629, 645, 684, 699, 706; U. S. Grant, *Memoirs*, 327.

65. Bearss, *Vicksburg*, 2:431–35.

66. *OR*, 24(1):32–33.

67. C. J. Durham Diary, May 11, 1863, 11th Indiana file, VNMP; Bernard Schermerhorn to Josie, May 5, 1863, Schermerhorn Papers, IHS; Calvin Ainsworth Diary, p. 37, UM; Bearss, *Vicksburg*, 2:437–38.

68. My discussion of Pemberton's quandary is partially based on the analysis in Daniel, "Bruinsburg."

CHAPTER 9

1. *OR*, 24(3):821–24, 826.

2. J. C. Taylor to S. W. Ferguson, May 4, 1863, Taylor to Major [Theodore] Johnston, May 8, 1863, RG 109, chap. II, vol. 60, NA; W. L. Sharkey to John Pemberton, May 6, 1863, ? Beard to Pemberton, May 3, 1863, G. Mayo to Pemberton, May 6, 1863, RG 109, Entry 31, Telegrams and Reports

Received, Department of Mississippi and East Louisiana, NA.

3. *OR*, 24(3):828, 830, Charles S. Howell to father, May 5, 1863, Howell-Taylor Family Papers, USAMHI.

4. *OR*, 24(3):828–31, 24(1):50, 656, 774, 24(2):314.

5. *OR*, 24(3):269–70, 272, 274, 276, 24(2):12, 133.

6. *OR*, 24(3):266, 277; W. H. Raynor Diary, May 8, 9, 1863, 56th Ohio file, VNMP; John V. Boucher to mother, May 6, 1863, Boucher Papers, USAMHI.

7. *OR*, 24(2):254, 24(1):758; H. S. Keene Diary, May 10, 1863, 6th Wisconsin Light Artillery file, VNMP; Bearss, *Vicksburg*, 2:450–51.

8. Bearss, *Vicksburg*, 2:452; Basler, *Works of Lincoln*, 6:210.

9. Bearss, *Vicksburg*, 2:453; *OR*, 24(3):834–36, 839–42; Larry J. Daniel, "Bruinsburg," 259.

10. *OR*, 24(2):69, 24(3):841–42, 24(1):259.

11. *OR*, 24(3):835, 839, 843–45, 850, 24(2):336.

12. *OR*, 24(1):84, 758, 761, 24(3):280; Samuel E. Sneier to sir, June 21, 1863, Sneier Papers, IHS.

13. *OR*, 24(3):280–84, 287–89; Bearss, *Vicksburg*, 2:465.

14. Asa E. Sample Diary, May 3, 5, 7, 1863, Sample Papers, IHS; J. A. Kincaid to sister, June 8, 1863, Hawley and Family Papers, LSU.

15. *OR*, 24(2):12, (3):292–93, 296, 24(1):762; Bearss, *Vicksburg*, 2:469.

16. *OR*, 24(3):296–97, 299, 24(1):146–47, 753, 24(2):31, 40–41, 118, 250.

17. *OR*, 24(1):259, 24(3):849, 852, 857, 863, 865. See Bearss, *Vicksburg*, 2:479–81.

18. *OR*, 24(3):851–66, 24(1):261; Bearss, *Vicksburg*, 2:480–81;

19. *OR*, 24(3):853, 24(1):737.

20. *OR*, 24(1):701, 737–41, 743, 746–47.

21. *OR*, 24(3):283, 287, 297, 24(1):701; Henry O. Dwight, "A Soldier's Story," *New York Daily Tribune*, November 21, 1886, clipping in Dwight Papers, USAMHI.

22. *OR*, 24(1):637, 645, 714, 731, 735, 739, 741, 743, 747.

23. *OR*, 24(1):108, 711–12, 740, 747; Bearss, *Vicksburg*, 2:495.

24. Dwight, "A Soldier's Story," Dwight Papers, USAMHI.

25. *OR*, 24(1):645–46, 716.

26. *OR*, 24(1):646, 741, 747, 708; Bearss, *Vicksburg*, 2:497.

27. Bearss, *Vicksburg*, 2:498; *OR*, 24(1):646, 715, 718, 728, 740, 748.

28. *OR*, 24(1):646, 716–17, 728, 741–46, 775, 782.

29. *OR*, 24(1):637, 646, 716–17, 721, 738–45, 775, 782; Anonymous to mother, May 26, 1863, 6th Ohio file, *Civil War Times Illustrated* Collection, USAMHI.

30. *OR*, 24(2):297; Bearss, *Vicksburg*, 2:511; S. C. Jones, *Reminiscences*, 33.

31. Joseph Bowker Diary, May 15, 1863, 42nd Ohio file, VNMP; John P. Davis Diary, May 13, 1863, Davis Papers, ISHL; Lavinia to Emmie, [June?, 1863], Crutcher-Shannon Papers, MDAH.

32. Letitia D. Miller, "Some Recollections of Letitia D. Miller," pp. 10–11, Miller Collection, UNCCH.

33. Asa E. Sample Diary, May 16, 1863, Sample Papers, IHS; George Hovey Cadman quoted in Grimsley, *Hard Hand of War*, 157.

34. See Bearss, *Vicksburg*, 2:512–13.

35. *OR*, 24(3):300–301, 24(1):638, 729, 735, 24(2):198; U. S. Grant, *Memoirs*, 332.

36. *OR*, 24(1):147, 753, 759, 767, 24(2):41, 250.

37. *OR*, 24(2):36, 255, 265–66, 281, 24(3):273.

38. *OR*, 24(1):739, 24(3):833, 853, 884, 873, 14:923, 925–26, 931; Dubay, *Pettus*, 169, 185; Ballard, *Pemberton*, 147.

39. Johnston, *Narrative*, 172, 174–75; *OR*, 24(1):215, 239, 260.

40. *OR*, 24(1):215, 239, 785; Johnston, *Narrative*, 175–76; U. S. Grant, *Memoirs*, 333.

41. *OR*, 24(1):775, 782, 785–87.

42. *OR*, 24(3):305, 307, 309, 24(1):638, 728–29, 735, 777, 782, 24(2):65; Bearss, *Vicksburg*, 2:533.

43. *OR*, 24(3):308, 707, 24(1):753, 767–68; Lavinia to Emmie, [June ?, 1863], July 1, 1863, Crutcher-Shannon Papers, MDAH.

44. *OR*, 24(1):753, 759, 762, 765–66, 770, 786, 24(2):284.

45. *OR*, 24(1):753–54, 759, 766, 760, 770.

46. *OR*, 24(1):638, 729, 756, 775, 777, 782, 786; Crawford McDonald to father and mother, May 25, 1863, in *Mishawaka Enterprise*, June 13, 1863, 48th Indiana file, VNMP.

47. *OR*, 24(1):639, 775, 780, 783, 786; William H. Van Meter, "A Condensed History of the 47th Regiment of Illinois Vol. Infantry," pp. 11–12, Cromwell Papers, ISHL.

48. F. Grant, "General Grant," *National Tribune*, January 27, 1887.

49. Ibid., February 3, 1887; U. S. Grant, *Memoirs*, 337–38; *OR*, 24(1):51, 639, 751, 754, 24(3):310; Feis, *Grant's Secret Service*, 162. For a general discussion of Grant's use of intelligence during the Vicksburg campaign, see ibid., 109–74.

50. *OR*, 24(3):881–84; Bearss, *Vicksburg*, 2:549.

51. Duncan McKenzie to uncle (Duncan McLaurin), May 14, 1863, McLaurin Papers, DU.

52. *OR*, 24(1):754, (24)2:251, 24(3):315; Grant, *Memoirs*, 338; John J. Pettus to Jefferson Davis, May 16, 1863, R. Maxey to Pettus, May 16, 1863, Governor John J. Pettus Papers, RG 12, MDAH; John P. Davis Diary, May 15, 1863, Davis Papers, ISHL.

53. Anonymous to mother, May 26, 1863, 6th Ohio file, *Civil War Times Illustrated* Collection, USAMHI; William McGlothlin Diary, May 14, 1863, William McGlothlin Papers, USAMHI; *OR*, 24(1):754; Sherman, *Memoirs*, 242; Scott, *Story of a Cavalry Regiment*, 85.

54. *OR*, 24(1):754–55, 759.

CHAPTER 10

1. *OR*, 24(2):116, 118, 24(3):873.

2. *OR*, 24(2):147, 24(3):877.

3. *OR*, 24(3):871–75, 24(1):261; Bearss, *Vicksburg*, 2:561.

4. Ballard, *Pemberton*, 154–55; *OR*, 24(3):877.

5. *OR*, 24(1):261, 24(2):125; Ballard, *Pemberton*, 155–56.

6. Lockett, "The Defense of Vicksburg," 487; Johnston, *Narrative*, 181; *OR*, 24(1):261, (3):876, 879.

7. *OR*, 24(3):882; Johnston, *Narrative*, 179–80; U. S. Grant, *Memoirs*, 338–39.

8. Lavinia to Emmie, [June ?, 1863], June 21, July 1, 1863, Crutcher-Shannon Papers, MDAH.

9. *OR*, 24(2):12–13, 31, 255, 24(1):616.

10. *OR*, 24(1):51, 646–47, 730, 776, 24(3):313–14.

11. *OR*, 24(1):262; Ballard, *Pemberton*, 158–59; William A. Drennan Diary, May 30–July 4, 1863, p. 4, MDAH.

12. *OR*, 24(2):74–75, 87, 90, 93,

107, 110–14, 124, 24(1):262; D. M. Smith, *Compelled to Appear in Print*, 96.

13. Calvin Smith Diary, excerpted from *Civil War Times Illustrated*, p. 22, 39th Tennessee file, VNMP.

14. Drennan Diary, p. 4, MDAH; James R. Binford, "Recollections of the Fifteenth Regiment of Mississippi Infantry, C.S.A.," p. 41, Henry Papers, MDAH. See also Bearss, *Vicksburg*, 2:576–77, and Ballard, *Pemberton*, 160.

15. *OR*, 24(1):48, 51–52, 24(2):13, 31–32, 40, 24(3):319–20; U. S. Grant, *Memoirs*, 339–41. The Jones plantation still exists.

16. *OR*, 24(2):32, 38, 87–88, 24(1):263.

17. *OR*, 24(2):75, 83, 91, 93–94, 24(1):263, 24(3):884.

18. *OR*, 24(2):104, 108, 110, 116; Drennan Diary, p. 4, MDAH.

19. *OR*, 24(3):316, 24(2):14, 22–25, 28–29, 108, 134.

20. Ballard, *Pemberton*, 159–60.

21. *OR*, 24(2):101, 104, 108; Lee, "Campaign of Vicksburg," 36.

22. *OR*, 24(2):32, 37–38, 75, 83, 88, 91, 110; E. McD. Anderson, *Memoirs*, 310.

23. Lee, "Campaign of Vicksburg," 37–38; *OR*, 24(2):101.

24. *OR*, 24(1):101, 104, (3):316–18.

25. *OR*, 24(2):94, 101, 104.

26. *OR*, 24(2):41, 42, 48–49, 53, 55, 57–58, 24(1):52.

27. *OR*, 24(1):639, 647, 709, 24(2):42; Samuel L. Ensminger to William T. Rigby, September 29, 1900, 11th Indiana file, VNMP; L. B. Jessup Diary, May 16, 1863, excerpted in letter to William T. Rigby, June 10, 1902, 24th Indiana file, VNMP; Charles Wood Diary, May 16, 1863, 29th Wisconsin file, VNMP.

28. Lee, "Campaign of Vicksburg," 40, 42; *OR*, 24(2):99, 101–5.

29. *OR*, 24(1):640, 647, 717; Samuel Gordon to wife, May 25, 1863, Gordon Papers, ISHL.

30. *OR*, 24(2):100, 24(1):717–18.

31. *OR*, 24(2):42, 49, 53–54, 105.

32. Lee, "Campaign of Vicksburg," 45; *OR*, 24(2):102, 24(1):640, 702; Alfred Cumming to Stephen D. Lee, November 3, 1899, Rigby Papers, MDAH.

33. *OR*, 24(2):55, 102; Lee, "Campaign of Vicksburg," 45; Frances G. Obenchain to William T. Rigby, July 14, 1903, Virginia Botetourt Artillery file, VNMP.

34. *OR*, 24(1):717–18, 24(2):75, 95, 100, 110, 122; U. S. Grant, "The Vicksburg Campaign," 511.

35. *OR*, 24(2):110–11, 116, 120–21; E. McD. Anderson, *Memoirs*, 311–12; Bevier, *First and Second Missouri*, 187–88; Bearss, *Vicksburg*, 2:608.

36. E. McD. Anderson, *Memoirs*, 312–13; *OR*, 24(2):49–50, 55–56, 110–12, 116.

37. A. H. Reynolds, "Vivid Experiences at Champion Hill," excerpted from *Confederate Veteran*, 19th Arkansas file, VNMP.

38. Byers, *With Fire and Sword*, 78–79; "Experiences of Lyman Baker," p. 9, Baker Papers, ISHL.

39. Bearss, *Vicksburg*, 2:613; *OR*, 24(2):102–3, 106; O. H. Oldroyd, *A Soldier's Story*, 23; M. D. Elliott to ?, May 27, 1863, from a newspaper clipping, 8th Michigan Light Artillery file, VNMP.

40. *OR*, 24(1):44, 718, 724, 730–31, 766, 783, 24(2):44, 50, 56, 65–66, 315.

41. *OR*, 24(2):15, 102, 106, 111, 116–17, 255, 24(1):731, 24(3):318.

42. Lee, "Campaign of Vicksburg,"

3:48; *OR*, 24(3):76, 79–80, 91, 126, 24(1):264.

43. Ballard, *Pemberton*, 163; E. McD. Anderson, *Memoirs*, 314; Bevier, *First and Second Missouri*, 190; *OR*, 24(2):15, 44, 50, 56, 63, 83–84, 88–89, 111, 117.

44. Kidd Memoir, n.p., n.d., OCHM.

45. Jasper Huffman to brother (Andy), August 4, 1863, in Erich Ewald, "Madison County's Civil War," in *Madison County Monthly*, March 1993, p. 40, 34th Indiana file, VNMP; *OR*, 24(2):15, 44, 50, 56, 63, 84, 88–89, 111, 117.

46. *OR*, 24(1):265, 24(2):76, 92; D. M. Smith, *Compelled to Appear in Print*, 135.

47. *OR*, 24(2):77.

48. *OR*, 24(2):32, 80–81, 24(3): 318; J. E. ? to Dr. Frank ?, December 31, 1905?, Mississippi–McClendon's Battery file, J. G. Spencer to F. H. Foote, September 18, 1910, 1st Mississippi Light Artillery file, folder b, VNMP.

49. *OR*, 24(2):102, 106, 112, 117, 24(1):265; Smith, *Compelled to Appear in Print*, 138.

50. Merrick J. Wald Diary, May 16, 1863, Orange ? Pasiet ? Diary, May 17, 1863, 77th Illinois file, VNMP; J. R. Reese, "Baker's Creek Battle," *Vicksburg Evening Post* clipping, October 4, 1902, 81st Illinois file, VNMP; John Hughes Jr., Diary, May 17, 1863, excerpts, 28th Iowa file, VNMP; Byers, *With Fire and Sword*, 82; Robert S. Finley to Mary A. Cabeen, December 18, 1863, Finley Papers, UNCCH.

51. [J. C. Mahan], *Memoirs*, 119.

52. C. M. Parker to Matilda Champion [n.d.], Sidney Champion to Matilda Champion [May 1863], Champion Papers, DU; Hobbs Diary, May 26, 1863, 99th Illinois file, VNMP.

53. *OR*, 24(1):53, 616, 718, 24(2):84, 100, 108, 135, 24(3):884–85; U. S. Grant, *Memoirs*, 349–50.

54. *OR*, 24(2):16, 24, 102–3, 108, 112, 116, 143, 24(1):151, 718.

55. *OR*, 24(1):151, 24(2):44; Asa E. Sample Diary, May 18, 1863, Sample Papers, IHS; U. S. Grant, *Memoirs*, 347–48. Grant does not specifically mention the Roberts house by name, but the home's location along the side of the road makes it the likely dwelling.

56. *OR*, 24(2):74, 77–78, 81, 89–90, 256; George H. Forney to Ma, May 27, 1863, Forney Papers, DU; B. J. Williams to William T. Rigby, June 30, 1905, 4th Indiana Cavalry file, VNMP.

57. *OR*, 24(2):7–10, 82, 86, 93, 99, 112, 120, 24(3):917; U. S. Grant, *Memoirs*, 349; Ballard, *Pemberton*, 165–66; Bearss, *Vicksburg*, 2:637–42.

58. Albert Chipman to Sophronia Chipman, May 15, 1863, Chipman Papers, ISHL.

59. *OR*, 24(1):266.

60. *OR*, 24(1):266, 24(2):113, 400–401.

61. Bearss, *Vicksburg*, 2:655–56.

62. *OR*, 24(1):266–67, 24(2):113; Bevier, *First and Second Missouri*, 182–83; Bearss, *Vicksburg*, 2:657; Johnston, *Narrative*, 185–86.

63. *OR*, 24(1):216–18, 241, 24(3):888; Johnston, *Narrative*, 186–87. Calhoun Station was in the approximate current location of Gluckstadt, Mississippi.

64. Grant, *Memoirs*, 349–50; *OR*, 24(2):32, 263, 265, 401, 24(3):322.

65. *OR*, 24(2):16, 46, 59, 60, 136, 250, 281, 24(1):151–52, 616, 640–41, 735, 770, 24(3):320, 465.

66. *OR*, 24(2):16, 18–19, 119, 136, 229, 24(1):152, 616, 24(3):322; Bearss, *Vicksburg*, 2:666.

67. Greene, *The Mississippi*, 163–64;

OR, 24(2):73, 401; Ballard, *Pemberton*, 164–66; Bearss, *Vicksburg*, 2:669.

68. OR, 24(2):32, 37, 39, 136, 235, 24(1):152, 24(3):596.

69. U. S. Grant, *Memoirs*, 350.

70. OR, 24(2):23, 119, 137.

71. OR, 24(2):119–20, 137; Bevier, *First and Second Missouri*, 194–95; J. G. Fox Diary, n.d., ISHL; Joseph W. Westbrook memoir, p. 4, Westbrook Papers, USAMHI.

72. I. H. Elliott, manuscript history of 33rd Illinois, p. 41, 33rd Illinois file, VNMP; M. A. Sweetman, "From Milliken's Bend to Vicksburg," clipping, newspaper identified only as *Tribune*, vol. 14, no. 47, n.d., 114th Ohio file, VNMP; F. Grant, "General Grant," *National Tribune*, February 3, 1887.

73. OR, 24(2):73, 24(1):268–69; Lockett, "Vicksburg," 488; E. McD. Anderson, *Memoirs*, 319.

74. Ballard, *Pemberton*, 3–4, 165–66; Lockett, "Vicksburg," 488.

75. Alison Diary, May 17, 18, 1863, UNCCH; Ballard, *Pemberton*, 167–68.

76. Joseph Bowker Diary, May 17, 1863, 42nd Ohio file, VNMP; OR, 24(2):27, 33, 132, 139, 205, 251, 24(1):617, 640–41, 648; Sherman, *Memoirs*, 352. See also Bearss, *Vicksburg*, 2:682–86, for discussion of Grant-Banks messages.

CHAPTER 11

1. OR, 24(1):271, 24(2):335–37, 375, 379–80; ORN, 25:6; Tunnard, *Southern Record*, 235–36; Louis Hébert, "An Autobiography of Louis Hébert," p. 13, Hébert Autobiography, UNCCH.

2. OR, 24(2):406–7, 24(1):271.

3. OR, 24(2):325, 358, 375, 400; Chambers, "My Journal," 269.

4. OR, 24(2):357; Thomas Waul to William T. Rigby, September 10, 1902, Waul's Texas Legion, 2nd Battalion

file, VNMP; Ballard, *Pemberton*, 167, 169.

5. Miller Diary, May 17, 1863, OCHM; Balfour Diary, May 16–31, 1863, p. 3, MDAH; Fremantle, *Three Months in the Southern States*, 116; Abbott, *History of the Civil War*, 2:292; Bevier, *First and Second Missouri*, 200; OR, 24(3):890.

6. OR, 24(2):343–44, 355, 398, 401, 405–6, 420, 474, 24(1):264, 271–72, 24(3), 890.

7. Bevier, *First and Second Missouri*, 429; Lockett, "Vicksburg," 484.

8. Lockett, "Vicksburg," 488; Bearss, *Vicksburg*, 3:740–42.

9. OR, 24(3):324, 24(2):139–40, 24(1):153, 596; F. Grant, "General Grant," *National Tribune*, February 3, 1887.

10. OR, 24(2):256, 263, 755, 24(3):256, 322; Sherman, *Memoirs*, 354; U. S. Grant, *Memoirs*, 354–55, 364.

11. OR, 24(1):272, 24(3):890; Ballard, *Pemberton*, 166, 169.

12. OR, 24(1):272–73; Ballard, *Pemberton*, 166.

13. OR, 24(3):887, 892; Johnston, *Narrative*, 187–88.

14. OR, 24(2):251, 256, 262–63, 266–67, 277, 375, 401, 406, 414; Sherman, *Memoirs*, 352–53.

15. OR, 24(1):273, 24(2):401–2, 406, 414; Hogane, "Reminiscences," 292.

16. OR, 24(2):251, 257, 263–64, 267, 281, 24(1):770; U. S. Grant, *Memoirs*, 353.

17. OR, 24(2):17–18, 27, 33, 229–33, 387, 24(1):153–54, 709.

18. OR, 24(3):329, 24(1):54; U. S. Grant, *Memoirs*, 354–55; Bearss, *Vicksburg*, 3:761.

19. OR, 24(2):267–68, 271, 274, 276, 414; E. McD. Anderson, *Memoirs*,

328–29; Committee of the Regiment, *Story of the Fifty-fifth*, 235.

20. *OR*, 24(2):263–64; Bearss, *Vicksburg*, 3:763; W. W. Gardner to Levi Fuller, May 25, 1863, published in *West Union Gazette* (Iowa), n.d., 13th U.S. Infantry file, VNMP.

21. *OR*, 24(2):281, 283, 406; R. M. Nelson to W. W. Gardner, February 2, 1902, 13th U.S. Infantry file, VNMP.

22. W. L. Foster to Mildred, June 20, 1863, W. L. Foster's Letter, Moore's Brigade, Forney's Division (C.S.A.) file, VNMP.

23. *OR*, 24(2):268; Committee of the Regiment, *Story of the Fifty-fifth*, 237–40; Bearss, *Vicksburg*, 3:766–67.

24. *OR*, 24(2):237, 266–67, 402, 406–7, (1):763; Anderson, *Memoirs*, 329; Bearss, *Vicksburg*, 3:768–69.

25. *OR*, 24(2):60, 67, 206, 292, 297, 299, 300, 24(1):709, 713, 718; Tunnard, *Southern Record*, 236–37.

26. *OR*, 24(1):17, 154, 230–31, 273–74, 24(2):13, 19, 33, 159–60, 229.

27. *OR*, 24(1):54–55; U. S. Grant, *Memoirs*, 355; Bearss, *Vicksburg*, 3:787–89.

28. *OR*, 24(1):731, 768, 776, 780, 784, 24(2):52, 139–40, 187–88; U.S. Grant, *Memoirs*, 355.

29. *OR*, 24(1):756, 24(2):251; Bearss, *Vicksburg*, 3:793.

30. *OR*, 24(1):709–10, 760, 24(2):262, 285, 300, 397, 407; Bearss, *Vicksburg*, 3:795–96, see especially 796 n. 20.

31. *OR*, 24(1):709–10, 719, 731–32, 776, 784, 24(2):206, 292–93, 370–71, 52(2):476.

32. Memoir, unidentified author, Illinois Light Artillery, Chicago Mercantile Battery file, VNMP.

33. *OR*, 24(2):19, 33, 140, 181, 229–30, 24(1):597–98, 617, 24(3):331.

34. *OR*, 24(3):331–32.

35. Bearss, *Vicksburg*, 3:807–8; *OR*, 24(2):301, 24(3):333–34; *ORN*, 25:21.

36. *OR*, 24(2):330, 402, 24(1):274, 24(3):370–71, 899, 901–4; Walker, *Vicksburg*, 171–72.

37. *OR*, 24(2):206–7; Crawford McDonald to father and mother, May 25, 1863, printed in *Mishawaka Enterprise*, June 13, 1863, clipping in 48th Indiana file, VNMP.

38. *OR*, 24(3):334–35, 24(1):171, 174–75.

39. *OR*, 24(3):334–35, 24(1):756–57, 24(2):257, 264, 269, 273, 282, 361, 407; J. W. Larabee statement on May 22 attack, Henry S. Nousse to William T. Rigby, November 9, 1901, 55th Illinois file, VNMP.

40. *OR*, 24(2):257–58, 264, 269, 282, 24(1):760; George Hildt to William T. Rigby, February 8, 1902, 30th Ohio file, VNMP; W. B. Halsey Diary, May 23, 1863, 72nd Ohio file, VNMP.

41. *OR*, 24(2):297, 300.

42. *OR*, 24(1):719; Tunnard, *Southern Record*, 239.

43. *OR*, 24(1):719; Oldroyd, *A Soldier's Story*, 31–32; Bearss, *Vicksburg*, 3:822.

44. *OR*, 24(2):67, 316, 24(1):732, 772–73, 776, 780.

45. *OR*, 24(2):140–41, 240, 351, 355, 357, (1):154; J. M. Pearson to Stephen D. Lee, May 17, 1902, 30th Alabama file, VNMP.

46. S. C. Jones, *Reminiscences*, 38.

47. *OR*, 24(2):141, 357; Merrick J. Wald Diary, May 22, 1863, 77th Illinois file, VNMP.

48. *OR*, 24(2):141, 24(1):128; Bearss, *Vicksburg*, 3:826; J. M. Pearson to Stephen D. Lee, May 17, 1902, 30th Alabama file, Jesse Sawyer to William F. Rigby, February 14, 1903, 77th Illinois file, VNMP.

49. *OR*, 24(2):387–88; Bearss, *Vicks-burg*, 3:828–29; excerpt from *Thirty-third Illinois*, p. 44, and Edward J. Lewis Diary, May 22, 1863, 33rd Illinois file, VNMP; T. J. Higgins to C. A. Hobbs, December 7, 1878, 99th Illinois file, VNMP.

50. *OR*, 24(1):388–89, 598, 24(2):33–34.

51. *OR*, 24(2):34, 420.

52. *OR*, 24(2):20, 27–28, 232, 240; M. A. Sweetman, "From Milliken's Bend to Vicksburg," clipping from paper with *Tribune* in title, vol. 14, no. 47, n.d., 114th Ohio file, VNMP.

53. *OR*, 24(1):55–56, 172–73.

54. *OR*, 24(1):757, 24(2):258, 297–98, 300, 415; Committee of the Regiment, *Story of the Fifty-fifth*, 243; Ramsdell Memoir, p. 67, WHSA.

55. *OR*, 24(1):757, 760, 768, 24(2):273, 415; Bearss, *Vicksburg*, 3:840–41.

56. *OR*, 24(2):251–52; Bearss, *Vicks-burg*, 3:843–44; Ainsworth Diary, pp. 42–49, UM; John W. Niles Diary, May 22, 1863, Alonzo Abernethy Diary, May 22, 1863, 9th Iowa file, VNMP.

57. *OR*, 24(3):341–42, 24(2):259, 264, 282.

58. *OR*, 24(1):598, 173, 617, 710, 720, 722, 732–33, 737, 777, 24(2):62, 67, 389.

59. *OR*, 24(2):7, 141, 238, 351, 357–58.

60. "Experiences of Lyman Baker," pp. 12–13, Baker Papers, ISHL.

61. Edwin C. Bearss, ed., "The Civil War Diary of Lt. John Q. A. Campbell, Company B, 5th Iowa Infantry," May 22, 1863, excerpted from *Annals of Iowa*, n.d., 5th Iowa file, VNMP.

62. *OR*, 24(2):21, 67–68, 141, 240, 302–3, 316, 358, 24(1):733, 776–77, 24(3):340, 908; *ORN*, 25:22; Bearss, *Vicksburg*, 3:853–56.

63. *OR*, 24(3):370–71, 24(1):56, 172–73, 177, 24(2):165.

64. *OR*, 24(3):914, 24(1):276–77.

65. Harvey D. Johnston Diary, May 24, 1863, 99th Illinois file, VNMP; Joseph P. Lesslie to wife, June 3, 1863, 4th Indiana Cavalry file, VNMP; J. C. Nottingham to William T. Rigby, December 12, 1901, 8th Indiana file, VNMP; L. B. Jessup Diary excerpts, May 25, 1863, in letter from Jessup to Rigby, June 10, 1902, 24th Indiana file, VNMP.

66. Tunnard, *Southern Record*, 240; T. T. Smith to children, February 17, 1899, p. 4, Sykes Papers, USAMHI; Phillips, *Some Things Our Boys Saw*, in *Civil War Times Illustrated* Collection, USAMHI; Henry Strong to family, May 23, 1863 (on letter initially dated May 15), Strong Papers, WHSA.

67. Hearn, *Admiral Porter*, 227.

68. Basler, *Works of Lincoln*, 6:226, 230–31.

CHAPTER 12

1. *OR*, 24(1):43, 84, 103, 159–70, 24(3):351, 419; Kiper, *McClernand*, 268–78; U. S. Grant, *Memoirs*, 360.

2. *OR*, 24(3):348, 24(2):170–71; I. Richards to all at home, June 15, 1863, 17th Ohio Light Artillery file, George Grindley to William T. Rigby, June 17, 1902, 56th Ohio file, VNMP.

3. J. B. to My Dear Kate, June 21, 1863, 72nd Ohio file, VNMP.

4. Bearss, *Vicksburg*, 3:886; William Camm to William Rigby, June 10, 1902, containing excerpts from May 26, 1863, entry of Camm's diary, 14th Illinois file.

5. *OR*, 24(2):291–92, 331, 345, 24(3):294.

6. Jenkin Lloyd Jones Diary, May 30, 1863, 6th Wisconsin Light Artillery file, VNMP; *OR*, 24(2):171–74.

7. Davis, *Jefferson Davis*, 505; *OR*, 24(2):172, 334, 403, 407–10.

8. *OR*, 24(2):172, 177, 189–93, 285, 332–33, 339, 407–10, 24(3):356; Committee of the Regiment, *The Story of the Fifty-fifth*, 251.

9. Bearss, *Vicksburg*, 3:901; *OR*, 24(2):192, 334, 376, 420–21.

10. *OR*, 24(2):172, 179, 199–200; Bearss, *Vicksburg*, 3:905.

11. *OR*, 24(2):155–57, 173, 176, 200–203, 207–9, 294, 312–13, 332–33, 363–65, 368, 372, 376–77, 411–13, 416, 438, 441; Tunnard, *Southern Record*, 246–48, 258; E. McD. Anderson, *Memoirs*, 345; U. S. Grant, *Memoirs*, 369–70; Hickenlooper, "The Vicksburg Mine," 539–40; O. J. Burnham to father and mother, June 12, 1863, and Anonymous diary, June 25, 1863, 6th Wisconsin Light Artillery file, VNMP; William Taylor to Jane, June 28, 1863, 100th Pennsylvania file, VNMP; William Lorimer Memoir, 17th Illinois file, VNMP; Robert W. McCrory to William T. Rigby, June 16, 1905, 31st Ohio file, VNMP; Jerome B. Dann to ?, March 3, 1902, and R. M. Springer to J. A. Edminston, March 18, 1902, 20th Illinois file, VNMP; William F. Crummer to W. T. Rigby, October 21, 1902, 45th Illinois file, VNMP.

12. *OR*, 24(3):410, 435, 24(2):174, 181–87, 332–34, 364–65, 390–91, 24(1):103, 107–8; W. H. Bently to William T. Rigby, February 18, 1903, 77th Illinois file, VNMP.

13. *OR*, 24(3):356, 24(2):107, 174, 193–97, 289–90, 356.

14. *OR*, 24(2):317–23, 342–43.

15. Seth Crowhurst to parents, May 31, 1863, Henry and Seth Crowhurst Papers, USAMHI; Anonymous Civil War Letter (by Union soldier) to brother and sister, June 19, 1863, LSU.

16. Elliott, *History of the Thirty-third*,

445; Joseph Bowker Diary, May 28, 1863, 42nd Ohio file, VNMP; R. M. Aiken to mother and father, June 24, 1863, and Sgt. J. M. Hobbs Diary, June 9, 1863, 33rd Illinois file, VNMP; Theo. F. Davis to William T. Rigby, March 31, 1902, 83rd Indiana file, VNMP; L. D. Baynes Diary, June 17, 1863, excerpts in 38th Iowa file, VNMP; G. W. Crosley Diary, June 12, 1863, 3rd Iowa (Colonel Aaron Brown) file, VNMP; "The Civil War Diary of an Iowa Soldier at the Siege of Vicksburg," Diary of Private Arch M. Brinkerhoff, Company H, 4th Iowa Infantry, 4th Iowa file, VNMP; Anonymous Diary, June 8, 1863, 6th Wisconsin Light Artillery file, VNMP; William R. Eddington, "My Civil War Memoirs and Other Reminiscences," p. 11, Eddington Papers, ISHL; Potter Diary, June 3, 1863, WHSA.

17. E. J. Irwin to mother, June 28, 1863, Irwin Family Papers, UM.

18. Joseph Bowker Diary, June 23, 1863, 42nd Ohio file, VNMP.

19. S. C. Jones, *Reminiscences*, 40–41; W. H. Raynor Diary, June 3, 28, 1863, 56th Ohio file, VNMP; Thomas Gordon Diary, June 29, 1863, excerpts in 1st Minnesota file, VNMP; James H. Lewis letter excerpt, June 5, 1863, 24th Iowa file, VNMP; Charles Schenimann to mother, June 26, 1863, 29th Missouri (Union) file, VNMP; S. H. Stephenson to parents, July 2, 1863, 48th Ohio, VNMP; E. J. Irwin to mother, June 28, 1863, Irwin Family Papers, UM; Thomas Beggs to Aunt Dollie, June 19, 1863, Beggs Papers, Charles ISHL; Henry Brush to father, June 26, 1863, Brush Family Papers, ISHL; Adolphus Engelmann to Mina, June 30, 1863, Engelmann-Kircher Family Papers, ISHL; Edward H. Ingraham to aunt, June 15, 1863, Ingraham

Papers, ISHL; John Harris to mother, June 15, 1863, Harris Papers, ISHL; Richard Hall to mother and father, July 2, 1863, Hall Papers, LSU; William H. Nugen to sister, June 23–24, 1863, Nugen Papers, DU; William Murphy to John Murphy, June 15, 1863, Murphy Letters, OHS.

20. N. M. Baker Diary, May 31, June 2, 1863, 116th Illinois file, VNMP; Pinckney S. Cone Diary, June 14, 1863, Cone Papers, ISHL.

21. Augustus G. Sinks, "Journal of the 46th Regiment, 1861–1865," pp. 40–41, Sinks Papers, ISL; John Travis to sister, May 25, 1863, Travis Family Letters, UM; Edward H. Ingraham to aunt, May 29, 1863, Ingraham Papers, ISHL.

22. L. B. Jessup Diary excerpts, June 17, 1863, entry, in letter from Jessup to William T. Rigby, June 10, 1902, 24th Indiana file, VNMP; Clark Whitten to wife, June 23, July 11, 1863, Whitten Papers, USAMHI; George Chittenden to wife, May 29, 1863, Chittenden Papers, ISL; Asa E. Sample Diary, May 20, 1863, Sample Papers, IHS; Charles Henry Brush to sister, June 14, 1863, Brush Papers, ISHL.

23. John V. Boucher to mother, June 7, 1863, to Mrs. J. V. Boucher, June 22, 1863, Boucher Papers, USAMHI.

24. Charles E. Lippincott to Newton Bateman, June 15, 1863, Bateman Papers, ISHL; on Vallandigham, see Klement, *The Limits of Dissent*.

25. John C. Dinsmore to Jane, June 8 [1863], Dinsmore Papers, ISHL; Joseph Willis Young to wife, June 19, 1863, Young Letters, IHS.

26. M. M. Lacy to James Keigwin, February 27, 1902, 49th Indiana file, VNMP; D. W. Reed, *Campaigns and Battles*, 124; Nathan Dye to friends, June 7, 1863, Dye Papers, DU.

27. Ainsworth Diary, p. 52, UM; "The Civil War Diary of an Iowa Soldier at the Siege of Vicksburg, Diary of Private Arch M. Brinkerhoff, Company H, 4th Iowa Infantry," June 4, 1863, 4th Iowa file, VNMP.

28. Edward H. Ingraham to aunt, June 15, 1863, Ingraham Papers, ISHL; unidentified author, diary, May 29, 1863, 17th Ohio Light Artillery file, VNMP.

29. William Taylor to Jane, June 16, 1863, 100th Pennsylvania file, VNMP.

30. Lewis Mathewson to father and mother, June 16, 1863, Mathewson Letters, OHS; Byron MacCutcheon, "Down the Mississippi: To Vicksburg," MacCutcheon Autobiography, UM; William J. Bolton War Journal, p. 140, 51st Pennsylvania file, VNMP (copy of original in Civil War Library and Museum, Philadelphia, Pa.).

31. William Taylor to Jane, June 18, 19, 21, 1863, 100th Pennsylvania file, VNMP; Tunnard, *Southern Record*, 232.

32. W. K. S. Hillhouse to John C. Hillhouse, June 26, 1863, 28th Iowa file, VNMP.

33. Edward H. Ingraham to Alice, June 25, 1863, Ingraham Papers, ISHL; Andrew J. Sproul to Fanny, June 9, 1863, Sproul Papers, UNCCH; John Harris to father, June 8, 1863, Harris Papers, ISHL.

34. Sarah Gregg Diary, June 10, 13, 1863, Gregg Papers, ISHL.

35. Church H. Smith Memoir, OCHM.

36. Nathan Dye to friends, May 18, 27, 1863, Dye Papers, DU.

37. Don Scott to mother, June 28, 1863, Scott Family Papers, UNCCH; S. E. Faunce Memoir, June 17, 1863, Dalton Papers, DU; Lewis Mathewson to father and mother, June 27, 1863, Mathewson Letters, OHS; David Poak

to Sister Sadie, July 10, 1863, Poak Papers, ISHL.

38. Andrew McCormack to friend, May 28, 1863, Sword Collection; William M. Reid Diary, June 1, 1863, Reid Papers, ISHL; Jose Stibbs to Pa, June 13, 1863, Stibbs Family Papers, TU; Joseph Bowker Diary, June 1, 22, 1863, 42nd Ohio file, VNMP; W. B. Smith Diary, June 12, 1863, 68th Ohio file, VNMP; Samuel Swain to mother, June 22, 1863, Swain Papers, WHSA.

39. John Fuller Diary, June 2, 10, 23, 25, 1863, 31st Louisiana file, Simeon R. Martin, "Facts about Company 'I' of the 46th Mississippi Infantry," p. 76, 46th Mississippi file, VNMP; Theodore D. Fisher (First Missouri Brigade), "A Confederate Veteran's Diary as Written during the Siege of Vicksburg — 1863," June 4, 12, 27, 1863, Missouri (Confederate) file, VNMP; Joseph W. Westbrook Memoir, pp. 5–6, Westbrook Papers, USAMHI; Henry Ginder to ?, June 12, 16, 1863, Ginder Papers, TU; Dill Diary, June 10, 1863, UNCCH; Leavy Diary, n.d., OCHM.

40. E. McD. Anderson, *Memoirs*, 337.

41. Edwin C. Bearss, ed., "Civil War Diary of John Campbell," May 30, 1863, *Annals of Iowa*, 5th Iowa file, VNMP; Bachman Memoir, n.d., n.p., OCHM; *Vicksburg Daily Citizen*, July 2, 1863, Lee Papers, UNCCH; Pepper Diary, June 13, 1863, MDAH.

42. Henry Ginder to ?, June 16, 1863, Ginder Papers, TU; Jefferson Brumback to Kate, May 25, 1863, 95th Ohio file, VNMP; Theodore D. Fisher, "A Confederate Veteran's Diary," June 6, 25, 27, 1863, Missouri (Confederate) file, VNMP; Dill Diary, May 30, 1863, UNCCH; Bachman Memoir, n.d., n.p., OCHM; Edward Higgins to Mrs. Eggleston, May 28?, 1863,

Eggleston-Roach Papers, LSU; Guion Diary, May 28, 31, 1863, LSU.

43. Sydney Champion to Matilda, [June 28, 1863], Champion Papers, DU.

44. W. R. McCrary Diary, June 7, 9, 26, 28, 1863, 43rd Mississippi file, VNMP.

45. Fisher, "Confederate Veteran's Diary," June 14, 23, 1863, Missouri (Confederate) file, VNMP.

46. O. J. Holland to Aunt Betsy, June 8, 1863, Roach and Eggleston Family Papers, UNCCH; W. L. Paulk Diary, June 9, 14, 25, 1863, 38th Mississippi file, VNMP; Frances G. Obenchain to William T. Rigby, March 8, 18, 1904, Virginia Botetourt Artillery file, VNMP; Oscar Cantrel Memoir, n.p., n.d., OCHM.

47. Henry Ginder to ?, June 28, 1863, Ginder Papers, TU; Edward S. Gregory, "Vicksburg during the Siege," clipping, and R. A. Jarvis, "Reminiscences of the Boys in Gray, 1861–1865," excerpt, OCHM.

48. W. L. Foster to Mildred, June 20, 1863, pp. 14–16, W. L. Foster's Letter, Moore's Brigade file, VNMP; W. H. McCardle to Surgeon E. W. Bryan, June 7, 1863 (2 messages), F. M. Stafford to Carter Stevenson, June 8, 1863, J. C. Taylor to S. D. Lee, June 8, 1863, Robert Memminger to R. Orme, June 17, 1863, RG 109, chap. II, vol. 60, Letters and Telegrams Sent, Department of Mississippi and East Louisiana, NA; Dill Diary, June 10, 1863, UNCCH; Tunnard, *Southern Record*, 267.

49. E. McD. Anderson, *Memoirs*, 341. See also Sumner, *Angels of Mercy*.

50. Tunnard, *Southern Record*, 237.

51. Mrs. Theodosia F. McKinstry, quoted in typescript, "Alabama," pp. 3–4, Alabama General File, VNMP.

52. William W. Lord, siege account from *Vicksburg Post Herald*, September 27, 1936, Journals/Diaries/Libraries Subseries of Vicksburg Campaign Series, VNMP.

53. Miller Diary, June 21, 1863, OCHM; Sara Stevens, "War Incidents," Stevens Papers, DU.

54. Annie Laurie Harris Broidrick, "A Recollection of Thirty Years Ago," pp. 11–18, Broidrick Memoir, UNCCH.

55. Tunnard, *Southern Record*, 260.

56. D. Rowland, *Jefferson Davis*, 5:502–3, 519.

57. Ballard, *Pemberton*, 172–75; W. A. Montgomery to sister, June 16, 1863, Bailey Papers, USAMHI; Rankin McPheeters to Annie McPheeters, May 17, 1863, McPheeters Family Papers, USAMHI; William H. Van Meter, "A Condensed History of the 47th Regiment of Illinois Vol. Infantry," p. 13, Cromwell Papers, ISHL; W. B. Britton to "Editors Gazette," July 4, 1863, 8th Wisconsin file, VNMP.

58. *OR*, 24(3):330, 361, 898, 905, 908–9, 930–31; *ORN*, 25:127–29, 147; Hearn, *Ellet's Brigade*, 163.

59. *OR*, 24(2):21, 209–13, 24(3):351, 356, 362, 24(1):88–89, 736; Bearss, *Vicksburg*, 3:1100–1102.

60. *OR*, 24(2):285, 302, 312, 435–36, 441, 24(3):352, 354–55, 361–63; Brigadier General J. A. Lightburn, General Orders No. 3, June 1, 1863, Ohio Infantry, 54th Regiment, Papers, USAMHI; Adams Diary, May 31, 1863, UI.

61. *OR*, 24(3):370–71, 934, 937–40, 978, 24(2):214, 325, 436–41, 24(3):373–74, 384, 946–47, 52(1):359; *ORN*, 25:57–58.

62. *OR*, 24(1):94, 24(3):387, 391–92, 396; Dana, *Recollections*, 82–83; Scott, *Story of a Cavalry Regiment*, 97;

Simpson, *Grant*, 207–8. On Milliken's Bend, see Bearss, *Vicksburg*, 3: part 11, chap. 59. General action in Louisiana during the Vicksburg campaign period is detailed in Winters, *Civil War*.

63. *OR*, 24(2):440, 442, 24(3):951, 953, 955–56, 978, 24(1):194, 224–28; Johnston, *Narrative*, 199; Bearss, *Vicksburg*, 3:1010.

64. W. A. Rorer to Cousin Susan, June 13, 1863, Willcox Papers, DU; Amanda Hall to Frank Hall, June 11, 1863, Lulah H. Clark Papers, H. P. Reynolds to [Edmund Kirby Smith], June 4, 1863, Edmund Kirby Smith Papers, UNCCH.

65. *Mobile Advertiser and Register*, June 9, 1863.

66. *OR*, 23(2):343, 358, 364, 857–58, 23(1):349–52; Bearss, *Vicksburg*, 3: part 11, chap. 59; John P. Davis Diary, June 15, 1863, Davis Papers, ISHL.

67. *OR*, 24(3):318–21, 376–77, 381–84, 398–99, 23(2):379, 384, 22(1):306–8.

68. *OR*, 24(3):368–69, 386, 24(1):244, 227–28.

69. *OR*, 24(3):965, 929–30; Johnston, *Narrative*, 199.

70. *OR*, 24(3):917, 929, 953, 958, 981, 987; Bearss, *Vicksburg*, 3:1079.

71. *OR*, 24(3):960, 24(1):244, 24(2):214; Johnston, *Narrative*, 194; Bearss, *Vicksburg*, 3:1085–86.

72. *OR*, 24(2):245–46, 24(3):427–28, 430–31, 439, 449; Bearss, *Vicksburg*, 3:1086.

73. *OR*, 24(2):533, 24(1):106, 24(3):971–72, 974, 980; Ballard, *Pemberton*, 33.

CHAPTER 13

1. *OR*, 24(1):281–84, 24(3):982–83; Pemberton, "The Terms of Surrender," 544.

2. *OR*, 24(1):285–86; Ballard, *Pem-*

berton, 180–82. Grant's account of the surrender is in his *Memoirs*, 375–81. See also Pemberton, "The Terms of Surrender," 543–46.

3. *Vicksburg Daily Citizen*, July 2, 4, 1863, Lee Papers, UNCCH; U. S. Grant, *Memoirs*, 379.

4. Bearss, *Vicksburg*, 3:1301, 1311; Grabau, *Ninety-eight Days*, 502.

5. U. S. Grant, *Memoirs*, 381; Basler, *Works of Lincoln*, 6: 350.

6. Barney, *Recollections*, 200; William P. Henderson to friend, July 11 [1863], 17th Illinois file, VNMP; O. J. Burnham Diary, July 4, 1863, 6th Wisconsin Light Artillery file, VNMP; [J. C. Mahan], *Memoirs*, 133; Edwin Dean, "Edwin Dean's Civil War Days, 1861–1865," Dean Papers, USAMHI.

7. Bevier, *First and Second Missouri*, 218; Tunnard, *Southern Record*, 273.

8. ? Bishop to wife and children, July 4, 6, 1863, 94th Illinois file, VNMP; Joseph Ray to Colonel ? Koch, July 20, 1902, 41st Illinois file, VNMP; Simeon R. Martin, "46th Mississippi Infantry," pp. 80–81, 46th Mississippi file, VNMP; Sylvester W. Fairfield to Tom ?, Fairfield Papers, IHS; William Montague Ferry to Jeanette, July 7, 1863, Ferry Family Papers, UM; Tunnard, *Southern Record*, 271–72.

9. J. L. Foster to Mildred, June 20, 1863, J. L. Foster's letter, Moore's Brigade file, Journals/Diaries/Letters Subseries of Vicksburg Campaign Series, VNMP.

10. *Chicago Daily Tribune*, July 9, 1863; *St. Louis Republican*, July 10, 1863; *Cincinnati Daily Commercial*, July 17, 1863; *New York Times*, July 8, 1863.

11. Gallagher, "Lee's Army."

12. Guion Diary, July 5, 1863, LSU; E. McD. Anderson, *Memoirs*, 359; Matilda Champion to Sydney Cham-

pion, July 10, 1863, Champion Papers, DU; J. Q. Anderson, *Brokenburn*, 230; Marszalek, *Diary of Miss Emma Holmes*, 278; Woodward, *Mary Chesnut's Civil War*, 459–60; Vandiver, *Civil War Diary of Josiah Gorgas*, 55.

13. *Richmond Whig*, July 9, 1863; *Richmond Examiner*, July 10, 1863; *Charleston Mercury*, July 9, 1863; *Macon Telegraph*, July 18, 1863; *Chattanooga Rebel*, quoted in *Macon Telegraph*, August 12, 1863; *North Carolina Standard*, July 29, 1863.

14. *OR*, 24(3):478, 481, 484.

15. F. Grant, "General Grant," *National Tribune*, February 10, 1887.

16. *OR*, 24(3):484; Tunnard, *Southern Record*, 278; Ballard, *Pemberton*, 181–82.

17. D. Rowland, *Jefferson Davis*, 5:555; Bearss, *Vicksburg*, 3:1207–45; Bearss, *Siege of Jackson*, 55.

18. *OR*, 24(1):57–58, (3):461–63, 470; Sherman, *Memoirs*, 358.

19. Byers, *With Fire and Sword*, 83–84.

20. William Taylor to Jane, July 11, 1863, 100th Pennsylvania file, VNMP; Willis Herbert Claiborne Diary, July 13, 1863, Claiborne Papers, UNCCH; John K. Street to Melinda Street, July 6, 1863, Street Papers, UNCCH; D. W. Reed, *Campaigns and Battles*, 128; MacCutcheon Autobiography, "Down the Mississippi," UM; J. W. Pursley to Mary Frances Pursley, July 28, 1863, Pursley Papers, DU.

21. Mrs. D. Rowland, *History of Hinds County*, 34; Hermann, *Pursuit of a Dream*, 41–42.

22. E. J. Irwin to mother, July 30, 1863, Irwin Family Papers, UM; ? Blackwell, "In the Tornado," pp. 103–7, 118–19, 33rd Wisconsin file, VNMP; William Taylor to Jane, July 11, 18, 1863, 100th Pennsylvania file, VNMP.

23. Johnston, *Narrative*, 205–6; Bearss, *Siege of Jackson*, map on p. 71.

24. Bearss, *Siege of Jackson*, 72–74; *OR*, 24(1):245; Johnston, *Narrative*, 207.

25. Bearss, *Siege of Jackson*, 81–82, 84–88; *OR*, 24(2):575.

26. Bearss, *Siege of Jackson*, 88–93.

27. Ibid., 93–95; *OR*, 24(2):541–42; Johnston's account of his retreat is in his *Narrative*, 211–52; Lash, *Destroyer of the Iron Horse*, chap. 3.

28. D. Rowland, *Davis*, 5:579; Bearss, *Siege of Jackson*, 97, 100–103, 105.

29. Anonymous Diary, 26th Illinois file, VNMP; William J. Bolton War Journal, p. 150, 51st Pennsylvania file, VNMP; A. J. Robinson, "Memorandum and Anecdotes of the Civil War, 1862–1865," p. 32, 33rd Wisconsin file, VNMP; Edward H. Ingraham to Alice, July 19, 1863, Ingraham Papers, ISHL; William R. Eddington, "Memoirs," p. 13, Eddington Papers, ISHL; Don Scott to mother, July 26, 1863, Scott Family Papers, UNCCH.

30. Basler, *Works of Lincoln*, 6:409. Good accounts of the Port Hudson siege are in Cunningham, *Port Hudson Campaign*, and Hewitt, *Port Hudson*.

31. *OR*, 24(3):546–47; U. S. Grant, *Memoirs*, 388–89.

32. Basler, *Works of Lincoln*, 6:326, 374.

33. U. S. Grant, *Memoirs*, 384.

34. *OR*, 52(2):833–34; Christ, *Papers of Davis*, 9:357–58.

35. Ballard, *Pemberton*, 182–86.

CHAPTER 14

1. Walker, *Vicksburg*, 203–4; Davis Manuscript, "Vicksburg: The Occupied City," VNMP; Currie, *Enclave*, 9; L. L. Reed, "A Woman's Experiences," 928.

2. Davis Manuscript, "Vicksburg," 92, 94; Walker, *Vicksburg*, 209; W. L. Rand to father, August 30, 186[3], 118th Illinois File, OCHM.

3. John Ruth to sister, June 11, 1863, Ruth file, OCHM; John G. Sever to Mrs. [Rachel] Piper, July 5, 1863, Israel M. Piper, 99th Illinois file, OCHM.

4. Howard [Stevens] to uncle, July 21, 1863, Marsh Family file, OCHM; Elizabeth Parkman to Mrs. McGahey [July 1863], (re: Alexander F. McGahey), 42nd Alabama Infantry file, OCHM.

5. *Vicksburg Daily Herald*, April 12, 1865, clipping in Cemetery Association-Confederate file, OCHM.

6. "Vicksburg National Cemetery" document, and George Macy to Colonel Chandler, March 17, 1868, Vicksburg National Cemetery File, OCHM.

7. Edward S. Gregory, "Vicksburg during the Siege," extract from *The Annals of the Civil War, Written by Leading Participants North and South*, in Deaths in the Court House during the Siege file, OCHM.

8. "A Brief History of the Work of Reburying the Confederate Dead in Vicksburg," undated clipping, and "A Ride to the Confederate Cemetery," in *Vicksburg Daily Herald*, April 23, 1868, both in OCHM; websites <http://www.nps.gov/vick/city_cem/sldrsrest.htm> and <http://www.nps.gov/vick/natcem/nat_cem.htm>.

9. Walker, *Vicksburg*, 208–9.

10. Currie, *Enclave*, 3–5.

11. Armistead Burwell to Abraham Lincoln, August 28, 1863, Lincoln Papers, LC, <http://memory.loc.gov/ammem/alhtml/malhome.html>.

12. Elizabeth Parkman to Mrs. Alexander F. McGahey, [July 1863], 42nd Alabama Infantry file, OCHM; *OR*,

22(2):482–84; Whittington, "In the Shadow of Defeat," 313–14.

13. Currie, *Enclave*, 10–13, 20; Walker, *Vicksburg*, 216; Davis Manuscript, "Vicksburg," 98; L. L. Reed, "Woman's Experience," 927.

14. Currie, *Enclave*, 56–57, 62–63; Walker, *Vicksburg*, 218; Davis Manuscript, "Vicksburg," 129–31.

15. Bigelow, "Vicksburg," 38–39; Basler, *Works of Lincoln*, 6:374; Hermann, *Pursuit of a Dream*, 44–46; Walker, *Vicksburg*, 211.

16. Currie, *Enclave*, 224, 229–30.

17. Terrence Winschel to author, February 4, 2003.

18. Grimsley, *Hard Hand of War*, 142–43.

19. See Ballard, "Yankees in the Yard," Author's Collection; Berlin, "Did Confederate Women Lose the War?" 188.

20. Sherman, *Memoirs*, 289–322; Hattaway and Jones, *How the North Won*, 690; Reyburn and Wilson, *"Jottings from Dixie,"* 197.

21. Grimsley, *And Keep Moving On*, 5–6.

22. Christ, *Papers of Davis*, 10:295–96; Woodward, *Mary Chesnut's Civil War*, 694.

23. For "Cuffee's War Song" and "Never Surrender Quick Step," search <http://scriptorium.lib.duke.edu/sheetmusic>; for "Vicksburg Schottish," search <http://levysheetmusic.mse.jhu.edu>; for "Grant's the Man," search <http://memory.loc.gov>. Wharton, *War Songs and Poems*, 35–36, 185–86; F. Moore, *Rebel Rhymes and Rhapsodies*, 272–73.

24. Woodward, *Mary Chesnut's Civil War*, 478, 568; Galbraith and Galbraith, *A Lost Heroine of the Confederacy*, 153; Christ, *Papers of Davis*, 10:129, 274, 443; Davis, *Jefferson Davis*, 529; Crabtree and Patton, *"Journal of A Secesh Lady,"* 546; Putnam, *Richmond during the War*, 232; Harwell, *Confederate Reader*, 243; *Mobile Advertiser and Register*, February 2, 1864.

25. The following biographical information is taken from sources cited above at the start of the Notes.

26. Hattaway, *General Stephen D. Lee*, 225–32; William T. Rigby information from the University of Iowa Libraries website under the description of "Papers of William Titus Rigby": <http://www.lib.uiowa.edu/spec-coll/msc/tomsc100/msc82/msc82.htm>. For general Park information, see the Park website, <http://www.nps.gov/vick>.

27. Newbill, *General Report*, 4, 23.

28. On the East versus West debate, see the entertaining and thought-provoking work by McMurry, *Fourth Battle of Winchester*. The author checked the website Amazon.com in September 2003 for the book subject areas of Gettysburg and Vicksburg; Gettysburg retrieved 476 hits and Vicksburg 88.

29. Gallagher, "Lee's Army."

Bibliography

MANUSCRIPTS
Author's Collection
    Ballard, Michael B., "Yankees in the Yard: Mississippi Women during the Vicksburg Campaign." Manuscript to be published by the University of Georgia Press in a forthcoming volume of essays on the history of Mississippi women.
    Lancaster, Gary. "Brierfield Arsenal and Supply Depot," unpublished manuscript provided courtesy of the author.
    Winschel, Terrence, e-mail to author, February 4, 2003.
Duke University, Perkins Library, Durham, North Carolina
    Champion, Sydney S., Papers
    Cockrell, Monroe Fulkerson, Papers
    Dalton, Harry L. and Mary K., Papers
    Davis, Jefferson, Papers
    Dye, Nathan G., Papers
    Gebbart, Noah L., Sr., and Emmanuel Martin, Papers
    Marrett, S. S., Papers
    McLaurin, Duncan, Papers
    Metz, George P., Diary
    Munford-Ellis Family Papers
    Nugen, William H., Papers
    Pursley, Mary Frances Jane, Papers
    Stevens, Frederick M., Papers
    Thompkins, Charles Brown, Papers
    Willcox, James W., Papers
East Tennessee State University Library, Johnson City, Tennessee
    Bowman Family Papers
Illinois State Historical Library, Springfield, Illinois
    Anthony, James W., and Charles E. Smith Papers
    Bailhache-Brayman Papers
    Baker, Lyman M., Papers
    Bateman, Newton, Papers
    Beggs, Thomas Benson, Papers
    Boyd, James P., Papers
    Brush Family Papers
    Burke, John W., Papers
    Chipman, Albert and Sophronia, Papers
    Cone, Pinckney S., Papers
    Cromwell, John Nelson, Papers

Davis, John P., Papers
Dillon, Isaiah T. and William L., Papers
Dinsmore, John C., Papers
Eddington, William R., Papers
Ehlers-Grebe Papers
Engelmann-Kircher Family Papers
Forrest, Joseph, Papers
Fox, James Garner, Papers
Funk, Isaac, Papers
Given, John G., Papers
Gordon, Samuel, Papers
Gregg, Sarah, Papers
Harris, John Lindley, Papers
Holmes, David N., Papers
Ingraham, Duncan G. and Edward H., Papers
Johnson, Frances Marion, Papers
Kellogg, Price F., Papers
Kennedy, William J., Papers
Lindsey, John Will, Papers
Marsh, William H., Papers
Matthews, John L., Papers
Packard, Thaddeus B., Diary
Poak, David, Papers
Rand, W. L., Papers
Reid, William M., Papers
Seacord, T. S., Papers
Smith, James W., Papers
Trefftzs, Louis, Papers
Indiana Historical Society, Indianapolis, Indiana
Bishop, Sylvester, Diary
Dean, Zacharia, Papers
Fairfield, Sylvester W., Papers
Ferree, John H., Papers
Grigsly, Bennet, Papers
McCarthy, Joseph F., Papers
Nelson, Charles F., Diary
Sample, Asa E., Papers
Schermerhorn, Bernard, Papers
Sneier, Samuel E., Papers
Stanfield, E. P., Papers
Thomas, William W., Papers
Young, Joseph Willis, Letters
Indiana State Library, Indianapolis, Indiana
Blasdell, John, Papers
Chittenden, George, Papers
Clark, William H., Papers

Marshall, George, Papers
McLaughlin, Mary, Papers
Moreland, David, Papers
Shields, Robert M., Papers
Sinks, Augustus G., Papers
Vanderbilt, James C., Papers
Library of Congress, Washington, D.C.
Lincoln, Abraham, Papers
<http://memory.loc.gov/ammem/alhtml/malhome.html>
Louisiana State University, Hill Library, Baton Rouge, Louisiana
Anonymous Civil War Letter
Chambers, Rowland, Diaries
Dixon, William Y., Papers
Eggleston-Roach Papers
Felton, H. H., Letters
Giles, G. W., Letters
Guion, Louis, Diary
Hall, Richard Alexander, Letters
Hawley, Orestes K., and Family Papers
Knighton, Josiah, and Family Papers
Smith, William H., Letters
Mississippi Department of Archives and History, Jackson, Mississippi
Balfour, Emma, Diary
Baxter, Francis Marion, Papers
Brown, Mrs. Calvin H. [Maude Morrow], Papers
Chambers, William Pitt, Collection
Crutcher-Shannon Papers
Drennan, William A., Diary
Henry, Patrick, Papers
Pepper, J. H., Diary
Pettus, John J., Papers, Record Group 27
Rigby, William T., Papers
Smith, M. J., Papers
National Archives, Washington, D.C.
Record Group 109
Chapter 2, vols. 57, 60
Entry 31
Ohio Historical Society, Columbus, Ohio
Brown, Ephraim, Papers
Heaton, Townsend, Letters
Mathewson, Lewis, Letters
Murphy, William, Letters
Old Court House Museum, Vicksburg, Mississippi
Adams, Matthew, Letter
Bachman, Robert L., Memoir
Bush, Andrew, Letters

Cantrel, Oscar, Memoir
Cemetery Association-Confederate file
Clippings re: Confederate Dead and the Confederate Cemetery
Clippings Scrapbook, "Civil War Incidents in Vicksburg"
C.S.S. *Arkansas* file
Deaths in the Court House during the Siege file
42nd Alabama Infantry file
Georgia file
Gregory, Edward S., Clipping
Hall, R. R., Diary
Jarvis, R. A., Reminiscence
Kidd, James T., Memoir
Leavy, John A., Diary
Marsh Family file
Marshall, Charles K., file
Miller, Dora, Diary
118th Illinois file
Ruth, John, file
Sanders, Jared, Diary
Smith, Church H., Memoir
Trowbridge, Silas, Autobiography
Vicksburg National Cemetery file
Wilson, Rev. R. A., file
Parrish, T. Michael, Collection (in the possession of T. Michael Parrish)
Golden, Gerald, unpublished history of 37th Alabama
Sword, Wiley, Collection (in the possession of Wiley Sword)
McCormack, Andrew, Letters
McWayne, Eugene, Letter
Tulane University Special Collections Library, Jones Hall, New Orleans, Louisiana
Ginder, Henry, Papers
Stibbs Family Papers
Wade Family Papers
United States Army Military History Institute, Carlisle Barracks, Pennsylvania
Bailey, Ann Sturdivant and Milton, Papers
Boucher, John V., Papers
Brown, William Leroy, Papers
Carnahan, Robert H., Papers
Chatfield, George H., Papers
Crowhurst, Henry and Seth, Papers
Dean, Edwin, Papers
Douglas, Thomas B., Papers
Dwight, Henry O., Papers
Howell-Taylor Family Papers
Hunt, Richard M., Papers
McGlothlin, William, Papers
McPheeters Family Papers

Morgan, Henry T., Papers
Ohio Infantry, 54th Regiment, Papers
Phillips, Lewis F., *Some Things Our Boys Saw in the War*, Gravity, Iowa, n.d., *Civil War Times Illustrated* Collection
Roberts, Luke R., Collection, Harrisburg Civil War Round Table Collection
Rounsaville, James B. and Thomas J., Letters, Civil War Miscellaneous Collection
6th Ohio file, *Civil War Times Illustrated* Collection
Smith, Fred, Letter, *Civil War Times Illustrated* Collection
Stone, Thomas R., Collection
Sykes, Columbus, Papers
Talley, Spencer Bowen, Memoir
Westbrook, Joseph W., Papers
Whitten, Clark W. M., Papers
Woodward, William, Papers
University of Iowa Libraries, Special Collections, Iowa City, Iowa
Adams, Henry C., Diary (microfilm)
Cady, Charles, Papers
Henry, Robert W., Papers
Palmer, David James, Papers
Rigby, William T., Papers
Thrall, Seneca, Papers
University of Michigan, Bentley Library, Ann Arbor, Michigan
Ainsworth, Calvin, Diary
Caldwell, William C., Papers
Ferry Family Papers
Irwin Family Papers
MacCutcheon, Byron, Autobiography
Robbins, Jerome, Journals
Travis Family Letters
University of Missouri–Columbia, Western Historical Manuscript Collection, Columbia, Missouri
Crider, Joseph, Papers
Nichols, William E., Papers
University of North Carolina at Chapel Hill, Wilson Library, Southern Historical Collection, Chapel Hill, North Carolina
Agnew, Samuel, Diary
Alcorn, James Lusk, Papers
Alison, Joseph Dill, Diary
Baker, Everard Green, Diary
Broidrick, Annie Laurie Harris, Memoir
Cadman, George Hovey, Papers
Claiborne, J. F. H., Papers
Clark, Lula H., Papers
Comstock, John Henry, Papers
Finley, Robert Stuart, Papers

Gale and Polk Family Papers
Hébert, Louis, Autobiography
Lee, Stephen Dill, Papers
Lockett, Samuel H., Papers
Miller, Letitia D., Collection
Niles, Jason, Papers
Quitman Family Papers
Roach, Mahala, Diary
Roach and Eggleston Family Papers
Scott Family Papers
Sheppard, Louisa C., Memoir
Smith, Edmund Kirby, Papers
Sproul, Andrew J., Papers
Street, John Kennedy, Papers
Thompson, Ruffin, Papers
Tracy, Edward Dorr, Papers
Whyte, Samuel Addison, Papers
Withrow, Adoniram Judson, Papers
Worthington, Amanda Doughtry, Diary
University of Texas at Austin, Center for American History, Austin, Texas
Simons, Maurice Kavanaugh, Diary
Vicksburg National Military Park Archives, Vicksburg Campaign Series, Vicksburg, Mississippi
Vicksburg Campaign Series
Davis, Betty Robbins, Manuscript
Journals/Diaries/Letters Subseries
Curtenius, F. W., Diary
Foster, W. L., Letter
Kreible, Karl, Letters
Lord, William W., Siege Account
Ruckman, John, Letters
Regimental Files Subseries
Alabama
Alabama (General File)
Infantry, 30th
Arkansas
Infantry, 19th
Georgia
Cherokee, Georgia, Artillery
Infantry, 40th, 42nd, 43rd
Illinois
Illinois Light Artillery, Chicago Mercantile Battery
Infantry, 13th, 14th, 17th, 20th, 26th, 31st, 33rd, 41st, 45th, 55th, 77th, 81st, 94th, 97th, 99th, 116th
Indiana
Cavalry, 4th

Infantry, 8th, 11th, 24th, 34th, 48th, 49th, 69th, 83rd
Iowa
    Infantry, 3rd, 4th, 5th, 9th, 24th, 28th, 30th, 38th
Louisiana
    Artillery, 1st
    Infantry, 27th, 31st
Michigan
    Artillery, 8th (Light)
Minnesota
    Infantry, 1st
Mississippi
    Artillery, McClendon's Battery, 1st (Light)
    Infantry, 31st, 38th, 43rd, 46th
Missouri
    Missouri (Confederate), General File
    Infantry, 3rd (Confederate), 29th (Union)
Moore's Brigade, Forney's Division (C.S.A.)
Ohio
    Artillery, 17th (Light)
    Infantry, 20th, 30th, 31st, 42nd, 48th, 56th, 68th, 72nd, 95th, 114th, 120th
Pennsylvania
    Infantry, 51st, 100th
Tennessee
    Infantry, 39th
Texas
    Infantry, Waul's Texas Legion, Second Battalion
U.S. Infantry, 13th
Virginia
    Artillery, Botetourt
Wisconsin
    Artillery, 6th (Light)
    Infantry, 8th, 11th, 14th, 23rd, 29th, 33rd
Vicksburg National Military Park Website for National and Confederate Cemeteries in Vicksburg
    <http://www.nps.gov/vick/city_cem/sldrsrest.htm>
    <http://www.nps.gov/vick/natcem/nat_cem.htm>
Wisconsin Historical Society Archives, Madison, Wisconsin
    Barney, John J., Papers
    Burdick, Samuel, Diary
    Clemons, Henry, Letters
    8th Wisconsin Infantry Reunion Papers
    Foster, Jacob T., Memoirs
    James, David G., Papers
    Jones, John G., Papers
    Norton, Joel, Letters

Potter, Edward N., Diary
Ramsdell, Daniel A., Memoir
Strong, Henry P., Papers
Swain, Samuel Glyde, Papers
World Wide Web Sites: Music and Poems
<http://scriptorium.lib.duke.edu/sheetmusic>
<http://levysheetmusic.mse.jhu.edu>
<http://memory.loc.gov>

PERIODICALS

Charleston Mercury, 1863
Chicago Daily Tribune, 1861, 1863
Cincinnati Daily Commercial, 1863
Macon (Ga.) Telegraph, 1863
Mobile Register and Advertiser, 1863
New York Times, 1863

North Carolina Standard, 1863
Richmond Examiner, 1863
Richmond Whig, 1863
St. Louis Republican, 1863
Vicksburg Daily Whig, 1860–1861

PUBLISHED SOURCES

Abbott, John S. C. The History of the Civil War in America . . . 2 vols. New York, 1873.

Abernethy, Alonzo. "Incidents of an Iowa Soldier's Life; or, Four Years in Dixie." Annals of Iowa, October, 1920.

Anderson, Bern. By Sea and by River: The Naval History of the Civil War. New York, 1962.

Anderson, Ephraim McD. Memoirs, Historical and Personal, Including the Campaigns of the First Missouri Confederate Brigade. 1868. Repr., Dayton, Ohio, 1972.

Anderson, John Q., ed. Brokenburn: The Journal of Kate Stone, 1861–1868. 1955. Repr., Baton Rouge, La., 1995.

Badeau, Adam. Military History of Ulysses S. Grant: From April, 1861, to April, 1865. 3 vols. New York, 1868–81.

Ballard, Michael B. Pemberton: A Biography. Jackson, Miss., 1991.

Barney, C. Recollections of Field Service with the Twentieth Iowa Volunteers . . . Davenport, Iowa, 1865.

Barron, Samuel B. The Lone Star Defenders: A Chronicle of the Third Texas Cavalry. New York, 1908.

Basler, Roy P., ed. The Collected Works of Abraham Lincoln, 8 vols. plus index vol. New Brunswick, N.J., 1953–55.

Bearss, Edwin C. Decision in Mississippi: Mississippi's Crucial Role in the War Between the States. Jackson, Miss., 1961.

——. Rebel Victory at Vicksburg. Little Rock, Ark., 1963.

——. The Siege of Jackson, July 10–17, 1863. Baltimore, Md., 1981

——. The Vicksburg Campaign, 3 vols. Dayton, Ohio, 1985–86.

Berlin, Jean V. "Did Confederate Women Lose the War? Deprivation, Destruction, and Despair on the Home Front." In The Collapse of the Confederacy, ed. Mark Grimsley and Brooks D. Simpson, 168–93. Lincoln, Neb., 2001.

Bettersworth, John K. Confederate Mississippi: The People and Policies of a Cotton State in Wartime. 1943. Repr., Philadelphia, Pa., 1978.

Bevier, R. S. History of the First and Second Missouri Confederate Brigades, 1861–1865;

and, *From Wakarusa to Appomattox, a Military Anagraph.* 1879. Repr., St. Louis, 1985.

Bigelow, Martha Mitchell. "Vicksburg: Experiment in Freedom." *Journal of Mississippi History* 26 (February–November 1964): 28–44.

Black, S. *A Soldier's Recollections of the Civil War.* Minco, Okla., 1911–12.

Boyd, Cyrus F. *The Civil War Diary of Cyrus F. Boyd.* Ed. Mildred Thorne. 1953. Repr., Millwood, N.Y., 1977.

Brieger, James F., comp. *Hometown Mississippi.* 2nd ed. Jackson, Miss., 1997.

Brown, Dee Alexander. *Grierson's Raid.* 1954. Repr., Dayton, Ohio, 1981.

Brown, Isaac N. "The Confederate Gun-Boat 'Arkansas.' " In *Battles and Leaders of the Civil War*, Robert Underwood Johnson and Clarence Clough Buel, 3:572–80. 1887–88. Repr., New York, 1956.

Butler, Benjamin F. *Private and Official Correspondence of Gen. Benjamin F. Butler, during the Period of the Civil War.* 5 vols. Norwood, Mass., 1917.

Byers, S. H. M. *With Fire and Sword.* New York, 1911.

Carter, Arthur B. *The Tarnished Cavalier: Major General Earl Van Dorn, C.S.A.* Knoxville, Tenn., 1999.

Castel, Albert E. *General Sterling Price and the Civil War in the West.* Baton Rouge, La., 1968.

Chambers, William Pitt. "My Journal." In *Publications of the Mississippi Historical Society, Centenary Series*, 5:227–386. Jackson, Miss., 1925.

Christ, Lynda Laswell, et al., eds. *The Papers of Jefferson Davis.* 10 vols. to date. Baton Rouge, La., 1971–.

Clark, Olynthus B. *Downing's Civil War Diary . . . , August 15, 1861–July 31, 1865.* Des Moines, Iowa, 1916.

Committee of the Regiment. *The Story of the Fifty-fifth Regiment, Illinois Volunteer Infantry in the Civil War, 1861–1865.* 1887. Repr., Huntington, W.Va., 1993.

Connelly, Thomas L. "Vicksburg: Strategic Point or Propaganda Device?" *Military Affairs*, 34 (April 1970): 49–53.

Cooling, Benjamin Franklin. *Forts Henry and Donelson: The Key to the Confederate Heartland.* Knoxville, Tenn., 1987.

Coombe, Jack D. *Thunder along the Mississippi.* New York, 1996.

Cozzens, Peter. *The Darkest Days of the War: The Battles of Iuka and Corinth.* Chapel Hill, N.C., 1997.

Crabtree, Beth G., and James W. Patton, eds. *"Journal of a Secesh Lady": The Diary of Catherine Ann Devereux Edmonston, 1860–1866.* Raleigh, N.C., 1979.

Crook, George, comp. *The Twenty-first Regiment of Iowa Volunteer Infantry.* Milwaukee, Wis., 1891.

Cunningham, Edward. *The Port Hudson Campaign, 1862–1863.* Baton Rouge, La., 1963.

Currie, James T. *Enclave: Vicksburg and Her Plantations, 1863–1870.* Jackson, Miss., 1980.

Dana, Charles A. *Recollections of the Civil War.* New York, 1898.

Daniel, Larry J. *Shiloh: The Battle That Changed the Civil War.* New York, 1998.

———. "Bruinsburg: Missed Opportunity or Postwar Rhetoric?" *Civil War History* 32 (September 1986): 256–67.

Daniel, Larry J., and Lynn N. Bock. *Island No. 10: Struggle for the Mississippi Valley.* Tuscaloosa, Ala., 1996.

Davis, William C. *Breckinridge: Statesman, Soldier, Symbol.* Baton Rouge, La., 1974.

——. *Jefferson Davis: The Man and His Hour.* New York, 1991.

Dubay, Robert W. *John Jones Pettus, Mississippi Fireater: His Life and Times, 1813–1867.* Jackson, Miss., 1975.

Duffy, James P. *Lincoln's Admiral: The Civil War Campaigns of David Farragut.* New York, 1997.

"During the First Siege of Vicksburg: From the Diary of a Kentucky Soldier." *Confederate Veteran* 2 (January 1894): 11.

Elliott, Isaac H. *History of the Thirty-third Regiment Illinois Veteran Volunteer Infantry in the Civil War, 22nd August to 7th December, 1865.* Gibson City, Ill., 1902.

Feis, William B. *Grant's Secret Service: The Intelligence War from Belmont to Appomattox.* Lincoln, Neb., 2002.

Fremantle, Arthur Charles Lyon. *Three Months in the Southern States: April–June, 1863.* 1863. Repr., Lincoln, Neb., 1991.

Galbraith, Loretta, and William Galbraith, eds. *A Lost Heroine of the Confederacy: The Diaries and Letters of Belle Edmondson.* Jackson, Miss., 1990.

Gallagher, Gary F. "Lee's Army Has Not Lost Any of Its Prestige: The Impact of Gettysburg on the Army of Northern Virginia and the Confederate Home Front." In *The Third Day at Gettysburg and Beyond*, edited by Gary F. Gallagher, 1–22. Chapel Hill, N.C., 1994.

Gift, George W. "The Story of the Arkansas." In *Southern Historical Society Papers*, 12:205–12. 1876–1959. Repr., Millwood, N.Y., 1977.

Gosnell, Harpur Allen. *Guns on the Western Waters: The Story of River Gunboats in the Civil War.* 1949. Repr., Baton Rouge, La., 1993.

Govan, Gilbert E., and James W. Livingood. *A Different Valor: The Story of General Joseph E. Johnston, C.S.A.* Indianapolis, Ind, 1956.

Grabau, Warren E., *Ninety-eight Days: A Geographer's View of the Vicksburg Campaign.* Knoxville, Tenn., 2000.

Grant, Fred. "General Ulysses S. Grant: His Son's Memories of Him in the Field." *National Tribune*, January 20, 27, February 3, 10, 1887.

Grant, Ulysses S. *Memoirs and Selected Letters: Personal Memoirs of U. S. Grant, Selected Letters, 1839–1865.* 2 vols. in 1. New York, 1990.

——. "The Vicksburg Campaign." In *Battles and Leaders of the Civil War*, edited by Robert Underwood Johnson and Clarence Clough Buel, 3:493–539. 1887–88. Repr., New York, 1956.

Greene, Francis Vinton. *The Mississippi.* 1882. Repr., Wilmington, N.C., 1989.

Grillis, Pamela Lea. *Vicksburg and Warren County: A History of People and Place.* Vicksburg, Miss., 1992.

Grimsley, Mark. *And Keep Moving On: The Virginia Campaign, May–June 1864.* Lincoln, Neb., 2002.

——. *Hard Hand of War: Union Military Policy toward Southern Civilians.* New York, 1995.

Grimsley, Mark, and Todd D. Miller, eds. *The Union Must Stand: The Civil War Diary of John Quincy Adams Campbell, Fifth Iowa Volunteer Infantry.* Knoxville, Tenn., 2000.

Harrell, Virginia Calohan. *Vicksburg and the River*. Jackson, Miss., 1982.

Hartje, Robert G. *Van Dorn: The Life and Times of a Confederate General*. Nashville, Tenn., 1967.

Harwell, Richard B., ed. *The Confederate Reader*. New York: 1957.

Hattaway, Herman L. *General Stephen D. Lee*. Jackson, Miss., 1976.

Hattaway, Herman L., and Archer Jones. *How the North Won: A Military History of the Civil War*. Urbana, Ill., 1983.

Hawkins, H. G. "History of Port Gibson, Mississippi." *Publications of the Mississippi Historical Society*. 14 vols. Oxford, Miss., 1898–1914. 10:279–99.

Headley, Katy McCaleb, comp. *Claiborne County, Mississippi: The Promised Land*. Baton Rouge, La., 1976.

Hearn, Chester G. *Admiral David Dixon Porter: The Civil War Years*. Annapolis, Md., 1996.

———. *The Capture of New Orleans, 1862*. Baton Rouge, La., 1995.

———. *Ellet's Brigade: The Strangest Outfit of All*. Baton Rouge, La., 2000.

———. *When the Devil Came Down to Dixie: Ben Butler in New Orleans*. Baton Rouge, La., 1997.

Henry, George. *History of the 3d, 7th, 8th, and 12th Kentucky, C.S.A.* 1911. Repr., Lyndon, Ky., 1970.

Hermann, Janet Sharp. *The Pursuit of a Dream*. New York, 1981.

Hess, Earl J. "The Mississippi River and Secession, 1861: The Northwestern Response." *The Old Northwest* 10 (Summer 1984): 187–207.

Hewitt, Lawrence Lee. *Port Hudson: Confederate Bastion on the Mississippi*. Baton Rouge, La., 1987.

Hickenlooper, Andrew. "The Vicksburg Mine." In *Battles and Leaders of the Civil War*, edited by Robert Underwood Johnson and Clarence Clough Buel, 3:539–42. 1887–88. Repr., New York, 1956.

Hogane, J. T. "Reminiscences of the Siege of Vicksburg." In *Southern Historical Society Papers*, 11:291–97. Millwood, N.Y., 1977, repr.

Howell, H. Grady, Jr. *Going to Meet the Yankees: A History of the "Bloody Sixth" Mississippi Infantry, C.S.A.* Jackson, Miss., 1981.

Hurst, Jack. *Nathan Bedford Forrest: A Biography*. New York, 1993.

Johnston, Joseph E. *Narrative of Military Operations, Directed, during the Late War between the States*. New York, 1874.

Jones, R. Steven. *The Right Hand of Command: Use and Disuse of Personal Staffs in the Civil War*. Mechanicsburg, Pa., 2000.

Jones, S. C. *Reminiscences of the Twenty-second Iowa*. 1907. Repr., Iowa City, Iowa, 1993.

Kelly, William Milner. "A History of the Thirtieth Alabama Volunteers (Infantry), Confederate States Army." *Alabama Historical Quarterly* 9 (Spring 1947): 119–89.

Kiper, Richard L. *Major General John Alexander McClernand: Politician in Uniform*. Kent, Ohio, 1999.

Klement, Frank L. *The Limits of Dissent: Clement L. Vallandigham and the Civil War*. Lexington, Ky., 1970.

Lash, Jeffrey N. *Destroyer of the Iron Horse: General Joseph E. Johnston and Confederate Rail Transport, 1861–1865*. Kent, Ohio, 1991.

Lee, Stephen D. "The Campaign of Vicksburg, Mississippi, in 1863, from April 15 to and Including the Battle of Champion Hills, or Baker's Creek, May 16, 1863." *Publications of the Mississippi Historical Society.* 14 vols. Oxford, Miss., 1898–1914. 3:21–53.

————. "Details of Important Work by Two Confederate Telegraph Operators, Christmas Eve, Which Prevented the Complete Surprise of the Confederate Army at Vicksburg." *Publications of the Mississippi Historical Society.* 14 vols. Oxford, Miss., 1898–1914. 8:51–55.

Lewis, Lloyd. *Sherman: Fighting Prophet.* New York, 1932.

Lillibridge, Laurence, ed. *Hard Marches, Hard Crackers, and Hard Beds: A Great Grandfather's Letters Written during the Civil War.* Prescott Valley, Ariz., 1993.

Lockett, Samuel L. "The Defense of Vicksburg." In *Battles and Leaders of the Civil War,* edited by Robert Underwood Johnson and Clarence Clough Buel, 3:482–92. 1887–88. Repr., New York, 1956.

Lumpkin, Martha Neville, ed. *"My Darling Loulie": Letters of Cordelia Lewis Scales to Loulie W. Irby during and after the War between the States.* Boulder, Colo., 1955.

Mahan, A. T. *The Gulf and Inland Waters.* New York, 1883.

[Mahan, James Curtis.] *Memoirs of James Curtis Mahan.* Lincoln, Neb., 1919.

Marszalek, John F. *Sherman: A Soldier's Passion for Order.* New York, 1993.

————. "Where Did Winfield Scott Find His Anaconda?" *Lincoln Herald* 89 (Summer 1987): 77–81.

————, ed. *The Diary of Miss Emma Holmes, 1861–1866.* Baton Rouge, La., 1979.

Maury, Dabney H. "A Winter at Vicksburg," *Philadelphia Weekly Times,* January 3, 1885.

McFeely, William S. *Grant: A Biography.* New York, 1981.

McGregor, John A. "Chickasaw Bayou." *National Tribune,* July 21, 1904.

McMurry, Richard M. *The Fourth Battle of Winchester: Toward a New Civil War Paradigm.* Kent, Ohio, 2002.

McPherson, James M. *The Negro's Civil War: How American Negroes Felt and Acted during the War for the Union.* New York, 1965.

Meyer, Steve. *Iowa Valor: A Compilation of Civil War Combat Experiences from Soldiers of the State Distinguished as Most Patriotic of the Patriotic.* Garrison, Iowa, 1994.

Moore, Frank, comp. and ed. *Rebel Rhymes and Rhapsodies.* New York, 1864.

————, ed. *The Rebellion Record: A Diary of American Events.* 12 vols. 1861–68. Repr., New York, 1977.

Moore, Glover. "A Separation from the Union, 1854–1861." In *A History of Mississippi,* edited by Richard Aubrey McLemore, 1:420–46. Jackson, Miss., 1973.

Morgan, George W. "The Assault on Chickasaw Bluffs." In *Battles and Leaders of the Civil War,* edited by Robert Underwood Johnson and Clarence Clough Buel, 3:462–70. 1887–88. Repr., New York, 1956.

Morris, Christopher. *Becoming Southern: The Evolution of a Way of Life: Warren County and Vicksburg, Mississippi, 1770–1860.* New York, 1995.

Newbill, Willard D. *General Report of the National Memorial Celebration and Peace Jubilee.* Washington, D.C., 1917.

Non-commissioned Officer, A. *Opening of the Mississippi; or, Two Years' Campaigning in the South-West, A Record of the . . . 8th Wisconsin Volunteers . . .* Madison, Wis., 1864.

Official Records of the Union and Confederate Navies in the War of the Rebellion. 30 vols. Washington, D.C., 1894–1927.

Oldroyd, Osborn H. *A Soldier's Story of the Siege of Vicksburg, from the Diary of Osborn H. Oldroyd . . .* Springfield, Ill., 1885.

Pemberton, John C. "The Terms of Surrender." In *Battles and Leaders of the Civil War,* edited by Robert Underwood Johnston and Clarence Clough Buel, 3:543–46. 1887–88. Repr., New York, 1956.

Popchock, Barry, ed. *Soldier Boy: The Civil War Letters of Charles Musser, 29th Iowa.* Iowa City, Iowa, 1995.

Porter, Admiral [David Dixon]. *Incidents and Anecdotes of the Civil War.* New York, 1885.

Putnam, Sallie B. *Richmond during the War: Four Years of Personal Observation by a Richmond Lady.* New York, 1867.

Read, C. W. "Reminiscences of the Confederate States Navy." *Southern Historical Society Papers,* 1:331–62. 1876–1959. Repr., Millwood, N.Y., 1977.

Reed, David W. *Campaigns and Battles of the Twelfth Regiment, Iowa Veteran Volunteer Infantry . . .* Evanston, Ill., 1903.

Reed, Lida Lord. "A Woman's Experiences during the Siege of Vicksburg." *Century Magazine* 61 (April 1901): 922–28.

Reyburn, Phillip J., and Terry L. Wilson, eds. *"Jottings from Dixie": The Civil War Dispatches of Sergeant Major Stephen F. Fleharty, U.S.A.* Baton Rouge, La., 1999.

Richard, Allan C., Jr., and Mary Margaret Richard. *The Defense of Vicksburg: A Louisiana Chronicle.* College Station, Tex., 2003.

Rogers, William Warren, Jr., ed. " 'The Prospects of Our Country Are Gloomy Indeed': Stephens Croom at Vicksburg (April, 1863)." *Journal of Mississippi History* 59 (Spring 1997): 33–51.

Rowland, Dunbar. *Military History of Mississippi, 1803–1898.* N.d. Repr., Spartanburg, S.C., 1978.

———, ed. *Jefferson Davis, Constitutionalist: His Letters, Papers and Speeches,* 10 vols. Jackson, Miss., 1923.

Rowland, Mrs. Dunbar. *History of Hinds County, Mississippi, 1821–1922.* Jackson, Miss., 1922

Russell, William Howard. *My Diary North and South.* Boston and New York, 1863.

Scott, William Forse. *The Story of a Cavalry Regiment: The Career of the Fourth Iowa Volunteers, from Kansas to Georgia, 1861–1865.* New York, 1893.

Sherman, William T. *Memoirs of General W. T. Sherman.* 1875. Repr., New York, 1994.

Simon, John Y., ed. *The Papers of U. S. Grant.* 22 vols. to date. Carbondale, Ill., 1967–.

Simpson, Brooks D. *Ulysses S. Grant: Triumph over Adversity, 1822–1865.* Boston, 2000.

Simpson, Brooks D., and Jean V. Berlin, eds. *Sherman's Civil War: Selected Correspondence of William T. Sherman.* Chapel Hill, N.C., 1999.

Slagle, Jay. *Ironclad Captain: Seth Ledyard Phelps and the U.S. Navy, 1841–1864.* Kent, Ohio, 1996.

Smith, David M. *Compelled to Appear in Print: The Vicksburg Manuscript of John C. Pemberton*. Cincinnati, Ohio, 1999.

Smith, Jean Edward. *Grant*. New York, 2001.

Sobotka, C. John, Jr. *A History of Lafayette County, Mississippi*. Oxford, Miss., 1976.

Soley, James Russell. "Naval Operations in the Vicksburg Campaign." In *Battles and Leaders of the Civil War*, edited by Robert Underwood Johnson and Clarence Clough Buell, 3:551–70. 1887–88. Repr., New York, 1956.

Still, William N., Jr. *Iron Afloat: The Story of the Confederate Armorclads*. Nashville, Tenn., 1971.

Sumner, Sister Ignatius. *Angels of Mercy: An Eyewitness Account of the Civil War and Yellow Fever*. Edited by Sister Mary Paulinus Oakes. Baltimore, Md., 1998.

Sword, Wiley. *Shiloh: Bloody April*. Rev. ed. Dayton, Ohio, 2001.

Symonds, Craig L. *Joseph E. Johnston: A Civil War Biography*. New York, 1992.

The Thirty-fourth Iowa Regiment, A Brief History. Des Moines, Iowa, 1892.

Tunnard, W. H. *A Southern Record: The Story of the 3rd Louisiana Infantry, C.S.A.* 1866. Repr., Dayton, Ohio, 1970.

Vandiver, Frank E., ed. *The Civil War Diary of Josiah Gorgas*. University, Ala., 1947.

Walker, Peter F., *Vicksburg: A People at War, 1860–1865*. Chapel Hill, N.C., 1960.

The War of the Rebellion: A Compilation of the Official Records of the Union and Confederate Armies. 128 vols. Washington, D.C., 1880–1901.

Weinert, Richard P. "The Neglected Key to the Gulf Coast," *Journal of Mississippi History* 31 (November 1969): 269–301.

Wharton, H. M., comp. *War Songs and Poems of the Southern Confederacy, 1861–1865*. Philadelphia, Pa., 1904.

"What Telegraph Men Did for Vicksburg," *Confederate Veteran* 10 (February 1902): 72.

Whittington, Terry. "In the Shadow of Defeat: Tracking the Vicksburg Parolees." *Journal of Mississippi History* 64 (Winter 2002): 307–30.

Willett, E. D. *History of Company B (Originally Pickens Planters): 40th Alabama Regiment, Confederate States Army, 1862–1865*. 1902. Repr., Jackson, Miss., 1963.

Winters, John D. *The Civil War in Louisiana*. Baton Rouge, La., 1963.

Woodward, C. Vann, ed. *Mary Chesnut's Civil War*. New Haven, Conn., 1981.

Wright, Henry H. *A History of the Sixth Iowa Infantry*. Iowa City, Iowa, 1923.

Index

Joseph E. Johnston, 116, 275, 409–10; visits Mississippi, 124, 126, 131; declares that both Vicksburg and Port Hudson must be held, 194, 256, 259, 325; during siege, 361–62, 388–89; and surrender of Vicksburg, 403–4, 412, 417; defends Pemberton, 412, 425; impact of surrender of Vicksburg on, 423–25

De Courcy, John, 135, 138, 139, 141, 142

De Golyer, Samuel, 240, 264, 265, 301, 366

Dennis, Elias, 242, 243, 263, 264, 265

Drumgould's Bluff, 140, 174

Duckport Canal operation, 193

Edwards (also Edwards Station), 283, 299, 304, 306–8, 310, 313

Ellet, Alfred, 49, 50, 56, 145; commands Mississippi Marine Brigade, 72; orders destruction of Austin, 389; and hard war, 389

Ellison house, 284, 287–88, 292–93

Ewing, Hugh: and Vicksburg operations, May–July 1863, 329, 339, 346

Ewing's Approach, 363–64

Farragut, David, 29, 30, 247; and 1862 river campaign against Vicksburg, 31–32, 35–36, 39, 42, 46–50, 52–56, 58–62, 198; leaves Vicksburg, 60; below Vicksburg in early 1863, 188; after Vicksburg, 428

Featherston, Winfield, 186, 187, 245, 292, 302, 304, 307–8

Ferguson, Samuel, 186, 187, 209–11, 319

Fontaine, Edward, 23–24

Forney, John, 116, 206, 217, 245, 260, 283, 284, 310, 312, 317, 319–20; and defense of Vicksburg, May–July 1863, 332, 340, 365; after Vicksburg, 426

Forrest, Nathan Bedford, 112, 125, 150, 207, 258

Fort Hindman, 115. *See also* Arkansas Post, campaign and battle

Fort Pemberton. *See* Yazoo Pass operation

Foster, James, 183, 189

Fox, Gustavus, 35, 36

French, Samuel: and siege of Jackson, 404, 407–8

Gardner, Franklin, 121, 167, 170, 192, 204, 205, 252, 256, 257, 405, 410–11

Garrard, Theophilus T., 230, 293, 302, 314

Garrott, Isham, 231, 232, 233, 236, 372

Gettysburg, 401–2, 430

Gist, States Rights, 273, 275

Gorman, Willis, 112, 147

Granbury, Hiram, 263, 267

Grand Gulf, Miss., 37, 42, 192, 225, 248, 251, 253, 257; battle of, 214–20

Grant, Fred, 200, 278–79, 316–17, 403

Grant, Ulysses S., 27, 54, 72, 129, 136, 137, 146, 147; relationship with Halleck, 70, 79, 80, 82, 83, 158, 315, 411; and guerrilla activity, 70–71; and Iuka and Corinth campaigns and battles, 74–79; North Mississippi campaign, 79–92, 101–28, 156; relationship with McClernand, 80–81, 83, 105, 114, 147, 150, 171–72, 193, 358–60; relationship with David Dixon Porter, 81; comments on logistics, 92, 248; sends Sherman downriver to attack Vicksburg, 111; order condemning Jewish merchants, 112–13; establishes local welfare system in North Mississippi, 113; reacts to Van Dorn's raid, 123, 126, 128; and Arkansas Post campaign and battle, 149, 150, 154, 155, 156; early 1863 operations of, 156–90; assumes field command of Vicksburg operations,

Osterhaus, Peter, 194, 195, 196, 197, 214, 215, 230, 231, 233, 253, 255, 272, 286, 289, 292–94, 302–3, 314; and Vicksburg operations, May–July 1863, 327, 335, 340, 343, 347–48

Oxford, Miss., 105, 108, 120, 126

Palmer, James, 32, 36, 40, 41, 42

Parke, John, 392; and siege of Jackson, 405, 408

Pemberton, John C., 82, 102, 155, 157, 191, 192, 193–94, 407; appointed to command in Mississippi and East Louisiana, 86–87; and North Mississippi campaign, 88–92, 104, 105, 106, 108, 111, 114–27; relationship with Joseph E. Johnston, 116; distrust of in Mississippi, 119–20; during Chickasaw Bayou and Arkansas Post campaigns, 131; during U. S. Grant's early 1863 operations, 166–72, 177–81, 186–90; caught between conflicting opinions of Jefferson Davis and Johnston, 169–70; disputes with Loring, 178–79, 292; actions during Grant's Louisiana march, 193–94, 203–6, 208, 212–13, 216–17, 220; and Grant's inland campaign, 224, 226, 243–46, 249–61, 271–74, 279–81; and battles of Champion Hill and Big Black, 282–85, 287–96, 298–300, 303–10, 312–15, 317–18; and Grant's May 1863 assaults, 319–22, 324–27, 336–37, 349, 351; and siege operations, 358, 360–62, 366, 373–74, 381, 383, 388, 393–95; and surrender of Vicksburg, 396–98, 401–5; meets with Johnston, 404; aftermath of defeat, 412–13, 418, 424–26

Pettus, John Jones, 8–10, 11, 16, 19, 44, 73, 166, 193, 245, 257, 273, 417

Phelan, James, 119–20

Pillow, Gideon J., 18, 77

Pook, Samuel, 28

Porter, David Dixon, 16, 24, 25, 47–48, 55, 80–81, 111, 157, 170, 191, 247, 250; and June 1862 attack at Vicksburg, 49, 50, 52, 53; transferred to Virginia, 55; named commander of Mississippi River Squadron, 72; relationship with U. S. Grant and Sherman, 81, 148; and Chickasaw Bayou campaign and battles, 112, 130, 134, 135, 139, 144, 145; and Arkansas Post campaign and battle, 148, 149, 151; dislike of McClernand, 148–49; at Yazoo Pass, 176–77; and Steele's Bayou–Deer Creek operation, 184–88; and Grant's Louisiana march, 195, 198–203, 206, 214–19; escorting transports past Vicksburg batteries, 198–202; and operations at Vicksburg, May–July 1863, 326–27, 336, 348, 350; after Vicksburg, 428

Porter, William, 59–60

Port Gibson, Miss., 170, 253; campaign and battle of, 222–40

Port Hudson, La., 66, 76, 77, 89, 92, 115, 116, 117, 121, 158, 167, 170, 173, 188, 191, 193, 198, 205, 248, 252, 256, 318, 393, 405, 410–11

Prentiss, Benjamin, 176, 177, 404

Price, Sterling, 61, 87, 88, 115, 167, 422; and Iuka and Corinth campaigns and battles, 73–77

Quinby, Isaac, 181, 183, 184, 188, 189; and Vicksburg operations, May–July 1863, 327, 334, 340, 344, 346–48

Randolph, George Wythe, 87, 88

Ransom, Thomas: and Vicksburg operations, May–July 1863, 327, 331, 339, 344, 364, 365

Ransom's Approach, 365

Rawlins, John, 102, 182

Raymond, campaign and battle of, 251–71; hard war during, 258, 270–71

Reynolds, Alexander W., 168, 246, 293, 306–7

Steele, Frederick, 102, 104, 111, 112, 130, 133, 134, 137, 142, 144, 272, 277, 326–27; leads Greenville Expedition, 204, 208–12; and Vicksburg operations, May–July 1863, 339, 345; and siege of Jackson, 405, 408, 410

Steele's Bayou–Deer Creek operation, 184–88

Stevens, Henry, 65, 67

Stevenson, Carter, 121, 144, 167, 177, 186, 187, 205, 206, 209, 244, 245, 246, 252, 255, 260, 310, 320; and Champion Hill campaign and battle, 282, 287–89, 291–300, 303–4, 307; and defense of Vicksburg, May–July 1863, 321, 361; and surrender of Vicksburg, 396; after Vicksburg, 426

Stevenson, John, 238, 240, 242, 265, 266, 267, 296–99, 306; and Vicksburg operations, May–July 1863, 339–40, 346

Stone, William, 227, 233, 234, 235, 237, 240

Streight, Abel: raid by, 207, 258

Stuart, David, 139, 143

Taylor, Richard, 69, 130, 391, 425

Taylor, Thomas, 304

Thayer, John, 142, 143; and Vicksburg operations, May–July 1863, 331, 345–46, 363

Thayer's Approach, 362–63

Third Louisiana Redan: mine explosions at, 367–69

Thirteenth U.S. Infantry, 329–30

Thompson, A. P., 277

Tilghman, Lloyd, 168, 178, 182, 189, 204, 205, 243, 244, 245, 246, 247, 252, 255, 258, 260, 292, 302–5, 308

Tracy, Edward, 225, 229, 230, 231, 233, 234, 246

Tupelo, Miss., 44, 73, 106, 120

Turner, J. J., 268

Tuttle, James, 213, 272, 277, 281; and

Vicksburg operations, May–July 1863, 327, 333, 339, 345, 363

Twiggs, David, 22

Union soldiers, 72, 158; and slaves, 70, 106, 107, 108, 161–62, 196, 197, 209, 286; in North Mississippi campaign, 82, 83, 84–85, 102–3, 106, 107, 108–11, 126, 127; in Chickasaw Bayou battles, 145–46; in Arkansas Post campaign and battle, 150, 152–54; in Grant's early 1863 operations, 159–64; at Lake Providence, 173–74; in Yazoo Pass expedition, 176, 180, 189; and Louisiana march, 194–98, 202, 215; at battle of Grand Gulf, 218; during Port Gibson campaign and battle, 223, 239, 241–42, 247, 248, 249; during Raymond and Jackson campaigns and battles, 254, 258, 263, 265, 269, 270–71, 280–81; during Champion Hill and Big Black campaigns and battles, 285–86, 301, 305–6; and operations at Vicksburg, May–July 1863, 329–30, 341–42, 345–47, 349–50, 368, 373–81, 390; and hard war outside Vicksburg during siege, 392; and surrender of Vicksburg, 398–400, 414; during march to and siege of Jackson, 405–6; and hard war during Jackson campaign, 406–7, 410

U.S. Colored Troops, 391, 419

Van Dorn, Earl, 34, 45, 57, 62, 63, 66, 68, 79, 87, 88, 150, 157, 244; appointed commander of Department of Southern Mississippi and East Louisiana, 44; and *Arkansas*, 45, 65; plans campaign against Baton Rouge, 63–64; and Iuka and Corinth campaigns and battles, 73–78; relieved of departmental command, 77; in North Mississippi campaign, 88–92, 104; leads cavalry raid against Holly Springs, 121–26; after Vicksburg, 426